P9-DXN-265

ROCOCO
Art and Design in Hogarth's England

16 May – 30 September 1984

THE VICTORIA AND ALBERT MUSEUM

This exhibition is sponsored by Trusthouse Forte

ROCOCO
Art and Design in Hogarth's England

Trefoil Books/Victoria & Albert Museum

List of abbreviations

M.   Married
b.   born
d.   died
c.   circa
l.   length
h.   height
w.   width
diam.   diameter
VAM   Victoria and Albert Museum
Dimensions are in millimetres, height, width, depth, unless otherwise stated.

Cover: *The Shudi Family*
         Attributed to Barthélémy du Pan (1712-1763), c. 1742
         The Broadwood Trust (Cat. B14)

Catalogue edited by Michael Snodin
assisted by Elspeth Moncrieff

Catalogue published in association with Trefoil Books
7 Royal Parade
Dawes Road
London SW6

Copyright © authors as listed, 1984

All rights reserved. No part of this publication
may be reproduced, stored in a retrieval system,
or transmitted in any form or by any means, electronic,
mechanical or otherwise, without the prior
permission in writing of the publishers.

Set in Baskerville by Words & Pictures Limited, London
and printed by BAS Printers Limited, Over Wallop, Hampshire.

ISBN 0 86294 046 X

MAIN LIB.
NK
928
R56
1984

Contents

The Friends of the V&A receive the following privileges:
Free and immediate entry to all exhibitions with a guest or husband/wife and children under 16
Free evening Private Views of major exhibitions and new developments within the Museum
Quarterly mailings of Museum literature and News Letters
The opportunity to participate in trips abroad with Keepers from the Departments
Discounts in the Craft Shop and on exhibition catalogues
Friends: £15 annually
Friends: (Concessionary) £10 annually for pensioners and full-time Museum staff
Corporate friends: £100 annually
Receive all the privileges offered to Friends, plus a fully transferable Membership Card
Benefactors: £1000 donation, which may be directed to the Department of the donor's choice

Corporate Friends
Alan Hutchison Publishing Company Ltd
Albert Amor Limited
The Antique Porcelain Company
Artists Cards Ltd
Ashtead DFAS
Asprey & Company
Bank of England Arts Society
Bankers Trust Company
Blairman & Sons Limited
British Petroleum
Cobra & Bellamy
Colnaghi & Co
Coutts & Co Bankers
Cyril Humphris
Doncaster Institute of Higher Education
Goldsmiths' Company
Hotspur Limited
John Keil Limited
Kennedy Brookes plc
Ian Logan Limited
London & Provincial Antique Dealers' Association Limited
Madame Tussaud's Limited
Marks & Spencer plc
Mendip DFAS
Barbara Minto Limited
W.H. Patterson Fine Arts Limited
S. Pearson & Son
Charles Pfister Inc.
Phillips Auctioneers
Phillips Petroleum
Pickering & Chatto
R T Z Services Limited
South Molton Antiques Limited
Spink & Son Limited
The Fine Art Society Limited

Stair & Company Ltd
The Wellcome Foundation Limited
Winifred Williams

Benefactor friends
Sir Duncan Oppenheim
Mr Garth Nicholas

ASSOCIATES

The Associates of the V&A are companies who pay a minimum of £500 annually, covenanted for four years, and who take a particular interest in the Museum and have a close involvement with it

Arthur Andersen and Company
B.A.D.A.
The Baring Foundation
Bonas and Company Limited
Christie's
Commercial Union Assurance plc
Granada Group
Charles Letts (Holdings) Limited
Mobil
Sir Duncan Oppenheim
The Oppenheimer Charitable Trust
S.J. Phillips plc
Rose and Hubble plc
J. Sainsbury plc
Mrs. Basil Samuel
Sotheby's
John Swire and Sons Ltd
Thames Television Limited

Honorary Associates and Benefactors
The Sirdar and Begum Aly Aziz

Foreword

The rococo, with its love of fantasy and ornament, has often seemed a puzzling phenomenon in the context of English art and design. 'So with the eighteenth century', wrote John Betjeman in 1933, 'we find an even greater restraint practised in England. There was hardly any *Rococo*'. Attempts to isolate and explain the style began in the 1950s, resulting in an exhibition planned for this Museum in the early 1970s, which unfortunately did not take place. The present exhibition, the first concerted exposition on the subject of the rococo in England, has been built upon the foundations of its predecessor, but has benefited enormously from recent scholarship, both published and unpublished, and from the clarity of vision that time inevitably brings.

Her Majesty The Queen, HRH the Prince of Wales, and a large number of institutional, public and private lenders both in Britain and abroad, have been extremely generous in their responses to our requests for loans. We are especially grateful to the National Trust and other owners of houses open to the public who have allowed us to show their treasures during the summer.

If this exhibition is anyone's child, it is my colleague's, Michael Snodin who worked on it with tireless energy and who orchestrated the other contributors both within and outside of the Museum. We owe its appearance to Brian Griggs, Head of Design Section, with graphics by Michael Martin. Its practical realisation is due to Garth Hall, Andrew Hiskens and Elspeth Moncrieff of the Exhibitions Section.

In these constrained days sponsorship has become an essential part of the staging of a major exhibition. We owe an enormous debt of gratitude to Trusthouse Forte, whose support has enabled this major event to take place.

ROY STRONG
April 1984

The following have contributed to the catalogue:

B.A.	Brian Allen	M.H.H.	Morrison H. Heckscher
M.A.	Michael Archer (VAM)	W.H.	Wendy Hefford (VAM)
C.B.	Claude Blair	G.J-S.	Gervase Jackson-Stops
E.B.	Elaine Barr	R.K.	Rose Kerr (VAM)
M.C.B.	Malcolm Baker (VAM)	M.J.H.L.	M.J.H. Liversidge
R.B.	Reinier Baarsen	R.W.L.	Ronald Lightbown (VAM)
S.B.	Dr. Sarah Bevan	J.V.G.M.	J.V.G. Mallet (VAM)
D.C.	David Coke	A.R.E.N.	A.R.E. North (VAM)
D.H.C.	Dr. David Caldwell	A.V.B.N.	A.V.B. Norman
P.C.	Dr. Philip Conisbee	M.S.	Michael Snodin (VAM)
L.M.C.	Lucy Cullen (VAM)	N.R.	Natalie Rothstein (VAM)
E.E.	Elizabeth Einberg	N.S.	Nina Stawski
R.E.	Dr Richard Edgcumbe	C.T.	Charles Truman (VAM)
P.G.	Philippa Glanville (VAM)	G.M.W.	G.M. Wilson
L.J.	Loftus Jestin	M.W.	Mary Webster
A.H.	Avril Hart (VAM)	R.W.	Roger White
J.H.	John Hardy (VAM)	R.H.W.	Dr. Rudolph H. Wackernagel
J.D.H.	Jean D. Hamilton (VAM)		

Acknowledgements

The Museum is indebted to a very large number of curators, librarians, scholars, and private owners, not only for their great generosity in lending their pieces and for generally smoothing the path, but also because of their willingness to share their knowledge, often in the form of unpublished manuscripts.

In the United States we are particularly grateful to Louise Belden, Catherine Jestin, David Kiehl, Clare Le Corbeiller, Timothy A. Goodhue, Herbert Moskowitz, Patrick Noon, William Rieder, Bruce Robertson and Kim Rorschach. In France we have been greatly helped by Peter Fuhring, Marie Noël de Gary, Gérard Mabille, Marianne Roland Michel and Monique Sevin, and in Germany by Peter Volk.

In Britain we owe a special debt to David Allan, Jane Baker, C.T. Barber, David Barker, David Beasley, Dr David Bindman, Marcus Binney, Marcus Bishop, David Brown, Anthony Burton, Terence Camerer Cuss, Sam Camerer Cuss, Robert Charleston, Julia Clarke, T.H. Clarke, Timothy Clifford, Robin Crighton, Geoffrey de Bellaigue, Shirley Bury, Martin Drury, E.S. Earl, Katherine Eustace, Jeremy Evans, Robin Faulk, Mary Fielden, Dr Celina Fox, Dr Terry Friedman, Mireille Gallinou, Giovanni Giachin, Christopher Gilbert, Dr John Gilson, Richard Godfrey, Richard Good, Antony Griffiths, Arthur Grimwade, Mrs P A Halfpenny, Dr Ivan Hall, Susan Hare, Helena Hayward, Amanda Herries, Ralph Hyde, Brand Inglis, Cedric Jagger, John Kenworthy-Browne, Alastair Laing, Edmund Launert, Emmeline Leary, Noel Mander, Sir Oliver Millar, Dr D McMichael, Tina Millar, Dr Jennifer Montagu, Arnold Mountford, Dr Tessa Murdoch, Charles Newton, Sheila O'Connell, Dr Nicholas Penny, Julia Poole, Anthony Radcliffe, Stuart Ramsdale, John Rowlands, David Rummery, Andrew Saint, the Earl of Scarborough, David Scrase, Jacob Simon, Kenneth Snowman, John Somerville, Lindsay Stainton, Kay Staniland, J S G Symonds, G Taylor, Gerald Taylor, Jane Tozer, Mrs J Turnbull, Michael Urwick-Smith, Nancy Valpy, Claire Venner, Justin Vulliamy, Peter Ward-Jackson, Philip Ward-Jackson, Giles Waterfield, Lavinia Wellicome, Dr Helen Whitehouse, Robert Williams, Tim Wilson and Eileen Harris and John Harris.

We are greatly indebted to Desmond Fitz-Gerald and his colleagues for the groundwork established by the first unstaged rococo exhibition.

We are extremely grateful to Peter Macdonald and his colleagues in the Photographic Studio for their help and support throughout the project.

The Department of Furniture and Woodwork archive has been invaluable. We are grateful to Jeannie Chapel for compiling the index, and to Melissa Denny who produced the catalogue for Trefoil Books.

French Paper Machee

To the Right Hon.ble

LORD BLAKENEY,

Grand President of the
Antigallican Associations,

and the rest of the Bretheren
of that most Honourable Order;

This Book
is most humbly Dedicated
by his Lordships
most Obedient
humble Serv.t
and Brother,
Tho.s Johnson.

Sold by
T. Johnson Carver,
At the Golden Boy,
in Grafton Street, St. Ann's
Westminster.

Publish'd by Act of
April 23.

Parliament
1758.

Dedication page. See cat. L44.

The English Rococo
Historical Background
Linda Colley

The French notion of England, wrote the poet James Thomson in 1732, was 'a cold, dark, dull, dirty country, where there is nothing but money'.[1] Thomson's claim tells us more about English francophobia than French bias, but burgeoning wealth, more widely-distributed than ever before, was indeed the most outstanding characteristic of mid-eighteenth century England. Its response to the Rococo was to be determined, more than anything else, by this pervasive, dynamic and blatant prosperity.

With only 5.3 million people in 1721, rising from the mid-1740s to some 6.4 million by 1771, England had only about a third of the population of her great rival France. But in the scale and diversity of her economic activity, she amply compensated for her size. In this same period – 1720 to 1770 – **English exports doubled in value** and agricultural and industrial production rose by 60 per cent.[2] For a tiny minority of peers and landed magnates this expansion meant unprecedented wealth; but the middling classes and some of the more fortunate artisans and workers may also have enjoyed a higher standard of living and more spare cash in this period than ever before.

Such prosperity was rooted in comparative political stability. After the Civil War and the Glorious Revolution of 1688 which expelled the last male Stuart monarch, James II, England achieved a large measure of dynastic security. In 1714 the first ruler of the House of Hanover, George I, succeeded to the British throne, and although the Stuart claimant James Edward (King James III to Jacobites, the Pretender to their enemies) attempted a violent Restoration in 1715 and 1745, the Hanoverians endured.[3] George II succeeded to the throne in 1727 and was in turn placidly succeeded by his grandson, George III in 1760. The contest between the Church of England and Protestant Dissent – one of the most dangerous and divisive issues of the seventeenth century – also ceased to be so contentious in the mid-eighteenth century. The majority of Englishmen and women remained remarkably devout, but Georgian society in general became more secular, more relaxed and much less austere in its religious behaviour.[4]

More settled at home, England could be far more assertive and successful abroad. Anglo-Scottish tensions were eased by an Act of Union between the two countries in 1707. A major war with Louis XIV of France which dragged on from 1689 to 1697 and again from 1701 to 1713 brought England substantial colonial and commercial gains as well as an enhanced European reputation. From 1713 to 1744 England and France were at peace, and this was crucial for England's initial acceptance of the rococo style and of French rococo artists like Hubert-François Gravelot who settled here in 1732. The next major Anglo-French conflict – the Seven Years War (1756-63) – was the most dramatically successful war England ever fought. Huge colonial gains in North America, India and the Caribbean sated national pride and enriched still further England's manufacturers, slave-traders and exporters. 'Commerce', as Edmund Burke trumpeted, had been 'united with, and made to flourish with war'.[5] High finance was no less buoyant. The Bank of England had been founded in 1694 to raise money for the war with France; in that decade and throughout the eighteenth century it did so triumphantly well, and London replaced Amsterdam as the financial centre of Europe and the world.[6]

The men who ruled this small, greedy and industrious nation were almost invariably wealthy landowners in their own right, and this, together with England's domestic and foreign success, ensured that political in-fighting – while always intricate and often vicious – took place within a certain degree of patriotic and social consensus. In the mid-eighteenth century the Whig party was in the ascendant. The Whigs were associated with support for religious toleration and the House of Hanover and had close links with the London money market. Their traditional opponents, the Tories, were committed to preserving the primacy of the Church of England and the sanctity of the royal prerogative. They were also deeply suspicious of the Whig financial interest in the City of London which, many Tories asserted, took the country too often and too long into continental wars for the sake of individual profiteering.[7]

Some contemporaries also believed, or claimed to believe, that the Tory party was tainted with Jacobitism. Almost certainly this belief was profoundly flawed, but it led both George I and George II to exclude Tories from political office.[8] Consequently, much of the political battle between 1714 and 1760 was fought out between men who all regarded themselves as Whigs. Successive Whig Premiers – Sir Robert Walpole, Prime Minister from 1722 to 1742, Henry Pelham, Prime Minister from 1744 until his death ten years later, and Pelham's brother the duke of Newcastle, premier from 1754 to 1756 and politically central into the 1760s – found themselves attacked by hybrid parliamentary Oppositions of Tory MPs and disgruntled Whig MPs. From 1736 to 1742 and again from 1746 to 1751 these dissident Whigs, who fought for a share of government office rather than ideology, found a prestigious if vacillating figure-head in George II's eldest son, Frederick, Prince of Wales.

Frederick presented himself and was represented in dissident Whig propaganda as a "Patriot Prince", a pure-minded and idealistic man compelled into opposition by love of his country and disdain for the corruption practised by the King's Ministers. But Frederick was also insecure and jealous, jealous of his father and, after 1745, jealous of his younger brother the duke of Cumberland, who vanquished the Jacobite army at the Battle of Culloden. Frederick also flirted with the Opposition in the hope that it would help him increase his annual parliamentary allowance of £50,000.[9] He was always in debt, and in the 1740s he claimed that it was this (largely self-inflicted) penury which hampered his role as an art patron and prevented him from fostering a national academy of art.[10]

This princely lack of cash is one of many factors which complicate an assessment of Frederick's role as a patron of the Rococo.[11] The suggestion that he encouraged and presided over an Opposition aesthetic which might rival the Palladianism favoured by the Whig Establishment, has to contend not only with the fact that Frederick's own architectural commissions were largely palladian in style and decoration, but also with the complex structure, ideologies and chronology of the Opposition.[12] Frederick never regarded himself as anti-Whig; rather, he and his immediate supporters claimed to be more purist in their Whiggery than the

Whigs holding government office. And, as has been argued, the Opposition was not uniform but an heterogeneous body of Whig and Tory politicians.

So what is the evidence at elite level for the Rococo as an Opposition aesthetic? It is certainly true that some of Frederick's political allies were among the most notable patrons of rococo-style town and country houses: Philip Dormer Stanhope, 4th earl of Chesterfield (Chesterfield House), Charles Wyndham (Petworth), and, arguably, Charles Calvert, Baron Baltimore (Woodcote Park).[13] But one has to remember that political allegiances in this period – especially among the Whigs – were always in flux. Baltimore had a fairly consistent record: he was Frederick's Gentleman of the Bedchamber from 1731 to 1747 and his Cofferer from 1747 to 1751. But Wyndham and Chesterfield were only in opposition with the Prince in the 1730s and early 1740s. By 1747 when Chesterfield commissioned Chesterfield House and by the 1750s when Wyndham presided over the re-decoration of Petworth, things had changed. Wyndham (a former Tory MP) had gone over to the Whig administration and Chesterfield was actually Secretary of State![14] And of course even if these men and others round the Prince (like his Treasurer, George Bubb Doddington, who employed the sculptor Henry Cheere at his villa in Hammersmith) did share an aesthetic of which the Rococo was a vital part, this may have been a tribute to their common acquaintance and exchange of information rather than a conscious expression of their political stance.[15]

What is striking if we look at the patronage patterns of England's political elite, particularly the Opposition, and what is still in need of research, is the large number of Tory MPs and Peers who supported rococo artists and craftsmen. Lord Scarsdale (formerly Sir Nathaniel Curzon, Tory MP for Derbyshire), William Drake, Tory MP for Amersham, Sir James Dashwood, Tory MP for Oxfordshire and, perhaps the party's greatest magnate, Charles Noel Somerset, 4th duke of Beaufort, were all important patrons of John and William Linnell.[16] In 1754 Thomas Chippendale dedicated his *The Gentleman and Cabinet Maker's Director* to the earl of Northumberland, formerly Sir Hugh Smithson, Tory MP for Middlesex. William Courtenay, Tory MP for Devon, was painted by Thomas Hudson and commissioned rococo-style plasterwork for his great house Powderham Castle.[17] Again, this may simply be a matter of men connected by party and friendship recommending artists to each other. But from 1747 to 1751 the Tory party was in formal political alliance with Prince Frederick and, since most of these Tory politicians were on the right wing of their party, it is just conceivable – one can say no more than that – that residual Stuart sympathies made them receptive to a decorative style that was associated with France.[18]

What is incontrovertible, however, is that in mid-eighteenth century England the market for art went far beyond the political and landed elite. There was no 'popular art market' in any widely democratic sense. But Daniel Defoe's seven-fold analysis of English society at this time shows that it had progressed far beyond a stark polarity between a minority of patricians on the one side and a vast majority of impoverished plebeians on the other:

1. The great, who live profusely.
2. The rich, who live plentifully.
3. The middle sort, who live well.

4. The working trades, who labour hard, but feel no want.
5. The country people, farmers etc. who fare indifferently.
6. The poor, who fare hard.
7. The miserable, that really pinch and suffer want.[19]

What enriched the eighteenth-century art market was the new prosperity and cultural awareness of Defoe's third category and, in the case of London, sections of his fourth.[20]

For London was a unique city. By 1750 it had 675,000 inhabitants, which meant that it held 11 per cent of the population and was about ten times bigger than the largest of eighteenth-century England's provincial towns. It was the home of an estimated 360 different trade groups, the centre of fashion, of luxury production and consumption, and a honey-pot of job opportunities.[21] It was also a haven for those middle class professionals whose occupations had blossomed in the late seventeenth and early eighteenth centuries – the bankers, the attorneys, the scriveners and the physicians. It was men of this type who were entering the art market seriously for the first time (Dr Richard Mead is one example) and who supplied artists like Francis Hayman with a multiplicity of modest but useful commissions.[22]

Much of this new middling class patronage derived from a snobbish if understandable desire to emulate the life-styles of the landed gentry and aristocracy. But more generally it reflected the increased supply of and wider access to cultural information. By 1760 London had four daily newspapers as well as six tri-weekly papers. The news these offered on foreign and domestic trends and events was supplemented by the periodical press, an innovation of the rococo period. The *Gentleman's Magazine* and the *Monthly Magazine* were both inaugurated in the 1730s, to be followed in 1747 by the *Universal Magazine*. These miscellaneous publications spawned other, more explicitly cultural journals. The *Monthly Review* was founded in 1749, and the *Critical Review* and the *Connoisseur*, which both devoted considerable space to questions of national and international taste, appeared in the 1750s.[23]

This growing press network not only propagated cultural information of all kinds, it also fructified art more directly. The periodical press, especially, created a wealth of new work for engravers and illustrators, as did the concurrent increase in the publication of pamphlets, ballads and novels. Cheap printed music scores also became much more widely available after 1730, an innovation which benefited Gravelot, for example, when he was commissioned to work on George Bickham's *Musical Entertainer* (1737-9).[24] Nor was this all. When Matthew Darly issued a trade card to advertise his wall-hangings business, he indicated some of the diverse and comparatively novel opportunities that were available for the decorative arts:

> Engraving in all its Branches, Viz. Visiting Tickets, Coats of Arms, Seals, Book Plates, Frontispieces, Shopkeepers Bills. In greater variety & cheaper than at any other shop in town.[25]

Quite evidently, Darly was appealing to an affluent society that was accustomed to the printed word and to design, a society that was becoming increasingly commercially-minded. Mid-eighteenth century Englishmen and women liked to sell as much as they liked to spend. Trade cards, which had been almost unknown in the seventeenth century, reached their peak between 1720 and 1770 and were just one aspect of an avalanche of commercial advertising which swept over Georgian England.[26] And, again, advertisements often required craftsmen-artists and an art style which could lend itself to a small-scale but flamboyant format. For this, the rococo was ideal.

One must not exaggerate the size or social depth of the audience for mid-eighteenth century art and printed ephemera. Over 70 per cent of Englishmen in this period lived in the countryside and, until the last three decades of the century, printing was largely confined to London and the major provincial centres. Newspapers cost an average 1½d a copy and periodicals sold for an average of 6d per issue, so their purchase was virtually confined to the middle classes and above.[27] In London, however, access to the printed word was uniquely extensive. By 1740 the City had some 550 coffee-houses. Like Old Slaughter's coffee-house in St. Martin's Lane, these served as clearing-houses for gossip and news, most of them purchasing newspapers, broadsheets and the occasional pamphlet for the use of their customers so as to attract clientele.[28] Coffee-houses and taverns were natural venues for a rich variety of clubs and societies. There were benefit clubs for tradesmen and artisans; debating and cultural clubs like the Society of Dilettanti; purely convivial clubs like the Sublime Society of Beef-Steaks which attracted Hayman and William Hogarth to its number; and a multiplicity of masonic and quasi-masonic clubs.[29] By 1768 England had 291 Masonic Lodges, eighty-seven of which were situated in London. They catered to a wide social spectrum from the elite (Frederick, Prince of Wales, for example, belonged to a highly-exclusive Lodge) to artist-craftsmen like Batty Langley and below.[29A] All of these clubs served to foster printing and the decorative arts, in some cases by direct commissioning. Clubs might need special illustrated song-books, engraved admission tickets, or portraits of their members. If they were affluent like the Honourable Board of Brothers, a Tory quasi-masonic society which met every Thursday at the St. Albans Tavern, they might even require special regalia and ornaments. The Board of Brothers commissioned a set of silver candlesticks for their club meetings from the Huguenot silversmith Paul De Lamerie.[30]

One historian has claimed that almost every male in Georgian London belonged to a club of some sort. But even those men (and the vast majority of women) who were not members of a club, who did not have access to printed ephemera or could not read them, were likely to be conscious that their world was becoming more visually exciting. The streets of London and the main provincial centres were becoming more elegant and shops more alluring to customers and spectators alike – the curved bow window with its enlarged display space became fashionable in this period. In their homes those who were moderately affluent or above were able to enjoy more colour and a greater variety of consumer goods than their seventeenth-century forbears. The rich could savour the sinuous curves and plasticity which porcelain china made available as earlier, coarser pottery had not. The merely prosperous could indulge in wallpaper, particularly coloured wallpaper. In 1713 197,000 yards of wallpaper had been sold in England. By 1785 the figure was over two million yards – a ten-fold increase.[31] For recreation Londoners might visit one of the sixty-odd pleasure gardens which mimicked fashionable Vauxhall and Ranelagh. Their provincial counterparts could sample the growing number of concerts held at the growing number of assembly rooms, or patronise the theatre which spread into major centres like Norwich, Birmingham and Bristol in this period.[32] In London, too, Covent Garden and Drury Lane increased their audience capacity by some 50 per cent between 1732 and 1762; theatre prosceniums became more ornate and elaborate and scene paintings more skilful and flamboyant. Everywhere in urban England the prosperous had access to a greater variety of organised leisure and luxury artifacts, and the provision of leisure, pleasure and consumer goods became a profitable business for a growing number of entrepreneurs, artists and craftsmen.[33]

The application of the Rococo to the decorative arts in England was one aspect of this revolution in consumer tastes and appetite. But having said that, we face an obvious question. Given pervasive English xenophobia (and particularly francophobia), how could a style that was openly acknowledged to be 'in the French manner' win wide social acceptance?[34] For the elite there were few problems. English politicians certainly disliked the French monarch's absolutism, his support for the Stuart Pretender, and his colonial ambitions which conflicted with England's own. But there was usually a marked divergence between such men's political responses and their cultural tastes. Until the last third of the eighteenth century most aristocratic Englishmen accepted the cultural and fashionable primacy of France: 'the whipped cream of Europe' as Voltaire called his country. French tailoring, French cooks and servants, French actors (and still more actresses) as well as the French fine arts were *de rigueur* for men who would almost certainly have taken in Paris on the Grand Tour. The Anglo-French wars made little difference to all this. Between 1763 and 1765 it was estimated that some 40,000 Englishmen had passed through Calais, eager for the direct contact with French culture and society of which they had been starved during the Seven Years War.[35]

Lower down the social spectrum it was different. The popular image of France was well conveyed by Hogarth in 1748:

> A farcical pomp of war, parade of religion, and bustle with little, with very little business. In short, poverty, slavery and insolence with an affectation of politeness.[36]

France was associated with 'papist superstition', with governmental tyranny, huge and oppressive standing armies and mass poverty. When a Naturalisation Act was passed in 1709 to facilitate immigration of foreign Protestants, including Frenchmen, into England, it was widely opposed and swiftly repealed. Further Naturalisation Bills in 1746-7, 1748 and 1751 were dropped by the government because of the outcry they provoked. Immigrants, it was believed, especially Frenchmen, put Britons out of jobs and imported lower living standards: 'No General Naturalisation! . . . No French Bottle-Makers! No Lowering of Wages of Labouring Men to 4d a Day and Garlick!'[37] When England and France were at war or near it, such prejudice could turn violent. In 1749 there was a riot in a London theatre where a troupe of French actors was playing; a similar and more destructive incident occurred in the City in November 1755. Given this plebeian anger one can understand Gravelot and his fellow French artist, Philip Mercier, leaving England in 1745-6 when France was lending aid to a Jacobite invasion.[38] Similarly his vaunted role as a 'Patriot Prince' and desire for popularity compelled Prince Frederick to make regular public announcements that his court would boycott French servants and French fashions.

So how did English rococo artists and craftsmen wanting to attract a wide custom vindicate their use of a French style? Most seem to have been oblivious to any contradiction between their patriotism and their work; it was indeed very much in their interest to deny any such conflict. Rococo art and craftsmanship was labour-intensive. It employed more workers and, when fashionable, often fetched higher prices than less ornate work. For the majority of craftsmen-artists this must have been rationalisation enough. By the 1750s, however, such complacency may have been under some strain. There was an increasing tendency in that decade for periodicals like the *Critical Review* to stigmatise French borrowings in English art and architecture, and, as the drift into the Seven Years War began, a bevy of polemicists led by John Brown argued that aristocratic and gentry emulation of the French and their 'vain, luxurious and selfish effeminacy' was enervating the British nation.[39] The rococo artists' response, insofar as they recognised the need to present one, was that by catering themselves for the public's taste for French fashions, they reduced the demand for French imports and thus advanced England's own fine art and decorative industries. As the hero of a novel published in 1757 *The Anti-Gallican* argued:

> Far be it from me to condemn my Countrymen for adopting any Invention in Arts or Sciences, which owes its Birth to the fertile Genius of our bitterest Enemies. – No – let us endeavour at raising ourselves to an equal, if not superior Pitch of Excellence, in every Science and Profession, to all the Nations of the Globe.[40]

Given this line of argument, it may have been no accident that many rococo artists and patrons were associated with the Anti-Gallican Society. Founded in London in 1745 this had as its explicit aim 'to extend the commerce of England and discourage the introduction of French modes and oppose the importation of French commodities'.[41] The Anti-Gallicans anticipated the Society of Arts in awarding premiums to inventive English craftsmen and while their connection with the craftsmen-artists of the English rococo has yet to be investigated, the available evidence seems suggestive at least. The Society's first Grand President was the London stationer and businessman, Stephen Theodore Janssen. He had extensive contacts and influence among printers and engravers as Master of the Stationers Company from 1749 to 1751, and his own French enamels factory at Battersea seems to have produced art work for the Anti-Gallican Society which combined strident patriotic symbolism with equally unabashed *rocaille*.[42] Janssen's sister was married to Lord Baltimore, the rococo patron. Another Grand President, Lord Carpenter, married his daughter to Charles Wyndham. In 1752 a pamphlet by Richard Parrott recommended increased immigration of French Protestant craftsmen so as to enrich England's manufacturing arts, and specifically praised the porcelain works of Sprimont of Chelsea, which 'will, I hope, be thought worthy of the Notice of the Patriot Society of Anti-Gallicans'.[43] We know that George Michael Moser was commissioned to produce some art work for the Society. And in 1758 the furniture-maker, Thomas Johnson, a member of the Anti-Gallican Society, 'an Englishman . . . who possesses a true Anti-Gallic Spirit' as he described himself, began his *Collection of Designs* with a splendid rococo cartouche and a dedication to the Society's current Grand President, Lord Blakeney.[44] Thus a style that was the quintessence of France became bizarrely reconciled with a chauvinist pressure group demanding greater cultural and manufacturing autonomy for England.

But such tensions could not be covered over for very long. Since Prince Frederick had confounded his supporters by dying at the age of 44 in 1751, it was his eldest son who succeeded to the throne as George III in 1760. In the first decade of the new reign the political scenario changed dramatically. Tories were re-admitted to political respectability and Whigs became more factionalised. More importantly, Britain's emergence from the Seven Years War as a mighty imperial power and her deteriorating relations with the American colonists made the stuff of politics more contentious, more dramatic and more ideologically-divisive. At home, escalating population growth, pioneering industrialisation and the radical activities of John Wilkes and his supporters increased social protest and unrest.[45] At one and the same time, Britain was more self-conscious in her greatness, more secure in her national pride and sense of cultural achievement, and more divided in her political debate and social structure. The foundation of the Royal Academy in 1768, the growing concern of artists like Sir Joshua Reynolds, Benjamin West and James Barry to celebrate British heroism in history painting, and Josiah Wedgwood's well-known disavowal of 'French and frippery' in 1769 were all signs of the times.[46] Not only were fashions in European art changing, but in purely domestic terms the rococo was also too foreign, too small-scale, and perhaps too frivolous for what was now no longer a small and peripheral European state, but a great and troubled empire.

What is Rococo?

Leda, Claude Duflos after François Boucher. See cat. A17.

18

A1 *Three cartouches*
Stefano della Bella (1610-1664). 1646
Etching; 235 x 191 (cut)
Lettered *Stef. Della Bella. in. fecit. F.L.D.*
Il Ciartres excud. Cum Privil. Regis. Chris.
Numbered *9*
VAM (28219.9)

From *Raccolta di Varii Cappricii,* 1646.

Lit: Berlin 1939, 567; de Vesme 1971,
1035
MS

A2 *Title-page of* Quinque
Sensuum descriptio
Anonymous, after Francis Clein
(1582?-1657/8). 1646
Etching; 90 x 196
Lettered with title and *In co picture*
genere. quod (Grottesche) vocant Itali.
F. Clein inv. 1646 and the address of
Thomas Hinde (replacing that of
Thomas Rowlett).
VAM (29688-80)

Lit: Berlin 1939, 52(2)
MS

A3 *Ewer*
Massimiliano Soldani (1658-1740).
Probably *c.*1695
Bronze; h.797
VAM (A.18-1959)

Decorated with Neptune and a Triton
riding a sea horse. One of two ewers
which are bronze versions of two vases
among the models of the Doccia
porcelain factory and listed in the
inventory as by Soldani (Lankheit
1982, pp. 126-7). They may well be
those vases which Horace Mann was
attempting to buy for Bubb
Doddington in 1759 (Honour 1964),
an example of 18th century English
taste for Florentine late baroque
sculpture (cf. Montagu in Florence
1974). In their use of freely modelled
figures to create the shape of each
vase, they contrast with compositions
by Fischer von Erlach (Lankheit 1962),
and Girardon (Montagu in Florence
1974, p. 128) and individual elements
might be described as proto-rococo,
among them the shellwork (though
this is appropriate to the marine
subjects) and the asymmetrical figure
compositions which are characteristic
of Soldani. However, the massive

quality of some details, such as the
gadrooning, and the overall form
remain fundamentally late baroque.

Prov: Scarlatti family, Florence (?);
Bubb Doddington (?); Stiebel, New
York
Lit: Florence 1974, p. 128; Lankheit
1958, pp. 159-63; Lankheit 1962,
pp. 146-8; Lankheit 1982, pp. 126-7;
Pope Hennessy 1964, pp. 588-9; Pope
Hennessey 1967, p 140.
MCB

A4 *Design for a stage set*
Attributed to Antonio Galli Bibiena
(1697?-1774)
Pen and ink and wash; 375 x 385
Inscribed *Apartamenti Terenni che*
corispondono a Reggi Giardini

The British Architectural Library, Drawings
Collection, RIBA

A characteristic *scena per angolo* of the
interior of a palace. From a domed
hall two grand staircases lead into an
arch on the left and a further hall; on
the right an arch leads to a garden.
The use of massed ribbed volutes and
mouldings was characteristic of
Antonio Bibiena's designs and is also
found in the work of Meissonnier
(Cat. A12).

Prov: presented by Sir John
Drummond Stewart, 1838-9
Lit: Jeudwine 1968, pl. 17; RIBA 1973,
cat. 7 (with bibliography)
MS

A5 *Design for plaster decoration*
over a window
Probably by a member of the
Bernasconi family. *c.*1750
Pen and ink and wash; 422 x 285
Private Collection

Above the arched window is a
cartouche containing two putti before
a trophy of standards, all within two
projecting walls with scrolled ends.
Through the window is a colonnade in
a garden, perhaps intended to be
painted. The design, vigorously
modelled yet entirely symmetrical, is
characterisic of the late baroque
mural and ceiling decoration of
northern Italy. The design is from a
group in various hands (of which this
is the most frequent) which belonged
to Giovanni Battista Bernasconi (1796-
1839), one of a number of Italian
stuccoists of that name who worked in

A4

England. They included Bartholomew
(d. 1786), Peter and John (Giovanni)
working in 1815, and Francis
(d. 1841), the most successful Regency
stuccoist. The Italian Bernasconis were
based at Riva S. Vitale near Lugano.
One of the drawings in the set is
inscribed *Primo disegno fatto in Bologna a
14 Agost 1741.*

Prov: Giovanni Battista Bernasconi;
Miss Alice Bernasconi by descent (d.
1964); Admiral Blackwell
Lit: Wunder 1975, p. 49 (erroneously
described as signed); Beard 1978,
p. 246; Gunnis 1968; p. 51; RIBA
1972, p. 77
MS

A6 *L'Embarquement pour Cythere*
Nicolas-Henri Tardieu (1674-1749)
after Jean-Antoine Watteau (1684-
1721). 1733
Engraving; 549 x 745
Lettered with title, privilege and
*A. Watteau pinxit. Tardieu sculp. Gravé
d'apres le Tableau original peint par
Watteau haut de 4 pieds sur 6 pieds de
large. Du Cabinet de Mr De Julienne* (also
in Latin) and with the address of the
widow of F. Chereau.
*The Visitors of the Ashmolean Museum,
Oxford*

From the *Oeuvre Gravé* of Watteau,
published by Jean de Julienne 1727-
1735. The single plate was announced
in the *Mercure de France* in 1733. The
original painting (Staatliche Museen,
Berlin-Dahlem) is a later version of the
painting in the Louvre, the subject of
which has been established by Michael
Levey as the embarkation *from* Cythera.
The latter was Watteau's *Morceau de
Reception* for the Academy in 1717 in
the records of which Watteau's title,
'Le pelerinage a l'isle de Cithere' was
substituted by 'une feste galante'; it is
the earliest example of the genre on
which Watteau's fame chiefly rested.
This print had an influence in England
(Cat. C6) but was preceded by Philip
Mercier's engraving, published in
London, of another version of the
Cythera theme (Dacier & Vauflart
1929, 155A).

Prov: Presented with other Watteau
prints by Mr Granville Tyser. Many
are from the Liechtenstein and
Furstenburg collection
Lit: Dacier and Vauflart 1929, 110;
Levey 1961; Parker 1931, 32 ff.
MS

A7 *Colombine et Arlequin*
Jean Moyreau (1690-1762) after Jean-
Antoine Watteau (1684-1721). 1729
Engraving; 516 x 320
Lettered with title, privilege, the
addresses of Gersaint and Surugue
and *Gravés d'après le dessein original
inventé et colorié par. A. Watteau Peintre du
Roi. Watteau Invenit. J. Moyreau Sculp.*

*The Visitors of the Ashmolean Museum,
Oxford*

Announced in the *Mercure de France* in
April 1729, and also published in the
Oeuvre Grave, Vol.I. The lattice-work
grotesque structure combined with the
lively Commedia dell'Arte figures
recalls the only surviving drawing by
Watteau for a grotesque panel, a
singerie for Marly which was painted in
1709 (Parker & Mathey 1957, 183;
Stockholm 1980, 568). While the
structure recalls those introduced into
French mural painting by Claude III
Audran (Watteau's master *c.* 1707-9)
the naturalistically-treated figures are
Watteau's own contribution. Many of
the 94 prints after Watteau's
ornamental compositions were
published after his death. They extend
the naturalistic treatment to the
grotesque structure itself, breaking
down its formality and symmetry.

Prov: see cat. A6
Lit: Dacier & Vauflart 1929, 64, 2nd
state
MS

A8 *Design, possibly for a wall decoration*
Jean-Bernard-Honoré Turreau, called
Toro (1672-1731). Perhaps *c.*1716-17
Pen and ink, grey wash, and pencil,
with a ruled border; 477 x 335
Private Collection

The drawing is suggestive of a *buffet*
but its exact purpose, as so often in
Toro's drawings, is unclear. In the
upper portion a large panel showing
Apollo and Daphne is flanked by
figures of Juno and Minerva. A
smaller panel in the base shows
Mercury receiving a scroll from Cupid
and a putto holding a flaming torch.
The drawing can perhaps be connected
with a group of six, formerly in the
Paignon-Dijonval collection, which
included a sheet of similar size and
format now at the National Gallery of
Scotland (D.933). It bears a dedication,
signed by Toro, to Robert de Cotte
(1656-1735) 'Premier Architecte de sa
Majesté' (a post he achieved in 1708).
Pierre Rosenberg has connected a
sheet at the Cooper-Hewitt Museum
with the set; he suggests that the
drawings may have been made during
Toro's only recorded visit to Paris in
1716-17.

Prov: (?) Paignon-Dijonval (1810),
No. 3355
Lit: Dimier 1928, Vol. I, p. 359,
cat. 35-49; Rosenberg 1972, p. 214
MS

A7

A8

A9 *Design for a ceiling cornice*

Anonymous, after François Roumier
(c.1701-1748). 1724
Etching; 70 x 182
Numbered *2*
VAM (E.2428-1909)

From the suite *Livre de plusieurs coins de Bordures,* Paris, 1724 (re-issued 1750).

Lit: Berlin 1939, 380
MS

A10 *Design for a silver centrepiece*

Claude II Ballin (1661-1754). *c.*1727
Pen and ink and wash; 380 x 540
The bottom of the drawing cut,
removing a long inscription
Musée des Arts Décoratifs, Paris (A 9625)

The main structure is, in effect, a
three-dimensional grotesque in the
manner of Jean Berain, combined
with mouldings and candle branches
characteristic of Régence interiors.
The scallop shells and bulrushes
(presumably salt cellars) are a foretaste
of the naturalism of English rococo
silver (Cat. G17)) and the musician
figures in their general type prefigure
the handles of the Kandler cistern
(Cat. B9). The centrepiece (Hermitage)
was made by Ballin in 1727-8.

Lit: Gruber 1982, fig. 255;
Connaissance des Arts 1965, p. 96
MS

A11 *A cartouche with emblems*

Gabriel Huquier (1695-1772) after
Gilles-Marie Oppenord (1672-1742).
1737
Etching and engraving; 321 x 219
Lettered with the privilege and
Oppenort in. Huquier Sculp. et ex. 6 A
VAM (E.3971-1907)

From the suite *Premier Livre de Différents morceaux,* which formed part of the
first group of Oppenord designs (the
so-called 'Moyen Oppenord'),
published by Huquier in 1737-8.
Oppenord was in Italy 1692-99, when
he took a particular interest in
baroque works, such as those by
Bernini and Borromini. This greater
sculptural sense was influential in the
part Oppenord played in the formation
of the Régence style (strictly 1715-23),
and is visible in this design emblematic
of the Arts, which is also markedly
asymmetrical.

Lit: BN: Fonds 1033-8; Berlin 1939,
383
MS

A12 *Three designs for a candlestick*

Louis Desplaces (1682-1739) after
Juste Aurele Meissonnier (1695-1750).
1734-8
Etching and engraving; 270 x 210, 269
x 210, 269 x 212
The title-page lettered *Chandeliers de
sculpture en argent Invanté par J.
Maissonnier Architecte en 1728. Desplaces
Sculpsit.* The plates lettered *Meissonnier*
*Architecte in. Desplaces Sculpsit. Avec
Privilège du Roi.* One also lettered with
the address of Huquier and numbered
2B 12. The other numbered *B 11.*
VAM (27988.C.1; E.1663 & A-1977)

These three prints, all views of the
same *genre pittoresque* candlestick,
epitomise the asymmetry of that style.
They probably formed part of the
group of 50 prints after Meissonnier,
published by the widow Chereau in
1734. The candlestick was copied for
the Meissen 'Swan Service' in 1739.
The thick parallel ribbing is very
similar to that employed by Antonio
Bibiena (Cat. A4). The title-page is of
the suite as published before
incorporation into the collected
Oeuvres in *c.*1749.

Lit: B.N. Fonds, 169-171; Berlin 1939,
3976; VAM 1983 2.3.i
MS

A13 *A Cabinet of Scientific Curiosities*

Jacques de Lajoue (1686-1761). 1734
Oil on canvas; 1194 x 1524
Sir Alfred Beit, Bart.

Originally executed as an overdoor for
a *'cabinet d'histoire naturelle'* in the Hôtel
du Lude, Rue Saint Dominique, Paris
home of the noted collector Joseph
Bonnier de la Mosson. His remarkable
collections of shells and other natural
specimens, architectural and
engineering models, scientific
instruments, and so on, was housed in
a suite of rooms designed in the 1730s
by the architect Jean Courtonne. For
these Lajoue painted decorative
cartouches and overdoors. Two of the
latter survive, Cat. A13 and another,
from the library, now also in the Beit
collection. While the architecture in
Lajoue's painting is imaginary, verging
on the fantastic, the palm motifs and
the asymmetrical cartouches echo
features of Courtonne's decoration of
the various *cabinets,* and some of the
scientific instruments and models
represented were in the actual
collection. The collection and its
original display and settings are
known from contemporary published
descriptions and from a suite of eight
drawings made by Courtonne's son in
1739 (Bibliothèque d'Art et
d'Archéologie, Collection Jacques
Doucet, Paris). These drawings were
probably originally made for

A10

A13

A14

FONTAINE GLACÉE

engravings, apparently never executed. Lajoue was one of the leading exponents of the *genre pittoresque* in painting, and the present work is typically rococo in its spatial richness and variety, its light, elegant and open architecture, the profusion of curling shapes, hollowed niches and bulging counters, and its use of asymmetry both in detail and in the overall design. The canvas was not originally rectangular, but slightly shaped to fit into the decorative panelling, which can be seen in one of the drawings by Courtonne *fils*.

Prov: Joseph Bonnier de la Mosson (d.1744); his sale, Paris, 8 March 1745, no. 869
Lit: Kimball 1943, pp. 170-1, fig. 227; Roland-Michel 1975; Roland-Michel 1979, pp. 9-10, 15-20; Royal Academy 1968, No. 372; Watson 1960, p. 163
PC

A14 *Fontaine Glacée*
Jean Baptiste Guelard (active 1733-1755) after Jacques de Lajoue (1686-1761). 1736
Etching and engraving; 365 x 203
Lettered with title and *Lajoue Del. Guelard Sculps.*
VAM (229678.3)

From the suite *Livre Nouveau de Douze Morceaux de Fantaisie,* described in the

Mercure de France, as 'des sujets de fantaisies singulières et très élégantes' (May 1736). This plate transforms the airy structures of Watteau into *treillages* receding in space; the frozen water becomes a kind of *rocaille*. The plates in the suite are even more imaginative than those of Meissonnier.

Lit: BN:Fonds 45; Berlin 1939, 414 (1); Kimball 1943, pp. 171, 2, fig. 226
MS

A15 *Title page:* Quatrieme Livre de Formes Ornées de Rocailles
François-Antoine Aveline (b. 1718, active 1762) after Jean Mondon (active 1736-1760). 1736
Etching and engraving; 228 x 179
Lettered with title and *Cartels Figures Oyseaux et Dragons Chinois Invente par Mondon le Fils et Grave par Antoine Aveline 1736,* and with the addresses of Aveline and Mondon and the privilege
VAM (E.359-1952)

These plates are the first to combine Chinese figures with *genre pittoresque* ornament. The titles of Mondon's suites of 1736 seem to have been the first examples of the use of the word *rocaille* in its rococo sense.

Lit: BN: Fonds 6; Berlin 1939, 403(D)
MS

A16 *The visual arts*
François-Antoine Aveline (b. 1718, active 1762) after Jean Mondon (active 1736-1760). 1736
Etching; 222 x 172 (cut)
Lettered *Mondon le fils Invenit A. Aveline Sculpsit.*
VAM (29342.2)

Plate 2 of the suite *Livre de Trophée.* Anounced in the *Mercure de France,* April 1736. A drawing master and his pupil before whom is a figure of the Farnese Hercules, holding down with one foot a sheet of paper on which is drawn a *rocaille* scroll. The pupil appears to be scratching his head. The rear screen wall and the foreground contain more scrolls. Mondon's intention may be satirical.

Lit: BN: Fonds 4; Berlin 1939, 403B
MS

22

A17 *Leda*

Claude Duflos (1700-1786) after
François Boucher (1703-1770).
Before 1738
Etching and engraving; 490 x 251 (cut)
Lettered *F. Boucher invenit. Duflos
Sculpsit.*
VAM (13685.1)

Formerly lettered with title. From a
suite of five designs for screens by
Duflos and Cochin *fils* after Boucher,
one of which is entitled 'Rocaille'
(Jean-Richard 1978, 872) and shows a
combination of shelly substances,
shells, coral and water very similar to
the present print. Both prints and the
Triomphe de Pomone (ibid. 518) were
adapted for decorations in George
Bickham's *The Musical Entertainer* 1738
(vol. I, pp. 81-84, vol. II, p. 37). The
upper framework and hanging canopy
of vegetation look back to the
grotesque compositions of Watteau.

Lit: Jean-Richard 1978, 874
MS

A18 *Candelabrum*

Maker's mark of Claude Duvivier
(1688-1747). Designed by Juste Aurèle
Meissonnier (1695-1750)
Silver; h.390
Engraved on the knop with a crest of a
lion rampant within a garter
Musée des Arts Décoratifs, Paris

Three branch candelabrum, the base
of which is cast with spiralling scrolls
and flowers supporting a stem formed
as a three-sided scrolling spiral
baluster hung with a garland of
flowers, a moth and a cartouche, from
which rises the nozzle. The three
branches are cast as swirling leaves
terminating in drip-pans below the
nozzles, each of which is cast in a
different pattern. The whole is
surmounted by a separate finial cast as
a cluster of leaves. The design for the
candelabrum is related to figures
73-75 from the *Livre de Chandeliers de
Sculpture en Argent* engraved by
Huquier after Meissonnier (*Oeuvre*
fol. 31-33). The designs are undated
and in the opposite sense to the
candelabrum. It is therefore probable
that either Duvivier was working from
a drawing, now lost, supplied to him
by Meissonnier, or that the engraving
(made no earlier than 1738) is after a
drawing of the candelabrum made
following its completion no earlier

A18

than 1734 and possibly not until 1737
or 1738. Either way, it shows a close
relationship between goldsmith and
designer. The practice of showing all
three sides of a complex piece had
been used by Meissonnier before
(Cat. A12) and it should be noted that
the engraving of the Duke of
Kingston's tureen, for which a drawing
exists, is also in reverse. Meissonnier's
choice of goldsmith is inexplicable
since at the same date he also used the
services of others (Cat. C7). Claude
Duvivier was apprenticed at the age of
13 to Claude Villain and entered the
maîtrise in 1720. It has been suggested
that the crest on the knop is that of the
Duke of Kingston. Indeed, in the
memorandum of plate acquired by the
Duke on 1 March 1737 in Paris
there appear '2 Grands flambeaux
avec leur girandoles a trois branches'
weighing 28 marks 4 grains. The
candelabra were supplied with fittings
for two branches as well. However, the
description is vague enough to make a
positive identification impossible and
indeed there is disparity in the weight
given in 1737 (equivalent to
approximately 3430 grams each
candelabrum and three branches and
fittings) and the present weight
(approximately 3620 grams). It must
be assumed, however, that the same
candelabra were included in the
inventory of the Duke's silver in 1755
and there it clearly states, beneath the

reference to '2 large Candelsticks & 4
(sic) Treble branches, 4 Tops for
ornament & 15 Sockets', 'NB each
piece is marked with No.1'. On the
present candelabrum each piece is
marked 'N 1' (Hawley 1978, p. 235
and appendix II and X). Work on the
candelabrum cannot have been begun
before 18 September 1734 the date
that the warden's mark found on the
piece was instituted and it may have
been completed by 1 March 1737, if it
is accepted that it is one of the pair
bought by the Duke of Kingston at
that date, or 3 October 1738, when
the charge and discharge marks found
on the candelabrum were replaced at
the Paris assay office.

Prov: Evelyn Pierrepont; 2nd Duke of
Kingston, 1737-1773; Paris, Hôtel
Drouot, March 1911; Gaston Le
Breton, (Galerie Georges Petit 6-8
December 1921, 266); David David-
Weill.

Lit: Connaissance des Arts 1965, pp.105,
114; Davis 1970, fig. 161; Honour
1971, p.175; Hawley 1978, pp. 325-6
& fig. 2; Kimball 1942, p. 30; Kimball
1943, p. 156; Messelet 1937, pp. 71-
73; Nocq II 1927, p. 148; Nocq,
Alfassa & Guerin, I (n.d.), p. 28;
Rosenberg IV 1928, p. 107
CT

A19 *Design for a chimneypiece and overmantel*

Pierre Chenu (b. *c.* 1718) after Juste
Aurèle Meissonnier (1695-1750).
1738-49
Etching and engraving; 543 x 348
Lettered *P87 J.A. Meissonnier inv. Chenu
Sculp. Cabinet de Mr le Comte de Bielenski
Grand Maréchale de la Couronne de Pologne
executé en 1734* and with the address of
Gabriel Huquier
The Duke of Norfolk

One of 14 sheets of prints from the
Oeuvres de Juste Aurèle Meissonnier
(published together by Huquier,
c. 1749) which are associated with 17
sheets from the *Grand Oppenord*.
Several of the suites are stitched together. The
Oppenord plate lettered 'RR CVII' is
inscribed in the hand of the 9th
Duchess of Norfolk (d. 1771) 'French
Designs [crossed out] of Finishings of
Rooms'. For the rococo interiors at
Norfolk House, see cat. B16. When
exhibited in an unspecified form at
the Tuileries in 1736, prior to the

23

Cabinet's removal to Warsaw, the *Mercure de France* described the room as 'D'une construction absolument nouvelle'. The elaborate combination of carving, modelling and painting, the broken and heavily sculptural mouldings and the trompe l'oeil painted ceiling with its simulated architecture are entirely opposed to the restrained and contained lines of contemporary French rococo interiors. A drawing for the ceiling is at the Cooper-Hewitt Museum.

Lit: Berlin 1939, 378; Kimball 1943, p. 159; Nyberg 1969, p. 21; Roland-Michel 1979, pp. 6, 7; Roland-Michel 1982, pp. 69, 71
MS

A20 *Design for a dining room or cabinet*

Nicolas Pineau (1684-1754). 1738
Pen and ink; 373 x 533
Inscribed with notes and *Fond de la salle à manger de Monsieur Boutin disposé ausy pour servir de cabinet.*

Musée des Arts Décoratifs, Paris (29.130)

In the left alcove is a wall fountain and in the right a small commode. A bed is shown through the open leaf of the centre door. Pineau was primarily responsible for the introduction of the *genre pittoresque* into French interiors from the early 1730s onwards; this is a comparatively restrained example, with only the main lines indicated. The rectilinear *boiserie* panels, alternately wide and narrow, which had been in use since the beginning of the century are here broken by free and graceful curved mouldings.

Prov: E. Biais (Lugt 1921, 363)
Lit: Deshairs n.d., No. 7331, pl. XXXVI; Kimball 1943, p. 169
MS

A21 *Design for a cartouche*

Pierre-Ědmě Babel (1720-1770). *c.* 1740
Engraving and etching; 300 x 192 (cut)
Lettered with the privilege, the address of Jacques Chereau and *Babel invenit et Sculpsit.* Numbered *4*
VAM (E.1905-1931)

From the suite *Cartouches pour estre acompagnés de Suports et trophées.* This plate may have influenced plate 7 of Matthias Lock's *Book of Shields,* 1747, (Heckscher 1979, pl. 15c).

Lit: BN: Fonds 55; Berlin 1939, 422 (4)
MS

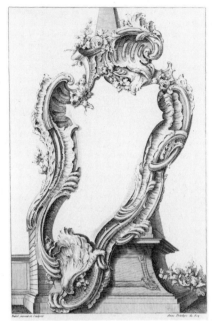

A21

A22 *Commode*

Hubert Hansen (maître-ébéniste 1747-1756). Paris *c.* 1750
Oak, veneered with kingwood; gilt bronze mounts; veined green and white marble top; h. 910, w. 1840, depth 730
Stamped *H.HANSEN* and *JME,* the monogram of the Guild. Bearing the trade label of the *marchand-mercier* Darnault
Private Collection

The commode, which contains two drawers in the front and cupboards in the splayed ends, is of unusual form. The standard French rococo commode contains two large superimposed drawers extending over its entire front, and is supported on relatively low feet. Cat. A22 almost has the character of a console-table serving to support the exceptionally thick and beautiful marble slab. It can be dated fairly accurately because Hansen only worked as a master cabinet-maker for a few years. The plain quartered kingwood veneers are slightly old-fashioned for the period. Much French furniture of the mid-eighteenth century is veneered with floral marquetry or Oriental lacquer. The gilt-bronze mounts, and especially the central keyhole escutcheon and the corner-mounts, are of highly asymmetrical design and of outstanding quality. The rules of the Guilds did not allow Parisian cabinet-makers to make their mounts themselves; they had to be made by the bronze founders who belonged to a separate Guild, and then be gilded by specialist gilders. The beauty of the mounts was one of the principal reasons why Parisian furniture was admired and acquired all over Europe throughout the eighteenth century.

Prov: Baron Mayer Amschel de Rothschild, Mentmore, Buckinghamshire; Earls of Rosebery; Sotheby's, Mentmore, 18-20 May 1977, 141, ill.
Lit: Mentmore 1884, Vol. I, p. 40, No. 21
RB

A22

I *Bureau cabinet.* German (Dresden). *c.* 1750. *Victoria & Albert Museum.* See cat. A25.

II *Capitano Cerimonia and Signora Lauinia*
Andien de Clermont
From a set of wall panels depicting
subjects from Jacques Callot's 'Balli di
Sfessania' etchings. 1742
Private Collection
See cat. C12

III *Teapot*
Anonymous 'A' marked group
*c.*1745-60
The scene after Hubert Gravelot *Songs
in the Opera Flora,* 1737
Victoria & Albert Museum
See cat. D2

IV *Ewer and basin*
George Wickes. 1735/6
Private Collection
See cat. C4

V *Self-portrait with his pug*
William Hogarth. 1745
The Tate Gallery
See cat. E3

VI *Covent Garden*
Peter Angellis. *c.*1726
*The Marquess of Tavistock and Trustees of
the Bedford Estates, Woburn Abbey*
See cat. E1

VII *Vauxhall Gardens*
Antonio Canaletto. *c.*1750
Private Collection
See cat. F14

VIII *Masqueraders*
Chelsea (Lawrence Street factory)
c. 1760-69
Private Collection
See cat. F43

A23

A23 *Title page:* Livre Nouveau
de Paneaux a divers Usages
Carl Albert de Lespilliez (1723-1796)
after Jean François Cuvilliés (1695-
1768). *c.* 1740?
Etching and engraving; 330 x 218 (cut)
Lettered with title, privilege and *invente*
par François Cuvillies Conseiller et Architecte
and with his titles and *C.A. de Lespilliez*
Scu Mon. N.6
VAM (24894.2)

The first suite after the designs of
Cuvilliés, principal architect to the
Elector of Bavaria, was published in
1737. This is the sixth suite. Although
he had been trained in France in the
1720s Cuvilliés' interpretation of the
genre pittoresque was markedly wilder
and more extreme than the French
version of the style, and may have
played a role in influencing the design
of English rococo carving.

Lit: Berlin 1939, 121 (6); Laran 1924,
p. 5
MS

A24 *Design for a vase*
Jacob Gottlieb Thelot (1708-1760)
after Christian Friderich Rudolph
(1692-1754). *c.* 1750
Engraving and etching; 280 x 175
Lettered *Einige Vases mit modernen*
Einfassungen untersschiedl. Liebhabern u:
Kunstlern zu Dienst. Christian Friderich
Rudolph Haered. Ier Wolffij inv. et excud.
Aug. Vindel. Jacob Gottlieb Thelot Sculps.
C.P.S.C. Maj.
VAM (E.1870-1948)

The comparatively modest title page
of a suite of vase designs of wild
asymmetry. This plate may have
influenced John Linnell (see Cat. G42);
the fantastic and spiky rococo
ornament in Augsburg prints is close
to English rococo carvers' designs.

Lit: Berlin 1939; 975(1); Berliner &
Egger 1981, 1386
MS

A25 *Bureau cabinet*

German (Dresden). *c.* 1750
Kingwood, inlaid with mother-of-pearl, brass and ivory, and decorated with ormolu mounts
2730 x 1270 x 740
Bearing the cypher of Augustus III, King of Poland and Elector of Saxony (1696-1763)
VAM (W.63-1977)

A cabinet with doors supported on a base, incorporating a slope-front bureau above four drawers. The cabinet interior is fitted with drawers and a central cupboard compartment above which are giltwood female figures holding a sceptre and sword (now missing) on either side of a cartouche bearing the AR cypher below a royal crown. The bureau section is fitted with drawers and a central revolving section, with one front ornamented with an ormolu balustrade incorporating another AR cypher. There are three important elements to the design of this piece: firstly, the asymmetrical twist given to the architectural elements such as the pilaster capitals (which are of the Composite order), the broken scroll pediment and the ornamental cartouches of the undulating facade; secondly, the abandoned naturalism of the sculptural ormolu, in which roses frame the strictly two-dimensional inlay of acanthus and flowers executed in shimmering pink-green mother-of-pearl on a trellis parquetry ground; thirdly, the palms and laurels of triumph and peace on the commode base and the interior, the cyphers and royal crown and the women holding the sceptre and sword, indicate that this is a piece of state furniture. It is likely to have been made shortly after 1750 for Augustus III, King of Poland and Elector of Saxony, and it has been attributed to the Court cabinet-maker Michael Kümmel. In terms of its sophistication of design, the variety of virtuoso technical skills involved, and its sheer expensiveness, this is the most outstanding piece of German rococo furniture. Its nearest rival is perhaps the bureau-cabinet produced by Christian Friderich Lehmann in 1755 for Frederick V of Denmark and which is now at Rosenborg Castle, Copenhagen.

Prov: Augustus III, Alexander Barker,

dealer; bought by Baron Mayer Amschel de Rothschild in 1835
Lit: Hase 1983, p. 291; Sotheby's 19 May 1977, 905
JH

A26 *Design for a mirror*

Johann Esaias Nilson (1721-1788). 1756
Pen and ink and wash, incised for transfer; 247 x 180
Signed and dated *inv: et dessiné p: J.E. Nilson 1756*
VAM (E.265-1946)

Engraved by Nilson with the title 'Trumeau de Glace Orné avec les quatres parties de la Vie humaine'. The feathery *rocaille* and the out-of-scale human figures are typical of the hundreds of rococo ornament prints published in Augsburg. For Nilson's influence in England see Cat. O48

Lit: Berlin 1939, 165 (X); Jessen 1924, pl. 140
MS

A27

A27 *Le Damier*

Charles-Germain de Saint-Aubin (1721-1786)
Etching; 182 x 277
Lettered with title
VAM (E.482-1982)

From the suite *Premier Essai de Papilloneries Humaines*. The character of the ornament strongly suggests a parody of German rococo prints (cf. Cat. A26). Saint-Aubin was primarily a designer of embroidered textiles.

Lit: de Baudicour 1859, 4
MS

A28 *Figure group*

German (Nymphenburg, modelled by Franz Anton Bustelli) *c.* 1759
Glazed white hard-paste porcelain; h. 273
Mark: the shield of the arms of Bavaria impressed on a scroll cartouche at the rear of a column
VAM (C.21-1946)

A picnic is taking place on a fantastic scrollwork mountain at the summit of which sits a lady in hunting clothes. She recoils from a man in a tricorn hat and hunting clothes who is carving a ham. Behind them is a column surmounted by an asymmetrical *rocaille* moulded base. At the base of the scrollwork mountain are three dogs and a dead roe-deer and hare. This piece represents in extreme form the refinement of South German rococo. Designed evidently as a table centre, it presents satisfactory views from all sides and the unusually elaborate scrollwork base encourages with its spiral movement a desire to explore these different viewpoints. The modeller, Franz Anton Bustelli, seems to have had a particularly close relationship with the engraver J.E. Nilson of Augsburg, who dedicated a print to him. The same extreme combination of naturalistic figures with formalised scrollwork settings is found in Nilson's work which was sometimes copied in England (Cat. A26). The only other two examples of this group that appear to be recorded both stem from the Royal Collection of Bavaria and are both white. One of them has a third figure of a huntsman blowing a horn. See Hoffmann 1921-3, vol. I, fig. 115, 116, and vol. III pp. 451-453. Hofmann says that this group was first delivered to the salerooms of the factory in 1759 and is recorded (in its three figure version) in the model list of 1760. It was not however listed in the 1767 price list.

Prov: Mr H.E. Bäcker. Bought with the Murray Bequest Fund
Lit: Hofmann 1921-3; Ruckert 1963
JVGM

English Rococo and its Continental Origins

Michael Snodin

The word rococo, like many designations of style, began life as a term of ridicule. Apparently devised in the studio of J.L. David in 1796-7 'pour désigner le goût à la mode pendant le règne de Louis XV', it was used in the same derogatory sense by Stendhal in 1828. As an adjective, in 1842, it denoted 'tout ce qui est vieux est hors de mode'.[1] Its career as an art-historical term began in the 1840s, and since that time, the word, the style it defines, and the origins of that style have been the subject of debate and disagreement. It is, however, generally conceded that rococo as an international style of architecture and decoration arose in the first half of the eighteenth century; the chief debates concern the origins of the national versions, in particular the influences of Italy in France and of France in Germany.[2] The shift of the word away from its perjorative sense, since the 1940s, has coincided with its expansion to cover painting, sculpture, literature and music, which from about 1700 onwards had begun to express a new mood of intimacy, elegance, colour and movement.

It is as a description of a style of decoration that rococo is most easy to define. The general lightening of the heavy baroque style of Louis XIV was signalled by the King himself in his statement to his architect Mansard in 1698: 'Il faut qu'il y ait de la jeunesse mêlée dans ce que l'on fera'.[3] The decorative painter Claude Audran lightened the ornament known as the grotesque, a Renaissance revival of an ancient Roman form, which, with its fantastic and illogical framework inhabited by human and other creatures was to be very influential in the rococo. The new mood of relaxation was most clearly expressed by Jean-Antoine Watteau, who further refined the grotesque (Cat. A7), and developed the genre of the *fête galante* (Cat. A6). These dream-like scenes of dalliance, essentially without subject, proclaimed an art determined not by rules but by sensibility, which set the tone for later rococo painting, and also for types of rococo ornament.

The *style régence* (a modern term), which is sometimes seen as a phase of the rococo, extended beyond the Regency proper (1715-1723) up to about 1730. Its principal painter was Watteau, but its chief designer of ornaments was Gilles-Marie Oppenord, who had studied in Italy in the 1690s, taking particular notice of the Roman high baroque of Bernini and Borromini. Many characteristics of the succeeding French style, known at the time as the *genre pittoresque*, were set in this period, including the development of the grotesque framework into C and S scrolls and its extension into furniture and other moveables (Cat. C10, A9, A10). Asymmetry, generally a rare phenomenon in ornamental art, also began to appear, first of all in cartouches which echoed their Italian baroque predecessors (Cat. A11).

The *genre pittoresque* (also called *le goût baroque*), has perhaps the best claim to be identified as rococo. It added two principal elements to the *régence* style, a protean rock-like watery and shelly substance known as *rocaille*, and an extreme use of asymmetry. It was this style, breaking all the rules of reason and restraint in ornament, which brought on the flood of criticism, beginning in 1731[4], which is our chief source of contemporary attitudes to the rococo.[5] Its major exponent was Juste Aurèle Meissonnier, a brilliant designer trained as a gold chaser. His candlestick of 1728 (Cat. A12), one of the earliest recorded examples of the *genre pittoresque*, exemplifies the style. Its asymmetry is such that it has to be shown in three prints, and the main stem and base are composed of one flowing mass of ribbed ornament close to *rocaille*.

The word *rocaille* was devised in the seventeenth century to denote the rocky materials used in the formation of artificial caves. The *rocaille* of the *genre pittoresque* was partly descended from the fleshy substance of the seventeenth century auricular style (Cat. G4), themselves associated with fishy and cave-dwelling creatures. Very similar forms were used in Italian late baroque metal and plasterwork (Cat. A3-5). The influence of the Italian baroque on the style of Meissonnier (whose earliest work was in Turin) was noted by his detractors, who linked him with the *bizarre* work of Borromini.[6] Meissonnier's designs for interiors (Cat. A19) were probably too extreme for native French taste. The *genre pittoresque* style in French interiors was set by Nicolas Pineau, who took to an extreme point the conception of a room panelled in *boiseries*, formed as a flowing, almost structureless, whole (Cat. A20).

The most characteristic production of the *genre pittoresque* was probably the ornamental print. The earliest suite to be published, Meissonnier's *Livre D'Ornemens* of 1734, (Cat. C17) represents an entirely new genre, the *morceau de fantaisie*, an ornamental print without overt practical purpose. At their publication the *Mercure de France* commented:

> Il paroit une suite d'Estampes en large, dans le goût d'Etienne la Belle [Cat. A1], qui doivent piquer la curiosité du Public et de Curieux du meilleur goût. Ce sont des Fontaines, des Cascades, des Ruines, des Rocailles, et Coquillages, des morceaux d'Architecture qui font des effets bizarres, singuliers et pittoresques, par leurs formes piquantes et extraordinaires, dont souvent aucune partie ne répond à l'autre, sans que le sujet en paroisse moins riche et moins agréable.[7]

This suite was succeeded by others, chiefly of *Morceaux*, after Jacques de Lajoue (1734, Cat. A14, C4), François Boucher (1736, Cat. A17), Jean Mondon (1736, Cat. A15, 16) and Pierre Edmé Babel (*c.*1740, Cat. A21). These prints of dream structures and cartouches in three dimensions often of illogical scale were derived not only from earlier French grotesques and Watteau, but also from Italian theatrical design (Cat. A4). They were extremely influential abroad, particularly in Germany, where the genre reached its highest expression (Cat. A28).

The 'effets bizarres singuliers et pittoresques' were soon to attract specific comment. In 1737 Blondel decried the 'amas ridicule de coquilles, de dragons, de roseaux, de palmiers et de plantes'[8] which appeared in interior decoration. The first major attack was that of the Abbé le Blanc published in 1745 and in English translation in 1747:

> A cupid is the contrast of a dragon; and a shell, of a bat's wing ; they no longer observe any order, any probability, in their productions. They heap cornices, bases, columns, cascades, rushes and rocks, in a confused manner, one upon another; and in some corner of this chaos, they will place a cupid in a great fright, and have a festoon of flowers above the whole. And this is what they call designs of a new taste.[9]

English rococo ornament was derived from the French *genre pittoresque*, but it was preceded by the adoption in England of several of the Continental movements discussed above. The role of immigrant craftsmen and artists was crucial. Some, like Huguenots, were escaping persecution, but others were invited or were simply exploiting the weakness of native talent and the wealth of English patrons. Italian late-baroque styles were imported by immigrant mural painters and *stuccadori*, theatrical designers, and architects who had visited Italy (Cat. B6). The pattern book of 1736-7 by the mural painter Gaetano Brunetti (Cat. B11), which is sometimes claimed to be the first English rococo pattern book is in fact in this Italian style. Other symptons of this taste for the baroque, reaching into the 1730s, were the re-issues of suites of Continental baroque ornament prints, (Cat. C3) and a fondness for monumental furniture (most of which was probably imaginary) in conversation pieces and state portraits (Cat. B7, B12).

The influential architectural style from 1715 onwards was, of course, Palladian, which, with its close adherence to rules and Italian models, earned the praise of the French detractors of the rococo (Cat. B2). The Palladian interior could be as controlled as the exterior (Cat. B3), but William Kent designed in the 1720s and 1730s furniture and decoration based on Classical forms with a strong admixture of the baroque (Cat. B8).

The influence of immigrant painters was widely felt in England in the first half of the century, and some of them imported the new intimate manner. The most illustrious was Watteau himself, who came in 1719 to consult Dr Mead, who later bought two of his paintings. Watteau's style was popularised in the 1720s and 30s by a number of lesser immigrant talents,[10] including Pieter Angillis, (Cat. E1), Andien de Clermont (Cat. C12), J.F. Nollekens, and Phillip Mercier (Cat. C2), and made a major contribution to the formation of the English genre of the conversation piece. At the same time large numbers of foreign, chiefly French, engravers arrived, starting with Nicolas Dorigny in 1711 (See Cat. C1).

It is against this background, and the constant English dependence on France for articles of fashion (Cat. C7, 15, 22, 24), that the first stirrings of rococo, known as 'modern' or 'modern French', should be seen. The earliest evidence, in about 1731,[11] is in the silver of Paul De Lamerie, a second-generation Huguenot. His version of the style, distinctly auricular in feeling, is not directly indebted to *genre pittoresque* silver, and may have been developed from French *régence* pieces now lost. George Wickes's basin of 1735/6 (Cat. C4), is the earliest evidence of the importation of *genre pittoresque* prints. Of the same date are the *genre pittoresque* cartouches, of original design but unknown authorship, which decorated Jean Rocque's maps from 1735 onwards (Cat. B2).

The French draughtsman and engraver Hubert Gravelot was endowed, according to Vertue (III, p. 105), 'with a great fruitfull genius for desseins inventions of history and ornaments', and was certainly a major influence in the English adoption of the *genre pittoresque*. He arrived in 1732, invited by Claude du Bosc to engrave his edition of Bernard Picart's *Ceremonies and Religious Customs of . . . the Known World*. His ornament in these volumes is *régence* in character. The change to *genre pittoresque* had occurred by about 1735, and his early version of the style, rather heavy and architectural, seems to have been indebted to Meissonnier's *Livre D'Ornemens* of 1734 (Cat. D7).[12] By 1738 Gravelot had developed a lighter ornamental style of gently-curved bands, often interlaced and leaf-fringed (Cat. D5). It survived, particularly in book decorations, long after his departure in 1745/6.

The French ornamental prints available in England in 1737 and 1738 are demonstrated by the headpieces in that brilliant work of plagiarism, George Bickham's *Musical Entertainer*. They included *genre pittoresque* prints by Boucher, Mondon, de Lajoue and Meissonnier (the *Livre D'Ornemens*) as well as prints by and after Watteau from the *receuil Julienne* and Boucher's illustrations to the 1734 edition of the works of Molière. It is possible that Bickham had contacts with the great French publisher Gabriel Huquier,[13] who issued most of the *genre pittoresque* suites and who made at least one plate used as a title page in England (Cat. C9). Also of 1737 are the cartouches in Edward Hoppus's *Gentleman's and Builder's Repository*, derived from de Lajoue and Brunetti as well as unidentified sources.[14]

Parallel with these ornamental developments was the gradual introduction into prints and book illustrations of elegant figures in the French manner. The chief influence was Gravelot, whose very early example, the View of the Hermitage in Richmond Gardens of 1735,[15] includes figures related to his costume prints. It was followed in 1736 by the extraordinary view of Richmond Lodge by J.B.C. Chatelain (Cat. C6) in which most of the figures and their composition are adapted from Watteau's *L'Embarquement pour Cythere* (Cat. A6). These prints, and those of other immigrant engravers such as Francis Vivares (Cat. D11) are examples of a new free etching style introduced in the 1730s.

Gravelot's easy and elegant handling and composition, both of which can be described as rococo in character, were probably his chief contributions to English art. Not only did he introduce a new type of figure (Cat. D15, 16), but placed it in French rococo settings (Cat. D18). His influence on painters and book illustrators was widespread, but was most strongly felt in his immediate circle, in the work of such artists as Francis Hayman and Thomas Gainsborough, and those who attended his drawing school in the Strand or the St Martin's Lane Academy.

The Academy in St Martin's Lane had been founded in 1735, 'principally promoted' by William Hogarth, who contributed the furnishings of the academy of his father-in-law, Sir James Thornhill. It met in the premises previously occupied by the academy of Louis Cheron and John Vanderbank, itself an offshoot of the first official art academy in Britain, that of Sir Godfrey Kneller, founded in 1711. The principal purpose of the St Martin's Lane Academy, as that of its predecessors, was the teaching of life drawing (Cat. E9), and until the foundation of the Royal Academy in 1768, it was the chief school for British artists. The extent to which the Academy went beyond this function is difficult to judge. An advertisement noted by George Vertue in 1745[16] described it as an 'Academy of Painting and Sculpture', listed 'Mr Hayman (History painter &c) Mr Gravelot (designer [i.e. draughtsman]), Mr Moser (chaser) Mr Rubilliac (Statuary) Mr Yeo (Seal Graver) Mr . . . (landskip painter) Mr Wills (portrait painter Treasurer)', and stated that the academy met 'for the study of drawing'. The list of names suggests that any ornamental drawing which was carried out was perhaps limited to sculpture and metalwork with a strong figurative bias and to the 'designing' of Gravelot. Apart from one nineteenth-century reference and the furniture in his book illustrations (which may be entirely fanciful) there is no evidence that Gravelot extended his designing beyond metalwork (Cat. H4, 5) and a single scheme for sculpture.[17]

There are, however, significant stylistic links between the work of the artists named, extending beyond the figures and composition (more or less influenced by Gravelot) to the rococo ornament used by Gravelot, Moser and Yeo. Numerous other links can also be made between teachers and pupils connected with the academy, such as Hayman, Moser and Grignion (Gravelot's pupil) (Cat. E16) and Roubiliac and another pupil of Gravelot (Cat. S6). The interior designs of the architect James Paine (Cat. M6) not only show a strong debt to Gravelot, but also the involvement of Francis Hayman. The same style is also evident in the ideal schemes of Samuel Wale (an Academy pupil) and James Gwynn, who were Paine's tenants.

The placing of many of these rococo artists and architects among the cosmopolitan habitués of Slaughter's Coffee House, also in St Martin's Lane (Cat. E10), was first expounded in a series of seminal articles by Mark Girouard.[18] The atmosphere at Slaughter's is brought out by such stories as that of Henry Fielding imitating Roubiliac's accent or Gravelot receiving a box on the face from Andien de Clermont for making slighting remarks about Clermont's patron Sir Andrew Fountaine. It is clear from these and other accounts that Gravelot was well aware of his artistic superiority. Girouard also set out for the first time the links with Vauxhall Gardens, which included Hogarth's key role, Roubiliac's 'Handel', Hayman's great series of supper box paintings, Gravelot's music sheets, Yeo's entrance tickets and Moser's design for the Music Room (Cat. E17). The last, is, however, one of the very few recorded architectural features of Vauxhall that can be described as rococo in a strictly ornamental sense; others were the pillared saloon and the Chinese pavilions.

After about 1740 the English rococo ornamental style underwent a marked change, which was probably unconnected with the Slaughter's set, indebted as it was to Gravelot for its ornament. Except for goldsmiths' work and prints, the French *genre pittoresque* had left English applied art of the 1730s largely unaffected. William Jones's *The Gentleman's or Builder's Companion* (1739) showed heavily-modelled pier-tables[19] which could be regarded as a sympton of the taste for the baroque already noticed. In 1740, however, Langley copied *régence* table designs by Pineau (Cat. C10), as well as late baroque German pieces, which probably show a desire to find new and novel styles.

The earliest evidence of the new manner is the goldsmiths's invitation card dated 1742 engraved by Henry Copland (Cat. D29c). Copland, who was almost certainly trained as a silver engraver[20], had produced a card in 1738 close to the manner of Gravelot (Cat. D29a). His new card, much more spiky and metallic in feeling is very much closer to French models, such as those of Babel. The new style was to dominate prints, and the applied arts until the 1760s, and was the basis of that extravagant carvers' work which is regarded as probably the most characteristic expression of the English rococo.

The earliest dated example of English rococo carving is a picture frame of 1742 by Paul Petit (Cat. L1). While showing the concern with animal life and symbolism ultimately derived from the grotesque that was so important in the English rococo, it is largely *régence* in style. Matthias Lock's *Six Sconces* of 1744 (Cat. L4) show the new English style as well developed, and already wilder, more extravagant and inventive than any French furniture model.

Lock's sources are complex, and include Oppenord, and in another context Jean Berain. The pattern books of Gideon Saint (Cat. L72), Thomas Johnson (Cat. L44) and Chippendale show that Berain, Boulle, Toro and other pre-rococo designers were much consulted, but the concept and example of the *morceau de fantaisie* often combined with a cartouche, the first English example of which was engraved in 1741 (Cat. C11), was obviously important, as Copland's suite of 1746 (Cat. L16) demonstrates. The closest Continental parallels lie in Germany, not only in existing pieces, but in prints, which began to appear in 1737 with the first sets after Cuvilliés (Cat. A3). Their role, however, is uncertain[21] and it is possible that the imaginative leap performed by Copland and the English carvers and craftsmen was an independent and largely native achievement.

The unprecedented outburst of pattern books, both general and specialised, which accompanied the new style was one expression of the enormous increase in the number of prints of all kinds which had begun in the 1730s encouraged by the copyright act of 1735, at first engraved largely by foreigners, and then increasingly in the 1740s by native engravers. The engravers of trade cards, using a fast etching technique calculated to resemble engraving, took full advantage of the new style. The same engravers and publishers, such as Francis Vivares, also sold and copied a wide range of foreign ornamental prints, and those of the second wave of foreign immigrant ornamentalists, such as Jean Pillement (Cat. R6) and Peter Babel (Cat. L22) and Peter Glazier (Cat. H16).

The complexity of the rococo style must have placed an unaccustomed burden on the drawing skills of the executant craftsmen. From the 1730s onwards there was not only an increase in the number of drawing manuals, but also in the number of drawing masters active in London, some of whom, like Thomas Johnson, were also craftsmen. Others, like Jacob Bonneau and Francis Vivares were engravers and print-sellers. From 1756 the Society of Arts, founded two years earlier, began to award premiums for drawings for manufacturers. These awards to 'children' (in fact girls and boys under 18) were deplored by Hogarth, but reflected an increasing concern with the importance of drawing in the improvement of manufactured goods, especially in the battle against imported French products. The surviving drawings for these early competitions (Cat. E21), are ironically, and perhaps significantly, copies of the latest French drawing-school prints. They include the most frequent craftsman's drawing exercise of the period, the raffle-leaf, a leaf with raffled or cut edges. Matthias Lock's exercise in this form (Cat. E19), dating from 1740s, had an ancestry in the *régence* and even earlier. Ince and Mayhew (Cat. M21), showing a very similar twisting leaf, connect it with Hogarth's *Line of Beauty*.

Hogarth's treatise (Cat. E6), conceived in the 1740s and published in 1753, was the first investigation of a theory of beauty based on observation of actual forms rather than abstract theory. Although the book is not a theory of the rococo, ignoring as it does the basis of the *genre pittoresque*, Hogarth nevertheless found in many of the manufactured objects around him support for his championship of the serpentine 'Line of Beauty and Grace': 'there is scarce a room in any house whatever, where one does not see a waving line employed in some way or other'. Hogarth's early training in baroque ornament, which he continued to employ in his paintings and designs (Cat. E7), must have made him sympathetic to rococo.

The first attack on English rococo coincided with Cochin's famous piece of 1755[22]. André Rouquet, the miniaturist and friend of Hogarth, noted:

The taste called *contrast*, a taste so ridiculous and whimsical, when applied to objects susceptible of symmetry, has reached as far as England, where it every day produces, as it does elsewhere, some new monster. This taste, which men of indifferent talents adopt without feeling, and apply without judgment, could never be borne, had it not been for the superior abilities of the famous artist [i.e. Meissonnier] that invented it.[23]

In the same year *The World* (Number CXVII) observed characteristically that 'there is no difficulty in being merely whimsical'. In 1756 the style was reproved by its secret admirer Isaac Ware (see Cat. M6) chiefly because it was the taste of the French, 'a frivolous people whom we are too apt to imitate': 'It consists of crooked lines like C's and ꓛC's, the *Gothick* is hardly more contemptible'.

In spite of Abbé le Blanc's statement that in England the greatest goldsmith was merely a craftsman whereas Meissonnier and Germain were architects and sculptors,[24] the main thrust of the French attacks on the rococo was that its irrationality was a reflection of its instigators, craftsmen and decorators who set themselves up as architects in the service of the ostentatious and tasteless. The precise composition of the English patrons of the rococo has yet to be fully determined, but it appears likely that the style was at least as popular, if not more so, among middle-class townsmen as it was among the country house-owning upper classes. It also seems probable that the impetus for its development in England may have been greatly encouraged by the craftsmen themselves, who would not only profit from the greater complication of works in the new style, but would also have little difficulty in creating new designs in a style which was essentially organic and fanciful.

Two other styles rose with the rococo in England: Chinese and gothic. The former, had, of course been popular in a restrained form since the previous century, but Chinese elements had been introduced into French *morceaux de fantaisie* (Cat. A15). In England the style appears to have become a popular craze about 1750, coinciding with its combination with *rocaille* and *genre pittoresque* elements. Gothic, which, like Chinese, also began in garden buildings and other structures, cannot in most of these cases be called rococo in the strict sense. In furnishings, however, it was combined by the 1750s with rococo forms to create a curious hybrid, often in conjunction with Chinese (Cat. R4).

The most complete conjunction of all these elements can be seen in the mid-eighteenth century garden, with its Classical, Chinese and gothic buildings ruins and grottoes, set in grounds in which asymmetrical elements and serpentine paths abound. Asymmetry, which had the appeal both of Classical and Chinese gardening precedent, was part of a conscious return to nature.[25] The serpentine path (Cat. B2) had appeared in English gardens by 1718, before the conception of the *genre pittoresque*, so cannot strictly speaking be called rococo.

There is no doubt, however, that these playful and yet serious gardens, can be seen as part of the taste which admired the *genre pittoresque*. The rococo was but one style set against a Palladian background. Very few English interiors were wholeheartedly rococo in style, but a man might have a rococo pier glass, a set of chairs, a coffee pot, or a book-plate, and could, as at Claydon, choose to sit in the gothic room, the Chinese room, or the French or rococo room.

Title page of *A New Book of Ornaments*. See cat. B15.

B1 *Frontispiece to Edward Oakley,* The Magazine of Architecture, Perspective and Sculpture

Benjamin Cole after Edward Oakley (active 1721-1756). 1730 (?)
Engraving and etching; 321 x 214
Lettered *A Practical Treatise on the 5 Orders of Ancient Architecture By A. Bosse. Beauty, Solid, Practice, Theory, Conveniency, Reason Above All Edwardus Oakley Delineavit. Benjamin. Cole Sculp.*

VAM (E.3026-1913)

An aedicule before which is an ionic portico. The architectural virtues, the exemplification of Palladianism, are, with the exception of 'Conveniency' and 'Reason Above All', represented as female figures. The latter is in the centre, beneath a figure of Minerva. Oakley dedicated the book to Sir Robert Walpole, and pursued a consistently Palladian line in the text.

Lit: Colvin 1978, p. 599
MS

B2 *Plan du Jardin & Vüe des Maisons de Chiswick*

Jean Rocque (d. 1762). 1736
Engraving and etching; 605 x 775
Lettered with the title, dedication to Lord Burlington, a publication line dated 1736 and *J. Rocque del: et Sculp.*
Dr Terry Friedman

One of a series of plans of parks published by Rocque from 1735 onwards, ten of which were published in Vitruvius Britannicus 1739, all of which have rococo title cartouches; those for 1736 (including Chiswick, Hampton Court and Richmond Gardens) being among the earliest in English prints. The lettering suggests that they were designed by Rocque, but other possible candidates are J.B.C. Chatelain and Hubert Gravelot. The cartouche on this plan contrasts curiously with the 13 views of garden buildings and the famous Palladian villa (built *c.* 1723-9) which surround it. The garden combines the straight avenues of the earlier scheme laid out before 1725, with the meandering serpentine paths introduced by Kent in the 1720s.

Lit: Nottingham 1973, 72; Orleans House 1982, 93; Vitruvius Britannicus 1739, pls 82, 83; Willis 1977, pl. 56
MS

B3 *A family in an interior*

Joseph Francis Nollekens (1702-1748). 1740
Oil on canvas; 863 x 1092
Signed and dated *J. Nollekens F. 1740*
Private Collection
See colour plate XVII

In the centre a young and an older man are playing cards with a woman, who is holding an open snuff box. Also present are six men, three women and an infant boy. The room is Palladian, with a Venetian window. The chimney-piece incorporates a painting, apparently of Pandora opening an urn, accompanied by Mercury, a youth (Epimetheus?) and a bearded man (Vulcan?), which should perhaps be connected with the open snuff box. This group portrait has been identified as Lord Tylney and his family and friends, on the basis of a document linking it with the sale in 1822 of the contents of Wanstead House (built *c.* 1714-20, demolished 1824), which was designed by Colen Campbell for Sir Richard Child, later the 1st Earl Tylney. Further support for this identification is lent by another version of the painting, with some different figures, in the possession of a descendant of the Long family, one of whom inherited Wanstead in 1784 through marriage with Lord Tylney's daughter. The room, however, cannot be connected with any at Wanstead, in which Venetian windows only occurred in the unexecuted tower additions designed by Campbell in 1720. Its decorative features nevertheless have parallels in a number of Palladian interiors, especially those designed by William Kent (*c.* 1726-31) at Campbell's Houghton (eg Rysbrack's figures of Peace and Plenty in the Saloon and the swags and panels in the Stone Hall) and the hall at Ditchley probably also designed by Kent (cf. also the 'Design for a Cube Room' in Kent 1727). Nollekens is here modifying his Watteauesque figure style to fit with that of the English conversation piece as it was popularised by Hogarth and Gawen Hamilton. Tylney was his chief English patron. Hogarth's well known *Assembly at Wanstead House* (1729-31, Philadelphia Museum of Art) appears to show the ballroom.

Prov: 1st Earl Tylney (?) (d. 1750);

Tylney family by descent (?); Wanstead House Sale, Robins, June 1822, 10th day, 318 (?): 'Nollekens – Interior of Saloon of Wanstead House with an Assemblage of Ladies and Gentlemen. A Conversazione'; Sir William Henry Salt, Bt.; Canon Arthur Evans; John Evans; Summer Fields School, Oxford; Arthur Tooth 1976
Lit: Country Life, 22 June 1967, p. 1612; Kimball 1933; Liversidge 1972, pp. 37-8, fig. 8
MS

B4 *A perspective view of the inside of the Grand Assembly Room in Blake Street York*

William Lindley. 1759
Engraving and etching and wash; 478 x 514
Lettered with the title, copyright line dated November 1759 and *Ld Burlington Archt. W. Lindley Delin. et Sculp*
York City Art Gallery

The Assembly Room, probably the most uncompromising English 18th century attempt to follow purely Classical ideas, was designed by Lord Burlington and built in 1731-2. It was based on Palladio's design for a hall 'suitable for festivals and entertainments', itself derived from an 'Egyptian' hall by Vitruvius. In order to preserve the effect of the columns the seats had at first been placed against the walls, but so narrow were the spaces between the columns that they led the Duchess of Marlborough to comment 'nobody with a hoop petticoat can pass through them'. In 1751 the seats were altered and placed in front of the columns. In 1754 the Assembly Rooms Committee was empowered to buy furniture and make improvements and ornaments. These included the addition of carved rococo 'Eschalop shells' and mouldings (by John Stavley) to the top of the seats, which are in the print, as well as the addition of more carved work by Stavley to the gallery. The seats were covered with silk and worsted damask, and the woodwork repainted (by Nathan Mason) and partly gilded (by Samuel Carpenter). Burlington's design shows the ceiling plan, but ceiling roses similar to those in the print are still present today, suggesting that the rococo mouldings in the print were actually executed. They may have been added in 1752 when John

Carr repaired the roof and 'stucco', or
during the improvement campaign of
1754-5.

Lit: York City Archives, Assembly
Rooms, Director's Minute Book 1730-
58, p. 263; Manager's Book, pp. 270,
291, 292, 294; Account Book 1729-
1883, p. 289; Nottingham 1973, cat.
37; Wittkower 1948, pp. 16-25
MS

B5 *Design for a stage set*

John Devoto (1708-1752). 1724
Pen and ink and wash; 230 x 207
Signed and dated *I.D. inv 1724.*
Inscribed with scale
*The Trustees of the British Museum
(1962-12-8-7)*

A magnificent building incorporating
a temple in which is the chariot of the
sun resting on clouds. This
symmetrical perspective design and
others by Devoto show that Italian
baroque scene-painting was established
in London theatres in the first half of
the century. Devoto, according to one
account born of Genoese parents in
France, was in England by 1708. He
was well known for his work in the
theatres of Lincoln's Inn Fields,
Goodman's Fields and the New Wells.

Prov: W.R. Jeudwine
Lit: Croft-Murray 1953
MS

B5

B6 *Design for the ceiling of St Martin-in-the-Fields*

James Gibbs (1682-1754). 1720-1724
Pen and ink and grey wash; 428 x 675
Inscribed *Ceiling for ye new Church of
St. Martin*
*The Visitors of the Ashmolean Museum,
Oxford (Gibbs vol IV, p. 31)*

Gibbs delivered the first design for
St Martin's in 1720; a design
substantially as built was submitted in
1721. In April 1724 he laid before the
Commissioners for Rebuilding two
'Designs for Frett Work of the Ceiling'
marked A and B respectively. B, the
richer of the two, was chosen and
Chrysostom Wilkins engaged to do the
plain work and 'Mr Bagutty' the 'Frett
Work and the Gilding' (Westminster
Public Library, St Martin-in-the Fields
papers 419/309). The ceiling was made
1724-6 by Giuseppe Artari and
Giovanni Bagutti, 'the best Fret-workers

B6

that ever came in England' (Gibbs 1728, p.v.). Whether the present design is A or B is uncertain as it is considerably more complex than the executed ceiling. It has close parallels with late baroque decoration of the type Gibbs would have seen in Rome (eg the Chapel of the Monte di Pieta in S.Salvatore in Lauro and the Church of SS Apostoli). Information supplied by Dr Terry Friedman.

Prov: James Gibbs; The Bodleian Library
Lit: Beard 1981, pp. 177-8; Friedman 1984, pl. 48; Turner 1927, fig. 308c.
MS

B7 *The Wollaston Family*
William Hogarth (1697-1764). 1730
Oil on Canvas; 990 x 1245
Signed and dated *Wm Hogarth: 1730*
The Trustees of the late H.C. Wollaston

One of Hogarth's earliest and most successful large figure groups, it represents William Wollaston (1693-1757, standing in the centre, dressed in black) of Finborough Hall, Suffollk , MP for Ipswich, surrounded by his relations by blood and marriage. Family tradition has it that it represents an interior at Finborough, or their town house in St James's Square, though the theatrical curtain on the left suggests an at least partly

imaginary setting. The room is still baroque, its pilastered walls suggesting it was built earlier in the century. The splendid silver tea-table has parallels in other conversation pieces by Hogarth. The painting aroused the enthusiasm of George Vertue, who praised it in December 1730 for all the best qualities expected of this kind of subject: '. . . a large Conversation . . . a most excellent work containing the true likeness of the persons, shape aire & dress – well disposd, genteel, agreable. – & freely painted & the composition of great variety & Nature.' – in short, he found it pleasantly informal in keeping with the increasingly relaxed bourgeois taste of the period. In this it contrasts sharply with Hogarth's almost contemporaneous *Assembly at Wanstead House* (Philadelphia Museum of Art) where the brief to portray the aristocratic Castlemaine family in the formal setting of their Palladian home (decorated by Hogarth's arch-enemy Kent, and including their most important works of art) resulted in stiffly old-fashioned grouping devoid of any hint of Rococo liveliness. The carved gilt frame, crowned with a plume of feathers, is in the manner of Kent.

Prov: Family possession since painted; lent by the trustees of the late

H.C. Wollaston to Leicester Museum
Lit: Beckett 1949, p. 47, fig. 31; Bindman 1981, p. 38, fig. 26; Paulson 1971, I, pp. 213, 218, fig. 79; Tate Gallery 1971, 30; Vertue III, p. 46; Webster 1978, p. 21, 24, 35
EE

B8 *Design for a table*
William Kent (?1685-1748). 1731
Pen and ink, pencil and wash;
156 x 286
Inscribed on the *verso* in the artist's hand *For Sr Rt Walpole at Houghton 1731 Novr:*
VAM (8156)

Beneath the table are sketches of two Cardinals. As in much of Kent's furniture, the table is composed of modified antique forms treated in a manner strongly influenced by the Italian baroque. The legs formed as two distinct units are characteristic of Kent and passed into the work of his followers (Cat. C18). Kent's rich internal decoration at Houghton Hall (carried out *c.* 1726-31) is in marked contrast to the Palladian austerity of Colen Campbell's exterior. The ceilings were described in 1731 by Sir Thomas Robinson as being 'in the modern taste'.

Prov: bought from E. Parsons, 1877
Lit: Beard 1975 II, p. 870; Vardy 1744, engraved, pl. 43; Ward-Jackson 1958, 18
MS

B9 *Delineatio Argenteae Cisternae*
Gerard II Scotin (b. 1698) after Hubert François (Bourguignon) Gravelot (1699-1773). 1735
Engraving and etching; 468 x 544
Lettered with the title and, in Latin, with dimensions, weight and *Henricus Jernegan Londini Invenit 1735. G. Scotin. Sculp.*
VAM (E.1594-1948)

A view, (with a detail of the relief on the hidden side), of the great wine cistern (Hermitage, Leningrad), made as a speculation by Charles Frederick Kandler for Henry Jerningham (begun 1730, hallmarked 1734-35). Jerningham was unable to find a buyer and in 1736 successfully petitioned Parliament for recompense on the grounds that the cooler

B7

'manifested that the sculptors and artificers of Great Britain are not inferior to those of other Nations'. It formed the chief prize in the 1737 Westminster Bridge Lottery. By 1740 it had passed from the winner to Empress Anne of Russia. In spite of the claim on this print (and in the Parliamentary petition) the cooler was in fact designed by George Vertue, whose sketch (Society of Antiquaries, presented in 1740) shows the handles as pairs of struggling male and female figures. Vertue's note with the sketch records that the handles and reliefs were modelled by J.M. Rysbrack, and that the silversmith was 'Kendelar a German' and was apparently 'the Modeller in Wax' referred to in the inscription. This print was probably used by Jerningham as a discreet and semi-public advertisement. A second state which is lettered in English, including 'now first published by Rt. Clee', and 'Now in the Possesion of the Empress of Russia' records Gravelot as the draughtsman. Gravelot also designed the medal, dated 1736, which accompanied the lottery tickets. The style of the cistern is characteristic of the baroque in use about 1730; the handles, however, reappear on rococo pieces (Cat. G40).

Prov: given by Lt. Col. the Earl Romney
Lit: Grimwade 1976, p. 567; Penzer 1956; Vertue III, p. 107
MS

B10 *Designs for hanging ornament and a cartouche*

Anonymous after Gaetano Brunetti (active 1731, d. 1758). Perhaps 1731
Etchings; 73 x 116, 73 x 115
Each lettered *G. Brunetti inv.*, the ornament numbered 3
VAM (29781.25; 29969 A 41)

These prints may be from an edition of 1731 (mentioned only in Berlin 1939) of Brunetti's 1736 suite (Cat. B11) The ornament is markedly better understood than in the 1736 suite.

Lit: Berlin 1939, 587
MS

B11

B11 *Designs for a chair, a picture frame and a cartouche*

Henry Fletcher (active 1715-1738) after Gaetano Brunetti (active 1731, d. 1758). 1736-7
Etchings; 166 x 115; 165 x 111 (cut)
Each lettered with a publication line dated 25 June 1736 and *G. Brunetti inv. et del. N. Fletcher Sculp.*
VAM (20329.8; E.295-1897)

From Brunetti's *Sixty Different Sorts of Ornaments ... Very useful to painters, sculptors, stone-carvers, wood-carvers, silversmiths etc.* (61 plates and title-page, engraved by Fletcher and Jean Rocque). The publication proposal was advertised in 1736 (*Daily Gazetteer,* 28 June); the suites were delivered to subscribers in 1737 (*Daily Post,* 16 May). Some plates are dated February 1737 within the design. This single cartouche was copied, with several others from the suite, by Augustin Heckel (see Cat. H2) and by James Paine on the pediment of the Doncaster Mansion House, 1745-8 (Cat. M2) Other plates were used for a Dublin silver coffee-pot of 1737 (Ashmolean Museum), and in later contexts (Cat. B13). The suite appears in Rocque's list of publications dated 1742. J.M. Rysbrack's copy is at the Avery Library, New York (information from Peter Fuhring). Most of the plates are based on mural decoration (the *Daily Gazetteer* connected them with Brunetti's painting at the town houses of the Duke of Chandos and the Duke of Tankerville and other houses), but there are six plates of furniture designs. As in the present case, they are very reminiscent of contemporary Italian examples. A chair in a very similar plate from the suite was copied for Cat. B12. Brunetti, a Lombard, whose earliest recorded English mural decoration was carried out 1730-31, worked in the north Italian style of *quadratura.* In 1739 he left England for Paris, where he died. Drawings for the suite are at Waddesdon Manor and the Ecole des Beaux Arts, Paris.

Lit: Berlin 1939, 587; Croft-Murray 1970, 176; Ward-Jackson 1958, 27
MS

B12 *George II*
Charles Phillips (1708-1747). *c.* 1740
Oil on canvas; 1094 x 875
Marble Hill House (GLC)

The King stands in an ante-room to a library; in the latter is a statue of Minerva. The bust of Queen Caroline (d. 1737) over the door represents J.M. Rysbrack's bust of 1738, which was in place in the New Library at St James's Palace in 1739. The throne behind the King is directly taken, but for the crest rail, from a print by Brunetti (see Cat. B11). Although such throne-like ceremonial chairs undoubtedly existed (eg a surviving example at Longleat), the throne and the curtain here establish the painting as a domestic variation of the baroque ceremonial portrait, such as Amigoni's portrait of Frederick Prince of Wales (1736, Raby Castle) in which late baroque Italianate furniture very close to Brunetti's plays a prominent part. A portrait of the 2nd Duke of Richmond (Goodwood), probably after Phillips, reverses the present setting, throwing doubt on the reality of both interiors. It includes a table after Brunetti and a figure of the Farnese Flora (Haskell & Penny 1981, 41) in the library. A gilt-lead Flora was in Kensington Palace by 1722 (Jourdain 1948, fig. 51) and a Flora in a niche flanked by pilasters forms pl. 54 of D'Aviler's *Cours D'Architecture,* 1738. Another version of the painting (Cirencester Park) appears to be a later copy after the same original. The figure of Minerva may be related to an engraving after Kent of a design for a cube room (Kent 1727).

Prov: Ashburnham collection; Lady Catherine Ashburnham, by descent; Sotheby's 15 July 1953, 132a; Anthony Hobson; Agnews 1971
Lit: Agnews 1971, 32 (as Dandridge); GLC 1975, 23; Marble Hill Supplement 1969, No. 23; Milan 1975
MS

B13 *Admission ticket to the Chester Music Festival*
By or after Miss Cunliffe, after Gaetano Brunetti (active 1731, d. 1758). 1783
Etching, printed in green; 64 x 94
Lettered with title etc. inscribed *99* and signed *J. Eltost* and *Thomas Huxley*

The Trustees of the British Museum (Banks C.2-267)

B12

For the evening concert, 19 September, 1783. One of a group of tickets for the Festival (16-20 September) collected by Sarah Banks on a mount inscribed by her 'All these tickets were designed by Miss Cunliffe'. Most of them are neo-classical; this one, however, is taken from Brunetti's *Sixty Different Sorts of Ornaments,* 1736. The Festival began with a performance of the Messiah in the Cathedral and included a masquerade.
MS

B14 *The Shudi Family*
Attributed to Barthélémy du Pan (1712-1763). *c.* 1742
Oil on canvas; 812 x 1340
The Broadwood Trust
(cover illustration)

The Swiss harpsichord maker Burkat Shudi (or Tschudi, 1702-1773) came to England in 1718 and by 1728 was running his prosperous business (the forerunner of the firm of Broadwood) from premises in Meard Street, Soho; this was conveniently close to the Court of St James's, the Prince of Wales's house in Leicester Fields and to many of his fashionable customers (including Handel) in the grand houses of the newly built Hanover and Cavendish Squares. The confident and prosperous figure of Shudi is seen here tuning a harpsichord. To his right are his elder son Joshua (1736-1754), his wife Catherine (d. *c.* 1759?) holding a large sheet of paper in her right hand and younger son Burkat (1737-1792?) nestling under the protective arm of his mother.

39

According to tradition, the picture was painted about 1744-45 to mark the completion of the opulent harpsichord seen here with its richly gilded ornate stand which Shudi, a staunch Protestant, allegedly presented to Frederick the Great of Prussia to mark the capture of Prague in 1744. However, there is no evidence to support this theory and the apparent age of Shudi's younger son would suggest that the picture was almost certainly painted *c.* 1742.

Shudi probably came to London in the first instance because Jakob Wild, from his native Schwanden, was already established in London as a merchant (perhaps a wood merchant) and could offer employment to a compatriot. Shudi later married Wild's daughter, Catherine, and his father-in-law probably underwrote the new business as Shudi's marriage portion. Jakob Wild died in 1741 and it is possible that the picture commemorates the inheritance of his father-in-law's estate through his wife for she appears to be holding some sort of document (possibly a will?). In October 1742, Shudi moved the family business and residence from Meard Street to nearby, but more fashionable, Great Pulteney Street. There the picture was placed above the fireplace in the little front parlour where it hung until the beginning of this century. If it was painted before October 1742 and then perhaps cut down to fit its new location that might account for its odd shape. There must be some explanation for the highly unusual truncation of the engraved portraits of Frederick, Prince of Wales and Princess Augusta and the landscape painting (supposed to depict Shudi's birthplace, Schwanden, in the canton of Glaurus). The presence of the portraits as symbols of patronage was not insignificant since Shudi had made a harpsichord for the Prince in 1740 (now at Kew) and his distinguishing trade sign displayed outside the Great Pulteney Street house was 'Ye Plume of Feathers', the Prince's crest. The authorship of this strikingly individual picture has puzzled art-historians for generations. It is stylistically incompatible with the work of any British painter and Sir Ellis Waterhouse's suggestion that it might be by Shudi's compatriot Barthélémy du Pan who known to

be in England by 1743, is the most plausible attribution to date. But whilst the rich, strong colours recall du Pan's palette in works like the large *Children of Frederick, Prince of Wales* of 1746 at Windsor, the crisp outlines and sharply modelled forms of the present work are not entirely consistent with those few works by du Pan known to have been painted in England which are softer and more overtly French in style. Only one other picture certainly by the same hand – *An English Couple in a Formal Garden* (Geffrye Museum) is known to the present author.

Prov: presumably painted for Burkat Shudi; by descent through Shudi's daughter Barbara (1749-1776) who married John Broadwood in 1769; by descent to the present owners
Lit: Dale, 1913, pp. 42-5, 65; Wainwright 1982, pp. 26-8; Waterhouse 1946, p. 152
BA

B15

B15 *Title page of* A New Book of Ornaments
Antonio Visentini (1688-1782) after Angelo de Rossi (1670-1742). 1753
Etching and engraving; 372 x 256
Lettered with title and description and *Invented by Angelo Rossi Florentine.*
Engrav'd by Ant. Visentini Venitian.
Publish'd Novr. 1st. 1753 by ye Proprietor F. Vivares

VAM (E.2109.1908)

A reissue of *Racolta di vari Schizi de Ornati,* Venice, 1747, in which Rossi is not mentioned and which is dedicated by Francesco Zuccarelli, who frequently collaborated with Visentini. The late-baroque *quadratura* style of this suite of designs for mural painting had largely passed out of use in England by 1753. The reissue of the Italian plates may be connected with Zuccarelli who came to England in 1752. Vivares was the first of many English publishers to issue prints of Zuccarelli's paintings (1753). See Cat. L30.

Lit: Berlin 1936, 588; McAndrew 1974, p. 7
MS

B16 *Door from the Great Drawing Room, Norfolk House*
Designed by Giovanni Battista Borra (1712-1736); carved by Jean-Antoine Cuenot (d. 1762). *c.* 1753-56
Carved wood, painted; w. of door and carving 328, max h. 3770
VAM (W4-1960)

Norfolk House in St James's Square was built for the 9th Duke of Norfolk by Matthew Brettingham senior between 1748 and February 1756, when a great gala was held to celebrate its completion. The celebrated 'monkey doors' are described in detail among the accounts sent in by the carver Jean-Antoine Cuenot between 1753 and 1756. But there is little doubt that, like the superb carved decoration of the Music Room (also acquired by the Museum), the designs were made by the Piedmontese architect, Giovanni Battista Borra. Closely related door cases by Borra survive in the Sala de Ricevimento at the palace of Racconigi near Turin, though with winged putti instead of monkeys. *Singeries,* derived from the designs of Watteau, Gillot and Audran, had already become popular in this country through the painted decoration of Andien de Clermont at Kirtlington, Langley Park, Syon and (most suitably) at the Duke of Marlborough's fishing temple on Monkey Island in the Thames. Borra may have adopted them, not only as a favourite rococo theme, but because they complemented the Gobelins tapestries in the Great Drawing Room, which Farington described as being ornamented 'chiefly with Beasts'.
GJ-S

France in England

An engraver working at his table, Jean-Antoine Watteau. See cat. C1

C1 *An Engraver working at his table*
Jean-Antoine Watteau (1684-1721)
Red chalk; 235 x 304
*The Trustees of the British Museum
(1874-8-8-2279)*

Goncourt records an inscription on the *verso*, now lost, in the hand of Hugh Howard: *M Baron, the graver, by A Watteau.* Bernard Baron (1696-1762) was among the most eminent of the many French engravers who came to England in the first half of the century. He was invited by Claude Dubosc in 1712, to assist with the engraving of the Marlborough House murals. Howard's suggestion is plausible, as it is very probable that Baron knew Watteau. He worked for Dr Mead, whom Watteau came to England to consult in 1719-20, and later engraved the Watteaus in Mead's collection for Jean de Julienne. It has also been suggested (Dacier & Vauflart 1929, p. 92) that the sitter is Sir Nicholas Dorigny, another French engraver who worked in London. The paper is French or Dutch. The engraver is shown at work beside a window, the light from which is filtered by a screen.

Prov: Hugh Howard (Lugt 2957); his sale, 1873; the Earl of Wicklow
Lit: Goncourt 1875, pp. 347-8; Hulton 1980, 54; Parker & Mathey 1957, 913
MS

C2 *Viscount Tyrconnel with his family*
Philip Mercier (1689-1760). *c.* 1726
Oil on canvas; 648 x 756
Signed *Ph. Mercier Pinxit*
The National Trust (Belton House)

The figures are, from left to right: the artist (seated), Viscount Tyrconnel (wearing the ribbon and star of the Bath), Miss Dayrell (on the swing, a cousin of the Viscountess), a black servant, the Viscountess Tyrconnel, (?) William Brownlow (the Viscountess's brother-in-law), Savile Cockayne Cust (pulling the swing), and, possibly, Mr Dayrell, Miss Dayrell's father. Sir John Brownlow was created Viscount Tyrconnel on the 23 June 1718 and made a Knight of the Bath on the 27 May 1725; William Brownlow died on the 28 July 1726. In the background is the family seat,

Belton House, built 1685-8. This conversation piece is a clear demonstration of the origins of the genre, that is the adaptation of the informal manner of Watteau's figure style and settings to a modern English setting. The figure which may be William Brownlow is very close to one of the etched *Figures de Modes* (Dacier & Vauflart 1929, 44).

Prov: Lord Brownlow, by descent
Lit: Cust 1909, pp. 191-2; Edwards 1954, pp. 58, 166 (80), pl. 121 (80); GLC 1965, 30; Waterhouse 1953, p. 141, pl. 115; York 1969, 12 repr.
MS

C3

C3 *A Compleat Book of Ornaments*
John Pine (1690-1756) after Jean-Bernard-Honoré Turreau called Toro (1672-1731), Paul van Somer II (*c.*1649-1694) and an anonymous engraver. 1728 or earlier
Title and 1 plate, etching and engraving; title-page 281 x 180
The title-page also lettered *consisting of a variety of compartments, shields, masks, frieze-work, moresk-work &c being very useful for Painters, Carvers, Watch-Makers, Gravers &c Invented & Drawn by some of the best Artists. Toro. in et del. Pine Sculp.*
and with the address of Thomas Bowles. The first plate lettered *Toro in. et del. J. Pine Sculp.*
The remaining plates lettered *P. Van*

Somer in fec et ex Londini (or variations thereof) *M* and numbered *3, 2* and *4.* Three plates bear traces of the address of J. Nicholls.
VAM (E.1451-6-1983)

The most complete recorded copy of this work (Winterthur, NK 1530. B.78) consists of this title and plates, with one addition, and 4 more suites, each with a title. They are made up of 27 plates by Van Somer, J.L. Durant, C. de Moelder, Mersonau after Berain and J.L. Durant after J. Mussard (including Berlin 1939, 344 (1), 753, 838). All the titles but two, and all the plates, are reissues of continental baroque plates, in most cases previously published in London by J. Nicholls. Two of the title-pages are made up by Bowles from elements taken from various suites by Toro. The present Toro plates are reversed copies of plates in *Cartouches Nouvellement Inventez par J.B. Toro* (Berlin 1939, 369 (12); Dimier 1928, 92.7). This title appears in John Bowles' *Catalogue of Maps, Prints, Books and Books of Maps*, 1728, p. 34
MS

C4 *Ewer and basin*
George Wickes 1698-1761
Basin London hallmarks for 1735-6; ewer maker's mark struck four times; both bear post-1893 French import mark
Silver-gilt; basin diam. 552, ewer h. 362
Engraved with 19th century armorials and monogram of William Stuart Stirling Crawfurd
Private Collection
See colour plate IV

Two of the most original and historically important pieces of early English full-blown rococo silver. Presented by the Common Council of the Corporation of Bristol to the City's Recorder John Scrope. Records of their manufacture and donation survive. French influence is clearly discernible. The left-hand cartouche on the centre of the basin derives from a print of Jacques de Lajoue published about 1734 (Cat. C5). The rococo details framing the profiles of the Caesars also owe much to Lajoue. No design books used by Wickes have come to light, but these pieces prove that he was in close touch with French trends. The ewer is remarkable for its avant-garde form; instead of the helmet outline popular at the time, Wickes used a graceful pear shape unknown even in the *oeuvre* of the great innovator Paul De Lamerie in 1735. Water and wine are represented by bulrushes and vines suggesting the vessel's dual purpose. Rococo elements predominate, but there still remain echoes of the baroque in the profiles of the Caesars on the basin; two such Roman profiles in the same frames appear that same year on the lids of a pair of tureens made by Wickes for Lord North. The female head on the handle possibly represents Britannia. The male mask on the body of the ewer appears to have been taken from a print after Gaetano Brunetti which must predate the edition of his suite issued in 1736 (see Cat. B11).

Prov: The Hon. John Scrope; the Fane Family; William Stuart Stirling Crawfurd; Asher Wertheimer; the Hon. Clive Pearson; Sotheby's 13 June 1983
Lit: Barr 1980, p. 10, fig. 4; Barr 1983, pp. 284-288; Bristol 1965; Jackson 1911, vol I, pp. 297-9
EB

C5 *A cartouche*
Gabriel Huquier (1695-1772) after Jacques de Lajoue (1687-1761). *c.* 1734
Etching and engraving; 222 x 185
Lettered with the privilege and *De la Joue in. Huquier Sculp B 10*

VAM (E.904-1905)

From the *Second livre de cartouches* published by Huquier. This print was used as the basis of one of the cartouches in the basin of cat. C4 and, also, for the engraving of the salver Cat. G35, made in 1754. It was copied in reverse in Edwards Hoppus's *The Gentleman's and Builder's Repository,* 1737 pl. LXVIII. Plates 2 and 3 of the suite are also copied by Hoppus, as well as other plates after Lajoue.

Lit: BN: Fonds, 818-28; Berlin 1939, 400 (2)
MS

C6 *Veüe de la Maison Royale de Richmond*
Jean Baptiste Claude Chatelain (*c.* 1710-after 1771). 1736
Etching and engraving; 441 x 556 (cut)
Lettered with title and *du Coté de la Tamise a 3 lieües de Londres 1736. Chatelain. inv. et. Sculp.* and with the address of J. Rocque and dedication to Lord Castlemain
Her Majesty The Queen

A view, from the Middlesex bank, of Richmond Lodge and its gardens. The ferry theme, the general treatment and most of the foreground figures, are adapted from Watteau's *L'Embarquement pour Cythère* (Cat. A6, published in 1733). The cow and one of the figures are after Watteau's *Veue de Vincennes* (Dacier & Vauflart 1929, 211) which may also have influenced the treatment of the Surrey bank. A reworked and altered state entitled *Richmond Ferry as it was* (Gascoigne 1978, 781; there was in fact no ferry at this point) is lettered 'Marco Ricci [d. 1730] pinxt, Goupy direxit Chatelain fecit'. It may be a third state, post-dating Richmond Bridge (built 1774-7), the lettering being perhaps derived from Chatelain's print 'Ruina di Memphio' after Ricci published by Goupy. A second, untraced state may be surmised, bearing the Royal arms as in the second state of the companion print showing the Lodge

from the other side (Vitruvius Britannicus 1739, 6-7; Gascoigne 1978, 780; Willis 1977, pl. 110a) which is similarly lettered. These prints are among the first to place elegant French figures in an English setting. Richmond Lodge was the favourite residence of Queen Caroline.

Lit: Vitruvius Britannicus 1739, 8-9; Willis 1977, pp. 101-105
MS

C7 *Tureen, cover and stand*
Makers' marks of Henry Adnet and Pierre-François Bonnestrenne. Designed by Juste-Aurèle Meissonnier (1695-1750). 1734-1740
Silver; overall h. 379, overall w. 456
Inscribed in the cover: *MEIS^{ER}.*
Inscribed in the tureen: *MEISSONIER.*
Inscribed on the stand, *FAI^{T} PAR-J-A-MEISSONIER-ARCHITECTTE*
Private Collection

Standing on an asymmetrical cartouche-shaped plateau, the borders of which are cast with scrolls, irregular shell-like fluting, celery leaves and salsify, the shell-shaped tureen rests upon cast and chased bunches of celery, cabbage leaves, an onion, a carrot and barnacles and is decorated with matting and an asymmetrical scrolling cartouche. The cover, is also shell-shaped and ribbed, and is set with a duck, a crab, a fish, an oyster,

C6

an artichoke, barnacles and foliage. Meissonnier's precise responsibility for this group is hard to estimate. He appears to have moved from Turin to Paris in about 1714, working as a medallist. In 1719, when Meissonnier took an apprentice in Paris, he describes himself as *ciseleur* and *dessinateur*. On the 28 September 1724 he was appointed to the Corporation des Marchands-Orfèvres-Joailliers by Royal *brèvet,* having completed ten years service at the Manufacture Royale des meubles de la Couronne at the Gobelins. This honour was subsequently confirmed by the guild on 19 October of the same year. In 1723 he is described as an 'ouvrier de Boîtes à montres' (information kindly provided by Peter Fuhring). His sponsor for the *maîtrise* was a seal cutter. Furthermore the duc d'Antin in 1729 wrote that Meissonnier's main occupation was as a chaser. It is therefore not unreasonable to assume that his skills as a plateworker would have been limited. Indeed only one piece, a gold and lapis lazuli snuff-box of 1728 bears his mark, a crowned fleur de lis, J O M and two *grains de remède* which he had registered on the 7 February 1725. However the signatures on this group of plate suggest that he maintained at least a supervisory role on work which was contracted to other goldsmiths. Meissonnier's choice of goldsmiths is, in this instance, surprising. The work of both Henry Adnet (1683-1745) and Pierre-François Bonnestrenne (1685-at least 1737/38) is rather undistinguished. A gold box in the Wallace Collection, London, is tentatively attributed to Adnet and a mustard pot by him of 1717-22 is in the Metropolitan Museum, New York. A mustard pot of 1737-38 by Bonnestrenne was in the collection of Mrs H.S. Firestone in 1956. There is no evidence, apart from the marks on this tureen, that the two goldsmiths collaborated or were in partnership. The dating of the tureen rests on the date of the introduction of the earliest warden's mark found on the pieces, that beginning on 18 September 1734, and the delivery of the tureen on 24 November 1740. It is clear from the presence of the discharge mark of Louis Robin that the tureen had not been completed until after 4 October 1738. The design of the present

tureen, and its pair (Cleveland Museum of Art), is related to a drawing in the Bibliothèque Nationale, Paris, signed 'J. Au. Meissonier', for a centrepiece and two tureens, and to an engraving by Huquier (*Oeuvres,* folio 72) for a similar group, but with a different centrepiece. The present tureen does not appear in either the drawing or the engraving, and indeed was not completed in 1735, the date given to the tureens in the print. Both the drawing and the engraving show both sides of the Cleveland tureen, in reverse in the engraving. Thus Meissonnier was not being strictly truthful when inscribing the engraving 'Projet de Sculpture en argent d'un grand Surtout de Table, et les deux Terrines qui ont été executés pour Millord Duc de Kinston en 1735'. However, given that the same makers made both tureens, and that the designs of both are so complementary, it would be unreasonable to suggest that the present tureen is not after Meissonnier's design. Clearly intended for *oglio,* that curious mixture of stewed meats which formed the usual main dish of the *premier service* in an 18th century dinner, Meissonnier has, in effect, turned the tureens inside out by displaying their contents in silver on the lid and body.

Prov: Evelyn Pierrepont, 2nd Duke of Kingston, 1740-1773; Elizabeth Chudleigh, Countess of Bristol and Duchess of Kingston 1773-1778; probably Alexander Andreievitch, Prince Bezborodko 1799; probably Ilia Andreievitch, Count Bezborodko 1815; Alexander Grigorievitch, Count Koncheleff-Bezborodko 1855; Alexander Polovtsoff, sold Galerie George Petit, Paris, 2 December 1909, 18 (Seligmann); J. Pierpoint Morgan; Christie's, Geneva, 8 November 1977 (No.2)
Lit: Carsix 1909; Dennis 1960, fig. 1; Detroit 1956, 533; Hawley 1978; Nocq I, pp. 1, 151, III, p. 225, IV, pp. 215-6, 232-3; Snowman 1966
CT

C8 *Invitation ticket, probably for the Grande Loge Anglaise de France*
Gerard Scotin after Hubert François (Bourguignon) Gravelot (1699-1773). 1737. Lettered with an invitation in French and *Studiomi F. Docris, Beaumont Magtri. Cura Frere G. Scotin sculp.*

C8
Trustees of the British Museum (Banks C.2-1037)

At the top a youth holding Masonic instruments and putting his finger to his lips is flanked by a beaver and a sphinx. At the base are a beehive and bees. The thick almost symmetrical cartouche is characteristic of the type being developed by Gravelot at this date. The figurative elements were re-used on a Masonic card engraved by *Fr. D. Fournier, G. Scotin inv. & del* (Banks C.2-1019). The whole upper part was engraved by George Bickham junior for a headpiece to 'The True Mason', 1738, lettered *Frater G. Bickham junr. sc.* in the *Musical Entertainer, vol II, no. I, p. 1.*
MS

C9 *Title page*
A Catalogue of Mr Samuel Paris's Collection of Paintings, Marble Bustos, Bronzes .&c. .&c. To be sold by Auction at Mr Cock's . . . the 2lst of this Inst. March 1738-9 Gabriel Huquier (1695-1772). 1737. The etched cartouche lettered *huquier in et fecit 1737*
The Trustees of the British Museum (Banks D.3-567).

The symmetrical scrollwork and *rocaille* recall the plates engraved by Huquier after Oppenord from 1738 onwards. An impression of this plate without the title letterpress is known (Banks 132.251); the blank sheets were presumably sent by Huquier for Cock's general use. They are the only recorded instance of this type of cross-channel traffic.
MS

C9

C10 *Two designs for a table*
Anonymous, after Nicolas Pineau
(1684-1754). 1732-9. Thomas Langley
(working 1739) after Nicolas Pineau.
1740
Engravings; 203 x 270, 144 x 218 (cut)
The first lettered *Mariette excudit* and
numbered 5. The second formerly
lettered *Marble Table Thos. Langley Invent
delin and sculp 1739* and numbered
CXLIII
VAM (E.5946-1908, E.1132-1888)

The French print is from Pineau's
*Nouveaux Desseins de Pieds de Tables et de
Vases et Consoles de Sculpture,* the English
from Batty Langley's *The City and
Country Builder's and Workman's Treasury
of Designs,* 1740 (later editions 1745,
1750, 1756, 1770) in which it is
described as being 'after the French
manner'. Thomas Langley's plates in
the volume include 6 tables after
Pineau and plagiarisms of prints of
furniture by Johann Jakob Schubler
and Johann Friedrich Lauch. A
number of English gilt-wood tables
after Pineau have survived, including
one (VAM W.3-1961) taken very
largely from this design. Its apron
does not follow the design.

Lit: VAM 1983, 2.2.f, 2.2.g; Ward-
Jackson 1958, p. 35
MS

C11 *Title-Page of the* First Book of Ornament
Francis Vivares (1709-1780) after
William De la Cour (active 1740, d.
1767). 1741

Etching and engraving; 293 x 214
Lettered with title, a dedication to
Lord Middlesex, a copyright line
dated 13 Nov. 1741 and *De La Cour
Invt. Vivares Sculp.*
VAM (E.731-1907)

A fantastic structure composed of
scrolls and columns, set in a wooded
landscape. It bears two chinamen, a
female figure, a dragon, the title and
the arms of Lord Middlesex. De la
Cour's *First Book* (title and 6 plates by
Vivares) was succeeded by the *Second
Book,* 1742, dedicated to the Earl of
Holderness (title and 5 plates by
Vivares); the *Third Book,* 1743,
dedicated to the Duke of Rutland (title
and 6 plates by De la Cour); the *Fourth
Book,* 1743, (title and 6 plates by De la
Cour, Charles Mosley and R. White);
the *Fifth Book, Useful for all manner of
Furniture and all other things,* 1743 (title
and 14 plates by R. White); the *Sixth
Book,* undated, (title and (?) 7 plates by
De la Cour); the *Seventh Book,* 1745
(title and (?) 6 plates, one by De la
Cour); the *Eighth Book,* 1747 (title and 6
plates by Jacob Bonneau). The only
complete set, in which the fifth and
sixth books are confused, is at the
Cooper-Hewitt Museum (1962-126-1
(1-56)). The three noble dedicatees
were all keen supporters of the Opera,
for which De la Cour painted scenery.

Lit: Berlin 1939, 261; Croft-Murray
1970, p. 199; Ward-Jackson 1958,
p. 34, No. 346
MS

C12 *Capitano Cerimonia and Signora Lauinia*
Andien de Clermont (active 1716/17-
1783). 1742
Oil on canvas; 1260 x 1320
Private Collection
See colour plate II

From a set of wall panels depicting
subjects taken from Jacques Callot's
Balli di Sfessania etchings (1621)
painted for the Scaramouche parlour
at Belvedere, the 5th Lord Baltimore's
villa in Kent. The house was enlarged
after 1751, rebuilt by James Stuart
c. 1775 for Sir Sampson Gideon Bart.,
and demolished *c.* 1860. The paintings
were seen at Belvedere by Mrs Lybbe
Powys in 1771 who commented 'the
rest of the house very small – two
small parlours, in one, panels painted
of monkeys, another *scaramouches,*

which the old Lord Baltimore used to
call the Monkey and Scaramouch
parlours'. The six narrow and six wide
canvases (one of the latter has been
divided) are now cut down and give
no clear indication of their original
arrangement. The panel showing
Mestolino is dated 1742 and is the
only surviving signed piece by
Clermont. The decorative elements of
most of the panels, excluding the
present example, are much indebted,
sometimes directly, to prints after
Watteau's grotesques, such as Cat. A7,
which with its use of *commedia dell'arte*
figures may have given the clue to the
whole series. Lord Baltimore (or
perhaps his heir) continued the
French taste in the *boiserie* interiors at
Woodcote Park, Surrey, perhaps
completed *c.*1755, elements of which
were taken from Blondel's *Maisons de
Plaisance* (Cat. M13). Clermont also
painted at Woodcote, probably by
1753.

Prov: Charles Calvert, 5th Lord
Baltimore; Sir Sampson Gideon Bart.,
later Lord Eardley; Lieutenant Colonel
F.D.E. Freemantle; Sotheby's Monaco
8 Feb 1980, 124, 2
Exhib: Stockholm 1980, 130
Lit: Croft-Murray 1970, pp. 192, 39,
41; Harris 1961; Lybbe Powys 1899,
p. 151; Sitwell 1945, p. 116
MS

C13 *Subscription ticket*
Anonymous. 1747
Subscription ticket to the Ecole de
Charité Françoise de Westminster.
Lettered with title etc. in French and
Par Souscription Commencée 1747 with
the partially erased lettering *[illegible]
sculp 1747.* Signed by E. Artaud
(treasurer), inscribed (?)*C. Grignion* and
dated 2 May 1793
*The Trustees of the British Museum (Banks
D.3-468)*

The card shows two charity children
and a cartouche in the developed
rococo style. An uninscribed
impression, also with the engraver's
name erased, is known (Banks 104.82).
For this Protestant School see
Proceedings of the Huguenot Society, II,
p. 464
MS

C14 *Trade Card of Richard Sidall, Chemist*

Robert Clee. *c. 1750?*

The Trustees of the British Museum (Heal 34.64.)

The celebrated scene of an alchemist in his laboratory on this famous card is a reversed copy after *La Pharmacie* engraved in 1738 by C.N. Cochin after Jacques de Lajoue (BN: Fonds, 250). Clee has altered the alchemist's head and has introduced the shop sign 'The Golden Head' (ie Glauber's head). Lajoue's original painting was one of a set of 13 painted for the Duc de Picquigny *c.* 1735, all of which were engraved and subsequently much repeated. Clee engraved a number of ambitious cards and was a friend of J.B.C. Chatelain.

Lit: Heal 1925, p. 70, Xl; Roland-Michel 1979, pp. 10-13
MS

C15 *Drawing of a* bureau-plat *and* cartonnier

John Vardy (d. 1765). Perhaps *c.* 1746
Pen and ink and wash; 162 x 270
Inscribed on the *verso* in ink *J. Vardy delin. at Mr Arundales* and with a scale

The British Architectural Library, RIBA

Long thought to be an original design by Vardy, this drawing is now known to show a Parisian *bureau-plat* and *cartonnier* of about 1745. The former, made by Bernard van Risenburgh II, is at Temple Newsam House. The pieces belonged to Richard Arundale of Allerton Park who held various state offices including that of Surveyor General to the Office of Works, in which Vardy was employed. A drawing by Vardy (VAM) for the enlargement of Allerton Park is dated 1746. Although it is known that Arundale had extensive Continental connections, the first record of the furniture is at the time of its removal from Allerton at his death in 1759. It is, however, probable that the drawing was made when Vardy was working at Allerton Park. The pieces are among the very few examples of French rococo furniture that can with certainty be said to have been in England before the early 1760s. The earliest dated *bureau-plat* by Van Risenburgh (1745) is a considerably more fluid design than this example, which could be dated stylistically

1740. Maker's marks on furniture were not introduced in Paris until after 1744.

Lit: Colvin 1978, p. 855; Gilbert 1973 I, pl. 4; Gilbert 1978, 561; Ward-Jackson 1958, 45
MS

C16

C16 *A Description of the Illumination, or Fire-Work, Intended for the Peace*

George Bickham junior (1706?-1771). 1748
Etching, engraving and letterpress; 456 x 240
The headpiece lettered *A Section of ye Building 1748 G.Bickham sc According to Act of Parlt.* Title and description in letterpress, concluding with an advertisement for an engraving by Bickham of Rubens *Horror of War*

The Trustees of the British Museum (1868.6.12.1167)

The firework building in the headpiece, 'a vast Hall, finely illuminated', is adapted from a plate in Meissonnier's *Livre D'Ornemens,* first published in France in 1734 and in England probably in 1737 (Cat. C17). Bickham used the same source in his *Musical Entertainer,* vol. II, p. 4, 1738. The spiky rock-work ornament over the top is taken from Watteau (Dacier & Vauflart 1929, 93) and had also been used in the *Musical Entertainer* (vol. I, p. 61, 1737). The Peace of Aix-la-Chapelle was celebrated in April 1749 with a firework display in Green Park, the structure for which, formed as a Doric temple, was designed by G.N. Servandoni.

Lit: Phillips 1964, p. 44; Snodin 1983, p. 359, figs. 7 & 8
MS

C17 *A fountain*

Laureolli (active 1734) after Juste Aurèle Meissonnier (1695-1750). 1734

Etching and engraving; 117 x 210
Lettered with the privilege and *Meissonnier Arci.te in. Laureolli Sculp.*
VAM (E.940-1905)

A 'Morceau de Fantaisie' from the suite *Livre D'Ornemens*, published after the widow of F. Chereau, announced, together with 50 other plates by Meissonnier in the *Mercure de France,* March 1734. The set was copied in reverse apparently in an edition published by Jean Rocque in 1737, and engraved by Vivares (Metropolitan Museum 58. 635.11) and was also adapted for plates in Bickham's *Musical Entertainer,* 1738-1739, for Sir Charles Frederick's decorations for Shaw's *Travels,* 1738 (Cat. D4 and Cat. C16).

Lit: Berlin 1939, 378 D; Kimball 1943, p. 161, fig. 209; Snodin 1983, fig. 8
MS

C18 *Design for a pier table and glass*

John Vardy (d.1765). Probably 1761-3
Pen and ink and wash; 448 x 213
The British Architectural Library, RIBA

Designed for the 5th Duke of Bolton at Hackwood Park, Hants., where Vardy was making alterations 1761-3.

C18

46

The central part of the table apron is taken from Meissonnier (Cat. C19) but this part was not used on the executed table (still at Hackwood) which has on the apron a motif derived from that at the bottom of the glass. Apart from this detail, the pieces show William Kent's style softened and made more fluid by the general influence of the rococo. The palmette frieze on the table and, possibly, the hanging husk garland, are neo-classical. The Hackwood furniture may have been carved by Vardy's brother Thomas.

Lit: Coleridge 1962; Coleridge 1968, pl. 78-80; Lever 1982, p. 42 repr; Ward-Jackson 1958, 43
MS

C19 *Design for a sofa*
Gabriel Huquier (1695-1772) after Juste Aurèle Meissonnier (1695-1750). 1738-1749
Etching and engraving; 316 x 362
Lettered *Canapé exécuté pour Mr Le Comte de Bielenski Grand Mal. de Couronne de Pologne, en 1735. J.A. Meissonnier inv. Huquier Sculp* and with the address of Huquier and the privilege. Numbered *Q.94*
The Duke of Norfolk

The lower rail of the back was used by Vardy for Cat. C18. From the *Oeuvre de Juste Aurèle Meissonnier,* published by Huquier *c.*1749. This type of seat furniture, in its smaller form as an armchair, had a considerable vogue in England where it was known as a 'French Chair'.

Prov: see Cat. A19
Lit: BN:Fonds, 1011
MS

C20 *Before*
William Hogarth (1697-1764). 1730-1
Oil on canvas; 372 x 447
After
Oil on canvas; 372 x 451
The Syndics of the Fitzwilliam Museum, Cambridge

C20

Antal was the first to point out the affinity of this pair to Jean-François de Troy's small *fêtes galantes* of the 1720s, which Hogarth may have known from engravings, or from examples in English collections like that of Dr Mead. There are particularly close parallels here, fortuitous or otherwise, with de Troy's *La Proposition* of 1725 (Wrightsman coll., exh. R.A. Winter 1968, cat. 669) whose theme of seduction, poses and even colouring it seems to echo. Yet it also shows the mental gulf that separates the exquisite urbanity of the French Rococo and the ablest English exponent of the style: while in de Troy the erotic intimacy of *After* floats as a desirable dream in the painted pastoral above the couple's head, in Hogarth it is given equal weight to

Before, in a sequence of moralizing cause and effect that takes a much less elegant view of human nature. Significantly, Hogarth soon repeated the subject in an indoor version (Getty Museum, Malibu) where all traces of French gracefulness and colouring were eliminated in favour of a plethora of ribald detail closer to a Dutch brothel scene – and which, incidentally, translated into a more 'readable' popular print.

Prov: (for the pair) commissioned in 1730 by John Thomson, member of the Commons Committee on prisons, but not collected; London art market 1832; H.R. Willett, of Shooter's Hill, London 1842; Locker-Lampson; Duke of Hamilton by 1907; bought by A.J. Hugh Smith 1919, and bequeathed, through the NACF, to the Fitzwilliam Museum, Cambridge, 1964

Lit: Antal 1962, pp. 95, 171; Bindman 1981, pp. 48, 49, figs 37, 38; Bordeaux 1977, 20, 21; Goodison 1977, p. 114, pl. 9; Munich 1980, 14, 15; Rosenthal 1980, p. 48, pl. III, 32; Tate Gallery 1971, 50, 51; Webster 1978, pp. 46, 47
EE

C21 *A Frenchman at Bow Street*

Marcellus Laroon (1679-1772). 1740
Pencil; 362 x 518
Signed and dated *M: Laroon F: 1740.*
Inscribed in the Colnaghi hand *A Curious and Interesting Drawing by Laroon of a French Gentn Brought at night before the Justice at Bow S.*

Her Majesty The Queen

A Frenchman brought before a magistrate, surrounded by a crowd of prostitutes, beggars and watchmen. This view of the mannered effeminacy of the French contrasted with the earthy directness of the English was widespread. The present title was given to the drawing in the 19th century; its original title, 'Night Walkers before a Justice of the Peace' is inscribed on a preliminary sketch (Yale center for British Art; Raines 1966, 93).

Prov: probably Samuel Scott sale, 13 Jan 1773, 90; Colnaghi, purchased for the Prince Regent 18 Jan 1813
Lit: Oppé 1950, 409, pl. 68; Raines 1966, 56, pl. 31
MS

C21

C22 *Pantin a la Mode*

Attributed to John June (active 1747-1752). 1748
Etching and engraving; 225 x 300
Lettered with title, a copyright line dated 7 September 1748, *for J. Wakelin,* and a verse. Inscribed in ink *From a painting of Hogarth's*

The Trustees of the British Museum (1859-8-6-374)

A satire on French fashions. An interior; two fops dressed in the French manner, ladies and a clergyman play with pantins, or puppets. The verse compares the beneficial influence of ancient Rome with the 'Gallic Influence' which 'Bid Foppery rise, and turn'd the Scale of Sense: / Now View that Ardour which in every Youth / Seraphic blaz'd, for Liberty and Truth / Quench'd by the false Delights of Ease and Dress'. A link is made with the rococo in the title frame, the chair and the pier table and glass, the glass being a simplified version of the type shown in Lock's *Six Sconces,* 1744, (Cat. L4, L5). Curiously, both appear in 1747 in the neutral context of a tavern scene, *The Sailors Fleet Wedding Entertainment* by June (BM: S2875). He also engraved three plates for Lock's *New Book of Ornaments for Looking Glass Frames, c.* 1752 (Heckscher 1979, pls. 35-7, 39).

Lit: BM: S 3017
MS

C23 *Badge of the Antigallican Society*

Possibly Battersea, probably Birmingham. *c.* 1750-60
Painted enamel, silver, glass and rock crystal; 139 x 73
The Trustees of the British Museum (H.G.161)

The enamel plaque is painted with a version of the arms of the Antigallican Society, St George on a horse spearing the flag of France, supported by a lion and a double-headed eagle surrounded by scrolls, flags, cannons and a mask, and is surrounded by silver foliate scrolls set with faceted rock-crystals and a scroll bearing the Society's motto: For Our Country. The badge is surmounted by a crown set with rock-crystals and incorporating five sails, and is hung with a pendant mounted in silver set with rock-crystals of reverse-painted glass showing Britannia seated with a shield, spear and olive branch. The reverse of the enamel and the pendant is a silver-gilt plaque engraved with designs similar to the obverse. The Society was founded about 1745 'to oppose the insidious Arts of the French Nation' and continued to be active until the Napoleonic Wars. The Society had a number of influential supporters, including the carver Thomas Johnson, who included the Society's badge on his dedicatory frontispiece to his collection of designs of 1758 (Cat. L44) and Stephen Theodore

48

Janssen, the owner of the York House, Battersea enamel factory. Janssen became Grand President of the Antigallicans and it has been suggested that the plaque is likely to have been made at his Battersea factory. However Janssen was also Vice-President of the British Herring Fishing Company and a plaque celebrating that Company has been convincingly attributed to Birmingham by Bernard Watney (1966, p. 66 ff). Furthermore the Battersea factory employed the technique of transfer printing, introduced by John Brooks in Birmingham in about 1751, and no plaque which is solely painted has been attributed to Battersea. Indeed where painting is used on enamels accepted as Battersea it is used to highlight the printing, not to hide it. The design of the badge celebrates the alliance of England and Austria encouraging the destruction of France.

Prov: Hull Grundy Collection
Lit: British Museum 1978, p. 10, pl. 2, Col. pl. III; Mew 1928, pp. 216-21; Watney & Charleston 1966, p. 66 ff
CT

C24 *The Imports of Great Britain from France*

Louis Philippe Boitard (active *c.* 1733-63). 1757
Etching and engraving; 250 x 352
Lettered with title, 'explanation', copyright line dated 7 March 1757, address of John Bowles & son, and *Humbly Addressed to the Laudable Associations of Anti-Gallicans, and the generous promotors of the British Arts and Manufactories . . . Invented & Engrav'd by L.P. Boitard.*

The Trustees of the British Museum

The quay at Billingsgate or the Custom House, with a French packet unloading. On the quay are French wines, cheeses and luxury goods. The French persons include an Abbé working as a tutor, dancing masters, dancers and actors, coiffeurs, and 'At a distance, landing, swarms of milliners, tailors, mantua-makers, frisers, tutoresses for boarding-schools, disguis'd jesuits, quacks, valet de chambres &c. &c. &c.' Although by an artist of French origin, this print is the most complex and sophisticated of the many satires on the French taste and manners of the upper classes.

Lit: Atherton 1974, pp. 46, 173; BM:S 3653
MS

C24

49

Gravelot and printmaking

Thomas Shaw *Travels*, 1738. See cat. D4

D1 *Wine cooler*

Paul Crespin (1694-1770). London
hallmarks for 1733/4
Silver-gilt, gilding renewed; h. 320
Engraved in cartouche with the arms
of Charles, 3rd Duke of Marlborough,
KG (succ. 1733, d. 1758) surmounted
by a cast ducal crown
*His Grace the Duke of Marlborough DL, JP,
Blenheim Palace*

One of a pair. Raised cast and chased.
The shape of the buckets can be
compared with a design for an
icebucket by Meissonnier
subsequently published by Huquier
entitled *Pour M. le Duc 1723 (Oeuvres,
suite I58)*. The elements and
treatment of the armorial shield are
derived from French Régence sources;
pairs of animated fauns occur widely
both in contemporary French
decorative painting, as in Boucher's *Le
Denicheur des Moineaux* after Watteau,
published in 1727 and occasionally in
silver; on a *surtout de table* by Jacques
Roettiers, a pair flank the central basin
(Germain 1748, pl. 71). The
asymmetrically-set applied cartouche
is among the earliest to appear on
English silver and may be traced back
to Toro's designs and the cartouches
of Brunetti (Cat. B10). Wave ornament
is found on a Paris-made tureen also
of 1733, by Thomas Germain (Dennis
1960, 167). Single-bottle buckets for
ice became customary in England
from about 1700, supplied in sets of
two or more; see Hayward 1959, 29;
Hackenbroch 1969, 125 and others
cited there. At least two English
noblemen, Sir Robert Walpole and the
Duke of Kingston, owned Paris-made
icebuckets, the latter purchasing four
in 1735 to accompany his dinner
service. However, very few sets made
in England in the rococo style are
recorded. Families already possessing
this item of sideboard plate did not
necessarily replace it when ordering
tableware in the new fashion; neither
buckets nor other sideboard plate
were included in the Leinster order
(Cat. G23).

Prov: The Dukes of Marlborough
Lit: Loan Ex. Old English Plate 1929,
275; Grimwade 1974, pl. 13
PG

D1

D2 *Teapot*

English ('A' Marked Group).
c. 1745-60
Semi-hard porcelain, enamelled in
colours; h. 114
Marks: a capital letter *A* in underglaze
blue and *X* and *41* incised
VAM (C.50&A -1961)
See colour plate III

Globular body, serpentine spout and
foliate handle; the lid with turned
acorn knop. On each side of the
teapot is a scene painted after an
engraving by George Bickham after
Gravelot from *Songs in the Opera Flora,*
London, 1737: on one side
Mr Friendly sings 'Liberty a Duette' to
Flora, the heiress whom he is courting
despite opposition from her uncle and
guardian, Sir Thomas Testy; on the
other side is a scene after the hasty
marriage of Mr Friendly to Flora, with
their respective servants showing signs
of copying their master and mistress,
while Sir Thomas walks off in a huff.
These scenes are framed by iron-red
scrollwork not found on Bickham's
engravings but nonetheless very close
in character to Gravelot's style. The
rare group of porcelains marked
sometimes in underglaze blue and
sometimes by incision with a capital
'A' present serious problems of
attribution and there are still those
who do not rule out an attribution to
continental Europe, probably in the
hinterland of Venice as suggested in
1958 by Arthur Lane. However, as
more pieces of the class have turned
up (all in England) and been
identified, the predominance of pieces
painted after designs published in
England after Gravelot's designs has
also expanded. For instance, the slop-
basin of the service to which the
present teapot belongs is painted with
a cricketing subject. Acorn knops and
knops in the form of a coiled Chinese
lion both suggest a link with
Staffordshire saltglaze. The paste,
however, is unlike any other known
ceramic body. A short-lived British
factory influenced not only by
Gravelot's prints but also by his style
of ornamental rococo scrollwork
seems indicated. One possibility, as
yet quite unproven, is that the 'A'
marked wares were examples of the
'porcelaine ware' which we now know
to have been advertised by Nicholas
Crisp and John Saunders at Vauxhall
on May 21, 1753.

Prov: Messrs P. and K. Emden;
Anthony Baer
Lit: Charleston and Mallet 1972 &
1973; Lane 1958, pp. 15-18; Valpy and
Mallet 1982
JVGM

D3

D3 *John Gay,* Fables

Vol. II, 1755, fifth edition, London,
J & P Knapton. 8vo
VAM (National Art Library)

John Gay (1685-1732) poet and
dramatist, was an indulged friend of
Pope, Swift, Steele, Arbuthnot and
other Augustan wits, and much petted
and patronised by the cultivated great
nobility. His most popular drama, *The
Beggar's Opera,* first produced on 29
January 1728, is one of the key works
of the rococo age in England. His
Fables, written in 1725 for Prince
William, later Duke of Cumberland,
were almost equally popular
throughout the 18th century, and
from their first edition of 1727,
illustrated with designs by John
Wootton and William Kent, were
issued repeatedly in finely illustrated
editions until the end of the century.
They give a lively, witty, contemporary
twist to the traditional moral lessons of
the fable, aided by the quick, jerky
rhythms of their octosyllabic verse.
Volume II, with title, vignette,
frontispiece and 16 plates by Gerard
Baptiste Scotin II after Hubert
Gravelot, was first published in 1738.
The plate exhibited, that for 'The
Man, the Cat, the dog, and the Fly'
(facing page 69) is characteristic of the
graceful naturalism of the illustrations.

52

The man's rococo chair, with its
elegant tapering cabriole leg and
rocaille shell on the back, is in advance
of contemporary English furniture.

Lit: Hammelmann 1975, p. 43
RWL & MS

D4 *Thomas Shaw,* Travels, or Observations relating to Several parts of and the Levant.

Illustrated with Cuts. 1738
First edition Oxford, folio
The Bodleian Library, Oxford

Open at the headpiece and initial
letter to Chapter I of Tome II, part I
designed and engraved by Hubert
Gravelot (size of plate 100 x 160). The
Rev. Thomas Shaw (1694-1751),
English chaplain at Algiers from 1720
to 1733, wrote a description of North
Africa, Egypt and Syria which is
notable for its acuteness and learning.
It is not an itinerary but a collection of
essays on the topography, antiquities,
ethnography and natural history of
these countries: the notes on natural
history being particularly novel and
important. Each of the book's four
parts has a headpiece consisting of a
motif enclosed in a cartouche frame in
a brilliant rococo style. Three were
engraved by Gravelot and Jean
Rocque after designs by Charles, later
Sir Charles, Frederick (1709-85), an
antiquary and amateur artist who 'was
eminently distinguished for his taste in
the polite arts and for his great skill in
drawing' (*Gent. Mag.* 1785, 2, p. 1010).
Frederick's headpieces contain many
elements skilfully adapted from
Meissonnier's *Livre D'Ornemens,*
published in England in 1737 (see cat.
C17). This headpiece is one of three
engraved by Gravelot; unlike those for
parts I and II it is entirely of his own
design. It is an ingenious
intermingling in a rococo cartouche of
motifs illustrating the principal themes
of the book, the antiquities of Egypt
(figured in the pyramids), the Arab
inhabitants of the Near East, the
plants and trees of the same region,
and its birds and animals (l), an eagle,
a camel, a lion, a serpent, (r) an ostrich
and crocodile. Below are insects. All
these motifs are rather fancifully
treated. Shaw's book was produced
with an expensive richness of
engraved maps, illustrations after his

own not very good drawings, and
headpieces. In the dedication to the
second edition (1757) he says that he
had been honoured with the
patronage of Queen Caroline
(d. 1737).

Lit: Hammelmann, 1975, p. 43
RWL & MS

D5 *Design for a border*

Hubert François (Bourguignon)
Gravelot (1699-1773). *c.* 1738
Pen and ink and wash, silhouetted;
375 x 609
Inscribed in pencil *Portion of a Design by
Van Dyck*
*The Cooper-Hewitt Museum, The
Smithsonian Institutions's National Museum
of Design (1946-2-2)*

On the right Britannia vanquishes
Envy, Superstition and Spain; on the
left Hypocrisy, Ignorance and Popery
fall before the true Religion. A
drawing for the surround to the
General Chart in John Pine's *The
Tapestry Hangings of the House of Lords,*
1739, for which Gravelot designed
borders for 9 of the 18 plates, all
engraved by Pine. The remaining
plates are after C. Lemprière, very
much in Gravelot's manner. The 17th
century tapestries depicted the defeat
of the Spanish Armada, a subject of
great popular interest during the war
with Spain, which began in 1739. The
long band-like scrollwork is similar to
that executed by Richards around
Hogarth's paintings in St
Bartholomew's Hospital (1735-6,
Croft-Murray 1970, p. 55)

Prov: Horace Walpole (?)
Lit: Berlin 1939, 1677; FitzGerald
1969, p. 145, fig. 25; Vertue VI, p. 195
MS

D6 *Plate*

Chelsea (Lawrence Street Factory). *c.*
1753-5
Soft-paste porcelain, the glaze
apparently slightly opacified with tin,
enamelled in colours; diam. 235
Mark: an anchor in red
Private Collection

Of wavy outline painted in colours in
the centre with the scene after
Gravelot of a boy flying a kite
accompanied by two others boys and
a dog above a puce scrollwork half-
frame with pendant garlands. The
border with flower sprays and the rim

D5

D6

D7

outlined in brown. Six plates from this service are recorded: five of them formerly in the Robert Gelston Collection illustrated together in Mackenna, 1951, pl. 53 and pp. 89-90, amongst which was the plate exhibited and two in the VAM (C. 119&A-1980). A sixth plate, formerly in the Alfred G. Hutton Collection, is illustrated in Blunt 1924, pl. 3, fig. 29 and is now in The Museum of Fine Arts at Boston (Honey revised by Barrett, 1977, pl. 8D). The anonymous painter of these plates can be recognised by the neat inverted 'U' strokes by which he indicates foliage, and by other characteristics such as his manner of stippling flesh in red, to be the painter of many landscapes and figure subjects on Chelsea from the period about 1753-6. His work is sometimes confused with that of his

contemporary, J.H. O'Neale. Cook (1946-52, p. 57 & 58, pl. 22 a & c) discusses the engraver Hancock's use of Gravelot's designs of *Jeux* engraved in England in 1738 and illustrates the subject *Le Cervolant* and the present hand-painted plate.

Prov: R. Gelston Collection
Lit: Blunt (ed) 1924; Cook 1946-52; Charleston & Towner 1977, pl. 121; Honey 1928, pp. 57-60; Severne Mackenna 1951
JVGM

D7 *Henry, Prince of Wales*
The portrait attributed to Arthur Pond (1701-1758) after Isaac Oliver (before 1568-1617). *c.* 1738. The ornamental surround by Hubert François (Bourguignon) Gravelot (1699-1773). *c.* 1739
Oil colour on a separate piece of paper pasted down, the surround pen and ink and wash over red chalk, indented for transfer; 371 x 231
The surround signed in ink *H. Gravelot inv et delin* and inscribed on the *verso* in another hand *General L*
The Visitors of the Ashmolean Museum, Oxford

The surround was engraved in 1739 by Jacobus Houbraken of Amsterdam for a portrait of General Lambert. The drawing of Henry, Prince of Wales, which was engraved by Houbraken with a different surround in 1738, has been applied at a later date to the present surround. Both prints formed

part of a series of 80 portraits published by J. and P. Knapton to illustrate Nicholas Tindal's *Continuation of Mr Rapin Thoyras's History of England,* for which the subscription opened in 1736. The prints, announced in 1737, could also be purchased separately. They were re-issued, eventually with 28 additional plates, as part of Thomas Birch's *Lives and Characters of eighty Illustrious Persons,* which was announced in 1742 and published in sets of four, then in two volumes (1747 and 1752) and finally in a collected edition entitled *The Heads of Illustrious Persons,* 1756. The 1752 title page states that the ornaments were invented by Gravelot and most of the plates are in his style. A number of designs by Gravelot, and his assistants survive, including 15 signed sheets by Gravelot at the Ashmolean. The earliest dated plate in Birch (no. 20), Thomas Howard, Duke of Norfolk engraved in 1735, already shows the heavily-modelled, often symmetrical, mixture of baroque and genre-pittoresque forms characteristic of the series. No plates are dated 1736, and the two plates dated 1737 are by George Vertue, who designed and engraved l0 in the series up to 1742. The main dated group begins in 1738 (when 22 were engraved). The plates dated between 1748 and 1750 are chiefly weak imitations of the manner of Gravelot, who left England by 1746. In this design a putto lifts a curtain to reveal a relief of a battle in the Civil War. Pond's role in the execution of the heads has been linked with his tours to country seats from 1737 onwards to copy portraits for the Knaptons. There is no convincing evidence to support the tradition that the young Gainsborough was involved with the design of the surrounds.

Prov: A. H. Sutherland; Bodleian Library
Lit: Birch 1756, no. 29 (the portrait), no. 63 (surround); Brown 1982, 1503, 1503A, pl. XXXIV; Hayes 1969 I, fig. 3; Hayes 1969 II, fig. 1; Lippincott 1983, pp. 36, 150-153. Vertue III, p. 9l.
MS

D8 *Aeneas and Anchises*

Hubert François (Bourguignon) Gravelot (1699-1773). *c.* 1739
Pen and ink and wash; 187 x 160
Inscribed . . . *Superat quoniam Fortuna, sequamur / Quoque vocat, vertamus iter . . .*
Private Collection

Perhaps the original drawing for a second, perhaps only projected edition (1739) of John Theobald's translation of Virgil's *Aeneid,* book II. The subject perhaps formed a tailpiece to canto 4, but no copy of the book has been found. T. Aris, who published Theobald's *Aeneid* book IV in 1739, moved to Birmingham in

1741. He may have been responsible for introducing the copper plate to the makers of ceramics and enamels (Cat. D9, D10). The plate appeared again in Sayer's *The Compleat Drawing Book,* 3rd ed. 1762.

Lit: Hammelmann 1975, pp. 42-3; Watney 1975, pp. 270-1, pl. 175(a)
MS

D9 *Plate*

Bow. *c.* 1756
Soft-paste porcelain containing bone-ash, transfer-printed in red and with border hand-painted in red;
diam. 197
Private Collection

In the centre is a transfer-print in red of Aeneas who, followed by his son and wife, carries his aged father Anchises on his back from the burning ruins of Troy. The whole scene is framed in a scroll and ribbon border. At the rim of the plate is a spearheaded pattern painted in red. The original design by Hubert François Gravelot, Cat. D8 in the present exhibition, is the same way round as the present Bow transfer-print. This would be due to the double process of reversal involved in first engraving and then transferring an impression to the porcelain. The version of the print published in the *Compleat Drawing Book* (3rd edition, 1762) is signed *H. Gravelot delin* and is, as one would have expected, reversed

from the original drawing (Toppin, 1948, pl. XCIV c). When this print appears on Worcester porcelain as on a black-printed bell-shaped mug in the VAM (C.83-1939) it is the same way round as on the Bow plate. The same print is found on a single recorded enamel plaque attributed to Birmingham (Cat. D10) also the same way round as the drawing and the transfer on the present Bow plate. Whereas the Gravelot pictorial design draws heavily on the 17th century baroque, the framing with its rather cartilaginous type of scrollwork, only very slightly asmmyetrical, is characteristic of the rococo style that Gravelot did so much to diffuse in England.

Lit: Adams & Redstone 1981; Cook 1948, Item 1; Gabszewicz & Freeman 1982, No. 118; Rackham Vol.I 1928, No. 111 & p. 10; Toppin Vol. 2, No. 10, 1948, pl. XCIV c & d; Watney 1975, pl. 175a; Sotheby's, 3 December, 1968, 152
JVGM

D10 *Plaque*

London or Birmingham. *c.* 1755-60
Copper, enamelled and gilt. w. ll5
Private collection

Cartouche-shaped plaque of copper printed and painted with Aeneas and Anchises with Julius fleeing Troy, mounted in a copper-gilt frame. The print on this apparently unique

D9

D10

plaque is after the drawing by Gravelot (Cat. D8) from a plate probably engraved to accompany a 1739 edition published by T. Aris, London, of John Theobald's translation of the *Aeneid,* book IV. The same plate was used to decorate porcelains made at Bow about 1755 and at Worcester about 1757-60. It is therefore uncertain where the present plaque was printed. However, when offered for sale in 1979, it was accompanied by four other plaques in identical frames, and the style of decoration of these four pieces suggests a Birmingham origin.

Prov: Sotheby's 23 October 1979, 42
Lit: Watney 1975, pp. 270-271, pl. 175a
CT

D11 *A landscape*

Francis Vivares (1707-1780). 1739
Etching; 94 x 154
Lettered *Vivares invenit sculpsit london Vivares, in. Sclp.* and with a copyright line dated 19 March 1739
The Yale Center for British Art, Paul Mellon Collection (b.1977.14.14228)

The copyright line is contained within a *rocaille* cartouche. This is an early example of the small landscapes, generally Dutch or Italian in character, which were often included in English drawing manuals. Similar subjects were etched after Watteau, eg *L'abreuvoir* (Dacier & Vauflart 1929, 137).

Prov: from an album compiled in the 18th century *a book of Sundry prints*
MS

D12 *Snuff-box*

English ('A' Marked Group).
c. 1745-60
Semi-hard paste porcelain, enamelled in colours and mounted in gilt base-metal; diam. 625, h. 350
Mark: a capital letter *A* incised in the interior of the base
National Museum of Wales, Cardiff (D.W.552)

Of circular section and slightly *bombé* form, the lid slightly domed. On the greyish-white porcelain are painted panels of polychrome flowers round the exterior of the base, a harbour scene in Meissen style and further flowers on the lid, all contained within iron-red scrollwork. The class of porcelain known to collectors as 'A'-marked because of the capital 'A' found sometimes incised sometimes in underglaze blue on many pieces, has a chemical composition unlike that of any other known porcelains. An origin in continental Europe, particularly in the region of Venice has been suggested by Lane (1958) and others, but Charleston and Mallet (1971) have argued strongly for an English origin. An argument for an English origin is the strong influence of Gravelot on the design of the scrollwork even when, as on this snuff-box, the scenes depicted do not derive from Gravelot prints.

Prov: De Winton Collection
Lit: Lane 1958, pp. 15-19, pl. II, figs. 7, 8; Charleston & Mallet 1971, pp. 80-121, pl. 69, figs a, b

D13 *The Races of the Europeans, with their Keys*

George Bickham junior (*c.* 1706-1771).
1740
Etching and engraving; 275 x 398
Lettered with title, etc. and *Geo. Bickham junr. invt. et sculpt.* and dated *1740*
The Trustees of the British Museum (1868-8-8-3642)

Described in the *London Daily Post* (20 March 1740) as 'A Curious Print, with a fine Border'. Many of the images in the four connected frames are derived from a series of prints by Charles Mosley and Phillip Overton using the metaphor of a horse race to satirise the state of Europe at the start of the War of the Austrian Succession. The very striking border, incorporating an asymmetrically placed satyr's head (re-used on Cat. J3) is the strongest of a number of intertwined frame borders ultimately indebted to Gravelot (eg BM:S 2440 dated 1740). Bickham's most imaginative work was in the field of satirical prints.

Lit: Atherton 1974, pp. 12, 15;
BM:S 2335
MS

D14 *William Shakespeare,* Works

Edited by Lewis Theobald, 1740, vol. 8. Second edition, for J. Lintot *et al.,* London, 12mo
VAM (Dyce 8941)

Open at the plate (150 x 75) by Gerard van der Gucht (1696-1776) after Hubert Gravelot, illustrating *Othello,* p. 229. The plates for this edition were designed by Gravelot, who also engraved eight of them himself. They show him practising the light and elegant French style evolved during the Régence and the 1730s. Rendered in engraving by light silvery tones, grey shadows and much use of white highlights, this style is deliberately sketchy and suggestive in effect. In this scene, illustrating Othello murdering Desdemona (Act V, Scene 2) Gravelot achieves a certain dramatic suggestiveness by virtue of this technique of sketchiness in spite of the mannered elegance of his figures. The setting is a French rococo bedroom, its walls hung with tapestries of landscapes, its chair, bed, footstools and candelabrum shaped by

D11

H.Gravelot in & del.   G.Vander Gucht Scul.
V.8.P.229

D14

dominant scrollwork motifs and ornaments. The candelabrum is a peculiarly violent early rococo invention with its irrational, asymmetrical forms, here adding an unexpected expressive element of violence to the scene. Ironically enough Gravelot's composition disregards Theobald's note (p. 329) to line 29 of the scene 'Put out the light, and then put out the light' that the players 'often commit an absurdity here, in making Othello put out the Candle; which 'tis evident, never was the Poet's Intention. *Desdemona* is discover'd in her Bed, in the dark; and *Othello* enters the Chamber with a single taper.' The setting, like many settings in illustrations to plays and novels, is enhanced by the designer's fancy much beyond reality; especially the reality of an English interior of *c.* 1740. There is an interesting record of what an author or publisher might expect to pay an engraver for such a set of plates in a letter from Thomas Cooke to Sir Thomas Hanmer of 1 May 1740 in which he says that to embellish the ten volumes of his proposed edition and translation of Plautus he wants a 'set of Copper plates for each respective volume; for which I have agreed with an eminent

Engraver, for two Guineas a sett' (Hanmer, *Correspondence*, 1838, p. 227). 13 of Gravelot's drawings for Theobald's Shakespeare are in the Albertina, Vienna; 15 are in the Huntington Library, San Marino, including that for the present plate (repr. Wark 1972). The engraver's medium has deepened the contrasts of light and shade, but van der Gucht has followed Gravelot very literally.

Lit: Hammelmann 1958; Hammelmann 1975, pp. 43-4; Merchant 1959, pp. 53-5; Wark 1972, pp. 26-8, 76
RWL

D15

D15 *A Gentleman Standing*
Hubert François (Bourguignon) Gravelot (1699-1773)
Chalk and stump; 335 x 196
The Visitors of the Ashmolean Museum

Both D15 and D16 represent the same model, although Gravelot's figure wears a sash. They were no doubt made during Grignion's period as a pupil of Gravelot, and one may be a copy of the other. A number of Gravelot's drawings of figures in fashionable costume have survived, one of which (British Museum) is of the same model as that shown from a different viewpoint in a drawing by Grignion. They can be related to the

sets of figures after Gravelot engraved by Truchy, Major and Grignion, which were published by John Bowles, 1744-5. All but one of the prints are probably derived from drawings of articulated dolls or lay figures, and most of the surviving figure drawings also suggest this technique. Three such figures, 2½ feet high, were in the sale at Gravelot's death. Roubiliac's figure (Museum of London) answers very closely to the description of Gravelot's figures (Preston 1983, 55; D'Oench 1980, pp. 13-14). It is also recorded that Gravelot made large-scale figure drawings for his book illustrations.

Prov: Francis Douce; Bodleian Library
Lit: Ashmolean 1979, no. 74; Brown 1982, 764; Parker 1938, 500
MS

D16 *A Gentleman Standing*
Charles Grignion (1721-1810)
Chalk and stump, heightened with white; 370 x 212
Inscribed in an old hand on the *verso, Grignon*
The Visitors of the Ashmolean Museum

See Cat. D15

Prov: presented by Miss Drummond, 1950
Lit: Ashmolean 1979, no. 41, Brown 1982, 814
MS

D17

D17 *The Grant Family*

Francis Hayman (1708-1776).
c. 1740-42
Oil on Canvas; 1028 x 1067
Private Collection

John Grant (d. 1747) with his wife
Margaret (d. 1787) and their children.
In 1746 the family lived in Smith
Street, Westminster where John Grant
kept one of the boarding-houses for
the boys of Westminster School.
Following his death, his widow
followed the custom then prevailing at
Eton and Westminster by continuing
to keep the house as a 'Dame'. They
are typical of Hayman's
predominantly middle-class clientele.
Although trained as a painter of
decorative history and stage-scenery,
very little of Hayman's early work
survives. His rise to prominence in the
early 1740s coincided with the
declining taste for decorative painting
and the rise of the conversation piece.
Hayman's reputation nowadays is
based on his informal group portraits
and *The Grant Family* is a
particularly good example of his
ability to anglicise the *fête galante* of

Watteau and his followers, adapting it
to the native propensity for portraiture
in the early 1740s. The lively
composition of the figures, which
owes something to the waspish
elegance of Gravelot, and the
naturalistic yet capricious landscape
backdrop is of the type developed to
great effect by the young Thomas
Gainsborough just a few years later.
The lively pose of the young boy on
the left with his sister may be adapted
from Van Dyck's well known double
portrait of *Lord John Stuart with his
brother Lord Bernard Stuart* of *c.* 1639,
now at Broadlands, and contrasts
sharply with the rigid formality of
similar groups by Arthur Devis.

Prov: probably painted for John Grant;
Mrs Grant; by family descent to
Mrs Maria Dixon (née Grant);
Mrs Caroline Webster Wedderburn
(niece of Mrs Dixon); Christie's
29 February 1896 (84) as by Hogarth
bt Colnaghi; Christie's 14 July 1911
(40) as Highmore bt. F. Harper
(dealer); Mr and Mrs Basil Ionides.
BA

D18 *Illustrations to Samuel Richardson,* Pamela

Hubert François (Bourguignon)
Gravelot (1699-1773). Before 1742
a) Pamela upsetting the table in her
haste to embrace her father (for
vol. II, p. 89)
b) Pamela's marriage to Mr B (for
vol. II, p. 175)
c) Pamela refusing to pour out wine
for Lady Danvers (for vol. II, p. 249)
Pen and ink, wash and red chalk;
130 x 78, 130 x 77, 130 x 77
d) Unfinished proof etching after (a),
touched with pencil; 131 x 80 (cut)
e) Unfinished proof etching after (c)
128 x 80 (cut)
f) Etching after (c), final state, 143 x 91
*The Trustees of the British Museum
(1888-6-19-26,25,23; 1875-7-10-5030,
5039, 5032)*

The first part of *Pamela* was published
by Samuel Richardson (1689-1761) in
1740. The story describes in a series of
letters how the artless heroine,
Pamela, a humbly born serving-maid,
by her virtuous resistance to his
attempts at seduction wins the
affections and becomes the wife of her
master Squire B –. It was immediately
popular, especially among women, of
whose rights to respect and chivalrous

D18

treatment Richardson was an ardent advocate. The book is the first masterpiece of the 18th century novel of sentiment and has survived the ridicule levelled at it by Fielding in his anonymous satire *Shamela* (1741) and *Joseph Andrews* (1742), not least because of its delicacy and acuity of psychological analysis. The sixth edition of *Pamela* (4 vols., 1742) was illustrated with etchings by Gravelot, 17 after his own drawings and two after Hayman. The interiors shown are only loosely connected with actual English examples. The viewpoints and the proportions of the rooms as well as details such as the overdoor painting in (a) recall the illustrations after Boucher in the *Oeuvres de Molière*, Paris 1734. These illustrations were certainly known to Hayman (see Cat. D19) and to George Bickham, who used them for headpieces in *The Musical Entertainer* in 1737. It has been suggested that Gravelot assisted Boucher with the illustrations in 1732 (Croft Murray n.d.). The chair in (c) with its interlace back also appears, in a modified form in the works of Hayman (Cat. D21) and has parallels in the prints of De la Cour (Cat. D22). No English chairs of this form appear to survive, and it is possible that they were entirely imaginary. No French parallels exist, the closest Continental equivalent being undated Venetian chairs. The motif of interlaced bandwork was much used by Gravelot (Cat. D13)

Prov: the drawings purchased from A.W. Thibaudeau
Lit: Binyon 1898, 5(e) (d) (b); Croft Murray n.d., 29-31; FitzGerald 1969 II; Hammelmann 1975, p. 44
RWL & MS

D19 *The Works of Mr William Shakespear Volume the Sixth. Consisting of Tragedies.*
Edited by Thomas Hanmer 1744
Oxford, printed at the Theatre
VAM (Dyce 8942)

Open at the plate engraved by Hubert Gravelot after Francis Hayman illustrating the lines from *Othello*, Act 4, Scene 6, in which Othello, deceived by Iago's letter, orders Desdemona 'Out of my sight'. *Left* are Lodovico *(front)* and Iago. The setting is adapted

OTHELLO. Act 4. Sc. 6.

D19

from a plate by Laurent Cars after Boucher illustrating *L'Avare* (Jean-Richard 1978, 436) in *Oeuvres de Molière*, Paris, 1734. Indeed Hayman's plate interprets the scene in a light style better suited to the illustration of French comedy than to its tragic motifs of treachery and betrayal. The dress, like the setting, is strictly contemporary, except for Othello's, which has one or two features of rococo historical costuming. Both setting and costume are perhaps intended to highlight the domestic nature of the tragedy; in the anachronistic treatment of this last of Hayman's designs for Hanmer's Shakespeare there seems to be something of a departure from the fuller historical costuming found in many of the other illustrations of Hanmer's Shakespeare. However, in these illustrations Hayman often fluctuates with true rococo insouciance between anachronism and attempted verisimilitude of setting and costume. The drawings for the plates to this edition of Shakespeare were commissioned from Hayman directly by Sir Thomas Hanmer. The agreement between them stipulated that the subjects of the illustrations were to be selected by Hanmer and that Hayman was 'to finish the same with Indian ink in such a manner as shall be fit for an Ingraver to work after them and approved by the said Sr Thomas Hanmer'. Hayman was to

receive three guineas per drawing, but only when the whole set had been finished, and the date of completion was to be Ladyday, 1741. In fact Hayman did not complete the work, for the illustrations to volume four were designed and engraved by Gravelot. The agreement, and all the drawings by Hayman and Gravelot, are now in the Folger Library, Washington, bound into a set of Hanmer's *Shakespear*.

Lit: Hammelmann 1975, p. 52; Merchant 1958; Merchant 1959, pp. 55-6
RWL & MS

D20

D20 *Le Lecteur*
Hubert François (Bourguignon) Gravelot (1699-1773). *c.* 1745
Oil on canvas; 311 x 234
Marble Hill House (GLC)

Gravelot very rarely painted in oil, although Vertue noted in 1733 that he had tried painting small pieces 'which gives some hopes of his succeeding in small histories or conversations'. The figure of the girl was engraved by Grignion in 1745 for the suite of figures after Gravelot published by Bowles. The whole composition was engraved in reverse by René Gaillard and published in Paris in 1756 with the title *Le Lecteur* and a verse beginning 'Oui, cette jeune Angloise...' It was also engraved in reverse in England by James Marchand with the title *The Judicious Lover* and a verse on the wooing of Celia: 'And what the Swain himself could neer have won / A single page of Ovid see has done'. The stiff pose of the girl is very suggestive of the use of an articulated doll. A close version, signed in monogram *H.G* is in the York City Art Gallery.

Prov: (?) artist's sale, Paris 19 May 1773; Mr & Mrs Eliot Hodgkin (bought in Paris); bought for Marble Hill 1968
Lit: Buck 1979, fig. 16; Edwards 1958; GLC 1968, 22; GLC 1975,11; Royal Academy 1968, 297; Vertue III, p. 67; Walker Art Gallery 1958, 8
MS

D21 *Mr and Mrs Richard Bull*
Arthur Devis (1712-1787). 1747
Oil on canvas; 1067 x 864
Signed and dated *A Devis fe 1747*
The Institute of Fine Arts, New York University

The couple are seated at a table in a stark, airy, and probably imaginary interior. On the mantlepiece is a row of Chinese porcelain, and on brackets on the wall male and female classical busts. Over the chimneypiece in an Italianate landscape in a frame taken from a plate in De la Cour's *Fifth Book of Ornaments*, 1743 (see Cat. C11). The top of the frame incorporates a cartouche bearing the arms of Bull. Richard Bull of Ongar (1721-1805) was a noted antiquary and print collector and a friend of Horace Walpole. D'Oench points out the influence of Gravelot in the relaxed pose of the man and of Hayman on the placing of the couple in the room. Devis repeated most of the setting and the poses in *Mr and Mrs Dashwood* 1750 (D'Oench 1980, list 45; Preston 1983, 18, repr.)

Prov: at North Court, Isle of Wight, purchased by Bull in 1795; by descent through owners of North Court; Christie's 9 July 1926, 22; Gooden & Fox; Jesse Isidore Strauss; Mrs Irma M. Strauss (d. 1970), bequest to the Institute
Lit: D'Oench 1980, 19 (includes full references)
MS

D21

D22 *Master's chair of the Fruiterer's Company*
Anonymous. 1748
Mahogany with leather upholstery
1645 x 850 x 825
Lady Lever Art Gallery, Port Sunlight

The acanthus cartouche on the arched crest rail depicts the Beadle of the Company making an annual presentation of fruit to the Lord Mayor. The figure-of-eight scallop-edged splat springs from the shell-shaped shoe and frames the charge from the arms of the Company: The Tree of Knowledge entwined by the serpent. Lions *couchant* are perched on

the arms, and a satyr-mask appears
within the cartouche on the seat
frame. The cabriole legs are headed by
men-of-the-woods masks and end in
lion paw feet. The design of the back,
with its scrolling structure, is taken
from a plate in William De la Cour's
Fifth Book of Ornaments (1743).

Prov: the Fruiterer's Company;
Mrs A.G. Storr, 1908; Christie's,
10 Dec. 1913, 59; bt by M. Harris &
Son; bt. by Lord Leverhulme, 1919
Lit: Foley 1911, Vol. II, p. 14; Gould
1912; Macquoid 1928, p. 198;
Macquoid 1928 I
JH

D23 *George Dance the Elder*

Francis Hayman (1708-1776). Late
1740s
Oil on canvas; 534 x 431
*The Syndics of the Fitzwilliam Museum,
Cambridge (PD.20-1951)*

George Dance the elder (1695-1768)
was Surveyor to the City of London
and is best known as the architect of
the Mansion House and a number of
City Churches. The picture can be
dated on the grounds of costume and
comparison with other similar dated
work to the late 1740s. The fact that
Dance sent his son Nathaniel to study
with Hayman *c.* 1749-50 may have
some connection with his choice of
painter. Hayman's portraits often
suffer from his tendency to make all
his sitters look alike, but this portrait
of Dance is uncharacteristically
forthright and individual. Hayman
shows Dance leaning against a curious
chair with cabriole legs and an
interlaced back, and another of these
is placed against the panelling in the
background. Hayman must have
owned a chair of this type for it
appears in several other portraits,
including *The Tyers Family* and *The
Bedford Family* (Cat. D17, M3). It has
been suggested (Fitz-Gerald 1969) that
the design of the chair is derived from
Hayman's close association with
Hubert Gravelot. The small landscape
on the wall is very close to the work of
the young Gainsborough and is a
reminder of the close connection
between the two artists about this time.

Prov: anon sale (Mrs Metges) Sotheby's
6 June 1935 4, bt. Agnew; purchased
later that year from Agnews by present
owners

D23

Lit: Fitz-Gerald 1969, p. 142; Geffrye
Museum 1972, no. 1; Goodison 1977,
pp. 99-101
BA

D24 *Illustration to Alexander
Pope's* Moral Essays

Epistle IV, of the use of Riches
Simon François Ravenet (1706-1774)
after Nicholas Blakey (worked 1749-
53). *c.* 1748-1751
Etching and engraving; 165 x 90
Lettered *What brought Sr. Visto's ill-got
wealth to waste? / Some Daemon whisper'd,
Visto! have a Taste. N. Blakey inv. et del.
Ravenet Sculp*

Private Collection

From Vol. III of Warburton's edition
of Pope's *Works*, 1751, 8o (Griffith
1962, 643). Blakey, who died in Paris

on 20 November 1758, was an Irish-
born designer, engraver and
illustrator. He was trained in Paris but
worked in London from *c.* 1748 to
c. 1753. He made designs for a
number of plates in this edition of
Pope's *Works*. The *Epistle* is addressed
by Pope to Lord Burlington, as the
arbiter of good taste. The wealthy
prodigal Visto is shown in a cabinet
awkwardly and pretentiously
decorated with a huge, richly framed
mirror hung above a chimneypiece on
whose mantlepiece stands an absurdly
designed rococo clock absurdly
flanked by naked figurines. On the
adjoining wall hangs another
pretentious decoration, a painting in a
ridiculously elaborate rococo frame of
a genre pittoresque garden staircase,
exemplifying the pompous barren

Plate XV.	Vol. III. facing p. 162.

N. Blakey inv. et del.	*Ravenet Sculp.*

What brought Sr Visto's ill-got Wealth to waste?
Some Dæmon whisper'd,Visto! have a Taste.
Ep: on Taste.

D24

formality Pope satirises in his description of the gardens of Timon's villa in this *Epistle*. To either side of the painting various disparate *bibelots* and curiosities are ranged ostentatiously on wall brackets, a Chinese pagod, a covered cup, a stuffed animal, a poleaxe and Roman sword, with, above, a barometer. Visto is seated on the left in a *robe de chambre*, holding his morning levée, with a drinking mug in his left hand. A footman stands behind holding a salver with breakfast things and a coffee or chocolate pot. As Folly whispers into Visto's left ear, he examines a painting and a medal proffered by eager dealers. Other dealers offer a mummy-case and huge ancient tomes, the 'Rare monkish Manuscripts' of Pope's text. Behind, an architect holds up a rule and the plan of an irregular building with a terraced garden beside it. The plan is inscribed 'Rupery' (?) no doubt to suggest 'Ripley'. Joseph Ripley (*c.* 1683-1758) was a second-rate architect patronised by Sir Robert Walpole, who made him Comptroller of the Public Works. His buildings earned him the contempt of Lord Burlington and drew down Pope's scathing satire in this *Epistle* (11.17-18): 'Heav'n visits with a Taste the Wealthy

Fool / And needs no Rod but Ripley with a rule', the motif precisely illustrated in Blakey's design. In the foreground a Canopic jar and antique bronze figurines represent types of Egyptian and Classical antiquities favoured by collectors, while a swordfish's 'sword' symbolises the natural curiosities and a broken sword and scabbard the strange weapons which were other standard features of 18th century collections of curiosities. In the right background is a sheet of music on a stand. The plate satirises the empty-headedness of fashionable rococo taste. It illustrates Pope's satire of the ignorant and vulgar Visto who collects without knowledge and builds and decorates in an absurd manner, overloaded with ornament and flouting the rules of art. 'A standing sermon, at each years expense, / that never Coxcomb reached Magnificence'. As Pope's *Epistle* was first published in 1731, Blakey has modernised the false taste Pope satirises – he has also Frenchified it. This volume of Warburton's great edition of Pope's *Works,* which had been in preparation from 1748, was published in June 1751. Blakey signed plate IX of this volume with the date 1748.

Lit: Colvin 1978, pp. 694-5; Hammelmann 1975, pp. 18, 53-54
RWL

D25 *Designs by Mr. R. Bentley, for six Poems by Mr. T. Gray.*
R. Dodsley, London, 1753, Imperial 4o. Engravings by Johann Sebastian Muller (b. 1715, d. after 1785) and Charles I Grignion (1721-1810) after Richard Bentley (1708-1782).
VAM (National Art Library)

Horace Walpole fostered, promoted and paid for the publication of this pioneering book. Bentley's unique innovation is the design of a particular frontispiece, headpiece, initial letter, and tailpiece for each poem. The counterpoint of word and image and placement of the text only on one side of the page make the whole an art work. The witty play of sister arts is announced by the title-page fleuron: a monkey (who apes reality) draws what an Apollonian poet sings. Melancholy is the dominant theme; many images (from Gray in the initial frontispiece to

D25

the expiring torch of the final tailpiece) recall Ripa's 'Malinconia'. Berain, Watteau, Picart, Gravelot, Hogarth, and Pine inspire Bentley's rococo art, influences happily shown in the frontispiece to the 'Long Story'. The strapwork recalls Berain; the canopy and ambience recall Watteau (eg *La Pellerine Altérée,* Dacier & Vauflart 1929, 89); Mr Purt, Lady Schaub, and Henrietta Jane Speed recall Picart in *Monument Consacré à la Posterité en Memoire de la Folie Incroyable de la XX. Annee du XVIII Siècle.* Reminiscent of Hogarth's wit, the muses below make a double portrait of the women. Doubly doomed, Gray is led to the closet in the garden and then mounted on the broken pediment above the gorgons in the tailpiece. The drawings carry the eye and mind through the text.

Lit: Hazen 1948, no. 42; Hazen 1969, no. 2044
LJ

D26 *The Entail: A Fable*
The poem by Horace Walpole. The decoration by Richard Bentley (1708-1782). 1755
Pen and ink. Headpiece and MS poem; 85 x 85, initial letter 30 x 30 and tailpiece 90 x 115 on separate pieces of paper pasted down
The Lewis Walpole Library, Yale University

Influenced by Croxall's *Aesop's Fables* (1722), Pine's *Horace* (1733), and rococo pattern books such as the *Livre d'Ornemens* by Juste Aurèle

D26

Meissonnier (see Cat. C17), Bentley's zoomorphic frame holds in balance irregular yet revelatory forms; this strategy duplicates the Gray. The headpiece unfolds first like a shell cartouche, then a rosebud, a snail's shell, or the page of the will itself. The opposition of the east facade of Strawberry Hill and the manor of the haughty insect makes the allegorical identity. The butterfly directs the caterpillar to pen 'In the name of God, Amen ...'; at the upper left a young fly is anchored by escutcheons that make a pun on 'entail'. To the right the caterpillar below and the snail above foreshadow ruin. In the web of the initial letter the butterfly dies just above the blank oval left for Walpole's arms. The tailpiece explicates the ironic doom that opens like a scroll beneath, on which the 'Entail' is written. The staircase and armoury at Strawberry Hill collapse in rubble; rain puddles stand in the hall; a bat flies; a rook nests. The 'wanton Boy' destroys the fly's castle, yet above, released from its entail, the offspring flies free. Walpole thought the boy too large. *The Entail* was published at the Strawberry Hill Press in 1758 as one of Walpole's *Fugitive Pieces*; though Bentley also designed a frontispiece for the book, none of the illustrations for it was engraved.

Prov: Walpole to Mrs Damer; to Sir Wathen Waller; Waller Sale, Christie's 15 Dec. 1747, 45; bt Lewis,

bequeathed by Lewis to Yale 1979
Lit: Lewis 1936; Lewis 1937; Hazen 1948, 11
LJ

D27 *Edward Ryland,* The Liturgy of the Church of England

Illustrated with Fifty Five Historical and Explanatory Sculptures; Engrav'd by Mess. Ravenett, Grignion, Scotin, Canott, Walker and W. Ryland
London, E. Ryland, 1 May 1755, 8vo
VAM (National Art Library, L.702-1983)

Allegorical frontispiece of the Church of England, engraved by Charles Grignion after Samuel Wale (1721?-1786). Title page, an engraved cartouche enclosing a title designed by William Chinnery (1708-91) (each 160 x 110). The *Liturgy* is shown as an example of English rococo applied to religious art. Except by some High Churchmen the Reformation proscription of figurative religious art in churches, particularly sculpture, was still fairly rigidly observed in the 18th century. Hence the rococo style could not become a functional or expressive part of the decoration or liturgy of churches as in Catholic Germany or Austria. Religious book-illustration did not fall under the same prohibition, and so art was allowed a role as an aid to devotion and in explanation of doctrine in the illustration of the Bible and the Prayer-Book. Samuel Wale, an assistant of Hayman, was the most prolific English book-illustrator of the third quarter of the century. His designs were invariably made for engraving by others. William Chinnery, designer of the title, was one of the leading London writing-masters of the 1750s and grandfather of George, the painter. It seems to be an unrecorded work. That the title should have been specially commissioned from him shows the publisher's anxiety to ornament the book. Here the *Book of Common Prayer,* as printed in Cambridge in 1751, contains 55 engravings after Wale illustrating the life of Christ, the principal feast-days of the Virgin and the Apostles, and the Sacraments, all enclosed in elaborate engraved frames.

Prov: given by the Earl of Kinnoul to

Charlotte Frances Johnstone, later wife of Lt. Gen. Sir John Burgoyne, Bt., when a child; later an heirloom in the family of Lord Ongley.
Lit: Hammelmann 1975, p. 91; Heal 1931, pp. 27-9, 186-7
RWL

D28 *Bureau cabinet*
Anonymous. 1735/6
Mahogany. The silver fittings stamped with the makers' marks of Richard Gurney and Thomas Cooke. London hallmarks for 1735/6.
2670 x 1220 x 640
Private Collection

The base of the cabinet is fitted with drawers and a slope-front bureau and the upper section is fitted with candle-slides and doors with mirror-fronted panels, set in serpentine borders and flanked by fluted composite pilasters. The cornice is surmounted by an owl, symbol of wisdom, and broken scroll pediments. The drawers and doors have silver escutcheons and back-plates which are formed as asymmetrical scrolled cartouches. The basic form of the cabinet had been popular since the beginning of the 18th century, but the asymmetrical rococo silver fittings reflect fashionable taste of the mid 1730s. It is rare to find silver mounts on furniture of this scale, although they were popular for items such as knife boxes or tea caddies. For instance the tea caddy with silver *equipage* (Cat. G1) by Paul De Lamerie dates from the same year as the cabinet.
JH

D29 *Trade cards and ephemera*
The Trustees of the British Museum (unless otherwise stated)
a) Benjamin Rackstrow, figure-maker. Henry Copland (d. 1753). 1738.
VAM (E.1646-1907).
Lit: Heckscher 1979, pl. 46A.

b) William Kidney, goldsmith. Henry Copland. *c.* 1738. *(Heal 67.247).*
Lit: Heckscher 1979, pl. 46B.

c) Admission ticket: the annual dinner of the rest of the Mystery of Goldsmiths, November 1742. Henry Copland. Stamped with the hallmark date-letter for 1742/3. *(Banks C.2.586).* The first dated example of Copland's developed rococo style.

d) William De la Cour, drawing master. R. White after De la Cour. *c.* 1743 *(Heal 89.45)*. See Cat. C11.

e) John Duncan, bookseller. Jacob Bonneau. 1743.
Westminster City Libraries Archives Department (b.63.44F).

f) Advertisement for Right Redstreak Cider. George Bickham junior. *c.* 1745? One of a group of advertisements for general use listed in Bickham's *Oeconomy of the Arts*, 1747, at 1d and 1 1½d each. This impression was published by T. Butcher at May's Buildings (also Bickham's address) in 1749. The style is close to Gravelot *(Banks 59.32).*

g) Admission ticket: the trials in Westminster Hall of the Earls of Kilmarnock and Cromertie and Lord Balmerino.
Anonymous. 1746. *(1858.4.17.608).*
Lit: Moger 1980, 12.

h) Admission ticket: the Babylonian Lodge of the Order of the Bucks. Anonymous. The inscription dated 1749. *(Banks 1873.8.9.483).* All the Bucks cards seem to derive from a card of Henry Copland dated 1748. *Lit:* Wyman 1979.

i) P. Hurst, linen draper and seller of tea, chocolate and coffee, Knutsford, Cheshire. Henry Copland. *c.* 1750.
Blaise Castle House Museum, City of Bristol Museum and Art Gallery.
This card seems to have been engraved in London for a provincial client.

j) John Bishopp, engraver. Probably by himself.
c. 1750? *(Heal 17.54).*
In the style of Copland, with whom Bishopp had worked (card of John Raynes, gold-chain maker, *c.* 1740). The heads are after Toro (see Cat. C3) and the top after Cat. L4, 1744.

k) John Fuller, bookseller and stationer.
Anonymous. *c.* 1750. *(Heal 17.54).*
One of a group of ten cards probably indebted to an original by Copland.

l) Henry Patten, razor-maker. Edward Warner; one of a group of twelve, all indebted to Copland. 1756 or earlier. *The Guildhall Library.*
Lit: Heal 1925, LXXX (showing the second state; this is the first).

m) Advertisement for Calvert's violet cordial. Charles (?) Sherborn.
c. 1755?. *(Banks 83.2).* In the style of Copland.

n) John Haynes, land surveyor. By himself. *c.* 1755? *(Heal 76*.4).*
Partly derived from Copland's card for the Society of Bucks of 1748.

o) David Crashlay, figure and ornament maker. George Bickham junior.
c. 1750? *(Heal 32.13).*

p) John Clark, lamp lighter. Possibly by George Bickham junior.
c. 1750? *(Heal 76.4).*
Lit: Heal 1925, L.

q) Bartholomew Valle and brother, Italian grocers. Possibly by George Bickham junior.
1750? *(Heal 89.156).*

r) Peter Bonneau, razor-maker. Jacob Bonneau. *c.* 1750?
Westminster City Libraries, Archives Department.

s) William Keeling, pastry cook. William Austin.
1750s? *(Heal 48.37).*
Inscribed with a bill dated 1767.
Lit: Griffiths 1980, pl. 119.

t) William Austin, etcher and engraver. By himself. Before 1756, *c.* 1750? *(Heal 59.3).* See cat. L43.

u) Mary and Anne Favell's Ladies' Boarding School, Eltham. Matthew Darly and George Edwards. *c.* 1755? Probably derived from an untraced Copland card of *c.* 1740, cf. Cat. D29a. *(Banks 104.32).*

v) John Hutchinson, ships' broker. H. Burgh. *c.* 1755? *(Banks 5.23).*

w) Samuel Foulger, nightman. Anonymous. *c.* 1770? On the back a bill dated 1783 for 'Emptying a Vault of a ton of soil' for Mr Windmill, hatter of East Smithfield. *The Guildhall Library.*

x) Midwifery certificate. William Tringham. *c.* 1760? Adapted in the 19th century and awarded to John Moore Bowman by John Haighton in 1809. *(Banks 1938.U.2303).*

y) Admission ticket: the annual feast of the Society of College Youths, a club of campanologists. T. Kitchin. For the feast of November 1766. Addressed to Christopher Pinchbeck. The interlaced scroll design is ultimately indebted to Gravelot (see Cat. D13) but the etching style (as often in the 1760s) and parts of the design are very close to plates in Thomas Johnson's pattern book of 1758 (Cat. L44). *(Banks C.2-402).*

z) Admission ticket: the Society of the Free and Easy round the Rose. F. Garden. For the dinner in March 1762. *(Banks C.2-299)*
MS

Hogarth and St Martin's Lane

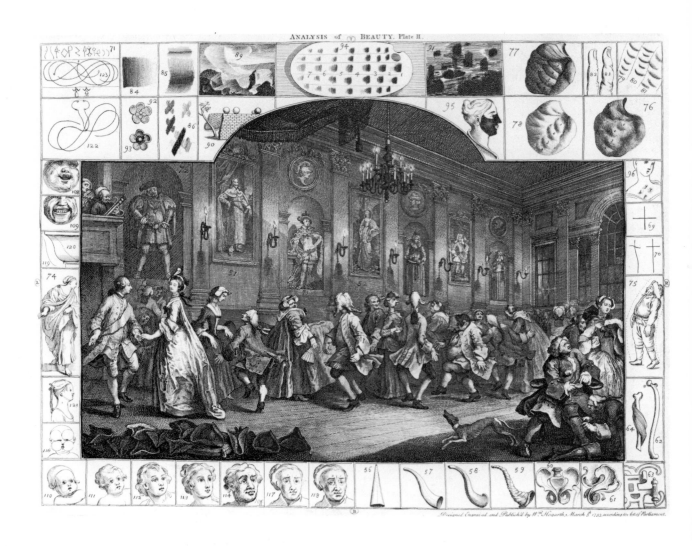

Analysis of Beauty. Plate II. William Hogarth. See Cat. E6.

E1 *Covent Garden*

Pieter Angillis (1695-1734). *c.* 1726
Oil on canvas; 762 x 1245
The Marquis of Tavistock and the Trustees of the Bedford Estates
See colour plate VI

A view of Covent Garden looking towards St Paul's Church. One of several surviving paintings by Angillis taken from the same viewpoint, one of which is dated 1726. They are connected with 'a curious Picture of Covent garden Markett. as it now appears. with persons in the habit of the time finely painted. A View of the North Side. & the Church front ... about 4f. by 3. done for Mr ... Walker Comiss. of the Customes by ... P. Angelles 1626 [sic]' noted by Vertue in 1726 (III, p. 31). The strongly emphasised back view of the woman in the foreground is probably indebted to the example of Watteau. Angillis, a Fleming, was in England *c.* 1713-1728. In 1726 he was living in Covent Garden which was not only a market but also 'the rendezvous of most of the most celebrated artists' (Vertue III, p. 27). He imported a style derived from Teniers, 'very free and light appearing rather too fair' (*ibid*, p. 25).

Lit: Plumb 1977, cat. 106
MS

E2 *William Hogarth*

Louis François Roubiliac (1702/5-62)
Terracotta, with plaster socle; h. (inc. socle) 711
National Portrait Gallery, London
(Reg. no. 121)

Presumably the 'Mr Hogarth very like' among the clay models seen by Vertue in 1741. The painter is shown *en negligé* wearing the informal dress with soft cap considered appropriate for artists and *virtuosi* but which by the 1740s was being adopted more widely. In addition to Coyzevox's *Prior* (cf. Cat. S29) Roubiliac was no doubt familiar with other French examples such as Guillaume Coustou's portrait of his brother, Nicolas (Souchal 1977, p. 151) and the sharp turn of the head recalls Coyzevox's *Robert de Cotte* (*ibid*, p. 211). Roubiliac's inventive use of this convention evolves from the *Hogarth*, which is closely comparable in form and scale to the *Handel* (1738; Royal Collection) and *Ware* (Cat. E15),

through the more broadly conceived *Folkes* (Cat. S11) to the *Wilton* (Cat. S36). The striking characterization of the sitter's alertness and energy makes this the most immediate and penetrating of the sculptor's early portraits, reflecting the close affinity between the two artists. Its freshness and wit are even apparent in the treatment of the socle, which, though in plaster, is shown (with the terracotta of *Trump,* cf. cat. E4) in an engraving of 1799 and is surely original. Socles bearing coats of arms were used by Scheemakers for the busts executed, probably in 1740, for the Temple of Friendship at Stowe (Whinney 1971, p. 60) and Hogarth's

cartouche with satyr head and palette may be a playful rococo gibe at this solemn Palladian convention.

Prov: sitter's collection; Mrs Hogarth's sale, 24 April 1790, 57, bt. John Hunter; Hunter sale, Christie's 29 Jan. 1794, 3rd day, 62, bt. Ireland; George Baker by 1809; by descent to Frances Hemming; bt. by W. Baker, 4 Feb. 1861; purchased by the NPG 1861
Lit: Burke 1976, p. 164; Esdaile 1928, p. 50; *Genuine Works* 1809, II, frontispiece; Ireland 1799, frontispiece; Kerslake 1977, pp. 143-4; Mallet 1967; Sainte-Croix 1882; Whinney 1964, p. 104
MCB

E2

65

E3 *Portrait of the Painter and his Pug*

William Hogarth (1697-1764). 1745
Oil on canvas; 900 x 699
Inscribed *W.H. 1745* and *The LINE of BEAUTY and GRACE* on palette (last two words overpainted, but now visible)
The Trustees of the Tate Gallery (112)
See colour plate V

Pentimenti show that Hogarth originally painted himself on the oval *trompe l'oeil* canvas in a full wig, white cravat and buttoned waistcoat, with the simple tools of his trade – a palette with brushes stuck through the thumb-hole – resting in front. It is not known when he decided to elaborate this conventional gentlemanly image of an artist into the much more forceful personal statement that we know, but some of the ideas may go back to his visit to Paris in May 1743, when he met French engravers and probably visited the studio of the only living foreign artist for whom he is known to have expressed admiration Maurice-Quentin de la Tour. (It has been noted that La Tour's lost self-portrait 'au chapeau borde', exhibited in 1742 and known only from G.F. Schmidt's engravings of 1772, bears numerous parallels in its organisation to Hogarth's self-portrait. We do not know, however, how much of this represents La Tour's ideas, or the engraver's). The conception of a portrait as an object within a still-life was well-known among French Baroque painters, and received great elaboration at the hands of French engravers as a play on dimensions between portrait and a *trompe-l'oeil* surround (or vice-versa), particularly in artists' portraits, from the 18th century onwards, as countless engravers' *morceaux de réception* for the *Académie* testify. The setting, the engraving tool in the foreground (which occurs only in the print) and the fact that the painting was engraved by Hogarth himself some time before 1749 as a frontispiece to his collected engraved works, shows that it was painted with engraving in mind. As such it was to become his best known official image and a visual statement of his artistic beliefs as expounded in his *Analysis of Beauty* (published in 1753, but already begun at the time this portrait was painted). Central to it was

the view that a serpentine curve – the 'Line of Beauty and Grace' – was at the basis of all that was beautiful in nature. The portrait rests on three volumes representing the works of Shakespeare, Swift and Milton, ie pinnacles of English comedy, tragedy, satire and sublime poetry, into whose tradition Hogarth wished his art to be ranged. His personal mascot, Trump, one of a succession of favourite pug dogs, sits guard over the whole assemblage like a benevolent *alter ego*, adding a typical note of irreverence to the solemnities of baroque drapery and artistic intent.

Prov: Mrs Hogarth's sale, 24 April 1790 (47), bt. by Alderman Boydell, and still with the Boydell family in 1795; J.J. Angerstein by 1814, acquired with his collection for the formation of the National Gallery in 1824; transferred to the Tate Gallery in 1951
Lit: Antal 1962, pp. 12, 14, 118, 250, n. 31, pl. 96b; Beckett 1949, p. 55, fig. 155; Bindman 1981, pp. 109, 151, 195, 203, fig. 119; Davies 1946, pp. 67, 68; Kerslake 1977, p. 148, pl. 391; Paulson 1971, I, p. 450, II, pp. 3, 4, 83 , 258, 259, 417, pl. 190; Tate Gallery 1951, 59; Tate Gallery 1971, 135; Webster 1978, pp. 126, 127, 203, fig. 119
EE

E4

E4 *Figure of Dog Trump*

Chelsea (Lawrence Street Factory) after a sculptural original by L.F. Roubiliac. (1702/5-1762) *c.* 1747-50
Glazed white glassy soft-paste porcelain; l. 265
Without factory mark, but inscribed in an indelible ink on the biscuit under the base *No. 33* and with further

indecipherable figures
VAM (C.101-1966)

The pug dog, which has a much longer muzzle than the modern breed, reclines on an irregular mound base, his right fore-paw extended, his head raised alert and swivelled to his left. The left rear paw is missing. Slip-cast. Identifiable as Hogarth's dog, modelled by the painter's friend, Louis François Roubiliac, by means of the engraving by Phillips (Ireland 1799, Vol. II, pl. 1, pp. 2-3). The dog Trump, *alter-ego* of the combative painter, appears seated in the foreground of Hogarth's self-portrait of 1745. A number of Chelsea models have in the past been attributed without justification to Roubiliac but this model, though not expressly made for the purpose, is the only porcelain figure that can be shown to be his. Nicholas Sprimont, manager of the Chelsea factory, stood godfather to Roubiliac's daughter Sophie in 1744, but even without this personal connection it seems likely that plaster casts of Roubiliac's figure of Trump were for sale in the sculptor's studio (Esdaile 1928, pp. 218-229). The original terracotta of Trump, sold on the death of Hogarth's widow in 1790 was last recorded at the Watson Taylor sale at Erlestoke Park in 1832. Meanwhile the plaster-cast seller, Richard Parker, was able in 1774 to sell Josiah Wedgwood a 'Pug Dog' for 10/6d, and by 1774 the model was being marketed by Wedgwood. An unmarked black basaltes example (Mallet 1974/5, fig. 3) is doubtless of Wedgwood's production. Other Chelsea examples of Trump are a reversed example in the collection of Mr Lionel Geneen and an enamelled example at Rous Lench. Cruder, smaller scale examples of Trump exist both in triangle period Chelsea and in black basaltes.

Prov: Christie's London, 24 Oct. 1966, 2
Lit: Clarke 1959, pp. 53-4, pl. 27; Esdaile 1928; Mallet 1967 III; Mallet 1974; Tilley 1957, pl. 1
JVGM

E5

E5 *James Quin, Actor*
William Hogarth (1697-1764). *c*.1740
Oil on canvas; 749 x 616
Signed *W. Hogarth* and dated 17... .
Inscribed *Mᵣ QUIN* in later script
The Trustees of the Talte Gallery (1935)

Quin (1693-1766) the illegitimate son
of a barrister, came to London from
Dublin in 1715, and soon established
himself as the leading tragic actor on
the London stage. He maintained his
position until his retirement to Bath in
1751, although in the last few years his
old-fashioned heroic declamatory style
was overshadowed by the new
naturalistic style of acting introduced
by Garrick. Hogarth, who painted
both actors at the height of their
careers, admirably reflects this contrast
in styles. While he strove to portray
Garrick in naturalistic action, Quin is
shown here in a rococo adaptation of
the formal baroque head-and-
shoulders portrait set in a carved stone
false oval, complete with upturned
inspirational gaze. At the same time it
is a particularly forceful character
study, typical of Hogarth's fresh
directness of approach to portraiture
at this period. The gold frogging on
the coat is composed of scrolls of
rococo character.

Prov: Gwennap of Lower Brook
Street 1817; Marquess of
Townshend by 1867, his sale
Christie's, 5 March 1904, 61,
bt. Agnew from whom purchased by
the National Gallery the same year;
transferred to the Tate Gallery 1951
Lit: Arts Council 1975, 17; Beckett
1949, p. 59, fig. 153; Davies 1946,
p. 73; Paulson 1971, I, p. 342, 454; II,

p. 24, 26, 27, 130, 427 n. 48, 425
n. 84; Tate Gallery 1971, 108; Webster
1978, pp. 97, 102 repr.
EE

E6 *Analysis of Beauty. Plate II*
William Hogarth (1697-1764). 1753
Etching and engraving; 385 x 514
Lettered with the title and figure
numbers and *Designed, Engraved, and
Publish'd by Wm. Hogarth, March 5th
1753,* and a copyright line
VAM (Forster 118 (125))

One of two plates illustrating
Hogarth's *Analysis of Beauty,* 1753. The
central ballroom scene, derived from
the ball in the series of paintings of the
Happy Marriage (*c.* 1745), in which the
dancing figures and other features
illustrate the text. In this 3rd state of
the print (re-issued in the 19th
century) the man in the elegant couple
on the left has been given the features
of George, Prince of Wales or,
possibly, George III. The serpentine
'Line of Beauty and Grace' had
appeared in Hogarth's self-portrait of
1745 (Cat. E3) and became the basis
of *The Analysis of Beauty.* It is specifically
linked with rococo forms in the
discussion of figs. 60, 61 & 63 (bottom
right) a pelvis, a *rocaille* scroll, and a
strapwork Jacobean cartouche: 'The
thigh-bone fig. 62, has the waving and
twisted turn of the horn, (58) but the
beautiful bones adjoining, called the
ossa innominata (60), have, with
greater variety, the same turns and
twists of that horn when it is cut; and
its inner and outward surfaces are
exposed to the eye. How ornamental
these bones appear, when the
prejudice we conceive against them, as
being part of a skeleton, is taken off,
by adding a little foliage to them, may
be seen in fig. 61 – Such shell-like
winding forms, mixt with foliage,
twisting about them, are made use of
in all ornaments; a kind of
composition calculated merely to
please the eye. Divest these of their
serpentine twinings and they
immediately lose all grace, and return
to the poor gothic taste they were in
an hundred years ago (63).' The first
illustration has as its main scene the
yard of the sculptor John Cheere.

Lit: Paulson 1970, I, p. 221 (3rd state);
II, fig. 211; Tate Gallery 1972,
pp. 74-5
MS

E7 *The President's Chair of the Shakespeare Club*
Mahogany with composition
medallion and leather seat;
1850 x 920 x 840
Probably designed by William
Hogarth. *c. 1756*
Folger Shakespeare Library, Washington DC

Of typically large proportions, and
standing on a plinth fitted with a
sliding platform. The high-arched
scrolling crest rail
surmounted by a 'dramatic' trophy
with a theatrical mask and supported
on outward-scrolling uprights
entwined with snakes, which face
towards a profile medallion of
Shakespeare framed by laurel and
hung from the trophy. The back filled
with floral trellis, and the base of the
splat carved with shells. The arms
terminating in bold scrolls. Another
shell carved in the centre of the bow-
fronted seat, which is fitted with an
upholstered frame and supported on
cabriole legs headed by satyr masks
with buskins and cloven feet. The
chair was designed for the Temple of
Shakespeare, built in 1755 in the
grounds of the actor David Garrick's
villa at Hampton, Middlesex, which
also contained L.F. Roubiliac's statue
of Shakespeare (1758). The chair,
without its crest, is depicted in
William Hogarth's portrait of
Mr and Mrs Garrick of 1756. It was
famous enough to be mentioned in
Horace Walpole *Anecdotes of Painting in
England,* 2nd ed., 1782, vol. IV, p. 180,
where he states 'Mr Garrick has several
of Hogarth's paintings, and the latter
designed for him, as president of the
Shakespeare club, a mahogany chair
richly carved, on the back of which
hangs a medal of the poet carved by
Hogarth out of a piece of the
mulberry-tree planted at Stratford
by Shakespeare.' The 'Shakespeare'
mulberry tree at New Place, Stratford-
upon-Avon, had been cut down in
1756, and some of it was used to make
souvenirs. Walpole was either
mistaken about the medallion being
carved in mulberry wood, or the
present composition medallion is a
later replacement. Garrick's mulberry
wood medallion for the Shakespeare
jubilee of 1769 (see Arts Council 1975,
cat. 51, repr.) shows a similar profile
head. An aquatint of the chair
executed by Jane Ireland was

published in Samuel Ireland *Graphic Illustrations,* vol. II, 1797. The initial inspiration for the trellis-back entwined with snakes may have come from François Boucher's engraving *Le Medecin Chinois* in his *Receuil de diverses Figures Chinoises...* published by Huquier between 1738 and 1745 (Jean Richard 1978, 12). Most of the decorative elements of this chair – the bold scrolling volutes, the trellis ground, the plant and shell ornament – indeed its whole character, are close to designs published by Gaetano Brunetti, *Sixty different sorts of Ornaments* (1736, Cat. B10). The trellis work is particularly appropriate to the chair's use in a garden temple. The chair, called 'emblematical' at the time, is full of literary allusions. The snakes, symbols of wisdom, gaze admiringly at Shakespeare, who is surmounted by a trophy which, with its dagger and sword, alludes to the tragedies (the mask closely resembles David Garrick himself), while the satyr masks, buskins and cloven feet of the legs refers to the Comedies. Richly carved, throne-like chairs occur frequently in Hogarth's work, from his print of *Henry the Eighth and Ann Boleyn* (1728-9) onwards. The chair in his portrait of William Jones (1740, Christie's 16 March 1984, 94) has scrolled arms close to the present example.

Prov: sold with Mrs Garrick's effects, 1823; Mr Rowland Stephenson's effects sold 1829; Mr P.P. Frith, left to widow who afterwards became Mrs Broadbent; 1861 Messrs. Puttick & Simpson sale; Baroness Burdett-Coutts, Christie's 10 May 1922, 150
Lit: Anon 1897, p. 267; Galbraith 1972, p. 47, fig. 3
JH

E8 *Trade card for Dr James's powder for fevers*
T. Kitchin. *c.* 1760?
Etching and engraving; 374 x 240
Lettered with the title etc. and
T. Kitchin Sculp. Clerkenwell Green

The Trustees of the British Museum (Banks 35.46)

Sold by John Newbery, the Bible and Sun, St Paul's Church Yard. One of the most impressive of all rococo trade cards. The scene of the Good Samaritan in the cartouche at the top is taken from Hogarth's painting at

E7

St Bartholomew's Hospital, finished in 1737. It was engraved in 1772. Newbery was at this address 1757-75; his chief trade was as a publisher.

Lit: Heal 1925, pp. 86-7, LXXIX
MS

E9 *A nude female figure*
William Hogarth (1697-1764). Before 1736
Black and white chalk, with ruled lines; 373 x 287
Inscribed *From Hogarth's Sketch Book* and, by Samuel Ireland, *The original Sketch from the life for the principal female figure in the picture of the Pool of Bethesda at St. Bartholomew's Hospital – by William Hogarth – this figure was drawn in St. Martins Lane – and given me by Chs. Catton Esqre. Nov. 21 1794. S.I.*

Her Majesty The Queen

E9

Although certainly used for *The Pool of Bethesda* in 1736, the character of this drawing suggests that it is a life-school study later taken up for the painting. Ireland's reference to St Martin's Lane may be correct. According to Vertue the 'Accademy for drawing from the Life' was started in St Martin's Lane in Winter 1735, 'Mr Hogarth principally promotes or undertakes it' (III, p. 76).

Prov: perhaps S. Ireland's sales, 6 May 1797, 135 and May 1801, 307; in the Royal Library before 1833
Lit: Nichols 1808, II, p. 190; Oppé 1948, 25
MS

E10 *Old Slaughter's Coffee House*
Thomas Hosmer Shepherd (active *c.* 1819-*c.* 1860)
Pen and ink and watercolour; 175 x 216
Signed *T.H. Shepherd* and inscribed *Old Slaughter's Coffee House S Martin Lane Taken Down 1843.* Numbered *1*

The Trustees of the British Museum (1880-11-13-3031)

Slaughter's (called 'Old Slaughter's' after 1740), demolished in 1843 for the formation of Cranbourn Street, was described by George Vertue in 1739 as 'a rendezvous of persons of all languages & nations Gentry artists and others' (III, p. 91) and by Baron Bielfield in 1741 as 'The rendezvous of all the wits and the greatest part of the men of letters in Town'. It was certainly frequented by Gravelot and other artists connected with the

St Martin's Lane Academy. The house on the right was that of Charles Beard, the celebrated actor and singer, and that on the left was remodelled in 1754 by the architect James Paine, who may have attended the Academy and was certainly closely associated with its members (see Cat M2). At the same time he designed and built three small houses at the back of his property, two of which were occupied by John Gwynn and by Samuel Wale who had attended the Academy. In 1755 they published a section of St Paul's which shows the influence of Paine. The cabinet makers Thomas Chippendale, John Channon and William Vile all worked in St Martin's Lane. The location of the Academy is not known.

Prov: the Crace Collection
Lit: Colvin 1978, pp. 372, 609; Harris 1969, fig. 7; Phillips 1964, pp. 107-113, fig. 128
MS

E11 *Tobacco paper*
Tom Harbin's Superfine Sweet-Scented York-River Tobacco
Henry Copland (d. 1753). *c.* 1750?
Etching and engraving; 72 x 98
Lettered with the title etc. and *Copland Sculp.*
The Guildhall Library

Addressed by Harbin to those 'choice spirits' who have 'honour'd him with

their friendship'. Surrounding the title cartouche are five scenes, one of which is indecent, with appropriate lettering. They exemplify the male society of the London clubs and coffee houses. Another state of the card is addressed 'In Sweetings Alley Royal Exchange'. The probable use of these small prints is shown in a portrait of an unknown man attributed to Stephen Slaughter (Sotheby's 14 March 1984, 34). He is surrounded by the bottles, glasses and pipes that appear on the card, and has before him two small tobacco packets each formed from a single sheet of paper, one side of which bears the words 'Hughes Virginian' within rococo scrolls (kindly drawn to my attention by Katharine Eustace).
MS

E12 *A London Potboy*
Louis Philippe Boitard (active *c.* 1733-1763). 1759
Watercolour with pen and brown ink on laid paper; 185 x 113
Inscribed with the title and dated *1759*
The Yale Center for British Art, Paul Mellon Collection (B.1977.14.4927)

Less a boy than a short fat man, seen from the back holding a tankard. One of a number of humorous drawings by Boitard of London characters (see also cat. H1).

Prov: Ponsonby Shaw, Dublin; Jonathan Eade, Stoke Newington;

E10

Colnaghi; Leonard G. Duke (one of 65 watercolours bought from Colnaghi's in the 1940s)
Lit: Hammelmann 1959, p. 357 repr.
MS

E13

E13 *Pair of candlesticks*
After George Michael Moser (1706-1783). *c.* 1740?
Silver; 370 x 170
VAM (M.329-c-1977)

One of two pairs. The cast and chased stems are formed respectively as a running figure of Apollo, holding the candle socket with one hand and reaching for an arrow with the other, and a running figure of Daphne, who holds the socket in both hands. The triangular bases are identical, composed on two sides of shells and *rocaille*, with a third bearing a blank cartouche. The separate nozzles are flower-shaped. The candlesticks can be viewed with the figures and cartouches facing the spectator, or with the figures seen from the side in the act of running, conforming to their ultimate source, Bernini's famous marble group at the Villa Borghese, and with the design for Daphne (Cat. E14). The influences lying behind the design and conception are complex (see VAM 1983, 2.3), but the candlesticks are fundamentally a synthesis of Bernini and a violently twisted composition, especially visible in the design, almost certainly derived from Meissonnier. Direct French influence, in both cases more evident in the design, is visible in the solid base and in the shell and garland on. the base. The shell and garland motif

is apparently taken from a reversed impression (perhaps from the set published in England in 1737) of a plate in Meissonier's *Livre D'Ornemens,* 1734 (no. D22 in *Oeuvre,* see Cat. C17). Flower-shaped candle-holders were used by Thomas Germain in 1734 (*Connaissance* 1965, p. 128) on figure candlesticks which were copied by George Wickes in 1744 (Barr 1980, fig. 42). Moser's contribution to the candlesticks beyond the design stage is difficult to estimate, but the alterations and weaknesses in the execution probably indicate that he had no hand in either the modelling or the chasing. The latter differs for each pair. The lack of marks indicates either that the pieces were never put on sale or that they are made from melted plate; the blank cartouches show no traces of erased engraving. These pieces are related to a group of figure candlesticks, chiefly with the stems formed as nymph and satyr demi-figures, which were apparently first made by Paul De Lamerie (Ashmolean Museum 1748, Grimwade 1974, pl. 74). Their twisted triangular bases, flower garlands and flower-shaped nozzles suggest that they ultimately derive from the present pair.

Lit: Bury & Fitz-Gerald 1969, VAM 1983, 2.3.a
MS

E14 *Design for a candlestick*
George Michael Möser (1706-1783). *c.* 1740?
Pen and ink wash; 350 x 200
Signed *G.M. Moser iv. & delt*
VAM (E.4895-1968)

The design differs in many respects from the executed candlestick (Cat. E13), not only in its more twisted composition and fluid handling but also in many details. Unlike the candlestick, the nozzle and socket are formed from Daphne's rising hair. Moser's skill in life drawing was mentioned by Vertue in 1745 (III, p. 123) but none of the many life studies in sales at his death have been identified. The composition of the figure seems to have been strongly influenced by a pilaster design engraved by Huquier after Oppenord in the suite *Quatrième Livre Contenant des Montans ou Pilastres* (plate D3

E14

BN:Fonds, p. 500) published in the Moyen Oppenord, 1737-8.

Prov: Richardson Simmons, New York; Christie's 12 Nov. 1968, 134; S.J. Phillips
Lit: Bury & Fitz-Gerald 1969; Grimwade 1974, pl. 94; VAM 1983, 2.3b, j
MS

E15 *Isaac Ware*
Louis François Roubiliac (1725/6-1762). *c.* 1741
Marble bust; (without socle) h. 520
Inscribed on the socle in gold capitals
ISAAC WARE
The National Portrait Gallery, London

The architect Isaac Ware (c. 1707-1766) was initially a disciple of Lord Burlington and well-versed in Palladian theory. By the 1740s, however, he was experimenting with rococo decoration, notably in several rooms in Chesterfield House (1748-9, Cat. M6). He was also a member of the St Martin's Lane Academy and a friend of Roubiliac who may have executed the caryatid chimneypiece now in the Metropolitan Museum of Art (Parker 1963), formerly at Chesterfield House. Although unsigned this marble may be identified with that engraved by J.T. Smith in 1802 and described as 'From a Bust by Roubiliac'. A bust of Ware is among several portraits by the

E15

sculptor noted by Vertue in 1741. However, the dating of the marble is complicated by an anecdote related by Nathaniel Smith and recorded by his son (Smith 1828, p. 207) which involves Ware's sitting to Roubiliac. If correct, this sitting must have taken place after 1755, when the elder Smith became Roubiliac's apprentice, indicating that the sculptor executed a second portrait of Ware. It need not be assumed, however, that this later bust is that engraved by the younger Smith and identifiable with the surviving marble. This latter bust is indeed wholly consistent in style with Roubiliac's early portraits. Ware's drapery follows a pattern seen in the Handel of 1739, while in its small, almost intimate scale, the bust recalls that of Hogarth (Cat. E2). Another version is at Ripley Castle, Yorkshire.

Prov: Throckmorton family (?); Lady Fitzgerald; by descent to Major Richard Wellesley; Christie's 4 Dec. 1973, 159; Cyril Humphris; purchased by the National Portrait Gallery with the assistance of the NACF
Lit: Beresford Chancellor 1909, p. 287; Colvin 1955; Esdaile 1928, p. 108; Kerslake 1977, pp. 293-4; Sainte-Croix 1882, p. 115
MCB

E16

E16 *Fables for the Female Sex*
Edward Moore and Henry Brooke. 1744
R. Francklin, London, 8vo
VAM (National Art Library)

Open at the frontispiece, engraved by Simon François Ravenet (1706?-77) after Francis Hayman (1708-1776), and the title-page vignette, a trophy of music, engraved by Charles Grignion (1721-1810) after George Michael Moser (1706-1783). In the frontispiece a young woman stays a satyr and reaches for the mask that he holds. He leads onwards, pointing in a direction reaching beyond a mirror in which she is reflected. Behind are other young women either masked or holding a mask. The allegory seems to be that foolish girls prefer to follow pleasure and wear folly's mask rather than to contemplate themselves in the mirror of truth. Such fanciful inventions for frontispieces were often submitted to the author's criticism and that of his friends or of the publisher's gentlemen advisors. Thus Shenstone writes in 1761 to Dodsley about the proposed design for a frontispiece for Baskerville's *Horace* (*Letters*, ed. M. Williams, 1939, p. 570): he had a high opinion of Hayman as a designer of frontispieces. In Fable I, dedicated to the Princess of Wales, Moore explains that his purpose is to 'weed out folly from the heart / And choak the paths that lead astray / the

wandring nymph from wisdom's way' by holding up 'With friendly hand ... the glass / To all, promiscuous as they pass'. Hayman probably embodied these themes in his design at Moore's request. His mirror is a notable piece of fantastic rococo design in itself; its leafy frame may be derived from Boucher's illustration to *Dom Garcie de Navarre* in the *Oeuvres de Molière* (1734, Jean-Richard 1980, 407); the wyvern(?) on its top is derived from a plate in Lock's *Six Sconces,* 1744 (Cat. L4), or possibly from the Oppenord plate which Lock used. The setting may also be related to the Molière illustrations (*Le Depit Amoureux*, Jean-Richard 1980, 403). His drawings for the plates he designed for this book are now at Waddesdon Manor, Bucks. This frontispiece is one of the first English engravings by the Paris-born engraver Ravenet, who came here *c.* 1745. Moser's vignette design is a Régence cartouche interpreted in rococo ornamental forms. Edward Moore (1712-57) a playwright and writer of fables, turned to literature after failing as a linendraper. A protegé of Lord Chesterfield, he became in 1753 editor of *The World*, a weekly periodical satirising the vices and follies of the fashionable. His verse fables were popular in the 18th century: in writing he was assisted by the Irish playwright and novelist Henry Brooke (1703?-83)

Lit: Hammelmann 1975, p. 52
RWL & MS

E17 *The Inside of the Elegant Music Room in Vaux Hall Gardens*
Henry Roberts (d. *c.* 1790) after Samuel Wale (?1721-1786). 1752
Engraving, coloured by hand;
290 x 435
Lettered with the title (and in French), the addresses of John Bowles and Carrington Bowles and *S. Wale delin H. Roberts sculp.*
Gerald Coke Handel Collection

The Rotunda which was 70 feet in diameter, was completed by 1749. The very elaborate festoons of flowers that decorate the ceiling were executed by a specialist in this sort of work called Morell (Yale 1983, p. 24n), and the plasterwork of the windows, mirrors and sculpture brackets was designed by George Michael Moser and

The Inside of the Elegant Music Room in VAUX HALL GARDENS. L'ordres de Concert Elegant aux Jardins de VAUX HALL.
Published according to Act of Parliament. June 24 1752.
Printed for the Vendors in S.t Pauls Church Yard & John Bowles & Son at the Black Horse in Cornhill

E17

'executed by French and Italians' (Vertue III, 150). Together with Hogarth's inspiring role and Hayman's paintings, it is one of the clear demonstrations of the involvement of the St Martin's Lane group at Vauxhall. The marked contrast between the exterior scene at the Gardens (eg Cat. F15) and this very elaborate interior was an effect often sought at Vauxhall, and one that was frequently noticed. Coming through the entrance to the Rotunda from the Grand Walk, the visitor could not help being amazed by the splendour that greeted him; this effect is echoed at the main entrance to the gardens themselves, and in the startling spectacle of the sudden illumination of the lamps at a certain time of the evening.

Lit: Girouard 1966, p. 58, fig. 1; Wroth 1896, illus. p. 302-3 (dated 1752); Yale 1983, no. 88, fig. 25, p. 22
DC

E18 *Designs for a pier table and glass and a bed*
John Linnell (d. 1796). *c.* 1755 & *c.* 1760
Pen and ink and wash; 294 x 189, 214 x 204
The pier table and glass inscribed in pencil *Plate 2*, the bed inscribed *Plate 5 No 1*
VAM (E.246, 152-1929)

E18

John Linnell, the eldest son of the furniture maker William Linnell, is the only craftsman who is recorded as having attended the St Martin's Lane Academy, where he was described as 'an excellent carver in wood'. As a draughtsman he was without parallel among furniture makers both in his graphic technique and in his sophisticated grasp of design, qualities

he may have developed at the Academy. He was also a painter and had his own 'drawing room' at the family firm's premises in Berkeley Square. The inscriptions on these drawings are connected with the scheme of the neo-classical architect C.H. Tatham to publish the drawings of Linnell, who was both his uncle and his drawing teacher. The pier table has beneath it figures of a stag and a doe probably derived from Francis Barlow. The glass carries figures of the Farnese Hercules (Haskell & Penny 1981, 46) and the Faun with Pipes (*ibid*, 38), then at the Villa Borghese. The vase at the top is closely related to that on cat. G37.

Prov: see Cat. L64
Lit: Hayward 1969, fig. 49; Hayward & Kirkham 1980, II, fig. 7
MS

E19 *Title page*
The Principles of Ornament, or the Youth's Guide to Drawing of Foliage
Matthias Lock (*c.* 1710-1746). *c.* 1765
Etching and engraving; 92 x 151
Lettered with the title and *By M. Lock Price 1s* and the address of Robert Sayer. Numbered *1*
VAM (16366.1)

Title page and 11 plates first issued *c.* 1746. The title page shows a raffle leaf, the theme of the suite, which contains developing exercises, with instructions, in progressing from a three-lobed leaf (each lobe being called a raffle) to a complex one of many raffles: 'Upon this simple principle [ie a three-lobed leaf] all kinds of Foliage is form'd & upon the well understanding these first eight Pages depends the knowledge of Foliage'. The third leaf is 'improv'd by breaking into more Raffles which enriches it sufficient for both embellishment of Ceilings Cornices &c. &c. &c.'. The final leaf is 'sufficient for any Ornament near the Eye, as ye Judicious Workman will discover'.

Lit: Heckscher 1979, IX, pl. 40A
MS

E20

E20 *A raffle leaf*
Gabriel Huquier (1695-1772) after
Alexis Peyrotte (1699-1769)
Etching; 331 x 480
Lettered *Peirotte in huquier Sculp et ex*
and with his address.
Numbered *B6*
VAM (E.1297.c.1886)

From the suite *Divers Ornemens Dédiés à
Monsieur Tanevot Architecte du Roi par son
T.H.S. Peyrotte, Second Partie*. It was
copied in Cat. E21.

Lit: BN:Fonds, 1672-1683; Berlin
1939, 439
MS

E21 *A raffle leaf*
Frederick Miller. 1758
Pen and ink, pencil and wash;
425 x 498
Inscribed in ink *Fredk Miller*, signed in
pencil *W Shipley* and inscribed in
pencil *P 48 1757*. The *verso* inscribed
Fredk Miller Under 18 Never learnt to draw
(formerly concealed under a piece of
blue paper) and *3d* and in pencil *under
18 years*
The Royal Society of Arts
Pasted into an album together with
other drawings submitted for the
premiums awarded by the Society for
the Encouragement of Arts and
Manufactures and Commerce. The
Society had been founded in 1754,
with William Shipley, a painter and
drawing master, as its senior founding
member. The first drawing
competitions (1755), for children from
under 14 to 17, were for 'the best
drawings of any kind'. The premiums
were won by Shipley's own pupils and
those of Jacob Bonneau (Dossie 1782,
p. 394-6). The first premiums for
drawings with a practical application
were awarded in 1756. The present
drawing won third premium in 1758
for 'the best drawings or compositions
of ornaments being original designs fit
for weavers, callico printers or any art
or manufactory, by youths under 18'.

Dossie, who misdescribes the class of
drawing, describes Miller as an
engraver of Dorset Court, Westminster
(1782, p. 408). He may have been
related to the engraver J.S. Muller
(also known as Miller). Up to and
including 1758 the premium drawings
were carried out in the Society's
premises under Shipley's supervision,
and he may have provided the print
(Cat. E20) which Miller copied.
Another drawing of 1758 in this
volume is copied from a print in the
same set. Most of the 1758 premium
winners, however, copied plates from
Gilles Demarteau's suites after Girard,
entitled *Dessins au crayon* and the
Troisième and *Quatrième Livre de Lecons
d'ornemens dans le Goût du Crayon* (Berlin
1939, 433). The first was registered at
the French Royal Library in June 1756
(information Peter Fuhring). The
French raffle leaf is close to English
examples, such as pl. II in Ince and
Mayhew's *Universal System of Household
Furniture,* entitled 'A Systematical
Order of Raffle Leaf from the Line of
Beauty'.

Lit: Allan 1968; Royal Society of Arts,
MS Minutes of the Committee for the
Polite Arts; Society of Arts 1778, p. 34
MS

E22 *Design for a trade card*
Thomas Johnson (b. 1714- d. after
1778). *c.* 1760
Pen and ink and wash; 65 x 97
Inscibed *Thos. Johnson Drawing Master:
at ye Golden Boy in Charlotte Street
Bloomsbury London* and the volumes
inscribed respectively *prospective,
lanskips, fig Dr* [illegible] *Archi*. A paper
inscribed *flowers*.
*The Trustees of the British Museum
(Heal 56.7)*

The card shows a pupil at a table in a
panelled room drawing, with a pair of
compasses; a volume is on the table,
others are on a shelf. No engraved
version of this card is recorded. It is
probably the only surviving drawing
that can with confidence be said to be
by Johnson.
MS

E23

E23 *A raffle leaf*
Attributed to Luke Lightfoot (*c.* 1722-
1789). *c.* 1765
Carved pine; 156 x 100
The National Trust (Claydon House)

From a shutter in the Paper Room (see
Cat. M27)
MS

Vauxhall Gardens

The Triumphal Arches, Mr Handels Statue &c in the South Walk of Vauxhall Gardens. See cat. F18

Vauxhall Gardens
David Coke

One of the earliest records of Vauxhall Gardens is in 1661, when John Evelyn 'went to see the New Spring Garden at Lambeth, a pretty contrived plantation'. On a plan of 1681 it is shown as laid out in walks, planted with trees, with a circle of trees and shrubs in the centre. In 1710 Zacharias Conrad von Uffenbach noted: 'It consists entirely of avenues and covered walks . . . and green huts, in which one can get a glass of wine, snuff and other things, although everything is very dear and bad'. The formal seventeenth century layout was to survive until the destruction of the gardens in the nineteenth century.

When the 21 year old Jonathan Tyers took out a lease on the Gardens in 1728, William Hogarth was only 31, with his famous series *The Harlot's Progress* still four years away, and with seven years to go until the founding of his academy in St Martin's Lane; the French engraver and illustrator Gravelot would not arrive in England for another five years, although Philippe Mercier had been in England for some time, and Watteau had visited briefly eight years before; it was also the year of John Gay's 'Beggar's Opera' and the arrival in this country of the young Frederick Louis, Prince of Wales, with the start of the reign of George II.

Little is known about Jonathan Tyers's early life or background, to explain why he took over a public garden, or what potential he saw in its exploitation. It was obviously a long-term venture, as the lease was for thirty years, and Tyers planned to inject a substantial amount of capital into the gardens.[1]

The first signs of Tyers's revitalisation of Vauxhall came in 1732: 'We hear that several Painters, and Artificers are employed to finish the Temples, Obelisks, Triumphal Arches, Grotto Rooms, etc. for the Ridotto Al' Fresco, commanded for the 7th of June, at Spring Gardens, Vaux-Hall.'[2] It has been suggested that William Hogarth gave the idea of the Ridotto to Tyers, but it is most unlikely that he would have actively encouraged the import of a foreign entertainment; his direct involvement cannot be postulated until later in the decade.

Some of the 'Temples, Obelisks, Triumphal Arches and Grotto Rooms' must have been temporary buildings erected for the Ridotto, but others were more permanent, and it was these that formed the basis of the later architecture. The only evidence so far discovered for the longer-term appearance of Vauxhall Gardens at this early stage is contained in a manuscript journal of a voyage to England, Holland and Flanders in the year 1728, by Pierre Jacques Fougeroux.[3] This fascinating document written in the form of letters to a friend, goes into great detail about the social life of the time. In the second letter, Fougeroux talks of Vauxhall – '. . . il consiste en un bois Coupé de plusieurs grandes allées avec une Cinquantaine de Cabinets Couverts de Tuilles et dispersez dans Le bois de manière que L'un ne va pas dans L'autre . . .' he goes on to mention that he went by water to dine there, and that the population of 'nymphes familières ont coutume d'orner ces Cabinets . . .'

By 1732, some form of classical style seems to have begun to dominate the gardens. In a satirical piece published in that year, in the form of a letter to Diana, goddess of Chastity from 'Sir John Meretrix,' the reader is ironically reproved for considering the Ridotto at Vauxhall merely an excuse for intemperance and dissipation; its 'real and genuine Design' he says, was 'to instruct both Sexes in *good Letters*, *good Manners*, *Writing*, *Needle-work* and a *nameless* Et cetera,' bringing it as near to the Academies of ancient Greece and Rome as anything before or since. The classical decoration, which, it seems, may have included didactic inscriptions, would without any doubt inspire a 'Love for *Wisdom*,' and the 'Spirit of Bravery of the Old Romans.'[4]

The earliest pictorial representation of the Gardens, on the Vauxhall Fan first published in 1736 (Cat. F5), backs up the Meretrix letter, showing three very simple structures, all basically Doric. The Colonnade of supper-boxes going around three sides of the grove date from after Fougeroux's visit of 1728 and may have been erected for the Ridotto. The central structure was the orchestra building, opened on 2 June 1735;[5] despite its prominence and obvious importance, we have no record of its architect; one source confidently states that 'Hogarth assisted with his pencil in the Decoration, he built an Orchestra, placed a statue of Handel by Roubiliac in a conspicuous part of the garden . . .',[6] but this is unsubstantiated elsewhere; a more likely candidate may be William Kent.[7] It is entirely possible that he could have become involved with the project at this early stage, particularly in view of its strong classical bias; the ground-landlord of the Vauxhall Gardens estate was the Prince of Wales, and Frederick Louis, whose interest in the Gardens was strong enough to merit the building of a large pavilion exclusively for himself and his entourage (illustrated on the reverse of the Vauxhall Fan), had employed Kent for the previous five years at Kew House, as well as on designs for masquerades and for his Royal State Barge (1732); the Prince may well have suggested Kent to Tyers as a suitable architect-designer. The 'Turkish Tent' erected shortly before 1744, discussed below, is certainly in his style. In 1737 an 'Elegant edifice' was built behind the Orchestra to house the organ.

Undeniably the most important single work of art commissioned for Vauxhall was also the earliest:

> We are informed from very good Authority; that there is now near finished a Statue of the justly celebrated Mr. Handel, exquisitely done by the ingenious Mr. Roubiliac, of St. Martin's Lane, Statuary, out of one entire Block of white Marble, which is to be placed in a grand Nich, erected on Purpose in the great Grove at Vaux-hall-Gardens, at the sole Expense of Mr. Tyers, Undertaker of the Entertainment there; who in Consideration of the real Merit of that inimitable Master, thought it proper, that his Effigies should preside there, where his Harmony has so often charm'd even the greatest Crouds into the profoundest Calm and most decent Behaviour.[8]

This article, published on the 15 April 1738 goes on to inform us that the cost of the commission must have been about three hundred pounds, and that Tyers bought fifty tickets at the Handel benefit concert (at the King's Theatre, Haymarket on the 28 March). Eight days later, the statue was carried 'over the Water' to the Gardens, and placed in its 'grand Nich' set into the range of boxes to the South of the Grove, where it is seen in Maurer's etching of 1744 (Cat. F13).

Whether or not Hogarth was involved in the Roubiliac commission is debatable, but it was almost certainly he who prompted Jonathan Tyers to decorate the supper-boxes around the Grove with large (all approximately 8' x 5') paintings by the members of his academy.[9] The actual terms of the commission are not known, and no evidence of payment has been traced, but the project was of demonstrable benefit to both parties; Hogarth and his followers gained an ideal outlet for their work with a huge captive audience and built-in publicity; Tyers had his gardens totally re-decorated and re-animated perhaps for a nominal sum or even free of charge. He acquired an extra attraction, and both he and Hogarth could further their common objective of encouraging contemporary English artists in defiance of the Old Masters and 'Exoticks.'

An important and fascinating series of articles published in The *Scots Magazine* in the summer of 1739 tells us something of the look of Vauxhall at this time, and about the company, the entertainments and the *mores* of the place. It is here that the first mention is made of paintings in the supper boxes. At a certain stage during the evening., 'in an instant they all fell down', enclosing the back of each box. Exactly how this worked is not clear; there seems to be no evidence of the surviving pictures having been rolled or folded in any way, and the technicalities of other methods of 'letting down' the pictures would appear to be complex, to say the least. Tyers though, was certainly fond of surprise effects and was clearly inventive and resourceful in achieving them; the lighting in the Garden and the serving of suppers, as well as the appearance of the paintings, were all achieved 'in an instant'.

The *Scots Magazine* articles were written in the form of three letters from a certain 'S. Toupée', each dealing with one hour's activities during a typical evening at Vauxhall. The first hour starts with the inevitable trip over the river that was, so we are told, part of the attraction of the place; after a brief description of some of the visitors, and their reactions to the excitement, the author continues:

> Being all landed, they proceed in cavalcade, through a lane of watermen, to the entrance of the gardens; where, (no dogs being admitted) after *Chlo* is huff'd by one passage-keeper, *Pug* beat by another, and *Pompey* scar'd by a third, they are all trusted to the care of their several watermen; and after shewing tickets, or paying money [the price of a single admission was one shilling], the Ladies and Gentlemen walk in, survey the coop made to keep the footmen in, just at the door, take a hasty circuit around the walks, the paintings not being yet let down, take a view of *Handel's* bust, curiously carved on a fine block of marble, and placed on one side of the garden, striking his lyre: – but before they have observed half its beauties, the musick striking up, the whole company crowd from every part of the gardens toward the orchestra and organ; which gives a fair opportunity of meeting one's acquaintance, and remarking what beaus, belles, and beauties are present . . .[10]

The second hour, from eight o'clock until nine begins with the overture:

> After the piece of musick is finish'd, a silence ensues, of a length sufficient to allow the company time to take a circuit of the gardens before another begins; which is the same before each piece; and those intervals are chiefly employed in visiting the walks, remarking the company, and viewing the paintings, which have been put up the last

spring to protect the Ladies, while sitting in the arbours, from catching cold in their necks by the inclemency of the evening breezes. – These paintings forming something like three parts of the square, the Prince's pavilion (so called in honour of his Royal Highness, who always honours that place with his presence when he visits these gardens) and the house belonging to the manager [Jonathan Tyers], form the fourth. In the middle of this square, which takes up about a fourth part of the gardens, stands a beautiful orchestra for the band of musick, which consists of the best hands upon every instrument in modern use: and from that a little bridge of four or five yards reaches to an elegant edifice, wherein is placed an excellent organ; which has lately been fitted to several new pieces of entertainment, particularly a *symphony of singing birds*, which never fails to meet with the loud applauses of all present. Many little novelties are contrived to yield a greater variety to the audience on the other instruments; and a *set of small bells* have been introduced in a tune which meets with a very favourable reception. The walks leading close by the front of the arbours, (each of which is large enough to entertain ten or twelve persons to supper) the paintings at the back of every arbour afford a very entertaining view; especially when the Ladies, as ought ever to be contrived, sit with their heads against them. And, what adds not a little to the pleasure of these pictures, they give an unexceptionable opportunity of gazing on any pleasing fair-one, without any other pretence than the credit of a fine taste for the piece behind her – To preserve these pieces from the weather, they are fixed so as to be in cases, contrived on purpose, from the close of the entertainment every night, to the fifth tune of the evening following; after which, in an instant, they all fall down; and, from an open rural view, the eye is relieved by the agreeable surprize of some of the most favourite fancies of our poets in the most remarkable scenes of our comedies, some of the celebrated dancers, &c. in their most remarkable attitudes, several of the childish diversions, and other whims that are well enough liked by most people at a time they are *disposed to smile*, and every thing of a light kind, and tending to *unbend the thoughts*, has an effect *desired* before it is *felt*![11]

The three salient facts about the paintings can be gleaned from this passage; they decorated 'the back of *every* arbour' (my italics), they matched in their subject-matter the pictures by Francis Hayman and his followers that are known to have decorated the supper boxes by the early 1740's, and they were stored away 'in cases', presumably incorporated into the roof of the boxes during daylight hours. Only as an afterthought does he mention that the paintings are 'well enough liked by most people' because they are enjoying themselves anyway.

The sheer quantity of paintings (fifty-three supper-box pictures of the series existing in the 1740s are recorded) is rarely mentioned, but it must surely be a major factor in their interpretation. Less than four years had elapsed between the founding of Hogarth's Academy and the recording of the paintings by *The Scots Magazine*. If, as seems possible, a new series of paintings was painted between 1739 and 1743, then an equally Herculean task faced the artists. The hunt for subject matter must have been frantic, and all possible sources would have been plundered, so any attempt to read into them grave moral messages, allegorical meanings, or, indeed, any particular continuity is probably misleading, and can also make us forget the original purely decorative purpose intended for them.

From all available evidence, it appears that Francis Hayman designed the vast majority of the compositions. Two were based on designs by Hubert Gravelot, at least two were copied from Hogarth, and four were by Peter Monamy. Apart from the Monamys, any attempt to attribute the finished paintings to a particular artist would be doomed to failure, and in the context of Vauxhall, would be meaningless anyway. Hayman's influence is very evident, but the sheer quantity of work points to the large-scale involvement of students and colleagues. The brush of Hogarth himself is not discernible amongst the surviving works, and he appears, after the initial period, to have stood aloof from the project, while 'allowing' two of his paintings to be copied.

A Discourse on the Dignity Certainty, Pleasure and Advantage of the Science of a Connoisseur, published by Jonathan Richardson in 1715, gives some idea of the arguments that would have been in Tyers's mind when he decided to go ahead with the decoration of the boxes with paintings:

> 'If gentlemen were lovers of painting, and connoisseurs, this would help to reform themselves, as their example and influence would have the like effect on the common people. All animated beings naturally covet pleasure, and eagerly pursue it as their chief good; the great affair is to chose those that are worthy of rational beings, such as are not only innocent, but noble and excellent . . . If gentlemen therefore found pleasure in pictures, drawings, prints, statues, intaglias, and the like curious works of art; in discovering their beauties and defects; in making proper observations thereupon . . . how many hours of leisure would have been profitably employed, instead of what is criminal, mischievous and scandalous! . . . We know the advantages Italy receives from her possession of so many curious works of art, fine pictures and statues; if our country become famous in that way, as her riches will enable her to be, if our nobility and gentry are lovers and connoisseurs, we shall share with Italy in the profits arising from the concourse of foreigners for the pleasure and improvement that is to be had from the seeing and considering such rarities.

Richardson goes on to assure his reader that an improvement in our artistic capabilities would certainly lead to an improvement in trade, and that the finest art, that of the painter, should be considered to be as respectable and as creative as our best manufacturing trades. 'Thus a thing, as yet unheard of, and whose very name, to our dishonour, has at present an uncouth sound, many come to be eminent in the world, I mean the English school of painting, and whenever this happens, who knows to what heights it may rise; for the English nation is not accustomed to doing things by halves.'

Although the painted decorations at Vauxhall received no critical acclaim, they became extremely popular with the ordinary visitor. A series of eighteen engravings after a selection of the paintings was published by Thomas Bowles in 1743/4: six of dramatic or literary subjects, six of childish amusements, and six of pastimes of maturity. The set ran to three editions, and various pirated versions, making the Vauxhall cycle, together with Hogarth's 'Harlot's Progress' and 'Rake's Progress', the best-known pictures in England. Although they could never be considered the summit of achievement in 18th century English painting, there can be little doubt that they did have a fundamental and far-reaching influence on the direction of the future of English art, affecting artists and patrons alike with their infectious charm, novelty and decorativeness.

Vauxhall seems to have drawn together a large body of young artists with new ideas and a strong feeling of reaction against their traditional academic background. Vauxhall Gardens, the St Martin's Lane Academy, and Slaughter's Coffee-house[12] were the meeting-points of an amorphous group of artists, craftsmen, writers, actors and others whose ideas and work all contributed to an anarchic, destructive and unbalanced movement in all the arts, almost an early form of Dada; they were intent on the destruction of the old dogmas and taboos, of stylisation and intellectualism, and on bringing in a new freedom and tolerance.

The ideal vehicle for the expression of this movement was Vauxhall. Tyers clearly wanted the publicity that controversial art inevitably attracts; he was always alert for new ideas, particularly in temporary structures and decorations, and it was in this area that the most avant-garde designs were produced. The garden quickly became very theatrical, with the architecture acting as scenery, and the visitors, particularly the nobility and royal family, as the players. By far the most perceptive comment about the whole spirit of Vauxhall at this time was made by B. Sprague Allen who referred to Vauxhall as the spot 'where the jazz spirit of eighteenth-century London was wont to manifest itself most hilariously.'[13] Certainly, the improvisation, spontaneity and impact of the gardens all accord well with the generally accepted characteristics of jazz, as do the foreign exotic sources of both.

The first clear sign of a more avant-garde attitude influencing the architecture of Vauxhall is in the "Turkish Tent", erected shortly before 1744. Intended as a shelter for diners, this fantastic structure introduced that element of frivolous impermanence which became so characteristic of Vauxhall; it draws elements from International Gothic, from Palladio, and from court pageantry and is close to the designs of William Kent. Its name derives less from its style than from its intention to evoke foreign climes.

It is hard to gauge the impact of this sort of building at the time; the only recorded comment is that the Turkish Tent and Orchestra building were "of such a Contrivance and Form, as a Painter of Genius and Judgement would chuse to adorn his landscape with.'[14] None of the Vauxhall buildings were ever taken seriously by contemporary commentators, but the likelihood is that, like the paintings, they came to be accepted as a new style, and infiltrated the establishment styles unperceived. Most of the external architecture would in any case not have been seen by the fashionable clientele, who would only have come after dark; to them, the buildings were merely frameworks for the illuminations, and protection from 'The nocturnal rheums of an aguish climate'.[15]

By the end of 1751, when the topography of the gardens was well recorded by various artists and by John Lockman (1751) the transformation from classical forum to rococo pleasure garden was complete (See Cat. F15). Each supper box is enclosed on three sides, semi-circular piazzas have been opened out on the north, south and west sides, and the Rotunda built (probably by 1749) and Pillared Saloon (1750), to the left beyond Tyers' house, are complete; the only building to be replaced later was the 'rustic music house' and organ, which was demolished in favour of a much more ornate Gothic structure, unveiled for the 1758 season.

The Rotunda, of all the buildings at Vauxhall, contained the most authentic rococo decoration, closely related to continental models. The inside decorations were 'designed by Mr. Moser Chaser – and Executed by French and Italians'.[16] The Rotunda does have something of the quality of Moser's gold-chasing; every available space is filled, and even the small remaining areas of flat wall are 'painted in Mosaic'.[17] The whole effect is rather that of a monstrously enlarged snuff-box turned inside out. Recent research has shown that the floral decoration of the ceiling was actually executed by a painter who was a master of this type of decoration, called Morell,[18] apparently, because of a tendency to over-indulge his love of 'ardent spirits', he had to be confined at Vauxhall until he had finished his work on the Rotunda, and some other decorations elsewhere in the gardens. His ceiling as seen in the engraving of 1751 (Cat. E17) relates closely to other art forms of the eighteenth Century, notably textiles and the decoration of porcelain. By 1769 the decoration was considered old fashioned, and was changed for a scheme involving musical emblems.

The engraving shows the Rotunda, looking from west to east, after the addition of the 'Pillared Saloon', which was not part of the original design. It was divided from the main body of the Rotunda by a 'Screen of Columns . . . embellish'd with Foliage, from the Base a considerable way upwards; and the remaining part of the Shaft, to the Capital (of the *Composite* Order) is finely wreath'd with Gothic Balustrade, where Boys are represented ascending it.'[19] The Italianate Mannerist detail of the acanthus bases, the 'gothic' spiral moulding and the classical capitals combine to give a very heavy result, which works against the much lighter plasterwork and painted decoration in the main body of the Rotunda. It is quite a relief to read that the columns were stripped in 1786 for the Vauxhall Jubilee celebrations, and repainted with a rose-coloured ground inlaid with silver, to imitate a certain rock.[20]

The end of the true rococo era at Vauxhall was signalled by the completion of the new gothic orchestra in 1758, which was also the year in which Tyers finally purchased the estate. No really significant additions were made after that year, although one project that was actually planned for the following year does help us to realise the significance of Vauxhall as a breeding-ground for new styles, as well as the depth of Tyers' insight, perception, and commitment. Robert Adam, writing to his brother James just after his return from the Grand tour in Europe, mentions that 'I am now scheming another thing, which is a temple of Venus for Vauxhall which Mr Tyers . . . proposes to lay out £5000 upon and is happy in my doing it. You shall hear more of this when I know of it myself; but you may easily judge that it is one of the most critical undertakings for a young beginner and requires more to be perfect than anything I know. For here the universe are judges, whereas in a private garden it is only the narrow public and clamour. However if I can satisfy myself and Paul Sandby and the proprietor, who has genius and fancy, I doubt not but it will please all and Sandby will make it public over all by Rooker and him engraving it . . .'[21] Nothing further is heard of this building, and the likelihood is that it was never actually put up.

The last word on Vauxhall and its attractions should go to the author of a letter from 'a Foreigner to his Friend at Paris': 'In spite of all the Refinements which the *English* have undergone, within the two or three last Centuries, Eating and Drinking are still the Ground-work of whatever they call Pleasure: which is not likely to suffer any Diminution by Fashions imported from *Germany*.'[22]

F1

F1 *Jonathan Tyers (1702-67)*
Attributed to Louis François Roubiliac
(1702/5-62) *c.* 1745-50.
Marble bust, h. 784, l. 495, w. 295
BirminghamCity Museums and Art Gallery

Tyers was the proprietor of Vauxhall
Gardens and a patron of both
Hayman and Roubiliac. In addition to
the Handel statue (Cat. F9 and F10) it
is likely that he also commissioned
from Roubiliac a lead figure of Milton
for Vauxhall (Esdaile, 1928, p. 40) and
a monument to Robert, 8th Baron
Petre for his garden, with its Temple
of Death, at Denbies (Penny, 1975;
Allen, 1982). Following a type that has
become standard by the 1730s, this
bust is unusually conventional for
Roubiliac, differing markedly from the
early portraits of Hogarth (Cat. E1),
Handle and Ware (Cat. E15) but
lacking the scale and originality of his
busts from the 1750s. However, the
use of the same drapery pattern on the
bust of John Ray (Esdaile, 1924,
pp. 12-13) and Tyers' patronage of
Roubiliac on other occasions together
make an attribution to him plausible.
Usually dated to about 1738 and
related to the Handel commission, the
portrait shows Tyers in early middle
age, indicating a date around 1745-50.

Prov: Tyers family; Tyers sale, 28 April
1830 (unsold); Brandon House sale,
1919; R. Levine; J. Rochelle Thomas.
Lit: Esdaile 1928, p. 41; Sainte-Croix
1882, p. 113; Whinney 1964, pp. 103-
4; Whinney 1971, p. 82.
MCB

F2

F2 *Jonathan Tyers and his family*
Francis Hayman (1708-1776). 1740
Oil on Canvas; 743 x 1028
Signed and dated (lower left corner)
F. Hayman 1740 P.
*The Trustees of the National Portrait Gallery
London.* (5588)

From the left the sitters are Thomas
Tyers (d. 1792), eldest son of Jonathan
in academic dress; Jonathan Tyers
(1702-1767) seated cross-legged at
table; daughter Elizabeth (1727-1802)
pouring tea, behind whom stands
Jonathan Tyers junior leaning against
the back of a chair; Mrs Elizabeth
Tyers (1700-1771), wife of Jonathan
holding a cup and saucer in her right
hand and finally Margaret Tyers
(1724-1786), who appears to have
been the eldest child. About the time
this group portrait was painted
Jonathan Tyers commissioned
Hayman to paint the celebrated series
of pictures for the supper boxes at
Vauxhall Gardens (of which he was
proprietor) and the Tyers family
remained Hayman's most consistent
patrons throughout his career. The
austere panelled interior, which
appears in several other indoor
conversation pieces by Hayman, is
almost certainly capricious but is here
enlivened by an elaborate chimneypiece and overmantel not unlike those
designed by James Gibbs in the 1730s.
It contains a profile medallion portrait
of Frederick, Prince of Wales who was

both ground landlord of Vauxhall
Gardens and its most prestigious
patron. This sculpted portrait almost
certainly never existed (John Ruch has
shown that it was based on a medal
struck in 1736 to commemorate the
Prince's marriage to Princess Augusta)
and it was presumably included as a
symbol of patronage.

Prov: Painted for Jonathan Tyers;
probably by descent through Tyers's
younger daughter, Elizabeth who
married John Wood *c.* 1750; by
descent to Mrs Skelton; Mrs Dorothy
Scobell Wood; Morton Lee (dealer)
from whom it was acquired by Robert
Tritton in 1949; Mrs Robert Tritton;
acquired by the present owners in
1983 from the estate of Mrs Tritton.
Lit: Ruch 1970, pp. 495-7.
BA

F3 *Admission Ticket*
John Laguerre (d. 1748). 1732
Engraving and etching; 235 x 192
Lettered. *The Ridotto Al' Fresco at Vaux
Hall on Wednesday June the 7th 1732.*
J. Laguerre inv.
Lambeth Archives Department.

This Ridotto marked the re-opening of
the gardens four years after Tyers had
taken the lease, and was not a
conspicuous success; the hundred or
so soldiers called in to keep order
were not greatly outnumbered by the
Company, estimated at around four

F3

F4

hundred. In Italy, the ridotto was a fancy dress ball, usually in the open air, with refreshments and entertainments provided, but at Vauxhall, the fancy dress idea was not taken up with any great enthusiasm, most guests arriving in ordinary dress or else in Dominoes and Lawyers' Gowns. Tyers' disappointment at this setback must have been greatly offset by the presence at the Ridotto, from ten until midnight, of the Prince of Wales and his entourage. The ticket appears to be a reversed copy, with modifications, of an Admission ticket to the Guildhall on Lord Mayor's Day 1723, (British Museum 1983.U.1815) a second, untrimmed state of which, for Lord Mayor's Day 1727, is lettered *C. Gardner Sculpst*. (Banks C-2-1738). Most of the design is taken from an arabesque by Pierre Giffart after Jean Berain (1638-1711) (in suite B of the *Œuvres*, Berlin 1939, 343).

Lit: Coke 1978, fig. 1.
DC, MS

F4 *Admission ticket*
Obverse: Virtus, wearing Chiton, Peplos, Aegis and helmet, standing facing, holding in her right hand a shield; beside her stands Voluptas in light drapery, with hair flowing, holding the left hand of Virtus. Beneath, in a scroll, FELICES UNA.
Reverse: Hogarth In perpetuam Beneficii memoriam (engraved)
Gold: 455 x 345
The Trustees of the British Museum (1913. 5-15-1)

William Hogarth's ticket of admission for life. It was possibly designed by Richard Yeo It was used as a pass until at least 1841.

Prov: F. Gye
DC

F5 *The Vauxhall Fan*
M. Harris 1736
Etching, printed in blue; 230 x 444
H.R.H. The Prince of Wales

The earliest reliable view of Vauxhall, as seen from the Proprietor's house. A proof before letters. Another impression (British Museum) is lettered with Harris's name and '12 March 1736'. The first of at least three editions. It shows the simple open supper-boxes, with the opening for the Handel niche to the right, the

F5

orchestra, and the tables and benches, with the statue of Aurora in the distance. The reverse showed The Prince of Wales's Pavilion. The editions of 1737 and 1738 are known only from advertisements; the former apparently illustrated 'The rural Harmony and delightful Pleasures of Vaux-Hall Gardens; with the different Air, Attitude and decorum of the company that frequent that beautiful Place . . . Whereon is shown the Walks, the Orchestra, the grand Pavillion [on the reverse] and the Organ' (unidentified Museum of London cutting). The 1738 edition added 'the Statue of Mr Handel' (unidentified Duchy of Cornwall Office cutting, July 28, 1738); both were available from Pinchbeck's Fan Warehouse. Amongst the fascinating detail on the fan, we see three examples of the 'smug Waiter, with his Apron blue; the painted Tin upon his rising Crest . . .', one of whom has dropped the chicken he was carrying to a customer. The satirical poem entitled 'A Trip to Vaux-Hall . . . by Hercules MacSturdy, of the County of Tiperary, Esq.' (London, A. Moore, 1737, quoted in full in Coke 1978), from which the reference comes, could almost be a description of the Vauxhall Fan.

Lit: Yale 1983, figs. 15, 16.
DC

Gravelot inv.   *G.Bickham jun. sculp.*

The Words (in 1735) by Mr. Lockman.   *Set to Musick by Mr. Boyce.*

F6 *The Adieu to the Spring-Gardens*

The headpiece by George Bickham junior (1706?-1771) after Hubert François (Bourguignon) Gravelot (1699-1773). 1737.
Etching and engraving; 325 x 200.
Lettered with title, music etc. and *Gravelot inv. G. Bickham junr. sculp. The Words (in 1735) by Mr. Lockman. Set to Musick by Mr. Boyce* and with a copyright line dated 17 August 1737.
Lambeth Archives Department.

A song sheet, no. XIII (p. 49) of vol. I of George Bickham's *Musical Entertainer*. The headpiece shows the Grove and the Orchestra, with a singer beneath the projecting sounding-board. It is the only view of this period to depict the Gardens in the artificial light by which they must most commonly have been seen. Seated at the table in the foreground is a figure wearing a garter ribbon who is very probably intended to represent Frederick, Prince of Wales, an identification which is supported by a satirical print (see Cat. F7). He is the only male figure in the foreground wearing a hat. Also seated at the table are two ladies and another man, while two gentlemen and a waiter are in attendance. The cloth of the table has been lifted to show its number, 33, which is also inscribed on a disc hung around the waiter's neck. The headpiece for 'The

Pleasures of Life' (*Musical Entertainer*, II, no. VI, p. 21), repeats most of the figure group (but not the Garter ribbon) and also shows the statue of Handel (copied from Cat. F11), the Orchestra and the Prince's Pavilion. The buildings in all these headpieces, and Cat. F8 may have been copied from lost versions of the Vauxhall Fan (Cat. F5), but it is likely that this example was taken from life. The scrolling surround with its asymmetrical *rocaille* is an early example of Gravelot's characteristic treatment of rococo ornament.

Lit: Snodin 1983, fig. 1.
MS

F7 *Spring Gardens, Vaux-Hall*

'M. Ramano', i.e. George Bickham junior (1706?-1771). 1741
Etching and engraving; 178 x 311
Lettered with title, explanatory verses, the address of George Bickham and *Printed, & Engrav'd, by M. Ramano, with Authority, May 1741*
H.R.H. The Prince of Wales

A social satire set in the Grove, showing (from left to right) the book-keeper, Jonathan Tyers, John Lockman with his hand in Tyers' pocket, Dawson the glass-maker, one of the Garden Chaplains, and Sir Robert Walpole. The group in front of the Orchestra includes a Knight of the Garter (probably Frederick, Prince of Wales), Lord Baltimore standing with his back to us, and a group of ladies, all under a canopy probably derived from Watteau. The trees and horn-playing women at the sides are taken from Claude Gillot's 'Diane' from the *Livre de Portières*, published in 1737. The principal figures, excluding those in the left foreground, are taken from Cat. F8 and the same composition was also published as one of an undated series of prints headed 'Royal Amusement, or a curious Representation of one of ye celebrated Paintings at Vaux-Hall done by ye Ingenious Mr HYMEN'.

Lit: BM:S 2465; Yale 1983 p. 12, Cat 86 frontispiece.
DC, MS

F7

Printed, & Engrav'd by M. Ramano, with Authority. May 1741.   SPRING GARDENS, VAUX-HALL.   *Publish'd by G.Bickham, at Vauxhall Gardens, & in May's Building, C. Garden.*

F8 *Rural Beauty, or Vaux-Hal Garden*

George Bickham junior (1706?-1771)
May 1737
Etching and engraving; 325 x 197
Lettered with title, music etc. and
Bickham sc. the words by Mr Lockman Set by Mr Boyce
Lambeth Archives Department

A song sheet, which later formed no. VI, p. 21, of vol. I of George Bickham's Musical Entertainer. The headpiece shows the Grand Walk, the Grove, the Orchestra and the organ building. It may have been derived from a lost version of the Vauxhall Fan (Cat. F5), but is in any case the earliest surviving view of the Orchestra and organ together. The framing of the music is copied from Gabriel Huquier's engraving after Watteau, *L'Autonne* (Dacier & Vauflart 1929, 92, published in 1734), which was used a number of times in the *Musical Entertainer*. The song itself is a good description of the Gardens, and mentions a grand pavilion, a temple, colonnades, chandeliers, 'glittring lamps in order planted', and nightingales. The theme is the conjunction of art and nature: 'Equal here, the Pleasures ravish,/Of the Court, and of the field'.
MS

F9 *George Frederick Handel*

By Louis François Roubiliac
(1702/5-62). 1738
Terracotta; h. 470.
The Syndics of Fitzwilliam Museum, Cambridge.

First mentioned by Vertue in 1751 as 'the Model in Clay bak'd of Mr Handel done by Mr Roubilliac – the same from which the statue in Foxhall Gardens was done as big as the life in Marble . . . an excellent statue [Cat. F10] – this Modell near 2 foot high is in possess" of Mr Hudson, painter'. It shows Roubiliac's composition almost fully evolved and is evidently the final version, presumably developed from various more freely modelled sketches. Nevertheless, certain modifications were apparently made when the marble was carved; the face appears slightly younger in the terracotta while in the marble the lyre not only has a somewhat different form, with the sun-mask made more prominent, but is now also tilted on one end to heighten still further the informality and momentary nature of the pose. The model's ownership by Hudson, who visited Italy with the sculptor and also possessed a terracotta of his Shakespeare statue (Esdaile, 1928, p. 124), is an index of the respect accorded to Roubiliac's work by fellow artists during his lifetime.

Prov: Thomas Hudson (by 1751); Hudson sale, 26 Feb 1785, 37; bought by Nathaniel Smith; given by Smith to Joseph Nollekens; Nollekens sale,

3rd July 1823, 60 (as Carlini); bought by Hamlet, goldsmith; given by Capt E.G. Spencer-Churchill MC to the Fitzwilliam Museum, 1922.
Lit: Smith, 1828, ii, p. 30, 127; Vertue, III, p. 157.
MCB

F10 *George Frederick Handel*

Louis François Roubiliac (1702/5-62).
1738
Marble statue, h. 1353
Inscribed 'L.F. ROUBILIAC/IN.[II] ET. SCUL.[II]
VAM, purchased with the assistance of the National Art-Collections Fund (A.3-1965)

First mentioned in the *Daily Post* of 15 April 1738, the statue was commissioned for Vauxhall Gardens by Jonathan Tyers who no doubt encouraged, and probably instigated, the various newspaper reports about it. By 18 April the figure was 'now finished' and, together with the 'grand Nich' in which it was to be set was said to have cost not 'less than Three Hundred Pounds'. It was first displayed to the public on 1 May and immediately became widely celebrated, playing the role of the gardens' presiding genius. The marble was originally placed beneath a 'triumphal Arch' surmounted by figures of Harmony and Genii, probably in stucco and based on an engraving in Ripa's *Iconologia* (English edition, 1709). However, by 1751 the niche had been dismantled (Cat. F18) and the Handel shown as a free-standing statue in a semi-circle where it remained until 1786. Although portrayed with a realism that greatly impressed contemporary commentators, the composer is given the mythological attribute of Apollo's lyre, an idea which according to J.T. Smith (1828, p. 94) was suggested to Tyers by Henry Cheere. Descriptions of the statue in the 1740s refer to Handel as both Apollo and Orpheus (to whom Apollo's lyre was given) and the ambiguity apparent even at this early date suggests that the imagery was always imprecise, perhaps referring to both myths. A topical allusion was also probably intended since the publication, in the same month as the statue's completion, of *Alexander's Feast* (the only named work among the scores above which Handel sits) has on its title page Gravelot's illustration of the lines,

'Timotheos plac'd on high/ . . . with flying Fingers touch'd the Lyre'. The statue and its setting employ features derived from various traditions, including garden sculpture, portraits of living persons in the guise of mythological figures, and theatre design while the putto is close to those in Houbraken's *Heads* (Cat. D12). Roubiliac's work is, however, wholly original in two important respects: it is the earliest life-size marble statue depicting a living artist (rather than a royal, military or mythological figure) and, furthermore, portrays the sitter in startlingly informal manner, boldly developing a convention formerly used only for busts. Equally striking would have been the virtuoso carving of the marble, the play of light on the crumpled drapery creating the essentially rococo effect of a transitory and momentary state. The presence of an iron dowel behind the viol and an indentation in the marble base indicate that a further instrument, not visible in engravings, originally belonged; an addition has apparently been made to the right hand side of the base.

Prov: Jonathan Tyers; by family descent to Dr Tyers Barrett; Tyers Barrett sale (Christie's, 28th April, 1830); Mr Squibb, Savile Row; purchased by Joseph Brown, sculptor, 1833; purchased by Sacred Harmonic Society, Exeter Hall, 1854; purchased by Henry Littleton, about 1880; purchased by Novello's, about 1900.
Lit: Allen 1982, p. i; Baker 1984 IV; Bindman 1970; Burke 1976, pp. 156-7; Esdaile 1928, pp. 36-9; Hodgkinson 1969 (lists earlier lit.); Pinkerton 1973, p. 277; Sainte-Croix 1882, pp. 70-81; Whinney 1964, p. 103.
MCB

F11 *The Invitation to Mira, requesting her company to Vaux Hall Garden*
The headpiece by George Bickham junior (1706?-1771) after Hubert François (Bourguignon) Gravelot (1699-1773). 1738
Etching and engraving; 328 x 199
Lettered with title, music etc. and *Gravelot inv. G. Bickham junr. sc. The Words by Mr. Lockman. The Musick by Mr. Gladwin. According to ye late act, 6 June, 1738.*
Lambeth Archives Department.

F10

F11

A song sheet, no. II (pl. 5) of vol. II of George Bickham's *Musical Entertainer*. The headpiece shows Roubiliac's statue of Handel (Cat. F10) firmly identified with Apollo (Pegasus leaps off Mount Parnassus in the background) and surrounded by dancers and musicians and by putti carrying hearts and torches. This is the earliest engraved view of the statue, being published a month after its unveiling in the Gardens. The first lines of the song are: 'Come, Mira, Idol of ye Swains (Se green ye Sprays, The Sky so fine) To Bow'rs where heav'n born Flora reigns, & Handel warbles Airs divine'.

Lit: Yale 1983, cat. 22
MS

F12 *George Frederick Handel*

Louis François Roubiliac (1702/5-62). *c.* 1759.
Terracotta portrait relief; diam 286.
VAM (A.11-1961)

This relief represents Handel late in life. Although unsigned, it may be confidently attributed to Roubiliac on account of both its vivid portraiture and the distinctive handling of the stretched drapery, a device varied and evolved by the sculptor over many years. With the monument, a plaster medallion in Sir John Soane's Museum and a terracotta bust (Baker

F13

1984 IV) the relief belongs to a group of late portraits by Roubiliac. Several variants are known in bronze (Cat. S45a) although the finish of the terracotta, its higher relief and other substantial differences in size and detail between this and the bronzes indicate that the latter cannot be modelled on this relief. In addition to these bronze 'basso relievos', of Handel and others the 1762 sale catalogue includes various 'plaister medals' of the same sitters but no 'medals' in terracotta. However, terracotta reliefs matching the Handel are known of Newton and Cromwell, the latter following Roubiliac's plaster bust in the British Museum, and Mallet has plausibly suggested that these terracottas 'formed a series parallel to, but quite independent of the bronzes'.

Prov: purchased from Messrs Peel and Humphris
Lit: Mallet 1962; *Musical Times* 1961; Kerslake 1977, p. 131
MCB

F13 *A Perspective View of Vaux-Hall Garden*

J. Maurer (*c.* 1713-61). 1744
Etching, coloured by hand; 235 x 407
Lettered with title, *J. Maurer delin et sculp.* and a copyright line dated 1744
Lambeth Archives Department (LP 14/581/3).

The Grand South Walk, showing the 'Grand Nich'. This print shows clearly the original setting for Roubiliac's Handel; the third edition of the Vauxhall Fan (Cat. F5) is known to

have shown the statue, presumably in the grand Nich built specifically for it, but no copy of this has yet come to light. Roubiliac certainly designed, on occasion, the architectural settings for his sculptures, and his early training would have prepared him for some architectural work; he would definitely have been closely involved in this particular design, as it had also to incorporate his group of 'Harmony and the Genii'. The very simple and somehow incomplete triple arch with its natural or grotesque decoration suggests that a model for the Nich may be found amongst the ruins of Ephesus, Palmyra or Baalbek. The placing of the Nich or something similar in the south walk must have been part of the original layout, as a gap was left for it in the western end of the range of boxes; this gap shows clearly in early views (the Vauxhall Fan, Cat. F5) and in maps of the period.

Lit: Hodgkinson 1965, p. 4 fig. 3; Yale 1983, p. 19 fig. 19
DC

F14 *Vauxhall Gardens, the Grand Walk*

Antonio Canaletto 1697-1768. *c.* 1751.
Oil on canvas; 510 x 768
Private Collection

The classic view of Vauxhall in its heyday, this painting shows the scene that would have greeted the visitor as he entered the gardens; in spite of the fact that the sunlight is coming from the wrong direction, and the scale of the architecture and walks is exaggerated, we can perhaps rely on the accuracy of Canaletto's detail; he had taken four careful studies of the Gardens for a series of engravings published by Robert Sayer in 1751, and this painting presumably dates from the same time. Almost ten years before, a rather fanciful writer had described the scene: 'Right before me extended a long and regular vista; on my Right Hand, I stepp'd into a delightful Grove, wild, as if planted by the Hand of Nature, under the Foliage of which, at equal Distances, I found two similar Tents, of such a Contrivance and Form, as a Painter of Genius and Judgement, would chuse to adorn his landscape with.' The Turkish (Dining) Tent beyond is described by the same author (possibly John Lockman) as 'Architecture, such as *Greece* would not be ashamed of', with 'Drapery, far beyond the Imaginations of the East.' In the distance, at the end of the Grand Walk, can be seen a gilded statue of Aurora, goddess of youth and recklessness.

Lit: Constable 1927, pp. 18-19, pl. IIB; Constable 1962, I, pl. 80, II pp. 390-391, No. 431; Jeannerat 1950
DC

F15 *A General Prospect of Vaux Hall Gardens, Shewing at one View the disposition of the whole Gardens*

Johann Sebastian Muller (1715-*c.*1785) after Samuel Wale (?1721-1786). *c.*1751
Engraving and etching , coloured by hand; 285 x 408
Lettered with title (and in French), the addresses of R. Wilkinson and Bowles & Carver, and *Wale delint. I.S. Muller sculp.*
The Museum of London (A6690 21c)

The whole layout, with the principal buildings. In the foreground, is the unassuming main entrance leading through the Proprietor's house, next to which is the back of The Prince of Wales's Pavilion; this, in turn, leads to a small gothic piazza in the style of Batty Langley. Beyond Tyers' house, the Rotunda and Pillared Saloon nestle in behind the gothic boxes. The Grand Cross Walk traversing the six hundred foot width of the gardens just beyond the Grove ends to the left in a scene of painted ruins; at the far end of the gardens, we see another large painted scene, the statue of Aurora, the Temple of Neptune, and an obelisk. According to Lockman (1751, p. 5), the visitor to Vauxhall after dark who looks back up the garden from this obelisk 'would perceive at the Extremity of this View, a glimmering Light, (that in the opposite *Alcove*) which might image to him an Anchoret's Cave; for instance that of the imaginary *Robinson Crusoe*.' The alcove mentioned was one of the supper-boxes strategically placed so as to allow the unwitting complicity of a group of diners in this innocent illusion.

Lit: Wroth 1896, illus. pp. 300-301; Yale 1983, p. 44 (No. 73).
DC

F16 *Vauxhall Gardens shewing the Grand Walk at the entrance of the Garden and the Orchestra with Musick Playing*

Johann Sebastian Muller (1715-*c.*1785) after Samuel Wale (?1721-1786). *c.*1751
Engraving and etching, coloured by hand; 315 x 442
Lettered with title (and in French), copyright line dated 25 Nov. 1751, the address of John Bowles & Son and *Wale delint Muller sculp.*
The Museum of London (5352/7)

The same view as is seen in Canaletto's painting (Cat. F14), but reduced to more realistic proportions, and showing the 'grand *Visto* or *Alley* about 900 Feet long, formed by exceedingly lofty Sycamore, Elm, and other Trees . . . a noble Gravel *Walk* throughout . . .' (Lockman 1751, p. 2). In the gothic boxes to the left, we may see how some of the paintings by Hayman and his students were hung, and how vulnerable they would have been. Of all the works of art that appeared at Vauxhall, only one can be said to have been unsuccessful. It may be seen in this engraving at the end of the Grand Walk; a commentator of 1740 (*Scots Magazine*, June 28, 1740, p. 363) informs us woefully that 'a hideous figure of *Aurora* on a pedastel *interrupts*, I cannot say *terminates* the view.' The author of this figure is unknown, but any connection with the very proficient and experienced Cheere family, as recently suggested (Yale 1983 p. 23n) should perhaps be discounted.

Lit: Yale 1983, p. 19 No. 74 fig 21
DC

F15

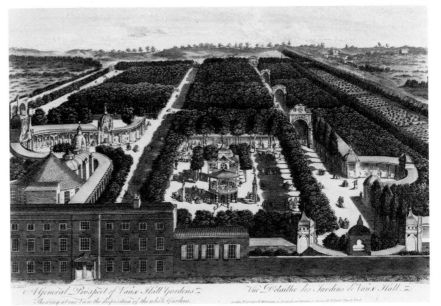

A General Prospect of Vaux Hall Gardens;
Shewing at one View the disposition of the whole Gardens.

Vue Détaillée des Jardins de Vaux Hall.

VAUXHALL GARDENS, shewing the Grand Walk,
at the entrance of the Garden, and the Orchestra, with the Musick Playing.
La Grande Allée a l'entrée des JARDINS de VAUXHALL.
L'Orchestra, et les Musiciens.

F16

F17 *A View of the Center Cross Walk & c in Vauxhall Gardens*

Edward Rooker (1711-1774) after
Antonio Canaletto (1697-1768). 1751
Engraving and etching, coloured by
hand; 229 x 388
Lettered with title (and in French),
copyright line dated 2 Dec 1751, and
Canaleti delint E Rooker sculpt.
Museum of London (5352/6)

This view reveals more than any other
of the true feeling of the gardens; it
shows the lattice-work fence enclosing
the 'wildernesses', stone urns at the
corners, the large painted scene of
ruins, and the end of the gothic
supper-boxes to the left. The illusion
given to visitors of having been
transported magically to some exotic
spot in a foreign land must have been
stronger here than anywhere else in
the gardens, particularly with the
addition of the sounds of distant
music drifting over from the Grove,
away to the left.
   'Verdant Vistos, melting Sounds;
   Magic Echoes, Fairy Rounds.
   Beauties ev'ry where surprize,
   Sure this Spot dropt from the Skies!'
The scene of ruins was probably in
place for no more than a season, to be
replaced the following year; it does not
appear to be the one mentioned in the
'Sketch', which apparently represented
'an *Alcove*; consisting of three Niches,
with *Flora* and *Genii* in them, all
pleasingly decorated.' Nor is it the
'landscape painting of ruins and

running water' mentioned by Hooper
(1762), even though both were
obviously of a similar type. George
Lambert (1710-1765), who worked
with Hayman as a scene painter at
Covent Garden Theatre has been
suggested as the author of other
similar 'Day Scenes' at Vauxhall.

Lit: Constable 1976, pp. 577-8
No. 748; Dobson 1892, p. 230ff; Yale
1983, p. 20 No. 90 fig. 22.
DC

F18 *The Triumphal Arches, Mr Handels Statue &c. in the South Walk of Vauxhall Gardens*

Johann Sebastian Muller (1715-c.1785)
after Samuel Wale (?1721-1786).
Engraving and etching, coloured by
hand; 279 x 410
Lettered with title (and in French), the
addresses of R. Wilkinson and
Carrington Bowles and *S Wale delint
I.S. Muller sculp.*
*The Trustees of the British Museum (Crace,
p. xxxv, sheet 45, 141)*

The second of the two parallel grand
walks, the Grand South Walk is
traversed by three triumphal arches
and terminated by a painted 'Temple
of Neptune'; the four structures, all
made of a wooden framework covered
with canvas, were intended to appear,
as here, as one grand building when
viewed from a particular spot.
Lockman (1751, p. 6) tells us that the
arches were 'design'd by an ingenious

Italian; but the Figures were drawn, as
well as coloured, by another able
Hand. These *Arches* are so finely
design'd and painted, and the
Perspective is so happy, that the whole
has the Appearance of a noble *Edifice*.'
Canaletto's version of this view gives
the piazza on the right eleven supper
boxes between the outer and central
temples; Wale indicates only ten.

Lit: Yale 1983, p. 20, No. 74, fig. 23.
DC

F19 *A View of the Temple of Comus &c. in Vauxhall Gardens*

Johann Sebastian Muller (1715-c.1785)
after Antonio Canaletto (1697-1768).
1751
Engraving; 231 x 387
Lettered with title (and in French), a
copyright line dated 2nd December
1751, *Canaleti delint. Muller sculp.* and
the addresses of Robert Sayer and
Henry Overton.
The Museum of London (5352/3 21c)

One of the set of four views of
Vauxhall after Canaletto's designs,
published by Robert Sayer; in this
case, and in his View of the Grand
South Walk, Canaletto shows
buildings that differ fairly substantially
from what is known to have existed
later; as it is unlikely that Canaletto
would have strayed too far from direct
representation in this sort of
commission, it must be assumed that
he is showing an intermediate stage of
the development of this part of
Vauxhall. In 1751, this piazza was in
'a noble Style of Gothic Architecture'
as shown in Wale's view (Cat. F20),
and as recorded in Lockman (1751)
which Canaletto's prints were
intended to accompany. The two
versions of the piazza are by no means
incompatible, one merely showing a
gothic skin superimposed on the
other, but this feature of the gardens
had existed for, at most, two years
when this print was published, hardly
allowing time for the demolition of the
original range of boxes, the
construction of this classical colonnade,
and its conversion.

Lit: Constable 1976 pp. 577-8,
No. 748; Yale 1983 p. 21, No. 72.
DC

89

F20 *A View of the Chinese Pavilions and Boxes in Vaux Hall Gardens*

Thomas Bowles (b. *c.* 1712) after Samuel Wale (?1721-1786). 1751
Engraving and etching, coloured by hand; 254 x 402
Lettered with title (and in French), the addresses of Thomas Bowles and John Bowles & Son, and *S Wale delint T. Bowles sculp.* Dated *1751.*
The Trustees of the British Museum (Crace, p. xxxv, sheet 45, 141)

The same view as Cat. F19 with the addition of the gothic ornaments, and a colonnade (apparently 500 feet long) in front of the boxes. Lockman's description of this piazza (1751, p. 18), which demonstrates the gothic revival at its most brash, explains some of the detail of sunbursts, terms, battlements, pinnacles, wreathed columns etc., as well as mentioning the 'whimsical Piece of Painting' in the central temple representing Vulcan catching Mars and Venus in a net, 'the whole drawn in the *Chinese* taste.' Hooper (1762) states that it is by 'Ricquet'. Several candidates have been suggested, including P.J. van Reyschoot a Flemish painter working in England whose name was variously spelled 'Rischoot' and 'van Risquet' (Waterhouse 1981, p. 307). A name not yet mentioned would bear some investigation: the Frenchman Louis-Rene Boquet (active 1760-1782) worked as a designer for the Opera, and for Court entertainments at Versailles and Fontainbleau, producing scenes of a very similar sort to the Mars and Venus, and in similar settings. A good deal of scorn has been poured on the 'pseudo-Gothic' pavilions with their 'fantastic exaggeration' of the medieval style, but serious comparison with English 16th Century architecture may give pause for thought; one close analogy with the type of decoration used may be found in the terracotta decoration of the entrance bay of Layer Marney Towers in Essex.

Lit: Allen 1937, pp. 81-2; Girouard 1966, p. 60, fig. 8; Hooper 1762; Yale 1983, No. 24, fig. 24
DC

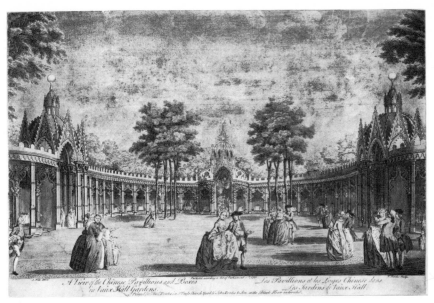

F20

F21 *Vauxhall Gardens*

Samuel Wale (?1721-1786) *c.* 1761
Black chalk; 83 x 140
Private Collection

The original drawing for the engraving by T. Simpson in James Dodsley's *London* of 1761. One of the clearest topographical studies of the gardens, this drawing shows the 'Gothic' boxes and Rotunda building on the left, the Grand Walk leading to the 'Grand Gothic Obelisk' three hundred yards away, the new orchestra with the Dining Tent behind, and Roubiliac's 'Handel' in the second version of its 'Grand Alcove'. This view, and its derivations, is the only one which shows this particular setting of the statue, probably a temporary structure left over from the celebrations for the accession of George III; Hooper (1762) describes the statue in its 'grand portico of the Doric order', mentioning also the group in the pediment above, made of lead figures and cloth drapery. The Gothic Orchestra was built in 1757-8, to replace the structure of the 1730s. The new building was an extraordinary conception, rather like a giant pulpit from a Gothic cathedral; its designer, apparently a carpenter named Maidman, has had to solve several problems in the one building, not the least of which was to house the organ, orchestra and singers under one relatively small roof, whilst still allowing for supper-boxes below. A good description of Vauxhall Gardens at this time appears in Oliver Goldsmith's *Citizen of the World*, 1760.
DC

F22 *The Old Garden Seat at Vauxhall in 1777*

Anonymous; 1777
Ink over black chalk; 107 x 118
Inscribed in ink *Old garden seat at Vauxhall in 1777, carved after a design of Mr Hogarth for J. Tyers Esq.* On the back is the family arms of Mr Tyers and the date 1763
The Trustees of the British Museum (1928-4-17-14)

A rough sketch of an elaborate garden seat, the back decorated with a coat of arms (indecipherable) supported by two reclining figures, the initials 'J T', and the date 1763. This is the only record of any such seat existing at Vauxhall; the use of Tyers' initials may indicate that it was placed either in a private part of the garden, or near the proprietor's house at the west end. Except for the date of 1763, the design of this seat may perhaps be attributed to William Kent, with its scallop shells, scroll arms and heavily decorated seat-rail. If 1763 is its true date, then it was certainly old-fashioned.
DC

F23

F23 *Vauxhall Gardens*

Thomas Rowlandson (1756-1827). 1784
Pen and water-colour over pencil;
483 x 749
VAM (P.13-1967)

The best-known image of Vauxhall, showing a large number of contemporary characters near the orchestra building, in which Mrs Weichsell's singing is accompanied by a full orchestra. Rowlandson's classic caricature of the later 18th century social scene. The persons depicted, which include the Prince of Wales and Doctor Johnson, are well enumerated elsewhere, except possibly Mrs Barry, 'The Old Bawd of Sutton Street', seen seated at the extreme right with two clients. The orchestra features strongly, with its decorative detail of pattern-book gothic, and the Covered Walk can be seen in the background with its scalloped cornice, 'and a draw-up Curtain on each Side, neatly painted.' The most striking feature of the drawing, however, is its use of contrast between horizontal and vertical, between nature and the artificial, between the coarseness of humanity and the elegance of the architecture, between the dark of the night and the light of the lamps, between the various classes and types of people, and even the implied contrast between the human orchestra and the music supplied by the 'Feathered Minstrels' that were such a feature of the place.

Lit: Coke 1978, No. 5; Mayne 1968 (gives full bibliography to date)
DC

F24 *Season Tickets*

The Trustees of the British Museum

a) Obverse: On a pedestal inscribed IOCOSAE CONVENIUNT LYRAE, three cupids, two supporting a garland of flowers, a third playing a lyre which rests on two books; on the left a tree, on the right a temple.
   Reverse: Mr Tho. Corner 726 (engraved)
Silver; 42. Example dated 1750 in Wilkinson 1825.
(Montague Guest 678).

F24

b) Obverse: Handel, seated playing a lyre, the statue by Roubiliac of 1738. At his feet a putto with music book records the music; behind, a colonnade. In the exergue BLANDIUS ORPHEO (Horace, Odes, I xxiv 13).
   Reverse: Sr. Jnᵒ: English Barnᵗ 592 (engraved)
Silver; 45
(Montague Guest 680; ex. Smith collection)

c) Obverse: Orpheus, wearing a laurel wreath and cuirass, seated facing, playing a lyre; near him are various animals (giraffe, bear, rabbit, dog, and a monkey playing a violin); behind is a tree on which is a squirrel.
   Reverse: Mr John Robinson No 68 (engraved). 1751 (cast in relief).
Silver; 41
(Montague Guest 684; ex collection A.W. Waters, 1898)

d) Obverse: Draped female figure of Spring reclining on clouds; her right elbow rests on a basket of flowers, her left hand holds a garland; above is the head of a winged Favonius; beneath in a scroll, GRATA VICE VERIS (Horace, Odes, I iv 1)
   Reverse: Mr Fran Plomer 518 (engraved)
Silver; 48
(Coins + Medals No. J3027)

e) Obverse: Female figure of Summer lightly draped, reclining on wheat sheaves beneath a spreading tree; her left hand supports her head. On the right is an avenue, the entrance to which is decorated with an arch of lamps; above, Cupid flying with a scroll reading FRONDOSA REDUCITUR AESTAS.
   Reverse: Mr Parris 256 (engraved)
Silver; 41
(Coins and Medals T 3028, Hawkins collection)

f) Obverse: Arion on a dolphin playing a small harp; in the left background a ship; above, in a scroll, AEVE SIT DULCIS MUSICA NOSTER AMOR. Border decorated with marine details.
Bronze; 41
(Montague Guest 676)
MS

F25 *See-saw*

Francis Hayman (1708-1776)
Oil on canvas; 1270 x 2415
The Trustees of the Tate Gallery (T.524)

An original supper-box decoration, placed originally in the southern row of boxes, just to the west of the Handel statue, and in the neighbouring box to 'Bird Catching' (Cat. F26). Three girls and four boys are playing on a makeshift see-saw in front of a ruined windmill and a classical building with wooden scaffolding. The engraving by Truchy gives the composition more height both top and bottom, adding a fallen section of column in the centre foreground. A very lively painting, in which the composition for once plays an important role; the asymmetrical S-curve adds to the dramatic imbalance. The various 'props' used in the painting leave us in no doubt as to the moralising intention of the artist; the second verse of the couplet accompanying the engraving reads 'But when the Nymph with Prudence unprepar'd / By pleasure swayed – forsakes her Honours Guard; / That slip once made, no Wisdom can restore. / She falls indeed! – and falls to rise no more.' The overt moral message has parallels with the participation work of Hogarth, and the strong modelling of light and shade with the full characterisation in the faces of the youths suggests that Hayman was closely involved in the actual painting. The combination of these two factors, perhaps gives grounds for the belief that 'See-Saw' was one of the earliest of the decorations to have been completed.

Prov: Lowther sale 1947 (1897); private collection, Blackburn; with Appleby Bros. 1960
Lit: Gowing 1953 p. 15 No. 41
DC

F26 *Bird Catching with a Decoy and Net*

Francis Hayman (1708-1776)
Oil on canvas; 1405 x 2335
Private Collection

One of the original supper-box paintings, showing a country landscape with distant hills; in the foreground, in front of some trees, a group of three children watch a decoy cage, whilst a fourth blows a bird-call; an adult

F25

F26

sporting gun lies across the front of the group. The boy blowing the whistle is closely derived from a picture of the same subject by the French artist, Nicholas Lancret. Lancret's 'Printemps' (Louvre) was engraved by Champollion in 1738, so would certainly have been known by Hayman and his students. Despite the similarity of that one figure, and of subject matter, Hayman has resisted the temptation to borrow wholesale from Lancret; in general terms, the pictures are very similar, but the emphasis and tone could not be more different. Hayman's studies from the life reinforce the impression given elsewhere in the Vauxhall pictures that we are eavesdropping on a moment of rural life, the composition and decorative quality coming a poor second. The painting of the landscape and trees compares closely with the

early work of artists like Richard Wilson and Thomas Gainsborough, but we would be treading on dangerous ground if we were to try to attribute any of the Vauxhall pictures to any of the known students or visitors at St Martin's Lane.

Prov: Christie's 9 July 1859, 104 as property of F. Gye; bt. Forman, thence by descent
DC

F27 *Hunt the Whistle*

Francis Hayman 1708-1776
Pen & ink and wash; 140 x 230
Inscribed in ink *Hunt the Whistle* the figures *3 Feet & 1 in*
The Courtauld Institute of Art (Witt 1469)

A central standing figure, surrounded by seven others seated or kneeling on the floor in a typical early 18th century interior; squared-up for enlargement.

Even though this subject would be the ideal vehicle for the use of Hogarth's Line of Beauty, Hayman ignores the opportunity, preferring to stick to the more naturalistic approach. In this drawing, Hayman is more interested in exploring the effects of light and shade over the various different surfaces and textures; the interplay of light and shade is matched by the relationships and tensions between the various protagonists. In common with other drawings in this series, the perspective is distinctly odd, the left-hand wall bearing absolutely no relationship with the back wall.

Prov: Sir Robert Witt
Lit: Gowing 1953, p. 11 No. 15 fig. 4
DC

F28 *The Play of Skittles*
Francis Hayman (1708-1776)
Pen and ink with bistre and grey wash; 143 x 233
Inscribed in ink *The enraged Vixen of a Wife*
City of Birmingham Museum and Art Gallery

In an inn garden, a man is being attacked by his (?) wife; the landlady marks up credit, and a pipe-smoking man and six others look on. Loosely related to a Lancret composition of the same subject (Berlin), this dramatic scene is very much a composite; the figures, part perhaps drawn from life and part derivative, do not really make a very satisfactory grouping. The perspective certainly does not bear close scrutiny, nor does the human anatomy. There is no doubt as to Hayman's authorship of the drawing, though, so this may be an early work, possibly dating from

c. 1740. It provides a perfect example of Walpole's rather unkind remark about the 'large noses and shambling legs' of Hayman's figures, as well as a strong hint of that humour with which he is known to have been blessed.

Lit: Gowing 1953 p. 15 No. 30.
DC

F29 *Flying a Kite*
Francis Hayman (1708-1776)
Pen & ink wash; 142 x 227
Inscribed in ink *The Figures 2ft 5In: or 6"*
The Yale Center for British Art, Paul Mellon Collection (B.1975.4.504)

A boy moves to the left, pulling the kite string, whilst a group of three others hold the kite prior to launching. Another in the series of children's games derived from the Continent, but anglicised in much the same way as 'Shuttlecock' (Cat. F30). All attention is centred on the kite, and it is made clear that there is enough wind to lift it, and that the kite itself is strong enough to fly. Hayman's children are quite capable of getting dirty, of tearing their clothes, losing their hats in the mud, and involving themselves completely in the game. For Gravelot's version of this subject see Cat. D6. Obviously, comparisons can easily be made between the subjects chosen for Vauxhall decorations and their continental counterparts; both derive in some degree from everyday life. However, in Europe it is the decorative element that is all important, closely followed by some secondary, but significant, inner meaning; at Vauxhall, Hayman wanted to show actual scenes of the

real world of mid-18th Century England.

Prov: H. Reitlinger (as by Highmore)
Lit: Gowing 1953 p. 11 No. 11; Yale 1983 No 50 fig. 33
DC

F30 *Shuttlecock*
Francis Hayman (1708-1776)
Pen & Ink wash; 142 x 227
The Yale Center for British Art, Paul Mellon Collection (B.1975.4.503)

A boy and girl playing at battledore and shuttlecock, with another girl, keeping the score, in a simple interior, with a Palladian fireplace, and a covered table and two cross legged stools to the right. Squared-up for enlargement. The subject had been a popular one for some time in the European repertoire, amongst the 'Jeux d'enfants' (see Cat. D6), eventually becoming no more than a compositional device; in Hayman's drawing, the game is the all-absorbing feature, giving it an immediacy and vitality which so often differentiates the English rococo from its continental counterpart. The details of the boy's rumpled clothing and the domestic paraphernalia give the definite feeling of a study from the life, a feeling totally lacking in the engraving of the painting, which, with its much more stylised figures and formal setting, displays a far closer relationship to the imported rococo style.

Prov: Sir Robert Witt (as by Highmore). H. Reitlinger
Lit: Gowing 1953 p. 11 No. 14; Kenwood 1960, No. 32; Yale 1983 No. 49, fig. 30
DC

F29

F30

F31 *Falstaff's Cowardice Detected*

Charles Grignion (1717-1810) after
Francis Hayman (1708-1776). 1743
Engraving; 267 x 346
Lettered with title, verses, the
addresses of Thomas and John
Bowles, *April 4th 1743* and *F. Hayman
Pinxt. C. Grignion after the Painting in
Vaux-hall Gardens*
*Lambeth Archives Department
(LP14/581/29B)*

An episode from Shakespeare's Henry
IV part I (Act II Sc 4), set in the Boar's
Head Tavern, Eastcheap. A static and
uninteresting scene, this picture was
perhaps more important as a theatrical
portait group than as a dramatic
illustration. The three actors who
regularly played the role of Falstaff in
the 1730s and early 1740s were Quin
(see Cat. E5), Giffard and Harper. One
of the few concessions to historical
realism is Falstaff's 'Old English'
costume.

Lit: Gowing 1953, p. 15, No. 36, fig. 7;
Yale 1983, No. 100, fig. 37
DC

F32 *The King and the Miller of Mansfield*

Nathaniel Parr (active 1742-51) after
Francis Hayman (1708-1776). 1743
Engraving; 280 x 352
Lettered with the title, the addresses of
Thomas and John Bowles and *Hayman
Pinx N Parr sculps from the Original
Painting in Vaux-Hall Gardens.*
*Lambeth Archives Department
(LP 14/581 29B)*

A play of this name, by Robert
Dodsley, was published in 1737, and a
popular song based on the same story

appears in Bickham's *Musical Entertainer*
(I, 40) in the same year. When
compared with 'Falstaff's Cowardice'
(Cat. F31), the drama of this scene
strikes us forcibly; if the painting does
show a scene from the theatrical
performance, then it is remarkably
naturalistic. The characterisation of
the two principal actors suggests that
they, too, may be portraits; at its
original production, the King was
played by Cibber, and the Miller,
John Cockle, was portrayed,
appropriately enough, by Miller.

Lit: Gowing 1953, p. 16, No. 61, fig. 9;
Yale 1983, No 80, fig. 38
DC

F33 *Quadrille*

Charles Grignion (1717-1810) after
Hubert Gravelot (1699-1773) and
Francis Hayman (1708-1776). 1743
Engraving and etching; 267 x 305
Lettered with title, the addresses of
Thomas and John Bowles, *4th April
1743* and *H Gravelot Invt F Hayman
Pinx C Grignion Sculps from the Original
Painting in Vaux-hall Gardens*
*Lambeth Archives Department
(LP 14/581 29B)*

A group of young ladies and
gentlemen playing cards, while a maid
and negro boy serve tea. This
composition is one of the cases in
which engraving can be compared
with a surviving painting; the latter
has, unfortunately, been heavily
overpainted, obliterating much of the
finer detail. The attribution to both
Gravelot and Hayman is one of only
two cases where the design is attributed
in this way, and the French content is
unmistakable; to the ordinary

Englishman of 1740, this interior, with
its 'boiseries', overdoor cartouche,
ionic pilasters, Turkey rug, elegantly
carved chairs and heavy curtains
would have seemed very avant-garde
and perhaps ridiculously over-
elaborate, even though it was, in fact,
only a very slight foretaste of things to
come. This picture, and some others
at Vauxhall, may, to some extent have
been responsible for the acceptance of
the rococo style in English interiors;
the Vauxhall paintings, seen as they
were by many thousands of people
every month, were ideal propaganda
for the emerging style.

Lit: Fitzgerald 1969, p. 141, fig 4;
Gowing 1953, p. 11 No. 4 fig. 23;
Henry 1958, No. 1; Yale 1983, No. 55
DC

F34 *Building Houses with Cards*

Louis Truchy (1721-1764) after Francis
Hayman (1708-1776). 1743
Engraving and etching; 254 x 365
Lettered with the title, the address of
Thomas Bowles and *4th April 1743 H
Gravelot Invt. F. Hayman Pinx L. Truchy
sculps from the Original Painting in Vaux-
hall Garden.*
*Lambeth Archives Department
(LP 14/581/25)*

A group of three men and two women
around a table, where one man is
trying to build a card house while
another blows it over. Two young girls
play with cards on a stool. A small oil
sketch attributable to Gravelot may
show more clearly than the surviving
supper-box decoration what the
original picture looked like. This
sketch, which gives in detail the figures
and in outline the background, was

F32

F33

probably the working sketch from which Hayman's academy students worked up the final painting; it may also have been used by Truchy as the model for the engraving. The Englishness of the very plain interior and the rather too sturdy table and chairs is in strong contrast to the formal and decorative poses of the French figures, making a rather unsatisfactory composition, and a transitional stage in the anglicisation of the Continental rococo vocabulary.

Lit: Fitzgerald 1969, p. 141, fig. 3; Gowing 1953, p. 11 No. 6 figs. 6 & 13; Kenwood 1968 Nos 30, 35, 52, 57, 73(a); Yale 1983, No. 98 fig. 34
DC

F35 *Sir John Falstaff in the Buck-Basket*

Charles Grignion (1717-1810) after Francis Hayman (1708-1776). 1743/4
Engraving and etching; 254 x 365
Lettered with the title, address of Thomas Bowles, *from the Farce, Merry Wives of Windsor, Feb 1st 1743* and *F. Hayman Pinx C Grignion Sculp from the Original Painting in Vaux-hall Garden*
Lambeth Archives Department (LP 14/581/24)

The famous scene from Shakespeare's Merry Wives of Windsor (Act III sc. 3), in which Mistress Ford and Mistress Page take their revenge on Falstaff; this same composition was used by Hayman for his illustration to the play in Thomas Hanmer's edition of Shakespeare (Cat. D19), so it is reasonable to assume that Hayman himself was responsible for its design. As in the other Falstaff scene (Cat. F3) the only concession to historical authenticity is Falstaff's costume; the decoration of Ford's room, with its rococo-patterned screen, modern paintings and classical door-frame, is the height of fashion for 1740, so increasing considerably the dramatic impact and immediacy of the scene for the audience of the time.

Lit: Gowing 1953, p. 12 No. 17; Henry 1958, No. 3; Yale 1983, No. 102
DC

F36 *Blind Man's Buff*

Nathaniel Parr active (1742-51) after Francis Hayman (1708-1776). 1743
Engraving; 292 x 356
Lettered with the title, the address of Thomas Bowles, *F. Hayman Pinx 1743 N. Parr sculp from the Original Painting in Vaux-hall Garden.*
Lambeth Archives Department (LP 14/581/23)

A group of three girls and three boys in front of a rustic cottage; one boy, blindfolded, is being taunted by another, and tickled with a feather by a girl; one of the girls looks on from behind a tree. All through the Vauxhall pictures, an underlying link with Watteau continually defies definition. The blindfolded boy in 'Blind Man's Buff' gives a rare opportunity to identify a direct connection; Watteau's painting 'Le Colin Maillard' from the first decade of the 18th Century, which was engraved by Brion in 1730, includes the same figure, along with others that relate closely to the Vauxhall picture.

Lit: Gowing 1953, p. 12 No. 27 fig. 12; Yale 1983, No. 81 fig. 27
DC

F37 *Madamoiselle Catherina*

Charles Grignion (1717-1810) after Francis Hayman (1708-1776). 1743
Engraving; 267 x 349
Lettered with the title and *Is a Puppet moved by Clockwork shown by the Savoyards for a Livelyhood. 4th April 1743* and *F. Hayman Pinx. C Grignion Sculp* and with the address of Thomas Bowles.
Lambeth Archives Department (LP 14/581/96)

A group of a gentleman, two ladies, a servant-girl and three Savoyards under a portico. One Savoyard demonstrates the automaton, which dances to the tune of a hurdy-gurdy played by his companion. One of the very few Vauxhall decorations which has no moral message ascribed to it, and one of the more original compositions, with some very interesting effects of light and shade. The group of two seated ladies and the two central Savoyards with the automaton re-appears in a decorative painting derived from Nicholas Lancret, formerly in the collection of Walter Gay in Paris, but the exact relationship between the two pictures cannot be satisfactorily explained without the more precise dating of both, and a more definite attribution of the latter.

Lit: Gowing 1953, p. 15 No. 32 fig. 11; Ingamells 1974, p. 315, fig. 1
DC

MADAMOISELLE CATHERINA. Engraved from the Original Painting in Vaux Hall Garden

F37

F38 Stealing a Kiss

Nathaniel Parr active (1742-51) after
Francis Hayman (1708-1776). 1743
Engraving; 267 x 305
Lettered with the title, the address of
Thomas Bowles, *4th April 1743* and
*F. Hayman Pinx N Parr sculp from the
Original Painting in Vaux-hall.*
Lambeth Archives Department
(LP 14/581/28)

A young woman kisses a sleeping
beau, watched by another woman in
an embroidered dress, while a negro
boy tries to save the upset tea-table,
and a serving-maid looks on in horror
from the doorway. The double allusion
in this picture to Hogarth's Harlot's
Progress (plate 2) and Rake's Progress
(plate 3) leaves us in no doubt as to
the moral content of this composition,
and provides the closest link in any of
the surviving Vauxhall decorations
with Hogarth; this relationship,
though, must be tempered by the
simplicity of the setting, which is
decidedly non-Hogarthian. The dining
chair with its looped splat, very similar
to the one in 'Mademoiselle
Caterina' (Cat. F37) is of a type that
became almost a trademark of
Hayman (see Cat. D23).

Lit: Gowing 1953, p. 15 No. 44
DC

F39 The Fortune-teller or Casting the Coffee Grounds.

Francis Vivares (1709-1780) after
Francis Hayman (1708-1776). 1743
Engraving; 251 x 368
Lettered with the title, the address of
Thomas Bowles, *4th April 1743* and
*F. Hayman Pinx. Vivares Fecit from the
Original Painting in Vaux-hall Garden*
Lambeth Archives Department
(LP 14/581/37)

Three young ladies around a tea-table
listen to a gipsy fortune-teller, watched
by a servant-girl and a boy; the group
is set in a romantic silvan landscape,
with a stone urn to the left and a
ruined castle in the distance; a spaniel
sits on an ornate carved and
upholstered stool. This is a subject,
like Blind Man's Buff, Card Houses
and others, taken directly from the
Continental repertoire, and treated in
a very French manner, with its dream-
like landscape, the Watteauesque
costume of the girl on the right, and
the spirit of the *Fête Galante*. 'The

Fortune-Teller' represents an early
and perhaps influential stage in the
development of a particular type of
18th Century outdoor conversation
piece of which the work of Wills,
Hudson, Gainsborough, Dance,
Zoffany, and others includes later
examples.

Lit: Gowing 1953, p. 15 No. 47; Henry
1958, No. 2; Ingamells 1974, p. 315
DC

F40 Sweet William's Farewel to Black Eyed Susan

Paul Fourdrinier active (1720-60) after
Peter Monamy (1689-1749)
Engraving; 295 x 360
Lettered with the title, the addresses of
Bowles and Carver and Robert
Wilkinson and *P Monemie Pinxt
Fourdrinier sculp. from the Original Painting
in Vaux-hall Garden.*
The Trustees of the British Museum
(1854-6-14-276)

One of the set of four engravings after
the marine pictures by Peter Monamy
(1681-1749) which decorated four of
the supper-boxes, the subject matter is
taken from the ballad by John Gay
published in Bickham's *Musical
Entertainer*. Although totally different
from all the other supper-box
decorations, Monamy's paintings do

conform with the spirit of nationalistic
pride prevalent throughout Vauxhall;
this particular scene would be one that
found a sympathetic audience among
the ordinary population, many of
whom would have had some
connection with the sea, and who may
have lost friends or relatives during
the wars with France and Spain. To
this extent, 'Sweet William's Farewel' is
just as much an illustration of an
aspect of the English life as, say, 'The
Milkmaids' Garland' or 'The Play of
Cricket'. When these pictures were
hung at Vauxhall, Monamy was
approaching the age of sixty; he was
past his prime artistically, and not in
good health, and probably financially
embarassed. His involvement at
Vauxhall was perhaps the result of
intervention by his old friend William
Hogarth.

Lit: Gowing 1953, p. 12 No. 22;
Harrison-Wallace 1983, No. 38; Yale
1983, p. 14
DC

F40

F41 *Vauxhall Gardens, the Orchestra partly demolished.*

J. Findlay, 1859
Water colour; 176 x 120
The Museum of London (A 6983/4/ 9a)

The 'gothic' orchestra building in Vauxhall Gardens shown during demolition works, various parts of it on the ground around its base. The building is the same as that seen in the Wale drawing (Cat. F21) of almost one hundred years before, but after substantial alterations. The antiquary John Fillinham commissioned Findlay and H.S. Barton to prepare a full record of Vauxhall as it was at its end, and this tragic little watercolour is the most evocative of the two dozen surviving drawings. A photograph of the orchestra at the same date is preserved at the Minet Library, Lambeth. *The Times* (26/7/1859) gives a rather biting account of 'The pathetic ceremony of leave-taking . . . between the public and the old-fashioned gardens, noting that 'In a few days will begin the work of destruction that will level to the ground . . . the wooden edifices that look like spectres of dead 'fun' to the travellers by the South-Western Railway . . .' At the auction sale of fittings on 22 August, the orchestra, symbol of Vauxhall for a century, realised £99.
DC

F42 *Punch bowl*

Bristol (painted by Joseph Flower).
1743
Tin-glazed earthenware painted in blue; h. 210, diam. 320
City of Bristol Museum and Art Gallery (G.1690)

This bowl is closely similar to one in the Ashmolean Museum, Oxford which is inscribed 'Joseph Flower Sculp 1743'. Flower was apprenticed to Thomas Frank at the Redcliff Backs pottery in Bristol. He finished his apprenticeship and became a Burgess in 1743. The four outside scenes are taken from illustrations at the headings of songs in George Bickham's *Musical Entertainer* of 1737-39, as follows: Cato's Advice or the Jovial Companions (vol. I p. 18), The Relief (vol. I, p. 17), Britons Strike Home (vol. II p. 98), Beauties Decay (vol. I p. 33). The interior shows a punch bowl on a table and two chairs.

Prov: purchased 1921.
Lit: Bristol n.d., 10, 11; Bristol 1979, G36; Britton 1982, 8.1; Ray 1965; Ray 1968, p. 162
MA

F43 *Masqueraders*

a) *Masquerader*

Chelsea (Lawrence Street factory).
c. 1760-69
Soft-paste porcelain containing bone-ash, enamelled and gilt; h. 199
Mark: an anchor in gold at the back.
VAM (C.32-1973)
See colour plate VIII

The young man shown hopping on his left leg on a scroll-edged mound base applied with flowers and with tree trunk support behind. He wears a tricorn hat with a pipe held by two loops at the front, a domino covering one side of his face, red waistcoat with a puce sash, puce breeches with gold bells at the knee and turquoise apron. A wreath is thrown over his shoulder and he plays a flageolet. At his left side are hung a lantern and a flask half full of wine.

Fourteen models from this series, recognizable by their scroll bases, their size and their subject-matter, have so far been identified, nine of which are in the present exhibition. Eleven models are in the collection at Colonial Williamsburg; the six at Luton Hoo (Wernher Collection) include two further models, while yet another model of a man holding a bird-cage is illustrated by Stoner, 1955, pl. 32. It has often been suggested (e.g. by Blunt, 1924, No. 251 and pl. 18) that these figures commemorate a masque held in honour of the Prince of Wales'

F41

F42

birthday given in Ranelagh Gardens on 24th May, 1759. However none of the figures correspond at all exactly to those shown in the engraving by Bowles after Maurer representing this ball (illustrated in *Apollo*, August 1969, p. 92, fig. 2). It is not even certain that the figures were intended to represent the well-to-do in fancy dress rather than Mountebanks or Mummers. A figure in clothes not unlike those worn by the flageolet player is shown performing outside a tavern in a drawing of 1755 by Paul Sandby, now at Windsor Castle (Oppé 1950, pl. 114, supplement No. 431). A pair of Chelsea gold anchor vases now at Luton Hoo is painted on each side with a figure somewhat similar in character to the three-dimensional figures here discussed (see Gardner 1940, p. 6, figs. VII and VIII). Examples of this series are illustrated in Blunt.

Prov: Mrs William Salting; Sir B Eckstein; Sotheby's 29th March, 1949 Colonial Williamsburg (sold as a duplicate).
Lit: Austin 1977; Blunt (ed) 1924; Blunt & Gardner 1924; Bradshaw 1981, pp. 117 & 294; Charleston & Towner 1977; Gardner 1940, pp. 3-6; Hayden 1932; King 1925; Lane 1961; Oppé 1950; Severne Mackenna 1952; Stoner 1955; Sutton 1969
JVGM

b) Masquerader
Chelsea (Lawrence Street factory); *c.* 1760-69
Soft-paste porcelain containing bone-ash, enamelled and gilt h. 219
Unmarked
VAM (C.33-1973)

He is dressed as a pilgrim with staff (repaired) striding forward on a mound base applied with flowers which climb up the tree-trunk support. He wears a pointed turquoise cap with flower-shaped rim, a puce cape, yellow tunic and red belt from which hangs his sabre. His moustachioed face is dappled with black patches.

For notes and literature see Cat. F43a. Sotheby's 1st February, 1946, lot 26; Colonial Williamsburg (sold as a duplicate).
JVGM

c) Masquerader
Chelsea (Lawrence Street factory); *c.* 1760-69
Soft-paste porcelain containing bone-ash, enamelled in colours h. 206
Mark: an anchor in gold at the back
VAM (C.184-1977)

She stands dancing with her left hand holding her flowered white apron, her right holding her puce-lined yellow skirt. Her underskirt of turquoise with red fringe. Her head turned to her left, she wears a puce cap and a mask.

For notes and literature see Cat. F43a. Sotheby's 26th July, 1977.
JVGM

d) Masquerader
Chelsea (Lawrence Street factory); *c.* 1760-69
Soft-paste porcelain containing bone-ash, enamelled and gilt h. 203
Mark: an anchor in gold at the back
The Wernher Collection by arrangement with the NACF (No. 1416)

He dances with his left foot forward his right hand swung across his body wearing a broad-brimmed hat, lilac coat and turquoise breeches.

For notes and literature see Cat. F43a.
JVGM

e) Masquerader
Chelsea (Lawrence Street factory); *c.* 1760-69
Soft-paste porcelain containing bone-ash, enamelled and gilt h. 197
Mark: an anchor in gold at the back
The Wernher Collection by arrangement with the NACF (No. 1416)

She holds a mask in front of her face and wears a scarf over her head. A hurdy-gurdy is slung from her waist over her yellow apron with flowered red border and her turquoise dress. Gardner (1940, p. 4, figs. III and IV) suggested rather implausibly that this figure was inspired by a painting by Murillo. For further notes and literature see Cat. F43a.
Gardner, July 1940, pp. 3-6
JVGM

f) Masquerader
Chelsea (Lawrence Street factory); *c.* 1760-69
Soft-paste porcelain containing bone-ash, enamelled and gilt h. 213
Mark: an anchor in gold at the back

The Wernher Collection by arrangement with the NACF (No. 1416)

He is dancing with his left leg raised, playing a violin. He wears a black domino, plumed hat, cloak, puce waistcoat and turquoise knee-breeches. For notes and literature see Cat. F43a.
JVGM

g) Masquerader
Chelsea (Lawrence Street factory); *c.* 1760-69
Soft-paste porcelain containing bone-ash, enamelled and gilt h. 213
Mark: an anchor in gold at the back.
The Wernher Collection by arrangement with the NACF (No. 1343)

She wears a black tricorn hat over a white scarf, her features hidden by a black mask. Her shoulders are covered by a puce coat which she holds in front of her with both hands. Her scarf is striped in iron red and lilac and she has a drum suspended from her waist.
For notes and literature see Cat. F43a.
JVGM

h) Masquerader
Chelsea (Lawrence Street factory); *c.* 1760-69
Soft-paste porcelain containing bone-ash, enamelled and gilt h. 197
Unmarked.
The Wernher Collection by arrangement with the NACF (No. 1416)

She wears a black mask and holds in either hand the hem of her puce coat. Beneath this is visible a red and green striped undergarment and a turquoise skirt.
For notes and literature see Cat. F43a.
JVGM

i) Masquerader
Chelsea (Lawrence Street factory); *c.* 1760-69
Soft-paste porcelain containing bone-ash, enamelled and gilt h. 203
Mark: an anchor in gold at the back.
The Wernher Collection by arrangement with the NACF (No. 1343)

He stands holding a barrel under his left arm, a gun slung from his shoulder. He is dressed as a hussar with fur-lined red cap, turquoise coat with a cloak worn over it and yellow knee-breeches.
For notes and literature see Cat. F43a.
JVGM

Silver

A Book of ORNAMENTS

Containing Divers elegant Designs, for the use of Goldsmiths, Chasers, Carvers &c.
Curiously Engraved by Chatelin &c from the Drawings of Mess.rs German Meissomer Sig.r Cattarello &c.
Printed for John Bowles at the Black horse in Cornhill.

Title page for A Book of Ornaments. *See cat. G46.*

Rococo Silver
Design
Elaine Barr

The rococo period in English silver is sometimes regarded as an aberration interposed between the simple grace of the first quarter of the eighteenth century and the calm restraint of its last three decades. The new ideas came incontestably from France where Juste-Aurèle Meissonnier had introduced the *rocaille* style in the early 1720s. The Duke of Kingston went straight to the fountain head in 1735 and was rewarded, after a five year wait, with Meissonnier's incomparable tureens (Cat. C7); the third Earl of Berkeley commissioned a magnificent dinner service from the Parisian goldsmith Jacques Roettiers in 1735.[1] The scarcity in our native collections of pieces bearing French marks suggests that only a few English purchasers of advanced tastes followed their example. Nevertheless the influence of the French *maîtres orfèvres* was immense. French designs reached English goldsmiths through their rich and noble clients returning from the Continent with portfolios of sketches and published prints. A pair of candelabra was made to a famous design of Thomas Germain by George Wickes in 1745.[2]

Whilst there was a dearth of native English designers at the beginning of the rococo period, there was no scarcity of good teachers in London to instruct would-be exponents of the style. Hogarth's school, the St. Martin's Lane Academy, was founded in 1735. Two of its tutors, the Swiss-born chaser and enameller George Michael Moser[3] and Hubert Gravelot,[4] a Frenchman, had close contacts with goldsmiths. They are known to have worked at Hogarth's Academy in 1746, possibly earlier; both had drawing schools of their own and were well versed in continental design trends.[5] At the auction sale of Moser's library in 1783 the catalogue listed prints by Meissonnier, Le Brun and Brunetti, all designers to whom Moser would have turned for inspiration during his years as a chaser.[6]

Engravings of Meissonnier's designs were available in Paris from 1734 and speedily found their way to London. Long before that date, however, the Huguenot goldsmiths, attuned to all things French, had begun to assimilate the new style. Paul De Lamerie may have made a tentative start as early as 1721, when he made a small waiter chased with naturalistic flowers in the angles of the inner border. In 1723 a feeling for movement is definitely apparent in the scroll border of his stand for a christening bowl at Althorp.[7] By 1732 De Lamerie's advancing grasp of the style is demonstrated in a covered cup decorated with festoons of fruit and flowers, shells and scale work, its extraordinary handles each surmounted by a putto leaning backwards, one foot poised in mid air.[8] He was one of the first to introduce into his work elements from Meissonnier's still-life compositions published in the *Livre de Légumes* (Cat. O6) using his famous crayfish on tureens which were themselves unmistakably French in outline (Cat. G2). De Lamerie was closely followed by his fellow Huguenots, notably Paul Crespin, and the German goldsmith Frederick Kandler. The satyr-handled silver-gilt wine coolers Crespin made for the Duke of Marlborough in 1733 (Cat. D1) are chased with sea-waves, grapes and a rococo cartouche supported by amorini.

The English goldsmiths apparently did not follow the example of the Huguenots until the mid 1730s and then, like them, they were not content merely to copy actual objects made by their French counterparts. Instead they adopted ornamental motifs drawn from engravings of designers like Jacques de Lajoue and Gaetano Brunetti. George Wickes borrowed motifs from both in 1735 barely twelve months after their prints became available in France (Cat. G23). In 1748 the publication of Pierre Germain's *Eléments d'Orfèvrerie* made available one hundred plates of designs fashionable on the Continent at the time, seven of them after the celebrated goldsmith Jacques Roettiers.

French opponents of the *genre pittoresque* never ceased to protest against its excesses. In his celebrated attack on the goldsmiths in the *Mercure de France* in December 1754 Charles-Nicolas Cochin commented scathingly on their absurdities and lack of logic. Such excesses were calmly accepted by the English protagonists of the rococo. Country squires like Leake Okeover (Cat. G26) took in their stride coffee pots with spouts formed as rearing sea-horses and grotesque beasts and reptiles crouching over the handles of sauceboats and cream jugs. The London goldsmiths vested these devices with a vitality often lacking in French work.

Although the rococo style is essentially unfettered, certain overall elements prevail in form and decoration, even in silver, where principles of utility are usually paramount. Asymmetry was largely Meissonnier's contribution; French and English goldsmiths, however, produced many pieces which although unmistakably rococo in style are perfectly symmetrical. The basis of Meissonnier's ornament was *rocaille*. A strictly literal translation of the word would limit it to rocks and stones whereas in the context of the rococo style it embraces grottoes and caves and also their denizens, the dragons and grotesque reptiles, and with them the snakes beloved of Paul De Lamerie.

Water – which lent itself so well to engraving and chasing – fascinated the rococo designers: streams flow over ledges and cascade from crevices providing not only a rich and varied series of ornamental motifs but often the very framework of an object as in the swirling sculptural base of the Wakelin candlestick of 1753 (Cat. G34). The sea becomes water personified, peopled by Poseidon and his attendant tritons and nereids; coral branches, seaweed and palm fronds mingle with reeds and bulrushes, while sea foam, delicate as lace, provides sport for dolphins which play a major role in this marine fantasy. The dolphins in the work of Crespin and Sprimont, who may have derived their treatment of the motif from the sculptured fountains of Liège,[9] create a spray as they pass through the waves which takes on the likeness of whiskers when translated into silver. This continues an architectural conceit familiar to Bernini. Four such dolphins on the Fishmongers' chandelier (Cat. G33), the pattern of which is described in the Company's Court Minutes as 'Dolphin', closely resemble those on Crespin's centrepiece (Cat. G17) and Sprimont's sauceboats (Cat. G17).

In this watery realm, many of the realistic silver shells and crustacea must have been cast from nature. Whilst no documentary evidence of such casting is available for the eighteenth century the technique was certainly practised in the early 1800s.[10] The shell motif was not limited to decoration: it provided the ideal rococo form for containers, sometimes with the upper part of the shell acting as a lid (Cat. G10). In De Lamerie's hands it became an elegant basket resting on dolphin feet (Cat. G21). The most notable shell salts are in the remarkable marine service made by Crespin and Sprimont for Frederick, Prince of Wales in 1741-3 (Cat. G17).[11] Sprimont was responsible for introducing man into this marine creation, using figures on the sauceboats in the same service. Dr. Tessa Murdoch has recently drawn attention to a possible link with the sculptor Roubiliac who received part of his training in Liège.[12] Sprimont's intimacy with Roubiliac was marked in 1744 by his sponsorship of the latter's infant daughter.

The rococo style was not restricted to marine motifs. Scrolls achieved a virtuosity unknown in the preceding period. The delicate tracery of the scrolling handles and chasing of the Phillips Garden beer jugs of 1754 (Cat. G36) are akin to contemporary plaster work. The heavier scrollwork on the Crespin centrepiece of 1741 (Cat. G17) proclaims a French origin.[13] The cartouche, which had served merely to enclose armorials in previous centuries, became a decorative motif in its own right, as in the Crespin wine coolers of 1733 (Cat. D1).

Frolicking amidst the scrolls and cartouches are the putti and amorini which ornament the work of Paul De Lamerie, garbed as miniature Greek gods (Cat. G12) or sitting astride the lids of cups holding aloft bunches of grapes. Vines in all stages and forms vie with naturalistic flowers and leaves in a sylvan world inhabited by butterflies, ladybirds, bees, lizards and small insects. Masks also find a place in this mêlée, sometimes leonine or auricular as in Paul De Lamerie's cup of 1737 (Cat. G3), often in the form of satyrs and the gods of antiquity,[14] and others emblematical of the four continents.[15] The plumed women's heads favoured by many rococo goldsmiths, including Wickes, probably have their origin in prints by Pineau and Berain.[16]

Chinoiserie, so popular in Caroline times, reappeared in the rococo period, the delicately engraved humans, birds and flowers replaced by bolder casting and chasing. Enthusiasm for all things Chinese was not tempered by a knowledge of the Orient or its art; it is hard to reconcile the chinamen and the palm tree on De Lamerie's tea caddy of 1744 (Cat. R1). The Jacques de Lajoue cartouche (Cat. C5) used by Wickes in 1735 (Cat. C4) and later by Wakelin, also appears on a Wakelin chinoiserie caddy of 1751, presumably only because of its parasol.[17] Epergnes fashioned as pagodas were *à la mode* in the 1750s and 60s (see Cat. R10). The last word on the great Chinese craze may perhaps be given to Horace Walpole, writing ironically (and anonymously) in *The World* in 1751. Our Chinese ornaments, he commented, 'are not only of our own manufacture, like our French silks . . . but, what has seldom been attributed to the English, of our own invention.'

Patrons and Craftsmen
Philippa Glanville

'Tho' whims and fripperies may have a run, one always returns to what is really handsome and noble and plain' Lady Holland, 1764.

The craft was largely dominated by Huguenot goldsmiths who, through intermarriage and taking one another's apprentices and journeymen, ensured a professional cohesion and continued sensitivity to their French roots.[1] In the 1730s, the years of stylistic inventiveness, three names predominate: De Lamerie, Paul Crespin, and an Englishman, George Wickes.[2] A leading goldsmith from the 1720s, De Lamerie ran a large retail business with many of the aristocracy among his account customers; appointed one of the royal goldsmiths in 1716, he contributed to the Russian court orders (which went exclusively to Huguenot goldsmiths) of the 1720s and 1730s. His mark is found on some of the earliest surviving tureens, breadbaskets and epergnes, although this is probably to some extent an accident of survival since other goldsmiths are known to have supplied them too. His patrons were markedly different from those of his Huguenot contemporaries, such as David Willaume father and son and Augustine Courtauld, who merely dabbled in the rococo style.[3]

The plate of both Paul De Lamerie (1688-1751) and Paul Crespin (1644-1770) shows the continued influence of successive waves of French engraved ornament. In De Lamerie's case, in the 1730s and 40s this was modified and diluted by both Augsburg and Dutch designs of a century earlier, particularly auricular (Cat. G6, G11 & G7). The extraordinary concentration of high-relief chasing and asymmetrical forms in De Lamerie's output between about 1735 and 1742 is explicable only if we assume that he was employing both a modeller and highly skilled foreign-trained chaser at that time. His silver of the later 1740s is noticeably less inventive and repeats earlier successful motifs, such as his dolphin-footed shell basket, and batwing motifs on tea silver (Cat. G21 and Goldsmiths' caddy Cat. R1), and he continued to mark quantities of standard plain wares virtually unaffected by the parallel passion for scrolls, shells and curves.

The skills of Paul Crespin, who was at least a second generation immigrant, were of a different order. Patronized by the English nobility, with whom he corresponded in French, he also had the honour of repeated orders from the King of Portugal and from successive Tsarinas of Russia in the 1720s. By 1733 Crespin numbered at least three dukes (Portland, Marlborough and Devonshire) the Earl of Leicester, Earl Dysart, Viscount How and Viscount Townshend among his English customers.[4] Crespin's designs are purer and more consistent than De Lamerie's, without the mixture of auricular and Augsburg motifs, and more closely related to current or recent French silver, as in the Blenheim ice bucket (Cat. D1) or a chamber stick of 1744, a literal copy of a design by Germain (VAM/M2-1980). He was evidently a superb craftsman in his own right, known from his earliest work (a box of 1720) for his detailed chasing. His constant technique was to cast and chase marine elements in shell festoons, like a teapot of 1740 or coral-like elements, as in the salts supplied to Charles, Viscount Townshend in 1747; some of his early shell-encrusted sauceboats, made for Lyonel Tollemache 4th Earl Dysart, in 1733, were copied 13 years later to make a set of four and were then accompanied by a trefoil spicebox formed of shells with a coral stem.[5]

George Wickes' abilities are apparent in the Leinster service and the ewer and basin of a decade earlier (Cat. G23 & C4). His responsiveness, whether to the auricular tradition or to contemporary French silver, is less marked than De Lamerie's or Crespin's and he was apparently more dependent on books of ornament. The rediscovery of ledgers for his clients and those of his successors Edward Wakelin and John Parker, analysed by Elaine Barr and Arthur Grimwade[6] have exposed the complexity of internal relationships in their craft. By 1766, the date of the earliest surviving Workmen's Ledger for Wickes' successors in trade, this successful business had sixty-six plateworkers, candlestick makers, jewellers, buckle and spoon makers and other specialists on its books.[7] In addition to these three makers, a handful of craftsmen stand out around 1740 for their innovative designs or highly-chased plate – John Edwards, Aymé Videau, Christian Hillan, Frederick Kandler and Pézé Pilleau – but these men have not left enough documented silver for us to comment on their output or clients, although each was responsible for distinctive contributions to the mainstream of rococo silver (Cat. G10 & G9).

The rococo style swept the shops so totally that by the 1750s, not only did second rank goldsmiths show on their trade cards that they carried stocks of standard wares but standard rococo forms were so generally recognised that they could be ordered across the Atlantic.[8] Neither De Lamerie nor Crespin was as directly imitative of current or recent French design as certain goldsmiths active in the 1750s (Cat. G34 & G43). Taste had moved on to heavy, curvaceous but restrained forms close to French silver[9] of the 1730s and later. A tureen by Thomas Heming of 1762, while retaining a high proportion of wrought work and a realistically modelled cauliflower finial, shows a French-inspired taste which was already apparent in William Cripps' tureen of a decade earlier and De Lamerie's Anson tureens of 1750.[10]

Many of the striking effects achieved in rococo silver depended on the skilled modellers and chasers who, with rare exceptions such as Moser, remain anonymous; they often registered no mark at Goldsmiths' Hall and were hardly ever cited in bills. Even for a piece as important and well-documented as the Jerningham Kandler winecistern, whose designer, modeller and silversmith are all identified, the chasers are merely referred to in passing. In addition, certain widely-used designs for handles, feet or finials owe their common features to suppliers of cast components to the trade, although again their identities are not yet known (Cat. G45).[11]

Because very few sets of plate, whether for dining or tea-drinking, have survived intact and because armorials appear less frequently on the elaborately-wrought English silver of this period than on earlier plate, it is easier to name the goldsmiths than the clients who ordered and paid. But since the charges for wrought plate were markedly higher, clients' preferences were crucial to the emergence of the style. By 1740 the standard components of the dinner service were firmly established. The term 'wrought' in bills and inventories, applied particularly to salts, sauceboats, breadbaskets, epergnes and tureens, indicates the significance attached to their appearance; as a direct result they were often charged at markedly more per ounce for 'fashion' or workmanship.[12] On small tablewares, the more fantastic the design (particularly those pieces by Kandler or Videau derived from mannerist sources) the more intrusive a coat of arms became. On only one of the eight sets of fantasy sauceboats illustrated by Grimwade are there armorials, and those are of a later owner.[13] In both tea and dinner plate common themes such as Chinese scenes, tea plants or marine subjects are detectable, despite later losses; the Leinster service and the Prince of Wales's marine theme service indicate the size and subject matter of other, vanished, orders (Cat. G23 & G17). Tureens, which took a dominant place in the first course table-layout and so were elaborately finished, normally incorporated the arms or at least the crest of the owner, often modelled as handles, like the pair with his griffin crest made by George Wickes for the Earl of Malton in 1737.[14] De Lamerie frequently repeated his teaplant, shell and serpent theme for tea canisters, creamboats and teapots between 1736 and 1742 (Cat. R1). Even on standing cups, par excellence made as presentation pieces, armorials were no longer given prominence in the design.[15]

Special commissions are hard to single out after about 1740, with the possible exception of Nicholas Sprimont's silver, eg Cat. G17, so generally acceptable had the style become. The pattern of purchasing shows that no client dealt exclusively with one goldsmith. Benjamin Mildmay, Earl Fitzwalter, for example, had a running account with De Lamerie from 1729 to 1751, the year of the goldsmith's death, but nine other goldsmiths are mentioned in his accounts and some received substantial orders.[16] Some major purchasers remained quite indifferent to the rococo style; George Booth, Earl of Warrington, who was buying silver extensively and continuously from about 1700 to 1750 from a dozen leading Huguenot silversmiths, including De Lamerie, apparently purchased nothing 'bizarre, unusual and *pittoresque*'.[17] Although the Goldsmiths' Company cheerfully paid a high price for their new ewer and basin from De Lamerie, the rest of their 1740/1 order is comparatively restrained, the 'contraste' confined to the cast borders of salvers.[18]

As noted above, some Englishmen ordered their rococo silver directly from the Paris goldsmiths. Apart from the commissions of the Duke of Kingston and Lord Berkeley, William, Viscount Bateman ordered a tea equipage from Germain in 1734,[19] while in 1769 Horace Walpole was prevented by English Customs Officers from importing French silver: 'Plate, of all earthly vanities, is the most impossible'.[20]

French silver was circulating on the London market in the 1730s: Earl Fitzwalter bought four French candlesticks from De Lamerie in 1736.[21] London goldsmiths also copied French pieces in English hands, such as Germain's candelabrum, discussed above. Another Germain design, for an elegant tripod caster like those in the Berkeley Castle service, was copied by Simon Pantin in 1740, to make a matching set for an unidentified English client (VAM M.114-1978). Although Rouquet commented on the small quantity of silver tableware in English homes: 'A choice collection of porcelane, more or less fine, according to the taste and fortune of the master, supplies the place of a richer service',[22] his opinion is not borne out by the plate holdings of the aristocracy which were being constantly refashioned but not reduced, nor by the statistics for silver taken for assay at Goldsmiths' Hall, which show a marked increase from 1740.[23]

Given these quantities of plate it is hardly surprising that standardised production and repetitious design flourished. Extensive use of casting enabled goldsmiths to combine motifs, as in the openwork borders of salvers or the legs and handles of tureens, and vary the finished pieces sufficiently.[24] The 'curious' element in rococo silver, its elaborate ornament and complex shapes, has protected much from the melt. Sideboard sets, like the Scrope ewer and basin (Cat. C4) were essentially display pieces, designed to enhance the standing of the owner and not subject to heavy wear, although frequently regilt.[25] More surprising is the survival of relatively large quantities of rococo tableware, elaborately cast and chased, given the abrupt shift in taste of the 1760s.

G1 *Tea equipage*

Paul De Lamerie (1688-1751). London hallmarks for 1735/6
Silver: h. of larger canister 118, l. of teaspoon 122
Engraved on all except nip and straining spoon with the arms of Boissier impaling Berchere for Jean Daniel Boissier and Suzanne Judith Berchere (m. April 1735).
Leeds City Art Galleries

Chased, cast and engraved. Comprising two canisters for tea and a third, larger, for sugar, cream boat, straining spoon, 12 teaspoons, sugar nips and a pair of knives in a silver-mounted mahogany box. The earliest complete English tea equipage preserved, although combinations of these components still in silver-mounted cases are known, eg sets also by De Lamerie of 1739 and 1741 (Phillips 1968, pl. XVII; Sotheby's 16 July 1970, 97) lacking the cream boat. The design for the cast handle appears on a kettle of 1736 in the Gilbert collection (Los Angeles 1977, No. 8) and the cabbage and snail feet on a sauceboat by De Lamerie of 1739 (Christie's archives). The canisters with fluted angles and sloping shoulders are an early departure from rectangular forms; cf. a pair of a year earlier (VAM M.156+a-1939). This became a standard shape used by De Lamerie and others in the later 1730s and 1740s. The intertwined handles of the teaspoons are close to those in cat. G16.

Prov: Boissier family until 1954; Temple Newsam House, 1974
Lit: Wells-Cole 1974, pp. 13-24
PG

G2 *Tureen*

Paul De Lamerie (1688-1751). London hallmarks for 1736/7
Silver; h. 330, diam. 270
Engraved with armorials
Private Collection

The exuberance of the rococo decoration does not completely camouflage an object essentially French Régence in character. The fluted bowl and basket work, also used by De Lamerie in 1734 for the Bobrinskoy centrepiece (Phillips 1935, pl. XCV), derive from French designs of the 1720s as does the winged cartouche which was part of the

G2

standard baroque repertoire. Many of the naturalistic motifs may have their origin in Meissonnier's *Livre de Légumes,* published in 1734 (cat. O6), though De Lamerie seems to have adapted these designs to his own purpose. It is possible, moreover, that he may have seen the famous tureen with boars-head handles and cauliflower finial which Thomas Germain fashioned in 1733-34. The shape owes much to the *pot à l'oille* in which was served a soup made of meat and game: the latter figures prominently in the cast and applied decoration on the lid and in the two bird heads which emerge from the bound reeding on the rim. The crayfish and the shell base resting on dolphin feet supply the marine elements essential to a rocaille piece, incongruously allied here to trailing vine leaves and grapes. An almost identical tureen was made by De Lamerie in the same year (Metropolitan Museum, New York, formerly Swaythling Collection).

Lit: Bristol 1965; Grimwade 1974, pp. 42-3; Goldsmith's Hall 1978, cat. 94; Phillips 1935, pl. CVIII
EB

G3 *Cup and cover*

Paul De Lamerie (1688-1751). London hallmarks for 1737/8
Silver-gilt, gilding renewed; h. 395
Engraved with the arms of Maynard for Henry, 4th Baron Maynard (d. 1742).
The Worshipful Company of Fishmongers

Cast, embossed and chased. The circular foot chased with panels of shells and articular masks with scalework between, the body with matted shellwork below two large shells with alternate flutes of guilloche, strap- and scalework. The handles moulded as serpents, their heads emerging above the shells. The cover embossed with scrolls and shells and auricular masks and surmounted by a grape cluster finial. Several cups by De Lamerie identical to this design are known, eg one formerly the property of Earl Cowper (1739, Jackson 1911, p.730), others of 1737 and 1738 at Christie's, 27 May 1953, 169 and 24 November, 1971, 35. The design for the entwined snake handles was re-used, eg on the unmarked cup purchased from George Wickes by Frederick, Prince of Wales, for presentation to the City of Bath in 1739, and on another, unmarked, cup in the Royal Collection, also purchased from Wickes, in January 1740 (Jones 1911, pl. XXXVIII).

Prov: Henry, 4th Baron Maynard; Countess of Warwick; Col. H.H. Mulliner; Fishmongers' Company 1949
Lit: Goldsmiths' Hall 1951, p. 225, pl. LXVII; Mulliner 1924, fig. 97; VAM 1954, p. 38
PG

G4 *A cartouche*
Daniel Rabel (1578-1637). 1632
Etching and engraving; 121 x 169
Numbered *12*
VAM (20321.1)

From the suite *Cartouches de differentes Inventions.* The ambiguous, fleshy and sometimes scaly substances with their suggestions of monstrous heads, which exemplify the 17th century auricular style, seem to have been particularly influential in De Lamerie's work in the 1730s (see cat. G3). This example of an elaborate and almost deliberately distracting frame contrasted with the calm landscape it encloses is characteristic of the auricular period; similar contrasts were very popular in English rococo design.

Lit: Berlin 1939, 309(1); Meyer 1983, pp. 11-12
MS

G5 *Designs for vases and a large country house*
Anonymous, after Johann Bernhard Fischer von Erlach (1656-1723). 1721
Etching and engraving; 296 x 420
Lettered *Une vase qui est dedié a la Deesse Galatée. Et celui-ci aux Tritons de la mer,* and in German, and *J: B: F: vo. E. inven:*
Numbered 2 No. 11.
VAM (17200)

From Book 5 of Fischer's *Entwurff Einer Historischen Architektur* which was written by 1712, published in Vienna in 1721, and published in London with the same plates and a translation by T. Lediard, in 1730. The fantastic baroque and 'Egyptian' vases which form Book 5 contain many elements which find echoes in the cups of De Lamerie, such as the use of marine forms and fleshy overlapping straps. Very similar vases were used in the gardens at Schloss Mirabell, Salzburg, made *c.*1689-90. The building in the background of this print is Fischer's project for a 'Grosses Landgebaude' of *c.*1690.

Lit: Aurenhammer 1973, p. 101, fig. 57; Brighton 1983, 24; Sedlmayer 1956, fig. 22 (the drawing for this print)
MS

G6 *Standish with bell, pounce pot and inkwell*
Paul De Lamerie (1688-1751): London hallmarks for 1738/9
Silver-gilt, gilding renewed; l. 300
His Grace the Duke of Marlborough DL, JP, Blenheim Palace
See colour plate VI.

Cast, chased and embossed. The stand formed as an asymmetrical cartouche, one terminal chased with a bag of wind, a cock and staff entwined with serpents (attributes of Mercury), the other with a cornucopia crowned with a pineapple. The side edges formed as broad curving ribbons, overlaid with palms. The pounce pot and inkwell are irregularly shaped with shell covers and bases, formed to fit shell sockets (one chased with a sealed letter). On each a serpent twines around and through the body, across deep-set chased scenes of travel by land and sea. The bell is chased with sea plants on a matted ground, rising to three chased shells; the handle is the bust of a boy. Rows of raised circles on matted strips (seaweed) surround the covers and bases of the pots and bell stand. A rare instance in English silver of a cartouche dictating the form of an object. The design of a standish was normally symmetrical – oval or oblong – dictated by the components, particularly the bell. But De Lamerie's stand is asymmetrical and layered with

G5

exuberant cast and chased ornament whose imagery, of messages and travel, is particularly suited to the standish's function. While there is no parallel for this design, it has links with German silver; the cartouche form appears, for example, in an Augsburg sconce on 1737/9 by J.L. Biller (Hernmarck 1977, pl. 536), and the shell boxes are clearly related to a contemporary German *rocaille* design, now known only in a later set of engravings; (see the suite of *rocaille* silver designs by C.G. Eissler, No. 311, 2, which were probably published no earlier than the mid-1740s). The combination of unique form and German ornament in this standish imply a marked preference on the part of the client, whose identity is not known. Another inventive standish by Paul Crespin (sold from Wanstead House in 1822, now at Chatsworth) adopts shell forms for the boxes but is otherwise regular in form, on dolphin feet, and De Lamerie's standish for the Goldsmiths' Company confines its asymmetry to the ornament.

Lit: Grimwade 1974, pl. 84
PG

G7 *Coffee-pot*

Paul De Lamerie (1688-1751). London hallmarks for 1738/9
Silver; h. 280
Engraved with the arms of Lequesne impaling Knight of Sir John Lequesne, Grocer of London, m. Knight, 1738
Private Collection

Raised, cast and chased. Spirally fluted pear-shape, with handle set asymmetrically and three shell feet. The body chased with two panels of putti with coffee plants and a negroid mask in foliage, superimposed on a shell and flower trellis, rising to a flowering coffee spray below the spout. On the cover, strapwork rolls over panels of scales and flowers, rising to a shell-clasped finial. Several of De Lamerie's 1738 coffee-pots adopt this twisting shape on three feet. Both elements derive from French design (cf. one from Louis XIV's silver service 1702; Hernmarck, pl. 340). The closest is chased with dissolving auricular masks in place of the putti (Dauterman 1965; Phillips 1968, CXXI). Another pot is plain with a putto and coffee plant finial (Carver and Casey, 1978). De Lamerie's earliest use of chased

G7

putti occurs in 1736 on a tea kettle for the same family as this coffee-pot (Jackson 1977); and on the rim of a basin made for Henry, 4th Baron Maynard (Hernmarck 1969, 688); but compare an outstanding, unmarked, ewer and basin attributed to De Lamerie and made for Stephen Fox Strangways (m. 1735 Elizabeth Strangways Horner; Jackson 1911, p. 585, pl. 805-6). By 1738 other goldsmiths were following him in setting putti around the rims of vessels; compare a pair of dishes by Archambo of that year, formerly at Levens Hall, Cumbria. Putti are found as finials on French silver a little earlier, for example on Thomas Germain's surtout of 1729-32 and two unmarked ewers of 1727-32 and 1734-5 (*Connaissance des Arts* 1965, p. 116, 140).

Prov: John Gabbitas 1929; Mrs Anna Thomson-Dodge; Christie's 23 June 1971, Christie's New York, 24 October 1983, 207
Lit: Grimwade 1974, pl. 60a
PG

G8

G8 *Basket*

Benjamin Godfrey (active *c.* 1731-
d. 1741). London hallmarks for 1738/9
Silver-gilt gilding renewed; h. with
handle 305, 1. of base 283
Engraved with the arms of Harley
impaling Archer for Edward (Harley)
4th Earl of Oxford (1726-1790) and
Susana, daughter of William Archer of
Welford, Bucks (m. 1751).
*Lent by the Museum of Fine Arts, Boston
Theodora Wilbour Fund in Memory of
Charlotte Beebe Wilbour*

Cast, chased and pierced. Oval,
spreading to broad rim with border of
cast and applied flowers among
irregular cartouches and openwork
scrolls. By 1738 this flaring basket
shape with a central swing handle had
more or less supplanted the older
straight-sided type. The increased
contemporary interest in the ornament
of tableware is particularly evident in
the design of baskets from -
c. 1735 to 1745. The cast bust and scroll
handle terminal appears also on
baskets by George Wickes of 1737
(Sotheby's 5 July 1972, 76), and by De
Lamerie of 1739 (Sotheby's 27 June
1956, 125). While the cast apron foot
and applied border are made up of
irregular cartouches and openwork
scrolls and festoons similar to
contemporary German rococo
ornament, the two masks centred on
the border are more rigidly
conventional than the versions found
on other baskets; often the Four
Seasons are represented with ears of
wheat and flowers. In inventories and
goldsmiths' bills these pieces are
invariably described, if at all, as bread
baskets. An earlier pair by De Lamerie,
at Woburn, shows an alternative
treatment of the border and apron
(Grimwade 1965, pl. 5).

Lit: Gruber 1982, pl. 314
PG

G9 *Sauceboat*

London, marks on underside of bowl
filed away. *c.* 1740
Silver; h. 205
Cartouche engraved with the arms of
Champneys, with Swymmer as the
16th of 18 quarterings for a son of
John Langley Champneys, possibly
Thomas, between his father's death
and 1767 (creation of baronetcy). He
married a grand daughter of Sir
William Coddington.
*The Visitors of the Ashmolean Museum,
Oxford*

One of a pair. Cast, chased and
embossed with cast dragon (or
wyvern?) handle, shaped incurving
rim, under lip a grotesque mask and
on either side of the body a bat's mask
and wing surmounting a cartouche.
Dissolving auricular masks and
shellwork on foot. Despite its distinctive
design, the maker of these sauceboats
cannot be named although the
silversmith and modeller, Charles
Kandler (Grimwade 1976, p. 567) is a
strong candidate. The handle may be
heraldic in reference to the
Coddington dragon crest but another
dragon-handled sauceboat with
Kandler's mark and hallmarked 1742,
recently on the London market, makes
this unlikely. Such dragon handles
were part of the French baroque
repertoire; cf. especially a lead vase of
1705 by Hardy (Souchal 1981, p. 117).
London sauceboats of the 1730s and
early 1740s frequently incorporate
other animal or beast handles.
Kandler's silver is marked out by its
sharp and distinctive figure-modelling,
as in the tea kettle of *c.* 1737 (VAM) and
he was the silversmith for the
Jerningham wine cistern, 1735 (Cat.
B9).

Prov: Asher Wertheimer
Lit: Starkie Gardner 1903, pl. CXVII,
fig. 2; Grimwade 1974, pl. 35A;
Jackson 1911, Vol. 1, fig. 326
PG

G10 *Cream boat*

Christian Hillan (active 1736-)
London hallmarks for 1740/1
Silver; h. 125
Engraved with armorials of Fowler
with Whadcock in pretence
Private Collection

The cow with her calf are at first glance
a natural choice of decorative motif for
a cream boat, but when associated
with the majestic heavily-bearded and
crowned mask beneath the lip it is
apparent that they depict the legend of
Zeus and Io. Zeus ravished Io, a
priestess of Hera, his wife. To protect

G9

G10

110

her from Hera's wrath, he turned Io into a heifer and she later bore him a son. The female head on the handle possibly portrays Hera. The ogee-shaped bowl with cut rim was raised and flat-chased with scrolls which frame the cast and applied figures. The three grotesque cast feet may represent the many-eyed monster Argos whom Hera set to watch over Io. The Greek myths were a favourite source of inspiration in the rococo period. Little is known of Christian Hillan and there is no record of an apprenticeship or freedom in England. His name suggests that he may have been a Scandinavian immigrant. An unusual sugar bowl and cover (Grimwade 1974, pl. 68A) made by him in 1739 is distinctly Scandinavian in style.
EB

G11 *Ewer and basin*

Paul De Lamerie (1688-1751). London hallmarks for 1741/2
Silver-gilt, gilding renewed; h. of ewer 485, diam. of basin 790 Arms of Goldsmiths' Company cast and applied on ewer, cast and bolted onto basin.
The Worshipful Company of Goldsmiths

Chased, cast and applied. The helmet-shaped ewer rises from a shaped foot with three C-scroll terminals and scroll panels containing a lizard, snake, shells and flowers. The foamwork stem is clasped by the tails of a mermaid whose torso is flanked by a clump of sea cabbage and a butterfly and tritons, against an ocean scene; a sea monster spouts below the handle. On the upper body, above a strongly-moulded horizontal rib, leopard's heads and festoons of flowers hang from the shaped rim, flanking and intertwining with the cast and applied coat of arms. The handle is modelled as a marine god twisting back towards the rim, terminating in a scroll with scalework and spume. The flange of the basin is set with four plaques of putti personifying Minerva, Hercules, Mercury and Vulcan, in asymmetrical cartouches, the outer rim chased with their attributes, eg adjacent to Mercury are Pan pipes, a bag of coins and a book of musical notation and by Hercules, the head, wing and tail of a serpent. Between the plaques are inset a lion, a falcon, a phoenix and a sea monster (earth, air, fire and water)

between panels of trellis, scrolls and flowers.

This ewer and basin, commissioned as display silver (hence the gilding, applied also to the four standing cups ordered at the same time), incorporates virtually all the various design traditions on which De Lamerie was drawing from the mid-1730s. French silver of the 1720s contributed the trellis and shell design, already well-established in De Lamerie's repertoire (although earlier engraved, not chased, as on the Walpole salver; 1728, VAM). Antwerp silver of almost a century earlier adopted similar inset plaques with asymmetrical frames, for example a dish by Jan Lutma (Hernmarck 1977, pl. 487) while the cartouches may derive from Toro.

Insects and marine monsters are motifs familiar in northern European mannerist silver. Other examples of De Lamerie layering elements from earlier designs are his basin for Henry, 4th Baron Maynard, of 1736 (Hernmarck 1977, 688) and a set very similar to the Goldsmiths' Company order, made for the Earl of Montrath (1742; Jones 1977, 17). More integrated is the unmarked set in the Ilchester collection (Jackson 1911, 585) which, although attributed to De Lamerie, shows greater control, also avoiding the design constraint imposed by cast armorials. A display

of rich sideboard plate, as Rouquet and other visitors noted, was important to the English and heraldic or personal references were almost invariably incorporated; De Lamerie brought in the Company's leopard heads both on this set and on their inkstand, which also bears figures of Mercury and Hercules. Broken borders with putti are found on plate by other makers; compare dishes by Archambo (1738, Levens Hall, Cumbria). The asymmetrical figure handle was used also on the Kandler cistern (Cat. B9) and on a cup by William Kidney (1740, Goldsmiths' Company).

The order, agreed a year earlier, specified a fashion charge of not more than 5 shillings an ounce, comparable with the cost of the Scrope ewer and basin (Cat. C4); Goldsmiths Company, Committee Minute Bk. 8, 27 November 1740, f 28/9). When delivered, a separate additional charge of £44. 2s (or about 11d an ounce) was made for chasing the ewer and basin and four standing cups 'with curious ornaments.' Gilding was also more expensive than the agreed rate, at 4 shillings an ounce. To enhance the display of their splendid new plate, the Company not only had their old plate re-gilt but ordered a new 'Beaufet' to be made in their Common Hall, for work on which the carver William

G11

Linnell was paid £24. 17s. 6d on 11 August 1742 (Committee Minute Bk. 8, 91 and 99).

Prov: purchased by the Goldsmiths' Company as part of an order replacing plate melted in 1666 and 1711. Delivered 3 December 1741; Goldsmiths' Company, Court Minute Book 14, of 379
Lit: Carrington and Hughes, pl. 61, Grimwade 1974, pl. 55, HPL 235, 236; Phillips p. 106, pl. CXXV & CXXIV
PG

G12

G12 *Cup and cover*
Paul De Lamerie (1688-1751). London hallmarks for 1742/3
Silver-gilt; h. 400
Engraved with the arms of Hodgson
The Metropolitan Museum of Art Bequest of Alfred Duane Pell, 1925

Cast and chased. The base with leopard masks between vines and scrolls; on the body scrolls and vines enclose two panels, one with an infant Bacchus picking grapes, the other making wine; on the cover are two Bacchic figures with a trumpet and bagpipes separated by scrolls, shells, grapes and vine leaves. The finial is a large cluster of grapes surmounted by a lizard. Moulded vine tendril handles each with a snail. Several cups are known, cast to this design by De Lamerie in 1742. Compare, for example, one in the Gilbert collection, Los Angeles and another in the Sterling and Francine Clark Institute, Williamstown, USA (Phillips 1968,

pl. CXXXVIII). The vine handles are to a design by Thomas Germain, found on a pair of ice buckets (Paris 1727/8; Musee du Louvre 1958). The cups differ only in their chased detail, eg in the landscapes on the body and in the treatment of the foot. The design retains a basic symmetry of form although by contrast with the snake-handle cup cat. G3 the surface is worked in deep relief and the ornament more profusely rampant.

Lit: Carver & Casey, 1978; Jones 1979, pp. 50, 51
PG

G13

G13 *Candlestick*
Anonymous, French.
Before 1749 Ormolu; 235 x 144
Stamped with a small crowned C (de Bellaigue, vol. I, p. 34)
The Marquess of Tavistock and the Trustees of the Bedford Estate, Woburn Abbey

One of a pair; the nozzles are missing. The crowned C duty mark was used on ormolu between 1745 and 1749, not only on new pieces, but also on pieces which were in stock when the edict was enforced in 1745. This common type of rococo candlestick has been connected with the Slodtz family, designers at the French court during the period when Meissonnier was also *dessinateur du Cabinet du roi*.

The attribution has been based on a drawing in the Bibliothèque Nationale (Champeaux nd, pl. 134) showing a not very similar candestick, in a volume (Res Hd 64) entitled *Receuil de Dessins pour meubles et pour ornements exécuté en Partie le Surplus Projette MDCCLII*. The volume contains drawings by many different hands, and even those recently connected with the Slodtz (Souchal 1967, pl. 72 et seq.) seem to be by several hands. The form of the ormolu candlestick is that of a Régence baluster candlestick which has been given a *genre pittoresque* twist and ornament. It can be seen as a moderate version of Meissonnier's candelabrum (Cat. A18). This type of candlestick was copied by De Lamerie in 1742 (Cat. G14) and by Thomas Gilpin 1744-6. A carved wooden model, perhaps for casting, is in an English private collection.

Lit: Watson 1956, F.76, 77, pl. 21
MS

G14 *Candelabrum*
Paul De Lamerie (1688-1751). London hallmarks for 1742/3
Silver; h. 390
Engraved with an unidentified crest
The Metropolitan Museum of Art, Untermeyer Collection

One of a pair, cast and chased. Shaped circular base and twisting triangular baluster stem, the base chased with panels of shells rising to foamwork. The stem chased with cartouches and shells. For the French origin of this design see cat. G13. An earlier set of four tablesticks of 1740 by James Schruder, lacking branches, was sold at Christie's (14 October 1959) and the design was used again by Thomas Gilpin in 1744 (at Althorp; Grimwade 1963, pl. 4) and by Paul Crespin in a set of four for Lyonel, 4th Earl Dysart, in 1750, sold in 1955 (Trevor 1955).

Prov: Major H. Meynell; Christie's 24 July 1946, 25
Lit: Hackenbroch 1969, pl. 86
PG

G15 *A fountain*
Attributed to Gillas-Marie Oppenord
(1672-1742). *c.* 1715?
Red chalk; 248 x 208
Inscribed on the verso *Le Brun*
*The Syndics of the Fitzwilliam Museum,
Cambridge (2893)*

The water spouts from a dragon
standing on a rock; below are two
tritons riding dolphins. The drawing
has been connected by Cailleux with
fountain designs by Watteau and
Oppenord; a slightly inferior version is
at Stockholm. Dragons, like snakes (see
cat. G3) were seen as part of the life of
the grotto and therefore appropriate to
a rocky fountain in which sea-creatures,
tritons and dolphins, are also present.
All three with rockwork appear in the
Frederick, Prince of Wales Service Cat.
G17.

Prov: given by A.A. Vansittart, MA
(1824-1882)
Lit: Cailleux 1967, fig. 8; Cormack
1970, pl. 126 ; Eidelberg 1968; K.T.
Parker, letter in *Burlington Magazine,*
Feb. 1969, p. 92 and Eidelberg's reply
in *Burlington Magazine,* April 1969, pl.
223.
MS

G15

G16 *Design for a salt-cellar and two spoons*
Attributed to Nicholas Sprimont
(1716-1771)
Pen and ink, ink wash and pencil; 140
x 190
VAM (2592)

This drawing has been attributed to

Matthias Lock because of its
association with drawings by him, but
the hand is not his and appears to be
that of Sprimont. Not only is the
general arrangement of the bowl, with
its shell-encrusted base and dolphin
supports similar to the centrepiece of
the Prince of Wales's Service (Cat.
G27), but one of the spoons is almost
identical to those supplied for the
service. The salt probably represents a
project for the service. In addition to
this example and cat. G18, only one
other drawing can be connected with
Sprimont, a signed design for a silver
cruet dish at the Society of Antiquaries
(MS 263, see Esdaile 1944). The
presence of this drawing in a collection
associated with Matthias Lock (see cat.
G40) raises several intriguing questions.

Prov: given (?) in 1862 together with a
collection of drawings by Thomas
Chippendale and Matthias Lock,
formerly in the collection of Lock's
descendant, George Lock (see Ward-
Jackson 1958, p. 39).
Lit: Grimwade 1974, pp. 4, 45, pl. 37C.
MS

G17 *The Service of Frederick, Prince of Wales*
Frederick Louis (1707-1751) was a
discerning patron of the Arts and from
1735 onwards he enriched the Royal
Collection with many fine pieces. They
were for the most part entered in the
ledgers of his goldsmith George
Wickes, but this service, with the
possible exception of the centrepiece,
was not recorded. Its identification
with Frederick dates from the
Inventory of Royal Plate made for
William IV.
Her Majesty The Queen

Centrepiece
Paul Crespin (1713-1770).
London hallmarks for 1741/2
Silver-gilt; h. 685

The evidence of Continental influence
(particularly the bearded head of the
merman) leads to the conjecture that
this piece was the work, at least in part,
of the Liègois goldsmith Nicholas
Sprimont although it bears the mark of
Paul Crespin. In spite of the
impeccable modelling (a feature of all
Sprimont's work), the overall design
suggests an uneasy alliance of ideas
and it lacks the serene homogeneity of

Sprimont's hallmarked sauceboats and
salts which, whilst establishing an
affinity with the centrepiece, pose no
such aesthetic problems. Poseidon, in
the pose of a Roman river-god,
presides over this marine fantasy. The
lid – itself a small masterpiece – shows
French Régence influence in the
strapwork; the festoons of shells, pearls
and seaweed have baroque precedents.
The small wind masks are particularly
fine. The bowl rests in a shallow shell
the more delicate for being raised and
chased instead of cast. The whole is
supported on the raised arms of a
merman and mermaid and on the
flared tails of four great stylised
dolphins stranded on an islet from
which the sea has receded leaving it
littered with shells. The broad S-scrolls
seem extraneous to the design – the
dolphins' powerful bodies in their
spiral surge have no need of such
support. In a typically rococo manner
there is a scant regard for scale:
Poseidon is dwarfed by his sea beasts.
Candle branches encrusted with coral
writhe and curve upwards, their
twisted sockets fitted with removable
lids capped with sea foam. In the
absence of a drawing of this object,
Sprimont's involvement cannot be
proved, particularly as the exact date
of his arrival in England is unknown.
The piece bears the assay date letter
for the twelve month period ending on
29 May 1742. The Liègois was
certainly in London on 13 November
1742 when he married Ann Protin at
Knightsbridge Chapel. The following
January he registered a maker's mark
at Goldsmiths' Hall giving as his
address Compton Street, Soho. The
rate books are incomplete, but those
that survive do not show him in
occupation in 1741. He may, however,
have been moving between England
and the Low Countries until he had
settled his affairs, staying meanwhile in
lodgings in London, perhaps in
Compton Street in the house of his
future near neighbour Crespin. The
well-known practice whereby pieces
wrought by goldsmiths not registered
at the Hall were marked by freemen,
dated from the Huguenots' early
struggles for recognition. It is even
possible that it is the costly 'surtout
compleat' entered by Wickes in the
Prince's account on 24 June 1742,
barely a month after the change of
assay letter. It was shipped abroad on

G17

G17

the same date (possibly to Liège for finishing), following its transfer (in itself an apparently unique occurrence) from the Prince's account to that of Ritzau, a minor member of his household. The troy weight which Wickes noted meticulously against each object was not in this instance recorded, effectively denying comparison and possible identification.

Lit: Barr 1980, pp. 164-166; Clayton 1971, pp. 233 & 244, pls. 454 & 485; Garrard Inventory 1911, 163; Grimwade 1969, pp. 126-8; Grimwade 1974, ppp. 22-23, 30-32, 47 & pl. 48; Grimwade 1976, pp. 478 & 668; VAM 1954

Sauceboats (2 of a set of 4)
Nicholas Sprimont (active as a goldsmith 1742(?)-1747): London hallmarks for 1743/4
Silver-gilt; h. 230
In contrast to the Poseidon centre-piece, the design of these sauceboats is uncluttered to the point of austerity. The elegant bowl – half shell, half boat – was fashioned by raising, whereas the two dolphins who lift it out of the waves were cast. They are clearly smaller versions of those on the Crespin piece. The modelling of the human figures is exceptionally fine. Posed momentarily, as though in flight, on the prows of the boats, they were possibly intended to represent tritons and nereids and relate closely to baroque fountain sculpture (see also Cat. O4).

Lit: Garrard Inventory 1911, 228; Grimwade 1974, pp. 16, 31, 44 & pl. 33A

Salts (2 of a set of 4)
Nicholas Sprimont. London hallmarks for 1742/3
Silver-gilt; crayfish w. 127; crab 175
Whilst the crayfish may well derive from Meissonnier's designs (Cat. O6), the stark rocks on the base are the inspired contribution of Sprimont: their fresh modelling is without parallel in rococo silver. Both the crayfish and the crab are so naturalistic that they may well have been cast from the shells of real crustacea. The salts foreshadow, in proportion as well as design, those which Sprimont was to produce when, forsaking silver, he turned his talents to the manufacture of porcelain (Cat. O7, see also cat. G16).

Lit: Garrard Inventory 1911, 208 & 209; Grimwade 1974, pp. 16, 31, 45 & pl. 37B

The marine service is completed with a set of four high rococo dishes. One pair, fashioned as a flat shell edged asymmetrically with small shells and sea foam, is supported by young tritons. The other is in the form of a more convoluted shell resting somewhat uneasily on the wings of a dragon. The four salts are unmarked; they have been attributed to Sprimont. Two copies of the marine service were made in 1780 by Robert Hennell; one,

commissioned by the 4th Duke of Rutland, is now in a private collection.
EB

G18 *Design for a tureen and cover*
Nicholas Sprimont (active 1742(?)-1747)
Pen and ink and ink wash; 260 x 432
Signed *N:s. Sprimont in & Del.*
Inscribed on the verso: *My full intention VAM (E.2606-1917)*

The ostriches which form the legs are a reference to the supporters of the coat of arms of Thomas Coke (1697-1759), the builder of the Palladian mansion of Holkham, who was created Earl of Leicester in May 1744. The cartouches on the body, surmounted by an Earl's coronet were perhaps intended for his arms and those of his wife, Margaret Tufton. No surviving tureen after this design is recorded. The double-curved gadrooned rim also appears on a basket by Sprimont of 1745 (Grimwade 1974, pl. 42A) but the design is in other respects unlike Sprimont's surviving silver. A tureen by Charles Kandler of 1735 has a very similar knop (loc. cit. pl. 24). The strong armorial emphasis of this piece suggests a date soon after Coke's elevation to the earldom.

Prov: given by A.G.B. Russell, Rouge Croix, through the NACF
Lit: Grimwade 1974, p. 5, pl. 96
MS

G19 *Sauceboat, stand and ladle*
Nicholas Sprimont (active
1742(?)-1747).
London hallmarks for 1746/7 stand
only)
Silver; h. of boat 159; l. of stand 298; l.
of ladle 206
Engraved with the arms of Thomas,
1st Marquess of Rockingham impaling
those of Mary, daughter of Daniel,
Earl of Winchelsea and Notttingham,
with an earl's coronet, for Thomas
Watson who inherited the earldom in
1745.

The Museum of Fine Arts, Boston, Jessie and
Sigmund Katz Collection

From a set now comprising six
sauceboats with four stands and ladles.
Conch-shaped body and shell-shaped
foot with alternate panels left plain and
cast and chased with shells, shaped
rim and scroll handle capped by a
serpent. Closely comparable to a pair
of 1746 by Paul Crespin (Christie's 26
March 1975) and an unmarked pair
(c.1745) with the arms of Thomas, 3rd
Earl of Scarborough, KB, d. 1752.
Encrusted shell-festoons are found in
the previous decade, eg a tureen by
John Edwards of 1737 and a teapot by
Crespin of 1740 (Grimwade 1974,
frontispiece and pl. 58B).

Prov: Jessie and Sigmund Katz
Collection
Lit: Grimwade 1974, pl. 32B
PG

G19

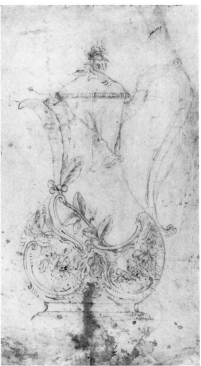

G20

G20 *Design for a coffee-pot or*
hot water jug
Anonymous. *c.*1750-60
Pencil; 235 x 156
VAM (9052.9)

Of bellied form with a leaf-shaped
spout; the body is decorated with
leaves, flowers and scrolls, with a

flower finial on the lid. It is a
characteristic rococo pot of the 1750s
and early 1760s. This drawing is an
example of a very rare survival, the
working drawing, perhaps made by
the silversmith himself. The stiff and
naive handling of the pencil can be
compared with other craftsmen's
drawings, such as those of Gideon
Saint (Cat. L72).
MS

G21 *Basket*
Paul De Lamerie (1688-1751). London
hallmarks for 1747/8
Silver; w. 355
The Visitors of the Ashmolean Museum,
Oxford (Farrer Collection)

Escallop shell with wavy gadrooned
border. Handle cast as a mermaid
rising from a wave, terminating in
entwined double tails above a cluster
of shells and seaweed. Three cast
dolphin feet. Saw-cut piercing in
alternating panels of scrolls and
diaper. A shape made by De Lamerie
from at least 1742 (eg Philadelphia
Museum of Art) until his death when
the moulds were apparently bought by
Phillips Garden, although other
goldsmiths, such as Edward Wakelin
in 1747, produced the design well
before De Lamerie's death. Minor
variations include cast shell borders
(Untermyer Collection basket, 1744)
and a horse-head handle (Thomas
Gilpin's basket, 1747). The dolphin
support was commonplace in mid-
17th century silver; see for example
three dolphins supporting scallop
shells in a salt by Johan Lutma, given
to the Fishmonger's Company in 1654.
Examples of dolphins as supports in
English rococo silver include cat. G17,
a tureen of 1736 by De Lamerie
(Metropolitan Museum of Art; Phillips
1968, pl. CVIII) and a triangular kettle
stand by John White of 1734 (Brand
Inglis, 1982); a plate in Brunetti (VAM
E. 942-1904) shows a similar dolphin,
tail raised, capping a cartouche. The
mermaid handle is a well-established
baroque motif, found considerably
earlier, for example on a helmet ewer
by David Willaume (1700, VAM) and
another by Harache (1697, Vintner's
Company) and was adopted as a
sauceboat handle by William Kidney
in 1739 (Christie's 29 Nov, 1961, 128).
The scallop form has a long history in
English silver, notably as sugar boxes

G21

and as ornament on flagons and standing cups in the late 16th century. De Lamerie was the first to consider it suitable for a bread basket. His immediate inspiration may have been Meissen porcelain, which was reaching London in the 1730s; an escallop-shaped dish by Heroldt of about 1728, whose painted diaper border is very close to the pattern of piercing on De Lamerie's baskets, is known (Illustrated in *Pantheon,* XV, 1935, p. 203). There were also French silver shell baskets; see a design (perhaps by Germain) reproduced by Diderot in *Encyclopedie Planches* vol. 8, *Orfevres Grossier* Paris 1771, fig. 5, pl. VI.

Lit: Starkie Gardner 1903, pl. CXIV; Grimwade 1974, pl. 42B; Jones 1924, p. 148, pl. LXXIX; Phillips 1968, pl. CLII
PG

G22 *Cup and cover*
Lewis Pantin (active 1734).
London hallmarks for 1744/5
Silver; 385 x 165
Engraved with armorials
The National Trust (Anglesey Abbey)

One of the charms of the rococo style is the plethora of incongruous decorative motifs. Vine leaves and grapes are an obvious choice for a cup

intended for wine although the shape evolved from the porringer in which gruel is served. The double-scroll handles rest on female masks and end in heraldic lion's heads representing the supporters of the owner's armorials. Flowers and foliage mingle with stylised shell work and the marine element essential to a rococo piece is present in the shape of a fierce looking dolphin thrusting its way through waves which swirl round the convoluted scrolled base. An asymmetrical cartouche frames the armorials and another above it is the setting for an allegorical scene in which Dike (Justice) is seated on books with her scales at her side. Eros

G22

sporting with Dike's sword symbolises Virgil's 'Omnia Vincit Amor' (*Eclogues* 10:69), a popular quotation of the day. Such figures would have been immediately intelligible to the 18th century cognoscenti reared on the classics of Greek and Roman literature.

Prov: 1st Lord Fairhaven
EB

G23 *The Leinster Service*
George Wickes (active 1722-1759).
London hallmarks for 1745-47
Silver
Engraved with the armorials of James Fitzgerald, Earl of Kildare (created Duke of Leinster in 1766)
Private Collection

On the evidence of Wickes's ledgers many fine dinner services were commissioned in the rococo period - this is the only one known to have survived virtually intact. The figures in brackets show the quantities orginally ordered. The simplicity of the domed dish cover (22) contrasts with the massive ornament in the French taste on the bombé tureen (2), the body slashed to reveal the liner within, the lid decorated with two waves which break at the edge with an inward curl. The piercing is seen again in miniature on the cruet stand (2). The pyriform container (4) is one of the earliest documented condiment urns, a form which replaced the caster. The covered sugar bowl (2) is en suite. Continental influence is seen in the rippled feet and elaborate scroll handle of the sauceboat (10). The motif which unites all the pieces in the service is repeated in the baluster candlestick (8): it takes the form of a serpentine threaded border bound at intervals with beaded strapwork and interspersed with shells of two types which interrupt the flow of the reeding. Cutlery apart, the order was completed by ninety plates, thirty dishes, four mazarines, eleven waiters, eight salts, two bread baskets, a dish ring, six escallop shells and a magnificent plateau and épergne based on a design of William Kent.

Lit: Barr 1980, pp. 197-205; Hawkins 1979, pp. 30-35
EB

116

G23

spouts fitted to ceramic pots and in wholly ceramic pots.

Lit: VAM Wickes/Wakelin Gentlemen's Ledgers, unnumbered vol., 1747-1750, f. 49, 2 June 1748 'To a Coffee pot £15.17s. To a Handle £3'.
PG

G26

G24 *Design for a centrepiece*

Peter Glazier (active 1748-54)
Etching and engraving; 177 x 245
Lettered with a copyright line dated August 16, 1754 and *Pr. Glisier inv. et fecit.* Numbered: *III.*
VAM (13694.3)

From an untitled set published in 1754 of which only this plate and another are known (VAM). The other plate also occurs in another fragmentary suite, published in 1748 which is probably an earlier, but differently numbered, edition of the same set (see Cat. H16). On the earlier set the designer is named Glazier. The centrepiece on this plate is more extravagant than any English examples which have survived.
MS

G25 *Coffee-pot*

Edward Wakelin (active1747-1784).
London hallmarks for 1747/8
Silver; h. 286
Engraved with the arms of Balch, for Robert Balch.
Private Collection

Chased with floral clusters, scrolls and shells, with the cast finial a shell. The spout a realistically modelled duck's head. At least one other pot to this design, although with a cone finial and flower-chased lid and the tube

missing, was sold by Wakelin in 1747-8, the first year of his partnership with George Wickes and the year in which he first registered his mark (Sotheby's, 18 March 1982). There is no making charge in Balch's account although the inclusive per ounce charge of 10 shillings allowed for a piece of more than ordinary elaboration. Robert Balch's complete order comprised thirty-nine items (excluding cutlery) of tableware. Four shell salts cost the most per ounce – 12 shillings; this making charge had a separate entry. By their form, these pots could be taken as French plate, marked here for retail, since the squat shape is otherwise extremely rare in English silver and the shell-centred floral border is French in feeling. The duck-head spout is also a feature of contemporary Parisian silver (cf. a teapot by Godin, Paris 1749; Hernmarck 1977 pl. 322), but fantastic bird and dragon spouts had been a recurring element in pots for hot beverages from the 1680s; cf. an English teapot of c.1686 (Museum of Fine Arts, Boston): two pots attributed to Willaume of 1717 and 1706 (Wilding Coll., British Museum; Assheton Bennett Coll., Birmingham) and Augsburg services of c.1700-1720 (Hernmarck 1977, pl. 308-10, 312); the bird spout also occurs both in metal

G26 *Coffee-pot*

James Shruder (active 1737-1749)
London hallmarks for 1749-50
Silver; h. 280
Engraved with the armorials of Okeover impaling Nichol for Leake Okeover (1701-1765), and his wife Mary Nichol
VAM (M312-1975)

The seahorse is the motif linking this high rococo object with the enamelled porcelain service (Cat. O2) made in China for Leake Okeover. Shruder's design source for the finely-modelled cast spout was the horse rearing up from the sea on the title page of Jacques de Lajoue's *Second Livre de Cartouches* (published in Paris about 1734). The dolphins and the chased boat with the sail cartouche enclosing the armorials were based closely on a Lajoue design (Cat. G28). The somewhat naively executed Poseidon may have been the work of the goldsmith, who designed his own trade card, cat. G29. The bat wing ornament above his signature and behind the C-scroll on the right hand side are echoed in the feathering on the feet of the coffee-pot. The sea foam on the lid was cast, as were the shells, but on the body it was achieved by fine matting on the crests of the waves. Unlike many rococo pieces, the inspiration here is wholly marine. A tea kettle of the same date made en suite is not exhibited (see also Cat. O1, O2).

Prov: Leake Okeover; Okeover family, by descent; Christie's 25 June 1975, 109
EB

G27 *Hot water urn and stand*
James Shruder (active 1737-1749).
London hallmarks for 1752-3
Silver; 559
Engraved with armorials
Part of the Folger Coffee Silver Collection owned by the Procter and Gamble Company

Jacques de Lajoue was to be once more the design source for James Shruder in this urn and stand made three years after the Okeover pieces Cat. G26. The sailing boat Cat. G28, in a slightly different form, still occupies a prominent position on the body of the object. The goldsmith then proceeded to translate the grotesque sea creature on the prow of Lajoue's boat into taps. The shell moulds used for Leake Okeover's order served for the spigots and finial and the coiled dolphin feet from the Okeover tea kettle stand, together with part of its handle embellished here with bulrushes were once more utilised (Shruder's bankruptcy in June 1749 may well have underlined the need for certain economies). The realistic lace effect of the sea foam is also repeated on the lid of the urn, reappearing in a

new and delicate guise on the apron of the stand. Shruder has once more achieved a pure marine fantasy, eschewing the rococo practice of incorporating popular conceits, however irrelevant.

Lit: Grimwade 1974, p. 50
EB

G28 *A ship*
Francois Joullain (b. 1697) after Jacques de Lajoue (1686-1761). 1734
Etching and engraving; 220 x 187
Lettered with the privilege and *De la Joue in. Joullain Sculp.* and numbered *A.10*
VAM (E.892-1905)

From the *Recueil Nouveau De differens Cartouches,* 1734. The suite was known in England by 1737, when plate 9 was copied by George Bickham in *The Musical Entertainer,* vol. I, p. 14 (Snodin 1983, fig. 2). Bickham used this ship design for a headpiece entitled 'The Dragon; or, the None Such Galley' on plate 119 of *The Universal Penman,* first published separately in 1738 and as a collected edition in 1741. This suite continued to be popular and pl. 12 was copied by François Vivares for the trade card of William Wapshare, land surveyor of Sarum (British Museum, Heal 76.7). Lajoue's drawing for the ship is at the Cooper-Hewitt Museum, New York (Wunder 1962, 75). For other uses of Lajoue's plates see cat. C4, G35.

Lit: Berlin 1939, 400(1); BN: Fonds, 809-817 (Huquier), 53 (Joullain)
MS
G28

G29 *Trade card of James Shruder, goldsmith*
J. Warburton after James Shruder; 206 x 157. *c.* 1750
The Guildhall Library (72763)
At the Golden Ewer in Greek Street. Cards were very rarely designed by the craftsmen themselves; in this case the rather ineptly handled **rocaille** ornament is very close to that on Shruder's coffee-pot, cat. G26.

Lit: Grimwade 1974, fig. 93A; Heal 1935, pl. LXV
MS

G30 *A Family being served Tea*
Anonymous, British School. *c.*1745
Oil on canvas; 1067 x 1397
Yale Center for British Art, Paul Mellon Collection

In a Palladian room three ladies, dressed in blue, grey and pink silk respectively, receive a gentleman. The tripod tea table is accurately shown, as is the tea salver, often itself known as a 'tea table' in contemporary documents, with its broken border. The tea service is entirely of oriental porcelain. A servant brings in a kettle, in order to place it on a burner stand in the corner; the artist is reflected in its shiny side. Various painters have been suggested, including Joseph van Aken. Formerly attached to the wooden frame was a wooden label inscribed 'The Carter Family'.

Prov: Sandy Martin; Colnaghi, 1964
Lit: Praz 1971, fig. 67; Yale 1965, 201
MS

G31 *Trade Card Elizabeth Godfrey, goldsmith and jeweller*
Anonymous. 193 x 142. *c.*1750?
The Trustees of the British Museum (Heal 67.167)

At the Hand, Ring and Crown, Norris Street. In the manner of Henry Copland. A very similar rock-work base was used by Henry Seton, engraver, for his own card, which is in turn indebted to Brunetti's *Sixty Different Sorts of Ornaments,* 1736 (cat. B10). Godfrey had a new card engraved when appointed goldsmith to the Duke of Cumberland. (Grimwade 1974, fig. 93B).

Lit. Heal 1935, pl. XXXXII.
MS

G27

G30

G33

G32 *Three teaspoons, decorated with putto, Apollo and Gilles*

Putto; maker's mark W.C., maker's mark only. Apollo; maker's mark J.J. surmounted by a unicorn. London hallmark for 1739-55. *c.*1750. Gilles; maker's mark J.L. London hallmark post 1756. *c.*1760
Silver and silver-gilt; l. 98, 117, 116.
Private Collections

In the 1730s cast or die-stamped ornament began to appear on the stems of spoons, the designs reflecting the current taste for rococo themes. Putti among scrolls and flowers, reminiscent of the delicate amorini of Boucher, were perennial favourites; they are also found on Vauxhall tickets (Cat. F24) and plaster ceilings. The preoccupation with Greek myths is personified by the full-length figure of Apollo with his lyre and bow, whose pose is taken from the Apollino (Haskell & Penny 1981, 7). The Gilles is possibly after Watteau's *Pierrot Debout* (Dacier & Vauflart 1929, 161). The acorn-shaped bowl of the putto spoon may have Jacobite significance.

Lit: Snodin 1974, pp. 42, 44
EB

G33 *Chandelier*

William Alexander (active 1743).
London hallmarks for 1752/3
Silver; h. 118
Engraved *In Grateful Remembrance of Sr. Thomas Knesworth Kt. A Principal Benefactor to the Worshipful Company of Fishmongers London 1752.*

The Worshipful Company of Fishmongers.

Following the discovery that their chandelier – made by William Gould in 1750 – contravened the strict regulations of the Goldsmiths' Company (it was 'loaded with copper' and only close-plated with silver), the Worshipful Company of Fishmongers commissioned a replacement from William Alexander. A committee examined several patterns submitted by him and selected one called 'Dolphin'. A favourite design motif since Classical times, the dolphin lent itself admirably to the rococo style. The dolphins vary subtly according to the artistic antecedents of the goldsmith; those entwined around the upper part of this chandelier are closer to the Liègois fountain sculptures which influenced Nicholas Sprimont

119

than to the French designs which inspired Paul De Lamerie. A cast gilt pineapple masks the suspension hook. The pendant is formed as a large shell with small applied shells clinging to it. In November 1761 when George III and the Royal Family were to be entertained at Guildhall, the Fishmongers' Company offered to lend their 'very grand silver chandelier'; it hung 'very near Their Majesties canopies where it was much admired'.

Lit: Clayton 1971, p.59 Pl. 119; Grimwade 1974, pp.19 & 57 Pl.81; Grimwade 1976, p.421; Metcalf 1977, pl. 96; Royal Academy 1934; VAM 1926.
EB

G34 *Candlestick*
Edward Wakelin (active 1747-d.1784)
London hallmarks for 1753/4
Silver; h. 286
Private Collection

From a set of four. Familiarity with French trends would have been one of the many benefits reaped by Wakelin during the years spent as apprentice and journeyman to the Huguenot John Le Sage. Meissonnier's oeuvre probably lies behind the form, but the nozzle appears to have been influenced by Thomas Germain's design for the gold candelabra he made for Louis XV in 1748 with sockets based on the calyx and petals of the sunflower (*Connaissance des Arts* 1965, p. 103). The spiral human form of the Moser Apollo and Daphne pair (Cat. E13), which was also favoured by De Lamerie and Kandler, has been replaced here by swirling drapes, garlanded with flowers, which flow into delicate open scrolled feet, so different from the architectural bases of the French exemplified by the Meissonnier/Duvivier candelabrum (Cat. A18). A pair of candelabra made by Wakelin in 1751 (Barr 1980, p. 70. fig. 34e) foreshadows this form.
EB

G35 *Tray*
Edward Wakelin (active 1747-d. 1784).
London hallmarks for 1754/5 Silver;
762 x 610
Engraved (after 1764) with armorials of Heathcote with Moyer in pretence
The Colonial Williamsburg Foundation

G35

Wakelin made this tray when he was employed by George Wickes as workshop manager. Set on four cast and scrolled feet, it is described in the firm's Gentlemen's (Clients') Ledger as 'a Large Oval Nurld [gadrooned] Table ornamented with vines'. It cost £119.18s.6d plus £10.10s for the engraving. The removable trailing vine cast ornament set below the rim creates an illusion of delicacy – typical of the rococo style – which is enhanced by the engraved border and superb cartouche in the centre. This follows closely a print by Jacques de Lajoue first published about 1734 (Cat. C5); it was also used by Wickes in 1735. The flattening of Lajoue's elegant elongated cartouche was possibly dictated by the shape of the armorials of the initial purchaser. The design is a reversed image of the original print, but it may have been taken from a reversed copy. Little is known about the engravers; documentation is scarce and signed examples of their work extremely rare.

Lit: Barr 1980, p.117 Fig. 72;Grimwade 1874, pp. 65-67
EB

G36 *Beer jugs*
Phillips Garden (active 1738-1773)
London hallmarks for 1754/5
Silver; h. 340
Engraved armorials of Sir Henry Hicks
Private Collection

It is doubtful whether Phillips Garden could have produced objects of this exceptional quality had he not bought the patterns and tools of Paul De Lamerie when they were auctioned following De Lamerie's death in 1751. The finely modelled mask (apparently Athene) under the spout is reminiscent of the Greek heads on the inkstand made by De Lamerie for the Goldsmiths' Company in 1741. Brewing was women's work and Athene the goddess of female skills; she was also associated with the art of the goldsmith (*Odyssey* VI, 233). Covered jugs are usually associated with wine, but the choice of barley instead of grapes as a decorative theme, together with the hop-bine decoration on the finial, clearly defines the purpose of these vessels. Their bucolic charm is enhanced by the putti and the insects and lizards on the lid, all high rococo motifs. German influence may be visible in the multi-scrolled handles for which there seem to be no English parallels.

Lit: Clayton 1971, Col. pl.31; Grimwade 1974, p. 38 & pl. 17B
EB

120

G36

G37 *Trade Card of Phillips Garden, working goldsmith and jeweller*

Probably engraved by F. Garden. 275 x 214. *c.* 1755?
The Trustees of the British Museum (Heal 67.156)

At the Golden Lion, St Paul's Church Yard. The view at the top is almost certainly an accurate representation of Garden's shop and is one of very few visual records of mid-eighteenth century shop interiors in the gothic style. On the left is the street door and the window filled with silver. On the right a gothic arcade leads into the back, perhaps to the workshops; the open door may be intended to emphasise Garden's statement: 'N:B: Work perform'd in my own house'. Garden's earlier card, an example of which (Heal 67.157) is dated 1749, is lettered 'F. Garden Scu.'. Their precise family relationship is unknown. A number of other cards by F. Garden are recorded.

Lit: Heal 1935, pl. XXX
MS

G38 *Sauceboat*

Philip Bruguier (active 1739-1773)
London hallmarks for 1755-6
Silver; h.145
VAM (M.94-1969)

The concept of organic naturalism in which plant or animal forms provide the structure as well as the ornament of an article became in the hands of the great French innovator Juste-Aurèle Meissonnier an art form for goldsmiths exemplified by the tureens he designed and made for the Duke of Kingston (Cat. C7). In the 1750s organic forms occur more frequently in English ceramics than in silver (Cat. O28). The genre has been mastered here, at least as far as the overlapping vine leaves and the gnarled stem handles are concerned. The body rests on tripod feet formed as twigs and leaves with clusters of grapes. The butterflies, bees and beetles (less finely executed) add to the realism.

Lit: Bury & Lightbown 1970, pp. 147-149
EB

G39 *Candelabrum (one of a pair)*

Lewis Herne (active 1757-65) & Francis Butty (active 1757-1776). London hallmarks for 1757-8.
Silver gilt; h.420; span of branches 356
The National Trust (Anglesey Abbey)

The rococo's preoccupation with naturalism is well illustrated by this candelabrum. The interlaced branches are pleached and would have been easily recognised as such in an age when much thought was given to landscaping and gardening. The candlestick itself is a delicate airy structure of scrolled tendrils rising from a base fringed with *rocaille* decoration and ending, like each of the two branches, in a flower calyx. Blossoms and leaves proliferate; a fly clings realistically to the outer edge of the openwork drip pan; ladybirds crawl over the foliage and the small bodies of caterpillars sway around the chrysanthemum finial. Butty, who later entered into partnership with the Huguenot Nicholas Dumée, may well have been of French extraction, his name possibly an anglicisation of Buteux.

Prov: The lst Lord Fairhaven
EB

G40 *Cup and Cover*

Thomas Heming (active 1745-d.1795-1801)
Silver-gilt; h. 394
Engraved (after 1790) with armorials of C.W.J. Shakerley (1767-1834)
VAM (M.41-1959)

An example of the rococo manner in one of its last stages of development. Baluster shaped spirally fluted body encircled with a cast and applied naturalistic design of vine leaves, tendrils and grapes harbouring snails, caterpillars and insects. The cast foot - its outline broken by scrolls - is decorated with grapes, lizards and foliage to which is applied a cast butterfly. The decorative vine theme – appropriate in a vessel intended to hold wine - is repeated on the conical cover which is surmounted by an infant Dionysus clutching a bunch of grapes. All these motifs were used extensively in the 1730s and 1740s (Cat. G36, 38, 39).
The handles cast as male and female terms, the former holding a bunch of grapes and a reed Pan-pipe, the latter a

121

tabor. Similar figures can be seen on the cup illustrated in the top left-hand corner of Heming's trade card Cat. G44. Although Heming used term handles with great effect (seven other examples by him are known made between 1753 and 1761) they are not original to him and appear on many earlier works by master goldsmiths, notably on the Jerningham wine cooler made by Kandler in 1734 (Cat B9).

Lit: Bury & Lightbown 1970 p. 150; Young 1983, pp.285-289
Prov: Goldsmiths & Silversmiths Company; Christie's 15 July 1925 given by the Esso Petroleum Co.
EB

G41 *Title page to* A New Book of Ornaments Useful for Silver-Smith's & c.
Gabriel Smith (1724-1783) after John Linnell (1729-1796). 1755?
Etching and engraving; 220 x 290
Lettered with the title and *Invented and Drawn by Jno. Linnell and Engraved by Gabl. Smith. Publish'd by Them according to Act of Parliamt. (price 3sh.) Sold by G. Smith at Mr. Wivils in Great Mays Buildings St. Martin's Lane*

Westminster City Libraries, Archives Department

From the suite of designs, chiefly for ewers and spouted pots, consists of a title and at least 5 plates, one of which, not recorded by Hayward, only survives in part (VAM 28860.21). The designs, which demonstrate an inventiveness in extreme rococo unmatched in contemporary English silver, have their closest parallels in the essentially graphic world of Augsburg prints, which may well have influenced them. Linnell's other sources for the suite seem to have included Meissonnier, Jean le Pautre, Stefano della Bella (see VAM 1983, 2.5.a) and in the case of the vase on the right of this plate, a French drawing-book plate such as cat. E21. Ward-Jackson (1958, p. 65) records an edition dated 1760; it is, however, unlikely that the undated edition is earlier.

Lit: Hayward 1970; Hayward and Kirkham 1980, p. 68, n.4, No. 314
MS

G40

G42 *Designs for ewers*
Gabriel Smith (1724-1783) after John Linnell (1729-1796). *c.*1755?
Etching and engraving; 222 x 300
Lettered with a copyright line and *J. Linnell Invt. et Delint. G. Smith Sculp.*
The Trustees of the British Museum (1913-12-16-28)

The ewer on the left can be compared with the vase on the title page of a suite by J.G. Thelot after C.F. Rudolph, *Einige Vases mit Modernen Einfassungen* (Berlin 1939, 975; Berliner & Egger 1981, 1386 repr.). Rudolph's title is especially close to another vase in Linnell's set (VAM 28860.21) unrecorded by Hayward. The putti forming the foot of the vases on the left may have been derived from a print by Jean le Pautre (1618-1682) which shows a fanciful ewer also held up by putti. The ewer on the right illustrates the legend of Pan and Syrinx.

Lit: Hayward 1970, figs 109, 110; Hayward and Kirkham 1980, fig. 318
MS

G43

G44

Gillois apparently specialised in tea canisters and other boxes, often chased with particularly delicate scrolled panels after designs by Lock & Copland (Cat. L16, L24; Copland 1762, title page & pl. 4, repr. Heckscher 1979, opl. 56A and 57A).

Prov: Queen Charlotte; Marquess of Cambridge; Richard Wagstaff Gibbs
Lit: Clayton 79, pl.44; Cooper 1979, p.135; Jourdain & Soan Jennins 1950, pl.126, 127 (for two other boxes)
PG

G44 *Tureen*

John Parker & Edward Wakelin (active 1747-d.1784). London hallmarks for 1765/6. Silver; 368 x 242
Engraved with armorials
The National Trust (Anglesey Abbey)

Apart from its outline, which is typically French, this tureen is remarkable for its beautifully modelled turnip finial, an original touch after the artichokes and cauliflowers which adorn so many rococo pieces. The body was raised from a flat disc of silver; the acanthus leaf feet and reeded handles were cast and applied. The chased ornament echoes a motif chosen by the celebrated Parisian goldsmith Thomas Germain in 1726 to decorate a toilet set made for Marie Leczinska, wife of Louis XV (Bapst 1887, pl.11). The bowl belonging to that set is of the same elliptical serpentine shape; it lent itself admirably to the tureen and was used to great effect in France, notably by Jacques Roettiers in 1735 for a pair in the Berkeley Service (*Connaissance,* 1965, p.142). The design appeared in *Eléments D'Orfevrerie* in 1748 cat.G47. The prints reached England by 1757, but the form was seldom used by English goldsmiths until the 1760s. It found favour with Thomas Heming whose tureen of 1763 (Campbell Museum Collection) is clearly based on the French print; it appears in Cat. G44.

Prov: 1st Lord Fairhaven
EB

G43 *Pair of tea canisters*

Pierre Gillois (active 1754-82). London hallmarks for 1763/4; the box Canton, *c.1760*
Silver-gilt; shell box; h. of canister 115
Engraved with the crowned cypher of Queen Charlotte (1744-1818)
Nottingham Castle Museum

Cast and chased. Gillois used this bombe shape for canisters at least from 1752; compare a pair of canisters in a lacquer box, formerly the property of Lord Talbot de Malahide (Christie's May 1974, 434). The box is carved with mythological scenes after unidentified English prints, with a border of cross-hatching and floral cartouches characteristic of the ornament in Chinese export porcelain. Two other carved shell boxes from the same workshop are recorded. Chinese lacquer and ivory boxes to contain silver tea canisters were imported from at least 1740; compare a set by Samuel Taylor (1744; VAM M.10a & b-1979).

G45

G45 *Flagon and chalice*

Francis Butty (active 1757-1773) and
Nicholas Dumee. London hallmarks
for 1766/7
Silver-gilt; chalice
h. 340; flagon h.270
The Dean and Chapter of Durham Cathedral

Engraved with the arms of the See of
Durham and of Dr John Cosin, Bishop
of Durham 1660-1672. The chalice
embossed and chased with floral
swags, spiral flutes and rusticated
foliage. From an altar service, each
piece of which is decorated en suite,
comprising pairs of flagons, chalices,
large and small patens, two-handled
cups (grace cups) pricket candlesticks
and an alms dish, purchased by the
Dean and Chapter of Durham
Cathedral in 1766 at a cost of
£296.18s, for approximately
613 ounces (Chapter Minutes, 8 Dec.
1766, 8 July 1767). When the Dean
and Chapter decided to refashion the
Cathedral plate in 1766 there was no
contemporary precedent for its design.
No church plate of any originality had
been commissioned in the previous
half century and no cathedral or
Chapel Royal had ordered plate since
the replacements of the 1660s.
Durham's existing set, a gift from its
post-Restoration Bishop, John Cosin,
was exchanged (presumably melted) in
1766. This was no doubt markedly
baroque and heavily embossed like his
Chapel plate at Auckland Castle and

the royal orders of the 1660s, on
whose design Cosin had advised the
Jewel House. But these precedents
were ignored as unfashionable in
1766; the altar set had to be designed
afresh, ignoring standard Anglican
plate of the 1740s and 1750s.
Inevitably the designs combined
elements familiar from rococo
domestic plate, by this partnership and
other makers. The pear-shaped flagon
follows a contemporary coffee-pot,
and is an unusual model for church
use; another by Butty and Dumee
(1768) is at Kirkby Mallory Church,
Leicestershire and an earlier version by
Ayme Videau (1757) is at Withland,
Leicestershire. The standard cast
handle on both grace cups and
flagons, is of familiar design, eg ewers
by Elizabeth Godfrey 1752. The
candlesticks are close to a Butty and
Dumee set of 1761. (Christie's 29 May
1963, 7; Brownlow collection).

Lit: Oman 1957, pl. 120, pp. 35-39;
Hernmarck 1977, pl. 862; Durham
n.d.
PG

G46 *Title page for A Book of Ornaments*

Jean Baptiste Claude Chatelain
(*c.* 1710- after 1771) after J.Cattarello.
Etching and engraving 298 x 208.
Lettered with title and *Containing Divers
elegant Designs for the use of Goldsmiths,
Chasers, Carvers &c. Curiously Engraved by
Chatelan &c from the Drawings of Messrs,
Germain Meissonnier Sigr. Cattarello &c. J.
Cattarello Inv. det delint. Chatelan fecit
aqua fortis Price 4s* and with the address
of John Bowles
VAM (3697.26)

A later edition of a *Book of Eighteen
Leaves,* published by Robert Clee in
1757 (Yale Center for British Art, Rare
Books L. 18.4°). All but four of the
plates are copied in reverse from plates
in Pierre Germain's *Eléments
D'Orfevrerie,* Paris, 1748. Of the rest,
two are after Meissonnier (the *Livre de
Légumes,* see cat O21, and the 'Terrine',
Oeuvres K62), and one is after Gravelot
(Cat. S2). The two Cattarello plates are
a rococo chimneypiece and the present
title, which shows a remarkable clock –
or, more probably, watch-stand –
which may be intended for execution
in ormolu, and has its closest parallels
in France. Nothing is known about

Cattarello beyond his appearance in
the present suite.

Lit: Ward-Jackson 1958, p. 13, f.n. 2
MS

G47

G47 *Designs for ewers and vases*

Probably by Jean Baptiste Claude
Chatelain (*c.* 1710-after 1771), after
Pierre Germain. 1757
Etching and engraving; 190 x 140 (cut)
Lettered *Pre. Germain in.*
VAM (29977.5)

Plate 4 in *A Book of Eighteen Leaves,* 1757
(see cat. G46) a state before numbers
and with the handles of the central
vase not yet added. The ewers and
vases are reversed copies of plates
by Pasquier after Pierre Germain, in
Eléments D'Orfevrerie, Paris, 1748 (pls 3,
4 & 13). The vine-handled ewer on the
left (after Germain, pl. 3) was used by
Thomas Heming, cat. G44 & 50, and
by Thomas Johnson, cat. G44.
MS

G48 *Design for a ewer and candlestick and bracket and a vase*

Butler Cowes after Thomas Johnson
(1714-active 1778)
Etching and engraving; 178 x 248
Lettered *Thos Johnson invt. et delin. B.
Cowes sculp.* and with a copyright line
dated 1761
VAM (29977.4)

First issued as plate 51 of Johnson's
untitled 'collection of designs' which
was published in parts from 1756 and

124

in a collected edition in 1758. This plate is from the second edition of 1761, *One Hundred and Fifty New Designs.* The ewer is adapted from a design in Germain's *Eléments D'Orfevrerie*, published in Paris in 1748 and in part in England in 1757 (Cat. G47). It was also copied by Thomas Heming (Cat. G44).

Lit: Hayward 1964, pp. 102-4
MS

G49 *Trade card of Thomas Heming, goldsmith*
Engraved by Robert Clee; 241 x 194. *c.* 1760
The Trustees of the British Museum (Heal 67.205)

At the King's Arms in Bond Street. On the verso of this card, taken from a very worn plate, is a bill dated 1770. Much of the silver is taken from identifiable sources. For the cup top left see cat. G40. The vase on the left, ewer on the right and cruet stand bottom right, are taken from Germain's *Eléments D'Orfevrerie* (1748), book I, pls. 14, 3 & 5, or its English derivation of 1757 (Cat. G47). The ewer was actually made in silver by Heming (Cat. G50). Heming was appointed Principal Goldsmith to the King in 1760.

Lit: Heal 1935, pl. XXXVIII; Young 1983, fig. 46
MS

G50 *Part of a toilet service*
Thomas Heming (working 1745, d. 1795-1801). London hallmarks for 1768/9
Silver-gilt, blue and gilt glass; h. of mirror 710
Engraved with the arms of Williams-Wynn impaling Somerset
National Museum of Wales

Tray, pin cushion, casket and scent bottle from a toilet service now comprising 29 pieces. Cast and embossed; some chasing, eg on salver, added possibly in 1827 when new snuffers were purchased. Its naturalistic flowering sprays represent the last stage of the rococo. Two years earlier Heming, as royal goldsmith, supplied an almost identical service to George III as a gift for his sister Caroline Mathilda, Queen of Denmark (Zahle 1960; Museum of Industrial

G50

Art, Copenhagen). Eighteen pieces are common to both and a box from another Heming service to this design is recorded. The Danish service, still accompanied by its travelling case, is differently composed, including two covered bowls (equelles) identical in design to that supplied by Heming to Queen Charlotte in 1763, a funnel and a bell. Heming's interest in French designs for goldsmiths' work of 30 years before is well known. The ewers follow a design published by Pierre Germain in 1748, Cat. G47, which Heming also used on his trade card of *c.* 1765-8, Cat. G44. The mirror frames are also taken from Germain's *Eléments D'Orfevrerie,* pl. 99. Both services were made up with items from stock, such as the snuffer trays by Emick Romer (1764/5); the candlesticks in the Cardiff set are caryatids (unmarked), virtually identical to one by Antony Nelme of *c.* 1680 in the Ashmolean Museum, whereas those in Denmark are clustered Gothic columns. Heming's

design sources were eclectic, as a recent article has demonstrated (Young 1982). No household account exists for this service, but Williams-Wynn was noted for his neo-classical taste, commissioning an important punchbowl to an Adam design from Heming two years later (Hughes 1973); it is worth noting that the engraved armorials are all set symmetrically, with the exception of those on the cartouche surmounting the mirror frame.

Prov: purchased by Sir Watkin Williams-Wynn, 4th Baronet (1749-89) for his wife to be, Lady Henrietta Somerset (m. 1 April 1769)
Lit: Hughes 1973, pp. 33-8; Grimwade 1956, pp. 175-8; London Museum 1937, pl. 87; Zahle 1960, pp. 14-34
PG

Gold Chasing

see Cat. H 1.

Gold Chasing
Richard Edgcumbe

'And 'tis surprising', wrote Ephraim Chambers in the *Cyclopaedia* of 1728, 'with what Beauty, and Justness . . . the Artist in this Kind will represent Foliages, Grottesques, Animals, Histories, etc.'[1] Chasing, the art of modelling metal with hammer and steel tools, was already established in London on the eve of the rococo as a fashionable means of decorating gold, not least the cases of some of the finest watches then being made in Europe. Yet the gold chasers did not lead the movement to discard the angles and symmetry of the baroque. In Paris Meissonnier's asymmetric design of 1728 for a candlestick was soon followed by such whole-hearted examples of asymmetric chasing as the gold flask of 1731–2 by Nicolas-Hilaire Vilain in the Waddesdon Collection.[2] But in London in 1738–9, despite the asymmetric decoration of silver by De Lamerie and his contemporaries, Augustin Heckel, George Michael Moser and John Valentine Haidt used the same symmetric cartouche (Cat. H3) which had been dominant on embossed London watchcases of the 1720s and 1730s. For Moser the change to asymmetry appears not to have come until the following year (Cat. H6).

London chasing was once again behind Parisian taste when neo-classicism replaced the rococo. The Baron de Grimm observed in 1763 that 'tout se fait aujourd'hui à la grecque': Svend Eriksen illustrates Paris boxes of 1762–3 which are entirely neo-classical.[3] In London in about 1760 Moser introduced a foliage whorl (Cat. I11) outside his rococo cartouches which was a harbinger of neo-classicism, but he signed a rococo chasing as late as 1768–9 and his earliest known chasing which is predominantly neo-classical is the box dated 1769 presented to Christian VII of Denmark by the City of London.[4]

While the scroll and shellwork of the London chasers became heavily indebted to Meissonnier and the French rococo, the figure scenes within the cartouches on boxes and watchcases remained predominantly classical, as they had been in the 1720s and 1730s. Biblical scenes are not uncommon, but *fêtes galantes*, *Commedia dell'Arte* scenes (Cat. H3) and chinoiserie (Cat. H21) are rare. Almost any print of a classical scene might be borrowed, and sometimes adapted (Cat. H17), by the chaser. Scenes were taken not only from such celebrated books as the Earl of Shaftesbury's *Characteristicks* (Cat. H25), but from prints by or after Italian and Flemish masters and a wide range of French masters from Vouet to Boucher (Cat. H17, I11) and Gravelot (Cat. I12).

The gold chaser could achieve both prosperity and the status of an artist. More than twenty chasers are known to have signed their work. In the rate books Henry Manly came to be dignified with the title of 'Esq.', while Augustin Heckel 'acquired a sufficiency' and retired to Richmond.[5] G.M. Moser appears to have arrived in London in the 1720s and worked at first for a coppersmith,[6] but in 1783 he was described by Sir Joshua Reynolds as 'the FATHER of the present race of Artists'[7] and was 'followed to his grave in grand funeral pomp by all the capital artists'.[8]

The wider recognition of chasers as artists owed much to Moser. He and John Valentine Haidt appear to have been the initiators of a small life school in the 1730s[9] and Moser later became a leading figure in the St Martin's Lane Academy. Probably due to his influence, chasing is consistently mentioned in the subsequent proposals for academies. In the scheme put forward in a letter originating in the St Martin's Lane Academy, dated 23 October 1753, it was proposed that the professors should include 'thirteen painters, three sculptors, one chaser, two engravers, and two architects'.[10] In the *Plan of an Academy*, published in 1755 by a committee including Moser and under the chairmanship of Francis Hayman, his former neighbour in Craven Buildings, Drury Lane, chasing is listed in similar company as one of the 'Performances, in which, Art and Genius, Elegance of Fancy, and Accuracy of Workmanship are confessedly united'.[11] In 1759 chasers were among those summoned by the resolution passed at the annual dinner of artists at the Foundling Hospital, which led to the birth of the Society of Artists.[12] Moser was named a director in the *Charter of Incorporation of the Society of Artists* granted on 26 January 1765[13] and became first Keeper of the Royal Academy in 1768. In the general ban on the exhibition of copies which was passed at the Academy in January 1769, it was specified that no chasing copied from another chasing could be included.[14]

In 1747 *The London Tradesman* declared that 'A Youth designed' for chasing 'must have a good Genius for drawing, and ought to be early learned the Principles of that Art'.[15] The drawing and modelling skills needed by chasers gave them versatility. Moser was an enameller, drawing master, designer and, almost certainly, modeller as well as chaser. G.D. Gaab was described in 1763 as a modeller and designer 'for Jewellers, &c' as well as a gold and silver chaser.[16] George Parbury exhibited wax models and later made models for coins and medals for Matthew Boulton,[17] but he had been apprenticed to learn chasing from G.M. Moser.[18] Jean-Nicolas Wieland and Richard Morton Paye were wax modellers as well as chasers, and Paye subsequently became an engraver and painter.[19] James Barenger was trained as a chaser (Cat. H14), but exhibited pictures of insects. Henry Pars[20] and perhaps Thomas Burges[21] appear to have been trained as chasers before they became drawing masters. In retirement Augustin Heckel executed fine engravings of flowers. The 'Beauty and Justness' of the best chasing become less surprising as more is learnt of the training, accomplishment and status of the gold chaser in mid-eighteenth century London.

H1 *A gold-chaser at home*

Louis-Philippe Boitard (active 1733-1765). *c.* 1750?
Pen and ink and watercolour;
208 x 280
The *verso* inscribed *Zoffany*
The Yale Center for British Art, Paul Mellon Collection (B.1975.4.1027)

Formerly described as a self-portrait of the artist with two young men, this drawing presents a number of oroblems of interpretation, not the least of which is the separation of the artist's satirical intention from the apparently accurate representation of a garret room. The hanging watch-like objects below the window, the leather apron, the vice and the pots on the bench containing tools (cf. drawing by Christoph Jamnitzer, VAM E. 2357-1928) all appear to indicate that the occupant of the room is probably a watch-case chaser. The prints or drawings pinned to the wall, which is covered with a cloth decorated with a pink zig-zag design, include the Sudarium, which perhaps indicates that the occupant is Catholic. The ladder-back chair has a parallel in plate three of Hogarth's *Harlot's Progress*.

Prov: probably Arthur Foxley; Norris; Sotheby's 19 Dec. 1962, 286, bought Appleby; Leonard G. Duke 4055; Cyril Fry, London 1971
Lit: Noon 1979
MS

H2 *Design for two cane heads*

Augustin Heckel (*c.* 1690-1770).
c. 1735
Pen and ink and wash; 187 x 154
Yale Center for British Art, Paul Mellon Collection (B.1975.2.681.i)

The handle on the left is surmounted by a female head in a loose collar, comparable with that on the handle of Cat. C4. The top of the handle on the right is formed as a helmeted head, with the attributes of Hercules lower down on the shaft. One of a group of 55 sheets of drawings at Yale formerly attributed to Gaetano Brunetti because it includes 10 sheets of copies after his *Sixty Different sorts of Ornament,* 1736 (Cat. B10). The remaining drawings comprise 23 sheets of grotesque masks and similar subjects, and 22 sheets of original designs for chased boxes, watch cases and etuis, the earliest of

H3

which probably date from the 1730s. The attribution of the whole group to Heckel is based on their general similarity of handling together with several certain connections with the drawings in the Heckel sketchbook. One of the drawings after Brunetti has on the *verso* a sketch for a watchcase of the 1740s.
MS

H3 *Watch*

Outer case: chaser Augustin Heckel (*c.*1690-1770). Case-maker mark indistinct. London hallmarks for 1738-9 (inner case). Gold cases; outer case diam. 51
Chasing signed *AH.* Movement bears the name of Richard Vick, London, no. 557
Private Collection

The outer case chased from in front and embossed. On the back, within a symmetric cartouche, a *Commedia dell' Arte* scene in which Harlequin surprises two lovers while Pierrot looks on. Outside the cartouche and on the bezel are flowers and

strapwork. At the junction of the cartouche four *Commedia dell' Arte* heads, perhaps Harlequin (north), Pantalone (east), lover (south), Pierrot (west). The scene may be a conflation of two compositions by Watteau engraved in 1729 by C.-N. Cochin. Harlequin, to the right, derives from a scene, *Pour garder l'honneur d'une belle,* in which the doctor surprises his daughter with a lover, who may also have suggested the lover in this version. The female figure could derive from the other scene, *Belle[s] n'écoutez rien,* although the conceit of the needle-threading is Heckel's addition. The cartouche is an example of the type most commonly found on watch-cases of the later 1720s and 1730s before the use of the asymmetric cartouche became general about 1739-40.

Augustin Heckel was born in Augsburg, the son of the goldsmith Michael Heckel (d. 1722). According to Captain Francis Grosse, joint executor with the watchmaker Edward Ellicott of Heckel's will, Heckel was brought up a chaser, worked in 'most of the capital cities in Germany', and travelled to Paris before he came to England. He was 'esteemed the best workman of his time, especially in those figures which required the representation of the human figure'. Surviving work suggests that he was in London by the early 1720s. In 1732 Vertue noted him in his list of leading chasers and in 1749 he praised him with Moser as being among the leading chasers who 'yearly produce works of Gold boxes watch cases – tweezers &c multitudes for their excellence not only admired here but sold for abroad to many parts of the World'. He retired to Richmond, Surrey, where he died.

Prov: Sotheby's 7 Feb. 1972, 197; Sotheby's 13 June 1980, 268
Lit: Public Record Office, Chancery Lane, P.C.C., PROB II/959, quire 298; Gentleman's Magazine xl 1770, p. 393; Seling 1980, no. 1813; Strutt 1786, ii, pp. 11-12; Sunderland 1971, pp. 90-93, nos 15-16; Vertue III, p. 62, 150
RE

H4 *Studies, including an etui*
Hubert François (Bourguignon) Gravelot (1699-1773)
Etching; 160 x 92

H4

Signed *H. Gravelot*
VAM (E. 2456-1932)

This sheet, a conscious tour de force of Gravelot's skill with the etching needle, shows an étui, a circular design of the abduction of Helen, perhaps intended for a watch, a finger ring, a sportsman with a gun, studies of heads and other studies. The design for the étui can with some confidence be placed in Gravelot's English period (1733-1744); it is not similar to surviving étuis, either French or English, but its ornament can be related to Gravelot's book illustrations of the late 1730s (eg Cat. D4, D5). The figure of Helen is similar to the figure in a plate of the same subject in Meissonnier's *Livre D'Ornemens* (Cat. C17). This plate recalls Vertue's observation in 1741: 'he practises etching or Stylography in which business he has done many curious plates from his own desseins masterly and free, and de bon gout' (Vertue III, 105).

Prov: given by Prof. E.W. Tristram
Lit: British Museum 1978, 1; Goncourt 1882, II, 31, no. 3, repr.
MS

H5 *Design for the lid of a gold box*
Hubert François (Bourguignon) Gravelot (1699-1773). *c.* 1740
Pen and ink; 159 x 193 (silhouetted)
Inscribed on the backing sheet in a nineteenth century hand *H. Gravelot.*

Private Collection

The design is for a gold box (Metropolitan Museum, New York) the chased scene on which is inscribed *G.M. Moser fecit London 1741.* It can be identified with Moser's 'large gold tobacco box of the Story of Musius Scaevola. with ornaments about it all over chased. the gold wt. about 70 guineas and the chaseing valud between 40 or 50 more – a most excellent work. to the Honour of this nation' (Vertue III, p. 107) which was seen by George Vertue in 1741. It cannot be the box presented to Admiral Vernon by the City of London, as rather doubtfully suggested by Vertue, because that box (National Maritime Museum) was made in 1740 by Jasper Cunst (Grimwade 1982, 482). The scene, which is probably in part derived from

a painting (1643-5) by Charles Lebrun of the same subject (Versailles 1963, 6), was repeated on a number of later English boxes and watch-cases. An attribution to Gravelot was first suggested by Timothy Clifford (British Museum 1978, 1). It can be upheld because of the similarity of the hand to that of other small-scale figure drawings by Gravelot which are markedly more graceful and subtle in composition and handling than those by Moser.

Lit: Watson and Dauterman 1970, snuff box 25; Watson 1976, fig. 34
MS

H6

H6 *Watch*
Outer case: chaser George Michael Moser (1706-1783). Inner case: London hallmarks for 1739/40 Gold cases and leather-covered protecting case; outer diam. 48 Chasing signed *Moser f.* Movement bears the name of Paul du Pin, London No. 1530
The Worshipful Company of Clockmakers

Outer case chased from in front and embossed. On the back within an asymmetric cartouche a scene of Vertumnus and Pomona. In the foreground an amorino tugs at a reluctant and semi-recumbant woman; her tambourine suggests that she may be Erato, muse of love poetry. Around the push, a characteristic Moser snake. Outside the cartouche and on the bezel, pierced, chased and engraved foliage, bandwork, shell and scrollwork. This is Moser's earliest datable use of an asymmetric cartouche around the central figure scene: a case of 1738-9 (T. Mudge 22) has a symmetric cartouche similar to that on Cat. H3.

Other versions of the Vertumnus and Pomona scene include a crudely chased watchcase, movement by J. Grontham (sic) (Walters Art Gallery, Baltimore), which has a similar cartouche. Both the Grontham chaser and Moser could have been using a design by a third party, but it seems more likely that the Grontham case is further evidence that Moser's designs, whether as drawings or as plaster casts of executed work, were in circulation in London.

Prov: purchased in 1818
Lit: Camerer Cuss 1976, p. 116, pl. 56; Clutton & Daniels 1975, no. 157
RE

H7 *Sketchbook*

Augustin Heckel (*c.* 1690-1770)
152 drawings in pen and ink, wash, red chalk and pencil on 156 pages with 65 sheets pasted in, full bound in parchment; 202 x 159 Signed on a drawing on p. 101 *A. Heckel.* Other drawings inscribed in English and German
VAM (E.2998-1948)

Most of the drawings, ranging from sketches to finished designs, are of figure subjects, chiefly Classical, in a circular format adapted to watch-cases. Also included are a design for a fountain (p. 15), a rococo clock (p. 17) and a gold box (p. 109). Some of the figure subjects are studies before adaptation of paintings or Classical sculpture. Unlike the Yale designs (see Cat. H2), ornament is infrequent and when present is of rococo character, ie of the 1740s or later. A circular drawing of Bacchus and Ariadne after Sebastiano Conca may be earlier as the subject also occurs on a design at Yale (B.1975.2.681) for a gold box of the 1730s (VAM 61-1871). A pair of drawings on p. 125 is also of earlier character. A design for a large watch-case is shown; it is washed in green, pink and gold, perhaps to represent differently coloured golds. Within the asymmetrical rococo cartouche is Venus taunting Cupid with his bow, taken from a well known Classical gem that was engraved by Claude du Bosc for George Ogle's *Antiquities Explained,* 1737, pl. XVII.

Prov: Appleby Bros., 1948
MS

H8

H8 *Designs for watchcases*

George Michael Moser (1706-1783)
a) *Classical Wedding*
Pen and ink and wash; diam. 56
Signed *Moser i.v. delin.*
VAM (D.142-1890)

The scene is close to that on Cat. H9. This design clearly reveals Moser's indebtedness to Gravelot for his figure style (cf. a wedding scene by Gravelot in Bruand 1960, fig. 4).

Prov: see below

b) *A military trophy within scrolls, with a dragon*
Pen and ink and wash; diam. 85
Signed *G.M. Moser* erased *delin.*
VAM (D.145-1890)

Prov: probably Dr J. Percy; Christie's, 18 April 1890, 849; E. Parsons 1890
MS

H9 *Watch*

Outer case: chaser George Michael Moser (1706-1783). Casemaker: John Ward (both cases marked). Inner case: London hallmarks for 1744/5
Gold cases; outer case diam. 49
Chasing signed *G. Moser: fec.*
Movement bears the name of George Graham, London, no. 826
The Visitors of the Ashmolean Museum, Oxford

Outer case chased from in front and embossed. On the back within a cartouche with a north-south axis symmetry, a classical wedding scene with a statue of Juno in the background. A snake around the push; pierced, chased and engraved foliage, bandwork, shell and scroll outside the cartouche and on the bezel. From the 1740s to the 1760s

H9

Moser's chased cartouches were predominantly symmetrical about the north-south axis: more than 20 examples are known, as opposed to only a handful of asymmetric cartouches. The pattern of the upper two-thirds of the cartouche on this case can be found repeated on many Moser watch-cases, including Cat. I 11 & I 12. It may be that Jean André Rouquet's praise of Moser in 1755 as being the one chaser 'whose abilities really deserve the attention of the curious, and the approbation of his profession', was founded partly on Moser's preference for the symmetric cartouche, rather than the 'contrast' or asymmetry that Rouquet deplored. The asymmetric cartouche is found more frequently in Moser's surviving designs, but the preference for symmetry in executed work must have been his own. It is clear that it was not the general preference because the great majority of embossed cases between 1740 and 1770 have asymmetric cartouches. Equally it appears not to have been the choice of his watchmakers because the Ellicotts, the most frequent employers of both Moser and Henry Manly, generally (but not always) received asymmetric cartouches from Manley and symmetric cartouches from Moser. The male figure is indebted to the Apollo Belvedere and Juno with her peacock, the altar, and the palm tree, may have been influenced by Nicolas Vleughel's *Solomon sacrifiant aux idolès* engraved by Edmé Jeaurat in 1723. There appear to be two distinct, but related, versions of the scene on this case. Examples of the first version include the present case and a Moser watchcase design Cat. H8. Examples of the second version include at least one signed chasing by Moser (*Ellicott 3895, c.* 1754). The scene in the second version shows the marriage of Alexander and Roxana, but the absence of military equipment and of Haephestion from the first version suggests that the scene should be seen simply as a Classical wedding. As with Cat. H6, the existence of watchcases chased with the scene within similar cartouches, but not from Moser's hand, suggests that his designs or casts were in circulation. Unless Moser dervied his figure scene from another's design, he may have had yet wider influence: the scene was chased on a gold box, apparently Swedish, of about 1766.

George Graham was the pre-eminent watchmaker of his day. In the 1720s and 1730s he frequently used Ishmael Parbury, a chaser described by George Vertue as 'above any other Englishman'. In the will made shortly before his death in 1746 Parbury appointed Moser as an executor and offered him 'my Gold Watch for his care and trouble'. Moser appears to have taken over the chasing of Graham's cases before Parbury's death: *G. Graham 826* is one of three signed cases for Graham dating from 1744-5. The casemaker's mark is that used by John Ward after the Plate Act of 1738 took effect in 1739.

Prov: bequeathed by Eric Bullivant, 1974
Lit: Goldsmiths' Hall: small workers' register A1. Public Record Office, Chancery Lane, P.C.C., PROB/II/751, quire 361. Brusa 1978, figs 522-3; Grimwade 1976, p. 308; Hercenberg 1975, no. 93; Rouquet 1755, pp. 85-6; Vertue III, p. 134; Christie's Geneva, 10 May 1983, 82
RE

H10 *Design for the lid of a snuff box*
Augustin Heckel (*c.* 1690-1770). 1740s
Pencil, pen and ink and wash;
187 x 154 (silhouetted)
The Yale Center for British Art, Paul Mellon Collection (B.1975.2.681.aaa)

Of wavy-edged but symmetrical outline. The centre shows a fantastic garden fountain formed as a semi-circular wall incorporating a domed pavilion at its centre. Between the wings is a fountain basin. Although

similar to French boxes of *c.* 1740 (Snowman 1966, fig. 177), this design seems in its details to be indebted to Meissonnier. The wall and its ends are probably derived from a plate (Cat. C17) in the *Livre D'Ornemens*, published in Paris in 1734 and, in reverse, in London in 1737. The central pavilion, with its double-curved dome characteristic of Meissonnier, may have been derived from a plate in *Cinquieme Livre D'Ornemens (Oeuvre* suite E.34; Kimball 1934, fig. 210), but also seems to be indebted to a large plate by Laureolli, probably published in 1734, of a firework structure celebrating the birth of the Dauphin in 1729 (*Oeuvres* 116; Souchal 1967, no. 50, pl. 55a). A gold box chased by Heckel (Sotheby's 7 Dec. 1970, 29, repr.) with a scene of Alexander and Roxana after Coypel on its lid, has on its bottom a fantastic boat and shell taken from another plate in the *Livre D'Ornemens (Oeuvres* D. 22). Unlike Moser (see Cat. E14) Heckel does not reverse the motif, so he may have been working from the French edition of the print.

Prov: see Cat. H2
MS

H10

H11 *Design for a watch-case*
Attributed to Augustin Heckel (*c.* 1690-1770). *c.* 1745
Pen and ink and wash; 136 x 137
The Yale Center for British Art, Paul Mellon Collection (B.1975.2.681uu)

The design for Cat. H13.

Prov: see Cat. H2
MS

H12 *Cast of the back of a chaise watchcase*
After Christopher Heckel (active 1745-1778). 1745-6
Plaster; diam. 147

The Syndics of the Fitzwilliam Museum, Cambridge (M.6-1981)

A cast of the cartouche and landscape on the silver case of Cat. H13. The cast appears to have been taken before the pierced and engraved sections were executed. Like Gérard Debèche in Paris, London chasers frequently took plaster casts of their finished work. Ishmael Parbury owned more than 400 casts at his death in 1746, mostly of his own work, but also including 'A Parcel of casts of *French* and *English* snuff boxes' and 'A Parcel of ditto, for snuff boxes, by Mr. *Moser.*' The first lot of 30 watchcase casts after his own work fetched 13s 6d. In 1783 more than 700 plaster casts were dispersed at Moser's death including multiple impressions of identified boxes. The casts served as a record for the chaser and as a means of disseminating designs, but they could also be exhibited. Moser showed 'Eight impressions from basso-relievo, chased in gold' at the Society of Artists in 1761; in 1767 T. Austin exhibited a 'cast in plaister' which appears to have

H11

H12

been taken from a City of London box presented to the Prince of Brunswick in 1765; in 1770 Henry Manly exhibited two pieces, each described as a 'Cast of a chasing'. The finest of surviving casts, discovered by Professor Jaffé and now in the Fitzwilliam Museum, is of the City of London Freedom Box chased by Moser and presented to the Duke of York in 1761. The Moser cast bears the name of Ellicott (possibly 'Jno') written on the reverse. Ellicott could have had or been given the cast for his own enjoyment, but the connection underlines the possibility that watchmakers could have shown casts of chasing to intending purchasers.

Prov: purchased 1981
Lit: Cock 1746; Graves 1907, pp. 17, 154, 179; Hutchins 1783, I; Hutchins 1783, II; Watson & Dauterman 1970, p. 167
RE

H13 *Chaise watch*
Inner case chaser: Christopher Heckel (active 1745-1778). Inner casemaker mark; *SA* within rectangular reserve. Inner case: London hallmarks for 1745/6
Silver inner case; leather-covered silver and base-metal protecting case; diam. (protecting case) 145
Chasing of inner case signed *C.H.* Movement bears the name of Joseph Martineau Senior, no. 1849.
Private Collection

Silver inner case chased from in front and embossed. Within a cartouche symmetric about its north-south axis, a classical landscape. Outside the cartouche and on the bezel pierced and engraved panels of foliage and bandwork between chased shell- and scrollwork. In 1770 Christopher Heckel of Covent Garden 'Chaser' was described as the cousin of Augustin Heckel in the latter's will. He received the interest of £1000 for life as well as wearing apparel, pictures, prints, books and household goods. He was presumably the Heckel 'At Mr. Pope's, in Little Russel Street, Covent Garden' who contributed a chased silver plate of the Crucifixion to the exhibition of the Free Society in 1778, in which year poor rate was paid on a property in the street by a William Pope. Christopher Heckel can be identified with the chaser 'C.H.' through links between the Martineau chaise watch-case, a group of plaster casts (including Cat. H12), and a gilt-metal plaque signed with the surname in full. A bronze cast apparently similar to the gilt metal plaque is also known.

Prov: Sotheby's 28 January 1977, 265
Lit: Victoria Library, Buckingham Palace Road, SW1: poor rate books of St. Martins in the Fields. Public Record Office, Chancery Lane, P.C.C., PROB II/959, quire 298. Graves 1907, p. 116. Sotheby's 28 April 1969, 66; Sotheby's 31 July 1980, 87
RE

H14 *Cane head*
Chaser: Barenger. *c.* 1740-1751
Gold; h. 77
Chasing signed *BARENGER.* Engraved with the arms showing a quartered shield (Hellier quartering Harris and Penn) and thereon an escutcheon of pretence (Huntbach quartering Cooke, probably, and Fowke).
The Visitors of the Ashmolean Museum, Oxford

Cane head chased from in front and embossed. Within borders of asymmetrically arranged scrollwork, a scene of the Good Samaritan, adapted from Hogarth's painting executed in 1737 at St. Bartholomew's Hospital. Michael Maclagan, Richmond Herald, has generously furnished an explanation of the arms, their origins and irregularities. They are those used without authorisation by Samuel Hellier, barrister, who married Sarah Huntbach in 1732, was High Sheriff of Staffordshire in 1745 and died in 1751. Consequently the chaser appears to have been an older relative of James Barenger, who, according to Redgrave , was born in 1745, 'brought up a chaser', and died in 1813. James Barenger married the sister of William Woollett, engraver to George III and secretary of the Society of Artists, exhibited paintings of insects at the Society of Artists and the Royal Academy, and was father of James Barenger, the painter. A third James Barenger was described as a freeman of the Cutlers' Company when he took on apprentices in 1747 and 1753.

Prov: Samuel Hellier; given by his son, Sir Samuel Hellier (d. 1784), to the Ashmolean Museum.
Lit: Public Record Office, Kew: IRI/18/55; IRI/19/147; College of Arms London, Howard, pp. 58-9; Shaw 1801, p.215; Ashmolean 1836, p. 175; Redgrave 1878, p. 22; Graves 1905-6, i, p. 112; Graves 1907, p. 21
RE

H15 *Designs for jewellery and snuff boxes*
Jacob Bonneau (active 1741, d. 1786) after William Delacour (active 1740, d. 1767). 1747
Etching and engraving; 294 x 211
Lettered *De la Cour invt. Bonneau sculpt.*
VAM (E.1387-1925)

From Delacour's *Eighth Book of Ornaments,* which consists of a title

H13

page and six plates containing 19 designs for jewellery, 22 for snuff boxes and five for watchcases. The designs for boxes, all rectangular, are remarkable for the use of the *à cage* technique, which was not apparently employed in England until the later 1750s or 1760s. The *à cage* work is essentially a flattened version of the type Morceau de Fantasie employed in Meissonnier's *Livre D'Ornemens* (Cat. C17). The watchcase designs in the suite are more closely related to this or a similar source. The stone-set breast ornament, which shows Delacour's ignorance of jewellers' practices is not unlike certain Mediterranean jewels in general design. This suite and Cat. H16 are the only English pattern books to show rococo gold chasers' work.

Lit: Snowman 1966, 44-46
MS

H15

H16 *Designs for gold chasing*
Peter Glazier (active 1748-52). 1748
Etching and engraving; 165 x 235
Lettered *Pr Glazier inv. et fecit. Plate. 3d. Pre. 6d.* and with a copyright line dated 4 April, 1748
VAM (12965.7)

Two watchcases, a box lid, an element for a chatelaine and five designs of uncertain purpose. The watchcase design on the right has a scrollwork frame of a type frequently used by Moser. The box, with its straight-hinged back has an outline more

extreme than most English boxes. The extensive use of putti in scrollwork is characteristic both of Glazier's designs for chasing and of the more modest type of small metalwork (eg Cat. H24, G32, F24), but not of the work of the better known chasers such as Heckel and Moser. This is one of two recorded plates from a suite of unknown title published in 1748. The other plate, the second of the suite (VAM 17518), shows scent bottles, cane handles, miniature frames and a clock. The present plate was reissued in 1754, numbered II, together with Cat. G24. A trimmed plate (VAM 24890.6) shows a chatelaine element and other chasing.

Lit: Snowman 1966, 47
MS

H17 *Watch-back*
Chaser: Henry Manly (active 1730s-late 1760s). Casemaker: *JB* incuse (John Beesly?). *c.* 1750
Gold; diam. 47
Chasing signed *Manly [The Trustees of the British Museum] (86, 5-11, 5)*

Watch-back chased from in front and embossed: within an asymmetric cartouche a scene of Diana and Endymion, adapted from Boucher's *Death of Adonis* engraved by Michel Aubert, 1733. The scene shows Manly's capacity for changing the divine attributes as well as the grace of which he was capable when following a French rococo source. The asymmetric cartouche follows a scroll pattern which can be found in Manly's cartouches. The casemaker's mark suggests the watch-back was probably cut from a case associated with an Ellicott movement dating from between 1739, when the Plate Act of 1738 took effect, and about 1760, when Ellicott ceased to use 'JB'. The mark used by John Beesly, a freeman of the Clockmakers' Company, before the Plate Act of 1738 has been found on *Ellicott 1016* (1728-9; Ashmolean Museum). Examples of a later mark, 'JB' incuse with the J in script, are found on Ellicott watchcases from at least 1741-2 until about 1760 and can reasonably be assigned to Beesly. Ellicott was the watchmaker for whom Manly most frequently worked, but no association earlier than 1748-9 has yet been recorded. Henry Manly's work is known from about 25 chasings

executed between the 1730s, or possibly earlier, and the late 1760s. He appears to have married Sarah Brawne on 13 August 1733 at St Benet's, Paul's Wharf, and to have taken on an apprentice, Daniel Disney, in 1744 for the substantial fee of £40. His name appears in the Roll Declaration of the Incorporated Society of Artists adopted in 1766 and in the list of members printed between the 1772 and 1773 exhibitions. He exhibited six pieces at the Society's exhibitions between 1769 and 1771, several of which can be related to surviving work. From 1737 certainly, and possibly from 1728, he lived in Knightsbridge, rising to the description of 'Esq.' in the rate books between 1753 and 1760. From 1759 to 1769 he appears to have been continually in arrears with his rates.

Prov: given by Augustus Wollaston Franks, 1886
Lit: Goldsmiths' Hall, small workers' register A1. Public Record Office, Kew, IRI/17/74. Victoria Library, Buckingham Palace Road, SW1: poor rate books, St Margaret's Westminster. Atkins 1931, p. 22; Graves 1907, pp. 154, 322; Grimwade 1976, p. 299; Harleian Society Registers 1911, 38; Jean Richard 1978, no. 191; Pye 1845, pp. 118-20
RE

H18

H18 *Outer watchcase*
Chaser: John Gastrell (active 1747, d. 1772). *c.* 1750
Gold; diam. 49
Chasing signed *J. Gastrill*
Private Collection

Outer case chased from in front and embossed. Within an asymmetric cartouche a scene of Perseus and Andromeda, adapted from a painting by Rubens (Hermitage). A snake around the push and flowers, shell- and scrollwork outside the cartouche and on the bezel. John Gastrell of the parish of St Martin's in the Fields was described as a 'Chasser' when he took on an apprentice John Darrene in 1747 for a fee of £8. He exhibited a chasing in gold of Britannia and Fame at the Society of Artists in 1761. He was buried on 28 May 1772. In the 1760s his work included figure scenes in very high relief, with elements modelled in the round. His son William Gastrell (b. 1746), who won premiums from the Society of Arts in the early 1760s, also worked in high relief.

Prov: Dyson Perrins Collection; Sotheby's, London, 11 Dec. 1958, 158; Sotheby's, Zurich, 16 Nov. 1973, 88
Lit: Public Record Office, Kew, IRI/18/75. Victoria Library, Buckingham Palace Road, SW1: parish registers of St Martin's in the Fields; Dossie 1782, pp. 403, 406; Evans 1921, p. 136; Graves 1907, p. 101; Musée de l'Ermitage 1981, no. 461, fig. 121
RE

H19 *Badge*

Anonymous. *c.* 1750
Silver, cast and chased: 68 x 58
Engraved on the reverse *Mr S Snape TREASURER To the Unanimous Mercurians From XMAS TO MID^R 1750*
VAM (M.733-1926)

Cartouche-shaped badge of silver, cast and chased with the figure of Mercury bordered by scrolling pilasters, flowers and shells. The Unanimous Mercurians have apparently disappeared without trace. Their choice of deity however suggests that this organisation was connected with commerce, or possibly the post. An inquiry in *Notes and Queries* (6th series, VII, 1883, p. 349) which probably refers to this badge, apparently did not elicit any information about the Society.

Prov: Croft-Lyons Collection
CT

H20 *Chatelaine*

Maker's mark *JJ* crowned, incuse.
London hallmarks for 1754/5
Gold; l. 145
The Visitors of the Ashmolean Museum, Oxford (Hanbury 41)

The hook plate symmetric about its north-south axis and cast and chased with a scene of Neptune. Beneath: three plaques of north-south axis symmetry cast and chased with a lady wearing a hat, two putti with festoons, and two putti with a portrait of a lady, the lower two plaques containing asymmetric scrollwork. The plaques are linked with chains, and two further chains with flat links chased with shell- and scrollwork hang from either side of the hook plate, one terminating in a chased gold flask with a seal engraved *'UN ME SUFFIT'*, the other terminating in a plain triangular swivelling seal. The maker's mark may have been registered in the lost small-workers' book for 1739-58. None of the possible users of the mark is completely convincing. The closest identified marks are two cameo marks entered by John Jacob in the large workers' register in 1739. Grimwade records that Jacob's mark has been found on rococo baskets, candlesticks and hollow-ware.

Prov: Mrs Hanbury
Lit: Grimwade 1982, no. 1433
RE

H21 *Box*

Chaser: George Daniel Gaab (active 1744, d. 1784). Boxmaker mark *AH* incuse. London hallmarks for 1756-7
Gold; h. 50, l. 96, w. 80 Chasing signed *GaB london* (top) *Gaab Lodon* (front side)
Musée du Louvre (OA 7971)

Box of cartouche shape, symmetric about its north-south axis. Both top and base are hinged and are mounted on the inside with miniatures. The box is chased with four large scenes within symmetric cartouches: on the top, putti personifying the Arts and Sciences; on the base, a garden; on the front side, the construction of a house; on the back, a port. Two pairs of scenes on the sides are set within asymmetric scrollwork: one pair shows grottoes and shells, the other birds and gardens. A departure from the more common classical subjects for

mild chinoiserie and contemporary dress. The cloud-borne deity on the lid is paralleled in one of the scenes chased by Gaab for the Brass Crosby Cup in 1772 (Mansion House, London). George Daniel Gaab was described on 1 February 1744 in his marriage allegation bond as a 'Gold and Silver Chaser' of the parish of St Martin's in the Fields and on the marriage allegation as a 'Batchelor aged above Thirty Years'. He married a widow, Ann Blakeway, on 6 February at St James's, Piccadilly. She was then living in New Belton Street and from 1745 to 1766 her name is replaced as ratepayer by that of Gaab, who appears at this address in the entry in Mortimer's *Universal Director* (see introductory essay). A Gaab is again recorded as ratepayer at this address from 1772-81, but in 1783 when Gaab exhibited at the Free Society of Artists, his address was 5 King Street, Seven Dials. He was recorded in the registers of St Giles in the Fields as a resident of King Street at his burial on the 7 April 1784. It seems possible that he could have been a member of the Gaap family of Augsburg goldsmiths of the same generation as Georg Lorenz Gaap III (1711-64).

Prov: bequeathed by Georges Heine 1929
Lit: St Giles in the Fields: parish registers. Holborn Library: rate books for St Giles in the Fields. Lambeth Palace Library: Faculty Office, Archbishop of Canterbury, marriage allegation bond and allegation. Victoria Library, Buckingham Palace Road, SW1: parish registers, St James's, Piccadilly. Bannister 1981; Franks & Grueber 1885, i, pp. 23, 72; ii, pp. 273, 458; Graves 1907, p. 98; Seling 1980, no. 2309; Grandjean 1981, no. 474
RE

H22 *Design for a watchcase*
George Michael Moser (1706-1783)
Pen and ink and wash; diam. 48
Private Collection

A design for enamel, in a plain
border; it is very close to the scene on
Cat. H23.

Prov: see Cat. I 9
MS

H23 *Box*
Chaser: George Michael Moser (1706-
1783). Not after 1761
Gold: l. 89
Chasing signed *G.M. Moser fecit* (lid),
Moser F. (base). Reverse of lid engraved
*Given by the Earl of Bute/To/Sir John
Pringle Bart, M.D, P.R.S. 1763*
Private Collection

Chased oval box. On the lid a scene of
Leda and the Swan; a plinth to the right
has a reserve containing Jupiter's
eagle. On the base within an
asymmetric cartouche a scene of
Cybele, wearing a mural crown,
holding a key, accompanied by lions,
and with a tambourine at her feet and
symbols of plenty around her. The
box sides are chased with foliage,
shell- and scrollwork, flowers and a
face. *Jupiter and Leda* and *Cybele,
daughter of Sol* were among the eight
'impressions' of chasings, probably
plaster casts, shown by Moser at the
exhibition of the Society of Artists in
1761. Also included were impressions
of the Wrightsman Mucius Scaevola
box (Metropolitan Museum). The
whole exhibit may have been lot 7 in
the Moser sale of the 21 May 1783: 'A
frame containing eight fine
impressions from boxes'. It seems
likely therefore that Moser originally

chased the box for Bute, who appears
in J.C. Fuessli's life of Moser as an
important patron, some years before it
was presented to Pringle in 1763. The
inscription must be a later record of
the presentation because Pringle,
distinguished for his advances in
military medicine, was not created a
baronet until 1766, or President of the
Royal Society until 1772. A line and
wash drawing of the scene of Leda,
her attendant, and the swan, within a
roundel, is among a group of
unpublished drawings by Moser
(see Cat. H22). The chasing of the
sides has been strongly influenced by
French chasing: compare, for
example, an oval box of 1736-7
bearing the mark of Jean Ducrollay
(Wrightsman Collection).

Lit: Blakemore 1976, fig. I 11; Dictionary
of National Biography 1921-2 pp. 386-
8; Fuessli 1774, IV, pp. 135, 137;
Watson & Dauterman 1970, nos. 2, 25
RE

H24 *Box*
English. 1761
Gilt metal; h. 28, l. 72, w. 55
Engraved on the base *AW/1761*
*The Syndics of the Fitzwilliam Museum,
Cambridge*

Rectangular box cast and chased: the
lid with a scene of two putti sending
hearts flying within an asymmetric
cartouche; each side with three
scrollwork reserves, two enclosing
foliage either side of a central reserve
enclosing a head; the base engraved as
above within asymmetrical scrollwork
with shell and flowers. Interior lined
with horn, the lid with a plain plate.

Prov: Spencer George Percival Bequest,
1922
RE

H25 *Watch*
Outer case chaser: Henry Manly
(active 1730s-late 1760s). Casemaker's
mark: *HT* incuse (both cases marked).
London hallmarks for 1762/3 (inner
case)
Gold cases; outer case diam. 49
Chasing signed *Manly fec.* Movement
bears the name of Ellicott, London,
no. 5141
Private Collection

Outer case chased from in front and
embossed. On the back within an

asymmetric cartouche a scene of the
Judgement of Hercules, after Paolo de
Matteis. Outside the cartouche,
flowers; on the bezel, flowers, shell-
and scrollwork. The triangular punch
marks next to the rim of the case are
commonly found in Manly's work.
Paolo de Matteis's painting
(Ashmolean Museum) was executed
under the direction of Anthony, Earl
of Shaftesbury, for the second edition
of the latter's *Characteristicks* (London,
1714), the plate being engraved by
Simon Gribelin. As part of one of the
most reprinted works on aesthetics in
the 18th century, the scene was
frequently copied. Versions include
jasperware jewellery, a chimneypiece
at Saltram House, Devon, and a
number of chasings. Moser's example,
T. Mudge & W. Dutton 816 (1768-9) was
one of his latest rococo chasings. The
scene is also found on two rococo
silver chaise watchcases chased by
Johann Bartermann II of Augsburg.
Another interpretation of the scene by
Manly is found on *Ellicott 3078* (1749-
50; Walters Art Gallery, Baltimore)
and on *Ellicott 6027* (1767-8;
Clockmakers' Company, London). A
further interpretation executed by an
unknown chaser in 1762 survives with
the original bill for the chasing from
the watchmaker Thomas Grignion to
the patron, Mr Price: 'the Story of the
Judgement of Hercules Viz Hercules
is represented as determining between
Virtue and Pleasure and gives the
preference to Virtue'. Cost: five
guineas.

Prov: Miss A.P. Belk; Sotheby's 2 May
1966, 132
Lit: Bramsen 1965, p. 221, Museo
Poldi Pezzoli 1974; Seling 1980,
no. 2326; Christie's 26 Oct. 1971, 107;
Phillips, Son & Neale 22 March 1977,
80; 14 Nov. 1978, 149
RE

Objets de Vertu

Design for a watchcase. George Michael Moser. See Cat. I 13.

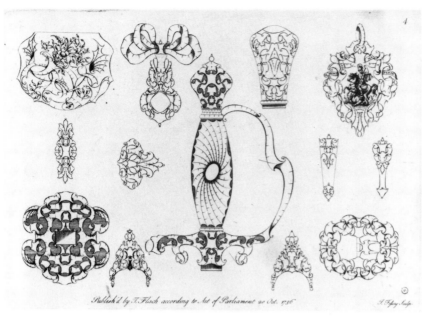

Publish'd by T.Flach according to Act of Parliament 20 Oct. 1736. *J.Fessey Sculp.*

11 *Designs for jewelled objects and jewellery*

J. Fessey after Thomas Flach. 1736
Engraving; 211 x 303
Lettered *Published by T. Flach according to Act of Parliament 20 Oct. 1736 J. Fessey Sculp.* Numbered *4*
VAM (E.3664-1904)

From *A Book of Jewellers Work Design'd by Thomas Flach in London,* sold at the Queen's Head and Star in St Martin's le Grand (Berlin 1939, 757; title and 5 plates). The plate shows gentlemen's equipment, including a sword hilt and mounts, a Garter badge, and a snuff box, all with precious stones in *pavé* settings. The marked asymmetry of the box decoration, also found on aigrette designs in the suite, is a feature of European jewellery from about 1720 onwards. Three of Flach's plates appear, probably as reissues, in *A Book of Ornaments useful for Jewellers; Drawn and Invented by Christian Taute. London* (title and 8 plates in the VAM). A design book of *c.* 1750 plausibly atttributed to Taute survives (VAM E.2041-1914). Except for Cat. H15, the other jewellery designs of the period published in England are also by Germans: Sebastian Henry Dinglinger's *A New Book of Designs for Jewellers Work,* 1751, engraved by J. Brooke (Berlin 1939, 758), and a suite by F. Loh engraved by Müller junior (4 plates without title in the VAM). A trade card of Sigismund Godhelp Dinglinger, jeweller at the

Diamond Cross, St Martin's le Grand, is also known (British Museum, Heal 67.121).
MS

12 *Table clock*

John Ellicott (1706-1772); *c.* 1740-50
Walnut mounted in silver-gilt;
h. 444, w. 195
The dial and back plate signed *John Ellicott London*
VAM (M.22-1970)

Rectangular walnut case, the arched top of which rises to form a plinth mounted in silver-gilt, and surmounted by a wrythen scrolling urn with a shell finial. The case is supported on four feet of silver-gilt cast with scrolls, water and shellwork rising to flowers and foliage, which are joined at the front and rear by festoons of shells and scrolls. The sides have floral swags of silver-gilt above and below glazed panels. The face is of silver-gilt with silver chapter-ring bearing the hours in Roman numerals and five minute intervals in Arabic numbers, above which are applied scrolls, flowers and pilasters supporting a small strike and silent dial. The back plate is engraved with foliated scrolls. John Ellicott junior was the most famous member of a distinguished family of clockmakers. He assumed control of his father's business in 1733 and took his son into partnership probably in 1757. During the period of his sole control he

appears to have signed his work 'John Ellicott London' as on the present example, whereas the signature 'Ellicott London' was used after 1757. Ellicott supplied three clocks and a celestial and a terrestrial globe to the Spanish court. One of the clocks (Palacio Real, Madrid) has very similar silver-gilt mounts to the present example.

Prov: traditionally said to have belonged to Catherine (II) the Great, of Russia; Percy Webster; Lord Kenyon; Ronald Lee
Lit: Foulkes, 1969, pp. 102-10
CT

13 *Ticket*

Daniel Piers (active 1746-58). 1746-56
Silver, engraved; h. 51
Inscribed on the obverse: *Opera Subscription, Kings Theatre.* and on the reverse *Mr Horatio + No 21 + Walpole Private Collection*

Silver ticket, shaped as a strawberry, the obverse bordered by engraved scrolls, and the reverse bearing the maker's mark of Daniel Piers and the lion passant London hallmark, which was replaced in 1756. The King's Theatre, Haymarket was built in 1705 by Vanburgh and was burnt down in 1781. Her Majesty's Theatre is on the original site. Horace Walpole, writing to George Montagu on 16 December 1764 said 'Of all the pleasures, I prescribe myself a very small pittance; my dark corner in my own box at the opera, and now and then an ambassador'. (Lewis 1936, p. 136). Daniel Piers, of Spur Street, Leicester Fields, entered his mark on 3 November 1746 and died in June 1758.

Prov: Paddy Green; Lady Dorothy Nevill; Frederick Charles Nevill (1936)
Lit: Grimwade, 1976, No. 625; Nevill 1919 p. 78
CT

12

14 *Pair of chatelaines with watch and etui*

Anonymous, London. *c.* 1755
Agate, gold, gilt metal and diamonds;
h. 200
The watch signed *Cabrier London 1780*
Private Collection

The chatelaines of gilt metal mounted
with plaques of grey striated agate set
a cage in gold pierced and chased with
Classical figures, foliage, pilasters and
scrolls. The outer case of the watch is
of agate covered with gold pierced and
chased with scrolls, foliage and
pilasters with a ship and a tree
flanking a scene of rape. The watch
chatelaine comprises three plaques of
agate mounted in gilt metal and

covered with gold pierced and chased
with figures reclining in foliage and
hook of gilt metal on the front of
which is a plaque of agate decorated
with Mars and Venus amid scrolls,
foliage and pilasters in pierced and
chased gold. A crank key and a
blackamoor's head seal hand from
chains on either side of the chatelaine.
The étui of tapering form is similarly
decorated with agate plaques and
overlaid with pierced and chased
scrolls and with a diamond thumb-
piece. The ornament is divided into
six reserves containing Classical
figures, pilasters and foliage bordered
by scrolls. The étui contains a mirror,
pencil, scissors, and a knife. The
chatelaine is composed of a hook and

pendant plaque of gilt metal decorated
with agate and pierced and chased
gold, and has a thimble case and scent
bottle case similarly ornamented. The
maker of the watch, Charles Cabrier,
was apprenticed in 1719, and became
free of the Clockmaker's Company in
1726. From 1757 until 1772 he was
Master of the Company.
(not exhibited)

Lit: Baillie 1929 p. 59
Prov: Christie's, Geneva 19 November
1982; Uto Auktion, Zurich
CT

15 *Combined scent-bottle and snuff-box*

English, anonymous. *c.* 1760
Agate set with diamonds, mounted in
gold, with enamel; w. 86
The collar lettered in gold *Fidele et
Sincere*
Arthur and Rosalinde Gilbert

Snuff-box of agate carved in the form
of a seated huntsman wearing a
tricorn hat, jacket, breeches and boots,
with diamond eyes and buttons, with
his dog, also with diamond eyes and
an enamelled collar. The head of the
dog forms the stopper of the scent-
bottle. The rim of the base is
decorated with gold chased in scrolls
and flowers and has a diamond-set
thumbpiece. The base, or lid, is
embellished with gold pierced and
chased with scrolls, shellwork, flowers
and a vase, around a huntsman astride
a dead stag. He is shown blowing a
horn, and holding a gun in his left
hand. The source for this scene would
appear to be an engraving in the style
of the South German artist
J.E. Ridinger. This box and scent-
bottle forms part of a small group of
hardstone boxes which clearly relate
to Chelsea porcelain toys of the 1760s.
It has been suggested that the stones
were carved by Italian craftsman but
there were several English ivory
carvers in the mid-18th century who
could have turned their hand to stone-
cutting. Other examples of the group
are found in the Museo Lazaro
Galdiano, Madrid, and in the VAM.

Prov: Enrico Caruso; Parke-Bernet
1949; Christie's 18 Dec. 1973, 193;
Christie's, Geneva, 8 May 1979, 118
Lit: Snowman 1966, pl. 455, pl. 94;
Habsburg 1983, No 17
CT

139

16 Trade cards
a) Joseph Creswell, toyman, 'At the Unicorn in Suffolk Street From Mr Chenevix'.
Anonymous, after Jean Rocque
240 x 150 (cut)
The Trustees of the British Museum (Heal 119.9)

The card derives from a cartouche on pl. LXXIII of Edward Hoppus, *The Gentleman's and Builder's Repository*, 1737, which is signed by Jean Rocque. The famous toyshop of Paul Daniel Chenevix (d. 1742) and his wife was on Cockspur Street, facing Suffolk Street (see Phillips 1964, p. 64). A Joseph Creswell entered a hallmark in 1767, but this card is almost certainly earlier.

b) John Wilmot, goldsmith and jeweller.
Anonymous. 170 x 130. *c.* 1760?
The Guildhall Library (94635)

The card shows jewellery, much of it asymmetrical in design. This card design was also used by four other jewellers and a linen draper.
MS

17 Etui
George Michael Moser (1706-1783)
Chased gold, set with six enamelled gold plaques, and with copper and steel fittings; h. 122, w. 42
The central enamel on the back signed *Moser F.* A tablet inscribed in pencil, *March ye 2nd 1787*
Private Collection

Gold étui, of tapering form chased on the front and back with three cartouches of scrolls, shells, masks and foliage, enclosing six enamelled gold plaques depicting, on the front Medicine, Literature, and Painting, and on the back Architecture, Music and Sculpture. The side panels chased with scrolls, flowers and foliage. The interior contains two ivory tablets held by a gold rivet, a gold combined toothpick and earpick, a pair of scissors with steel blades and gold handles, a pair of tweezers in gold combined with a steel nail-file, a gold bodkin, a gold pencil holder and a gold penknife with a steel blade. The painting emblematic of Music is apparently taken from a gem illustrated in Gori's *Museum Florentinium* (1731-62, Vol. II, fig. 8) and Agostini's *Gemmae Antiche Figurate*

(1686, pl. 7) both of which Moser possessed. It is possible that the other figures were adapted from engravings of gems also in the artist's collection.
CT

18 Snuffbox
Probably George Michael Moser (1706-1783)
Gold, chased and enamelled set with emeralds and rubies; 1. 860
The watch movement signed *Dan. De. St. Leu, London, 564.*
Arthur and Rosalinde Gilbert

Rectangular, containing nine panels painted in enamel with scenes from the adventures of Don Quixote bordered by gold chased with scrolls, shells and pilasters. The centrally divided lid reveals twin containers for snuff, and the base conceals a watch, the enamelled dial of which is set with emeralds and surrounded with rubies, mounted in a panel of gold chased with scrolls, shells and trophies of the Sciences. The scenes are after Charles Coypel's illustrations to Pierre de Hondt's edition, *Les Principales Aventures de l'Admirable Don Quichotte*, Paris, 1746, except those of the front which are taken from Dr Smollet's translation with engravings after Francis Hayman (London, 1755, Vol. II, pp. 284 and 458). The enamels and the chasing of the gold are in the style of G.M. Moser (cf. a design for a watchcase by Moser, also after Hayman Cat. I 9). Moser appears to have turned to enamelling when 'adorning plate, cane-heads and watch-cases became unfashionable'. Claude Blair (Wartski 1971) has deduced that this must have been about 1760 for in 1755 André Rouquet referred to Moser as only a chaser whereas he is recorded in 1763 as a 'Chaser and Painter in Enamels'. It is evident that Moser abandoned the rococo in favour of neo-classicism about the mid-1760s for a box enamelled by him dated 1764 contains a purely neo-classical scene within (Metropolitan Museum 1974). An enamelled watch-case of approximately the same date (Schweizerisches Landesmueseum Zurich, LM 49072, Zurich 1971, pp. 23, 24) may be compared with the present box. Daniel de St Leu (active 1753-97) specialised in watches for the Turkish market, as well as working for the Spanish Court.

Prov: Traditionally given by Louis XVI to M. de Vougelot, French Ambassador to the Court of St James; Viscount Bearsted MC; Messrs. S.J. Phillips
Lit: Habsburg 1983, No. 16; Norton 1938, pp. 82-83; VAM 1962; VAM 1968
CT

110

I9 *Design for a watch-case*

George Michael Moser (1706-1783)
Pen and ink, water and body colour
on vellum; diam. 62
At the bottom a cut inscription
Private Collection

The central scene, intended to be
enamelled, is taken from Grignion's
engraving after Francis Hayman in
Smollett's translation of *The History and
Adventures of the Renowned Don Quixote*,
1755, vol. I, p. 196: 'Cardenio and his
companions surprise Dorothea
bathing her feet in a stream'. Moser
reverses the figures of both the
engraving and the original drawing
(British Museum) and adds a
mountain in the distance. The mild
eroticism of this scene, which would
have passed unnoticed in France, was
unusual in England. In the outer
compartments of the rim are
enamelled flowers. The meaning of
the red lines on a grey ground in the
other areas is uncertain; they may
indicate engraving or chasing. This is
one of a group of 39 designs by Moser
for watch-cases, boxes and a medal of
George III. Most are circular studies
of Classical subjects; many are for
enamelled pieces.

Prov: Mary Moser, the artist's
daughter; Daniel Cubitt Nichols; by
descent
MS

I10 *Design for a watchcase and chatelaine*

George Michael Moser (1706-1783).
c. 1766?
Pen and ink and body colour;
209 x 60
Inscribed on the *verso* in pencil *Molford Col*
The Metropolitan Museum of Arts, gift of Janos Scholz 1949

The chatelaine elements are enamelled
with putti emblematic of the
Elements. The watch, with its scroll
surround to an enamelled scene of
Apollo and the Seasons is very close to
Cat.I 11. This is the only recorded
design by Moser for a watch and
chatelaine together; a design for an
enamelled chatelaine is in a private
collection. In both cases body colour
is used to imitate the effect of enamel.

Prov: (?) R.S. Holford
MS

I11 *Watch*

Outer case chaser and enameller;
George Michael Moser (1706-1783)
Casemaker mark; *HT* incuse
(associated inner case). London
hallmarks for 1766-7 (inner case).
Gold cases outer case diam. 49.
Enamelling signed *G.M. Moser*
Private Collection

Outer case chased from in front,
embossed and enamelled: on the back
within a cartouche with north-south
axis symmetry an enamelled scene of
Apollo and the Four Seasons: Ceres
with a wheatsheaf personifying
Summer; Flora with flowers
personifying Spring; Boreas with grey
hair and beard, and a fire, personifying
Winter; and Bacchus, holding a
thyrsus, personifying Autumn.
Around the push, a Moser snake.
Outside the cartouche and on the
bezel pierced, chased and engraved
foliage between shell and scrollwork.
For a design by Moser including a
similar scene, see Cat. I 10. Another
version by Moser is in the Taft
Museum, Cincinnati, and chased
versions by a number of hands,
including Moser, are also known. The
figure of Apollo appears to be
indebted to the frontispiece for the
*Tombeau de Charles Sackville, comte de
Dorset* engraved by Michel Guillaume
Aubert after an illustration by Boucher
for E. Mac Swiny's *Tombeau des Princes,
des Grand Capitaines et autres Hommes
illustres . . .*, published in 1741. The
looping scrollwork in the bottom third
of the figure scene cartouche and the
foliage whorls outside the cartouche
are typical of Moser's chasing in the
1760s.

Lit: Taft Museum, no 387; Jean
Richard 1978, no 194
RE

I11

112 *Watch*

Case chaser and enameller: George Michael Moser (1706-1783); *c.* 1768-9
Gold and enamel case, interior lined with unmarked gold plate; diam. 51
Enamelling signed *G.M. Moser* (further letters indistinct). Movement bears the name of Conyers Dunlop, London, no. 3383
The Worshipful Company of Clockmakers

Case chased and enamelled: on the back within a cartouche with north-south axis symmetry, an enamelled scene, after Gravelot, *Hannibal at nine Years of Age, Swearing Enmity to the Romans.* Outside the cartouche and on the bezel panels of tracer-work with rosettes, shellwork, scroll and a foliage whorl. The numbering of Conyers Dunlop's movements might suggest that the movement could be as early as 1760, but the style of the chasing, especially the regular panels of tracer-work makes the case transitional from rococo to neo-classicism and a date in the late 1760s more likely. A number of watch-cases derive their figure scenes from book illustrations by Gravelot. This scene is adapted from the frontispiece to the first volume of Charles Rollins' *Ancient History* published in London in 1738. Chased versions closer to Gravelot's illustrations include one by Henry Manly, Ellicott 3579, *c.* 1752, and Ellicott 6369, *c.* 1770.

Prov: purchased by the Clockmakers' Company in 1898
Lit: Clutton & Daniels 1971, figs 276-8; Clutton & Daniels 1975, no 319; Weiss 1982, fig. 62; Sotheby's I Nov. 1965, 160; Sotheby's 29 Nov. 1979, 66
RE

113 *Design for a watchcase*

George Michael Moser (1706-1783)
Pencil, pen and ink and wash; diam. 57
Signed *Moser: iv*
VAM (D.143-1890)

Two putti bear up a flower basket, surrounded by scrolls which are set with precious stones. The putti can be compared with those on Cat. H23.

Prov: see Cat. H22
Lit: Girouard, 1966, III, fig. 2
MS

114

114 *Design for a watchcase*

Hubert François (Bourguignon) Gravelot (1699-1773)
Pencil, pen and ink; 99 x 53
The Metropolitan Museum of Art (44.66.1); gift of A.S.W. Rosenbach 1944

Plan and section of an *à cage* watch-case set with moss-agates, which can be compared with English *à cage*-work pieces (eg Cat. I 19). The interlaced pattern is very similar to the linked scrollwork characteristic of Gravelot's English satirical prints (see Cat. D13). This is one of several undated designs by Gravelot for boxes, watches and jewellery in the Metropolitan Museum, the Ashmolean Museum and the British Museum.
MS

I15 *Necessaire*

John Barbot (active 1726-*c.* 1780).
c. 1765-70
Gold, agate and precious stones, surmounted by a watch;
239 x 63 The watch signed *Jn. Barbot*
The Metropolitan Museum of Art (45.164.1)

115

Necessaire in the form of a cabinet on stand, the legs of which are comprised of chased scrolls surmounted by masks, above which is the rectangular cabinet of agate plaques mounted *à cage* in gold chased and pierced with scrolls, flowers and spirally fluted columns, between which are swags and vases of gem-set flowers. The top of the cabinet is surmounted by four asymmetrical gold vases set beneath a gold putto with an hour-glass and a serpent. Very little seems known about John Barbot. On 16 July 1726 he entered a mark as a small worker. That he was still working in 1765 is indicated by a gold-mounted necessaire signed *J Barbot, London, fecit 1765* (Christie's New York, March 28 1979, 236), and the neo-classical ornament on one of three clocks by him in Peking suggests that he continued working until about 1780. The architectural details of the cagework on this necessaire may be derived from Meissonnier. The scrolling arch is a regular feature of his *oeuvre* but does not appear in conjunction with spirally fluted or solomonic columns. The scrolling vases at the corner are clearly related to English porcelain vases of the late 1750s while the watch holder is probably French in origin.

Lit: Grimwade 1982, pp. 88, 430
CT

116 *Scent bottle*

James Cox (active 1749-1791). 1766-72
Blue glass cut on the wheel mounted
in gold, set with diamonds, garnets, a
compass and watch; h. 135, l. 55,
depth 30
The movement of the watch signed
J. Cox London 125
Musée du Louvre (DA 8024)

Of pilgrim-bottle form, the scent
bottle comprises a facet-cut blue glass
bottle, mounted in a cagework of gold
scrolls and swags of flowers enclosing
architectural caprices, and set on one
side with a watch and on the other
with a compass both surrounded by
garnets. The base of the bottle is set
with diamonds and opens to form a
patch box with a mirror. The stopper
is encrusted with facetted garnets.
Complex pierced patterns of scrolling
cagework are a characteristic of
English rococo goldsmith work and it
is clear that Cox was not alone in
dealing in pieces in this style. Indeed
it is probable that the gold mounts of
this scent bottle are by an anonymous
out-worker to whom work was sub-
contracted by Cox and other toymen.
An identical example was sold at
Christie's London 18 November 1969,
73.

Prov: Georges Heine, 1929
Lit: Grandjean 1981, pp. 322-4
CT

117 *Cabinet*

James Cox (active 1749-1791). 1766-72
Agate mounted in gold, set with a
watch, pearls and paste jewels; h. 308
The enamel watch-face signed *Jas Cox*
London
Metropolitan Musuem of Art; gift of Admiral
F.Q. Harris 1946 in memory of his wife
Dena Sperry Harris (46.184a-c.)

This cabinet, or a very similar one,
was described by James Cox in the
Descriptive Inventory of the several exquisite
and Magnificent pieces of Mechanism and
Jewellery. . . ; For enabling Mr James Cox,
of the City of London, Jeweller, to dispose of
his Museum by way of Lottery (London
1773): 'Piece the Seventeenth. A
superb Cabinet. Of the finest and
most beautiful red onyx; it is overlaid
and mounted in every part with
ornaments of gold, richly chased in
festoons of flowers and other fine
designs. In the front are folding doors
lined with mirrors, which when

117

opened discover the draws of the Cabinet; these draws are fronted with chrystal finely cut and overlaid with gold to correspond with the Cabinet; the upper draw contains a great number of fine instruments and essence bottles mounted in gold; the under draw contains a key of a most curious timepiece, which when wound up gives motion to a sphere of gold, revolving on its axis during the going of the time-piece. At the corners of the Cabinet are golden vases fill'd with flowers of Pearls and jewellers work, above which spiral springs of temper'd gold, are insects that move with the smallest touch as if hovering over the flowers; above the sphere is a larger nosegay suitable to those at the corners and terminating the whole. In the bottom part of the Cabinet is a most curious chime of bells, playing various tunes; at the four corners are four bulls that support it; they stand on a gilt rock, in front of which is a cascade and running stream of artificial water, where Swans are seen swimming in contrary directions; at the corners of the rocks are Dragons with extended wings. The cabinet stands upon a pedestal of crimson velvet, with a glass shade, the frames both of the shade and pedestal are covered with silver, by which the whole is kept from air and dust.' The base of gilt rockwork, water, swans and dragons, has now disappeared but it very probably resembled the base of a Gothic pagoda by Cox sold by Messrs Phillips, London, 30 September 1980, 31. Watches by various makers set into necessaires in the form of miniature furniture indicate that Cox was not alone in commissioning such pieces. The designs are clearly derived from contemporary English furniture although the extravagantly *bombé* form of the lower part of the present example shows Continental influences. It is interesting to note that although using the standard canon of English rococo – scrolls, naturalistic flowers and asymmetrical motifs, the goldsmith who constructed this piece has arranged the ornament perfectly symmetrically. The design of the interior of the upper part is identical to the interior of a cabinet on stand with a watch by Cox in the Collection of H.M. The Queen, and the bulls which support the present example

are matched by those supporting cabinets in the Loup and Strogonoff collection.

Prov: probably James Cox's Spring Gardens Museum 1773
Lit: Le Corbeiller 1970, fig. 1
CT

118 *Trade card*
James Cox, goldsmith
Anonymous; 210 x 162
On the verso a bill dated 1751
The Trustees of the British Museum (Heal 67.99)

At the Golden Urn, Racquet Court, Fleet Street. A maker of toys and automata (see Cat. I 17) who is first recorded in 1749. In 1769 he bought the Chelsea porcelain factory from Sprimont but quickly disposed of it to William Duesbury of Derby. He had died by 1792. The design of this card, one of the strongest of the period, probably derives from Henry Copland. It was used at least seven times, by four identifiable engravers, including the card of the engraver John Spilsbury.

Lit: Heal 1935, XVIII; Le Corbeiller 1970
MS

119 *Snuff-box*
Probably James Cox (active 1749-1791); 1766-72
Gold set with moss agate plaques, glass, a watch and two automata; l. 178
Arthur and Rosalinde Gilbert

Rectangular gold box with plaques of moss agate mounted *à cage* in scrolls of gold, and set on the front with a watch flanked by a regulator and an open balance all behind glass. The rear panel opens to show a landscape with two revolving panels. Another snuff-box containing an identical watch, signed *Jas Cox London,* with a double automaton, and with the same gold borders (Christie's Geneva, 12 May 1981, 444) indicates that both pieces emanate from James Cox's toyshop at 130 Shoe Lane, Fleet Street. The interlaced scrolls which form the cagework to three sides of the box appear to relate to a design by Hubert Gravelot for a watchback (Cat. I 14). Although Gravelot had returned to France before the probable date of this box, we know from George Vertue that he produced a number of designs for goldsmiths while in England and it is possible that this type of interlaced cagework is ultimately derived from his designs.

Prov: Sotheby's, London, 17 May 1956, 95; A la Vieille Russie, New York
Lit: Berry Hill 1953, p. 112, ill. 89 & 90; Habsburg 1983, no. 19; Le Corbeiller 1966, no. 287
CT

IX *Standish with bell, pounce pot and*
inkwell
Paul De Lamerie. 1738/9
His Grace the Duke of Marlborough DL, JP,
Blenheim Palace
See cat. G6

X *Design for a watchcase*
Augustin Heckel. *c.*1741
See cat. H7

XI *Etui*
The enamels by George Michael
Moser. *c.*1760
Private Collection
See cat. I17

XII *Commode*
Pierre Langlois. 1760
*The Marquess of Tavistock and Trustees of
the Bedford Estates, Woburn Abbey*
See cat. L53

XIII *Console table and pier glass*
Matthias Lock. *c.* 1745
Victoria & Albert Museum
See cat. L10, L12

XIV *Armchair*
Attributed to John Bladwell
Gilt wood with tapestry upholstery.
The tapestry from the workshop of
Danton. 1755-60
The National Trust (Uppark)
See cat. L29

XV *Door to the French Room at Woburn Abbey*
The design attributed to Giovanni Battista Borra. ? After Nicolas Pineau.
1747-*c.*1757
The Marquess of Tavistock and Trustees of the Bedford Estates, Woburn Abbey
See cat, M14

XVI *Design for the side of a room*
John Linnell. *c.* 1755
Victoria & Albert Museum
See cat. M15

XVII *A Family in an Interior*
Francis Joseph Nollekens. 1740
Private Collection
See cat. B3

Arms and Armour

Flintlock double-barrelled sporting gun. See Cat. J7.

J1 *Claymore and scabbard*
The hilt by Charles Frederick Kändler.
London hallmarks for 1740-41
Silver hilt, leather scabbard with silver
fittings; hilt and blade l. 960, hilt
l. 120 The blade etched on the outside
within a circle on a false-watered panel
Ne me/tire Pas/sans/Raison (draw me not
without reason) and on the inside on a
similar panel *Ne me/Remette/Point sans/
honneur* (sheath me not without
honour)
*The Sword is part of the Clanranald Collection
of family and Jacobite relics bequeathed to the
National Museum of Antiquities of Scotland
by the late Angus Roderick Macdonald, 23rd
Chief of Clanranald*

Basket guard, cast in a single piece,
decorated with figures of warriors, one
of whom is mounted and in classical
armour, a naked boy beating a drum,
a captive, and trophies of arms, all in
high relief amid pierced rococo
scrolls; on the front a figure of a
woman, symbolic of War, seated on a
cloud, her head forming the
projecting 'beak' of the hilt; the wrist
guard or rear quillon formed like a
crouching lion. The pommel, through
which the tang is riveted, is formed as
a horned owl. The grip is of wood
covered in white ray-skin with silver
wire Turk's head ferrules, and has a
spiral binding consisting of two bands
of wire, lying side by side, twisted in
opposite directions to give a herring-
bone effect. The light blade is back-
edged almost to the point and has a
broad fuller for almost its full length.
The surface is partly etched and gilt.
On each side there is the figure of a
man in pseudo-classical armour
holding a sword above which is
written the name 'hanniball'. A foliage
scroll runs some way up the spine.
The scabbard is of unlined black
leather, decorated with blind tooling
with saltires and marks like deer slots.
It has a silver locket incised on the
front with rococo scroll-work and
foliage, and on the back with a trophy
of arms amid rococo scrolls. The belt-
hook is decorated with acanthus
foliage. The silver chape has an
invected upper edge incised to match
the locket. Another scabbard
associated with the sword was made in
Edinburgh in June 1838.

Prov: George IV (B. Jutsham's Ms.
Carlton House Catalogue, No. 381,
where the tradition that this weapon

J1

belonged to Prince Charles Edward
Stuart is recorded); given by him
c. 1820 to Reginald George
Macdonald, Chief and Captain of
Clanranald (Mudie 1822, p. 210)
Lit: Grimwade 1976, 567, no. 691;
Proc. Soc. Antiq. Scot., CVIII, 1944-5,
pl. 178 & pl. XXII, Norman 1967
AVBN

J2 *Silver mounted targe*
English? *c.* 1740
Wood, covered with pigskin;
diam. 485
Mottoes (on silver escutcheons):
*Premitur. Non. Opprimitur; Deo Iuvante;
Pro Rege et Patria: Rursus Orietur Ad
Gloriam* and (on cap badge of trophy of
arms) *Gang Warily*
*National Museum of Antiquities of Scotland
LN 49*

The front is elaborately decorated with
chased silver work, shields, trophies of
arms, trumpets and drums, scrolls and
sunflower rosettes surrounding a
Medusa's head in whose mouth is the
threaded socket for a screw-in spike
(now missing). One sunflower rosette

has been replaced by a stud decorated with filigree of Scottish work. The back is covered with leopard skin. The targe is said to have belonged to Prince Charles Edward Stuart and to have been lost by him at Culloden. If this was indeed the case it is unlikely to have been a presentation piece from admirers as a near identical targe is preserved at Warwick Castle. More probably it is one of a group commissioned by an individual to give as presents to Jacobite leaders. The presence of the Drummond motto 'Gang Warily' might suggest an association with the Jacobite Duke of Perth. There is some doubt as to its place of manufacture; France being suggested by previous commentators. It is not unreasonable, however, to link it with other British-made rococo silverwork associated with Prince Charles, the basket hilted sword elsewhere in this exhibition and a canteen of cutlery by Ebenezer Oliphant, Edinburgh, 1740-1.

Prov: Sotheby's 23 May 1928, 101
Lit: Proc. Soc. Antiq. Scot. lxxix, 1944-5, 178-9
DNC

J3 *The Butcher*

George Bickham Junior (1706?-1771). 1746
Etching, coloured by hand; 321 x 197
Lettered with title and *Taken from ye Sign of a Butcher in Butcher Row* and with a verse. Dated *Decemr. 1746*
The Trustees of the British Museum

The butcher, an ox with a calf's head dressed as a butcher holding a bloody cleaver, stands before a burning house and a gibbet. The figure is the Duke of Cumberland who was believed to have ordered the barbarous treatment of the Jacobites after the Battle of Culloden. The frame is closely related to Cat. D13 and includes the same satyr's head. Also incorporated are burning torches and a dying thistle. The opposite view of Cumberland is taken in 'The True Contrast. The Royal British Hero – The Fright'nd Italian Bravo' of 1749, engraved by Anthony Walker (BM:S 2790) which has a sophisticated rococo frame. Its second edition was published in 1750 by Peter Angier.

Lit: BM:S 2843
MS

J4 *Air-gun*

Johan Gottfried Kolbe. *c.* 1743
Walnut stock mounted in cast, chased and engraved silver, the barrel of brass formerly silvered; barrel l. 1015; overall l. 1357
Engraved on top of barrel *Kolbe fecit Londini,* the lock engraved *Kolbe VAM (494-1894)*

This is undoubtedly one of the finest silver-mounted firearms in existence. A detailed examination of this gun was made in 1973 at the workshops of the Tower Armouries when all the silver mounts were removed. No marks of any kind were discovered. Dr Hayward pointed out that although the chiselling of the lock-plate is characteristically German, the silver mounts could well be English. The similarity in style between the chasing on the mounts and the work of contemporary watch-ca...makers has been noted. Certain elements of the design especially the carved rococo cartouche on the stock seem to be copied from the designs of De Lacollombe published in 1730 and 1743 by his pupil Gilles de Marteau as *Noveaux Desseins d'Arquebuserie.* Johan Gottfried Kolbe whose signature appears on the lock and barrel worked in Suhl in Thuringia, an important centre of the gunmaking trade. He is known to have worked in London between 1730 and 1737, and was celebrated as an engraver and steel-chiseller. Although the lock appears to be a conventional flint-lock, a catch on the tumbler operates a valve to allow compressed air into the barrel. The space between the barrel and outer brass sleeve forms the air-reservoir and the pump is set within the stock. Another air-gun of similar construction by Kolbe is in the Keith Neal Collection, and several other firearms signed by him are recorded including a fine garniture made for Charles III of Spain in the Capodimonte Museum, Naples. The allegorical figures on the stock appear to represent protagonists in the War of Austrian Succession: Prussia, Great Britain and France. The scene on the butt-plate may be intended for either Prague or Munich both of which surrendered during the campaign. George II led an allied army including Prussian troops against France in the campaign of 1743 which culminated in the battle of Dettingen. The allegorical references lend weight to the suggestion that this air-gun was made for George II just after the Dettingen campaign of 1742. It is not without significance that the page of designs from which the rococo cartouche on the stock is taken is also dated 1743.

Prov: Alexander Davison sale, Mr Farebrother, 21 April 1817, 592 'An unique air-gun formerly in the possession of George II'; acquired from Messrs. J. Sassoon & Co. in 1894
Lit: Blackmore 1965, pl. 736; Hayward 1963, p. 330.
AREN

J5 *Small-sword*

The knuckle guard marked *P.M.* in script and with London hallmarks for 1744/5 The shell guard also marked. The blade possibly German
Silver hilt: steel blade: overall l. 940
The Armouries, H M Tower of London (IX 2246)

Silver hilt of conventional form with all-metal grip. The pommel, grip, shell guards and quillon-block bear low relief ornament cast and chased in the rococo style. The decoration consists of writhen flutes enclosing panels of asymmetrical shell-work and sprigs of naturalistic flowers centred on musical and classical trophies. On the shell towards the blade are cascades of sea shells of various kinds. At the centre of the knuckle-guard is a diagonal panel chased with a design of asymmetrical shell-work flanked by swags of flowers. The slender knuckle-guard terminates in a small scroll where it joins the pommel, and *rocaille* ornament adorns both sides of the lobed end of the quillon. The straight, hollow-ground, three-edged blade tapers rather rapidly from the hilt for some eight inches. It is etched in fine line near the hilt with panels of strapwork interlace and scroll-work which flank an oval containing a roughly drawn tree with, beneath, a dog giving chase to a rabbit. The design runs over the spine of the blade on one side and is repeated on the broadest face inside the hand. The hilt-maker's mark is so far unidentified. It is first recorded on a sword-hilt in 1739-40, and was probably entered in the missing 1739 Small-workers' Book. This hilt is interesting because it represents a

dated British example of a class of
rococo hilt which was frequently cast
in gilt-brass and generally classified as
German.

Prov: Christie's, 17 Feb 1964, 118;
Christie's, 14 May 1975, 40, pl. 2; R.
Wiggington Esq., purchased
September 1982
Lit: Southwick 1982, p. 70, no. 163
SB

J5

J6 *Small-sword*

Anonymous. The hilt by I.R. *c.*1750
Hilt of cast and chased silver, the
shells decorated with punch work
Leather scabbard with silver mount;
overall l. 995, c. of hilt 165; w. of
shell-guard 73
Scabbard mount inscribed *Hervett
Temple Barr*. The maker's mark *I R*
stamped on the end of the knuckle-
bow and on the hook of the scabbard
mount
VAM (140+A-1978)

The decoration consists of fluted
designs overlaid with leaves and
acorns. The knuckle-bow, pommel
and shell-guard are decorated with
radiating flutes, the quillon block is
chased with a prominent rococo
cartouche in relief, the down-turned
quillon terminating in a grotesque
head. The blade of hollow triangular
section bears faint traces of etched and
engraved decoration. The maker I R
seems to have specialised in hilts
decorated with flutes overlaid with
leaves and acorns as another silver hilt
of this design was sold at auction in
1970. English silver hilts in this ornate
rococo style are unusual, the majority
from this period are decorated with
simple spiral fluting. Hervett was a
retailer and is not otherwise recorded.

Prov: acquired in 1978 from a dealer
Lit: Norman 1980, pp. 206, 207;
North 1982, pl. 48
AREN

J7 *Flintlock double-barrelled sporting gun*

William Bailes. The silver trigger
guard and butt plate marked JA.
London hallmarks for 1764-5.
Flat lockplates. The rounded cocks are
later replacements. Gold-lined pans.
Walnut half-stock inlaid with silver
wire and engraved silver plate. Mounts
of cast silver. Side-by-side browned
barrels octagonal from the blued false-
breech for approximately one third of
their length, and then round to the
muzzle. Silver bead foresight; scooped
backsight to the tang of the false-
breech. Wooden ramrod with a horn
tip; l. 1390. Calibre .626 in (19 bore)
The lockplates engraved *W. Bailes*. The
top flats inlaid in gold *William Bailes/
London*. Stamped on the underside of
the breech with the proof marks of the
London Gunmakers' Company as
used for those who were not Freemen

of the Company.
*The Armouries, H. M. Tower of London.
(XII-4669)*

This elegant sporting gun is unusual
in being partly decorated in the
Chinese style which was rarely used by
English gunmakers. One side of the
shoulder stock is decorated with
Chinoiserie figure scenes, and the
other with a more conventional scene
of a stag hunt against a background of
classical and castellated ruins. The
engraved decoration on the lock and
the cast decoration on the silver
mounts include a mixture of rococo
and classical motifs. For instance, the
maker's name engraved on the
lockplate is surrounded by a frame of
rocaille scrollwork, while the silver
escutcheon is in the form of a classical
bust of Minerva beneath a baldachin.
The maker of this gun, William Bailes,
worked in Bloomsbury from about
1745 until his death in 1766. A pair of
flintlock holster pistols by Bailes
(Tower of London Armouries, Inv.
XII 1649-50), have similar Chinoiserie
decoration on the stock, and it is
possible, therefore, that Bailes
specialised in this form of fashionable
ornament. The mark on the mounts is
so far unidentified.

Prov: The Earl of Eglinton; A.R. Dufty,
Esq FSA; purchased by the Armouries
1979
Exhib: Willmer House Museum,
Farnham 1962; the Art of the
Armourer, VAM 1963, Cat. No. 186;
Arms and Armour at the Dorchester,
Nov. 1982, Cat. No. 11
Lit: Hayward 1963, II, pl. 70a-b;
Blackmore 1965, pl. 204-5
GMW

J8 *Bill: Jonathan Stanton, gun maker*

J. Pack. The bill dated 1763
The bill-head 89 x 146; the sheet
131 x 166
The Guildhall Library (65380)

'Nephew & Successor to the late
Mr Turvey next Furnivals Inn
Holborn'. The bill (cut) is for cleaning
guns for 'Wych esqr.' The design was
re-used for an invitation to the Court
of Assistants of the Gunmakers'
Company 1835 (Museum of London,
77.82/117).
MS

Base Metal

Rich Iron Gate.

Design for a gate, J. Jores after Gabriel Huquier. See Cat. K2.

K1 *Lock*

Anonymous. *c.* 1742
Cast brass; 114 x 178
The Trustees of Sir William Turners Hospital

One of a pair of pew-locks from the chapel of Sir William Turner's Hospital, Kirkleatham. The Hospital, an almshouse, was almost completely rebuilt from 1742 onwards by Cholmley Turner. The Chapel, the interior of which was completed in 1748, was very possibly designed by James Gibbs, who designed the Turner mausoleum attached to the nearby parish church. Several of the chapel fittings may have come from Gibbs's chapel at Canons House, Middlesex (built 1716-20, demolition sale 1747), but they could not have included the very remarkable flame-shaped rococo pew-locks, which appear to have no parallels either in Britain or the Continent. Their vigorous modelling probably places them in the 1740s. The rococo lock of the Codrington Library, All Souls College, Oxford, which is more conservative in design, was supplied in 1751.

Lit: Cornforth 1977, fig. 10
MS

K2 *Design for a gate*

J. Jores after Gabriel Huquier. 1759
Etching; 282 x 205
Lettered *Rich Iron Gate* and numbered *10*
VAM (E.4698-1907)

From *A New Book of Ironwork . . . Design'd by J. Jores,* published by Robert Sayer, 1759 (title and 20 plates). The first twelve plates are revised copies after suites F and G of Gabriel Huquier's *Nouveau Livre de Serrurerie* (Berlin 1939, 1360; BN:Fonds, 428-487). This print is after suite G (*Livre de Grilles à divers usages*), plate 2. The French origin of the plates is carefully disguised; a design for a Grand Garden Gate (pl. 8) is one of several taken from Huquier's projects for ironwork in the choir of Amiens Cathedral. The remaining plates in the book, chiefly of sign irons in the Chinese, Gothic and 'Modern Taste', show the much less extreme rococo style then in use in English ironwork.

Lit: Harris 1960
MS

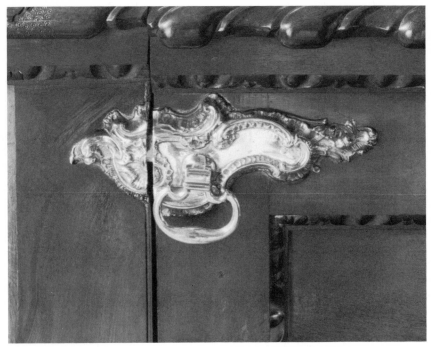

K1

K3 *Trade cards*

The Trustees of the British Museum (Heal 130.24; 85.93; 85.83)

a) Thomas Winspear, distiller and tobacconist. Anonymous. *c.* 1750?; 194 x 155 (cut). Winspeare's sign, the Angel and Still is shown hanging from an elaborate rococo sign-iron.

b) Anthony Dyckhoff, tin plate worker. Gabriel Smith (1742-83) probably after John Linnell (*c.* 1737-1796). *c.* 1755; 195 x 152 (cut). Dyckhoff was at this address after 1748 and before 1761. The scrolling ornament recalls Smith's etchings after Linnell (Cat. G41) as well as some of Linnell's drawings (eg VAM E183-1929). The Chinese pavilion over the door approached by the lamp lighter is very close to Linnell's bed made for Badminton, 1752-4 Hayward & Kirkham 1980, pl. 1.

c) Edward Denby and William Crook, founders and smiths. Simon Hennekin. *c.* 1765; 120 x 157. The founder on the left holds a hall lantern and a rococo girandole; the oval cartouche is neo-classical in feeling. Hennekin, a carver and gilder, also engraved his own trade card (Heal 32.31).
MS

K4 *Design for a clock*

William Herbert. 1759
Pen and ink and wash; 35 x 44 (drawing)
Inscribed on the *verso* in pencil *an Invention of Ornament under 20 Class 59 No. 1 Wm. Herbert at Mr Vivares Newport Leicester Fields.* The clock lettered at the top *Quebeck Taken 1759*
The Royal Society of Arts

A mantlepiece clock on four legs. The framing of the dial is baroque, but the scrollwork elseqwhere is wilfully asymmetrical and rococo. On the left is an English rural scene with a huntsman and on the right Roman ruins with mythological figures, perhaps an allusion to the passing of time or to the growth of England's Empire. At the top are French trophies. The design won the second prize of five guineas in its class: 'For the best Drawings or Compositions of Ornaments, being original Designs, fit for Weavers, Callico-Printers, or any Art or Manufacture, by Youths under the Age of Twenty'.
MS

K5 *Stove plate*
Abraham Buzaglo. 1765
Cast iron; 572 x 350
Lettered *Buzaglo fecit 1765*
Claude Blair

Rectangular, decorated in relief on
one face with a rococo cartouche, set
between foliated rods and framing a
vase of flowers; at the top the
inscription divided by a swag. A rare
example of English rococo ironwork,
it is all that remains of one of the
household stoves patented by Buzaglo
(1716-88), a Moroccan Jew, in 1765
and which became celebrated for the
relief of gout. Only two complete
stoves are known: one, rococo, dated
1770, at Williamsburg, Virginia,
whither it was sent for the Governor,
Lord Botetourt; the other, neo-
classical, and dated 1774, at Knole,
Kent. Records of stoves exist in the
archives at Winchester College and
Cambridge University the latter
including an elaborate trade bill with
engravings of all the different designs,
which were sold at premises 'facing
Somerset House'. Buzaglo became an
authority on the gout, on which he
wrote a treatise, and was satirised by
Francis Grose and Paul Sandby in
1783.

Prov: bought in Framlingham, Suffolk
Lit: Roth 1971
CB

K4

K5

K6 *Coffin plate and escutcheon with handle*
Supplied by Thomas Chippendale
(1718-1779). 1772
Brass; 406 x 305 x 184 x 267
The plate engraved *Bridget Heathcote.
The Widow & Relict of Sir John Heathcote
Bart. Died May the 5th 1772. Aged 68
years* and with her coat of arms. The
plate stamped on the back BW
crowned, in a circle
The Chippendale Society

From a a coffin at Normanton
Church, Rutland. Chippendale took
charge of all the arrangements for the
funeral of the Dowager Lady
Heathcote. The 'Brass plate of
Inscriptions with the Coat of Arms
neatly Engrav'd and Gilt & C'cast. £4.
The handles, together with the outside
coffin, £17.' The rococo style survived
in coffin furniture long after it had
ceased to be fashionable elsewhere.
The fittings were almost certainly
obtained from a specialist
manufacturer.

Prov: given by the Earl of Ancaster
Lit: Gilbert 1973, pl. 38B, 40A; Gilbert
1978, pp. 249-52, pl. 511
MS

K6

151

K7 *Watch stand*

Anonymous, probably Birmingham. *c.*
1770 or later(?)
Cast brass; h. 321
City of Manchester Art Galleries

A figure of Time, holding an hour-
glass, sits on top of the asymmetrical
cartouche which forms the frame for
the watch. The base is composed of
three swirled feet, in the manner of
silver figure-candlesticks. This stand
differs from the more common type in
which Time sits at the bottom. This
latter type is shown in a number of
brass-founders' pattern books
together with the two other types of
watch stands, the putti and an owl,
and a shepherd and shepherdess, the
last being perhaps derived from a
plate in Cat. L16. The pattern books
which are believed to have been
produced for Birmingham
manufacturers, contain both rococo
and neo-classical designs and should
probably be dated to the later 1760s
or even later. There is evidence to
suggest that the conservatism of the
designs is a reflection of the
importance of the tastes of the foreign
market for which the catalogues may
have been principally intended.

Lit: Gentle & Field 1975, pl. 186;
Goodison 1975, cat. 3, 4, 6
MS

K7

Furniture and Carving

6

Cat. L5

153

Rococo Furniture and Carving
John Hardy

'I am really a very pretty connoisseur in furniture',[1] claimed the architect William Chambers (1714-85) when criticising some drawings by Thomas Chippendale (1714-79), and indeed, the design of furniture was an important branch of the architect's profession in the 18th century. On the other hand, upholders like Chippendale, who employed an army of cabinet-makers, carvers, upholsterers, glass grinders, mercers, smiths and other tradesmen, considered that it was they who were the true connoisseurs in the fitting up and furnishing of a house. Whereas a tightly controlled guild system in France had led to greater specialisation and superior craftsmanship, in England there tended to be a general free-for-all, so that we find architects, upholders and carvers all providing designs for ceilings and wall-elevations as well as for individual pieces of furniture.

Throughout the first half of the century it was primarily France that set the fashion for grand English furnishings. The baroque style created by Jean Berain (1640-1711), Le Brun (1619-90), Pierre Lepautre (1648-1716) and others for Louis XIV was made available in England by the architectural publications and engravings sold by bookshops and print-sellers, and in particular was promoted by the Huguenot Daniel Marot (c.1660-1752), who was architect and designer to William and Mary and whose *Œuvres Du Sr. D. Marot*, 1702 was republished as late as 1727.

The large numbers of foreign artists and craftsmen working in London helped to propagate the French taste in furnishings, which flourished in spite of the attempts by Richard, 3rd Earl of Burlington (1694-1753), William Kent (1685-1748) and others to 'correct' English taste by laying down rules for a classical style of interior decoration. This was influenced by the designs of the Italian architect, Andrea Palladio (1508-80), of the English architect, Inigo Jones (1573-1652), and combined with Italian baroque ornament. Kent, who acquired the post of Master Carpenter to the Board of Works in 1726, created an 'Italian' style of interior decoration and furniture, which mingled bold architectural forms with vigorously sculpted three-dimensional ornament – fat acanthus leaves, scallop shells, classical figures, putti, and animals. His heavy classical style was later made available in publications by Isaac Ware and John Vardy in the 1730s and 1740s[2] and therefore ran parallel with the introduction of the rococo style. The Palladians' severe architectural approach to interior decoration tended to drive a wedge between the architect's furniture designs and those of the upholder and carver, who generally preferred to follow the contemporary French style, which had abandoned 'regular' forms in an attempt to lighten, enliven and add variety. From the 1730s irregularity and assymmetry combined with elegance and lightness were considered the essence of beauty. The new decorative style was compounded of a 'medley and a contrariety'[3] of curved mouldings, sculptural forms and a profusion of ornaments that tended to dominate rather than be governed by architecture. Making architecture 'speak nonsense'[4] was one of the important ingredients of the rococo style. For instance the form of a pediment or cornice on the exterior of a building was limited by its function of throwing off rain water, whereas on furnishings they merely served a decorative purpose, and could be broken, scrolled or infinitely varied and ornamented. A light-hearted touch was the application of watery ornament, such as on the cornice of the Petworth bed-head (Cat. L49).

French pattern-books and engravings flooded into London, and as the style evolved on the continent, the designs came also from Italy and Germany. The catalogues of booksellers show that the designs of Le Pautre, Poilly, Rossi, Boucher, Cuvilliés, Babel, Toro, De la Joue and Watteau were all available and were ransacked not only by craftsmen but also by publishers.[5] The 1750s scrap book of the carver Gideon Saint (Cat. L72)[6] includes engraved designs and drawings after Jean Berain, François Roumier, André Charles Boulle, Jean Mariette and Nicolas Pineau.[7]

During the second quarter of the 18th century, as fashionable London expanded westwards into Mayfair, St Martin's Lane took over from the area around St Paul's Churchyard as the centre of the cabinet-making and upholstery industry and became the breeding ground for the new style. In particular the St Martin's Lane Academy, founded in 1735, appears to have played an important role in introducing artists, architects, sculptors and other craftsmen to the *Régence* and early Louis XV styles. The French artist, Hubert François Gravelot, who taught at the Academy as well as at his own school in the Strand, helped to introduce the beautifully sculpted serpentine line that was such an important element of the rococo style.[8] William Hogarth, a prominent member of the Academy, was the person to devise a rationale for the rococo. In his *Analysis of Beauty*, 1753 he said that the straight line was 'unnatural' and that a beautiful design should have a serpentine line, which curled in all three dimensions to give the outline a novel variety as well as expressing motion. He also stressed the fact that nature could provide all the range of ornament that was needed by the artist or designer. The main structure of many designs was provided by the acanthus leaf which was so important to classically designed ornament; but in the rococo it is no longer confined stiffly to the capital, frieze or bracket, but breaks out with its scrolling stem. Indeed, an important element of rococo is the triumph of nature, and this was not confined just to furniture and works of art: rather as vegetation veiled the ruins of man-made classical architecture, so the 'unnatural' formal gardens of earlier times were swept aside to bring the landscape park with its trees, plants, serpentine rivers or lakes, its animals and birds, right up to the house. The parks were viewed as Arcadia, and the architects improved their picturesque quality by ornamenting them with temples, seats, gazebos, grottoes, sculpture and trelliswork. The garden buildings not only served as menageries, aviaries and hot-houses but were used as outdoor drawing-rooms and eating-rooms and were furnished accordingly. Amongst the many published designs for garden furniture were rustic seats made from the roots or branches of trees.[9] George Edwards and Matthias Darly in their *New Book of Chinese Designs*, 1754 (Cat. R9) issued engravings of Chinese chairs made from contorted roots, while Robert Manwaring, in *The Cabinet and Chair-Makers Real Friend and Companion*, 1765 illustrated chairs, 'Executed with the limbs of yew, apple or pear trees, ornamented with leaves and blossoms, which if properly painted will appear like nature'. Of these hundreds of pleasances, and the furniture made for them, only a fraction has survived distorting our view of rococo furniture production.

Nature also triumphed inside the house, where flowers and foliage provided the principal decorative motifs for the furnishings and furniture. For example, on the mirror frame (Cat. L19) the most admired ornament of any park – the ancient oak beside water – was brought indoors and miniaturised, bending over the glassy surface. Just as architecture had been made to 'speak nonsense', so scale was often ignored and the natural proportions of carved plants, animals or birds, were varied as much as those on Anglo-Indian textiles or Chinese wall-papers. The real or imaginary inhabitants of the woods, parks and grottoes, also invaded the house, and satyrs and nymphs, shepherds and shepherdesses, hunters and huntresses together with moralising animals from Aesop's Fables and strange figures from Ovid's Metamorphoses, were no longer confined to canvas but inhabited the furnishings. Certain figures or ornaments were appropriate for the various rooms of a house: bacchic figures and vines might appear in the dining room, musical trophies and flowers in the drawing room, and cupids, doves and amorous trophies in the bedrooms and dressing rooms. All these fantastic carved and gilded concoctions, which comprised a true mingle-mangle of architectural elements, foliage and figures, must have come alive by candlelight.

The rococo domination of architecture by ornament and its rejection of the 'correct' rules caused the 'French' style to be considered in much the same way as the Chinese and Gothic. Variety became the crucial element in a fashionable house and led to each room or set of apartments being treated in different styles. Thus the carver Luke Lightfoot (c. 1722-89) at Claydon House, Buckinghamshire created rooms in the classical, gothic, chinese and french tastes.[10] In turn the ornaments of the various styles often came to be fused on a single item, such as the Master's chair of the Joiner's Company (Cat. R4).

In France and Germany the rococo was a wholly interpenetrating, organic style, which embraced architecture and furnishings, but in England, rooms with French style *boiseries* and furniture, were comparatively rare: the majority mixed classical and rococo decoration. This is best understood by looking at two rooms in detail. Both are picture galleries, one devised for Henry, 7th Viscount Irwin at Temple Newsam House, Yorkshire around 1740 and the other for Lord Littleton at Hagley Hall, Warwickshire in the 1750s. At Temple Newsam House the 'continued' chimneypieces were modelled on a classical design by William Kent,[11] but the furniture was executed in the rococo style, with acanthus scrolls and rocaille ornament. The frames of the table (Cat. L8) and candlestands (Cat. L7) were carved in allusion to Arcadia, the paradise of pastoral poets, ruled over by Pan, the God of flocks and herds, and they depict a scene from Ovid's Metamorphoses. The wall-sconces (Cat. L9) were carved with hunting scenes of hounds attacking stags, and heads of hounds also appear on the arms of the settees, which were upholstered in floral needlework.

At Hagley a long gallery was created giving fine views over the old park, which was greatly admired at the time. The walls were hung with ancestral portraits set in mahogany frames ornamented with fruit-wood carvings of acanthus and oak foliage. The furniture comprised pier-glasses, girandoles, wall-lights and candlestands (Cat. L45) and was carved with trees, craggy branches, windmills and dripping rock-work etc., and painted to resemble old wood that was slowly being petrified. This 'landscaped' gallery then led into the 'garden' drawing room, whose walls and seat furniture were covered with brilliantly coloured floral tapestries and the carved and gilded pier-glasses and tables were ornamented with baskets and festoons of flowers.

Who were the inventive minds behind English rococo furnishings?[12] An early and influential pattern book was by the Italian artist Gaetano Brunetti (Cat. B10, B11), whose *Sixty Draughts of Different Sorts of Ornaments in the*

Italian Taste, appeared in 1736. This was followed by William De la Cour's eight *Books of Ornaments* (1741-8 (Cat. C11)), which, like Brunetti's publication, illustrated chairs, tables and mirrors, and the wildly asymmetrical cartouches, which were such an important feature of the new style. Asymmetrical cartouches comprised of rocaille and garlanded acanthus scrolls also appeared in the engraver, Henry Copland's *New Book of Ornaments*, 1746 (Cat. L16), where they were accompanied by pastoral figures, a triumph of Neptune, putti and a dragon.[13]

The architect, Isaac Ware, in his *Body of Architecture*, 1756 (Cat. M6), made it clear that any young architect who wanted employment had to be able to design in the curvilinear French style, and laid down rules for drawing elegant and airy rococo ornament with continuous curves composed of forward and backward 'Cs', foliage and flowers. The Palladian architect, John Vardy[14] designed furniture ornamented with richly scrolling foliage, but it lacks the extravagant contours and free-flowing sculptural frame-work that can be seen in the furniture designed by the architect, James Paine (1718-89). Paine, more than any other architect, reflects the teaching of Gravelot and the St. Martin's Lane Academy (see Cats. L26, M10). Amongst the craftsmen, Matthias Lock (*c.*1710-65), a master carver and teacher of ornaments was the most important exponent of the rococo style in furniture. His furniture label of 1746 (See cat. L17) displays a light fanciful cartouche combining sweep cornices, garlanded acanthus scrolls, branches, bulrushes and rocaille inhabited by a dragon and a bird. These motifs, together with trellis work, emblematic trophies and scroll terms with rustic heads, such as appear on the Hinton House furniture (Cat. L10, L12) are published in his *Six Sconces*, 1744 (Cat. L4) and *Six Tables*, 1746 (Cat. L5). The latter were intended to accompany the sconces, and comprised patterns for console table frames, stands and wall-brackets. The acanthus leaf and asymmetrical cartouche, which provide the essential structure of these designs, formed the subject of three pattern books dating from around 1746 – *Principles of Ornament or the Youth's Guide to Drawing of Foliage* (Cat. E19), *A Book of Shields* and *A New Drawing Book of Ornaments, Shields, Masks etc.* In the early 1750s Chinese elements played an increasingly important role in his publications, first in *A New Book of Ornaments for Looking Glass Frames, Chimney Pieces etc. in the Chinese Taste*, and then in *A New Book of Ornaments*, 1752 (Cat. L24), which was issued in conjunction with Henry Copland and illustrated designs for chimneys, sconces, tables, stands, girandoles, chandeliers, clocks, etc. His talents as a draughtsman were mentioned in a letter written by the upholder James Cullen to Lord Hopetoun in 1768. 'The Enclosed Drawings are valuable being designed and drawn by the famous Mr Matt. Lock lately deceased who was reputed the best Draftsman in that way that had ever been in England'.[15]

Thomas Johnson (1714-*c.*1778), master carver and teacher of drawing and modelling followed in Lock's footsteps as a publisher of furniture pattern books.[16] His *Twelve Girandoles*, 1755 are in a lighter and more fanciful style than Lock's and combine a mixture of architectural fantasy with rocaille and spiky vegetation inhabited by birds, animals and rustic figures. He followed this with designs for carver's work, which were issued monthly and then appeared as an untitled suite in 1758 (Cat. L44). They ranged from ceilings and wall-elevations to organs and clock cases, and were dedicated to Lord Blakeney, Grand President of the Anti-Gallican Society, which had been founded in the mid 1740s in an attempt to promote British Manufactures by 'preventing the importation of the insiduous arts and fashions of the French Nation'.[17] One such art was the manufacture of *papier mâché* frames and ornaments, which threatened the carver's market, and on his title page Johnson drew the carver's figure of 'genius' setting fire to scrolls of 'French paper machee'. In 1760 Johnson issued *A New Book of Ornaments* (Cat. L48). This included patterns for mirrors, tables etc. as well as for 'continued' chimneypieces, one of whose overmantel frames combined a mirror, painting, busts, and candlebranches merged together in true rococo spirit. Chimneypiece tablets and friezes provided the subject of another *New Book of Ornaments*, 1762 (Cat. L48) which included rural vignettes as well as swirling foliage and dragon heads.[18]

Both Matthias Lock's and Johnson's furniture appears to have been marketed through the leading upholders' firms: for example, in Johnson's case George Cole of Golden Square probably supplied his furniture to Corsham Court and Blair Castle (L46).[19]

Matthias Darly (active *c.*1750-78) is well-known because of his role in engraving the majority of the plates for Chippendale's *The Gentleman and Cabinet-Maker's Director*, (1754) (Cat. L32) but he had an independent career as well.[20] He was an ornamentalist and engraver and at one time styled himself 'Painter of Ornaments to the Academy of Great Britain'. His speciality was providing drawings for 'Gentlemen, mechanics etc.' designing trade cards and publishing rococo pattern books for furniture. The first of these, *A New Book of Chinese, Gothic and Modern Chairs*, 1750/1 (Cat. L21) illustrated chairs with elaborately fretted and scrolled backs, in the manner of those in William De la Cour's, *Fifth Book of Ornaments*, 1743.[21] During 1753 he shared a house with Chippendale in Northumberland Court, and it has been suggested that he served as Chippendale's drawing master. At this time he was engaged in engraving the plates for *A New Book of Chinese Designs*, which he issued in collaboration with George Edwards (1694-1773) in the following year, and was also preparing many of the plates for the *Director*, to which over three hundred people subscribed, and which helped to found Chippendale's towering reputation. In the late 1750s he was involved in engraving plates for two other major rococo furniture pattern books, firstly for William Ince and John Mayhew's *Universal System of Household Furniture* (Cat. M21), which was published in parts between 1759 and 1763, and secondly *Household Furniture in Genteel Taste for the Year 1760 by a Society of Upholsterers, Cabinet-Makers etc.*, which was issued by the print seller Robert Sayer and contained designs by Johnson, Chippendale, Ince & Mayhew, Robert Manwaring and others.[22]

The publication of the *Director* was first announced in March 1753 as 'Being a New Book of Designs of Household Furniture in the Gothic, Chinese and Modern Taste, as improved by the politest and most able artists'. The significance of the *Director* was that, with its 161 plates, it was the first furniture pattern book to cover the entire range of household furniture. It was intended, 'To assist the one [i.e. the patron] in the Choice, and the other [i.e. the craftsman] in the Execution of the Designs; which are so contrived, that if no one Drawing should singly answer the Gentleman's taste, there will yet be found a Variety of Hints, sufficient to construct a new one.' Its success led to a second edition in 1755 and a revised and enlarged edition in 1762, included a number of neo-classical designs together with an increased use of emblematical ornament and figures.

Furniture design in general, and the design of chairs in particular, was affected by the fact that tough, close-grained mahogany replaced walnut as the fashionable wood during the second half of the century. The new wood could take far more stress than walnut, so that the splat of a parlour chair, for instance, was pared away and contorted into a variety of shapes rather like wrought iron balusters. At the same time the various elements of the chair frame began to be merged together to produce serpentine forms such as appear in the portraits of Francis Hayman in the 1740s.

The upholstered drawing-room chair also underwent a change and tended to grow broader. It was often given a scrolled cartouche back, framed on four sides, and contracted in the 'French' manner so that there was a gap between the base rail and seat frame (Cat. L38), in the manner of chairs illustrated in prints after Meissonnier. Even more than chairs, mirrors probably gave the rococo designer the greatest scope for invention. Because English rooms tended to be hung with textiles or paper, and carved woodwork like that in the *Régence*/rococo music room at Norfolk House (Cat. B16) was comparatively rare, the pier-glasses and overmantel mirrors were nearly always treated as loose fittings, rather than incorporated in the woodwork as in France. Picture frames similarly provided endless opportunity for creative designs and, following a long tradition, their ornament was often related to the subject of the painting or the rank, heraldry, occupation or interests of the sitter (Cat. L1). In general, heraldry was a rich source of ornamental ideas.

In a grand drawing-room, the pier glass was generally accompanied by a marble-topped table, its frame usually en suite with it. During the second quarter of the century the console table form, with one or two legs, and its frame fixed to the wall, became increasingly popular (Cat. L10). The window pier of a library might be occupied by a desk, while that in a bedroom or dressing room might take a mahogany chest of drawers, or a 'French' commode fitted with doors. In accordance with the rococo style their forms became increasingly serpentine or bombé, and their frames were decorated with carving or applied mounts, and sometimes inlaid with marquetry of various woods or with brass in the French manner. Amongst the sale of stock of a cabinet-maker in St Martin's Lane in 1735 were 'Buroes richly inlaid and ornamented with bronze . . . in the finest French taste'. John Channon, who was one of the leading cabinet-makers in St Martin's Lane in the 1740s, is credited with having produced the mahogany desk (Cat. L2) with its undulating form enriched in the French manner with brass inlay and ormolu mounts.

Commodes in the French taste were the speciality of the *ébéniste* Pierre Langlois (active 1756-*c*.76), who traded at the 'Sign of the Commode Table' in Tottenham Court Road. His elaborate rococo trade card (Cat. L34) was illustrated with a floral marquetry chest of drawers, a small table, a bracket clock and ormolu candlebranches, and it stated that he made 'All sorts of fine cabinets and commodes . . . inlaid in the Politest manner with brass and tortoiseshell and likewise all rich ornamental clockcases and inlaid work mended with great care'. A particularly fine example of his work is the Louis XV style marquetry commode, (Cat. L54) decorated with flowers and a trophy of pastoral music, which he supplied to John, 4th Duke of Bedford in 1760. Langlois was also famed for his ability to mould lacquer panels, and in 1763 supplied a pair of serpentine-fronted and lacquer-mounted commodes for Horace Walpole's gallery at Strawberry Hill.[24]

But the role of the craftsmen who, like Lock or Johnson, remained specialist carvers, or even the successful cabinet-maker, Langlois, was much less important than that of the upholders, who, as mentioned earlier, were capable of the entire fitting up and furnishing of a house. They ran large workshops and also acted as middlemen for other craftsmens' work. Among the most important ones in mid 18th century London were James Whittle, Samuel Norman, William Mayhew and John Ince, William and John Linnell, Thomas Chippendale and James Rannie, John Cobb and William Vile. Messrs. Vile and Cobb were cabinet-makers and upholsterers to George II and George III, and they supplied the jewel cabinet for Queen Charlotte in 1761 (Cat. L60). Norman was in partnership with his father-in-law, Whittle, in 1755 and they worked as master carvers, before setting up as upholders with Mayhew in 1758. In 1762 he held the posts of Master Carver in Wood to the Office of Works, sculptor and carver to their Majesties [George III and Queen Charlotte] and 'Surveyor of the curious carvings at Windsor Castle'.[25] He supplied furniture for Woburn Abbey (Cat. L55) as well as to Charles Wyndham, 2nd Earl of Egremont. The Petworth bed (Cat. L49), which is attributed to his firm, is perhaps the grandest rococo state bed produced in England. Mayhew was only in partnership with Norman and Whittle for a few months, before he went into partnership with the cabinet-maker Ince and set up an upholstery, cabinet-making and carving business at Broad Street, Carnaby Market.[26] They almost immediately launched their 'Universal System of Household Furniture', (Cat. M21) for which Ince produced most of the designs. William Linnell, who began his career as a master carver, acquired large new premises in Berkeley Square in 1754, and set up as an upholder with his son John. John Linnell had been trained at the St. Martin's Lane Academy and executed the large collection of late rococo drawings for carving, upholstery and cabinet-maker's work, now at the VAM (Cat. E26). Among them are his designs of 1761 for the grandest suite of seat furniture produced in the 18th century – the four gilded merfolk settees supplied for Kedleston Hall, Derbyshire.[27] In 1754, the same year that the Linnells moved to Berkeley Square, and the *Director* first appeared Chippendale went into partnership with the upholder James Rannie (d. 1766) and moved to new premises at The Cabinet and Upholstery Warehouse in St Martin's Lane. They traded at the sign of the chair, which was no doubt a 'French' chair similar to that depicted on their trade card/label[28] and of which a number of patterns were illustrated in the *Director*. Some of the designs in the *Director* had already been executed before its publication including the parlour chair with a 'ribband' splat, of which, according to Chippendale, 'Several sets have been made, which have given entire satisfaction'. But comparatively few rococo pieces have been traced among over a thousand items documented to the firm; of these some fine examples are the furniture supplied to Dumfries House (Cat. L36, L37). The major episode of Chippendale's career as a furniture maker however was to come in the neo-classical period.

During the 1760s, many of the rococo pattern books were reissued; however, there was a gradual return to the 'true' style of interior decoration, as suggested by Isaac Ware in 1756. This was assisted by the revolutionary neo-classicism of architects such as William Chambers and Robert Adam (1728-92). The battle of the fashionable styles is evident in 1766 when David Garrick and George Colman mock at the rococo in *The Clandestine Marriage*: 'Ay, here's none of your straight lines here – but all taste – zig-zag – crinkum-crankum – in and out – right and left – so and again – twisting and turning like a worm'.

L1 *The Shooting Party*

John Wootton (?1683-1764). 1740
The frame by Paul Petit (active *c.* 1740-45). 1742
Oil on canvas; 889 x 740
Signed and dated *JW 1740*
Her Majesty The Queen

One of Wootton's most important portrait groups, painted for Frederick, Prince of Wales, who is shown seated on the right, wearing the ribbon and star of the Garter. The other figures are (centre) Charles Douglas, 3rd Duke of Queensberry (1698-1778), Gentleman of the Bedchamber to the Prince, and (left) John Spencer (1708-46), favourite grandson of Sarah, Duchess of Marlborough. He succeeded her as Ranger of Windsor Great Park in 1744, but died soon afterwards, it is said of a surfeit of brandy, small beer and tobacco. As the leading sporting painter of his day, Wootton was extensively patronised by the Prince of Wales and his circle from the 1730s onwards, and a series of impressive canvases, concerned with the Prince's activities in the hunting field, are still in the Royal Collection. Wootton's retirement sale of 12-13 March 1761 shows that he kept versions of several of his royal commissions in his studio throughout his working life, including one of this group (lot 97, possibly the version now at Drumlanrig).

   The rectangular frame is ornamented with hunting trophies amongst scrolled and lambrequined mouldings. The side scrolls entwine a hunting sword, powder flask, bow and quiver of arrows together with oak leaves and bulrushes. A dead snipe and duck lie on the cornice, and a hawk stands astride a dead bird on the base rail, where hound's heads emerge from the watery scrolls at the corners. On the crest rail a lion's head supports the Prince of Wales's coronet and feathers. The carver Paul Petit's bill to Frederick Prince of Wales, dated Oct 6 1742, includes 'A rich picture frame carved with birds richly ornamented neatly repair'd [prepared] and gilt in burnished gold to a picture of His Royal Highness painted by Mr Wootton . . .£21.'

Lit: Edwards 1974, p. 414, fig. 19;
Millar 1963, cat. 547, fig. 195
JH & EE

L1

L2 *Desk*

Attributed to John Channon (active *c.* 1733-83). *c.* 1740
Mahogany with ormolu mounts and brass inlay; 890 x 7240 x 575
VAM (W.4-1956)

This serpentine and *bombé* desk is decorated with brass inlay and elaborate ormolu mounts. The fitted frieze drawer is linked to corner trusses, which support it when open. The pedestals of drawers flank a recessed nest of smaller drawers, within an arched niche. Similar arched recesses and carrying-handles appear on the side of the desk. The corner mounts comprise winged satyr heads on scallop-shell shoulders from which water drips over palm and laurel sprays to form watery splashes at the feet, where scalloped acanthus cartouches conceal the castors. Framing the central recess are heads of water nymphs with acanthus-scroll shoulders from which water drips onto open scallop-shells garlanded with shell- and rock-work. Winged dolphins frame the acanthus cartouche on the apron, while the escutcheon on the frieze drawer is framed by palm and oak branches and garlanded with shell- and rock-work. The backplates of the large handles are formed of winged cartouches with acanthus foliage. It is possible that this and a similar desk (missing some of the mounts and without the nest of drawers; sold Sotheby's 12 Feb. 1965) were provided for William, 1st Viscount Courtenay's (1710-62) library

L2

at Powderham Castle, Devon. Two brass-inlaid library bookcases at Powderham have similar dolphin mounts and bear plaques engraved 'J.Channon 1740'. John Channon traded at the Sign of The Cabinet in St Martin's Lane, and was one of the subscribers to *The Director*, (1754). Amongst related furniture attributed to Channon are a bureau-cabinet surmounted by figures of Venus and Bacchus (ill. Coleridge 1968, fig. 64). The two corner mounts with their fountain/cascade ornament can be compared to the patterns for shields 'of a new invention', copied by Edward Hoppus and published in *The Gentleman's and Builder's Repository*, 1737, pl. LXXIII. The very naturalistic shell and rock-work garlands can also be seen on contemporary silver by Huguenot silversmiths such as Nicholas Sprimont (1716-1771) and Paul Crespin (1694-1776).

Prov: Possibly from Powderham Castle, Devon. By tradition William Beckford Collection; and Peter Admiral Walcott Collection; H.Blairman & Sons Ltd
Lit: Coleridge 1968, fig 61; Hayward 1965, I, no. 1, fig. 5; Symonds 1965

L3

L3 *A Classical landscape with ruins*
John Wootton (?1683-1764)
Oil on canvas, in a carved and gilt frame; 940 x 864
The Mapledurham Collection

Although early in his career Wootton prospered chiefly as a 'horse-painter', he was also the first British painter with a genuine bent for landscape, which, either in the topographical or classical mode, is a dominant element in his best sporting pieces. Later he was more frequently identified as a landscape painter and as such

evidently applied himself seriously to the study of the classical masters, for as early as 1722 Vertue describes him as a distinguished landscape painter in the manner of Gaspard Poussin. His pure landscapes tend to be decorative pastiches of 17th century Italianate works, whose picturesque ruinscapes and intensified light-effects formed an agreeable adjunct to classicising interiors, chiefly in architectural positions such as chimney breasts and overdoors. The painting has been linked with 'a Ruen by Wooton in Ditto [a gold frame]' which was in the Little Parlour of Alexander Pope's Villa at Twickenham in 1744 (MS inventory of the Villa, probably made for probate at the poet's death, see Notes and Queries, 6th series, 13 May 1882, pp. 363-5). Also at Mapledurham are a Flemish landscape and a mirror, both in frames *en suite* with that of the present painting. The latter may be the 'Large Glass in a gold Frame' in the Great Parlour of the Villa. All the frames are in the heavy style characteristic of the first phase of rococo carving in the early 1740s.

Prov: Alexander Pope; bequeathed to Martha Blount; by descent
Lit: GLC 1980, pp. 7, 23; Tate Gallery 1982, cat. 6, repr.; Vertue I, p. 101
MS & EE

L4 *Design for a pier glass*
Matthias Lock (*c.* 1710-1765). 1744
Etching; 238 x 160
VAM (27811.6)

From Lock's *Six Sconces,* 1744, the first rococo carvers' pattern book to be published in England. The extreme asymmetry of this design is perhaps deceptive as the print was probably intended to show two designs, each of which could be read by placing a small frameless mirror down the centre. The eagle at the top is taken from plate 6 of suite A of Gabriel Huquier's set after Oppenord, *Livre De Differents morceaux* (from the 'moyen Oppenord') Cat. A11. A pair of winged heads representing the winds appear at the base of the title cartouche of Lajoue's *Receuil Nouveau De differens cartouche* (Cat. G28), which may have influenced this plate. Matthias Lock was apprenticed to his father, also called Matthias, in 1724

L4

for eight years (Joiners' Company Apprentice Binding, vol. 4, p. 141). He married Mary Lee at St Paul's Covent Garden in July 1734, when he may already have been living in Long Acre, where he was from at least 1746 until 1750. In 1752 he was in Tottenham Court Road.

Lit: Heckscher 1979, pl. 3; Ward-Jackson 1958, 51
MS & NS

L5 *Design for a pier glass*
Matthias Lock (*c.* 1710-1765)
Etching; 249 x 155
Numbered *6*
VAM (E.3381-1938)

From Robert Sayer's edition, 1768, of *Six Sconces*

Lit: Heckscher 1979, pl. 6
MS

L6 *Design for a chimney-piece and picture frame*
Edward Rooker (1711-1774) after Abraham Swan (active 1745-1768). 1745
Engraving; 345 x 197 (cut)
Lettered *Ab. Swan in et de. E Rooker sc.* and with a copyright line dated 26 Jan 1745.
VAM (29476.164,165)

Plate 49 of Swan's *The British Architect: or, the Builder's Treasury of Staircases,*

L6

1745 (republished 1750, 1758). Swan's designs for chimney-pieces and frames represent an early and rather unhappy attempt to apply vigorous *rocaille* ornament to Palladian forms. This frame is described (p. 13) as 'a very rich Frame; the Ornament on the Top is represented something in the Form of a Pediment'. Picture frames after plate 48 were made probably in 1757 for Blair Atholl, when Swan also designed a staircase for the house.

Lit: Colvin 1978, p. 799; Ward-Jackson 1858, 38
MS

L7 *Two candlestands*
James Pascall (active 1723-d. 1747). 1745
Gilt pine; walnut. 1260 x 660 x 660
Leeds City Art Gallery

The triangular top with acanthus-scroll cornice is supported on a stem of garlanded bulrush fronds incorporating a bust of the nymph Syrinx, framed by watery sprays. The tripod feet are carved with watery *rocaille* and acanthus foliage springing from scroll toes. They are part of a set of eight stands, which are listed in a bill to Henry, 7th Viscount Irwin

L7

(1691-1761), dated 16 August 1745, from James Pascall (active 1723-d. 1747), carver, gilder, and frame-maker, 'For a rich pair of carved stands gilt in burnished gold . . . £26.0.0'. The other six stands were listed between June and August 1746. They were all supplied for the gallery at Temple Newsam House, Yorkshire, and flanked two pairs of tables. The ornament of the stands and tables is inspired by the story of Pan and Syrinx as recounted in Ovid's *Metamorphoses*. Syrinx, pursued through arcadia by Pan, god of woods, leaps into the river Ladon and prayed to be transformed, with the result than Pan found himself clutching an armful of reeds. The scene was watched by putti holding torches. Pan masks are carved on the large side tables, now at Floors Castle, and the putti are alluded to by the masks on the console tables (Cat. L8).

Prov: Temple Newsam House, Leeds; removed to Hickleton Hall, Yorkshire in 1922 and sold by Lord Halifax (Hollis & Webb, Leeds) 18-22 March

1947; W. Waddingham (Antiques), Walter P. Chrysler, Jnr; Warrington, Virginia; Chrysler sale (Parke-Bernet, New York) 29-30 April, 1960, 383; Needham (Antiques); Leonard Knight Ltd., John Fowler (Antiques); The Hon. Michael Astor, Bruern, Oxford; Temple Newsam House (1976)
Lit: Gilbert 1968, pp. 84-8; fig. 8; Gilbert 1978, p. 293; Hill 1981, pp. 26-32; Hill 1981 II, pp. 70-74, fig. 49-56
JH

L8 *Console table*

James Pascall (active 1723-d. 1747).
1745
Gilt mahogany and pine.
900 x 1220 x 640
Leeds City Art Gallery

The gilt gesso slab is carved with acanthus ornament together with garlands, foliage, bulrush fronds and trellis-work. The garlanded frame is carved with a sunburst framing the head of a putto, and is supported on scroll console legs, ornamented on the knees with acanthus foliage and terminating in scalloped *rocaille* toes. In the centre of the shaped plinth is one half of a scrolling broken pediment, which echoes those of the wall-sconces (Cat. L9). It is one of a pair of console tables supplied by James Pascall for Henry, 7th Viscount Irwin's (1691-1761) gallery at Temple Newsam House, Leeds, and listed in

his bill dated July 8 1745, 'For two Neatte Carved and Gilt tables in burnished gold with Mahogany tops, because they shant warp . . . £34.0.0'. They are *en suite* with the stands (Cat. L7), the wall-sconces (Cat. L9) and a pair of large tables, now at Floors Castle, Kelso. A console table of similar character with garlanded frame and legs formed of opposed acanthus scrolls, appears in William Jones's engravings for tables published in *The Builder's Companion,* 1739, pl. 31.

Prov: Temple Newsam House, Leeds; removed to Hickleton Hall, Yorkshire in 1922 and sold by Lord Halifax (Hollis & Webb, London) 18-22 March 1947; Charles Thornton (Antiques); W. Waddington (Antiques); presented by Councillor F.E. Tetley to Temple Newsam House
Lit: Edwards 1964, p. 589, fig. 43; Gilbert 1968, pp. 84-88, fig. 7; Gilbert 1978, p. 450; Hill 1981 I, pp. 70-74, figs 49-56; Lenygon 1914, pl. 210; Moss 1910, p. 321; Royal Academy 1955-6, 130
JH

L9 *Wall sconce*

James Pascall (active 1723-d. 1747).
1745
Gilt pine; 2110 x 1520
Leeds City Art Gallery

A spray of garlanded bulrushes supports two tiers of scrolling candle-branches, each fitted with three brass

L9

nozzles and pans. A snarling hound, standing on a shaped bracket with a scalloped *rocaille* stem, bounds up to attack an exhausted stag, which is suspended astride and half-hidden behind a scrolled and acanthus-tipped broken pediment. The asymmetrical elements are counterbalanced by those of the second girandole. These are listed in James Pascall's bill to Henry, 7th Viscount Irwin (1691-1761), dated 16 August 1745, 'Two Rich Gerandolls with two branches and six lights Gilt in burnished gold . . . £50.0.0.' They formed part of the furnishings of the gallery, together with the candlestands (Cat. L7) and the console tables (Cat. L8). In an accompanying letter Pascall stated that although their cost had exceeded the estimate, they were nevertheless, 'Five pounds a pease cheaper than I could have Charged or that many would have done . . .' as 'I am ye Maker my Self and does Everything at ye first hand'. Pascall also supplied the seat furniture for the gallery including settees whose arms were carved with hounds' heads. A hunting scene and a related wall-bracket appear in Lock's *Six Tables,* 1746, pls. 3, 4.

Prov: see Gilbert 1978, II
Lit: Coleridge 1968, pl. 114; Edwards 1974, p. 430; Edwards & Jourdain 1955, fig. 73; Gilbert 1968, pp. 844-8, fig. 5; Fitz-Gerald 1969, pp. 145-6, fig. 24; Gilbert 1978 II p.156; Hill 1981 I pp. 16-32; Hill 1981, pp. 70-74, figs. 49-56; Lenygon 1914, pl. 34; Temple Newsam 1938 (237)
JH

L8

L10 *Console Table*

Matthias Lock (*c.* 1710-1765).
c. 1745
Gilt wood with agate veneered slab.
840 x 1290 x 710
VAM (W.35-1964)

The rectangular frame, with a guilloche and feather frieze, and a winged lion mask cartouche in the centre, is supported on acanthus-scroll legs which curve inwards to the base plinth. The front legs are formed as term caryatids with heads of a man- and woman-of-the woods draped with garlands of fruit and flowers. The console table was supplied by Matthias Lock for John, 2nd Earl Poulett's drawing room at Hinton House, Somerset, and is *en suite* with the pier glass in cat. L12. His workshop sketch for the table (Cat. L11) indicates that the legs were originally linked by stretchers supporting a basket of flowers. The flanking tripod candlestands (now in a private collection) are carved with similar caryatid figures. Designs for console tables with related features had been published by the French sculptor, J.B. Toro, *Livre de Tables de diverses formes*, *c.* 1716 and by the French architect Nicolas Pineau, *Nouveaux Desseins de Pieds de Tables* (Cat. E10), as well as the English architect William Jones's, *The Gentlemens' and Builders' Companion,* 1739 and Batty Langley, *The City and Country Builder's and Workman's Treasury of Designs,* 1740.

Prov: Hinton House, Somerset,
Mrs Rhodes of Thorpe Underwood
Hall, Yorkshire
Lit: Hayward, 1980, pp. 284-286

L11 *Sketch of a pier table and account*

Matthias Lock (*c.* 1710-1775). *c.* 1745
Pencil, pen and ink and wash; 113 x 93
Inscribed *A Table in ye Tapestry Roome/ Joyner £1 5s 0d/Carving £21 0s 0d/Days 89 in all/Lock 15/Lomar 20/ Mill 10 Wood [?] 15 the othr [?] time &c*
VAM (2602)

A record drawing and account for cat. L10.

Prov: See cat. L28
Lit: Hayward 1961; Ward-Jackson
1958, 61
MS

L11

L12 *Pier glass*

Matthias Lock (*c.* 1710-1765). *c.* 1745
Gilt pine wood. 2620 x 1270
VAM (W8-1960)

The dominant feature of the boldly sculpted frame is the man- and woman-of-the-woods caryatid terms with acanthus-scroll supports crowned by baskets of fruit and flowers. A baldachino frames the hare's head in the centre of the cornice and is flanked by pediment scrolls, which once supported birds. Trophies of rustic pipes and hunting weapons are held by scroll clasps below the caryatids. At the base, within clusters of fruit branches, a bird is attacked by a hound, while its companion feeds, oblivious of two more hounds emerging towards it from the side rosettes. Winged dolphin heads support the corners of the frame. This pier glass, with its celebration of hunting, nature's fruitfulness, and the rustic life was supplied by the carver Matthias Lock for John, 2nd Earl Poulett's (1708-1764) drawing room at Hinton House, Somerset. It was designed *en suite* with the console table (Cat. L10) and a pair of candlestands (now in a private collection). Lock's workshop sketch for the left side of the mirror (Cat. L13) indicates that there were originally garlands of flowers draped across the joint between the two panels of glass. A frame support with a scroll-caryatid figure like the ones on this pier glass was published by Lock in *Six Sconces,* 1744 (Cat. L4, L5). Lock may have been influenced

by a design for frames by Jacques de Lajoue (1687-1761), which Huquier engraved in *Livre de bordures d'écrans à la chinois,* 1737. The hunting trophy may have been inspired by an engraving after Jean Baptiste Oudry (1686-1755) *L'arret du cigne.*

Prov: Hinton House, Somerset
Lit: Coleridge 1968, fig. 91; Hayward, 1980, pp. 284-286
JH

L13

L13 *Sketch of a pier glass, and account*

Matthias Lock (*c.* 1710-1765). *c.* 1745
Pencil, pen and ink and wash;
136 x 90
Inscribed *138 Days in all / Lock 20 / Lomar 40 / Wood 15 / Loo 14 the other by &c / Charged for Carving £34 10s 0d / for Joyneurs & stuf £1 15s 0d / A Large Sconc in the Taptstrey Roome*

VAM (2587)

A record drawing and account for Cat. L12

Prov: see Cat. L28
Lit: Hayward 1961
MS

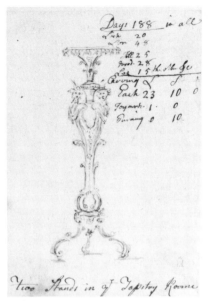

L14

L15

L14 *Sketch of stand and account*
Matthias Lock (*c.* 1710-1765). *c.* 1745
Pencil, pen and ink and wash;
132 x 88
Inscribed *Days 188 in all / Lock 20 / Lor [for Lomar?] 48 / Hill [?] 25 / Wood 28 / Loo 15 the othr &c / Carving each £23 10s 0d / Joyneurs £1 0s / Turning £0 10s /Two Stands in ye Tapstrey Roome.*

VAM (2588)

A record drawing and account for the stands made for Hinton House, now in a private collection.

Prov: see Cat. L28
Lit: Hayward 1961
JH

L15 *Console table*
Anonymous *c.* 1745-8
Pine wood, originally gilded, with verde antico slab. 960 x 1370 x 660
A carved ribbon fixed to the frame is inscribed *John Sanderson's gift*
The Thomas Coram Foundation for Children

The rectangular frame is supported by an oak tree, whose foliage decorates the frieze. Below the tree, a naked child sits astride a reclining goat and holds one of its horns, while reaching up to tear a branch from the tree. His companion lies on the plinth alongside the goat.This remarkable sculptural piece was supplied *en suite* with a gilded oval pier-glass carved

with foliage and palm fronds, and stood in the Foundling Hospital's Court Room, which was fitted up between 1745-8. The room was hung with paintings of biblical subjects, representing the rescue of children, and with tondo canvases of the London hospitals, set in oak-garlanded frames. The overmantel bas-relief by Rysbrack shows Charity with some children, in the act of securing a floundering ship to an oak tree with Hope's anchor. Both Rysbrack and Hogarth, who devised the iconographic programme for the room as well as a crest for the Hospital, may have been involved in the design of this piece. John Sanderson (active 1730-1771) was the architect entrusted with the building of the hospital to the designs of Theodore Jacobsen.

Prov: The Foundling Hospital, now named The Thomas Coram Foundation for Children
Lit: Cornforth 1967, p. 1260, fig.4; Nicolson 1972, pl. 17, 47; Nichols & Wrey 1935, pp. 261, 263
JH

L16 *A New book of Ornaments*
Henry Copland (d. 1753). 1746
Etchings; average 121 x 172
VAM (E.669-678-1927)

Title and nine plates, published by Copland and Bucksher in Gutter Lane, Cheapside. A second edition bears Copland's name only. This suite, and Copland's trade cards, seem to have established his manner as the first fully developed rococo style used on English printed ephemera. Of Bucksher nothing is apparently known. Copland is discussed in *English Rococo and its Continental Origins*.

Lit: Hecksc her 1979, XI
MS

L17 *Trade cards*
The Trustees of the British Museum (Heal 59.103; 100.32)

a) Matthias Lock, carver. Matthias Lock. 1746. From his address in Tottenham Court Road. The card was devised for his address at Nottingham Court, Castle Street, Long Acre (Heckscher 1979, III (1) (B)). The unusually small size of this card (78 x 91) suggests that it was intended to serve as a label on Lock's work.

b) Peter Griffin, map and print seller. Anonymous. 1747-9? The card shows a number of prints, including a watch-paper of Lord Lovat (BM:S 2816,

L17

1746), profiles after Sebastian le Clerc, and the title page of Matthias Lock's *A Book of Ornaments* dated 1 Feb. 1747, formerly only known in its later state (Heckscher 1979, pl. 14A, entitled *A Book of Shields)*. Peter Griffin died in 1749 (Lippincott 1983, p. 189, n. 51). This card was later used by Elisabeth Griffin and with modifications by Michael Jackson and George Pulley.
MS

L18

L18 *Designs for tables*

Matthias Lock (*c.* 1710-1765). 1746
Etchings; 175 x 287; 262 x 176
VAM (27811.2; 12957.23)

From Lock's *Six Tables,* 1746. In the first plate, the base of the pier table incorporates a dog attacking a dragon. The other plate shows a pier table (which incorporates a head indebted to Toro and a dragon probably derived from Pineau), and eight other details for tables. The underlying form of the second table has its origins in French prints such as those after

Pineau (see Cat. C10), but the table in the first print is entirely asymmetrical and looks forward to the creature-inhabited carvers' work of the 1750s.

Lit: Heckscher 1979, II, 8b, 10; Ward-Jackson 1958, 50
MS

L19

L19 *Pier glass*

Attributed to Matthias Lock
(*c.* 1710-1765). *c.* 1750
Gilt pine wood. 1980 x 1070
The Methuen Collection

This frame has been concocted of acanthus scrolls, and ornaments from the landscape park. It is formed like an archway with paired and angled pilasters, entwined by gnarled oak trees, supporting a trellis-work cornice and acanthus-husk balustrades. A large exotic bird on the crest stands astride a grotto from which water drips through the broken sweep cornice and forms a watery spray below the gothic arcade which runs across the base-rail. This mirror was designed *en suite* with the console table Cat. L20 for Paul Methuen (1723-95) at Corsham Court, Wiltshire. Although no documentation for them has been found, it is possible that they originally stood in the Cabinet Room. Many of the elements of this mirror appear in patterns for rustic

chinoiserie frames published by Matthias Lock and Henry Copland, *A New Book of Ornaments*, 1752, pls. 5-7 and in Thomas Johnson, *Collection of Designs*, 1758, pls. 1-4. The inset glass borders enable the size of the mirror to be enlarged, without the additional cost of purchasing a large main sheet of glass, and at the same time they helped to lighten the structure.
JH

L20 *Console table*

Attributed to Matthias Lock
(*c.* 1710-1765). *c.* 1750
Gilt pine wood with Sicilian jasper slab; 760 x 1290 x 680
The Methuen Collection

The serpentine frame with a foliage lambrequin apron is supported by acanthus-scrolled uprights around which a gnarled tree stretches its branches. Water oozes from beneath the tree and falls over the mouth of a cavern formed by the scroll supports terminating in rockwork feet. The table was designed *en suite* with the pier glass Cat. L19 for Paul Methuen at Corsham Court, Wiltshire. Many of the elements of this table appear in a pattern for a rustic chinoiserie table, with figures below a tree set on a pagoda-shaped plinth, which was published by Matthias Lock and Henry Copland in *A New Book of Ornaments,* 1752, (Cat. L24) pl. 2. Patterns for tree-supported table-frames were also published by Thomas Johnson in *Collection of Designs,* 1758 (Cat. L44) pls. 20, 24.

Lit: Edwards 1978, fig. 44, pl. 589; Hayward 1964, pl. 36
JH

L21 *A New Book of Chinese, Gothic, & Modern Chairs*

Matthew Darly (active 1741-1773). 1751
Engravings; *c.* 102 x 186 (cut)
The title page lettered with title and *with the manner of putting them in Perpsective according to Brook Taylor. Price 1s 6d. M Darly Invt. et Fect.* Plate 3 dated *1750.*
VAM (E.216, 219, 220, 223-1911)

Title and seven plates (title and plates 3, 4 and 7 shown here). Each plate shows two chairs in sharp perspective, which from this date becomes the standard viewpoint for chair designs.

L20

L21

The gothic chairs on plate 7 are the earliest to appear in an English pattern book. The chair on plate 3 with a fan-shaped back may be intended to be Chinese; a similar chair was provided for the Chinese Pavilion at the Shakespeare Jubilee, 1769 (Gilbert 1978, pl. 136). The chair on the left of plate 4 may also be intended to be Chinese, but that on the right, with its swirling raffle-leaf back is certainly 'modern' – that is rococo. A similar spiral motif is characteristic of, and peculiar to, the engravings of Pierre-Edmé Babel, published in Paris in the 1730s and 1740s (Kimball 1943, pl. 193, figs 253, 255). The suite was re-issued, with slight modifications, in Robert Manwaring's *Chair-Maker's Guide,* 1766.

Lit: Gilbert 1975, pp. 34-5, pls. 69, 70, 73; Ward-Jackson 1958, 46, 47
MS

L22 *Title-page of* A New Book of Ornaments
George Bickham junior (1706?-1771) probably after Pierre-Edmé Babel (1720-1770). 1752
Etching; 203 x 245
Lettered with title and *for Glasses, Tables, Chairs, Sconces, &c with Trophies in ye Chinese way Drawn for ye use of Artificers in General by Babel of Paris G. Bickham according to Act of Parliamt. P. Babel Invent. 1752*

Private Collection

The suite consists of a title and at least five plates. That the designer can probably be connected with the French wood carver and designer Pierre-Edmé Babel is strongly suggested by a comparison between Babel's *genre pittoresque* suites (probably of the 1740s) and this suite and Dominicus Negri's trade card (Cat. L52). Not only is the rather wild and individual treatment of *genre pittoresque* elements very similar, but specific links can also be made such as between the water-spouting swans on the trade card and those on plate 4 of the suite *Fontaine Decorée* (Berlin 1939, 422 (2)) and several other pieces by Babel, and between the cockerel on the table in the English suite and that on the page ('Avis au lecteur') after Babel in Charpentier's edition of *Vignola,* 1747. The same French plate incorporates shell motifs which also occur in an untitled set of prints *(VAM E.36.A-D-1981)* engraved by P. Benazech after Babel and published by Vivares. Vivares announced a *New Book of Ornaments, from Babel* and *A New Book of China Ornaments* in 1753. Peter Babel 'Designer and Modeller, Long Acre . . . – one of the first Improvers of Papier Mache Ornaments for Ceilings, Chimney-pieces, Picture-frames &c, an invention of modern date imported by us from France and now brought to great perfection' is listed in Thomas Mortimer's *Universal Director,* 1763.

Prov: Godfrey's Bookshop, York; Geoffrey Beard
Lit: Beard 1975, pl. 61
MS

L22

L24

L23

L23 *Design for a girandole*
Matthias Lock (*c.* 1710-1765). *c.* 1705?
Pencil, pen and ink, and wash;
281 x 127
VAM (2550)

At the top a hound attacks a stag;
below is another hound. The whole
girandole is formed as a scroll.

Prov: see Cat. L28
Lit: Ward-Jackson 1958, 58
MS

L24 *Designs for wall clocks, a bracket and a frame*
Matthias Lock (*c.* 1710-1765). 1752
Etching and engraving; 250 x 177
Lettered with a copyright line dated
Nov. 12 1752
VAM (E.2810-1886)

From an edition of *A New Book of
Ornaments with Twelve Leaves . . . by
M. Lock and M. Copland,* published in
1752 by Lock and Elizabeth Copland,
and re-issued in 1768 by Robert Sayer.
Copland's contribution seems to be
limited to the right half of one plate
(Heckscher 1979, pl. 25). Lock's
designs mark the establishment of a
carvers' style that was to survive into
the 1760s. This plate is from a set

(VAM E.2804-2811-1886) probably
originally stitched together, composed
of three plates from the original suite
together with five plates which are
copies of the original suite but bear
the same date. They include copies
from plates re-used by Sayer in 1768,
so this unrecorded set may represent a
pirated edition.

Lit: Heckscher 1979, VII, pl. 32
MS

L25 *Armchair*
Matthias Lock (*c.* 1710-65). *c.* 1755
Gilt wood with damask upholstery, the
seat and arm-pads close nailed.
430 x 660 x 640.
VAM (W.1-1973)

The moulded and pierced frame to
the cartouche-shaped back is carved
with acanthus scrolls and flower sprays
and is fitted with an upholstered
panel. The seat frame is decorated in a
similar manner with fish-scale panels
framing the open cartouche and is
supported on cabriole legs, which
have acanthus foliage on the knees
and terminate in lion paw feet. A
drawing by Lock of this chair is at the
VAM. No designs for chairs were
published in Lock's various pattern
books, and the earliest engraved
designs for this type of 'French' chair
are dated 1759, and appeared in *The
Director,* (3rd ed. 1762). Lock's chair
appears in a number of portraits
executed in the 1770s by the artist
Richard Cosway (1742-1821), and it is

L25

thought to have served as his sitter's chair.

Prov: Richard Cosway *c.* 1775; Messrs. Asprey
Lit: Hardy 1973, pp. 705-6; Hayward 1973, pp. 268-271
JH

L26 *Overmantel mirror*

Designed by James Paine. Carving attributed to John Bladwell (active *c.* 1725-68). *c.* 1752
Gilt wood 1020 x 1630 x 150
The National Trust (Felbrigg Hall)

The elongated cartouche-shaped frame consists of bold scrolls with acanthus foliage springing from the central cabochons at top and bottom and from scroll-brackets at the lower corners. The sides support palm branches and the top a garland of flowers. The small central head-glass is surmounted by an acanthus scallop-shell with drip-work ornament. The mirror was designed (see Cat. M10) by

the architect James Paine for William Windham (1717-61) and was intended to hang above a chimneypiece at Felbrigg Hall, Norfolk. Its design and ornament is closely related to the overmantel frame, which Paine designed for Windham's Cabinet Room, to incorporate a mirror surmounted by a landscape painting of the Cascade at Tivoli. The carving of the mirror is attributed to John Bladwell, who supplied a large quantity of furniture for Felbrigg in the 1750s, and it may be the 'chimney glass in a gilt frame', which was recorded in the North Dressing Room in the 1764 inventory.

Lit: Jackson-Stops 1980, p. 20
JH

L27 *Pier glass*

Attributed to John Bladwell (active *c.* 1725-68). *c.* 1752
Beechwood, painted white and gilded.
2130 x 1120 x 150
The National Trust (Felbrigg Hall)

Like the mirror from Corsham Court (Cat. L19) this rectangular frame is conceived as trelliswork garden ornament combined with the ubiquitous acanthus scroll. The *rocaille* sides are overgrown by sinuous fronds springing from rocky mounds on the base rail, whose central cartouche is surmounted by a 'pagoda-sweep' husk. More fronds cross the mirror to conceal the joint with the head-glass. A perspectival trick is played with the angled cornices at the top to suggest that they jut forward, and the whole

L26

L27

crest is garlanded with flowers. The mirror is thought to have formed part of the bedroom furnishings supplied by John Bladwell to William Windham. In April 1752 William Windham wrote to his agent Robert Frary about some mirror designs, 'I have ordered at Bladwell's . . . two white and gilt frames for the two oval glasses and would know whether no. 4 would not do for the pier in our bedchamber'. In 1756 John Bladwell, carver and upholsterer of Bow Street, Covent Garden was paid nearly £1000 for goods sent to Felbrigg.

Lit: Jackson-Stops 1980
JH

L28 *Design for a pier glass*
Matthias Lock (*c.* 1710-1765). *c.* 1752?
Pencil, pen and ink and wash;
394 x 137
VAM (2583)

Half the design is shown. On the side are the head of a chinaman and a ho-ho bird. At the top is a pair of kissing doves, with a bow and quiver, and a flower basket flanked by palm branches below. All these elements

except for the bow and the ho-ho bird occur in the same relationship in a design for a mirror on pl. 5 of Babel's *A New Book of Ornaments,* 1752 (Cat. L22, Ward-Jackson 1958, 70). It is perhaps more likely that Lock was using the print rather than Babel the drawing. Kissing doves were particularly popular motifs for the crestings of French mirrors and appear on a mirror at Woburn Abbey copied from Blondel (see Cat. M13). The particular arrangement used by Lock, with bow and quiver, also appears on pl. 201 of Vol. II of Charles Etienne Briseux's *L'Art de Bâtir de Maisons de Campagne,* 1743. Four other designs by Lock in the VAM carry similar crestings. Babel's mirror design is a wilful distortion of the standard English rococo pier glass form.

Prov: from a group of 77 sheets of designs by Lock, Thomas Chippendale and others bought by the South Kensington Museum in 1862 from George Lock of Edinburgh, a descendant of the artist
Lit: Ward-Jackson 1958, 66
MS

L29 *Two armchairs*
Attributed to John Bladwell (active *c.* 1725-68) the tapestry from the workshop of Danthon. *c.* 1755-60
Gilt-wood, with tapestry upholstery
1070 x 710 x 710
One cover signed *Danthon*
The Treasury (on loan to the National Trust, Uppark)

These have serpentine crest rails and seat rails carved with light relief acanthus leaves on incised trellis backgrounds. The cabriole front legs have a cabochon and leafy fan on the knee and terminate in scrolling toes fitted with castors. The back tapestries depict scenes from Aesop's Fables, (a) The Hare and the Tortoise, (b) the Leopard and the Fox, set within floral frames; and the seats have set-piece fruit and flower arrangements. These are from a set of eight armchairs and a settee, which may have been carved by John Bladwell, who provided furniture for Sir Matthew Fetherstonhaugh (1714-74) for Uppark, Sussex, between 1725-68. The ornament of acanthus-lapped trellis on the frames was dictated by the borders of the tapestry

panels. The tapestry scenes with animals were copied from Francis Barlow's Aesop's Fables (1666 and 1687) have three different rococo surrounds with asymmetrically placed flowers associated with three seat designs. Barlow's Fables were much admired in the 18th century appearing in the 1760s in a Nixon plate-printed cotton, and as isolated animals on a plate in Sayer's *Ladies Amusement.* It is uncertain which member of the Danthon family, working in London from before 1707, supplied tapestry to Sir Matthew Fetherstonhaugh. His account book records tapestry bought from Paul Saunders in 1761 and from Mr Browne in 1760. Saunders is unlikely to have supplied Danthon's work; but Browne might have been Danthon's agent.

Lit: Coleridge 1967, pl. 161, fig. 10;
Hefford 1984
WH & JH

L30 *A Classical landscape with peasants fording a stream*
Francesco Zuccarelli (1702-1788)
Oil on canvas; 560 x 822
The National Trust (Shugborough)

Both the painting and the carved and gilt rococo frame are slightly concave, are from a pair and were probably intended to hang in one of the bows added to Shugborough by Thomas Wright in the 1740s. The park at Shugborough was noted for its Classical and other ruins, some of which were designed by Wright. The fondness of the English for Zuccarelli's light and pleasant Italianate landscapes resulted in two long visits to England, 1752-1762 and 1765-1771. The frame of this painting probably dates from the 1750s (see also Cat. B15).

Prov: Thomas Anson (1695-1773); by descent
Lit: Levey 1959
MS

L31 Chair

John Gordon (active *c.* 1750-*c.* 1776).
1756
Mahogany with needlework
upholstery, 940 x 710 x 610
*His Grace the Duke of Atholl's Collection,
Blair Castle*

The rectangular back and seat are
upholstered in needlework mostly
worked by Jean Drummond, wife of
the 2nd Duke of Atholl and depicting
cornucopia with flowers. The shaped
seat rails are carved with fish-scales
and a rosette within the central
pointed arches, and the legs are also
decorated with fish-scales and
acanthus foliage within trefoil arches
on the toes, which are fitted with
castors. It is one of a set of eight chairs
supplied for Blair Castle, Perthshire,
and listed in a bill from John Gordon
of Swallow Street to James, 2nd Duke
of Atholl and dated 17 June 1756,
'8 Mahogany chairs carv'd frames in
fish scales with a French foot and
carv'd leaf upon the toe . . . £31.8.0
. . . To making an addition to your
Grace's needlework . . . £2.5.0.'. A
similar suite of 24 armchairs and two
settees was supplied to Ditton Park,
Surrey (ill. Coleridge 1968, fig. 85).

Lit: Coleridge 1960, p. 252-3;
Coleridge 1968, fig. 87
JH

L32 Designs for chairs

Thomas Chippendale (1718-1779).
c. 1754
Pen and ink and wash; 205 x 335
Inscribed *No.12* and *3*
The Chippendale Society

Three chairs, but made of composite
parts comprising six designs for legs,
two for splats and four for uprights to
the backs. The original drawing
engraved by Matthew Darly for
Chippendale's *Director,* first edition,
1754, pl. XII, and reissued as plate
XIV of the third edition, 1762. The
design on the left includes the very
popular splat used on Cat. L33, L34.
The drawing once formed part of the
Chippendale albums now in the
Metropolitan Museum, New York.

Prov: Thomas Chippendale; 4th Baron
Foley; William Fowkes; John Marks;
Sotheby's 20 April 1972, 33;
O.F. Wilson (Antiques) Ltd.
Lit: Gilbert 1972, I, p. 101, II, pl. 129
MS

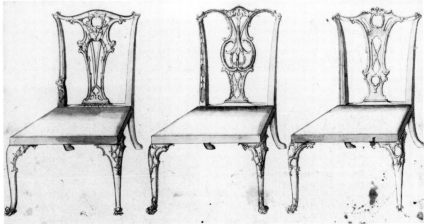

L32

L33

L33 Chair

Attributed to Thomas Chippendale
(1718-79). *c.* 1754
Mahogany with upholstered seat;
970 x 560 x 560
The Trustees of the Nostell Settled Estate

The chair back has a pierced splat
composed of acanthus-ornamented
scrolls, gothic fretwork at the base and
an open acanthus cartouche at the
top. The crest rail is bowed and
terminates in acanthus scrolls above
the shaped and moulded uprights.
The rectangular seat is fitted with a
loose upholstered frame and is
supported on straight legs united by
stretchers. both the splat and the crest-
rail appear in Thomas Chippendale's
engraved patterns for 'parlour' chairs
published in the first edition of *The
Gentleman and Cabinet-Maker's Director,*

(1754) pl. XII, and reissued in both
subsequent editions (1755 and 1762).
This is one of a set of 12 chairs
thought to have been supplied by
Chippendale for Nostell Priory,
Yorkshire, but not mentioned in the
incomplete surviving accounts.
Straight chair legs were cheaper to
produce than the ornamented cabriole
legs, illustrated in the *Director* plates.
The design of the splat was one of the
most popular produced by
Chippendale, and appears on a
number of other chairs (eg Cat. L34)
none of which, however, can be
documented to Chippendale.

Lit: Coleridge 1968, fig. 169; Gilbert
1978, fig. 131; Temple Newsam
House 1951, cat. no. 30
JH

L34 Chair

Anonymous *c.* 1754
Mahogany with leather upholstery;
945 x 590 x 565
VAM (W67-1940)

One of a set of six 'parlour' chairs,
whose splat is based on the same
Director design as that of Cat. L33, but
the crest-rail has been varied by the
addition of pointed sweep cornices
and rounded ends. In addition the
seat-rail is bowed in front and the
upholstery is close-nailed. A pencil
inscription on the 'shoe' beneath the
splat of this chair reads: '6 pedestals
for Chipendel's backs', which
probably implies that the splats were
copied from the engraving in the
Director. Because of its undistinguished
quality, it is unlikely that this chair
stems from Chippendale's workshops.

L34

L35

Prov: formerly owned by the Tomes family
Lit: Bolling Hall 1979, cat. no. 13; Edwards 1951, fig. 26; Gilbert 1978, fig. 132, p. 290
JH

L35 *Chair Attributed to Thomas Chippendale*

(1718-79). *c.* 1754
Mahogany with upholstered seat; 950 x 600 x 560
Branded *T.P.*
The Duke of Norfolk

From a set of six. The arched corners of the chair-back are carved with acanthus leaves, which scroll inwards towards the central cartouche of the shaped crest-rail. The pierced splat is formed of acanthus-scrolls, which frame two trefoliated gothic arches, one above the other. The bow-fronted seat is fitted with a loose upholstered frame and its shaped apron is carved with foliage. More foliage is carved on the knees of the cabriole front legs and springing from the scroll toes. The various elements of the chair-back and legs appear in the patterns for parlour chairs published in the *Director* (1754) pls. IX, X & XII. The chairs are thought to have been supplied to Edward, 9th Duke of Norfolk, who was among the 308 subscribers to the *Director.* Although Chippendale played endless variations on the splat-back parlour chair in his three editions of the Director, no example in the rococo style can be proven to be by

him, all the documented chairs being in the neo-classical taste. In his description of such parlour chairs, Chippendale stated that they looked best when upholstered over the seat-rails rather than fitted with a loose seat, as in this case. The craftsman responsible for making the chairs has not been identified.

Lit: Coleridge 1968, fig.167; Edwards & Jourdain 3rd ed. 1955, fig. 106; Edwards 1964, pl. 147; Jervis 1978, pl. 210
JH

L36 *Armchair*

Thomas Chippendale (1718-79). 1759
Mahogany, upholstered in damask, close nailed. 990 x 710 x 710
Private collection

The upholstered back has a bow-shaped top, which is echoed by the seat front, whose apron is carved with foliage within the central pointed arch. The cabriole legs are carved on the knee with a sunk trefoil panel, framing an acanthus leaf, and terminate in scrolling whorl toes on pedestals, which conceal castors. One of a set of 14 drawing-room chairs supplied by Chippendale to William, 5th Earl of Dumfries for Dumfries House, Ayrshire and described in his bill dated May 5, 1759, '14 Mahogany Elbow chairs wt. stuff'd Backs and Seats Cover'd & brass nailed the Elbows & fronts of the seats richly carv'd & scrol feet and castors . . . £63'. The chair was supplied en suite

with the pair of card tables (Cat. L37) and was originally upholstered in blue damask to match the window curtains. The chairs must have been ordered when Lord Dumfries visited Chippendale's warehouse in February 1759. This pattern of cabriole leg appears in a design for a 'French commode table' published in the *Director,* (1754), pl. LXIV.

Lit: Gilbert, 1978, pl. 18, fig. 139, pp. 132-3, 137
JH

L37 *Card table*

Thomas Chippendale. (1718-1779). 1759
Mahogany; 740 x 890 x 460
Private collection

The moulded top with bow front and rounded corners has a hinged flap and baize-lined interior. The concertina-action frame is supported on cabriole legs, which are a stretched version of the legs of the chair Cat. L36. This is one of a pair of card tables supplied by Chippendale for William, 5th Earl of Dumfries for Dumfries House, Ayrshire, and described in his bill dated May 5, 1759, 'A pair of mahogany card tables of fine wood lined wt. superfine green cloth the knees carvd & scrol toes to match ye chairs . . . £11.' They took the place of pier tables, and stood under gilt mirrors in the drawing room; as was usual in such cases, they were designed en suite with the chair frames.

Lit: Gilbert 1978, pp. 133, figs. 402-404
JH

L38 *Armchair*

Anonymous. *c.* 1759
Mahogany, upholstered in red damask, close nailed seat and arm-pads; 1070 x 740 x 740
VAM (W47-1946)

The cartouche-shaped back is fitted with an upholstered panel and its moulded frame is comprised of counterpoised 'C' and 'S' scrolls ornamented with acanthus foliage. The bow-fronted seat rail is carved with a central acanthus cartouche and the cabriole legs are carved on the knee with acanthus sprays and

L37

L38

terminate in scroll toes on plinths fitted with castors. The design of the chair is based on an engraving dated 1759 in the *Director* (3rd ed. 1762) pl. XXII, where it is described as a 'French' chair. Chippendale recommended that there should be an open space between the lower rail of the chair-back and the seat in order to lighten the general effect, and indeed it is this lightness and the cartouche back which do give the chair its French appearance. With its padded back, this is the drawing room equivalent to the parlour chair. While the latter had leather or horsehair seats, most of the former were

upholstered in damask or tapestry. Owing to the poor quality of the carving, the chair is thought to be of provincial make. The chair is en suite with a settee and an armchair at the Metropolitan Museum, and is reputed to have been supplied to William Plummer (1688-1767) of Gilston Park, Hertfordshire.

Prov: traditionally from Gilston Park, Hertforshire; Brigadier W.E. Clark collection
Lit: Coleridge 1968, fig. 179, p. 96; Edwards 1951, pl. 74; Edwards and Jourdain 1955, pl. 178, fig. 110; Edwards 1974, p. 151. fig. 136; Hackenbroch 1958, figs. 141, 142
JH

L39 *Pair of candlestands*
Thomas Chippendale (1718-79). 1758
Gilt pine (originally painted white); 1340 x 350 x 350
His Grace the Duke of Atholl's Collection, Blair Castle

The tripartite stem is formed of elongated 'S' scrolls, surmounted by 'C' scrolls, which support the hexagonal top with its fretted gallery. The 'C' scrolls are linked by trefoil headed brackets, and the stem frames a central hexagonal finial, perched on small scrolls. Another finial appears at the top of the scrolling tripod legs,

which terminate in volute toes ornamented with acanthus foliage. The candlestands were supplied by Thomas Chippendale to James, 2nd Duke of Atholl for Blair Castle, Perthshire and are listed in his bill of 1758: 'A Pair of large Candlestands neatly carv'd and painted white . . . £7.7.0'. They provided the pattern for four cheaper stands, which were supplied by John Thomson of Edinburgh in 1760. Here Chippendale has almost eliminated the acanthus ornament to create a light and elegantly curved structure, each scroll counterbalancing another. Two similiar candlestands, attributed to Chippendale, were published in the compendium of various designers' work entitled *Household Furniture in Genteel Taste* and issued by A Society of Upholsterers in 1760, pls. 73, 74.

Exhib: Thomas Chippendale & His Patrons in the North, Temple Newsam, 1968
Lit: Coleridge 1960, fig. 12, pl. 256; Coleridge 1968, fig. 288; Gilbert 1978, vol. 2, fig. 378; Oswald 1949, pl. 1508
JH

L40 Pole screen

Thomas Chippendale (1718-79). 1759
Screen panel probably Moorfields
Mahogany with knotted woollen pile
panel; 1700 x 790
Private collection

The pole has a pine-cone finial and a
turned baluster stem, ornamented
with acanthus foliage and trefoil-
headed blind fret. It is supported on
tripod feet with arched toes on
scalloped plinths. The panel design
came from the Gobelins or the
Savonnerie, brought to London by
defecting workmen. Several pile and
tapestry versions survive, probably
made both in the Fulham
manufactory of Peter Parisot,
dispersed in 1755, and by Thomas
Moore at Moorfields. A rococo
surround was sometimes added. The
surround on a panel in the
Metropolitan Museum looks likely to
be from a French model, perhaps
woven at Fulham. The simpler
Dumfries House surround appears

much more English, and that,
together with an improvement to the
squirrel's tail, could be alterations
made at Moorfields. Two similar
panels in French collections may be
the result of Moore's foreign trade.
The pole screen was supplied for one
of William, 5th Earl of Dumfries's
bedroom fireplaces and was one of a
pair described in Chippendale's bill,
dated May 5, 1759, 'A mahog: frame
to a Firescreen . . . and a
mahogany pillar and claw richly
carv'd'. The pair cost £8, and a similar
pole screen with 'lustring' backing to
the panel cost £4.4.0. The decoration
of the stand picks up the ornament of
the *trompe l'oeil* tapestry frame with its
foliage and scallop shells. *The Director*,
1754, was the first work to include
designs for 'pillar and claw'
firescreens, and pl. CLVI provides
patterns for rounded toes and
acanthus and scallop ornament.

Lit: Gilbert 1969, pp. 663-77; Gilbert
1978, pl. 3, pp. 134-5; Hefford 1977,
pp. 840-849; Standen 1983, pp. 251-
256
WH & JH

L41 Hall chair

Anonymous. *c.* 1758
Mahogany; 1040 x 560 x 600
The Most Hon. The Marquess of Hertford

The fretted back bears an acanthus-
scroll cartouche painted with the head
of a Blackamoor, representing the
supporters of the Hertford crest, set
within the Garter and surmounted by
a Marquess's coronet. The arched
crest-rail is supported by gothic
mouchette uprights and acanthus
scroll brackets. The frame of the
dished seat is carved with bands of
gothic quatrefoil blind tracery, and is
supported on tapering pedestal legs
which terminate with inward scrolling
toes. The chair is part of a suite of
twelve chairs and four settees made for
Francis, 1st Marquess of Hertford
(1719-94), after he had been installed
as a Knight of the Garter in 1757, and
they were placed in the hall at Ragley
Hall, Warwickshire. Designs for chairs
with fretted backs combining gothic
motifs and acanthus scrolls, were
published in the 1740s by Henry
Copland, *Designs for Hall Chairs*, (n.d.)
(q.v. Heckscher, 1979, p. 6, figs. 58a-
59c) and also by Matthew Darly, in

1750/1, see Cat. L21.
JH

L42 Commode

Anonymous. *c.* 1760
Mahogany veneer with ormolu
mounts and engraved gilt brass
panels; 890 x 1310 x 790
VAM (W32-1977)

The serpentine top is rimmed by
foliate gilt brass mouldings, and the
frame has curved keel-edged corners
which are mounted with ormolu
acanthus scrolls on the shoulders
linked by husk-trails to the scrolled
foliage of the feet. The two doors are
fitted with pierced brass grilles backed
by silk and their shaped aprons are
mounted with acanthus gadrooned
borders and a central scalloped
cartouche. The grilles are ornamented
with neo-classical rosettes framed by
roundels and with acanthus-scroll
spandrels. The interior is fitted with
trays for clothes. The pair to this
commode is at Temple Newsam
House, Yorkshire. It is of similar form
and has some related mounts to a
commode in the possession of
H.M. The Queen (illustrated Anthony
Coleridge 1968, fig. 58). The latter has
brass ornament inlaid in its top and is
related to a design by Chippendale at
the *VAM* (D737-1906). Referring to the
ornaments of a 'French Commode
Table', published in the *Director*
(3rd ed., 1762) pl. CXXII,
Chippendale states that they can be
'Brass, or Silver, finely chased and put
on; or they may be cut in Filligree-
work, in wood, brass or silver'.

Prov: by tradition owned by William-
Wyndham Grenville (d. 1834), then
inherited by Hon. George Matthew
Fortescue (d. 1877) of Boconnoc,
Cornwall. Ethy House, Cornwall.
Lit: Christie's 1977, p. 55; Gilbert
1978, fig. 223a.
JH

L42

L44

L43 *Broadsheet*
James Kirk and William Austin (1721-1820) after Thomas Johnson (b. 1714, d. after 1778). 1755
Etching, engraving and letterpress; 130 x 280 (headpiece), 255 x 295 (sheet)
Lettered *Proposals* (within a cartouche) and *Jas. Kirk Sc. Willm. Austin Sculp. T. Johnson invt. & delin* and in letterpress *For Publishing by Subscription, a new Book of Ornaments* and other details.
The Trustees of the British Museum (1872-6-8-543)

The subscription advertisement for Cat. L48. The pieces are described as being in the 'Chinese, Gothick, and Rural Taste'. Although the cartouche, engraved by Kirk, is in Johnson's style, it may be suspected that the conception of the title on a ruinous wall set in an Italianate landscape reminiscent of Zuccarelli (see Cat. L30) is due to Austin, who etched the rest of the plate. It can be compared with Austin's own trade card, which incorporates a pointing figure (Cat. D29t), and a subscription plate by Austin for one of his plates after Zuccarelli. In this present print the figure pointing out the cartouche is Chinese and his companion, who carries a mallet and chisel, evidently a carver. A similar conceit was used by Johnson in the title page of Cat. L24 with its figure of a carver carrying a frame. Part of the plate was used in plate 16 of Cat. L48, in a frame etched by Butler Clowes. Austin who etched

Johnson's *Twelve Gerondoles* in 1755, also etched a storm scene (plate 36) and the whole of plate 52 for Cat. L48.

Lit: Hayward 1975, fig. 95
MS

L44 *Dedication page and designs for pier tables*
Butler Clowes after Thomas Johnson (b. 1714, d. after 1778). 1758
Etchings; 245 x 179, 249 x 175
The table designs lettered *T. Johnson inv del B Clowes sculp* and with a copyright line dated 1757.
VAM (E.3717-1903)

From Johnson's untitled suite of 52 plates with a letterpress preface, published in 1758, and with modifications and additions, in 1761 with the title *One Hundred and Fifty New Designs*. The designs were probably prepared in 1755 and were first issued in sets from 1756 onwards (Cat. L43). The dedication page names Lord Blakeney, President, and the members of the Antigallican Association. Above the figure of Britannia, who holds a shield bearing the arms of the Association, flies a putto labelled 'Genius', who sets fire to a strip of linked scrolls labelled 'French Paper Machée'. A figure of Envy, carrying a paper bearing fleurs de lys, lurks behind a wall. The designs for pier tables incorporate figures taken from Francis Barlow's illustration of 1687 to Aesop's Fables No. XX, The Fox and the Cat. As is often the case with

Johnson's designs, no attempt is made to modify the borrowed figures. The majority of plates in the suite are for carvers' work, but they also include designs for silver (Cat. G49), ceilings, and a wall (Cat. M18).

Lit: Hayward 1964, pl. 1, 58-62.
MS

L45 *Candlestand*
Thomas Johnson (1714-78) *c.* 1757
Painted pine with brass nozzles and pans. 1590 x 940 x 560
VAM (W9-1950)

The stand is painted brown and stone colour to give the impression of partly petrified wood, and is carved with aquatic ornament. Water drips from stalactites below the scalloped rim of the top, while winged dolphins slobber over the sweep cornices of an open grotto framing a fountain [replaced]. The tails of the dolphins are entwined round the shaft of a rusticated pilaster with flanking demi-pilasters. The small pilasters support acanthus brackets from which emerge gnarled candlebranches. The tripod feet are formed of inverted scroll brackets ornamented with rocaille and stalagmites. This is one of a set of four candlestands, which were supplied to flank two tables in George, 1st Lord Lyttelton's gallery at Hagley Hall, Worcestershire. They correspond with other 'rustic' furnishings, including pier glasses, girondoles and wall-brackets. The general form, and much

of the decorative ornament of the candlestand, appears in two patterns for stands published by Thomas Johnson, *150 New Designs*, 1758, (Cat. L44) p. 13, and this stand is thought to have been executed in his workshops. The winged and feathery tailed dolphin, a popular feature of Baroque fountains, appears as ornaments for candlestands in an engraving published by Cuvilliés in 1745. Thomas Johnson (1714-78) of Grafton Street, Soho was a carver, but in addition taught drawing and modelling and published various pattern books.

Prov: By descent to Viscount Cobham; Sotheby's 17th March 1950, 134. Two are now at the Philadelphia Museum of Art (50-83-3-4) and the fourth is at Temple Newsam House, Yorkshire.
Lit: Jourdain 1950, pp. 8-10, fig. IV; Leeds 1950, p. 8; Leeds 1957, pp. 19-21
JH

L46 *Wall-bracket*

Anonymous. *c.* 1760
Gilt pine wood. 460 x 350 x 250
His Grace the Duke of Atholl's Collection, Blair Castle

Beneath the serpentine platform with scalloped border, an exotic bird with outstretched wings is shown emerging from an acanthus-scroll cartouche with weeds hanging from its long bill. A watery rocaille band pours from the cartouche and drips from the base of the scroll stem. This is one of a pair of wall-brackets supplied for James 2nd Duke of Atholl (1690-1764) at Blair Castle, Perthshire. It is a simplified version of a design published in Thomas Johnson, *Collection of Designs*, (1758), p. 42. Designs for related brackets, which served to support busts, candlesticks, porcelain or clocks, were first published in England in the *Director*, 1754.

Lit: Edwards 1974, p. 70, fig. 7
JH

L47 *An Emblematical Girandole. Earth*

Thomas Johnson b. 1714, d. after 1778). 1760
Crayon-manner etching, printed in red; 450 x 298
Lettered with title and *T. Johnson inv: delin & Sculpt; Published by act of Parlimt. decr. ye 16th. 1760 & sold Pr 1s: by ye Proprietor at the Golden Boy in Grafton Street St: Anne's Soho London where this & all other Ornaments are Carv'd & Gilt*

The Trustees of the British Museum (1862-11-8-219)

The only recorded impression of this print, which was perhaps part of a set of The Elements from which no other prints are known (I am indebted to Antony Griffiths for drawing it to my attention). It is a characteristic example of the type of girandole which was popular in the 1750s and 1760s, which incorporates rural figures and ruins ultimately derived from Italian landscape paintings.
MS

L48 *Design for a chimney-piece and overmantel*

Thomas Johnson (b. 1714, d. after 1778). 1760
Etching; 139 x 85 (cut)
Formerly lettered *T.I. fecit* and numbered *3*
VAM (2607)

L48

From *A New Book of Ornaments* (title and seven plates), published by Johnson on 27 December 1760. The plates are an example of Johnson's experiments with etchings in imitation of ink and wash drawing, which resemble the aquatinted plates in his book *A Brief History of Free Masons*, the second edition of which was published in 1784 (British Museum Print Room). Johnson was an active Mason, being Clerk of the Charlotte Street Chapel, Pimlico, as well as Tyler and Janitor to several other Lodges.

Lit: Hayward 1964, pl. 151
MS

L49 *Bed*
Attributed to James Whittle (active 1740-65) and Samuel Norman (active 1752-64) *c.* 1758
Oak and pine, gilded and painted white. Upholstered in red damask; l. 2300. w. 1830
Lord Egremont

The bed is conceived as a bower with garlands of flowers pouring down over the swelling dome from the gnarled oak tree finial inhabited by a squirrel and birds. The curving outline is continued with the nodding arched cornices and their upswept corners terminating in carved plumes. The cluster-column gothic posts are set on rock-work plinths. The inside of the

dome is also overlaid with carved and upholstered garlands. The swept and arched headboard is overlaid with elaborately pierced and carved rocaille and acanthus scrolls. The hangings are largely replaced to the original design of flowers and acanthus which echoes the ornament of the woodwork. The newly fashionable reefed curtains add to the curvilinear quality of the bed. It was supplied for Charles Wyndham, 2nd Earl of Egremont (1710-63) to stand in 'The King of Spain's bedroom' at Petworth House, Sussex, and was listed there in the 1763 inventory. James Whittle and Samuel Norman supplied most of the important furnishings, but the bed is not listed in the surviving accounts. Although it includes nothing specifically chinoiserie, the very daring curves of the cornices would be inconceivable without the influence of the pagoda. For the rest, the ornament is eclectic, combing naturalism, gothic and the most frothy, *mouvementé*, rocaille scrolls possible. For designs of squirrels and birds see, for example, Robert Sayer, *A Book of Birds and Squirrels, etc. from Barlow, c.* 1760.

Lit: Dickson 1978, p. 183; Jackson-Stops 1977, p. 362, fig. 13; Jackson-Stops 1982, p. 54
JH

L50 *Armchair*
Attributed to Samuel Norman (active *c.* 1752-65). *c.* 1760
Virginia walnut. 950 x 390 x 620
The Marquess of Tavistock and Trustees of the Bedford Estates, Woburn Abbey

The rectangular back is carved with plaited strapwork tracery. The bow-fronted seat is dished in the centre and its shaped apron is decorated with acanthus scrolls. The cabriole legs are carved on the knees with fronded quatrefoil cabochons and terminate with inward-scrolling volutes. The suite of four armchairs and four stools has been attributed to Samuel Norman, and was provided for John, 4th Duke of Bedford for Woburn Abbey, Bedfordshire. Related geometric looped backs appear in engravings published by William de La Cour, *Fifth Book of Ornaments*, 1743; Mathew Darly, *A New Book . . .*, 1750/1; and Robert Manwaring, *The Chair-Maker's Friend*, 1765. A set of similar

armchairs, supplied to the 4th Duke of Beaufort, is in Worcester Lodge, Badminton House, Gloucestershire (ill. 'Badminton, Gloucestershire III, *Country Life*, LXXXVI, 9 Dec. 1939, p. 601, fig. 4). Wooden seated chairs of this type were considered suitable for halls, passages and garden buildings.

Lit: Pinto 1955, pp. 202-6
JH

L51 *Chair*
Supplied by Samuel Norman (active 1752-64) 1760
Virginia walnut, partly gilded, upholstered and brass nailed; 106 x 63 x 68
The Marquess of Tavistock and Trustees of the Bedford Estates, Woburn Abbey

The upholstered back has a bowed crest rail with indented corners and the moulded frame is carved with foliage and bead and reel ornament. The seat frame has a bowed apron carved with foliage and a central asymmetrical cartouche, the cabriole and fluted front legs are ornamented with acanthus-bordered cabochons on the knees and terminate in scrolling volute toes. This is part of a suite of fourteen chairs, two armchairs, a large 'easy' chair and a sofa, supplied for John, 4th Duke of Bedford's (1732-71) Grand Saloon at Woburn Abbey and described in a bill dated 1760 from Samuel Norman, 'For fourteen neat carved Virginia walnut chairs partly gilt and varnished, stuffed backs and seats in Linen Quilted and covered with Your Grace's silk damask, for materials and backing do. in the French manner, with fine crimson serge finished complete with the best double gilt nails . . . £58.16.0., for 14 scarlet check petticoat cases to do . . . £5.5.0., for 14 fine flannel cases to do . . . £3.17.0.' This type of upholstered chair with serpentine frame was described as 'French' in Chippendale's *Director*, 1754, where he states that, 'Both the back and Seats must be covered with Tapestry, or other sort of Needlework'. Plate XIV illustrates patterns for chairs with scroll toes, and acanthus cabochon ornament.

Lit: Edwards 1965, pp. 449-61
JH

L52 *Trade card of Pierre Langlois*

Engraved by François-Antoine Aveline (b. 1718, active 1780). *c.* 1760?
Etching and engraving; 234 x 164
Lettered *F A aveline Scul.* and with title etc. in English and French
The Trustees of the British Musuem (Heal 28.121)

In Tottenham Court Road, 'Makes all Sorts of Fine Cabinets and Commodes made & inlaid in the Politest manner with Brass and Tortoishell. & Likewise all rich Ornamental Clock casses, and Inlaid work mended with great Care. Branch chandelier, & lanthorns in Brass at the lowest prices'. The French text makes it clear that he sold ormolu and specialised in 'Meubles, inscrulez de fleurs en bois'. This card, with its putti at work and a figure of Fame bearing up a clock case, strongly recalls vignettes in French architectural books, such as those by P.E. Babel and others in Charpentier's edition of *Vignola*, 1757. The date of Aveline's arrival in England is not known, but he engraved a suite after Pillement, (Berlin 1939, 449, band 6) which, as often with Pillement's designs was published both in Paris and in London in 1759. He also designed the vignettes in the London edition of the *Contes de Fontaine*, 1780, and engraved two prints (BN: Fonds 65) published from the London address of Thomas Major, who returned to England from Paris in 1753. Aveline engraved Mondon's earliest *genre pittoresque* suites in the 1730s.

Lit: BN: Fonds, I, p. 285; Heal 1953, p. 94; Rieder & Thornton 1971, part I MS

L53 *Commode*

Pierre Langlois (active *c.* 1759-81). 1760
Kingwood with marquetry of various woods and ormolu mounts;
844 x 1441 x 635
The Marquess of Tavistock and Trustees of the Bedford Estates, Woburn Abbey

The serpentine top has a reeded brass border and the bombé frame has curved corners and short splayed legs, richly mounted in ormolu with acanthus foliage springing from scroll toes. The centre of the serpentine apron is mounted with a Louis XIV style Zephyr mask with acanthus wings. The five shaped panels on the front are veneered with marquetry of flowers, butterflies, insects and a parrot, set within narrow foliate brass frames, which conceal four drawers and a door to a central compartment. The sides are similarly decorated with roundels and corner spandrel panels, while the top is veneered with a garlanded pastoral music trophy and theatrical mask within a central cartouche flanked by panels portraying flowering branches with birds. The commode was listed in a bill sent to John, 4th Duke of Bedford, and receipted by Pierre Langlois on

December 10 1760, 'In full for a large Inlay'd Commode Table . . . £78.0.0.'. Langlois, a French *ébéniste*, was established at Tottenham Court Road in the late 1750s, and had considerable success with his ormolu-mounted marquetry furniture executed in the French style. He traded at the 'Sign of Commode Tables' and a floral marquetry commode appears on his florid trade card (Cat. L52). This is the earliest of his documented commodes. A number of similar features appear on commodes, by, or firmly attributed to him, including a commode supplied to Croome Court, Worcestershire in 1764 (now in the Metropolitan Museum of Art), a commode at the *VAM* (W8-1967)

Prov: Woburn Abbey, Bedfordshire.
Lit: Coleridge 1968, fig. 50; Edwards 1965, pp. 449-61; Rieder & Thornton 1972, p. 105; Scott-Thomson 1949, p. 53
JH

L54 *Commode*

Attributed to Pierre Langlois. (active *c.* 1759-81) *c.* 1760
Japanned frame partly veneered with Chinese lacquer, ormolu mounts and portor marble slab. 880 x 1210 x 630
Private Collection

The serpentine front is fitted with two drawers which are veneered with black and gold lacquer panels, portraying

L54

Chinese landscapes and buildings, and the sides are japanned to correspond. The curved front corners and splayed feet are elaborately mounted in ormolu with garlanded and winged female scroll caryatids, ornamented with acanthus foliage and scallop shells and linked by palmette sprays to the scroll toes. The drawers fitted with brass foliate rims, female mask escutcheons and handles with scrolling foliage backplates. A design, attributed to Pierre Langlois, for a commode with some similar mounts is in the collection of Sir Francis Dashwood at West Wycombe Park, Buckinghamshire. Langlois was renowned for his skill in moulding lacquer, and in 1763 supplied two commodes and four corner cupboards for the gallery at Strawberry Hill, Twickenham, which were made from a Chinese lacquer screen belonging to Horace Walpole (1717-97). The corner mounts on this commode are attributed to the French emigré metalworker Dominique Jean (active *c.* 1760-1807). One mount bears a stamped 'C' with a crown, which was the mark used on French bronzes around 1745-9. However the mark is blurred and the mount is thought to have been cast from a French model. The pair to this commode is in a private collection in Ireland and there are commodes with some similar features and mounts in the Royal Collection and at Aske Hall, Yorkshire.

Prov: Kenure Park, Rush, Co. Dublin; sold Kenure Park, 21st Sept. 1964, lot 304
Lit: Rieder & Thornton 1972, pp. 105-12
JH

L55 *Library steps*
Attributed to Luke Lightfoot
(*c.* 1723-77) *c.* 1760
Mahogany. 1900 x 1140 x 580
Sir Ralph Verney, Bart

The ends of the treads are ornamented with acanthus scroll brackets, above which are four different patterns of balusters. Each baluster is comprised of a pair of elongated pilasters, entwined by acanthus scrolls, which support a central pilaster. The end baluster is composed of acanthus scrolls, which frame a trelliswork panel. The balusters may have formed part of a

staircase in the East Wing of Claydon House, Buckinghamshire, and are attributed to the carver and amateur architect Luke Lightfoot. They were executed for Ralph, 2nd Earl Verney (1712-1791). The library steps, together with a reading stand, were made up from a collection of balusters which were found in an attic at Claydon at the end of the 19th century.

Lit: Clouston 1904, pp. 12-34, 243-63
JH

L56 *The Ludford tea-chest*
Thomas Sharp. 1760
Mulberry wood with silver mounts;
170 x 270 x 170
Private Collection

The rectangular chest contains two cannisters of mulberry wood and is carved with acanthus scrolls, rosettes and vases of flowers. The top of the hinged lid is fitted with a silver carrying-handle with an open scroll-work back-plate, and the front has a similar scroll-work escutcheon. Thomas Sharp, carver of Stratford-on-Avon, made the box from the mulberry tree, which William Shakespeare was reputed to have planted at New Place, and which was cut down in 1756. The tea-chest was presented by the Corporation of Stratford-upon-Avon to the town's Deputy recorder John Ludford of Ansley Hall, Warwickshire in 1760. Sharp's bill dated 2 Aug 1760,

together with John Ludford's letter of thanks to the Corporation, is in the archives of the Shakespeare Birthplace Trust.

Prov: By inheritance Mrs. Lucy Champneys
Lit: Deelman 1964; Halliwell 1864
JH

L57 *Designs for chandeliers*
Thomas Chippendale (1718-1779)
c. 1760
Pencil, pen and ink and wash, on four sheets pasted together; 221 x 345
Inscribed *Chandeliers for halls &c N 155 T Chippendale Invent et delin Published According to act of Parliament Hulet sculpt*
VAM (2601)

The original drawings for pl. CLV of the 3rd edition of the *Director*, 1762, engraved in reverse by Hulett, 1760. Some elements have been added in the engraving. This assembly of sheets, with inscriptions close to the final lettering on the print, demonstrates Chippendale's method of making up his more complex plates, and also the degree of control he exercised in their production.

Prov: see Cat. L28
MS

L57

L58 *Design for a toilet table*
Thomas Chippendale (1709-1779)
c. 1761
Pencil, pen and ink and wash,
indented for transfer; 335 x 155
Inscribed in pencil *Design Toylet Table*
and numbered *118*. Signed
T. Chippendale.
VAM (D.701-1906)

The original drawing for the *Director,*
3rd edition, 1762, pl. CXVIII,
engraved in reverse by W. Foster,
1761. Chippendale comments (p. 14)
'The Ornaments should be gilt in
burnished Gold; or the whole work
may be japanned, and the Drapery
may be Silk Damask, with Gold
Fringes and Tassels'. This type of
drapery would have echoed that of the
bed.

Prov: bought, with 142 other sheets,
from Messrs Parsons in 1906; the great
majority are by Chippendale, and
many intended for the 3rd edition of
the *Director.*
Lit: Gilbert 1978, I p. 59, II pl. 411;
Ward-Jackson 1958, 95
MS

L59 *Designs for two pier glasses*
Thomas Chippendale (1718-1779)
c. 1761
Pen and ink and wash: 334 x 202
Inscribed *Designs for Pier Glasses* and
No. 173. Signed *T. Chippendale.*
VAM (2598)

The original drawing for pl. CLXXIII
of the 3rd edition of the *Director*, 1762,
engraved in reverse by W. Foster,
1761, described as 'Two Architrave
Frames, with Heads'. The form of the
lower half is that of an ornamented
Palladian frame. The glass on the left
is symbolic of the Arts, and that on
the right of War. One of several
Chippendale drawings which probably
came into the hands of Matthias Lock.

Prov: See Cat. L28
Lit: Ward-Jackson 1958, 96
MS

L60 *Jewel-cabinet*
William Vile (active *c.* 1750-67) and
John Cobb (active *c.* 1750-78). 1761
Mahogany, veneered with tulipwood,
amboyna, rosewood and ivory;
1080 x 813 x 559
Her Majesty The Queen

The rectangular cabinet with
serpentine frame is fitted with doors,
concealing a nest of drawers, and a
frieze compartment with a hinged lid.

The stand is fitted with a drawer and is
supported on cabriole legs with
stretchers. The cabinet and stand are
carved in mahogany and inlaid in
ivory with acanthus scrolls and floral
garlands together with rocaille and
scallop shell ornament. A 'victorious'
trophy comprising a palm-frond,
wreath and trumpet, and a trophy of
'plenty' with inverted cornucopias full
of flowers and pearls are inlaid within
cartouches on the doors, while the top
is inlaid with the Royal arms of King
George III and Queen Charlotte. This
cabinet was supplied for Queen
Charlotte's apartments in St. James's
Palace to contain her jewels, including
the Coronation jewels that had been
given to her as a wedding present by
the King. It is listed in Vile and Cobb's
bill of 1761 as 'A very handsome jewel
cabinet, made of many different kinds
of fine wood on a mahogany frame
richly carved, the front, ends and top
inlaid with ivory in compartments
neatly engraved . . . £138.10.0.'. Most
of the decorative elements of the
cabinet can be found in the *Director*,
1754, and the inlaid ivory can be
compared to that on a theorbo (*VAM*
9-1871), which is signed by Michael
Rauche of Chandos Street and dated
1762.

Prov: St. James's Palace; Mary, Duchess
of Gloucester; Marquess of
Cambridge, H.M. Queen Mary
Lit: Clifford-Smith 1931, pp. 73-4;
Edwards & Jourdain 1955, p. 53, figs.
62, 63; Edwards 1964, p. 101, fig. 32;
Gilbert 1978, p. 23, fig. 12; Pinto
1959; The Queen's Gallery 1962,
cat. no. 43
JH

L61 *Armchair*
Attributed to William Gomm (*c.* 1698-1765) *c.* 1761
Gilt wood, upholstered in silk;
1080 x 710 x 620
Private Collection

The cartouche-shaped back has a moulded and pierced frame carved with scrolls and acanthus foliage. Acanthus leaves grow out from the fronded cartouche surrounding the bell-husk in the centre of the crest rail, and meet 'C' scroll brackets perched on the rounded corners. The seat rail is treated in a similar manner with leaves unwinding from a central cartouche. The legs are carved on knees with acanthus sprays and terminate in inward scrolling toes. The back and seat are fitted with upholstered frames and the arm-pads are close nailed. William Gomm's sketch book (Henry Francis du Pont Winterthur Museum) dating from 1761 contains a design for an armchair which incorporates many of the features of this chair. It formed part of the proposed furnishings for a room together with a pier table and mirror and a girandole. His brother and partner Richard Gomm was one of the subscribers to the *Director*, 1754, which contained a number of designs for 'French' chairs whose frames had open-fretted cartouches.

Prov: Kenure Park, Ireland
Lit: Boynton 1980, pp. 395-400, 706; The Burlington Magazine 1978, p. Lxxii; Hardy 1973; Sotheby's December 1978
JH

L62 *Design for a chimneypiece tablet*
Thomas Johnson (b. 1714 d. after 1778). 1762
Crayon-manner etching;
200 x 347 (cut)
Lettered *T. Johnson invt: & delin Sold at ye Golden Boy in Grafton street St: Anns Soho London* and with a copyright line. Numbered *3*
VAM (E.422-1975)

From *A New Book of Ornaments by Thomas Johnson, Carver. Design'd for Tablets & Frizes for Chimney-Pieces; Useful for Youth to draw after,* published 28 August 1762 (title and five sheets). The prints in this suite are the most accomplished examples of Johnson's exercises in the crayon manner (see also Cat. L47). They include large raffle-leaves and were probably inspired by similar drawing exercises published in France (eg Cat. E20). The bull-baiting scene in the centre of this chimney-piece tablet was copied on a design for a Venetian stove in W. and J. Welldon's *The Smith's Right Hand,* 1765. In Robert Sayer's list of 1774 the suite was to be had 'printed either in Red or Black'.

Lit: Hayward 1975, pl. 98
MS

L63 *Organ (part of case)*
The case attributed to William Vile and John Cobb (active 1750-65). The organ by John Crang (active 1744-1773). *c.* 1765
Pine, originally painted white;
5590 x 5180 x 3660
VAM (W13-1980)

The case has a serpentine front with central tower and corner turrets and concave splayed sides. The upper section is filled with pipes and the lower one fitted with doors. The case is ornamented with acanthus foliage, floral garlands, palm, laurel and oak branches together with musical trophies suspended from ribbons. The central doors are carved with rose bushes bearing a book of music inscribed with the National Anthem. The case was originally surmounted by a figure of Fame. The organ was made for Alderman William Beckford, Lord Mayor of London (1709-70) and stood in the organ hall at Fonthill House, Wiltshire. This is one of the grandest chamber organs produced in the 18th century and the superb quality of its carving has been compared to some of the cabinet-pieces produced by the firm of Vile & Cobb and their specialist carver Sefferin Alken.

Prov: Fonthill House sale, Philipps, 1801, August 19, 46. Presented by Earl Pomfret to Towcester Church, Northamptonshire in 1817
Lit: Britton 1801, p. 214; Freeman 1937, pp. 818, 819; Pevsner 1973, fig. 44; Wilson 1968, p. 18
JH

L64 *Design for an armchair*
John Linnell (1723-1796). *c.* 1765
Pen and ink and water-colour;
170 x 109
Inscribed in pencil *No. 5*
VAM (E.93-1929)

The design is close to, but not exactly the same as Cat. L65 and another chair of the same type at Arundel Castle. The frame is gilt, the upholstery of red damask.

Prov: One of a group of designs bequeathed to the artist's nephew, Thomas Tatham; his brother, Charles Heathcote Tatham, who pasted them into an album in 1800, with a view to publication; Julia Richmond (née Tatham); Richmond Family; James Chance
Lit: Hayward & Kirkham 1980, fig. 50
MS

L64

L65

L65 *Armchair*
William and John Linnell. 1723-96
c. 1760
Gilt wood with green damask upholstery, the seat and arm-pads close-nailed; 1035 x 740 x 580
VAM (O.P.H.88-1949)

The cartouche-shaped back is fitted with an upholstered panel and its frame is carved with reeded mouldings wrapped round by acanthus leaves, which emerge from the watery cartouches flanking the central scallop shell on the crest-rail. The bow-fronted seat-rail has incised panels on either side of the central scallop-shell cartouche, and the cabriole legs are carved with pointed leaves on the knees and acanthus foliage on the inward scrolling toes. This is one of a set of eight armchairs and two settees which are thought to have been supplied by the firm of William and John Linnell for Francis Child's (1735-1763) drawing room at Osterley Park House, Middlesex. A watercolour by John Linnell for a 'French' armchair of similar character survives (Cat. L64). The acanthus-wrapped reeding links the chair back to the ornament of the frieze of the chimney-piece, originally part of Francis Child's furnishings of the Drawing Room. The acanthus carving also links the frame to the damask pattern of its upholstery.

Lit: Fowler and Cornforth 1974, pp. 154, 155; Hayward & Kirkham 1980, fig. 51; Tomlin 1972, pp. 48, 49
JH

L66 *Design for a chair*
John Linnell (1723-1796). *c.* 1765
Pencil and wash; 162 x 127
VAM (E.113-1929)

Very close to Cat. L67.

Prov: see Cat. L64
Lit: Hayward & Kirkham 1980, fig. 45
MS

L67 *Chair*
John Linnell (1723-96). *c.* 1765
Mahogany, upholstered in leather, close nailed; 960 x 580 x 560
Dr Eric Till

The splat is formed as a pair of interlocked figures-of-eight, and supports a dished acanthus-fringed scroll in the centre of the shaped crest-rail. The rectangular seat is supported by straight front legs carved with rosettes and bead ornament and linked by stretchers. This is one of a set of twenty four 'parlour' chairs thought to have been supplied by John Linnell to Robert Child (1739-82) of Middleton Park, Oxfordshire. Linnell's drawing (Cat. L66) is for a closely related chair. Entwined-loop chair-backs were published by William de la Cour in his *5th Book of Ornaments* (1743), but Chippendale in the *Director*, 1754, pl. XVI was the first to publish designs for chairs with looped splats.

Prov: Robert Child: by inheritance to the 9th Earl of Jersey and sold in the 1930s
Lit: Hayward and Kirkham. 1980, pp. 78, 101, 116, figs. 46, 47
JH

L68 *Desk*
Attributed to William Ince (active *c.* 1755-1803) & John Mayhew (active *c.* 1755-1811). *c.* 1760
Satinwood with marquetry decoration and ormolu mounts; 1020 x 960 x 510
The Earl Waldegrave, KG, GCVO, TD, DL

The sloping desk-top, with hinged fall-front, is set on a table frame fitted with three drawers and standing on cabriole legs. The front and sides are concave, while the sweep and arched cornices of the fall-front are echoed by the shaped apron. Ormolu foliate mounts are applied to the top corners

L68

and the shoulders and toes of the stand. Marquetry sprays of flowers ornament the top and the drawer-fronts and are also framed within scroll-cartouches on the fall-front and sides. In addition there are musical trophies on the sides, while the fall-front is embellished with the arms of Walpole impaling Waldegrave for Maria, Countess Waldegrave. The desk is reputed to have been presented by Horace Walpole to his niece following her marriage to James, 2nd Earl Waldegrave, in 1759. A desk of this form, but with more restrained ornament, at Burghley House, Licolnshire, has been attributed to Ince & Mayhew (information gratefully received from Mr. Hugh Roberts) and it has been suggested that they also supplied this desk. The base of the desk follows the traditional *bureau-plat* shape, such as that drawn by John Vardy *c.* 1745 (see Cat. C15). This form of *bureau en pente* is thought to have been first manufactured in England by Pierre Langlois in the late 1750s.

Prov: Chewton House, Somerset
Lit: Coleridge 1968, fig. 49; Rieder & Thornton 1972, p. 30, fig. 1
JH

L69 *Candlestand*
William Ince (active *c.* 1758-1803) & John Mayhew (active *c.* 1755-1811).
1768
Gilt wood with brass nozzles;
1830 x 530 x 530
Burghley House Collection

Bold 'S' shaped acanthus scrolls form the tripartite stem and support a pineapple framed within watery rocaille borders. Clusters of pineapple leaves emerge from the scroll brackets at the top and support a pineapple finial which is entwined by three twisted candlebranches. The stand is wrapped round by floral and fruit garlands and is supported on tripod acanthus legs with lion paw feet. This is one of four tripods supplied by William Ince and John Mayhew to Cecil, 9th Earl of Exeter (1725-93) for

Burghley House, Lincolnshire and listed in their bill of 1768, 'Four tripods for the hall very richly carved with lamps to ditto gilt and varnished . . . £120' (information gratefully received from Mr. Hugh Roberts). Ince and Mayhew, cabinet-makers and upholsterers of Golden Square, were one of Chippendale's principal competitors, and authors of a rival publication to *The Director*, called *The Universal System of Household Furniture*, 1762, (Cat. M21). Among the designs for candlestands was one formed as a tree, which the authors claimed had, 'Gained great applause in the execution'.
JH

L70 *Night Table*
James Cullen (active *c.* 1750-79).
c. 1768
Mahogany with inlaid chequer bands and ormolu mounts; 810 x 410 x 410
The Hopetoun House Preservation Trust (Not exhibited)

The drum-shaped frame has splayed corners supported on cabriole legs, which scroll up to form brackets and are linked to the extended corners at the top. The legs are mounted with ormolu acanthus-scrolls at top and

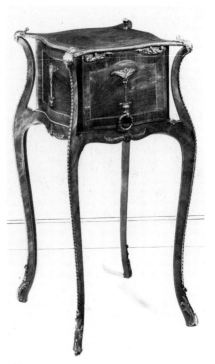

L70

bottom linked by husk-trails, and the front and sides are mounted with potted palm trees in the centre, and acanthus sprays on the serpentine aprons. The arched-top panel fitted in the front is hinged and can be opened and pushed back under the top. One of a pair of tables (the other is now at Lauriston Castle, Edinburgh) en suite with a pair of large *bombé* commodes decorated with Chinese brass escutcheon plates, which James Cullen supplied for John, 2nd Earl of Hopetoun's (1704-81) state bedroom at Hopetoun House, nr. Edinburgh. Designs for the commodes were included in a letter sent from London by Cullen to the Earl on the 25 February, 1768, 'Herewith are the designs for the Commodes in the Grand Bedchr. one of which is intended to introduce different colloured woods which with good brasses has an effect that is generally approved here . . .'

JH

L71

L71 *Scrapbook*
49 pages in paper covers, containing 54 engravings and drawings; 258 x 194
Inscribed on the cover *Ornaments by Lock . . . Vivares and Others 1757*
The Chippendale Society

The pieces include: 6 plates by Matthias Lock, 1752 (see Cat. L24);

4 plates of Chinese grotesques by François Vivares; 6 plates from a set mistitled *A New Drawing Book of Ornaments Shields, Masks &c* (Berlin 1939, 260; Heckscher 1979, p. 17) with plates by Vivares and Anthony Walker dated 1752; plate 7 of Lajoue's *Second Livre de Cartouches* (Cat. C5); two cartouches by Gravelot; 4 plates from J. Collins, *A New Book of Shields*, engraved by J.S. Muller, Sayer's edition (Berlin 1939, 267); a French Baroque print of a trophy; 2 vases, reversed copies after Charles Eisen (Berlin 1939, 440, 441, dated 1752, 1753); title and 4 plates of *A New Book of Hunting Trophies Engrav'd from the Designs of the Celebrated Monsieur Huet properly adapted to the New Manner of Ornamenting Rooms & Screens with Prints*, engraved by P. Angier, published by Vivares, 1757, (Berlin 1939, 447, after 446, they were also copied in a suite published by Regnier of Newport Street); 15 fragments of borders for print rooms published by Vivares, dated 1754, 1767 and 1768. Also included are two late 18th century trade tickets, a drawing in reverse of a Baron's coat of arms and a sketch of a putto pointing to an inscription.

Prov: The Boydell family; Sotheby Beresford Adams, Chester, 27 May 1981, 31
Lit: Friedman 1981, figs. 5, 6
MS

L72 *Carver's album of ornamental designs*
Gideon Saint (1729-1799). *c.* 1760
Drawings and etchings on paper; 343 x 216
The Metropolitan Museum of Art Harris Brisbane Dick Fund (acc. 34.90.1)

The vellum-bound volume has 364 numbered pages, each sheet with the same mid-18th century English watermark. Pasted to the inside front cover is an engraved trade card within whose rococo cartouche is the legend: *Gideon Saint Carver & Gilder, at the Golden Head in Princes Street, near Leicester Fields*. The book is divided into twelve sections, each with a finger tab marked with the name of a specific furniture form. On the pages within each section are pasted illustrations of the particular form, either etchings from pattern books or original drawings. In addition, a number of

designs by Gideon Saint himself are drawn directly on the pages. The album exemplifies the intimate connection between the French Huguenot community in England and the rococo style there. Gideon Saint was born of French parents, apprenticed to a Huguenot carver, and married to a Huguenot woman; he was an official of a French church and a French school in London. Between 1763 and 1779 he ran his carving and gilding establishment in Princes Street. He began filling his scrapbook with Régence-style French engravings (by Berain, Boulle, Mariette, Pineau, and Roumier), but soon switched exclusively to English designs (by Lock, Copland, and Johnson) in the fully developed rococo manner. The scrapbook also graphically documents how Georgian craftsmen worked. First, they 'mined' published books for ideas. Here, inexpensive cahiers of carvers' designs were cut up, the parts rearranged by type of object, and numbered, providing a library of anonymous designs to show would-be clients. Second, they made full-scale drawings of the ornament to be carved. Two such drawings, for a picture frame, survive with the scrapbook. On each, one half of the design was drawn on a folded sheet which was then pricked with a pin to duplicate the pattern on the other side.

Lit: Heckscher 1969
MHH

L73 *Chest of drawers*
Thomas Chippendale, (1718-79). *c.*1772
Mahogany with ormolu handles; 840 x 1320 x 610
The Earl of Harewood

This chest of drawers is serpentine in all its profiles. All four corners are delicately carved as elongated 'S' scrolls with acanthus leaves and husks on the shoulders and rosettes and pendant husks on the sides. Three graduated drawers are fitted with ormolu handles with acanthus-cartouche back-plates, and the bottom drawer incorporates the apron. The chest of drawers is thought to have formed part of Chippendale's furnishings supplied to Daniel Lascelles (1714-1784) for Goldsborough Hall, Yorkshire.

L73

Although no bills survive, a Day Work Book records several visits by Chippendale's foreman William Reid to Goldsborough Hall between 1771 and 1776. This pattern of serpentine-fronted chest of drawers is called a 'French commode table' in the *Director*. The elimination of a top pair of drawers, common in earlier pieces, the restrained ornament and the 'French scroll toes' reflect Chippendale's more refined style of the late 1760s, and indeed the rosettes on the shoulders introduce a neo-classical feature. Chippendale stated in the *Director* (3rd ed. 1762) that the ornament on such 'commode tables' could be executed in brass rather than carved in wood. Carved decoration, however, remained popular for mahogany veneered furniture, whereas brass mounts predominated on marquetry pieces.

Prov: Goldsborough Hall; by descent Harewood House, Yorkshire
Lit: Gilbert 1978, fig. 225, 226, p. 259
JH

L74 *Armchair*
Anonymous. *c.* 1770
Beechwood with cane seat and back painted green and white;
920 x 630 x 660
The National Trust, (Uppark,)

The moulded frame of the cartouche-shaped back is carved on the crest rail with a spray of flowers and foliage. Similar sprays decorate the centre of the serpentine seat rail and the knees of the slender cabriole legs, which terminate in scrolls carved on the toes. It is one of a set of sixteen chairs and four armchairs supplied to Sir Matthew Featherstonhaugh (1714-74) for Uppark, Sussex. Such easily moveable chairs for everyday use, sometimes called 'rout' chairs, were known in France as '*chaises au courant*' as opposed to the richly upholstered and more expensive '*chaises meublants*' which lined the walls. The light cabriole leg with floral ornament continued to be fashionable into the 1780s, and can be seen for instance in Hepplewhite, *The Cabinet-maker and Upholsterer's Guide*, 1788, pl. 16.

Lit: Coleridge 1967, p. 161, fig. 11
JH

L75 *A View of Cheapside, as it appeard on Lord Mayor's Day Last*
John June (active 1747-52). 1761
Engraving; 238 x 343
Lettered with title, copyright line dated 16 Nov 1761, the address of J. Smith and *June Invt. et Sculpt.*

The Trustees of the British Museum

The young George III and his Queen, together with the Duke of Cumberland and the Duke of York, watch the procession. The Lord Mayor's State Coach, first used in 1757, had been made by Joseph Berry, with painted panels by Giovanni Battista Cipriani. Marcus Binney (1984) has suggested that the design of coach may be connected with Sir Robert Taylor.

Lit: BM:S 3819; Wackernagel 1983, pp. 403-404
MS

L76 *Design for the decoration of the side of a coach*
Charles Crace (1727-1784). 1754
Pencil, pen and ink and wash;
90 x 180 (the drawing)
Inscribed *Charles Crace 1754*
The Cooper Hewitt Museum, The Smithsonian Institution's National Museum of Design (1948-40-185)

A design for painting the side of a Berlin coach with an overall asymmetrical design of rococo scrolls incorporating the arms of a Duke supported by lions, and two crests. Attached to the drawing are two cuttings from newspapers, one of which advertises the coach painters Thomas Greenwood and William Taunton. The other, inscribed '1756' advertises the practice of Charles Crace, designer of coaches and carriages, 'who has designed and drawn for the Trade several years, and has just finish'd a complete Collection of the same, particularly some new Designs in the French and Chinese Taste'. Crace published in 1750 a set of plates for coach designs (Metropolitan Museum of Art, see *The Carriage Journal*, IV, no. 3, 1962). He was the son of Thomas Crace, citizen and coachmaker, and married Susannah Newman, the daughter of a German cabinet maker living in Brownlow St., Drury Lane. John Crace & Sons, the well-known 19th century firm of decorators, was descended from Charles Crace's brother Edward, who started as a coach designer. J.D. Crace owned a scrapbook of Edward's coach designs and a few of Charles's (see Crace MSS, VAM).

Prov: The Crace family; from a group of drawings chiefly for the firm of John Crace and Sons. Purchased in Memory of Annie Schermerhorn Kane MS

L77 *Model for the State Coach of King George III*

Sir William Chambers (1723-1796) (designer); Giovanni Battista Capezzuoli (active *c.* 1755-*c.* 1782) and John Voyez (active *c.* 1760-1773) (sculptors); Giovanni Battista Cipriani (1727-1785) (painter). 1760/61
Wood, beeswax, and iron, gilt and painted; l. 1240, w. 432
The Worshipful Company of Coach and Coach Harness Makers

The model, used for the construction of the coach completed in 1762, follows Chambers' final design for the whole coach, dated 1760 (WCRL 17942; Harris 1970, 134) except that it hangs in elbow springs (see the variant design, Soane Museum, Arch. Libr. Dr. 3, sect. 6, fol. 23). Chambers's

design was the result of several artists' projects, including those of Robert Adam and John Linnell. Such models had been used since the 16th century. For ceremonial reasons State coaches for solemn entries followed the French *grand carosse* design of the 1680s. The broken contours of their bodies concealed steps to facing seats. Instead of the usual single driver's perch of the *carosse* this model and the coach have two perches, a characteristic of the more recent Berlin coach, which became the new state coach type in the 1760s. Also unique are the earliest recorded crane-necks of the perches, shown by Chambers, and by Linnell in the latter's baroque co-project with the coach builder Samuel Butler (Harris 1970, 138). A variant design by Linnell shows the Berninesque tritons used by Chambers in the model and coach, replacing the fore and hind-standards of the Soane design. The Tritons are closely derived from designs by Joseph Wilton, the King's State Coach Carver. The modern carriage and straight flat-sided body emphasise the neo-classical aspects of Chambers' original ideas and motifs, which are now more evident in the model than the coach, which was altered in the nineteenth century. The hammer-cloth on the model is modern. The designs discussed by Harris (1970, 63, WCRL 13999, 14000) are for the print of the Roman state coach of Lord Castlemaine, published in 1687.

Lit: Harris 1970, no. 63, figs. 134-8; Hayward and Kirkham 1980, p. 58; Pitkin 1979, pp. 4-7; Wackernagel 1983, pp. 380-3
RHW

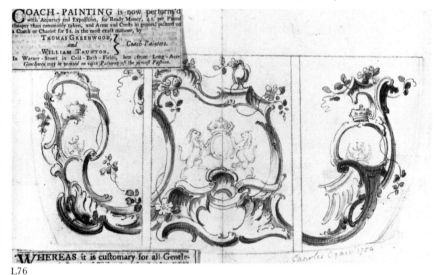

L76

L77

L78 *Two designs for sedan chairs*
Anonymous. *c.* 1770
Pen and ink and wash;
248 x 412; 249 x 417
*The Cooper-Hewitt Museum, The
Smithsonian Institution's National Museum
of Design (1900-1-15,17)*

No. 17 is rococo chinoiserie in style,
and carries a Baron's coronet and the
letter H. The poles, however are
decorated with neo-classical husk
ornament. No. 15 is neo-classical in
style but for the small window and the
owner's armorial cartouche. The
colour range of pinks, greens, lilacs
etc, is probably a reflection of the
influence of the interior decorative
work of the Adam brothers.
MS

L79 *Trade cards*
*The Trustees of the British Museum, unless
otherwise stated*

B. Philpott, painter. Thomas Scarlett
(active 1743). *c.* 1745? (Heal 90.89).
Philpott painted coaches, funeral
escutcheons, houses, signs and floor
cloths. The asymmetrical and freely-
etched design showing Philpott's wares
is without parallel; Scarlett can
perhaps be linked with 'Mr . . . Scarlett
Optician & Spectacle Maker' (Vertue
III, p. 117) who was collecting pictures
in 1743. An etched cartouche by
Scarlett, dated 1743, is in the British
Museum.

William Cochran and Jonathan
Cartwright, coachmakers of Davy
Gate, York. Anonymous. *c.* 1770?
(Heal 43.5). The foliage is probably
indebted to prints after Jean Pillement.

William Welsh, coach and harness
makers, near College Green, Bristol.
William Milton (active 1740-1790).

Blaise Castle House Museum
A cartouche on wheels; the right-hand
border is taken from the subscription
plate of Gaetano Brunetti's *Sixty
Different Sorts of Ornament,* 1736
(Cat. B10). Milton was a local engraver
of very spirited and imaginative
rococo trade cards; A book of his
designs survives in the Bristol
Reference Library (Braik. Coll. 10124).
MS

Architecture and Interiors

Design for the Dining room at Kirtlington Park. John Sanderson. See Cat. M4.

Rococo Architecture and Interiors

Gervase Jackson-Stops

In a celebrated passage in his *Analysis of Beauty*, Hogarth writes 'it is no wonder this subject should have long been thought insoluble since the nature of many parts of it cannot possibly come within the reach of mere men of letters'.[1] A clear definition of the rococo style is almost as difficult for 'mere men of letters' to establish as the principle of beauty itself, because, as Hogarth was at pains to point out, the style involved a direct means of artistic expression – without the supporting machinery of Baroque mythology and allegory – and was thus essentially abstract, even if it was ultimately based on the observation of natural forms.

This very abstraction does help, however, to explain why the rococo was never adopted for external architecture in this country. Even on the continent, what Henry-Russell Hitchcock has described as works of 'atechtonic' architecture – buildings in which the structural elements have been generally eliminated – are largely confined to the façades of Parisian town houses, garden buildings like the Amalienburg and the pilgrimage churches of southern Germany and Austria, whose exteriors are uncomfortably contrived to suit internal plans of great originality, often based on interlocking circles, oval and ellipses.[2] As Anthony Blunt put it, 'Rococo architecture reaches its most complete expression in works on a small scale and in rooms which are essentially intimate'.[3]

In England, Lord Burlington's rediscovery of the classical architecture of Palladio was so perfectly matched to the aspirations and the practical needs of the great Whig landowners that it was to remain unchallenged until Robert Adam's return from Rome in 1760: the villas of the Brenta were not only transported to the banks of the Thames, but, much enlarged in scale, dominated the broad-acred parks of East Anglia, Yorkshire or the West Country, their symmetrical wings and pavilions no longer barns and farm-workers' quarters but chapels, libraries, private family apartments, or household offices. Perhaps too much has been made in the past of the divisions between the official Palladian architects of the Office of Works and the second generation of designers, centred on the St Martin's Lane Academy, who promoted the rococo. Convinced Burlingtonians like John Vardy and the elder Matthew Brettingham could produce (or connive at) highly rococo interior designs for Milton Abbey or Petworth; while Isaac Ware and James Paine could construct the most conventional and static Palladian shells, as at Chesterfield House or the Mansion House at Doncaster, to contain some of their wildest rococo fantasies (Cat. M2).

To a large extent rococo in fact became the official style of interior decoration, particularly for smaller and more intimate rooms, among this new generation of Palladians in the 1740s and 50s, but posed no threat to the established conventions of exterior architecture. The canted or semicircular bows favoured by Ware and Paine (for example at Wrotham and Stockeld), and adopted by Thomas Wright of Durham at Shugborough and Horton, gave some movement to their façades. But these can hardly be described as true rococo features, and the influence of Gravelot and

1   Design for a British Museum.
Cornelius Johnston. 1754.
Guildhall Library, City of London.

Brunetti makes itself felt only in the froth of carving surrounding the cartouche of family arms in a pediment, like that at Nostell Priory or Gopsall (Cat. M16). The one unmistakably rococo design for a large building is Cornelius Johnston's ambitious proposal for a British Museum, engraved in 1754, and like the *residenz* of a German elector, with echoes of Paine and Hayman in the cross-section showing its interior (Fig. 1). The work of a painter, attempting to express the high ideals of the St Martin's Lane Academicians, it found no followers stylistically, though an interesting milestone on the road to the founding of Reynolds' Royal Academy.[4]

Ironwork, which one might have thought a fruitful field for rococo experiment, after the technical achievements of Tijou and his English followers, was equally a lost cause – partly perhaps because cast-iron could increasingly be produced more cheaply than wrought-iron, though only in much simpler form. Engravings from Huquier's *Nouveau Livre de Serrurerie* were stolen by J. Jores for his *New Book of Iron Work* of 1759 (Cat. K2), and other equally rococo designs from Blondel's *Maisons de Plaisance* found their way into W. and J. Welldon's *The Smith's Right Hand* of 1765. But neither pattern-book seems to have evoked a response among London or provincial craftsmen.[5]

Rococo garden buildings are a different story. The watercolours of Thomas Robins (Cat. R8), Wright's *Arbours and Grottoes* (the first engravings in Europe to show buildings in naturalistic surroundings), and what

2 Congreve's Monument at Stowe. William Kent. 1736.

3 Design for a cascade at West Wycombe. Attributed to Maurice-Louis Jolivet. *c.* 1752. *Sir Francis Dashwood, Bart.*

Walpole called the 'Sharawadgi taste' of amateurs like Richard Bateman, Philip Southcote and Philip Spence, come half way between the Baroque layouts of Bridgeman and the natural landscapes, with picturesque classical buildings after Claude, supplied by Capability Brown.[6] Their serpentine paths are the equivalent of the C and S-scrolls of rococo carving and plasterwork, and their whimsical ornaments – seats, arbours, temples, wooden gates and pergolas – are likewise Chinese, Gothick or naturalistic in the manner of Thomas Johnson's ornament: bark and root houses, pebble alcoves, grottoes with false stalactites, menageries filled with exotic birds and beasts. Monkeys, straight out of the *singeries* of Christopher Huet and Andien de Clermont, can be found on Congreve's Monument at Stowe (Fig. 2), or flanking the cascade (Fig. 3) and the suggestive oval entrance to Sir Francis Dashwood's Temple of Venus at West Wycombe – designed for him by another Frenchman, Maurice-Louis Jolivet.[7]

Gothick follies, like William Halfpenny's garden house at Frampton and his villa at Stouts Hill, Uley, show a typically rococo interest in the style simply for its exotic qualities and sentimental associations, not for the sort of antiquarian and archaeological reasons which were later to gain vogue at Strawberry Hill. Chinese pavilions and bridges, like those at Shugborough, Wallington and Wootton, were derided by Sir William Chambers for the same reasons, that they were 'mere inventions', copied 'from the lame representations found on porcelain and paper hangings'.[8] His own pagoda at Kew, based on drawings made as a young man on a voyage to China, may have been more accurate but was equally light-hearted in intention – its nodding dragons and tinkling bells summoning the royal party into tea. Though Kew also boasted an Alhambra and a Mosque (probably designed by J.H. Muntz), and there were Turkish tents at Painshill and Stourhead, *turquerie* was not as popular in England as in Germany and Austria, where the Danube still provided a trade route to Constantinople. Here by contrast, ever-increasing trade through the East India Company kept up a steady interest in the Orient.

Despite this plethora of follies and eyecatchers, pure rococo buildings in the continental sense are virtually unknown in the English landscape garden. Only the Trianon-like Queen's Temple at Stowe, its niches once containing garlanded serpentine urns, or the oval domed temple on a lonely hill-top in the park at Allerton (surely by James Paine), give one a taste of the Watteau *fête-champêtre*. To find the true rococo architecture in England we have to retrace our steps indoors, and to approach the achievements of the *stuccatori*, which still enliven the walls and ceilings of so many country houses, through that of their predecessors – the decorative painters.

The first stirrings of the rococo in English architectural decoration long predate the arrival of Gravelot in London or the opening of Slaughter's Coffee House. In 1707, the 4th Earl (later first Duke) of Manchester returned to England from his embassy in Venice, with the painters Antonio Pellegrini and Marco Ricci. After working at Kimbolton (Fig. 4), the Venetian painters decorated the hall and saloon at Castle Howard in 1710, collaborating here with the plasterers, Bagutti and Plura.[9] Whether the latter were also brought to England by the Earl of Manchester, by Gibbs or by Leoni, is uncertain. But what is clear is that this team of artists and craftsmen together produced a 'proto-rococo' scheme of decoration which was to have immense consequences for the future. In place of the

4 Staircase at Kimbolton Castle.
   Painting by Antonio Pellegrini.
   After 1710.

5 Detail of the painted ceiling in the
   Monkey Room, Kirtlington Park.
   Andien de Clermont. c. 1745.

heavy feigned architecture, ponderous allegory and dark Baroque tones of
Verrio, Laguerre and Thornhill, the Venetians substituted lighter colours,
and a softer texture, paying far less attention to subject matter. Still more
important they avoided painted architecture all together, leaving the
plasterers to frame their air-borne goddesses with sinuous cartouches
formed of shells and scrolls, or flanked by winged caryatids supporting
baskets of flowers.

Pellegrini's later work at Narford is still more rococo in feeling. His
serpentine *trompe-l'oeil* vases derived from Polidoro, and his elegant
trophies of musical instruments, are just the sort of ornament which
plasterers of the 1730s and 40s would be rendering in three dimensions.
Of Pellegrini's successors, Antonio Bellucci, who worked at Canons,
Giacomo Amiconi and Andrea Casali display an increasing softness and
lightness of touch, prefiguring Hayman in their subject matter, and leaving
Sleter at Moor Park and Mereworth almost isolated in his liking for heroic
deeds and Roman *gravitas*, derived from the Carracci. But it was only with
the emergence of Andien de Clermont in the 1730s (previously he is
thought to have been a designer in Joshua Morris's Soho tapestry
manufactory), that a truly rococo style of painted decoration was born in
this country. De Clermont's wall and ceiling paintings ultimately derive
from the grotesques of late 17th century *ornemanistes* such as Berain,
Audran and Gillot, with their Commedia dell'Arte figures (Cat. C12),
fantastic orientals and outlandish birds and beasts. His trophies of war at
Wilton are consciously satirical, with a flapping goose replacing the
Imperial eagle and a dog's head on the marshal's baton; at Wentworth
Woodhouse he is capable of charming *scènes galantes* in the manner of
Watteau; but it is his *singeries* at Kirtlington and elsewhere which come
nearest to the vigour and playfulness of Vauxhall Gardens rococo (Fig. 5).
These monkeys mounted on greyhounds and shooting at hares larger than
themselves, look back to Christopher Huet's *singeries* at Chantilly, and may
ultimately be due to the import of Indian chintz palampores with a design
of monkeys aiding Vishnu against his demon adversaries. But their
significance in a rococo context is that they represent the comedy of
manners: La Fontaine's Fables, and later books such as Julien de la
Mettrie's *L'Homme Machine* of 1748, re-established animals as intelligent
beings, differing only from man in their degree of organisation.[10] With
rational enquiry leading to a new interest in the observation of nature, this
kind of humorous allegory was bound to be more popular than the heavy
symbolism of Ovid and Homer.

Natural forms, and the attributes of everyday life, became increasingly
popular in plasterwork as much as in decorative painting. Just as a small
band of Venetian artists held the field in England in the 1720s and 30s, so
the leading plasterers of the period, usually called Italians, in fact came
from a small area of the Ticino – in what is now Italian-speaking
Switzerland. Bagutti, the first recorded, came from Rovio near Lugano; the
two Artari brothers from the nearby village of Arogno; the Vassallis and the
Bernasconis (see Cat. A5) from Riva San Vitale and the Francinis from
Mendrisio.[11] With such a close-knit circle of constantly shifting partnerships,
it is, not surprisingly, difficult to differentiate these *stuccatori* on stylistic
grounds. To add to the problem, it is seldom clear from the accounts
whether they were working to their own designs, or merely following the
detailed instructions of an architect. James Gibbs' meticulous drawings for

6 Saloon at Ditchley Park. Plasterwork by the Artari brothers, Vassalli and Serena. 1725.

7 Detail of the ceiling of the saloon at Carton, Co. Kildare. Plasterwork by Paolo and Filippo Francini. *c.* 1740.

8 Ceiling of the King's Bedroom at Compton Place, Eastbourne. Plasterwork attributed to Charles Stanley and John Hughes. 1728-9.

ceilings at Fairlawne in Kent, and Gubbins, Herefordshire, suggest that he was responsible for designing most of the outstanding work carried out for him by Bagutti and Artari in the 1720s – including Orleans House, Twickenham, St Martin's-in-the-Fields (Cat. B6), and the Senate House at Cambridge. The Saloon at Ditchley (Fig. 6) is more Italianate, and more nearly rococo, than anything we know of Gibbs', but just to confuse matters, no less than four plasterers are recorded here – Giuseppe and Adalbertus Artari, Francesco Vassalli and Francesco Serena, who later worked at Ottobeuren under the great Bavarian stuccoist, Joseph Anton Feuchtmayer.[12]

Yet another possibility cannot be ruled out: that instead of either architect or plasterer, an *ornemaniste* (like Daniel Marot at an earlier period) could be called in to design wall and ceiling decorations. Gaetano Brunetti was perhaps the most influential of these during the development of the rococo in England. As a *quadraturista* (or specialist in architectural painting) he had collaborated with Amiconi on the staircase of Lord Tankerville's house in St James Square, and probably also with Sleter at Moor Park – where the borders to the *Seasons* in the Saloon are close to engravings in his *Sixty Different Sorts of Ornaments*, published in 1736.[13] (Cat. B10)

But the plaster ceiling in the hall at Clandon (convincingly attributed to Bagutti and Artari) repeats so many of the painted motifs at Moor Park as to suggest Brunetti had a hand in its design too. On the borderline between Baroque and rococo, it seems to show the very moment of explosion, with the architectural elements blown apart, figures clutching disembodied fragments of entablature, their legs trailing over the cornice like the angels in a Counter-Reformation *trasparante*.

The subject matter at Clandon is still heroic, complementing Rysbrack's bas-reliefs of Hercules above the chimneypieces, and this remained the standard treatment for halls – whose decoration was intended to provide a transition from external architecture to the more comfortable and intimate rooms beyond. At Stoneleigh, medallions of the labours of Hercules decorate the walls and his apotheosis is represented on the ceiling – probably by Vassalli. Extraordinarily old-fashioned pattern-books were often used for these scenes, a favourite being Cesare Ripa's *Iconologia* of 1630 (published in France at various later dates), the source for some of

the plasterwork by Paolo and Filippo Francini at Riverstown House, Co. Cork.[14] Elsewhere the brothers were to copy Poussin ceilings, cameos and gems taken from del Pozzo, or muses from Reinach and de Rossi, interpreting these seventeenth-century academic subjects with a rococo grace and lack of drama (Fig. 7). Others were to use Francis Barlow, a still more unlikely source, for his depictions of Aesop's Fables – Thomas Roberts in plaster medallions at Kirtlington and Nuthall Temple, Sir Henry Cheere in chimneypieces at Picton Castle and Sandbeck.

The relations between sculptors and plasterers in the rococo period deserve a closer study than they have yet received. Charles Stanley the Dane, who worked under the stuccoist C.E. Brenno at Fredensborg and Clausholm, and then under Jan van Logteren in Amsterdam, came to England in 1727 where he studied with the sculptors Delvaux and Scheemakers. As well as carving church monuments in marble, he was almost certainly concerned with the plasterwork at Compton Place, Eastbourne (Fig. 8), and later in 1742 worked with Thomas Roberts of Oxford on the decoration of the Radcliffe Camera 'according to a drawing made by Mr. Gibbs'.[15] Stanley, and later William Collins, who worked with James Paine, must have provided valuable cross-fertilisation between the two disciplines. The young Joseph Wilton too must have learnt from his father, the plasterer William Wilton, who was responsible for the highly rococo ceilings at the Foundling Hospital, about 1740.

If the treatment of halls remained sculptural, plasterwork in other rooms expressed their uses too. Dining rooms like that at Hagley were given garlands of vines and Bacchic emblems, goatskins and satyr masks, or trophies of the chase to complement paintings by Snyders at Easton Neston. Bedrooms might have *amorini* on billowing clouds, turtle doves and cupid's bows; drawing rooms, festoons of flowers and musical instruments. Long in advance of his time, Sir Roger Pratt had recommended ceiling panels depicting 'airial nature, such as birds,

9   Saloon at Edgcote, Northamptonshire. Plasterwork by John Whitehead. 1753.

10

12

11

10 & 11 Staircase at Powderham
     Castle, Devon. Plasterwork by John
     Jenkins and William Brown. *c.* 1755.
12 Drawing Room at Heath Hall,
     South Yorkshire. Plasterwork by
     Joseph Rose the elder. 1758.

cupidons, fairies, both in regard of the place which is supposed to be the sky, and likewise for that they are so represented in their natural positions.'[16] Purely abstract rococo ceilings were also popular, however, particularly among the native plasterers, who followed the lead of the Italian *stuccatori*, but relied on the pattern-books of Delacour and Brunetti, or even Parisian engravings sold by London booksellers – Blondel and Huquier. These were often men of high ability, like the London plasterer John Whitehead, who worked at Edgcote in Oxfordshire in 1753 (Fig. 9). But they could also be provincials like John Jenkins and William Brown, whose eccentric and crowded compositions at Powderham in Devon now please more by their naïvety than their skill (Figs. 10 and 11). Isaac Ware, as part of his anti-Gallican stance, condemned such pattern-book ceilings as 'straggled over with unmeaning C's and O's and tangled semi-circles', advocating a return to naturalism with 'the flowers of our country, wind instruments . . . and the representation of books of music'.[17]

Perhaps the most talented of all the native plasterers outside London were the Perritt and Rose families, based at York and Doncaster. The elder Joseph Rose (at first in partnership with Thomas Perritt) carried out most of Paine's designs for plasterwork, in just the spirit advocated by Ware, at Nostell Priory, Felbrigg and Cusworth. On other commissions – for instance working under Carr of York at Heath Hall, Wakefield (Fig. 12) he most probably made his own designs, in the most assured rococo manner, and there is even evidence that he visited Italy in the company of Richard Wilson, long before his more celebrated son. William Perritt, Thomas'

13 Dining Room at Farnborough Hall, Warwickshire. Plasterwork by William Perritt, framing pictures by Canaletto. 1750.

14 Dining Room at Hartlebury Castle, Worcestershire. Pâpier maché ceiling and wall decorations. *c.* 1759.

elder brother, was responsible for the outstanding plasterwork at Farnborough in Warwickshire (Fig. 13), and later assisted the leading Scottish stuccoist Thomas Clayton at Blair Castle.[18] The extraordinary mobility of leading craftsmen such as these is also suggested by the fact that Clayton's eldest son was christened 'Thomas Varsallis', apparently after Francesco Vassalli.

It has been suggested that the Italian plasterers brought the art of true stucco to England, mixing marble dust instead of sand and hair with the slaked lime. In fact this much harder plaster was occasionally used for special purposes such as chimneypieces, or for exteriors. Vassalli used scagliola for the background to plasterwork in the Temple of the Winds at Castle Howard, and at Hall Place, Maidenhead, where the hall is more likely to be by him than Charles Stanley. But by and large the traditional methods of lime and hair plaster laid on to oak laths prevailed until the invention of fibrous plaster at the end of the century. *Papier-maché*, a cheaper but less long-lasting form of ornament, did however, become popular, after its introduction from France (see Cat. M29), and the saloon at Hartlebury Castle is a rare example of complete wall and ceiling decoration in this medium (Fig. 14).

The scientific analysis of early colour schemes is still in its infancy, but it does seem that ceilings were very rarely coloured, and that architect's drawings like James Paine's for Gopsall may only employ different washes in order to emphasise the relief:[19] hence, also, the novelty of Robert Adam's proposals to introduce colour in the ceilings at Nostell Priory in 1765. Certainly plasterwork before his time was usually three-dimensional enough to cast light and shade without the help of paint. The French taste was for white and gold, as d'Aviler, and later Blondel, both make clear – the white interpreted as a warm pearl or stone grey. But then the English never adopted the ubiquitous French fashion for *boiseries* – partly because their picture collections, fuelled by the Grand Tour, looked best against the crimson, blue or green damasks shown in the conversation pieces of Zoffany (Cat. M3) and Hogarth; partly because their London houses and

15 White and Gold Room at Petworth, West Sussex. Attributed to Samuel Norman and James Whittle. 1753.

16 Detail of a chimneypiece in the Chinese Room at Claydon House, Buckinghamshire. Wood carving by Luke Lightfoot. *c.* 1766.

country seats generally lacked the height and proportions of the apartments in a Parisian *hotel*.

A small group of English *boiserie* rooms do exist, but they are exceptions to the rule, and conscious expressions of French taste. The finest of them, the Music Room from Norfolk House (now in the Victoria and Albert Museum), has been convincingly attributed to the Turinese architect Giovanni-Battista Borra, though the recent discovery of a series of Huquier engravings at Arundel endorsed by the Duchess of Norfolk 'French Designs of Finishing of Rooms' (see Cat. A19) suggests that pattern-books were also consulted. Less convincing is the association of Borra with the other rooms in the group. The *boiserie* room from Woodcote Park (now in the Museum of Fine Arts, Boston) and the Yellow Drawing Room and Sporting Room at Woburn (see Cat. M14) include direct quotations from Blondel's *Maisons de Plaisance*. Isaac Ware, who was the architect at Woodcote, was almost certainly responsible for the extraordinary rococo interiors at Chesterfield House, one of which survives in part at the Bowes Museum, and is closely based on the engraved designs of Nicholas Pineau. The White and Gold Room at Petworth (Fig. 15) – probably by Samuel Norman and James Whittle – and a room at Stratfieldsaye, are different in feeling again, with their less crowded arrangement of trophies in panels and arched doorcases. Interesting as these rooms are for their totality of rococo decoration (disproving Fiske Kimball's contention that the style was applied only to furniture in this country[20]) they cannot be regarded as more than an interesting by-product of the movement nurtured in St Martin's Lane.

At the centre of the web remain the carvers, cabinet-makers and upholsterers whose premises lay within a stone's throw of the academy and the coffee-house. It is no accident that Thomas Johnson, John Linnell or Ince and Mayhew should produce schemes for whole rooms (see Cat. M18, M15); that carvers like Timothy Lightoler could branch out into architecture (Cat. M22) or produce ceiling designs for plasterers;[21] or that the office notebook of a virtually unknown craftsman like Gideon Saint (Cat. L72) should be an encyclopedia of ornament applicable to every sphere of the decorative arts. This was the age of the decorator, and as climax and a postscript to this age, there could be no more appropriate figure than the maverick Luke Lightfoot at Claydon (Fig. 16 Cat. M28, R11, E23) receiving Sir Thomas Robinson in 1770 (the year of Adam's greatest triumphs) 'with his Hat on his head, an austere look, fierce as an eastern Monarch', a 'knave, with no small spice of madness in his composition', yet the begetter of 'such a Work as the World never saw'.[22]

M1 *Roger Hesketh and his family*
Arthur Devis (1712-1787). *c.* 1742-3
Oil on canvas; 1016 x 1270
Roger Fleetwood Hesketh

Roger Hesketh (1711-91), High Sheriff
of Lancashire, his wife Margaret
Fleetwood and their children
Fleetwood (b. 1738) and Sarah
(baptised Jan. 1742). They are in a tall
pilastered room, from which two
more rooms are visible. The entire
setting is imaginary and perhaps made
up from architectural pattern books; it
recurs with small changes of detail in
Children in an Interior (Yale Center for
British Art). Included in both is the
large cartouche on the wall of the first
room which incorporates kissing
doves and a lion, and was perhaps
intended to be in relief. Although
clumsily composed, it displays a
knowledge of French or German *genre
pittoresque* prints. Although no precise
source has been established, similar
compositions can be found in the
cartouches in Edward Hoppus's
Gentleman's and Builder's Repository 1737
(most of which are copied from
French sources) as well as in the early
suites after Cuvilliés (see Cat. A23) and
the cartouches of P-E Babel, such as
Cartouche Pittoresque (Berliner & Egger
1981, 1305). In the Yale painting a
mirror in the second room also has a
pittoresque frame. The gilt furniture,
which occurs in a number of Devis's
paintings of this date, may be derived
from prints after Gaetano Brunetti
(Cat. B10).

Prov: Roger Hesketh; by descent
Lit: D'Oench 1980, cat. 7 repr (with
full literature); Preston 1983, cat. 11
repr.
MS

M2 *Chimney Side of the Banquetting Room*
Edward Rooker (1711-1774) after
James Paine (1717-1789). Before 1751
Engraving; 257 x 357. Lettered with
title and *James Paine invt. et delin. Edwd.
Rooker Sculpt. XX*

VAM (National Art Library)

From *Plans, Elevations, Sections and other
ornaments of the Mansion House of
Doncaster,* 1751. Except for his work at
Nostell Priory, the Doncaster Mansion
House, built in 1745-48, was Paine's
first important commission, and the

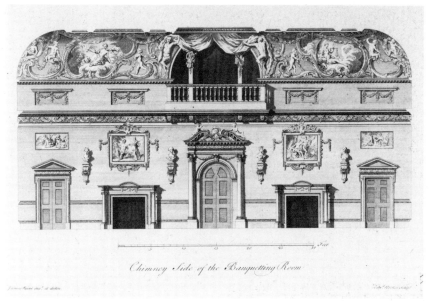

Chimney Side of the Banquetting Room

M2

public building that above all
launched his career on a national
scale. He published his designs in a
splendid folio volume in 1751, with
his portrait by Francis Hayman as the
frontispiece, and Hayman (his friend
from St Martin's Lane Academy days)
also seems to have designed the
paintings shown set into the walls and
ceiling of the banqueting room. The
paintings were never executed, but the
plasterwork by Thomas Perritt and
Joseph Rose the elder influenced a
whole generation of native as well as
immigrant *stuccadores* in the 1750s.

Lit: Girouard 1966, p. 190; Beard
1975, pp. 233, 237
GJ-S

M3 *The Bedford Family*
Francis Hayman (1708-1776). *c.*1747-8
Oil on Canvas; 635 x 762
*Royal Albert Memorial Museum, Exeter
(71/1939)*

Traditionally called *The Walpole Family*
the sitters were in fact friends of the
Walpoles; Grosvenor Bedford (1708-
1771), his wife Jane (1712-1759), and
their son Charles (1743-1814). In 1732
Sir Robert Walpole had appointed
Grosvenor Bedford to the sinecure of
Collector of Taxes at Philadelphia and
in 1755 he became Horace Walpole's
deputy at the Exchequer, both posts
being held until his death. A date of
c. 1747-8 is suggested not only by the

apparent age of the young boy and
stylistic criteria but also by the
presence of the book held upright by
Mrs Bedford on her lap which is
lettered on the spine SPE TAT, surely
a volume of that symbol of middle-
class morality *The Spectator.* This is not
entirely insignificant since the eight
volumes of the 1747 edition,
published by Bedford's friends
Tonson and Draper, were embellished
with frontispieces designed by
Hayman. The stark panelled interior is
enlivened, as in *The Tyers Family*
(Cat. F2), by a fanciful veined marble
chimneypiece with its curvaceous
mantel surmounted by oriental
porcelain. To the left, the folding
screen with its oriental decorations is,
like the chair with the interlaced back
and cabriole legs on which Grosvenor
Bedford leans, a studio prop which
Hayman used in several other
pictures.

Prov: Earl of Rosebery; his sale
Christie's 5 May 1939, 53, bt. Sutch;
acquired later that year by Exeter
Lit: Edwards 1955; Kerslake 1977,
vol. I, p. 137
BA

M3

M4 *Design for the dining room at Kirtlington Park, Oxfordshire*

John Sanderson (d. 1774). *c.*1747-48
Pen, brown and grey ink and wash over pencil, with four attached flaps;
444 x 508
Inscribed *Section of the Dineing Roome with different Specimens of Sides & Ceilings the Ornaments of plaister*

Metropolitan Museum of Art, New York (Rogers Fund 1970. 674.1)

Sanderson completed the building of Kirtlington for Sir James Dashwood, Bt., after the death of the original architect, William Smith, in 1747. He probably designed the wings and was certainly responsible for the interior decoration of the main rooms in a highly accomplished rococo manner. Neither this drawing nor its companion (Cat. M5) shows the room exactly as executed, though the eagles with outstretched wings above the pier glasses were finally adopted both here and on the opposite wall. The plasterer is thought to have been Thomas Roberts of Oxford, perhaps in collaboration with Charles Stanley, with whom he worked at the Radcliffe Camera in 1744. The room was dismantled and sold in 1931, and is now in the Metropolitan Museum, New York. Comparisons with the

contemporary rococo decoration here and at Kimberley Park in Norfolk suggest that John Sanderson was also responsible for the interiors at Hagley, where he worked under the architect Sanderson Miller in the same decade. The main elements of his rooms – doorcases and chimneypieces, pedimented overmantels and compartmented ceilings – are unashamedly Palladian in character. But the ornament within these confines, beautifully drawn, shows an interesting amalgam of the Italian Baroque motifs used by Artari and Bagutti with the looser, more French, vocabulary being pioneered by the members of the St Martin's Lane Academy. Beneath the flaps over the left and right walls and the ceiling are alternative designs in a much more extreme rococo style. On the right wall is a very wild asymmetrical cartouche. The alternative ceiling centre is a flamboyant rose. The left wall has two flaps.

Lit: Beard, 1974, pp. 236, 247, plates 72-73; P. Remington in MMA Bulletin, xiv, no. 7 (March 1956)
GJ-S

M5

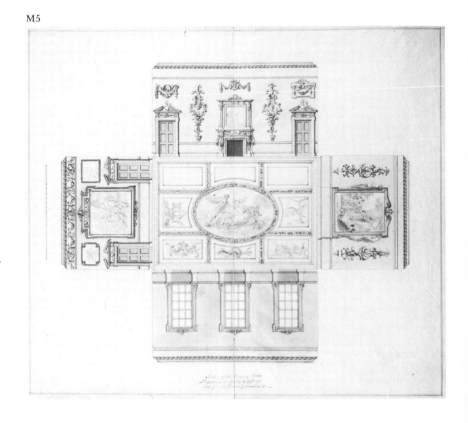

M5 *Design for the dining room at Kirtlington Park, Oxfordshire*

John Sanderson (d. 1774). *c.*1747-48
Pen, brown and grey ink and washes;
456 x 520
Inscribed *Section of the Dineing Rome with Pictures in ye sides & Ceiling and plaister frames & Ornaments*

Metropolitan Museum of Art, New York (Elisha Whittlesey Fund 1970/706)

See cat. M4. A slightly less elaborate alternative without pier glasses, this shows pictures in the large panels at either end, and a bas-relief of Apollo driving the chariot of the Sun in the centre of the ceiling. A third drawing for a more conventional ceiling, with a purely ornamental centre oval, is also in the Metropolitan Museum (1970.675), and is closest to the final solution.

Lit: see Cat. M4
GJ-S

M6 *The Drawing Room at Chesterfield House*

Photograph by Bedford Lemere, 1894
National Monuments Record

Chesterfield House, which until 1937 occupied a prominent site in South Audley Street, Mayfair, was begun for the francophile 4th Earl of Chesterfield in 1747 and unveiled to an admiring public in 1752. Although the exterior and some of the interior was a restrained and dignified essay in English Palladianism, a considerable stir was caused by the fact that a number of the principal rooms reflected the client's determination to decorate 'à la Françoise'. His architect, Isaac Ware (d. 1776) contrived to give the impression in *A Complete Book of Architecture* (1756) that he complied with Chesterfield's dictates under protest. His gloss on the design for the Music Room ceiling (pl. 81, 82) after talking apologetically of the need to satisfy the fancy of the proprietor at the expense of propriety, goes on to recommend ways in which the English architect might improve upon the French model by instilling order and simplicity into the mazes of 'unmeaning ornament'. The wall panels in the drawing room are derived from a plate after Pineau in Jean Mariette's *L'Architecture Françoise*, III, 1738 (Mariette 1929, pl. 503) and the overdoors are probably also from

the same work (*ibid.* pl. 481) as is part of the ceiling cornice (*ibid.* pl. 537). Whether produced under duress or not, the interiors at Chesterfield house did not give the impression of piecemeal composition and are easily the most authentic evocation of French models achieved during the English Rococo. It is not known if, as at Norfolk House, foreign craftsmen were used; Ware merely states that the ceilings and chimneypieces were 'all by the first artists in their several professions'. Parts of the drawing room have been re-erected at the Bowes Museum, Barnard Castle.

Lit: Country Life, 25 Feb., 4 March 1922; Harris 1961, fig. 14
RW & MS

M7 *Matrimonial fisticuffs*

Attributed to Paul Sandby (1725/6-1809). *c.* 1750?
Pen and ink and wash; 66 x 116
The Yale Center for British art, Paul Mellon Collection (B1977.25.2631)

A young couple engaged in fisticuffs, their headgear discarded on the floor. They are watched, perhaps approvingly, by an older man and woman; on the wall is a portrait of John Braughton, the famous prize-fighter. The room has plain walls, a chair rail, and one splat-back parlour chair. In the fireplace is a vase of flowers, and on the mantleshelf of the plain chimneypiece another vase and some Chinese figurines. Their presence is perhaps intentional, as similar Chinese ornaments had been used by Hogarth in *Marriage à la Mode* scene II to symbolise both bad taste

and barbarity and to emphasise the atmosphere of domestic discord. This drawing is very close in hand, format and general character to two etched prints perhaps by Paul Sandby in the British Museum (vol. 189.B.2, p. 113)
MS

M8 *Design for a state bed in an arched alcove*

James Paine (1717-1789). *c.* 1750
Pencil; 414 x 241
Signed bottom left *J.Paine* in sepia ink and with the inscription top left *N.B. The Alcove is 7ft 6ins wide a 9 feet long*

The Rt. Hon Lord St. Oswald MC (Nostell Priory Archives C3/1/4/163)

Paine's ground plan of Nostell Priory printed in Woolfe and Gandon's *Vitruvius Britannicus* of 1767, shows that the present State Dressing Room with its south facing Venetian window was originally intended to be the State Bedchamber. An alcove with two small closets either side is also shown here on the plan, so the drawing was almost certainly made with this room in mind. In 1770 the Bedchamber was altered by Adam, who enlarged the alcove, removing Paine's arch, and who probably also designed the new, highly neo-classical bed which Chippendale delivered in May of the following year. Whether a bed designed by Paine was ever made for this position is not known. The pencil sketch, remarkably free in style, has analogies with Chambers's state bed at Woburn, and is of interest in being one of Paine's few known furniture designs. A more finished, but less ambitious, pen and ink drawing for a

M7

M8

domed bed-tester (also shown in an arched alcove) exists in the Nostell papers (C3/1/4/161) and may suggest an alternative treatment for the same bed. The elaborately scalloped upper and lower valances and the reefed curtains, bunched up and tied with large tassels, show Paine at his most theatrical, and compare with his design of the musicians box in the ballroom of the Doncaster Mansion House (Cat. M7). The drawing also demonstrates how important pieces of furniture were already considered within the architect's domain, and how the details of bed hangings and curtains were not always left to the upholsterer.

Prov: commissioned by Sir Rowland Winn, 4th Baronet; thence by descent
Lit: Jackson-Stops 1974, pp. 26-27, 34, plate 13
GJ-S

M9

M9 *Design for a pier glass with plasterwork decoration*
James Paine (1717-1789). *c.* 1752
Pen, ink and grey wash; 247 x 191
The Rt. Hon. Lord St. Oswald MC (Nostell Priory Archives C3/1/4/66)

This drawing was almost certainly intended to be carried out in plaster by Thomas Perritt and the elder Joseph Rose, who decorated the two staircases and other rooms at Nostell Priory under Paine's direction in the late 1740s and early 1750s. The composition is very similar to the series of pier glasses which Paine designed for the dining room at Felbrigg in 1752 (Cat. M11). In the Nostell dining room, completed in the same year, vines are the predominant theme, appearing in the frieze, overmantel, overdoors and sideboards (for which another drawing by Paine exists). It seems hardly possible that this pier glass design could form part

of the same scheme of decoration, and it must have been either an early idea for the room which was abandoned (and adapted for Felbrigg soon afterwards), or have been intended for some other room at Nostell – perhaps one of those remodelled by Adam after 1765. The drawing is a good example of Paine's fluid draughtsmanship, and the treatment of the cartouche in particular is reminiscent of Van Vianen silver and the 17th century 'auricular' style. Busts on brackets are one of Paine's favourite decorative motifs, helping to give a more three-dimensional effect than is usual in the work of contemporary Italian and English plasterers.

Prov: commissioned by Sir Rowland Winn, 4th Baronet; thence by descent
Lit: Jackson-Stops 1974, pp. 26-27
GJ-S

M10 *Design for a chimneypiece and overmantel mirror*
James Paine (1717-1789). *c.* 1752
Pen and ink, grey and sepia washes; 143 x 111
The National Trust (Felbrigg Hall)

William Windham II employed James Paine to remodel many of the 17th century rooms at Felbrigg between 1749 and 1756, and the architect's surviving drawings at the house are among his most fluid rococo designs. The overmantel mirror shown here survives in the Red Bedroom, though shorn of its garlands of flowers and two candle-branches; the chimneypiece, if executed, was replaced by a plain marble surround in the early 19th century. The sculptor Thomas Carter was responsible for the original marble chimneypiece in the Cabinet, and it has previously been thought that this design was intended for the room. But the relatively small size of the fireplace makes it more likely to have been a proposal for a bedchamber or dressing room and executed entirely in carved wood.
Lit: Jackson-Stops, 1980, pp. 20, 32
GJ-S

M11 *Design for the dining room at Felbrigg*

James Paine (1717-1789). 1752
Pen and ink, grey and sepia washes,
372 x 518
Inscribed (probably in William
Windham's hand): *NB instead of the
ornament over the Center Door there is
pictures intended & of which I will . . .*
[passage missing] *also observe that the
Glass frames that is on the right hand peir is
to be executed . . .*

The National Trust (Felbrigg Hall)
(Cat. no. 22)

The dining room at Felbrigg was
created by James Paine for William
Windham II in 1752, occupying the
site of William Samwell's 17th century
staircase. The plasterwork very closely
follows Paine's design and was carried
out by Joseph Rose the elder (the
uncle of Adam's celebrated plasterer),
with assistants including one George
Green. A full scale working drawing
for one of the brackets supporting
John Cheere's bronzed busts was also
sent down to Felbrigg, which shows
the care he took over the smallest
detail. It is likely that the ceiling was
also executed to the architect's design,
though Windham wrote to his agent at
the end of April, 1752, that he had
'chose casts of the four seasons for the
corners'. The trophies of the chase
(which Windham chose to have over
the doors flanking the chimneypiece,
rather than on the end walls) are
reminiscent of Oppenord, and
suitably Bacchic decoration for a
dining room. But the most unusual
features are the slender links of chain,
looped or crossed, which appear to
support the pier-glasses and the oval
mirrors on the opposite wall –
perhaps a reference to the fetterlock of
the Windham crest. Similar oval
mirrors framed by palm-branches, a
favourite Paine motif, are to be found
at Wallington and Callaly in
Northumberland, and suggest that it
was he rather than the Francini
brothers who designed the plasterwork
in these houses, and in others he was
commissioned to build or remodel.

Lit: Jackson-Stops 1980, pp. 10-12
GJ-S

M12

M12 *Design for a chimneypiece and overmantel*

Peter Glazier (active 1748-52). *c.* 1752?
Pencil, pen and ink and wash, scored
for transfer; 190 x 134
Signed *P. Glazier inv. delin.* The *verso*
inscribed *No.11857* and *No. 28 Mar 12
80*

The Leeds City Art Galleries (35.7/76)

The drawing for the title page of
*Ornaments in the modern French & Chinese
Taste Consisting of Various designs for
Mantles and Chimney Pieces,* title and five
plates, engraved by J. Couse and
Henry Roberts after Glazier,
published by John Bowles (Guilmard
1880, 519.20; Metropolitan Museum
of Art, New York, 29.58.19). It is listed
in Bowles's catalogue of 1764, and
(probably) Francis Vivares's catalogue
of the 1760s, but probably dates from
the 1750s. The overmantel consists of
a (?) mirror surmounted by a large
framed landscape painting. Also at
Leeds is a signed design for a pier
table; the other Leeds drawings are by
another hand. These two designs are
similar to Glazier's other signed
design (for a chair, Henry Francis du
Pont Winterthur Museum, 69.194)
and to Glazier's title page to Lock's *A
New Book of Ornaments for Looking Glass
Frames c.* 1752 (Heckscher 1979,
pl. 34). They differ considerably in
feeling from Glazier's prints for
chased work (Cat. H16). Glazier,

about whom nothing biographical is
known, seems to have been a general
designer.

Prov: Private collection, Dublin;
Sotheby's Belgravia 23 March 1976, 1;
bt. from C. Powney 1976
Lit: Friedman 1981, p. 13; Gilbert
1978, II, no. 653 repr.
MS

M13

M13 *Jacques-Francois Blondel* De la distribution de maisons de plaisance

Vol.II, 1738, Paris, Charles-Antoine
Jombert, 4°.
VAM (National Art Library)

This work is the source of at least two
attempts to adapt the French *boiserie*
interior to English tastes. Plate 72 was
used for the doors at Woburn Abbey
(Cat. M14) and plate 64 for a mirror in
the same house. Plate 83 is the source
of one of the most complete English
attempts at the style, the rooms at
Woodcote Park made for Lord
Baltimore (see Harris 1961). Many of
Blondel's plates are unacknowledged
borrowings from Nicolas Pineau,
whose designs were also used for the
panelling at Chesterfield House
(Cat. M6).

Lit: Kimball 1943, pp. 168-9
MS

M14 *Door*

The design attributed to Giovanni
Battista Borra (1712-1786) after (?)
Nicolas Pineau (1684-1754).
1747-c. 1757
Carved and painted wood;
2130 x 1050
*The Marquess of Tavistock and Trustees of
the Bedford Estates, Woburn Abbey*

Henry Flitcroft's remodelling of the
west front of Woburn for the 4th Duke
of Bedford was begun in 1747, but the
decoration of the rooms in the north
wing continued throughout the
following decade, adopting more up-
to-date rococo forms in place of
Flitcroft's somewhat stolid
Palladianism. Borra's hand has been
seen in the Palmyra ceiling of Queen
Victoria's Bedroom (he had
accompanied Wood and Dawkins on
their recent expedition to Palmyra),
and in the ceilings and carved doors of
the Sporting Room and Yellow
Drawing Room beyond. The ceilings
in particular, bear comparison with
those at Norfolk House (where he is
known to have worked on the
interiors, under another Palladian
architect, Matthew Brettingham) and
at Stratfieldsaye. The doors, however,
and mirror frames above them (which
once contained landscape paintings)
are conceived as *boiseries* although the
walls are covered in damask rather
than panelling. They are directly
derived from a plate in Blondel's *De la
Distribution de Maisons de Plaisance, 1738*
(Cat. M13). The French door is two-
leaved; the English copy is a single
door imitating the central division but
with an empty space in the centre
where Blondel shows the lock. At
present in the State Dressing Room is
a gilt overmantel mirror also taken
directly from Blondel (pls. 64 & 90)
which may have been intended for the
Sporting Room or Yellow Drawing
Room.
GJ-S & MS

M15 *Design for the side of a room*

John Linnell (1723-96). *c.* 1755
Pen, ink and watercolour; 260 x 265
VAM (E.263-1929)
See colour plate

Nothing is known of the client for
whom Linnell executed this delightful
watercolour, though the comparatively
low ceiling suggests that it may have
been intended for a London house. As
a design for a whole interior, it is
something of a rarity among Linnell's
drawings, which are generally for
individual pieces of furniture, but it
gives an idea of the wide range of his
firm in this decade, after the success of
the Badminton and Woburn
commissions. Upholstery, carving,
gilding, and every other form of
furniture-making and wall-decoration,
came within his province, and here he
can be seen usurping the role
architects like Kent (and later Robert
Adam) would consider to be their
own. The red damask of the settee is
echoed by the colour of the wall-
hangings, with particularly elegant gilt
borders. The picture framed in the
overmantel, in the style of Dobson or
Van Dyck, has not proved identifiable,
but could be a fanciful portrayal of
Inigo Jones pointing to a plan, for the
leaders of the rococo did not always
consider themselves enemies of the
Palladians. The wall-clock, which also
acts as an *étagère* for porcelain, is close
to the naturalistic designs of Thomas
Johnson, as is the right-hand
alternative proposed for the picture
frame. The chimney surround and left
side of the overmantel are more
recognisably in Linnell's own brand of
controlled French rococo, perfectly
balanced and abstracted in the
manner of Gravelot's engraved frames.

Lit: Hayward & Kirkham 1980, pp. 20,
61 & col. pl. 3
GJ-S

M16 *Design for the dining rooom
at Gopsall Hall, Leicestershire*

William Hiorne (*c.* 1712-1776) and
David Hiorne (d. 1758). *c.* 1757
Pen and ink wash; 355 x 42
*The British Architecture Library (RIBA
Drawings Collection K10/11/18)*

The Hiorne (or Hiorns) brothers
succeeded the Smiths as the leading
masons and architects in Warwick in
the mid-18th century. Gopsall Hall,
which they built for Charles Jennens,
Handel's librettist, in the 1750s, was
demolished in 1951, and it is unclear
how many of the interiors were
decorated in accordance with their
detailed drawings for the house, now
in the RIBA. The design for the dining
room is particularly interesting in
showing how provincial architects
could still depend on an old-fashioned
pattern book like Gibbs's *Book of*

Architecture of 1728 for the Corinthian
pilasters, doors, doorcases and panels,
while filling the voids with rococo
ornament in a quite different vein – in
this case apparently borrowing the
table in the alcove, and the pier glass,
from Chippendale's *Director* (pls. CXLI
& CXLVIII in the 1754 edition). The
drawing of the south front (also at the
RIBA) is a typical example of how
little the rococo style affected the
stolid Palladian facades of English
country houses in the 1750s. Only in
the pediment, comparable with James
Paine's at Nostell Priory of the
previous decade, is there a hint of the
riotous decoration, the 'C' and 'S'
scrolls, the flowing acanthus and
asymmetrical cartouches that lie
within.

Lit: RIBA Drawings Catalogue (G-K),
1973, pp. 130-131
GJ-S

M17 *William Halfpenny* The
Modern Builder's Assistant
1757

Published by J. Rivington, J. Fletcher
and Robert Sayer, London
VAM (National Art Library)

Open at plate 76, 'Section of a Saloon'
engraved by J. Miller (probably
J. S. Muller) after Timothy Lightoler
(active 1758-1775). One of the best
known pattern books of the mid-18th
century, still found in large numbers
of country house libraries, *The Modern
Builder's Assistant* was a collaboration
between William and John Halfpenny,
Robert Morris and 'T. Lightoler
Carver' as he is described on some of
the plates. Some copies bear the date
MDCCVLII, which has been read as
1742, mistaking the V for an X. But
this would almost certainly have been
too early for the participation of the
younger Halfpenny and of Lightoler
and for the style of the designs, and
the most probable explanation is a
typesetter's error, corrected before the
whole edition was printed. Lightoler's
designs are the most markedly rococo
in the book and reminiscent of his
drawings for plasterwork at Burton
Constable of about 1760. In this plate,
the influence of Cuvilliés is apparent,
particularly in the cove with its
graceful *chinoiserie* scenes and
'frostwork' dripping over into the
entablature. The painting in the

overmantel is very much in the style of the Richard Wilson landscape, included in Lightoler's design for the dining room at Platt Hall in Lancashire (see Cat. M22). Two closely related drawings in the Metropolitan Museum, New York, showing a similar rococo room with a deep coved ceiling, have been attributed to Lightoler on stylistic grounds.

Lit: Hall 1982, pp. 1278-9, 1358-59; Harris 1971, p. 131 & pl. 94
GJ-S

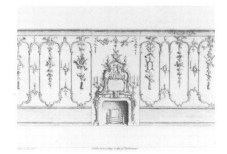

M18

M18 *Design for the side of a room*
(?)Butler Clowes after Thomas Johnson (b. 1714, d. after 1778). 1758
Etching and engraving; 177 x 248
Lettered with a copyright line and *T Johnson invt delt* and *plate 25*

VAM (E.3717-1903)

Despite the fact that the first untitled edition of Johnson's collected designs appeared in 1758 dedicated to Lord Blakeney, Grand President of the Antigallican Associations, and despite the fact that its author described himself in the foreword as 'one who possess a truly Anti-gallic spirit', the plates it contained were to a large extent influenced by French *ornemenistes* such as Bérain, Cuvilliés and Toro. Moreover plate 25 (renumbered as plate 10 in the 1761 edition), is one of the only English engravings of the period to show a scheme for carved *boiseries* with trophies of musical instruments in a full-blown Parisian manner perhaps derived from Pineau. In fact the handling is crude compared with the small group of *boiserie* rooms which survive in this country – those from Norfolk House and Chesterfield House in London, and those at Petworth, Woburn and Stratfieldsaye. Johnson treats the panels as mere surface ornament, rather than as

architectural elements, and the most successful feature is the combined chimneypiece and overmantel mirror drawn in his characteristically spiky and jagged style. A cockerel surmounting the clock, and the figure of Father Time accosting a naked woman below, add an equally typical touch of humour to the composition.

Lit: Hayward 1964, fig. 76
GJ-S

M19 *Trade cards*
The Trustees of the British Museum (unless otherwise stated)

a) Masefield's wallpaper manufactory. Perhaps by George Bickham junior. *c.* 1758. Inscribed by Sarah Banks 'Engraved about the year 1758' *(Banks 91.20)*. The central cartouche depicts the interior of the shop, with stacks of wallpaper rolls in box compartments. The vendor unrolls a length of paper for his customers (there were no pattern books); each pattern was displayed to show its full repeat, one wall of the shop being fitted with mirrors and brackets so that the effect could be judged. Masefield specialised in 'mock India' papers, ie European *chinoiserie* or imitations of hand-painted Chinese papers, although the pattern in the vignette seems to be one of the popular 'chintzs' (Heal 1925, p. 33; Sugden & Edmonson 1926, fig. 43)

b) Matthew Darly, wallpaper manufacturer. Matthew Darly. *c.* 1755? Inscribed by Sarah Banks '1791 (old)' *(Banks 91.7)*. Darly, who also had many other business interests (see Cat. R9), specialised in paper hangings in the 'Chinese taste'. The card shows rolls of wallpaper 'Painted or Printed from Copper Plates or Wood'. The *chinoiserie* papers were almost certainly printed from copper plates, and may have been etched by him. Other papers depicted have gothic or *chinoiserie* fretwork patterns and both stylised and naturalistic floral designs. Also specified is 'Paper for Exportation and Sketches or Designs for Gentlemen's Different Fancies', indicating that he undertook special decorative schemes. He also produced borders for print rooms in the 1760s (Heal 1925, LXX; Sugden & Edmonson 1926, fig. 44).

c) James Rodwell, upholsterer and sworn appraiser. Anonymous. *c.* 1765?

The Guildhall Library. At the Royal Bed and Star, Moorfields. At the top is a scene in perspective of a rococo state bedchamber. Such scenes were customary on the trade cards with this shop sign. As well as furniture, Rodwell sold cabinet and braziery goods and paper hangings.
MS & JDH

M20 *Design for a drawing room*
Thomas Paty (1713-1789). *c.* 1760
Pen and ink with brown wash within an inscribed border; 357 x 465
City of Bristol Museum and Art Gallery

This study belongs to a series of ten designs for the interiors of two rooms apparently drawn by Thomas Paty, the most gifted member of a Bristol family that operated a successful business as builders, ornamental masons, carvers and surveyors. Their attribution to Paty rests upon similarities in draughtsmanship to the very few other drawings that survive from his hand (Eustace 1982, 95, 24a-c) and correspondences between some details in their ornament and the plasterwork decoration of the Royal Fort in Bristol. The house was designed by James Bridges and built between 1758 and 1760 for Thomas Tyndall, a prominent local banker: its principal rooms and staircase were decorated in the rococo taste by the plasterer Thomas Stocking together with some richly ornamental woodcarving probably supplied by Thomas Paty who also provided exterior stonework embellishments. The drawings display a more ostentatiously fanciful vocabulary than the relatively conventional rococo idiom used for the Royal Fort interiors. Their style is puzzling and their purpose uncertain in so far as they cannot be identified with any recorded building or project. However, their attribution to Paty may be inferred from technical affinities with securely attributable drawings, as well as from the congruity of certain details with features in the Royal Fort.

Prov: Christie's 24 March 1982, 94
Lit: Gomme, Jenner & Little 1979; Parker 1929; Avray Tipping 1916
MJHL

(illustration overleaf)

M20

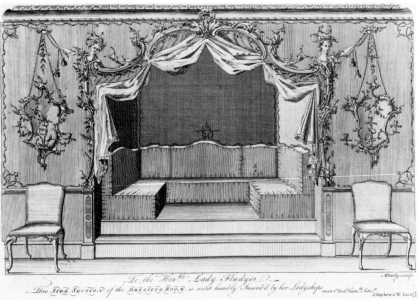

To the Honble Lady Fludyer
This SIDE SECTION of the DRESSING ROOM is most humbly Inscrib'd by her Ladyships most Obed.^t ham.^{le} Serv.^{ts}
J. Mayhew & W. Ince

M21

M21 *The Universal System of Household Furniture*
William Ince & John Mayhew, 1762
Robert Sayer, London, folio
VAM (National Art Library)

Open at plate LXV, a side section of a dressing room, engraved by Matthew Darly. Ince and Mayhew's *Universal System* was issued in parts betweeen 1759 and 1762, evidently to rival the third edition of Chippendale's *Director*, which was appearing serially in the same period – Matthew Darly being employed as engraver for both books. The only plate in the *Universal System* to be signed by both partners, the design for a dressing room, is also the only one to be dedicated to a particular client, the Hon. Lady Fludyer, wife of Sir Samuel Fludyer who was Lord Mayor of London in 1761. Although the note to the plate does not specifically mention that the scheme was ever executed, the implication must be that it was – and almost certainly in a London house. The caryatids, playfully holding back the tassels of the flanking girandoles, are unmistakably Chinese in the manner of Thomas Johnson, though the alcove itself is described as 'compleat with cushions in form of a Turkish Soffa' with 'a Drapery Curtain in front'. The nearest surviving equivalent to such an interior is Luke Lightfoot's Chinese Room at Claydon, where the alcove must have been used for the appropriately Oriental pastime of making tea. Mayhew had been in partnership with Samuel Norman until 1758, and the carved (and presumably gilded) framework to the alcove has similarities with the pier glass supplied by Norman and Whittle to Petworth in the early 1760s.

Lit: Edwards 1960, pp. e-j
GJ-S

M22 *Design for the dining room at Platt Hall, Leicestershire*
Timothy Lightoler (active 1758-1775).
1764
Pen and black ink with brown, grey and blue wash, annotated with dimensions in red ink; 357 x 500
Signed (bottom right corner)
T. Lightoler
City Art Gallery, Manchester
(1961.165.A/1)

Lightoler is thought to have been a native of Lancashire, and was probably born at Ollerton-in-Withnell, near Blackburn. About 1763 he was commissioned by John Worsley to design Platt Hall near Rusholme, outside Manchester. Earlier alterations for the house by William Jupp and John Carr of York, dated 1760 and 1761, seem to have been abandoned in favour of Lightoler's – a version of which is shown here, together with the album of his drawings for the interiors of the house. The strictly Palladian exterior is, typically, at variance with the elaborate rococo decoration proposed within. Unfortunately the dining room is the only one of the principal rooms to survive with its original decoration intact, including the overmantel picture by Richard Wilson variously entitled *A Summer Evening* or *On the Arno*, sent by the artist to John Lees, the builder of Platt, in December 1764. During recent restoration, the green-painted walls which were apparently chosen to complement the painting have been reinstated. Lightoler's pier glasses with their frames of oak branches in plasterwork also continue the pastoral theme.

Lit: Colvin 1978, p. 521; Johnston 1970, p. 535, figs. 58-60
GJ-S

M23 *Album of drawings*
Thomas Farnolls Pritchard (1723-1777). *c.* 1765-69
Sepia pen and ink; 210 x 170
Library of the American Institute of Architects, Washington DC

Pritchard's reputation as the leading architect working in Shropshire and neighbouring counties in the 1760s has only been re-established comparatively recently with the discovery of this book of designs from his office in Shrewsbury, complete with records of the time spent on each commission, the names of the carvers, and costs. The page displayed shows a variety of different decorative features, all interpreted by Pritchard in an accomplished rococo style that is close in style and draughtsmanship to the work of James Paine. The 'candlestick bracket' and the mahogany shield for the cresting of the bookcase was designed for a house in Mardol, Shrewsbury, belonging to Mr and Mrs

Benjamin Bather and were carved by the sculptors John Nelson and Alexander van der Hagen; the chimneypiece was carved by Danders, another craftsman regularly employed by Pritchard, for Richard Corbet of High Hatton in Shropshire; and Nelson's 'modell for a machine grate for Colbrook Dale' was for a cast-iron stove which still exists in the hall at Shipton Court in the same county. The stove was made by Abraham Darby, for whom Pritchard was later to design the celebrated Iron Bridge at Coalbrookdale – an interesting connection between the rococo style and the early Industrial Revolution.

Prov: A. Lawrence Kocher; American Institute of Architects
Lit: Harris 1968, p. 17-24 & fig. 8b
GJ-S

M24

M24 *The Chimneypiece Maker's Daily Assistant*
Vol I, John Crunden (*c.* 1745-1835), with Thomas Milton and Placido Columbani. Printed for Henry Webley in Holburn, near Chancery Lane, 1766. Frontispiece designed by Isaac Taylor, engraved by R. Pranker
VAM (National Art Library)

Open at the frontispiece. The simple Palladian shape of the chimney surround being erected by the joiner in this engraving, and the inclusion of

Rysbrack's famous bust of Inigo Jones (reversed as in Knapton's portrait of Lord Burlington), but placed on a rococo bracket, and with a rococo ceiling above, shows that the world of the St Martin's Lane Academy was not always at war with the 'official' Palladianism of Kent, Flitcroft and the Board of Works. The figures of the architect with his measuring rod and the patron examining his drawing are strongly influenced by Gravelot. Crunden was also to become a proficient architect in the neo-classical manner, designing Boodle's Club in St James's in 1775-6, while his collaborator, the plasterer Placido Columbani, later worked for the Earl-Bishop of Bristol at Downhill and Ickworth. The chimneypieces in this book and vol. II are in both the neo-classical and rococo styles.
GJ-S

M25

M25 *Pair of wood-carvings from the cresting of a doorcase*
Luke Lightfoot (*c.* 1722-1789). *c.* 1769
Carved wood, painted white; 940 x 1142
The National Trust (Claydon House)

The rococo decoration carried out for the 2nd Earl Verney at Claydon between 1757 and 1771 was largely the achievement of a builder and carver of genius named Luke Lightfoot. Lightfoot remains one of the most mysterious figures of the period, having no other known patrons. His extraordinarily elaborate designs for the interiors of the house were all to be carried out in carved wood rather than plaster, and his finest surviving room in this manner is the North Hall. When the architect Sir Thomas Robinson saw work in progress here in 1769, he wrote to Lord Verney that 'Mr Lightfoot's design for furnishing the great Eating Room shock'd me so much and is so much the ridicule of all who have seen or heard of it that it ... will indeed be what he expressed very justly – such a Work as the World never saw'. The great ho-ho birds perched on scrolling foliage come from the cresting of the conventional classical doorcase that once led from the North Hall through to the rotonda and ballroom beyond – demolished after Lord Verney's death. But this may not be their original position, as old photographs show them grained and standing on the sideboard. It is possible that they were among the carvings which Robinson advised Lord Verney to remove from Lightfoot's workshop in Southwark, having engineered the latter's dismissal in 1770, before the room was complete. Very much in the same spirit as the ho-ho birds and 'C' and 'S' scrolls round the niches on the opposite wall, they are obviously influenced by the engravings of Thomas Johnson, though more lifelike and less stylised in execution.

Lit: Boynton 1966, pp. 11-13; Jackson-Stops 1978, pp. 9-11

GJ-S

M26 *Design for one wall of a room*
Anonymous. *c.* 1765
Pencil; 320 x 380
Sir Ralph Verney, Bt., KBE

The drawing appears to be related to a ceiling design for the 'french room' at Claydon (Cat. M27), and to be in the same hand as a third drawing for a papier-maché ceiling (Cat. M29). At first sight the proposal would seem to be for a scheme of carved rococo *boiseries* in an advanced French style, not unlike those surviving at Petworth, Stratfieldsaye and Woburn (see Cat. M15). But it is possible that, as with the ceilings, the light and insubstantial looking ornament was intended to be carried out in papier-maché. The drawing is still of great importance in being one of the very few known designs for an English room in the full-blown Parisian taste of the 1750s. The delicate draughts-manship of the chimneypiece and the oval mirror frame above it is not unlike some of the Matthias Lock drawings in the VAM, but the overdoors with garlands of roses twisted round the edges of the panels

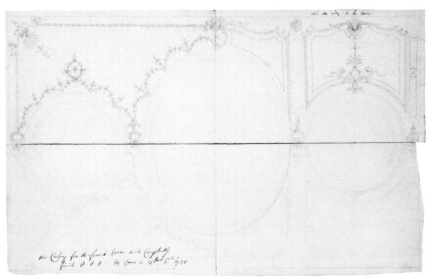

M27

could well be taken from Huquier and Pineau enravings, and perhaps suggest the hand of a French *ornemeniste*.

GJ-S

M27 *Design for a ceiling*
Anonymous. *c.* 1765
Pencil; 304 x 492
Inscribed *this ceiling for the French Room Compleatly finish 8.0.0 the Room is 31 feet 6 ins by 20* and *this side to be done*

Sir Ralph Verney, Bt., KBE

The drawing and inscription are in the same hand as that for a papier-maché ceiling (Cat. M29) and for a wall-elevation with rococo *boiseries* (Cat. M26) also in the Claydon Collection. The articulation of this ceiling and the wall-elevation suggest that they may both have been intended for the 'french room', and the inscription 'this side to be done' on the ceiling design (perhaps in Lord Verney's hand) implies that the scheme was indeed executed. A visitor to Claydon in 1768, whose diary has survived in the Bodleian Library at Oxford, described the 'lesser rooms' in the house as being 'furnished in all tastes, as the Chinese Room, the Gothick Room, the French Room etc.' The obvious candidate for the latter is the present Paper Room, which adjoins the Chinese and Gothick Rooms on the first floor of the west front. It also has three shallow saucer domes in the ceiling, a large central oval and two circles just as in

the drawing, though without ornamentation. However, the dimensions of the room are quite different from those shown on the ceiling design, and the chimneypiece wall is much longer than that shown in the elevation.

Lit: Jackson-Stops 1978, pp. 25, 29

GJ-S

M28 *Design for a doorcase*
Attributed to Luke Lightfoot (*c.* 1722-1789). 1770
Pen and ink; 300 x 182
Inscribed *Recd at Claydon Jan.ry 27, 1770* and *5 feet 6 inches in the clear of the Stone* (indicating the width), and *12 feet high;* in the left margin *i want this hight* (possibly in Lightfoot's hand)

Sir Ralph Verney, Bt., KBE

This is the only one among the drawings at Claydon which can plausibly be attributed to Lightfoot on grounds of style and date; he was not to be dismissed by Earl Verney until later in the same year, 1770, and he is known to have constantly sent for measurements from Claydon (instead of working on site) up till this time. The caryatids are similar in spirit to those in white marble flanking the chimneypiece in the North Hall, though the latter are demi-figures with arms – one of which is outstretched to support a basket on the head, filled with fruit and flowers. It is possible that the drawing represents Lightfoot's intention for the doorcase on the opposite wall leading to the rotunda and ballroom, which is roughly of these dimensions though of a more conventional Palladian form, probably designed by Verney's architect, Sir Thomas Robinson.

Lit: Jackson-Stops 1978, pp. 9-11
GJ-S

M29 *Drawing for a papier-mache ceiling*

Anonymous. *c.* 1770
Pencil; 565 x 430
Inscribed *this ceiling compleatly finisht and put up £18.0.0,* and on the *verso No. 5/Papier Machee Ceiling*

Sir Ralph Verney, Bt., KBE

Papier-mâché was a material quite commonly used for rococo ceilings though, lacking the durability of plasterwork, few examples now remain. That in the Spenser Room at Canons Ashby has four profile heads of the Seasons, not unlike the Claydon drawing, and during recent restoration work numbers were found on the backs of all the component parts, implying that ceilings were made up of pre-fabricated garlands, husks, acanthus scrolls or other ornaments. The prime papier-mâché suppliers in London in the mid-18th century were René Duffour at The Golden Head in Berwick Street, Soho, and Peter Babel in Long Acre. That such foreigners posed a threat to native plasterers and carvers is clear from the title page of Thomas Johnson's *One Hundred and Fifty New Designs* (see Cat. L44) when a flying putto sets a firebrand to a scroll inscribed 'French Papier Machée'. The Claydon drawing is in a transitional style, combining wholly rococo cartouches at the corners with an oval patera at the centre, including husks and anthemions in a distinctly neo-classical vein. It is also an interesting example of a 'rubbed' design, drawn in soft pencil, folded in four and then pressed or rolled so as to give the impression of the whole with only a quarter of the labour. The measurements do not seem to correspond with any of the main rooms at Claydon, but the drawing could have been intended for the east wing or for Earl Verney's London House in Curzon Street.
GJ-S

M30 *Mrs Abington in* The Way to Keep Him

Johan Zoffany (1733-1810). 1768
Oil on canvas; 990 x 1130
The Treasury on loan to the National Trust

Frances Abington (1737-1815) as the Widow Bellmour in Arthur Murphy's popular comedy *The Way to Keep Him* (Act II (later III) scene I), a role she made famous, and which she played on the occasion of her benefit at Drury Lane on 6 April, 1768. The scene Zoffany has painted takes place in 'a Room at the Widow Bellmour's, in which are disposed up and down, several chairs, a Toilette, a Bookcase ...' and begins with the Widow reading aloud from a volume of Pope. The moment depicted is when on finishing her reading she says to her maid, 'Here, Mignionet, put this Book in its Place'. But Zoffany has painted a celebration of Mrs Abington in the role she made her own, not a record of the scene as it took place on the stage, where the set would have been considerably simpler. He has adapted his earlier conversation group of the young Queen Charlotte seated by her sumptuous lace-covered dressing table with her two eldest sons. The three Derby china vases on the chimneypiece are of a type not made before 1768. The paintings hanging on the wall, *Diana and Actaeon* over the chimneypiece, and *Danae* to the left, were undoubtedly an allusion to the attractions of the sitter.

Prov: probably bought by the 3rd Earl of Egremont from W. Smart 1823; by descent
Lit: National Portrait Gallery 1976, 43; Webster 1976
MW

M31 *The Dutton Family*

Johan Zoffany (1733-1810). 1771-2
Oil on canvas; 1200 x 1275
The Hon. P. M. Samuel

Seated behind the card-table is James Lennox Naper (1712-76) of Loughcrew, Co. Meath, who assumed the surname and arms of Dutton. His second wife, Jane Bond, is seated by the fire looking at a hand of cards held out to her by their eldest son James Dutton (1744-1820), MP for Gloucester, 1780, 1st Baron Sherborne 1784. At the left, impatiently awaiting

play to resume, is the youngest daughter, Jane (1753-1800), who married in 1775 Thomas Coke of Holkham, the agriculturalist, later Earl of Leicester. The elegant veneered card-table dates from the 1760s, as probably does an oval mirror with a frame of rococo design which hangs on the wall; the breakfront chimney-piece with its swags and mask is a variation on a type that occurs in a number of Zoffany's conversation pieces of the 1760s. The scene is said to be set in the drawing room of Sherborne House, Gloucestershire, a mid-17th century house reconstructed in the late 1820s.

Prov: Lord Sherborne; Christie's 28 June 1929, 72; Daniel H. Farr; 2nd Viscount Bearstead; by descent
Lit: Park Lane 1930, 134; Praz 1971; Royal Academy 1907, 143; Royal Academy 1954-5, 100; Sitwell 1936, p. 94, pl. 29; Washington 1976, p. 76
MW

M32 *The Court of Equity or Convivial City Meeting*

Robert Laurie (*c.* 1755-1836) after Robert Dighton (1752-1814). 1779
Inscribed with title and *Published as the Act Directs by J. Smith Cheapside 1779*
The Trustees of the British Museum

A state before letters; the print was published by John Smith, printseller, Cheapside, 1 Nov. 1779. The scene is a meeting of a typical club in the upper room of a tavern. The members have been identified: they include a silver spoon maker, a printer, a sausage maker, an attorney, a bricklayer, a broker, an auctioneer, the artist (top right) and the publisher of the print (in the Windsor chair left). The motto of the club, 'Mirth with Justice' appears on the neo-classical coat of arms above the chairman. According to Smith (1883) the club met at the Bell Savage, Ludgate Hill, but the Globe, Fleet Street has also been proposed (BM:S). The furnishings are very simple, with the exception of the carved rococo wall sconce, which is still in favour well into the neo-classical period.

Lit: BM:S 5530; Phillips 1964, fig. 64; Pickford 1983, p. 27, figs. 13, 14; Smith 1883, II, p. 803
MS

Textiles and Dress

Plate impression for a printed textile: 'Birds'. See cat. N26.

Rococo in Textile Design

Natalie Rothstein

To define a style in words when it is composed of colour, line and texture is almost an impossibility. The quintessential features may be grasped only to slither away, for 'rococo' influenced different types of textile at different times, and considerations other than pure style affected the result. Style in textile decoration is subordinated to the use to which the textile must be put, to the technique by which it is made, and to its cost if it is to sell commercially.

Further difficulties bedevil an exhibition as opposed to an essay. The display of key pieces may be prevented by their intrinsic fragility, and the size of the exhibition area may exclude whole classes of material whose presence is needed for any discussion. Thus there are no carpets or tapestries to be seen. The carpets of the 1750s made in Exeter are too large to show, as are the tapestries. The tapestries, which should be here and are not, were themselves ousted as furnishings in all but the grandest state apartments during the 1730s. They were displaced by wallpaper, not other textiles.[1] Some textiles cannot be included because there is no *suitable* large space, an embroidered coverlet needing a glazed bed or an air-conditioned gallery. Then, too, some types of textile no longer exist or, like block-printed cottons, survive only in a few fragile and fragmentary examples. Woven carpeting by the yard, at first imported from France and then made in England from the 1740s, has not survived for the relevant period, although we have one design from 1753. Other textiles have been omitted from the exhibition when their date and attribution depend more on curatorial expertise than on firm documentation. This is a study of English rococo. Apart from the coarsest domestic products, table-linen was made in Scotland and Ireland, not England. Dutch, Flemish and German table-linen was widely used. The tablecloth shown in the Vauxhall box is almost certainly German.[2] Similarly the lace worn with English silks was likely to be Flemish.

Our attempt to define the English interpretation of rococo in textiles is therefore presented to the public almost exclusively in two media – the silks for fashionable dress and the plate-printed cottons (or fustians[3]) used mainly for furnishings. These are not however, contemporaneous. The silks date from the 1740s, the cottons from the 1750s, 1760s, or even later. There will obviously be changes in the treatment of cotton motifs over 30 years. The total desired effect may be quite different. We shall attempt to assess in the essay the objects which cannot be shown in the exhibition as well as those which are and to sum up our impressions at the end. The spectator may well disagree but if we have provoked such discussion our efforts will have been worth it.

There are important parallels in other media but they must not be overstressed. Two disparate objects ten years apart in date but apparently similar in style may, in fact, provide evidence of an alien influence – French or German – between the first and the second. Alternatively, 'The taste of the Nobility and Gentry at the Present Time'[4] (for we are talking of a fashionable world), may draw whatever appeals from a variety of disparate sources and ignore those features which seem of greater significance to later generations. While we shall discuss the favourite devices in the rococo repertoire it is also possible to take a classical ruin, for example, and treat it in a thoroughly rococo manner. Equally, even at the height of rococo influence there were customers who were old-fashioned or simply individual in their tastes and wanted something different.

Fig. 1 Tapestry, Joshua Morris. 1720s. *VAM (T.32-1979)*.

Fig. 2 Tapestry from a set signed Bradshaw, after paintings by Watteau and Pater. 1740s-50s. *Ham House*

Fig. 3 Tapestry with an ewer full of flowers. Bradshaw? 1730s-40s. *VAM T.46-1918*

Fig. 4 Chair-back with the fable of the Hare and the Tortoise (photo before conservation). Signed Danthon. c. 1755-60. *Uppark House, National Trust*. See colour plate XIV

Fig. 1

Tapestries and Carpets

Wendy Hefford

Fig. 2

Fig. 3

Fig. 4

It is debatable whether English rococo tapestry exists, in that designs during the first half of the eighteenth century were extremely dependent on French art. Tapestries made in England do, however, have a certain charming naiveté which might be considered an English colouring to the more sophisticated French taste. Arabesque designs woven in the workshop of Joshua Morris in the 1720s (Fig. 1), though still heavy with strapwork and acanthus, look forward to more rococo forms in their accent on the uncertain spatial rôle of the frame, and by positioning flowers and birds to lend lively touches of asymmetry. Edward Croft-Murray[6] suggested that these tapestries might have been the work of Andien de Clermont, (see Cat. C12) painting in England from 1716/17; but details in the tapestries seem rather more robust than his somewhat enervated designs.

Dependence on French design is illustrated by an advertisement in the Public Advertiser[7] of 1755, in which George Smith Bradshaw and Paul Saunders offered 'Eight complete Sets of curious Tapestry Hangings, from the designs of Baptist, Watteau, Laforce, etc.' The '3 sets of Conversations after Watteau' probably included the designs of the tapestries signed 'Bradshaw' at Ham House (Fig. 2), with figures taken from paintings by Watteau and Pater. The floral paintings of Jean Baptiste Monnoyer inspired most of the flower painters in England of the 1720s and 1730s, including Peter Casteels, an artist of printed cotton designs from c.1735 to 1749, whose ornate urns and ewers filled with flowers may have provided the chief motif for the delicate rococo tapestry in the Victoria and Albert Museum (Fig. 3). This was probably made either in the workshop of William Bradshaw or in that of his successors George Smith Bradshaw and Paul Saunders.

Tapestry-woven screen panels and chair covers, from which many small workshops made a precarious livelihood, tended to show vases of exquisitely woven flowers, or birds and small animals in vague landscapes with stylish rococo surrounds. Some of these designs, especially those used in the workshops of Peter Parisot and Thomas Moore (see Cat. L40) may have come direct from the Gobelins or the Savonnerie, brought over by dissident workers who sought employment in England.[8] By contrast with the surround on a screen in the Metropolitan Museum the surrounds on the chairs with tapestry-woven covers at Uppark (Cat. L29) seem likely to be English (Fig. 4) as is the design of a pole screen panel at Hopetoun signed DANTHON. Danthon's family, though originally from Aubusson, had been tapestry weavers in England since at least 1707. On the whole, however, no exciting display of specifically English rococo can be seen in either tapestries or carpets of the period.

The few surviving carpets woven in England in the 1750s and 1760s owe much to the design of Savonnerie carpets and may well be after designs brought from France. The dog on the cushion in the centre of the 1757 Exeter carpet (Cat. N35) is, however irrelevant, a purely English touch. The fresh colouring and the particular tone of blue in the field are distinctive. Its lively appearance stood out in the Council of Europe exhibition held in Munich in 1958.

Silk Design

Natalie Rothstein

The period in which the elements of rococo in English silk design unfold, flourish and decline can be precisely defined to 1742–1752 after which new influences predominate – although some of the motifs continued in use much longer. This precision is possible because of the survival of over a thousand of the dated silk designs of Anna Maria Garthwaite (1690–1763) from 1726–1756. She was a leading designer at a time when there were only two or three important designers.[10] Crucial for this study are her designs for 1743 and 1744 acquired by the Museum as recently as 1971. Since we are looking at trends through her eyes alone we must try to extract the essential features from her own idiosyncracies. Moreover, there seems every reason to believe that she was 'a certain woman who has neither skill nor fancy' who 'has been for many years the principal source of the coloured designs employed in this manufacture' described earlier as the 'famous manufacture at Spittlefields'.[11] The reasons for the intense dislike shown by André Rouquet lie, we argue, not so much in Garthwaite's deficiencies but, in Pevsner's phrase, in the 'Englishness of English Art'.[12] Precisely those qualities admired by Hogarth are those which mark the difference between French and English rococo.

Garthwaite was the well-educated daughter of a Lincolnshire parson (who had had hopes that she too would marry a parson) who came to London about 1730 with her widowed elder sister.[13] Although one of her early designs of 1726 was inscribed 'in York before I came to London' by 1733 she was living in a house on the corner of Princes Street and Wood Street.[14] They were joined by a ward, Mary Bacon, daughter of Vincent Bacon originally from Grantham, and they lived there until both sisters died in 1763.[15] How or where Garthwaite got the necessary technical training remains a mystery after 25 years research. She came from an educated English provincial family yet chose to live her entire life surrounded by foreigners, indeed the Camparts down the road were her 'good friends'.[16]

Garthwaite showed an increasing interest in botany from 1741 onwards. Her use of some newly introduced flowers[17] suggests that she was in contact with the naturalists of the day. She used in her designs several varieties of aloe – not the most obvious motif for silk design –and the Royal Society have a volume of Ehret's drawings of aloes bought in 1737. Unfortunately, the Society has no visitors' book which might show that she saw this, nor has any reference to her been found in the papers of any contemporary naturalist. Yet she must have been an unusual as well as a hard-working and successful designer. She produced and sold an average of 80 designs every year and bound fair copies in two volumes with an index giving the names of her customers and the types of silk. Only her last designs of 1755–6 show a decline in creative ability, by then she was 65. If, as we think, she was the author of the article on silk designing in Smith's Laboratory[18] it was Garthwaite who said that the silk designer 'ought to follow the principles Mr Hogarth gives in his Analysis, observing the Line of Beauty, so as to make it the foundation and support of all his designs, in ornaments, flowers, branches, leafs etc.'[19] A little earlier we learn that the

Fig. 5 Anna Maria Garthwaite. Silk design dated 14 October 1743. *VAM T.392-1971 p. 93*

Fig. 6 Silk woven by Captain Baker from a design by Anna Maria Garthwaite (VAM T.373-1971 p. 17). 1744. *Sherborne Museum.*

designer's 'fancy ought to be unlimited, neither strictly tied to or swerving entirely from nature'.[20] Hogarth attacked the 'giving of premiums to those that design flowers &c for silks and linens let it be recollected that the artisans copy the objects they introduce from nature' which he regarded as a pretty sure guide.[21]

The first dramatic change took place half way through 1742 when Garthwaite changed from using large-scale three-dimensional but non-naturalistic floral motifs to using flowers of a botanical size and shape. The emphasis on botanical realism was further developed in 1743. Since a naturally drawn flower is asymmetrical it lent itself nicely to rococo taste, as we can see in the silks from Sherborne Museum (Fig. 6),[22] in Cat. N7, also dating from 1744, and in the dress (Fig. 7) in Birmingham Museum and Art Gallery too fragile to exhibit.[23] The latter is not Garthwaite's but shows how the naturalistic style had spread to all the designers of the time. The Line of Beauty first appears in a tentative form in a design of October 14 1743 (Cat. N3). The balanced curve to which Rouquet drew attention[24] is essential to silk design for each warp thread must travel the same distance in the warp or be wound on a separate bobbin. Each intersection of the weft in one area of the repeat must be balanced by another elsewhere to avoid an uneven tension. By 1744 we have the fully developed serpentine line (Cat. N8 and Fig. 5) in fact a double line with a brocaded pattern in counterpoint to a self-coloured pattern in the ground. The contrasting texture of bright coloured flowers with a textured pattern in the ground became part of the designer's vocabulary of the 1740s. The superb

Fig. 7 Gown: brocaded silk. English. 1742-4. *Birmingham Museum and Art Gallery.*

Fig. 8 Dress of Brocaded silk. 1744-5. *Museum of London.*

215

brocaded silk dress from Colonial Williamsburg (Cat. N9) can be dated by reference to Garthwaite's design. Moreover, the robings of the dress echo the serpentine line of the silk. Another splendidly curvaceous line can be seen in a very popular silk known from three examples[25] (Fig. 8). As in Garthwaite's design this silk has a double Line of Beauty carried by the ground pattern as well as the brocaded one. We can even see the same scheme in the fan (Cat. N36) which has a wavy stem of well-drawn honeysuckle and other flowers contrasting boldly with the stamped paper pattern between. Garthwaite's designs are all earlier than even the earliest version of Hogarth's self-portrait. It can at least be argued that he admired Spitalfields and its products. He tossed out as an analogy 'as the mechanic at his loom may possibly give as satisfactory an account of the materials and the composition of the rich brocade he weaves as the smooth-tongued mercer surrounded with all his parade of shewy silks'[26] and he chose indeed 'Spittlefields'[27] for his study of Industry and Idleness.

From 1743 onwards each characteristic feature of rococo taste can be distinguished. The "C" scrolls reversed upon each other appear in 1743 in Garthwaite's designs and can be seen in the dress from Platt Hall (Cat. N15). Asymmetrical cartouches appear in 1744,[28] and by 1745 actual *rocaille* and shells. The dress from the Lynn Museum combines asymmetrical cartouches with shells and may date from 1746–7[29] (Cat. N15). The silk from Boston Museum of Fine Arts (Cat. N16) uses shells to form a wavy line. The 1740s are the decade in which brocaded silk, brocaded gold and silver in several textures and the open ground of the material, be it a shining lustring or a satin, are in a harmonious balance (as Smith's Laboratory article said they should be).[30] One of the most impressive silks is the waistcoat from the Metropolitan Museum (Cat. N12) woven by Mr Peter Lekeux from Garthwaite's design. The use of metal thread can surely be compared in this instance to the decoration of contemporary silver. The sparkle of the metal thread is set off by the fresh silks and the rich blue ground. The colour scheme is typical and the motifs in metal are undoubtedly rococo. Yet there is a total lack of French influence.

Only four pieces were usually made from a design and each piece may have been about 50 yards long. There were approximately 14 yards to a sack-back dress of the time of half-ell wide material (19–21 inches wide) so not many examples of each design were made.[31] The repeats of these designs were long – from about 28 inches to 44 inches – when they take the full length of the sack. There were two seasons: spring and autumn and continuous subtle changes appear. At first the brocaded motifs lie on top of the pattern in the ground, then the two are linked so that some parts of the pattern are carried by the brocaded silks and some by the self-coloured pattern in the ground. This last can be seen in VAM T.146–1973 and in the silk of the dress from the Boston Museum of Fine Arts (Cat. N17). Grounds became increasingly elaborate in the late 1740s as attention shifted from the floral decoration. The asymmetrical panels of Cat. N18 are typical of this later phase of design. These panels were to occur again in the printed cottons and again in the perforated pattern on the fan (Cat. N36). In the silk from Worcester Art Museum (Cat. N19) the Line of Beauty has been entirely transferred to the background while the brocaded pattern has been reduced to roses. In the final stage while the flower heads remained life-size the stems of the flowers are cut short (in contrast to those of 1740–44 when Garthwaite even drew the roots).[32] The central cartouche of Cat. N22

XVIII *Susanna Beckford*
Sir Joshua Reynolds. 1756
The Tate Gallery
See cat. N24

XIX *Dress silk*
Designed by Anna Maria Garthwaite
1744
Victoria & Albert Museum
See cat. N7

XX *Design for a brocaded damask*
Anna Maria Garthwaite. 1744
Victoria & Albert Museum
See cat. N8

Mr Vautein. June 16. 1794

Mr. Ledoux. Octr. 23 1747

Dark Yellow plate
Light Yellow plain
Gray Frostso

XXI *Design for a 'silk and silver waistcoat'*
Anna Maria Garthwaite. 1747
Victoria & Albert Museum
See cat. N11

XXII *Sleeved waistcoat*
The silk designed by Anna Maria
Garthwaite. 1747
Metropolitan Museum of Art
See cat. N12

XXIII *Plate decorated with a botanical fantasy*
Chelsea, *c.*1755
Private Collection
See cat. O10

XXIV *Sauceboat in the shape of a fluted shell*
Derby, *c.*1753
Victoria & Albert Museum
See cat. O22

XXV *Teapot and cover, the body in the shape of a melon*
Staffordshire. *c.*1755-60
Victoria & Albert Museum
See cat. O28

XXVI *Model for the monument to George Frederick Handel*
Attributed to Louis Francois Roubiliac.
*c.*1759
Gerald Coke Handel Collection
See cat. S47

remains asymmetrical however and the design preserves all the grace of rococo ornament. This type of design was successful commercially. Garthwaite first tried it in 1749[33] and there are two dresses which relate to it. One is that worn by Lady Sarah Fermor in her portrait by Vishniakov in the Russian Museum in Leningrad, the other is a dress worn by Hannah Allen of New York and now in the Museum of the City of New York.[34]

The changing nature of fashion must be emphasised. A few pieces were woven and sold and then a new design took their place. These patterned silks were not kept in stock and in the fashionable world a rich silk lasted no longer 'que la fraîcheur des couleurs qui la décorent, elle est faite pour parer et non pour l'usage'.[35] They were certainly altered, passed down to companions and favourite servants or children, or even sold, but in the fashionable world they were not worn when out of fashion. This world not only included such towns as Bath or Cheltenham and the Cities of Dublin and Edinburgh but also the rich merchants, the aristocracy in effect, of the American Colonies. The latter wanted fashionable goods,[36] the Boston Gazette advertised them and portraits show them being worn. The American demanded good quality, was well able to judge and, perhaps, even influenced production. While exports of silks as merchandise formed only a tiny proportion of the Customs figures[37] compared with worsteds and cottons, it is the silks which were ordered for the merchant's own use and for his friends and family which constituted an important market for the English master weaver. The frugality of the American merchant also ensured that many have been preserved in the eastern states, often with a firm American provenance – and several were woven from Garthwaite's designs.[38]

Rouquet, the Frenchman, may not have liked them but the English liked their own silks (and so did the Americans!) and were proud of them. Spitalfields had grown into an elegant suburb by the mid eighteenth century inhabited by the master weavers both English and Huguenot – the latter no longer unpopular foreigners.[39] With the greatest port at hand for both imports and exports, with the full backing of the Weavers' Company, the medieval guild, with access to government when necessary and with both the greatest financial centre of the world next door and a large and growing market in the fashionable world on their doorstep, the London industry was in a favoured position to respond to the demands of this fashionable world. French influence had been important in the 1730s and would again take precedence in the 1760s but in the 1740s they could do without it. John Sabatier looked back in 1765 to the period 1748–50 as the best he had known and he had entered the silk industry in 1721.[40] The dislike between French and English was mutual. When a correspondent to the *Gentleman's Magazine* in 1749 admired the 'beautiful disposal of colours and flowers in patterns of brocade . . . exhibited to view at our silk mercers' he said that they were indeed 'indebted to the skill of foreigners'. He provoked a fierce editorial response. English silks were exported to Vienna 'and many other foreign courts where the excellence of English brocades is distinguished and applauded'. 'This excellence arises from the judicious disposition of light and shade, the elegant designing and correct drawing of the model or pattern for the loom, which is the work of an *English* and even a female hand. Our incomparable countrywoman by the force of mere natural taste and ingenuity has made the English loom vie with the Italian pencil, very different from the gaudy patterns of the French, who have never yet with all the assistance of their drawing academy been able to exhibit *true proportion* or just colouring, on silks or linen in any single flower, much less to arrange a number of leaves and flowers, and other ornaments, so that each shall have apparent relation to the other; and from an union and harmony of part produce an whole.'[41] This passage, too, may refer to Garthwaite.

Embroidery

The styles of drawloom woven silks at this time determined those of high quality worsteds, of block printed cottons, and of professional embroidery. The first page of Barbara Johnson's Album has some printed cottons in the same style as those of the silks on the same page.[42] The album represents a chance survival of the textiles worn by one private customer. The reporters who commented upon the styles of silks worn at court commented equally upon woven and embroidered silks. Mrs Delany and other diarists and letter writers did likewise. The waistcoats turned to the viewer in the portraits of the time are sometimes embroidered and sometimes woven. There is no reason to be vague about the dating and style of professional embroidery. The picture is complicated, however, by the traditions of domestic embroidery and by the lack of dated embroideries – apart from samplers which are both domestic and follow traditional patterns quite rigidly. Chair seats may be copied from treasured models – especially if they were worked to complete a set. Certain types of embroidery pattern of which the 'flame-stitch' is the most notable example lasted from the seventeenth to the nineteenth century.[43]

In seeking rococo we must turn to professional embroidery. A coverlet belonging to the Marquis of Bath follows a traditional form for such grand embroideries but the basket of casually disposed and naturalistically rendered flowers in the centre (Fig. 9) and the border of diapered panels surmounted by shells suggest the 1740s rather than an earlier date. The effect is not too far removed from that of the brocaded metal thread in Garthwaite's waistcoat of 1747 (Cat. N12). An equally interesting example of shells upon a diapered ground with natural flowers can be seen on an embroidered Torah Mantle in the Jewish Museum. This came from the Hambro Synagogue, one of the old City of London synagogues.[44] Much closer to the silks of 1742–4 is a skirt bequeathed to the Museum of London[45] which has yet another version of the popular auricula and other flowers combined with the semi-naturalistic forms of the late 1730s. It makes use of the same colour scheme and the shading is by *points rentrées*, although these are not limited to a horizontal plane as they would be in a silk. The embroidery panel from a dress[46] displays a slightly uncertain use of rococo motifs (Fig. 10). The open ground, naturalistically drawn flowers and the botanical choice can be compared with the woven design with which it was in competition. The combination of real flowers with textured panels in gold thread is found in each. Once more, the auricula makes a striking appearance. This is not an easy flower to grow yet Ehret painted a masterly series of water colour studies of it.[47] We have thus a botanical fashion which, for a time, became a part of English rococo.

Fig. 9 Embroidered coverlet. 1740s. *The Marquis of Bath*

Fig. 10 Skirt panel. *VAM T.179A-1959*

218

Printed Textiles

There is no neatly defined period of years in which the rococo as a style arrived in English printed textiles, flourished, and departed. There were two major techniques for the printing of textiles, wood-block and copper-plate printing, both of which give very different results. The earliest copper-plate printing on fustian dates from 1752. Thus at the time when rococo can be discussed in silk design it is only possible to do so in relation to block-printing. Very few early English block-printed textiles have survived and even fewer which are known to date from the 1740s. The survivors include the early samples in Barbara Johnson's album and the Holker samples in Paris,[48] the latter the labours of an industrial spy who collected his samples about 1750. Both sets of samples show a strong allegiance to English silk design with naturalistically rendered flowers strewn casually across the textile. Some details like the vertical stripe in Holker's sample no 89 are lifted directly from warp-patterned silks. As the author of the Laboratory article wrote of the designs for printed textiles '. . . they are for the generality in imitation after the fashions of the flowered silk manufactory'.[49] With the 'whole chints' the calico printers could 'imitate the richest brocades with a great variety of beautiful colours: these make the best appearance on an open white ground. The fashion of late as with the brocaded silks has run upon natural flowers stalks and leafs . . .' An example of such a style is illustrated in Fig. 11.

Fig. 11 Printed lining to a child's Banyan. 1740s. *Mrs Cora Ginsburg.*

Few of the designers of printed calicoes are known even by name. The most dominant figure of this period was probably John Baptist Jackson who trained abroad, worked for a calico printer in 1745, and set up his own wallpaper business briefly in Battersea in 1752. Fig. 12 shows a detail from one of his paper impressions and Fig. 13 has been attributed to him on the basis of his own description of wallpapers: '. . . antique statues . . . surrounded with a mosaic work in imitation of Frames or with Festoons and garlands of Flowers'.[50] Given his training abroad, the rococo of this textile owes much more to French than English models. The flowers are subordinated to the decorative scheme, the birds are pattern-book birds. It is a splendid textile despite its condition but the predominant effect is French. The paper impression (Fig. 12) is quite different. There is plenty of air, and space with asymmetrically arranged, natural flowers. His work can certainly be compared with the Holker samples which are English by definition.

Copper-plate printing revolutionised design through the large size of the repeat and the accurate definition which became possible. With some notable exceptions copper-plate prints were monochrome. Their designers could and did make use of both decorators' manuals and publications on natural history. Fortunately, several books of impressions have survived from English factories[51] and a few others are printed with inscriptions and thus it is possible to determine which textiles are English. The printing of all cotton cloth became legal in 1774[52] but until 1812 such cloth had to be woven with three blue threads in the selvage to distinguish it from foreign cloth and this is a great help to any would-be connoisseur of the subject. English textile printing was extremely successful, technically, commercially, and aesthetically. Very large numbers of printed cottons were exported, especially to the American colonies and the new United States and also all

Fig. 12 Paper pattern of printed textile. John Baptist Jackson. 1745-55. *VAM (E.4538-1920).*

Fig. 13 Block printed cotton. John Baptist Jackson. *c.* 1750. *VAM (T.243-1979).*

over Europe. As Peter Floud found in his pioneering research in the 1950s[53] some of the most important English cottons are still in the former colonies. Selection for the present exhibition has been difficult because of the quantity from which to choose.

The valance (Cat. N27) combines flowers with the characteristic scrolls of rococo forming an asymmetrical frame. A similar bold frame can be seen on a fan believed to be English[54] as well as on carpet designs. Even bolder but most characteristic is 'Birds' (Cat. N26). We should emphasise again the massive size of the plate – a yard square which allows the designer the maximum freedom of expression. By this time, about 1755–1760, the vocabulary of rococo is used with assurance. Many of the features were those first seen in silks such as the variously diapered fillings of the scrolls and panels. It is odd that the author of the Laboratory article continued his (her?) description of the calico prints of 1756 by saying that designs were 'sometimes intermixt with ornaments after the French taste'[55] for these diapered fillings resemble English silks much more than any French decoration. 'Large Flowers' (Cat. N28) makes an interesting comparison with Garthwaite's 1744 design (Fig. 7) and the related silks. The double Line of Beauty is common to both but the difference in technique gives a totally different appearance. In this plate the ubiquitous auriculas have turned into a massed bunch and the convolvuli have acquired extra lines as though they had grown older. It is such details which mark the slightly later date. The choice of peonies and many-petalled roses rather than flowers with a simpler outline is indicative of the newer taste.

The Bromley Hall pattern book (Cat. N25) spans 45 years. The page we have chosen owes much to French silk designs of the 1760s. At this period these consisted almost exclusively of such diapered curving ribbons crossed by bunches or branches of roses.[56] Yet this is unmistakably English. The diapered fillings are much more varied and the flowers wander at will rather than marching in tidy bunches up the repeat. The scale allows for plenty of light. In contemporary French silks variously patterned effects in the ground may fill the space entirely.

The fancies of *chinoiserie* although despised by Hogarth[57] and by John Baptist Jackson lent themselves very readily to rococo taste. It must, however, be remembered that *chinoiserie* can be recognised in the seventeenth century and has continued until the twentieth century, it is not synonymous with rococo. 'Chinese figures' (Cat. R12) after Pillement is essentially French *chinoiserie*, a delicate, unified composition with a graceful sense of movement. Through Sayer's *Ladies Amusement* Pillement greatly influenced English taste. By contrast 'Pagoda' inspired by Edward Darly's *New Book of Chinese Designs* of 1754 has a much more English interpretation (Fig. 14). The figures are friendly naïve little mannequins. The irregular motifs are left in space without any attempt to join them visually. The bird perches on the small pagoda in a natural birdlike way which makes the design all the more absurd. The tree growing by the lowest pavilion is a real tree. Just as in 1733–4 the English silk designers turned the nightmarish vegetation of the Lyon silk designers into proper sturdy English trees[58] so we see in this cotton the same wish to regularise the fantastic. The urn of flowers sits in a solid fashion on its improbable rock. There is no unity of space, style, or conventional treatment yet the design is thoroughly successful in its own terms, amusing and well-printed.

As we look at the later plate-printed cottons other influences increasingly

Fig. 14 'Pagoda'. Plate-printed.
c. 1760. *Musée de l'impression sur Etoffe du Mulhouse.* 954.270.1.

overlay the recognisably rococo motifs. The outward forms are there: 'C' scrolls, shells, and even the asymmetrical cartouche but they are used as part of an eighteenth century *Grammar of Ornament* rather than to achieve a unique sense of space, air, and grace. The Line of Beauty was an early casualty. Such printed cottons were highly successful but suited to a different taste. *Don Quixote* after Hayman (Cat. N32), is a narrative and romantic scene, albeit framed in rococo decoration with shells in the foreground. 'Peacock and Hen' from Bromley Hall (Cat. N29) is unmistakably English taken from the frontispiece of Sayer's *New Book of Birds*. Peacocks at this date seem always to have drooping tails, even appearing on the fan mentioned earlier[54] as well as in the important print by Robert Jones of 1761.[59] The drooping tailed peacock of the 1760s seems to be the successor of the auricula of the 1740s and 1750s. It is this type of rococo in which a massive frame of 'C' scrolls dominates the composition which appealed to the taste of the 1740s as much in silver as in textile design.[60] The birds, pears, roses and peonies are well-drawn but are combined in such profusion that their individual characteristics are lost in a plethora of decoration dominated rather than supported by the scrolls. Such textiles made splendid bed-hangings, their long repeats and grand scale being entirely suited to their purpose. Since these are monochrome designs they are not overpowering. In our last textile Nixons 'Birds' (Cat. N26) the style is almost played out. The scrolls are there but one has turned unexpectedly into a cornucopia. The ringed doves are a long way after any ornithological treatise, the reversed scrolls are flattened, and the garlands look as though they have been unhooked from some neatly tied neo-classical decoration and allowed to droop. They are printed on fustian and therefore likely to be before 1774. This textile probably represents, however, the routine commercial production in a style already displaced by neo-classical taste on the one hand and by the richly inventive and colourful block-printed textiles on the other. Some rococo flavour still remains and the textile helps in the summing up of what are the essential features of rococo in English textile design.

Conclusion

French influence was paramount in certain fields especially in the design of English tapestries. It was very strong in the design of English hand-knotted carpets as far as we can tell from the few surviving examples. From the 1760s French sources had a role in the design of English plate-printed textiles but the latter remain unmistakably English. Any confusion has arisen because earlier scholars like Clouzot mistook English printed cottons for French.[61]

Between 1742 and about 1760 not only was rococo the paramount style but we think we can determine a peculiarly English version. The Line of Beauty appeared in English silks before Hogarth rationalised its importance. It had technical advantages but these were not why it was used. The contrast with silks of the 1730s and even up to 1742 was dramatic. The few dated French silk designs show nothing comparable.[62] Secondly, this phase in design coincided with a renewed and passionate interest in natural history – hence, apart from his artistic merits, Ehret's long stay in London. His way of rendering the details of flowers is the closest to Garthwaite's but no connection has been found, so far. The desire to use natural forms in a realistic way extended both to professional embroidery and to printed calicoes by the mid-eighteenth century. The latter could at last compete technically with drawloom woven design. Since a flower is seldom symmetrical (dahlias are a bit dull aesthetically!) the use of natural flowers in their proper colours created a feeling of space and delicacy. These flowers suited the asymmetrical cartouches which were part of the universal vocabulary of rococo. Thirdly, while the devices of rococo, 'C' scrolls, diapered asymmetrical panels, *rocaille*, shells and the like are used freely they never dominate. The fan we chose has a 'brocaded' naturalistic wavy line of flowers supported by a sub-pattern. Its perforated diapered pattern is comparable to those on the printed cottons. After 1760 the cast of English silk design was once more closer to France (and not specially rococo) while in printed cottons the rococo framework came to dominate the floral details. With the advent of neo-classical taste the rococo details decline in importance altogether. What is common throughout is firstly the choice of colour. Wherever possible the English designer chose fresh outdoor colours seen by daylight and not the subtler pastel shades considered by the French to be more tasteful.[63] It is the colouring of the Exeter carpet which makes it look English. Secondly, there is always a sense of space and air. The white ground of the cotton and the sheen of the silk are exploited. English silks stand out in foreign collections because of their colour scheme and every contemporary writer agreed about the excellence of their dyes, even Rouquet. In the eyes of the foreigner the English designers may have seemed naîve but they were bold in their choice of motif, and, in the case of woven and embroidered design, masterly in their handling of the various types of metal thread. They did not overload their silks as Rouquet claimed, unless ordered to do so by the customer. The spaniel on the Exeter carpet is surely an English conceit, a French customer would surely have required a coat of arms or at least a lion? The solid trees in a fantastic design are an English quirk. Rococo was essentially a light-hearted and ephemeral style. While it lasted it was fun – and won markets for the English. It coincided fortuitously with a number of favourable factors which gave Anna Maria Garthwaite an immortality denied to her rivals and set the printing of English cottons on a course of increasing prosperity and popularity which lasted until the twentieth century.

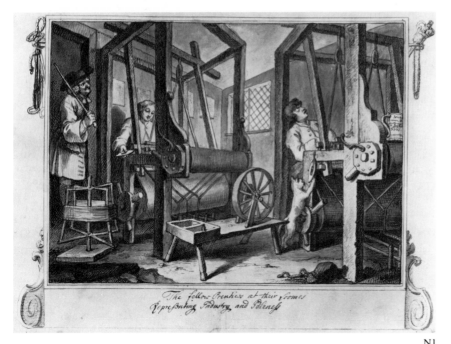

N1 *The Fellow 'Prentices at their Looms*

William Hogarth (1697-1764). Before 1747
Grey wash, pen and ink over black chalk or lead (?), indented for transfer; 275 x 353
Inscribed *The fellow Prentices at their Loomes Representing Industry and Idleness.*

The Trustees of the British Museum (1896-7-10-2)

The finished drawing for plate 1 of print series Industry and Idleness, published in October 1747. The two apprentices are at the looms of a Spitalfields silk weaver (indicated by the tankard lettered 'John . . . Crown a[nd] . . . in Spittle Fields'). The master appears angrily at the door brandishing a stick (his hat suggests that he is a Quaker); Francis Goodchild works diligently while Tom Idle sleeps at his loom. The series of prints, which was in Hogarth's words 'calculated for the use and instruction of youth', shows Goodchild's rise to the position of Lord Mayor and Idle's descent to the gallows. Clearly and vigorously etched, to reach the popular market, the series sold particularly well at Christmas. The looms and other weaving equipment are very much simplified.

Prov: Horace Walpole; Strawberry Hill Sale, Robins, 23 July 1842, 1311; Henry Graves & Co.; H.P. Standly; Christie's 21 July 1845, 1099; Colnaghi (?) or 'Anderson' (?); Edward Cheney, 1846 (?); P. & D. Colnaghi
Lit: Croft-Murray n.d., no. 25; Binyon 1898, 1; Nichols 1808, I, p. 67; II, p. 396; Oppé 1948, p. 41, pl. 42; Ayrton & Denvir 1948, p. 78, no. 34, pl. 34; Paulson 1970, p. 194, no. 168
MS

N2 *A Tailor's Shop*

Louis-Philippe Boitard (active 1733-1763) and (?) George Bickham junior (1706?-1771): *c.*1749.
Pencil, red chalk, pen and ink wash; 207 x 296.
Inscribed *Gravelot*
Her Majesty The Queen

Engraved in reverse by Bickham with the title *The Merchant Taylors, 1749*. In the foreground the Master, in nightcap and dressing gown, carries out a fitting. Through a window he can supervise the eleven seated tailors in the workroom, also visible through open folding doors. They are lit by a row of large windows, clearly on an upper floor. The main drawing is in brown on a pencil base. The border has been added by another hand in grey on a red chalk base. It is one of the few surviving drawings that can reasonably be attributed to Bickham; similar bound-cloth decoration appears on his trade card (Cat. N34a)

Lit: Oppé 1950, 71, pl 33
MS

N3 *Pattern book*

Anna Maria Garthwaite (1690-1763). 1743 Designs for woven silks (43 on 30 sheets), with a manuscript index, thread sewn and quarter bound with marbled boards, a label on the front cover inscribed in ink *Patterns for Capt. Baker &c 1743.* Pencil, ink and watercolour; 490 x 300.
VAM (T.391-1971)

Garthwaite sold 80 designs in 1743, a typical number, and bound the fair copies with an index of customers and the designs she sold them. She produced two volumes each year and this contains her work for a variety of customers including Captain John Baker (his rank in the City Trained Bands). The introduction of the serpentine Line of Beauty to her work can be dated to October-November 1743, hence the book is open at this page. Patterns were drawn half-size. Silks identified from this volume include page 55, a damask pattern sold to Mr Julins. This was woven and exported to the American Colonies, where it was worn by Mrs Charles Willing when she sat for her portrait to Robert Feke in 1746 (Henry Francis DuPont Winterthur Museum, Delaware). A wide botanical range appears in these two books including some quite unusual plants, eg the pink *Kalmia Latifolia* introduced to this country in 1734 (Cat. N4, p.3) and other interesting flowers such as the orange spotted white *Lilium Auratum* (Cat. N3, p. 109), a yellow spotted fritillary (Cat. N3, p. 99) and several different *Dicentra*. Flowers on page 107 include purple and yellow Heartsease (of which Garthwaite was very fond) and pink native dianthus. Mr Carr, whose name appears on some of the patterns, was the mercer Robert Carr of the Queen's Head, Ludgate Hill (1707-1791), senior partner in one of the most important firms which existed from 1727 until the 1750s when they were among the unpaid creditors of the Prince of Wales. They gave evidence to Parliament in 1765 and commissioned at least 30 of Garthwaite's designs. Mr Gobbe, who also appears, is probably Daniel Gobbe (before 1690-1758) of Princes Street, Spitalfields, one of a large contingent of Huguenots from Bas Poitou, and a loyal member of both the Weavers Company of London and the Vestry of Christ Church Spitalfields.

He gave evidence to Parliament in 1750 and offered 70 men to fight the Young Pretender in 1745.

Prov: purchased with the help of Marks and Spencer Ltd., the Pasold Fund Ltd., Courtaulds Ltd., The Wallpaper Manufacturers Ltd., Crossley Carpets Ltd., Parker-Knoll Textiles Ltd., Heal Fabrics Ltd., Liberty & Co. and the Worshipful Company of Weavers.
Lit: King 1980 (Ed), Vol I, pl. 234.
NR

N4 *Pattern book*

Anna Maria Garthwaite (1690-1763). 1743 Designs for woven silks (37 on 26 sheets), with a manuscript index, thread sewn and quarter bound with marbled boards, a label on the front cover inscribed in ink *Patterns for Mr Vauteir &c 1743.* Pencil, ink and watercolour; 490 x 300.
VAM (T.392-1971)

The second of her books of designs for 1743, chiefly those that she sold to Vautier, her best customer. Several silks have been identified from these two books including page 49 'a bro[caded] lut[estring] strawberries'. The silk woven from this design forms a dress in the Gallery of English Costume, Platt Hall, Manchester (1947-827). The book is open at a typical page with botanical flowers upon a pattern of meandering scrolls in the ground. Garthwaite has made use of a purple striped crocus, orange celosia and blue convolvulus tricolor. This is one of four complete volumes; all the rest, possibly 21 volumes, were dismembered when acquired in the 19th century by the South Kensington Museum and the designs for 1746 and most of 1750 are still missing. Some indexes are also missing so that the precise number of volumes is unknown. Some of the designs may never have been bound. The designs have been squared up in pencil by the designer to transfer to the draft from which the loom is entered.

Prov: see cat. N3
NR

N5 *Design for a brocaded silk*

Anna Maria Garthwaite (1690-1763). 1745 Pencil, ink and watercolour; 480 x 299 Inscribed in ink *Mr Vauteir.*
October 11. 1745
VAM (5983.22)

Described in the manuscript index as a 'bro[caded] lut[estring] one shade' (see cat. N3). The whole design depends upon a *rocaille* motif and there is a silk very similar to this design brocaded in silver thread and coloured silks on exhibition in the Students' Room of the Department of Textiles and Dress (100 Frame BB 14), given to the VAM by the Cooper-Hewitt Museum, New York. This motif was not a favourite of Garthwaite's although she used another half-rock, half-root in 1747 (VAM 5985.3).

Lit: King 1980 (Ed), Vol I, pl. 197 & p. XXVII.
NR

N6 *Design for a brocaded satin*

Anna Maria Garthwaite (1690-1763). 1744 Pencil, ink and watercolour, squared in pencil; 482 x 299 Inscribed in ink *Mr Gregory. April 22. 1744.* Inscribed in pencil with colour notes.
VAM (5982.10)

Although she sold 40 designs to the weaver 'Mr Gregory' between 1742-45 he cannot be identified. He wove this design into cat. N7 changing the leaves and stems from brown to green. The strokes on the bottom left indicate the number of shuttles needed.

Lit: King 1980 (Ed), Vol. I, pl. 190 & p. XXVII
NR

N7 *Dress*

Silk designed by Anna Maria Garthwaite (1690-1763). 1744 Satin brocaded in coloured silks; h. of repeat 580, width between selvages 527.
VAM (T.264-1966)
See colour plate XIX

The silk was sold to the master weaver Mr Gregory, on the 22 April 1744 (see Cat. N6). Brocaded in coloured silks with flowers including rose buds, morning glory and auricula. Described in the design catalogue as a brocaded satin. The dress has been re-made in the 1770s.

Prov: given by Mrs Olive Furnivall in whose family it has descended since the eighteenth century.
Lit: King 1980, Vol I, pl. 191 & p. XXVII.
NR

N8 *Design for a brocaded damask*

Anna Maria Garthwaite (1690-1763). 1744 Pencil, ink and wash and watercolour; squared in pencil; 482 x 298. Inscribed in ink *Mr Vauteir June 16. 1744*
VAM (5982.16)
See colour plate XX

For 'Mr Vauteir' (probably Daniel Vautier) see cat. N3. This design shows Garthwaite's fully developed use of the serpentine Line of Beauty, a year before Hogarth's self-portrait, with the brocaded pattern echoing that of the ground. Many silks may be compared with it, including that of the dress cat. N9, and a silk of which three examples are known; in the Cooper-Hewitt Museum, New York, the Heritage Foundation, Deerfield, Mass., and in the Museum of London (see fig. 8).

Lit: Rothstein 1964
NR

N9 *Gown and petticoat*

English; *c.*1745
Silk brocaded in coloured silks and gold thread with part of the design carried by self-coloured motifs in the ground; h. (neck to hem) 1430, w. (across shoulders) 330.
Colonial Williamsburg Foundation (1968-646)

The stomacher is original. The use of a double serpentine line may be compared with Garthwaite's design cat. N8. The theme is echoed in the robings.
NR

N10 *Dress*

The silk English; *c.*1745
Taffeta brocaded in coloured silks and three types of gold thread; h. 1498, repeat h. 965, w. (loom width) 517
City of Manchester Art Gallery (1947-2071)

The scrolls and flowers are evenly balanced in importance. Such designs may be compared with later printed cottons. The dress has been re-made in the 19th century, possibly in the 1840s.

Prov: Dr Willet Cunnington's Collection
NR

N9

N10

N11 *Design for 'a silk and silver waistcoat'*

Anna Maria Garthwaite (1690-1763).
1747
Pencil, ink and watercolour; squared
in pencil; 486 x 302
Inscribed in ink *Mr Lekeux Octor 23
1747* with details of threads to be used
VAM (5985.13)
See colour plate XXI

Garthwaite has explained her colour
code to the weaver, Peter Lekeux
(1716-1768): *plate* (light yellow)
indicates a plain metal strip, *plain*
(dark yellow) is a metal strip wound on
a silk or linen core, *frosted* (grey) is a
thread in which one component is
more tightly wound than the other to
give a crinkly yarn. This reflects the
light at different angles giving a
sparkling or frost effect. A similar code
is used on many other silk designs,
although grey may indicate other
effects. This design was
described in the manuscript index as
'a silk and silver waistcoat'. For a
waistcoat woven from this design see
cat. N12.
NR

N12 *Sleeved waistcoat*

The silk designed by Anna Maria
Garthwaite (1690-1763): 1749
Blue silk with figured effect in
extended tabby, brocaded in three
types of silver and with coloured silks.
The upper part of the sleeves (which
would not normally show) are made
from high quality glazed worsted; h.
(shoulder to hem) 965, w. (across the
chest) 1054.
*The Metropolitan Museum of Art (Irene
Lewison Bequest Fund 1966) (c.166.14.2)*
See colour plate XXII

The silk was sold to the master weaver
Peter Lekeux, October 23 1749. The
waistcoat is woven to shape, the
adjustment for the wearer being made
at the back by his tailor. Peter Lekeux
(1716-1768) was the third of his name
in the English silk industry. His father
and great uncle were key figures in
their day. Capn. Peter (died 1743) was
one of the first Huguenots to enter the
Court of Assistants of the Worshipful
Company of Weavers, the oldest
Livery Company in London, signing
the ordinances in 1737 with the
designer and manufacturer James
Leman (1688?-1745). Peter Lekeux III

reached the highest office in the Company, Upper Bailiff, in 1764 and gave evidence to the crucial Parliamentary Select Committees on the industry in 1765 and 1766. He retained his father's house and business in Steward Street, Spitalfields (now demolished), and was a respected citizen serving on the Jury which condemned no. 45 of the North Briton, thus precipitating the political crisis over John Wilkes. Both father and son bought a number of designs from Garthwaite. Peter III bought 16 between 1743-48 but both seem to have specialised in the richest silks for men's wear. Mrs Polaire Weissman, Curator Emeritus of the Costume Institute, recognised this waistcoat and sent a photograph to the V & A in 1966.
NR

N13 *Sir Richard Lloyd*

Thomas Gainsborough (1727-1788). Later 1750s Oil on canvas; 762 x 635. *National Museum of Wales (49.303)*

Lloyd wears a red velvet coat with gold buttons and a splendid waistcoat brocaded probably in gold thread and woven to shape, as in cat. N12. The waistcoat seems to date from the mid-1740s.

Prov: Sir Richard Lloyd (1698-1761); R.H. Lloyd-Anstruther; Hintlesham Hall sale, 16 June 1909, 374; F. Anstruther; Sir Gerald Ryan, 1915; Hintlesham Hall sale 10 Dec. 1937, 1315; Vicars 1947; C. Marshall Spink 1949; bought 1949
Lit: Bordeaux 1977, 8; Waterhouse 1958, 453
MS

N13

N14 *Children of Sir Edward Walpole*

Stephen Slaughter (1697-1765). 1747 Oil on canvas; 870 x 1093 Signed and dated *Stepn. Slaughter pinxit 1747* and inscribed *Sir E. Walpole's Children, 1747 The Minneapolis Institute of Arts. Gift of Mrs Eugene J. Carpenter and Olivia Carpenter Coan in memory of Eugene J. Carpenter (31.106)*

The girls are, from left to right, Laura (*c.*1734-1813) who m. the Hon. F. Keppel, later Bishop of Exeter, Maria (1736-1807), and Charlotte (1738-1789) who m. the 5th Earl of Dysart. The boy, Edward (1737-1771) d. unmarried. They were the children of Anne Clement, Sir Edward's mistress. Maria, who was the particular favourite of her uncle Horace Walpole, was firstly m. (1759) to the 2nd Earl Waldegrave (see cat. L68) and secondly in 1766 to the King's brother, the Duke of Gloucester. Laura wears adult clothes, an open robe in a highly fashionable brocaded silk of strongly naturalistic flowers. The other girls are in simpler children's clothes. Edward wears a velvet suit of adult type. This is Slaughter's most ambitious recorded work.

Prov: Walpole family, Norwich; Messrs Asscher & Walker, London; Howard Young Galleries, New York
Lit: Lewis 1961, pp. 26-9, no. 9 repr.; Minneapolis 1971, 27; Ribeiro 1983, 54; Sewter 1948, pp. 13-14, fig. xi; Waterhouse 1981, p. 348 repr.
MS

N15 *Gown*

The silk English. *c.*1745-7 Woven silk, brocaded with coloured silks; h. (at centre back) 1460. *Kings Lynn Museum (KL 131-972-CD 243)*

The gown was originally worn by Mrs Frances Fysh m. 1742, d. 1760. Asymmetrical cartouches containing shells are obvious rococo motifs. The basket of flowers and fruit appear in Garthwaite's work in 1745 (VAM 5984.2) and is carried by ladies in contemporary paintings such as G. Knapton's portrait of Lucy Ebberton in Dulwich Art Gallery. There are many asymmetrical cartouches in Garthwaite's work from 1744 onwards, but using small brocaded motifs to

N14

N16

N15

form the cartouche in reverse first
occurs in designs of 1747. This silk is
not, however, in her style and is
obviously the work of a rival. The
dress has been altered in the 1750s,
1780s and 1880s, the last time for
fancy dress.
NR

N16 *Woven silk, panel from a dress*

English; *c.* 1745-8
Tabby, brocaded in coloured silks
with a flush pattern in the ground;
1045 x 505
*Museum of Fine Arts, Boston, Gift of Miss
Amelia Peabody and Mr William S. Eaton
(46.279)*

Garthwaite sold a design for a
brocaded tabby 'holly leaves' in May
1743 (VAM T.392-1971 p. 31) to Mr
Vautier, commissioned by the mercers
Palmer and Halsey, and the motif was
popular with other designers in the
mid 1740s. Holly leaves and other
recognisable flowers are superimposed
upon a meander composed entirely of
shells. There is a dress of the same silk
in the Metropolitan Museum of Art,
American Wing (L.37.33), thought to
have an American provenance.
NR

N17 *Gown and petticoat*

English. *c.* 1745-50
Lustring brocaded in coloured silks; h.
(neckline to hem) 1295, waist 670, h.
of repeat of design 782.
*Museum of Fine Arts, Boston, Elizabeth Day
McCormick Collection (43.1639 & A)*

From the mid 1740s silk designs were
constructed from a combination of
brocaded and self-coloured motifs.
The brocaded flowers represent the
current botanical interest while the
linking self-coloured devices form an
asymmetrical framework. The silk may
be dated by comparison with
Garthwaite designs, but is not by her.
The dress is one of the most splendid
of its type. There is a version of the
design on a white ground in the VAM
(T.186-1963, King 1980 (Ed), Vol II,
pl. 2).
NR

N18 *Woven silk*

English. *c.*1747-50
Tabby brocaded in coloured silks with
a self-coloured pattern in the ground;
23036 x 508
VAM (723B-1905)

Peter Cheveney, a pattern-drawer, told
the Parliamentary Select Committee of
1765 that 'Brocades upon a white
ground were in greater perfection here
than at Lyons'. This silk is a typical
example.
NR

N19 *Woven silk*

English. *c.*1747-53
Tabby ground brocaded in coloured
silks with an elaborate flush pattern in
the ground; w. 445, repeat 505
*Worcester Art Museum, Massachusetts
(1919.342)*

The Line of Beauty has been
subordinated to the diapered patterns
of the ground, an indication of the
later 1740s or early 1750s. The
restricted botanical choice contrasts
with silks of a year or two before.
Roses, rosebuds and carnations were
to dominate the 'flowered silks' of the
next two decades. The silk may be
dated by reference to Garthwaite
designs of 1748 and 1749 (VAM
5986.3, 1 and 2, and 5987.2).
NR

N19

N20

N20 *Eleanor Francis Dixie*

Henry Pickering (active 1740-d. *c.*1770).
*c.*1753
Oil on canvas; 1440 x 1200
Nottingham Castle Museum (94.112)

The brocaded silk of the sack back
gown can be compared with cat. N19
which dates from 1747-1753. The
gown is here worn as formal dress,
with elaborate sleeve ruffles, gloves
and a straw hat over a small linen cap.
The Dixie family seem to have been
among Pickering's most frequent
customers. His full-length portrait,
also at Nottingham, of Eleanor's
father, Sir Wolstan Dixie (1701-1767),
4th Baronet, of Bosworth Hall, Market
Bosworth, Leicestershire, is dated
1741. The Dixie Family Group
(Sotheby's 29 May 1963, 134;
Christie's 18 March 1977, 105) is
dated 1755.

Prov: given by J. Henry Jacoby, 1894
Lit: Ribeiro 1983, 74 repr.; Thornton
1965, pl. 90B; Waterhouse 1981,
p. 282
MS

N21 *Design for a 'double comber brocaded tabby' pattern*
Anna Maria Garthwaite (1690-1763)
1752
Pencil, ink and watercolour; sight size 617 x 261
Inscribed in ink *Mr Sabiteir June ye 6: 1752*
VAM (5989.26)

This design, described in the manuscript index as a 'double comber brocaded tabby' was sold by Garthwaite to the master weaver 'Mr Sabiteir', probably John Sabatier (*c.*1702-1780). The watered tabby in cat. N22 was woven from this design. She drew a similar design in 1749 (VAM 5987.3) for another weaver.

Lit: King 1980 (Ed), Vol. I, pl. 245; Rothstein 1964, illus 7, p. 19
NR

N21

N22 *Woven silk*
Designed by Anna Maria Garthwaite (1690-1763)
Woven by 'Mr Sabiteir', probably John Sabatier (*c.*1702-1780) in 1752 from cat. N21
Brocaded watered tabby; 117 x 470
VAM (T.10-1962)

Tabbies could be watered or unwatered. The watering was produced by passing the folded silk through heated, engraved rollers. Such silks very often had point repeats. This alone produces a symmetrical pattern diminishing the rococo effect. Garthwaite sold a very similar pattern in 1749. Although the central cartouches remain asymmetrical and the flowers are treated naturalistically, their stems are cut short and their form subordinated to the general structure. These two patterns mark the passing of the rococo phase in English silk design. They can be compared with a dress in the Museum of the City of New York with an American provenance (60.9.1b), and with the dress worn by Lady Sarah Fermor in the painting by Vishniakov in the Hermitage, Leningrad. John Sabatier bought 90 of Garthwaite's designs between 1742 and 1756. The family came – unusually – from Lyon. He was an important figure, three times called to give evidence to Parliamentary Select Committees on the state of the silk industry. In 1766 he recalled the best years as 1748-50. He was a man of capital, buying his own raw silk and having it thrown, employing up to 400 men and even exporting woven silks to Ireland. Latterly, however, he worked only on commission. He held important local positions and retired eventually to Chichester.

Prov: given by Mrs M.H. Eden and Reading Museum and Art Gallery
Lit: Rothstein 1964, illus 7a & b, 31-34

N23 *Two ladies walking in a high wind*
Paul Sandby (1725/6-1809). *c.*1751-2
Red chalk; 190 x 137
Her Majesty The Queen

The ladies, seen from behind, are wearing a sack back and an English-fitting tight gown. The wind catches against the wide fashionable hoops at the ladies' hips, enhancing the flowing rococo lines of this beautiful drawing.

Lit: Oppé 1947, 263; Ribeiro 1983, 65
MS

N22

N23

N24

N24 *Portrait of Francis Beckford*
Sir Joshua Reynolds, PRA (1723-1792); 1756
Oil on canvas; 1270 x 1000

Portrait of Susanna Beckford
Oil on canvas; 1270 x 1000
Inscribed *J.R. 1756*
Trustees of the Tate Gallery (5798/9)
See colour plate XVIII

The sitters are Francis (d.1768), sixth son of the Hon. Peter Beckford, Governor of Jamaica, and his wife Susanna (d.1803), daughter and heiress of Richard Love of Basing Park, Hants. They were married in 1755 (she was his second wife), and these are evidently their marriage portraits. They sat to Reynolds several times throughout December 1755 and early 1756, usually one after the other, for about two hours each. Reynolds, by now a well-established painter in his early thirties, with a rapidly expanding practice, was still overshadowed as a painter to the establishment by the more French-inspired Allan Ramsay, whom he consciously tried to rival. Susanna Beckford's elegant pose is a repetition in reverse of one Reynolds had used some two years earlier (*Mrs Bonfoy*, ill. Waterhouse 1941, pl. 23), and it remained a favourite, with increasingly 'Grand Style' drapery, for the rest of his career. Mrs Beckford wears a splendid blue and silver watered silk gown with a matching stomacher and serpentine robings; the ruffles, handkerchief and ruff are of blue silk lace. Both portraits are in their original wavy-edged open-work gilded wood frames.

Prov: (for the pair) Mrs Kirby, Winchester; Agnew & Son, from whom purchased 1947
Lit: Buck 1979, fig. 6, 11; Ribeiro 1983, 75; Waterhouse 1941, p. 40; Waterhouse 1968, p. 142
EE

N25 *Pattern book*
Anonymous, for Foster & Co., Bromley Hall, Middlesex. *c.*1755-1800
Volume containing 223 impressions pasted in, of 144 engraved copper-plate designs for printing on textiles. Full bound in calf with two bronze clasps, with labels on front and back covers lettered *Foster's Bromley*, 559 x 356. Many designs inscribed *Talwin & Foster* with short titles for pictorial designs and others numbered from P.1 to P.185 in a broken series. Inscribed in ink throughout the volume with numbers, titles, notes etc. open at pp. 94-95, the design inscribed *P.8, Talwin & Foster 8d.*
VAM (E.458(1-223)-1955)

In this pattern, the rather stiff, formal meanders of lace fillings which repeat their designs without any technical necessity, are influenced by silk designs of the 1760s and probably indicate that this design was for dress material. Their late, clumsy version of the Line of Beauty and overdecorated fillings are lent a rococo lightness by the thin trails bearing naturalistic flowers, which cross at random. Many of the 141 different designs in this book contain rococo elements, scrolls, rocaille and graceful meanders, often with natural flowers. Designs in this book represented in this exhibition include cat. N26, 28, 29 & R12. Another fine chinoiserie pattern in the book, *Pagoda*, is based on plates in Edward's and Darly's *New Book of Chinese Designs* of 1754. Bromley Hall was in the hands of the Olive, Talwin and Foster families from at least the 1740s. The firm was called Talwin & Foster from 1785 to 1790; Foster & Co. from 1790 to 1823. Good designs were kept in production for as long as they would sell.

Lit: Montgomery 1970, pp. 232-249; VAM 1960, pp. 22-25
WH

N26 *Plate impression for a printed textile: 'Birds'*
Bromley Hall; *c.*1755-60, in use through to the 1780s
Ink on paper, from an engraved copper plate; 1040 x 1000
Inscribed on the back *Birds 10d Talwin & Foster*
Musée de l'Impression sur Etoffes de Mulhouse (514/0051)

N25

One repeat is shown. Opposed C-scrolls with crisp rocaille ornament spring in taut arabesques from corner to corner of this completely asymmetrical design, forming perches for posturing birds and supports for gracefully hanging flowers, exquisitely engraved. The naturalism of individual flowers and birds contrasts with the mannered elegance of the design as a whole. The same inscription is on another copy of this design in the Bromley Hall pattern book cat. N25. It is a pity that the manufacturer did not choose to record the name of the unknown artist who created this powerful design, making full use of the yard-square surface of the copper plate. Barbara Morris puts this design as late as 1770, but the style and quality suggest a date nearer to French and English engraved ornament of the 1730s and 1740s. Such exuberant rococo forms are lacking from contemporary French printed textiles, which tend to the pretty rather than the strikingly decorative.

Lit: Montgomery 1970, pp. 212-238, fig. 224; Morris 1957 II; VAM 1960, cat. 94.
WH

N27 *Valance*

*c.*1755-60
Cotton, plate-printed in red; 337 x 2210
The Cooper-Hewitt Museum, The Smithsonian Institution's National Museum of Design New York (1951-105-38)

Entwining scrolls form a repeat of three large, asymmetric cartouches almost covered by sprays of naturalistic flowers springing from the scrollwork. The area outside the cartouches is filled with little dashes, or 'mosaic'

work. No other record is known of this magnificent design. The valance was probably intended to accompany hangings similar to the Bromley Hall 'Birds' cat. N26, which also has bold flowers twined round powerful C-scrolls. The mosaic filling recalls designs of wallpaper and printed textiles of the late 1740s and 1750s by John Baptist Jackson, and carpet designs of the 1750s.
WH

N28

N28 *Printed cotton, probably for dress: 'Large Flowers'*

Bromley Hall; *c.*1755-60
Cotton printed from an engraved copperplate; 1372 x 775
The Cooper-Hewitt Museum, The Smithsonian Institution's National Museum of Design New York (1957-153-1)

Hogarth's Line of Beauty has run wild in a bold, convoluted meander emphasised by the large flowers of the title. The line of this meander is almost the same as that on a brocaded silk of 1744 cat. N8, suggesting both that this was intended as a dress material and that it was likely to have been one of the earlier plate-printed cottons, a novelty of the 1750s. A further indication that this was probably a dress material is seen in the half-drop repeat, not required by the technique, bringing the scale of the design more into conformity with contemporary dress silks and block-printed cottons. The flowers, in spite of different varieties growing from one stem, are individually in the tradition of English naturalism. Similar peonies were inscribed 'Drawn from Nature' and initialled *J:B:J* for John Baptist Jackson in a scrapbook of that designer which dates from the 1740s.

Lit: Floud 1957 II; Montgomery 1970, fig. 233; VAM 1960, cat. 98
WH

N29 *Printed furnishing cotton: 'Peacock and Hen'*

Bromley Hall. Design *c.*1765-70
Cotton, plate-printed in 'China blue'; 2520 x 2260
G.P. & J. Baker Ltd., London (Z.060)

Four birds stand framed in three asymmetric cartouches formed by opposed C-scrolls entwined with naturalistic flowers and fruit. The peacock and hen are copied from the frontispiece of *A New Book of Birds,* published in 1765 by Robert Sayer, cat. N30. The design of the printed cotton, though striking, lacks the springing tension and crisp detail of the C-scrolls in 'Birds', cat. N26. This may be due simply to a different designer; but later date may also be a factor. It was this heavier type of English rococo which was avidly imitated by the designers of the 1840s.

Lit: Farnham 1982, cat. B4;

N27

Montgomery 1970, figs 219, 221;
Morris 1957 II; VAM 1960, cat. 92
WH

N30 *Title page:* A New Book of Birds

Anonymous. 1765
Engraving; 348 x 247
Lettered with the title, the address of
Robert Sayer and *Pubd. Acod. Act. 1765*
VAM (16532.1)
MS

N31 *Printed fustian furnishing*

Nixon & Co.; *c.*1765-74
Linen and cotton, plate-printed in red;
1620 x 890
*The Henry Francis du Pont Winterthur
Museum, Delaware (66.104)*

A light inconsequential arrangement
of garlands and a cornucopia of
flowers, with C-scrolls half
metamorphosed into airy pergolas,
sets off perched and flying birds less
well drawn than in 'Peacock and Hen'
or 'Birds' cat. N29 and N26. Rococo is
still the dominant style, but it has lost
much of its strength in this design.
Two manufacturer's impressions
survive of this design, both numbered
'104'. The impression at Mulhouse is
inscribed '@ 10d Nixon & Co'; the
other is in a pattern book stamped
'Nixon and Co' belonging to G.P. &
J. Baker (VAM 1980). It was Francis
Nixon who brought the art of plate-
printing from Drumcondra in Ireland
to England in 1752-56, making
possible the use of finely engraved
design on so large a scale. English
rococo textile design was allowed an
additional lightness of touch in
designs which could spread to a yard
wide and stretch up to 39 inches, as
here, before needing to repeat. After
Nixon's death in 1765, the firm
operated as Nixon & Co. until 1789.
The use of a fustian suggests that this
textile was printed before regulations
concerning printed cottons were
relaxed in 1774.

Lit: Montgomery 1970, fig. 227, pp.
231-2; Morris 1957 II
WH

N32 *Plate impression for a printed textile: 'Don Quixote vanquishes the Knight of the Mirrors'*

After Francis Hayman. 1755
Used in the manufactory of Robert
Maxwell, 1780-83, and later at
Bromley Hall
Ink on paper, from an engraved
copper-plate; 1040 x 1000
Inscribed *No. 81*
*Musée de l'Impression sur Etoffes de
Mulhouse (514/0044)*

Don Quixote stands menacingly over
the sprawling Sampson Carrasco,
whose 'squire' kneels by him, while
Sancho Panza clings to the branch of a
tree. The scene is framed by a ruin,
scrolls, rocaille, a rustic fence and urns
on pedestals. The figures are taken
from G. Scotin's engraving in *The
History and Adventures of the renowned
Don Quixote . . . with Twenty-eight new
Copper-plates designed by Hayman,*
(London 1755, see also cat. I8, I9).
The designer of the larger copper-
plate added this landscape with flying
birds and the dramatic surround, the
latter with juxtaposed ornament
reminiscent of plates in William de la
Cour's *Second* and *Fourth Books of
Ornament* of 1742 and 1743. The
textile may have shown a second scene
on another copper-plate. The inking
shows this impression to be from the
workshop of Robert Maxwell, at
Merton Abbey from 1780 to 1783. But
he may have acquired the design from
some earlier manufactory, such as that
of Robert Jones of Old Ford, sold in
1780; just as many of Maxwell's plates
were purchased for use at Bromley Hall.

Lit: Floud 1957 I; VAM 1960, cat. 87
WH

N32

N33

N33

N33 *A Lady's Maid Soaping Linen*

Henry Robert Morland (?1719-1797).
Early 1760s?
Oil on canvas; 740 x 610

A Laundry-Maid Ironing Shirt Sleeves

Henry Robert Morland (?1719-1797).
Early 1760s?
Oil on canvas; 740 x 610
The Trustees of the Tate Gallery (1402 & 1403)

The pair is typical of the elder Morland's narrow range of popular 'fancy subjects' – wholesome, sometimes mildly erotic, servant maids, ballad-singers, oyster-girls etc – in which he specialised (at about 12 gns apiece) throughout his career, in a tradition derived from Philip Mercier's very similar domestic fancy subjects of the 1740s. He exhibited this particular pair, or close replicas, at the Free Society of Artists no less than five times between 1768 and 1782 (at present some seven replicas of the first and three of the second are known, all apparently autograph). The pair could have entered his repertoire well before the first date of exhibition, as some of his later stock subjects in oils were first exhibited as crayon drawings in the early 1760s, and could have formed part of his stock-in-trade even before that. The persistent tradition that these were portraits of famous contemporary society beauties is a romantic invention of the 19th century. The maid ironing is wearing a gown of printed linen or cotton. The pattern, in monochrome with delicate outlines, looks as though it derives from a plate-printed textile; but the artist has added areas of shading that presumably copy his original crayon drawing. He may have sketched a block-printed fabric which he either adapted or forgot when he came to reproduce his work in oils. The maid washing wears a painted silk gown. Both patterns and dresses date from the early 1760s. Neither dress, being of expensive material, would have been worn by a laundry-maid.

Prov: purchased by the National Gallery from P & D Colnaghi & Co. in 1894. Transferred to the Tate Gallery 1919
Exh: (this or close replicas) Free Society of Artists 1768 (B164), 1769 (A163), 1774 (A209, B215), 1775 (A169, 174B), 1776 (A250, B251), 1782 (A108, B40)
Lit: Dawe 1909, pl. LIV, f.p. 120, pl.

LV, f.p. 124; Graves 1907, pp. 175-6; Williamson 1904, pp. 2, 3
EE & WH

N34 *Trade cards and ephemera*

The Trustees of the British Museum (unless otherwise stated)

a) *Robert House, shoemaker.*
Probably by George Bickham junior. Dated on the sign in the design: *1746.* Such dating is unusual and its meaning unclear, although it is a feasible date for the design. Attributable to Bickham on grounds of similarity of the sign cartouche to cat. N34c and to a plate in *The Musical Entertainer,* which both ultimately derive from Meissonnier's *Livre D'Ornemens* (Heal 18.72).

b) *Francis Flower, haberdasher.*
Anonymous, possibly by George Bickham junior. The bill, for Mrs Hucks, is dated 1753.
The Museum of London (A 15219)

c) *Norris & Co., importers of Irish Linen.*
George Bickham junior;
*c.*1750? (Heal 80.248)

d) *Abraham North, milliner.* Anonymous; *c.*1755? He also sold straw, cane and turnery goods. (Heal 72.276)

e) *Trade label for the South Sea and Exeter Company.* Anonymous; c.1760? Lettered in Spanish for west-country woollen serge. This crudely-engraved label represents a type of rococo ephemera that has very largely disappeared.
The Guildhall Library (38433)

f) *Bill for Adam Digby, breeches maker.* William Austin; c.1760. Inscribed with bill dated 1767. *VAM (E.127-1943)*
MS

N35 *Carpet*

Exeter, Passavant's factory; 1757 Woollen pile, woollen warp (white, every 20th thread brown) woollen weft, 80 Turkish knots to sq. inch. The carpet is tightly woven and the warp lies on two levels; 3660 x 4600. Woven with the incription *EXON: 1757 VAM (T.78-1946)*

Passavant's factory was established in Exeter after the closure of Parisot's factory at Fulham in 1755. Some of Parisot's workers transferred to the new enterprise. Passavant won a premium from the Royal Society of Arts in 1758 jointly with Thomas Whitty of Axminster, possibly for the carpet now at Petworth which is entirely French in style and colouring. Passavant's carpets were expensive and the factory closed in 1761. One other carpet survives at Dumfries House, dated 1759.

Lit: Tattersall 1934, pp. 63, 93, pls. VI and XVI; Verlet 1982, p. 145
NR

N36 *Fan*

Probably English. 1750s
The leaf is of paper which has a ground wash of grey watercolour (see fingerprint in top left hand corner) subsequently hand painted in watercolour, trimmed with gilt paper and finally stamped. The perforated pattern appears to be the result of using a custom-made punch or stamp applied to the leaf after the decoration is completed but before the leaf is attached to the sticks. The sticks and guards are of carved and pierced ivory, the guards are backed with gilt paper. The stud and washer are of mother of pearl; 276 x 482.
VAM. Given by Her Majesty Queen Mary (T.214-1959)

N35

N36

The overall simplicity of the decoration and the clarity of its style suggest that the fan may be of English manufacture. The choice and naturalistic treatment and colour of the flowers is typical of English design. The diapered decoration and reversed C-scrolls of the stamped areas can be compared with printed cottons of the 1750s and woven silks of the 1740s.
AH

Porcelain

See Cat. O6.

Rococo in English Ceramics

J.V.G. Mallet

Nowhere in Europe did ceramics, glass or enamels – *les arts du feu* – play a leading role in the development of the rococo style. The potter, the glass-maker and the commercial enamellist (we are not here concerned with enamel as an adjunct to jewellery or as a medium for miniature painting) had to accept for his products a subordinate role in a decorative environment controlled by architects, cabinet-makers and upholsterers, all of whom worked on a larger scale. Gold- and silversmiths, whose expensive materials commanded respect and dictated a more immediate response to the whims of fashionable patrons, were also normally a step ahead of their ceramic *confrères* in adopting the new style; so too were the designers of silks. Nonetheless, when we think of the rococo today, it is not long before one particular material springs to mind: porcelain.

This refined ceramic substance can gleam whiter than stucco or be gilded and enamelled to a brilliance beyond the scope of the frescoist or the practitioner of scagliola; its imperishable colours outlast those of the textiles with which it once had to harmonise; it can be moulded or cast, if throwing will not suffice, into almost any irregular shape that the silversmith or the sculptor can devise and, before firing, crisp detail can either be applied or incised with the modelling-tool. After some three centuries of more or less unsuccessful experiment, at the dawn of the rococo era in the late seventeenth and early eighteenth century, the Europeans were able to produce on a commercial scale a substitute for the porcelains of China and Japan. The spread through Europe of porcelain-making and of the rococo style chanced to happen in the same years.

The period 1699-1712 when Pierre Lepautre was making his crucial contribution to the evolving rococo style in French architecture overlaps the period between 1694, when von Tschirnhaus can be shown to have begun his practical experiments in porcelain-making, and 1710 when Böttger had carried those experiments to a point that made possible the foundation of the Saxon porcelain factory at Meissen. Böttger's was a lime-porcelain not too dissimilar from the hard paste of China that was the object of imitation by all would-be porcelain-makers in Europe, and by the early 1730s, after Böttger's death, Meissen was able to produce a true hard paste. The secrets of the Meissen factory spread to Vienna in 1719 and from thence by degrees to other parts of Europe though not to England, where the serious manufacture of a true, hard paste porcelain had to wait until 1768, following independent researches by William Cookworthy. Meanwhile between 1693 and 1702 an artificial porcelain compounded not of kaolin and china-stone but of other white-burning clays blended with the ingredients of glass, had been developed at St Cloud, possibly following yet earlier experiments at Rouen. Other French soft paste factories followed: Chantilly in 1725; Vincennes in 1745; Mennecy in 1748. Vincennes has especial historic importance since it soon became the French Royal factory and was transferred to Sèvres. Technically the earliest English factories used soft paste processes somewhat similar to those of France even at times when, in point of style, the influence of the hard paste German factory at Meissen predominated. A consequence of this is that the sharp mouldings of Meissen wares, the mordant wit of Kändler's figure models, look blunted in their English counterparts as a result of the thicker glaze adapted to soft paste bodies, in which fine detail tends to be drowned. The charm of English rococo porcelain depends instead on its seductively melting appearance and the wide range of enamel colours obtainable at its comparatively low firing-temperatures.

1745, the year that saw the foundation of the Vincennes factory, seems also to mark the start of serious porcelain production in Chelsea, which at first made a glassy soft paste porcelain. Others were not far behind. Limehouse in East London may have pioneered between about 1745-48 the practical soap-rock or steatitic soft paste formula on which production at Lund's Bristol (1749-52), Worcester (founded 1751) and some of the Liverpool factories was to depend. Also in East London was the Bow factory, which took out its first patent in 1744, though commercial production probably did not get under way until 1747. Bow introduced the use of bone-ash to English porcelain, an ingredient later made use of by other soft paste factories before being adopted as the distinctive ingredient of modern 'bone-china' properly so called. The early 'dry-edge' Derby porcelains of about 1750-54 and Longton Hall porcelain from Staffordshire (about 1749-1760) were both of the glassy soft paste type. More mysterious in attribution, date and composition are the curious 'A Marked' porcelains (Cat. D2, D12).

It is here proposed to give a short account of the principal personalities who affected design in these English porcelain materials, and indeed also in other ceramic bodies, enamel and glass, before attempting some chronological account of the rococo style as it passed from factory to factory.

André Rouquet, whose observations were presumably made before he left England in 1752, wrote of the Chelsea factory: 'A rich private individual sustains its finances; an able French artist supplies or directs the models of everything that is manufactured there'.[1] Strong grounds exist for believing that these two men were respectively Sir Everard Fawkener, a merchant who had become secretary to the Duke of Cumberland, and Nicholas Sprimont, a silversmith born and trained in Liège.[2] Sprimont was that *rara avis* in mid-eighteenth century England, a craftsman who knew how to draw (Cat. G16, G18), and it is significant that Rouquet, himself an admirable portaitist in enamels, described him as an 'Artist'. If Sprimont ever read the Abbé Le Blanc's *Lettres d'un François* (1745) he would have agreed with many of the Abbés strictures on English art, but would surely have thought himself the exception to the statement that London goldsmiths were mere craftsmen, whereas in Paris Meissonnier and Germain were designers and sculptors. It was precisely the role of a Germain that Sprimont seems to have set out to play when he settled as a silversmith in Soho. Even when he had transferred his energies to the Chelsea porcelain factory Sprimont is likely in the early days to have done all the modelling and designing, as Rouquet says, until administration of a growing business forced him to lean heavily on the skills of a fellow Fleming, the sculptor Joseph Willems. Both Rouquet and Horace Walpole[3] thought of Sprimont as a Frenchman, but it is worth recalling that this designer and entrepreneur, like several of the other foreigners who led the rococo movement in England, came from the periphery of the French-speaking world, in Sprimont's case a Prince-Bishopric in what is now part of Belgium but was then linked to the Germanic world of the Holy Roman

Empire. Like Gravelot, Moser and Roubiliac, though his skills seem to have been acquired abroad, his reputation was made in England. With premises in Compton Street, Soho until 1748, he spent his silversmithing years in the very heart-land of the English rococo: he stood godfather in 1744 to a daughter of Roubiliac, and one of his earliest porcelain figures was cast from the sculptor's portrait of Hogarth's pug (Cat E4).

Thomas Frye, one of the principal partners in the Bow porcelain factory from the experiments preceding the abortive patent of 1744 until ill-health forced him to retire in 1759, has even stronger claims than Sprimont to be considered an artist: at the age of twenty-eight he was commissioned to paint Frederick Prince of Wales for the Saddlers' Company, and his mezzotints and rare surviving miniatures suggest that had he not broken his career as a painter for fifteen years to experiment with and later manufacture porcelain, labouring 'among Furnaces, Till his Constitution was near destroyed'[4], he would today hold a very high place indeed amongst the artists of his time. Even as it is, his influence on English porcelain did not stop at Bow: a Liverpool print after his portrait of Queen Charlotte will be seen on the Worcester mug (Cat O36). And yet the wares of Bow do not, even in the years of Frye's association with the factory, show much consistency either in design or in execution. Splendid models like the wildly rococo early sphinxes (Cat. O17) alternate with lumpishly conceived wares and with figures almost wholly lacking in style. After the earliest years at Bow there is much copying from Chelsea rather than from the Eastern or Meissen originals that Chelsea itself had copied. When allowance has been made for the fact that Bow aimed at a cheaper market than Chelsea, it is nevertheless clear that Frye's taste cannot have predominated at Bow to the extent that Sprimont's did at Chelsea.

This may have been because Frye was only one in a fair sized partnership, as was also the case with the Worcester factory's Dr Wall, who was an amateur artist of sorts. Wall may have captured too large a share of attention from modern collectors; we have no evidence that he had more influence on the design of early Worcester porcelain than may have done, for example, the local silversmith, Samuel Bradley, who was one of his partners. Silver- and gold-smithing were probably a better training for porcelain design than painting and drawing; at least one porcelain factory, Derby, was run in its earliest days by a man trained in London as a goldsmith, Andrew Planché. Many 'dry-edge' Derby figures and wares attributed to Planché's factory show what, for England, are precociously rococo features (Cat O22). This does not however mean that Planché necessarily acted as his own modeller any more than did his successors at Derby, the two William Duesburys, father and son. Surviving correspondence of theirs shows that they employed a number of different modellers, some of whom furnished models for the Derby factory without ever quitting London. A similar picture emerges from the archives of Josiah Wedgwood's Staffordshire pottery firm. Wedgwood boasted as late as 1779 that he had taken up his modelling tools again,[5] but in general he restricted himself to exercising tight control on all models issued by his factory, whether they were commissioned from outsiders or designed in house by specialist modellers such as Hackwood. William Greatbatch (1735-1813), another Staffordshire master-potter, began life as a modeller for Thomas Whieldon and after setting up on his own apparently continued to make his models and even to engrave his own copper-plates for transfer-printing. John Brooks was in 1751 himself an engraver and pioneer of printing on enamels and ceramics, but he soon had to give up his independence and move from Birmingham to work as one of a partnership for the Battersea enamel factory. Instances of designers also being proprietors are few indeed.

If we must look beyond the proprietors of firms, who then were the people responsible for the forms and decoration of the ceramics, enamels and glass? Few indeed of them have earned a place in our modern biographical dictionaries of artists, but they included sculptors, block-makers, enamel-painters and engravers, all of whom in turn drew on a variety of design sources.

We do not know the names of the modellers responsible for such figures as the Bow *Kitty Clive* and *Woodward* (Cat. O14, O16), the dry-edge Derby Chinoiserie groups of *The Senses*, or of such a thoroughly rococo group as the Longton Hall *Britannia* and its pedestal.[6] The only porcelain modeller active in England before 1770 of whose personality and work we can form any clear idea is Joseph Willems (1715-1766).[7] Willems was born in Brussels and is first recorded at Chelsea in the first half of 1748,[8] remaining until 1766, when he returned to Flanders to take up the posts of modeller at the Tournay porcelain factory and Professor at the town's Academy, though in the event he died soon after arrival there. At Chelsea Willems seems at least latterly to have enjoyed a certain independence of the Factory, exhibiting sculpture at various London societies of artists between 1760 and 1766 and allowing his talents as a teacher of drawing and modelling to be advertised in *Mortimer's Universal Director* of 1763, which also tells us he had 'modelled for the Chelsea China Manufactory for many years'. From surviving terracottas we can judge that he was a competent sculptor whose style varied considerably according to whether he was modelling heavy-limbed peasants in the manner of Teniers or adapting to the third dimension an airy print by Boucher; when working on a large scale for porcelain he could turn to baroque sources such as the sculpture of Roubiliac's master, Nicholas Coustou,[9] or to engravings after Rubens (Cat. O9). We can infer that practically all the figure-sculpture at Chelsea was modelled by him from at least 1749-1766; what we do not know is whether he also made moulds for the wares, as Kändler and his modelling workshop did at Meissen, or whether all the rococo borders of plates, scroll-handles and so on were the work of his silversmith employer, Sprimont, or of some third party.

Few links can be established between major English sculptors of the mid-eighteenth century and the porcelain factories. It is true that John Bacon was apprenticed in 1735 to the jeweller, Nicholas Crisp, at a time when the latter was in partnership with the Vauxhall delftware manufacturer, John Sanders, for the production of porcelain.[10] As a founding member of the Society of Arts, Crisp had interesting connections: he even sat in 1757 alongside the painter, William Hogarth and the sculptor, Henry Cheere, on one of that Society's committees intended to promote cultivation of the silk-worm in Georgia. But we have no certainty as to what the young Bacon did for Crisp's business, nor do we know what the porcelain Crisp launched on the market in 1753 was like, though the unattributed 'A Marked' porcelains, several of which bear Gravelot-inspired enamelling, could conceivably be his (Cat. D2, D12).[11] As for Bacon's later ceramic figure-modelling, it was neo-classical in style and need not detain us here.

There was one branch of the statuary trade that helped, often unwillingly, to diffuse sculptural models through the ceramic factories: the plaster-cast-sellers. Prince among these was John Cheere,[12] brother of Henry, but there were others like Hoskins and Grant, who sold in plaster form many of the library busts and figures that Wedgwood subsequently issued in black basaltes ware, or Richard Parker, whose sale to Wedgwood in 1774 of a plaster pug dog presumably explains the issue in black basaltes later that year of Roubiliac's old model of Hogarth's Trump.[13]

Through the plaster-cast shops models from continental Europe by such sculptors as the seventeenth century 'il Fiammingo' percolated to the ceramic manufacturers. But we must not overlook the possibility of direct intervention by other foreign sculptors besides Willems. Take for instance J.C.L. Lücke (ca. 1703-1780), a sculptor with unique experience in porcelain-modelling, having been present at the very birth of the European porcelain figure at Meissen in 1728-29, then at Vienna from *c.* 1749-51. Around 1757-61 Lücke was in London: is it pure coincidence that two figures of *putti* that had earlier appeared on a Meissen clock of the late 1720s suddenly feature on a single example of the Bow clock-case (Cat. O20) made to commemorate the death in 1759 of Lücke's fellow German, Handel? If the Bow factory did have direct dealings with von Lücke it was no doubt discouraged from further use of him by the dilatoriness that had caused his dismissal from Meissen.[14]

The commonest source of design for ceramic figures and wares was however direct copying of foreign prototypes. Writing in the *World* for February 8th, 1753, Horace Walpole affected astonishment that 'Jellies, biscuits, sugar plumbs, and creams have long since given way to harlequins, gondoliers, Turks, Chinese and shepherdesses of Saxon China'. By degrees, he noted, unified themes in porcelain spread themselves over the whole dinner-table, and even these were 'sinking into disuse . . . Gigantic figures succeed the pigmies . . .'. This was humorous exaggeration, but Chelsea, Bow and Derby scrambled to compete in such a lucrative market. Ideally foreign porcelain prototypes were borrowed through an influential patron, as Sprimont managed to borrow in 1751 Meissen figures and wares that had been presented to our Minister at the Court of Saxony and Poland, Sir Charles Hanbury Williams. Yet as so often happened, the items borrowed were not in the very latest fashion. A factory, too, might have strong links with a retailer who stocked foreign wares: was Bow influenced by the Doccia service contained in 1764 in John Crowther's stock?[15] Was James Giles's own studio affected by the Nymphenburg and Meissen he sold in 1774?

In considering the form of vessels and figures we should not forget one further category of designer: the block-makers. Blocks were the convex master-moulds, usually made of salt-glazed stoneware or other ceramic materials but occasionally of metal or even alabaster. From them were taken and renewed the concave plaster moulds in which the handles, spouts or bodies of vessels could be shaped. A wheel-thrown body or a strap-handle needed no such mould, but as soon as the saltglaze manufacturers of Staffordshire began to seek novelty of form for their tea-wares, specialist block-makers appear on the scene. The most influential of these seem to have been Aaron Wood (1717-85) and William Greatbatch (1735-1813). Of Aaron Wood's style around 1760 we can form some idea from two dishes later enamelled with inscriptions by his son, Enoch Wood.[16] Both have dry, meticulously accurate relief border patterns, in one instance a rice-grain design interrupted by wavy engine-turned lines and by basket-work, in the other 'mosaic' patterns interrupted by scrollwork. On the basis of the latter dish I have attributed to Aaron Wood a sauce-boat block (Cat. O29) and hence the design of the resultant saltglaze sauce-boat (Cat. O30). Aaron's son Enoch tells us his father 'was modeller to all the potters in Staffordshire at the latter end of the time that white ware or white stoneware was made'. Nor did matters stop there, because such blocks could be acquired not only in Staffordshire by the Longton Hall factory (Cat. O31) but even by that at Bow (Cat. O32). The Liverpool, Worcester and Lowestoft porcelain factories also used moulded patterns evidently derived from Staffordshire blocks. Aaron's brother, Ralph Wood, is sometimes also credited with having designed blocks, on the strength of several incised before firing with his name or initials, but this may indicate prospective ownership rather than his authorship. Thanks to the Wedgwood archives and an archaeological dig[17] it is however now becoming possible to form an idea of William Greatbatch's contribution to rococo design. Like Aaron Wood before him, Greatbatch worked for a time at Thomas Whieldon's potworks before setting up on his own. Josiah Wedgwood dissolved his partnership with Whieldon in 1759, at about the same time that Greatbatch left, and subsequently for several years a mutually profitable understanding existed whereby Greatbatch supplied Wedgwood with half-finished ware for Wedgwood to complete by adding the then fashionable green and 'tortoiseshell' glazes. Greatbatch also seems to have sold blocks to Wedgwood (and probably to other potters) besides manufacturing ware on his own account. It matters little who actually made the Flora cornucopia in this exhibition (Cat. P10); it is clearly from a block by Greatbatch, as was probably most of the Staffordshire pottery of about 1760-65 moulded as pineapples, cauliflowers (Cat. P8) and other fruit and vegetables. A creamy-coloured body and colours that flowed in the glaze made the degree of naturalism practised in Longton Hall porcelain (Cat. O28) out of the question. Instead Greatbatch developed a stylised manner in which crisp raised detail caused the glaze to 'break', emphasising the underlying pattern. His wares in this style must be reckoned one of the most distinctive achievements of the English rococo. Greatbatch also modelled blocks in the Chinoiserie taste. His attempts at a later date to engrave subjects for transfer-printing are sadly amateurish.

The painters who decorated pottery and porcelain often came and went between these and other trades. The Limehouse porcelain factory advertised in October, 1746 for 'POT, Fan, or Box Painters'.[18] Sprimont of Chelsea claimed to employ '. . . thirty lads, taken from the parishes and charity schools, and bred to designing and painting – arts very much wanted here, and which are of the greatest use in our silk and printed linen manufactures'.[19] William Beilby, the foremost enameller of rococo designs on glass (Cat. Q6) had been apprenticed to the Birmingham enameller John Haseldine in 1755,[20] while Thomas Craft, who lived at Battersea and presumably worked for the enamel factory there around 1753-55, was a painter at the Bow china factory after 1756 and by 1771 owned a considerable calico-printing business.[21] Painters could and sometimes did move from one factory to another. Others might take employment in an establishment such as that of James Giles in London, which enamelled mainly on Worcester but also on Bow or on Chinese porcelain. The eclecticism of this workshop is shown by its advertised ability to copy 'the Pattern of any China with the utmost exactness, both with respect to the Design and the colours, either in the European or Chinese taste.'[22]

The transfer-printers, too, could cross the barriers between one factory and another. Wherever Thomas Hancock may have lived, his prints are found mainly on Worcester (Cat. O34) but also on Bow (Cat. O18) and on enamels. John Sadler of Liverpool, who ran the most prolific transfer-printing workshop of all, was not an engraver but an employer of engravers, decorating tin-glazed tiles (Cat. P16) and Liverpool and Worcester porcelain. He also, by agreement, did all the transfer-printing Josiah Wedgwood needed to have done on his creamwares, continuing to do so until just short of the year of Josiah's death; and not until 1770 did Wedgwood become critical of the unabashedly rococo elements in the transfer-prints Sadler offered him. The subjects engraved for transfer-printing could be in any style, but rococo artists and designers such as Watteau (Cat. O34) or Gravelot (Cat. O9) enjoyed especial popularity.

It may be worth concluding with a summary of the way in which certain rococo themes filtered through the ceramic and enamel trades in England. A crude awareness of the rococo style shows in some of the Staffordshire salt-glaze commemorating Admiral Vernon's victory at Portobello (1739) and Fort Chagre (1740),[23] but the Chelsea goat-and-bee jugs of 1745 (Cat. O3) mark the real launching of rococo in English ceramics. Until about 1750, when England began to be flooded with Meissen wares and figures, Sprimont struggled to establish at Chelsea a rococo style based partly on French silver and porcelain, but also to a considerable extent autonomous. The sudden influx of Meissen wares and figures that occurred from around 1750 made even Chelsea change tack. For the next ten years the raised border patterns of Meissen, the figures of Harlequins and shepherdesses, latterly with scroll-edged bases, were relayed from Chelsea to Bow and elsewhere until they found a down-market echo in Staffordshire 'Whieldon ware' and saltglaze. Cut-flower painting on English porcelain of the 1750s follows, with a lapse of several years, fashions started by Meissen, and seems uninfluenced by contemporary textile design. Transfer-printing, a technique little used abroad, provided some of the few opportunities for Great Britain to escape the tyranny of Meissen fashions. From about 1755 coloured grounds, especially the dark Mazarine blue copied from Vincennes and Sèvres began to influence Chelsea (Cat. O39) and the makers of enamel snuff-boxes. After 1760 such blue grounds were commonplace at Worcester and elsewhere, their reserved panels filled with flowers, figures or exotic birds, and framed with gilt scrollwork. A variant much used by Giles, the outside decorator, and by the Worcester factory itself, broke the ground colour up into a field of neat, scale-like brush-strokes derived from the *Mosaik* borders initiated at Meissen, perhaps by Frederick the Great himself (Cat. O37).[24]

From about 1770 the tide of the rococo in English ceramics began to ebb. But even Wedgwood never wholly abandoned the style in his creamwares; it is surely fair to talk of a rococo survival before revival makes its tentative appearance around 1811-13.[25] When the Napoleonic Wars ended in 1815 the proprietors of the Meissen factory were astonished to find the London China dealers begging them to drag out and re-use the old rococo moulds of Kändler and his school: revival was under way.[26]

O1

O2

O1 *Design for a plate*

Anonymous *c.*1738.
Ink and body colour. The sheet is backed with another sheet of paper and stuck to a thin oak panel of the same size; 253 x 235
Inscribed in a contemporary hand on the *verso* of the panel. *The armes of Leake Oakover Esqr of Oakover near Ashbourn in the Peak in the County of Staffordshire a Pattern for China plates. Pattern to be returned.*
Private Collection.

The design for cat. O2. The marine motifs which dominate this design are not connected with the coat of arms and their meaning is unclear, but they do reappear on Okeover's silver (cat. G26). A print by Stefano della Bella (cat A1) may have influenced both the conception and some of the details of the central cartouche, such as the sea horses and the mantling, which is similar to the horses' manes. The thick scrollwork, however, is in the late baroque Italian style close to that used by Gaetano Brunetti, whose *Sixty Different Sorts of Ornament*, 1736 (Cat. B10) could have influenced the designer, although no precise parallel can be made. A comparison can be made between the upper cartouche on the rim of the plate and the title page, with its dolphin supporters, of Meissonnier's *Cinquième Livre D'Ornemens* (*Œuvre suite* E.28) probably published in 1734. A bill of *c.*1746 from Arthur Devis to Okeover for 'finishing' (perhaps furnishing) 'a pattern for a china service' and 'finishing (furnishing?) a pattern of a Plate' (D'Oench 1980, p. 51, list 274) is difficult to relate to the present design because of its date. The design is the work of a very competent heraldic painter, probably based in London.

Prov: Leake Okeover; by descent
Lit: Howard & Ayers 1978, vol. II, fig. 413a
MS

O2 *Plate*

Chinese, 1740 or 1743.
Porcelain painted over the glaze with enamel colours; diam. 228.
Painted with the arms and crest of Okeover, quartering Byrmingham (probably), Pettus, and Leake impaling Nichol. On the rim is the monogram *L.M.O.* and another Okeover crest.
VAM (FE.47-1982) Given by Alfreda and Peter Rochelle-Thomas

The quarterly arms are of Leake Okeover (b. 1702) and impale those of his wife Mary Nichol (married 1730). It was probably 1738 when he first ordered a porcelain service from China, sending a painted pattern (cat O1). In 1740 and 1743 two deliveries were made, the first dated 16th January 1740, listing '70 plates and 30 dishes' and costing £99.11s.0d. The second is dated 1743 and reads 'from ye Jerusalem Coffee House, Change Alley, a consignment of 50 plates and 4 large dishes with your arms' and is addressed to 'Leake Okeover Esqre.' by Joseph Congreve, Commander of the ship *Prislowe*. A total of not less than 120 plates and 34 dishes was delivered, many of which survive today. The price of £1 each reflects their very high quality, and is expensive even by the standard of armorial porcelain which cost around 25% more than ordinary China ware. The Okeover service is unique in that the original painting from which it was copied survives. Given the complex design, the Chinese copy is remarkably accurate. Large services like this one would have been decorated in a workshop in Canton by a number of artisans whose ignorance of European armorial bearings was absolute, and thus the skill of the copied design varies from plate to plate. On this piece the inaccuracies include a misunderstanding of the grotesque masks among the scrollwork on the rim, and the failure to fill in the blue in one of the scallops round the well. See also cat G26.

Prov: Sale given by Alfreda and Peter Rochelle-Thomas.
Lit: Howard 1974, p. 398; Howard and Ayers 1978, pp. 413-415
RK

O3 *Cream Jug*

Chelsea (Lawrence Street Factory)
1745.
Glassy soft-paste porcelain, slip-cast
and enamelled in colours; h. 105
Marks: A triangle and *Chelsea 1745*. All
incised.
*The Wernher Collection by arrangement with
the NACF*

Of upright form, with handle formed
as a simulated branch with applied
oak-leaves; the lower part of the body
moulded with two goats; beneath the
lip spout an applied bee climbs up a
moulded and brightly enamelled
flowering shrub. Though displaying
the characteristic C-scrolls almost
imperceptibly just above the goats, the
so called 'goat-and-bee-jugs', the
earliest dated examples of Chelsea or
indeed any English porcelain, are
rococo in their asymmetry and their
whimsical blending of functional
shape with naturalistic detail. The
motif of the two goats, placed parallel
but facing in opposite directions, is
reminiscent of Sprimont's silver
Centrepiece of 1747 (VAM M46-1971).
Among other dated examples is a
white jug, formerly in the Mackenna
Collection, now in the Pillow Collection
at the Beaverbrook Art Gallery,
Fredericton, Canada, whose date has
been read as '1743'. That date is two
years earlier than any other
documentation of activity related to
the porcelain factory at Chelsea, and
though the piece is genuine, it seems
likely that the incised line that has
been read as the top stroke of the
date's final digit may have been
caused before firing by some
accidental means. All known silver
versions of 'goat-and-bee-jugs' appear
to be of 19th century date. Not all
genuine Chelsea porcelain examples
have the bee. Some few are decorated
in underglaze blue and manganese,
while many were left white.

Lit: the Lord Fisher 1944, pp. 136-8;
Hayden 1932, no. 128, pl. 57; Mallet
1965, p. 29, pl. 1A. Severne Mackenna
1944, pp. 136-8; Severne Mackenna
1948, pp. 6, 23, pls. 1 & 54
JVGM

O4 *Salt-Cellar or Sweetmeat-Dish*

Chelsea (Lawrence Street Factory)
1746.
Glassy soft-paste porcelain. h. 970
Marks: a triangle and the date, 1746,
all incised
The Museum of London (A5 346).

In the shape of a stylised shell
supported on two dolphins. The paste
is greenish-yellow by transmitted light
and shows numerous 'pin-hole'
bubbles. Somewhat stained and
having a firing blemish on one side.
The shape is closely related to two
pairs of silver-gilt sauceboats in the
Royal Collection bearing Nicholas
Sprimont's hall-mark for 1743/4 and
1744/5 (cat. G17). The porcelain is
very probably from a model by
Sprimont himself. The mould for the
shell appears to have been re-used in
combination with a seated figure of a
Turk in the Barclay Collection.

Prov: Hilton Price Collection, Sotheby's
1911, London, Museum of London.
When acquired, apparently in 1911, it
was registered as 'Found in London'.
Lit: Jones 1911, p. 100, pl. L1; Mallet
1965, I, p. 29, pl. lc; Oman, 1954
fig. 11
JVGM

O5 *Pair of Sphinxes*

Chelsea (Lawrence Street factory). *c.*1747
Glazed white glassy soft-paste
porcelain; h. 117 & l. 106 112
Mark: incised under the base of the
right-hand sphinx, an indistinct
triangle
VAM (C.108+A–1977)

Each sphinx reclines on a scrollwork
base with paws folded in front of her
above a grotesque mask. A piqué
saddle-cloth covers their backs while
the human torsos are dressed in loose-
sleeved garments. They have frills
round their necks and wear caps on
their heads. The necks have been
broken through and parts of the caps
are missing. These unique Chelsea
rococo sphinxes appear from their
early-looking paste to pre-date the
arrival of the modeller Joseph Willems
at the Chelsea factory. They were
probably modelled by Nicholas
Sprimont himself, since pieces of his
silver show a similar use of rococo
scrollwork and the same nervous
sensibility of spirit. See also note to
cat. O17.

Prov: T.A. Hall Collection. E. Allman
Collection
Lit: Mallet 1977, p. 225, fig. 6; Tait
1960 II, p. 184
JVGM

O5

O6

O6 *A crayfish, reeds and a shell*
Jean-Baptiste Claude Chatelain (?)
(*c.*1710 – after 1771 (?)) after Juste
Aurèle Meissonnier (1895-1750). 1757
Etching; 130 x 89 (cut)
VAM (29564.121)

Part of plate 15 (actually printed from
two copper-plates) in *A Book of Eighteen
Leaves*, 1757 (Cat. G46), consisting of
copies in reverse after four plates by
P.Q. Chedel in the *Livre de Légumes*
after Meissonnier (BN: Fonds 35;
Œuvres, suite C 14, 15, 17, 18). The
Livre de Légumes may have formed part
of the first issue of almost fifty prints
after Meissonnier published by the
widow Chereau in 1734. These prints
of naturalistic vegetables and game
ornamentally arranged seem to have
had an influence on English silver and
the crayfish probably influenced
Sprimont's silver and porcelain (Cat.
G17, O7).
MS

O7 *Salt Cellar*
Chelsea (Lawrence Street factory)
*c.*1745-49
Soft-paste porcelain, the undecorated
white glaze opacified with tin oxide.
l. 130.
Mark: a triangle and the numeral 3
incised
The Trustees of the British Museum II.18

Formed as a shell, with a crayfish to
one side on the rock-work base. The

crayfish appears to have been cast
from the life. The model originated in
Sprimont's silver (Cat. G17) of 1742-3.
The idea was probably taken from an
engraving contained in Meissonnier's
Œuvre (see cat G6), which shows a
crayfish amongst shelly rock-work and
bulrushes. Chelsea porcelain crayfish
salts range in date from the Triangle
Period to the early Red Anchor
Period. They are still to be found in
the 1756 Chelsea sale catalogue (day 2,
lot 22 and five similar entries). Chelsea
crayfish salts are not altogether
uncommon and those of different
periods may be distinguished not only
by their different marks, including an
example with an underglaze blue
triangle (Austin, 1977, No 7) and Red
Anchors eg VAM (C.73-1938) but also
by their different paste, glaze and in
some cases enamel decoration. They
appear originally to have been used in
sets of two. The pair of which the
present example is one are believed to
be those described by Horace Walpole
in his description of Strawberry Hill as
'two white salt cellars, with crawfish in
relief, of Chelsea china.'

Prov: Strawberry Hill Collection (?)
Lit: Austin 1977; Blunt 1924; British
Museum 1910, p. 91, fig. 98; Gardner
1939, pp. 27-30, pls. Xa & b; Hobson
1905, p. 31, no. 11.18, fig. 22; Severne
Mackenna 1948, p. 79, figs. 2, 109
JVGM

O8 *Dish*
Chelsea (Lawrence Street factory)
painted by J H O'Neale. *c.*1753-4
Tin-glazed soft-paste porcelain
enamelled in colours; l. 135
Private Collection.

Of oval form fluted in a manner
somewhat similar to a scallop shell
and with auricular moulding at either
end. The centre painted with the fable
of the Tiger and the Fox in an
extensive landscape with a lake,
mountains and trees, the border with
scattered sprays of flowers and insects.
This shape was used by Nicholas
Sprimont for the stands of some silver
sauceboats now in the Katz Collection
at the Museum of Fine Arts, Boston
(see cat. G19). The porcelain examples
(which also seem sometimes to have
been used as stands for sauceboats)
were introduced during the Raised
Anchor Period, 1749-1752, such early
pieces normally having a flat

underside without any foot-ring. The
shape continued in production
throughout the succeeding Red
Anchor Period, 1753-1758, and Gold
Anchor Period, 1758-1769. During the
Raised and early Red Anchor Periods
some of the finest fable painting
attributable to Jefferyes Hamett
O'Neale was executed on pieces of
this form. Another oval dish of this
type decorated with the same subject
but showing the leopard in a tangled
wood was sold at Sotheby's July 16,
1946, 53. The late Major W. H. Tapp
attempted to trace the biography of
O'Neale, who exhibited between 1763
and 1772 at the Society of Artists of
Great Britain, the Free Society of
Artists and the Incorporated Society of
Artists. A number of plates from
different editions of the *Ladies
Amusement* are either signed or
attributable to him. An undated
edition of the *Ladies Amusement* in
private hands contains on pl. 111,
which is signed *O Neale delin: S. Sparrow
Sculp:*, a vignette of the leopard
wounded with an arrow in almost
exactly this attitude but accompanied
by only a single fox. The same fable
was later issued at Chelsea in three-
dimensional form as a bocage
candlestick. O'Neale seems to have
substituted a leopard for the Tiger of
the Fables who boasted of the
toughness of his hide, on hearing
which a huntsman shot him. Mrs
Aphra Behn, in the 1687 edition of
Aesop's Fables illustrated after Barlow
gives the following moral: 'So the
young Hero on his strength relying,/
Renderd him more remark'd and
worthyer dying.'

Prov: Selwyn Parkinson Collection
(Sotheby's October 11 1966, 241);
Christie's November 19 1979, 203.
Lit: Tapp 1937, pp. 71-9; Tapp 1938;
Tapp 1941 I, p. 14, 5-9; Tapp 1941 II,
pp. 119-122, 154-157
JVGM

O9

O9

O9 *Two Perfume Pots*

Chelsea (Lawrence Street factory);
1755
Soft-paste porcelain enamelled and
gilt. h. Meleager 393, Atalanta 401
*The Trustees of the British Museum II 27
and 1930-4-19, l*

Each perfume pot of vase form set on
an irregular scroll-edged rococo base,
one with Meleager clothed in armour
and holding the boar's head, the other
with Atalanta seated and accompanied
by greyhounds. The pieces each with a
pierced cover surmounted by
porcelain flowers and moulded with
scrollwork and shell-like ornament
picked out in gilding, both the vases
and the bases further ornamented
with panels containing cut flowers
painted in enamel colours. On the
ninth day of the Chelsea sale catalogue
of 1755 lots 58 and 59 read: 'A
LARGE BEAUTIFUL PERFUME POT
chased and gilt, enamell'd with flowers
with a figure representing
MELEAGER WITH A BOAR'S HEAD.
ONE DITTO with a figure representing
ATALANTA and her dog.' Two
similar items also appear on the
thirteenth day. A Chelsea-Derby
example without cover is illustrated
Godden, 1974, Colour pl. IV facing
p. 144 and pl. 149. This was
presumably made from the models
taken over by William Duesbury of
Derby at the time when he purchased
the Chelsea factory from James Cox in
1770. The style of modelling suggests
the work of Joseph Willems (1715-66)

and no European prototypes for these
figures appear to be recorded,
although for some reason Solon (1903,
pl. VII) considered the Atalanta to be
'in the Dresden Style'. In an English
context they are very advanced for
their date in their asymmetry and in
the way that scrollwork is allowed to
dominate the figures. As pointed out
by King (1942) the figures of Meleager
and Atalanta on these groups seem to
be very freely adapted from a print
after Rubens, a characteristic choice of
source for a Flemish modeller working
for a factory run by a Walloon. These
two pot-pourri groups may not
originally have been a pair since they
were acquired by the British Museum
from different sources and at different
times.

Lit: Godden 1974; Hobson 1905,
p. 34, No II, 27, fig. 32; King 1931;
King 1942, pp. 47-48; Mallet 1969;
Solon 1903
JVGM

O10 *Plate*

Chelsea (Lawrence Street factory);
about 1755.
Soft-paste porcelain enamelled in
colours; diam. 242
Private Collection
See colour plate XXIII

The plate with wavy rim edged with
brown enamel, the whole upper
surface decorated with a botanical
fantasy apparently not recognisable as
any particular species, with a dragon-

fly, a bluebottle and an Arctid moth
of South American appearance. The
present plate is an unusually lively
example of the botanical style as
introduced at Chelsea, giving a false
impression of scientific accuracy while
in fact aiming at decorative effect and
rococo irregularity of design. There is
one reference in a Dublin auction
advertisement of 1758 to a porcelain
service decorated 'in curious Plants,
with Table Plates, Soup Plates, and
Dessert Plates, enamelled from Sir
Hans Sloan's plants . . .'. Sir Hans
Sloane was a major landowner at
Chelsea and in 1722 saved the Chelsea
Physick Garden by granting a
favourable lease on it in perpetuity to
the Society of Apothecaries. The
presence of this botanical garden and
of the scientists concerned with it
probably stimulated production of
Chelsea's botanical style of porcelain
decoration. Patrick Synge-Hutchinson
(1958) has identified a number of
Chelsea botanical wares as being
copied from botanical illustrations
after G.D. Ehret. It is possible that
certain flowers and leaves may also
have been obtained for copying from
the Physick Garden, but Synge-
Hutchinson's suggestion that Ehret
would have lent his meticulous
drawings for copying by the Chelsea
artists seems implausible because the
Chelsea plates are invariably the same
way round as the engravings and not
reversed as they would be if they had
been copied from Ehret's drawings. In
a recent paper to the *English Ceramic
Circle*, not yet published, Dr Paul Riley
has shown that very few of the insects
on Chelsea plates are accurately
represented.

Lit: Gardner No. IV, 1932; Gardner
1937, I, Gardner 1937 II; Mallet 1965
II, pp. 15-29; Mallet 1980, pp. 12-15;
Synge-Hutchinson 1954; Synge-
Hutchinson 1958
JVGM

O11 *Looking-Glass-Stand for a Dressing Table*

Chelsea (Lawrence Street factory);
about 1758
Soft-paste porcelain containing bone-
ash, enamelled and gilt. Mirror h. 286;
stand h. 235.
VAM (C.214+A-1935)

Comprising a curved-topped container

with simulated flowered cloth thrown over it and partially concealing a star-like group of piercings at the front. At the side and front are two apertures suggesting that the piece may once have contained a clockwork movement or musical box. At the back is hinged an ormolu door with a piqué floral design, above a gilt-metal drawer. The sides of the container are decorated with flowers. The whole is set on a platform of complex form with concave and convex sides on which are further painted flowers, moulded and gilt scrollwork and, at the front, a duck-pond with three modelled and painted water-fowl. At the front of the platform are one large and two smaller porcelain-faced gilt-metal drawers. The whole is raised on six scroll feet. A separately formed porcelain looking-glass frame rests in two sockets on the platform and leans against the container. The frame of the glass rises to a *rocaille* crest incorporating a concave area probably intended to hold a small watch, above which are a pair of billing doves. An olive branch and weeds trail over this part of the frame. The frame is of white porcelain with elaborate scrollwork picked out in gilding and, immediately surrounding the glass, a gilt-metal border. The back of the looking-glass is finely painted at the top with flowers in the Meissen style and has a gilt-metal back-plate attached by screws with flower-shaped nuts. It does not appear to have been previously suggested that this looking-glass-stand might be the model referred to in the Chelsea factory's sale held by Burnsall in March 1763, of

which the announcement lists: 'a Lady's Toilet with a Looking Glass and Gold Instruments'. (Nightingale, 1881, p. xxi). Another of these curious objects, though lacking the mirror and the drawers, is in the Schreiber Collection in the VAM. This other example is decorated with gilding and a dark mazarine blue ground compatible with a date around 1763. The present example is more likely to be the one which, so Mrs Nancy Valpy tells me, is mentioned in a sale announcement of 9 March, 1758. These two stands are amongst the most elaborately rococo objects produced at the Chelsea factory. No other examples appear to be recorded.

Prov: Herbert Allen Collection
Lit: Nightingale 1881; Rackham 1923, pl. 16, no. 54; Rackham 1928, pl. 29, No 208
JVGM

O12 *Plaice sauceboat, cover and stand*

Chelsea (Lawrence Street factory).
*c.*1756
Soft-paste porcelain enamelled in colours. Sauceboat and cover h. 140; stand l. 292
VAM C.1451-B-1924

The sauceboat and cover formed as the flat fish, the body somewhat unnaturally deepened and the mouth extended to make room for a spoon (missing). The cover realistically painted with the fish's scales and reddish spots, a simulated spray of sea-weed forming its handle. The tail

of the fish curved upwards for use as the sauceboat's handle. The oval stand painted blue at the bottom to simulate water and moulded at the sides with bivalve shells and sea-weed, all naturalistically coloured. Lot 79 on the fifth day of the Chelsea factory's auction in 1756 reads: 'A beautiful pair of *plaice sauce boats*, with spoons and plates.' A plaice sauceboat and cover, without the stand or the spoon in the British Museum is illustrated by Mackenna (1951), pl. 40, fig. 82, pp. 25 & 92. A pair complete with stands but lacking the spoons is at Erddig and these are probably the pieces described in an inventory of 1789 as '2 Stands and two Carp Sauce Boats 6 pieces in all' (See Mallet 1978 pp. 44-45 and fig. 11). The only examples still with their ladles appear to be a pair at present on loan to the National Museum of Wales, Cardiff. A pair without stands is illustrated by Rice 1983, fig. 127 and pp. 57 & 202, as being from the Derby factory, *c.*1760-65. If this identification as Derby is correct, it seems more likely that the pieces should be dated after 1770, when Duesbury acquired the moulds and other stock of the Chelsea factory.

Prov: given by Mr and Mrs D. MacAlister.
Lit: Mallet 1978; Rice 1983; Severne Mackenna 1951
JVGM

O12

O13 *Sauceboat*

Bow. *c.*1750-55
Soft-paste porcelain containing bone-ash; l.197
The Trustees of the British Museum VIII.2

The boat with sides moulded with floral garlands and raised on an oval foot also moulded with flowers. The handle is formed as a dragon, its neck and head projecting well above the level of the boat. Banister (1983) compares a pair of silver sauceboats by Edward Wakelin, dated 1755, with a pair of dragon-handled Bow sauceboats. However her statement that the silver boats are 'in porcelain style' seems unjustified, and the resemblance is in any case unremarkable. Detached handles like these on the Bow sauceboats would have been extremely vulnerable and would therefore have made better sense in metal. The Bow model was also made with the more conventional scrollwork handle. (Compare Gabszewicz, 1982, Nos. 35 and 36).

Prov: Given by Henry Willett Esq, F G S.
Lit: Banister 1983; Gabszewicz & Freeman 1982; Hobson 1905, no. VIII.2, p.113.
JVGM

O14 *Figure of Kitty Clive*

Bow. *c.*1750-52
Glazed white soft-paste porcelain containing bone-ash; h. 267.
Geoffrey Freeman Collection of Bow Porcelain on loan to Pallant House Gallery, Chichester

Shown as 'the Fine Lady' from Garrick's farce *Lethe*, wearing a mob-cap and holding a spaniel under her right arm. On low square base. The model is copied from an engraving by Charles Mosley published in 1750 after a watercolour by Thomas Worlidge. The actress, Kitty Clive joined the Cast of *Lethe* in 1749. A white example in the Fitzwilliam Museum at Cambridge has a taller square base with a trophy at the front and is incised *1750* underneath. The majority of Bow Kitty Clive figures and their companions of Henry Woodward (cat O16)) are however on low square bases such as that of the present figure. Three rather crude examples of the Kitty Clive are known with flat, star-shaped bases, and these

O14

O16

are now generally believed to be early Derby of the 'dry-edge class. Several coloured examples of the Clive and Woodward figures are known, some at least of these probably having been enamelled in the workshop of William Duesbury, since there is an entry in his London account book 'for enamelling Mrs Clive three shillings'. After her retirement Mrs Clive lived in a cottage on Horace Walpole's Strawberry Hill estate, so it is not surprising that in his inventory, compiled in 1764, appears the entry: 'Mrs Catherine Clive, the excellent commedian, in the character of FINE LADY in LETHE: in water colours by Worlidge'. The Bow figures of Kitty Clive and Henry Woodward are probably the earliest full-length portrait figures in English porcelain,

Lit: Adams & Redstone 1981, pp. 134-6, pl. H; Charleston & Towner 1977, no. 135; Gabszewicz & Freeman 1982, pl. 186; George 1982, no. 62; Hackenbroch 1958, fig. 241 & pl. 76; Mallet 1964, no. 1, pl. 5; Tait 1959, nos. 40-43; Tait 1960 I, 40-44, figs I-III
JVGM

O15 *Henry Woodward as 'The Fine Gentleman'*

Francis Hayman (1708-1776). 1748-(?) 1757
Pencil: 322 x 223
The Syndics of the Fitzwilliam Museum, Cambridge (PD. 5-1962)

The drawing is probably for the print by James McArdell entitled 'Mr Woodward in the character of Ye Fine Gentleman', which was sold by Elizabeth Griffin (see cat. L17). Woodward appeared as 'the Beau' in the first production of David Garrick's mythological burlesque *Lethe* performed at Drury Lane in 1740. At this Drury Lane revival of 1748, Woodward was cast as 'The Fine Gentleman', and in a production of 1757 he played the part of 'Daffodil'.

Prov: Ronald A. Lee: bought from the Perceval Fund, 1962
Lit: Goodwin 1903, 103
MS

O15

O16 *Figure of Henry Woodward*
Bow. *c.*1750-52
Glazed white soft-paste porcelain
containing bone-ash and showing
traces of unfired gilding; h. 267.
Mark: a star incised underneath the
base
*Geoffrey Freeman Collection of Bow
Porcelain on loan to Pallant House Gallery,
Chichester.*

Shown as the 'Fine Gentleman' from
Garrick's farce *Lethe*, wearing tricorn
hat, sword and elaborately fashionable
coat and waistcoat on which details are
picked out in oil-gilding. The model
forms the companion to Kitty Clive
(see cat. O14) though it is likely that
the present two figures did not
originally go together, since the
Woodward is gilded and the Clive is
not. The model for Woodward derives
apparently from an undated mezzotint
by James McArdell after Francis
Hayman (see cat O15). The white
example of Woodward (on low base
with canted corners) at the Metropolitan
Museum, New York (Hackenbroch

1958, fig. 241 and pl. 77) bears the
incised date 1750.

Lit: Gabszewicz & Freeman 1982, 187;
and see lit for cat. O14
JVGM

O17 *Pair of Sphinxes*
Bow. *c.*1750-54
Glazed white soft-paste porcelain
containing bone-ash; l. 140.
*Geoffrey Freeman Collection of Bow
Porcelain on loan to Pallant House Gallery,
Chichester.*

In the form of two sphinxes with
bodies naturalistically modelled like
lions with saddle-cloths, and torsos
and heads like women wearing caps
and necklaces. They recline on
scroll and *rocaille* bases. Already in the
1885 Edition of the *Schreiber Collection
Catalogue,* No 143, Lady Charlotte
Schreiber says of her pair of this
model: 'said to be portraits of Peg
Woffington'. Hugh Tait (1960, p. 183)
points out the improbability of this
identification and shows how popular
naturalistic sphinxes with
contemporary clothing were in early
18th century France. The present
writer, however, finds improbable the
idea tentatively put forward by Tait
that the Bow sphinxes may even
antedate the triangle period Chelsea
pair (cat. O5). The Chelsea sphinxes
by reason of their triangle marks may
almost certainly be dated before 1749,
and their paste and glaze suggest that
they may be a year or two earlier than
that. Bow sphinxes of the class here
exhibited usually resemble in paste,
modelling and applied details the
Kitty Clive and Woodward figures,

O17

one of each of which is dated 1750
(cat. O14 and O16). There is, however,
a further pair of Bow models of
sphinxes whose design follows rather
closely, though with the omission of
the grotesque masks, that of the early
Chelsea pair, but whose paste,
modelling and decoration suggest
dates between 1754-60. Examples of
these later, Chelsea-based Bow
sphinxes are a single white example in
the VAM (*c.*110-1977) and two
enamelled examples (Tait 1960, figs. X
& XI). Arthur Lane (1961, p. 89)
makes the interesting suggestion that
the Bow sphinxes of both models
'perhaps owe their well developed
Rococo scroll bases to the fact that
they were copied from contemporary
bronze ornaments'. Certainly the
pricked effect found on the saddle-
cloths of both the Chelsea and the
earlier Bow models is uncommon on
porcelain but often encountered on
18th century bronzes and ormolu.

Lit: Gabszewicz & Freeman 1982, no.
189; Lane 1961, p. 89; Tait 1960 II,
pp. 183-5; Savage 1952, pls. 38, 39
JVGM

O18 *Plate*
Bow. *c.*1756
Soft-paste porcelain containing bone-
ash printed overglaze in brownish-red
the border further painted in
enamels; diam 200
VAM C.216-1940.

The centre is transfer-printed with
L'Amour from an engraving after
Cochin showing a gallant seated with a
lady on a bench in a garden and
kissing her hand, while a chaperon

O18

O19

standing behind raises her hand in astonishment. In the background is a fountain with Neptune, in the foreground a rococo urn, a garden roller and a dog. The narrow border is enamelled by hand with a floral border derived from the Japanese 'Kakiemon' wares, but with the additional colour, rose. The origin of the subject *L'Amour* is a print by Charles Nicolas Cochin (1715-90) which appears to have been re-engraved in England by W. Elliott (see Toppin, 1948, p. 271 and pl. XCVII a). The subject first appears as a transfer-print on ceramics at Bow in about 1755. Later versions of this print on Worcester, dating from about 1759 onwards, are sometimes signed by the engraver Robert Hancock and bear the anchor rebus of Holdship. The Bow versions may also be by Hancock though the early large version which appears on the present plate is of finer quality. Both on Worcester and on Bow the subject is sometimes found reversed and without the chaperon. (See Watney, 1971, p. 214, pl. 165c).

Prov: Arthur Hurst Bequest
Lit: Adams & Redstone 1981, p. 150, pl. 72; Charleston & Scheurleer 1979, pl. 60; Cook 1948 Item 2; Gabszewicz & Freeman 1982, p. 82, no. 117; Toppin 1948; Watney 1972 III
JVGM

O19 *Wallpaper*

Anonymous *c.*1760
Colour print from wood blocks; 816 x 543
Stamped on the *verso* with a Georgian excise duty stamp
VAM (E.474-1914)

On a blue ground frames enclose landscapes (a large landscape seen on more complete sheets is not present on this fragment) and a scene of lovers on a bench, copied from a print by or after C.N. Cochin the younger which was published by Francis Vivares. The subject was also used on transfer-printed porcelain and enamel (Cat. O18). This type of wallpaper, with its images in separate framed compartments was probably intended to imitate the effect of a print room,

i.e. wall decoration made of separate prints with cut-out printed borders pasted directly onto the wall which became fashionable in the 1750s. This paper may be connected with the major alterations carried out at Doddington Hall 1760-64. The predominant colour of the wall coverings and panelling at Doddington was blue.

Prov: Doddington Hall, Lincs; given by Mr. G.E. Jarvis
Lit: Cook 1948, fig. 3, item 2; Oman & Hamilton 1982, 134; Wells-Cole 1983, 44
MS

O20 *Clock-case*

Bow. 1759
Soft-paste bone-ash porcelain enamelled in colours; h. 312
Mark: *T°* impressed
Geoffrey Freeman Collection of Bow Porcelain on loan to Pallant House Gallery, Chichester

The aperture for the clock is set near the top of a violin-shaped case with rococo scroll-moulding. Surmounting the case sits a figure of Father Time, and below him on either side of the clock sits a naked putto. A cockerel stands centrally at the front of the base. The front is painted in crimson with the score of a 'Minuetto' and with two butterflies. On either side of the clock is a trophy of musical sheets.

O20

The left side has sheets inscribed *A Cantata, Handle* (sic), *by Lorv* (or Lon?) and a sheet inscribed *Haymakers* and bearing a musical score. The trophy on the right of the clock comprises a sheet headed *A Song*, another headed *Sonata IV* and what appears to be a letter headed *Nov 5 1759*. The main sheet bears a score and is inscribed *A Minuet*. Three other Bow clocks of this form are recorded: at the Cecil Higgins Museum, Bedford; formerly in the possession of Messrs D.M. and P. Manheim; formerly in the possession of the Antique Porcelain Company. On all of these, figures of less sophisticated modelling have been substituted for those on the example exhibited, while an owl is substituted for the cockerel. The figures of children on the Freeman Handel Clock derive from those on a Meissen clock of different shape, formerly in the Von Klemperer Collection, probably modelled by J.G. Kirchner or J.C.L. Lücke (see introduction) around 1732. (See Von Carolsfeld 1928, no. 480 and pl. 44.) The figure of Father Time was not present on the Von Klemperer clock, which instead had one of three female figures of Fates seated on its crest. In addition to

the Handel clocks several Bow examples of rococo vases surrounded by singing putti bear inscriptions relating to Handel. These and the clocks all seem to have been made to commemorate the great German composer, who died in London on April 14 1759.

Prov: Mrs Donald J. Morrison Collection, Nova Scotia, Sotheby's, London April 3 1973, 194
Lit: Adams and Redstone 1981, pp. 178-180, fig. 106; Charleston and Towner 1977, no. 132; Detroit Institute of Arts 1954, no. 205; Gabszewicz and Freeman 1982 no. 139; George 1982, no. 46; Tait 1962, I, pp. 384-390
JVGM

O21

O21 *Pair of wall-pockets*
Bow. *c.*1760
Soft-paste porcelain containing bone-ash, enamelled and gilt; h. 279
Geoffrey Freeman Collection of Bow Porcelain on loan to Pallant House Gallery, Chichester.

Of cornucopia shape with shell-like grooved moulding and flamiform outline, the flat backs pierced with two holes for suspension, the fronts of each picked out in puce and other colours and with a central zone sparsely decorated with floral sprays. Wall-pockets were probably intended for suspending from a wall and filling with flowers somewhat in the manner shown in a print by J. June after C. Fenn (reproduced in the

1966 reprint of the *Ladies Amusement*, pl. 18). That these wall-pockets were intended for flowers is also indicated by the presence of a bust of Flora on the Staffordshire example modelled by Greatbatch (Cat. P10).

Prov: Sotheby's, London, 16 October 1962, 34; Phillips, London, 7 November 1979, 168
Lit: Gabszewicz and Freeman 1982, no. 147; Seyer *c.*1758-62.
JVGM

O22 *Sauceboat*
Derby ('Dry-edge' class). *c.*1753
Glassy soft-paste porcelain enamelled in colours; h. 130, l. 183
VAM (C.277-1976).

In the shape of a fluted shell, the handle formed as a piece of green and turquoise sea-weed attached to the back of a crayfish or small lobster which is painted red as though cooked. The shell is white except for sea-weed-like encrustations. The whole rests on a base formed by sea-weed clad rock to which are attached tellins and other bivalve shells as well as red coral. The use of rocks, shells and other natural forms for a useful vessel is characteristic of the rococo and can be found, for instance, in the engraved designs of Meissonnier. This piece forms an interesting comparison to certain early Chelsea wares, with which the model has in the past been confused.

Prov: Earl Spencer Collection, Althorp
Lit: Charleston 1967, p. 11, fig. 14; Jewitt 1878, Vol. I, p. 328, fig. 706; Savage 1952, pl. 65a; Watney 1967, p. 19, figs. 34. 36
JVGM

O23

O23 *Pair of wall-brackets*

Derby ('Dry-edge' class, probably
from a factory directed by Andrew
Planché). *c.*1750-55
Glassy, glazed white soft-paste
porcelain; h. 159
VAM (C.60+A-1968)

Each in the shape of an identical
cornucopia, its entire front surface
moulded with a medley of scrolls and
shelly *rocaille* motifs. The unglazed
upper surfaces (one with circular
aperture) bowed at the front, provide
flat platforms for the objects to be
displayed. The flat backs, also
unglazed, each have two holes for
suspension. These wall-brackets were
probably designed to support small
rococo vases of porcelain, though the
earliest surviving Derby examples of
such vases seem a little later in date
than the brackets (cat. O24). Vases are
shown supported on two 'consolles' of
much this form engraved *c.*1753 by
François Cuvilliès the elder (Mallet
1969, fig. 14). Larger brackets may
have been intended to support busts
(cat. O27) or other sculpture. Watney
(1967, p. 16) suggests that these Derby
wall-brackets may have been directly
copied from ormolu examples. The
attribution to Derby seems first to
have been made by Glendenning
(1931, p. 81, pl. XVII) who also
illustrates a Derby wall-bracket of
more baroque shape.

Prov: collection of Mr A.F. Green
Lit: Glendenning 1931; Mallet 1969,
pp. 107-8; Rice 1983, pp. 30, 182, pl.
39; Watney 1967, p. 16, pls. 31, 32
JVGM

O24 *Vase*

Derby. *c.*1758-60
Soft-paste porcelain enamelled in
colours. h. 201.
VAM C.76-1967

Of exaggerated asymmetrical form
with leaf-like mouldings on the
circular foot and neck, the shoulders
slanting from the horizontal, the
upper shoulder ending in a leafy
flourish, both sides with further
mouldings of organic appearance.
One of the bellied sides painted with a
fishing scene with three figures in a
landscape all in crimson, the other
with polychrome flowers. Some of the
leaf and organic mouldings picked out
in turquoise or in crimson. This rare
and rather early model, more
asymmetrical than the Derby models
that replaced it, is crisp but a little stiff
in form, raising the possibility that it
was made from a carved wooden
master-model. Such wooden models
were not unknown at Meissen and in

England John Coward was employed
by Josiah Wedgwood to carve wooden
patterns, some of which survive at
Barlaston today (H. Barnard, 1924, p.
219 and pl. facing p. 218). A pair of
rococo vases of the same model,
decorated with flowers and with
butterflies, was sold by Sotheby's,
Florence, Palazzo Capponi, October
25, 1974, 383 and illustration. The
present piece is illustrated and
discussed by Mallet (1969, p. 107,
cover and fig 12) where it is dated
*c.*1756-58, which now seems a little
early, and by Rice, 1983, pp. 59, 67
and pl. 143, where it is dated *c.*1765,
which seems too late.

Prov: Dr Bernard Watney Collection
Lit: Barnard 1924; Mallet 1969; Rice
1983
JVGM

O24

O25

O25 *Pair of candlesticks*

Derby. *c.*1758
Soft-paste porcelain enamelled in
colours and gilt; h. 229 & 226
VAM (C.192+A-1935).

In the form of seated naked bacchic
boys each holding a cup of wine and
wreathed round with fruiting vine.
Each sits on a simulated tree-stump
rising from a circular base, painted
with 'cotton-stalk' flowers and edged
with moulded and painted scrolls.
From the head of each putto springs a
section of tree trunk. Screwed to the
top of this is a flower-shaped candle-
nozzle with drip-pan in the form of
leaves. It is a surprising feature of
these groups that on each the gilding,
which would probably have
necessitated a separate firing, is
applied only to the very rim of the
wine cups. Bradshaw points out that
the bacchic figure of the boy on these
candlesticks is from a mould used
earlier in the 'dry-edge' period of
Derby for Autumn, from a set of
Children as Seasons (Bradshaw 1981,
p. 194, pls. 95+107). For another
white set of 'dry-edge' Child Seasons
in the VAM see (Twitchett 1980, fig.
18.) The figure is not well integrated

into the design of the candlesticks and
the modeller who adapted it for this
purpose had a less thorough grasp of
the European rococo idiom than the
predecessor who modelled the 'dry-
edge' chinoiserie candlesticks.

Prov: Herbert Allen Collection
Lit: Rackham 1923, no. 29, pl. 4;
Rackham 1928, Vol. I, no. 293; Savage
1952, p. 222, pl. 296
JVGM

O26 Bust: VAM Sch. I 126

O26 *Bust of George II and socle*

Liverpool (Chaffers factory). *c.*1757-60
Glazed white steatitic soft-paste
porcelain. h.390
Leeds City Art Galleries

The King is shown in his later years,
wearing a wig, his head turned to his
left. He wears an asymmetrically
arranged cloak, buckled at the front
and partly concealing the star of the
Order of the Garter, and armour
embossed with rococo scrollwork. The
socle rectangular but with bowed
front, with floral and geometrical
moulding at the border in the front.

The date of this model may be
deduced not only from the age of the
Monarch but also from the patriotic
and victorious emblems on the wall-
brackets (see cat. O27) that seem to be
associated with them, which would
suggest a time of victories such as
those of 1757-9. 1759, the *Annus
Mirabilis,* was followed by George's
death in 1760, so it is possible that the
model was made in the last two years
of his reign or even to commemorate
his death. It is futile to invoke, as has
sometimes been done in the past, the
names of either Rysbrack or Roubiliac
as creator of the model; the
composition is too clumsy and
conforms with the style of neither,
even allowing for a loss of subtlety in
modelling during the process of
translation into porcelain. More
possible as the author of this bust is
John Cheere, whose name has been
suggested (Friedman and Clifford,
1974, p. 19). He had a liking for
embossed scrollwork detail on armour
and drapery that was probably
encouraged by study of the Coysevox
bust of Matthew Prior in Westminster
Abbey. John Cheere's models reached
a number of ceramic factories,
including Josiah Wedgwood's,
through the medium of plaster casts
which he sold from his premises at
Hyde Park Corner. However the
rather unsubtle arrangement of the
cloak on the Liverpool George II
seems without parallel in the work of
John Cheere, let alone in that of his
brother, Henry. The socles of the
Liverpool busts (other examples are
plainer than the one exhibited) are not
unlike the characteristic form
employed in John Cheere's workshop,
though they lack the heavily protruding
moulding at the top. (Compare
Friedman and Clifford, 1974, pls. 12,
16, 17, 18, 19, 20, 21, 24, 28, 29).
Friedman and Clifford state in a
corrigendum note to p. 14 that some
brackets of plaster painted white and
gilded, belonging to the set of plaster
busts by John Cheere originally at
Kirleatham and now at York (see cat.
S30, S3), comprise rococo cartouches
and figures; this might have a bearing
on the attribution of the model for the
porcelain bracket, Cat. O27. These
porcelain busts of George II have in
the past been attributed to almost
every known English eighteenth
century porcelain factory, but are now

believed by most authorities, following Watney (1968), to be from the Chaffers factory in Liverpool. Fourteen examples were located by Delevingne (1963), who illustrates the incised markings found on a few of them. Watney (1968) p. 48 mentions the existence of two more. Apart from the present example, whose socle is unusual and whose bust is fashioned somewhat differently to the others at the point of truncation, The British Museum example, (Hobson, 1905, p. 36, no. II.33 and illustrated by Solon 1903, pl. 7) is remarkable for possessing most of its original unfired oil-painted decoration. The example in the National Gallery of Ireland in Dublin (illustrated, Watney, 1971, pl. 177a) is remarkable in being associated with a bracket of the same model as Cat. O27 below, though Rackham (1928) states that the one was not originally made for the other, presumably because they do not fit well. However the reason for the poor fit must be that the socle which should separate bust from bracket is missing from the Dublin example.

Prov: Mrs Radford Collection (by 1924, when illustrated by Blunt). Sold Sotheby's November 3-5, 1943.
Lit: Blunt 1924; Burt 1816; Delevingne 1963 pp. 236-248; Friedman and Clifford 1974; Hackenbroch 1957, fig. 10. pl. 4; Hobson 1905; Severne Mackenna 1942; Severne Mackenna 1946, pp. 101-102, pl. 46, fig. 80; Severne Mackenna 1972, no. 22; Rackham 1928 no. 126; Solon 1903, Watney 1968 pp. 48-58; Watney 1972 II; Willet 1899
JVGM

O27 *Wall-bracket*
Liverpool (Chaffers factory). *c.*1757-60
Glazed white steatitic soft-paste porcelain h. 279
VAM C.53-1931.

Of flattened cornucopia shape edged with scroll and shell-like mouldings. At the front, seated on a conquered dragon, is a figure of a child dressed as Britannia holding a shield with the British flag. To the left is a further figure of a nude child as Fame saluting her and depositing a wreath on her lap. Illustrated and described as 'highly phosphatic' with the implication that it was probably Bow,

by Glendenning (1931 p. 81 and pl. XVIIa). The bust and the wall-bracket have different provenances and have merely been brought together for the purposes of this exhibition, but it is suggested that some at least of these busts were originally sold with such supports, whose paste and glaze seems compatible with theirs. A similar example is in the British Museum (Wallace Elliot, 1938, 3-14, 76). For further discussion and bibliography see cat. O26.

Lit: Glendenning 1931, pp. 80-82
JVGM

O28 *Teapot and cover*
Staffordshire (Longton Hall factory). *c.*1755-60
Glassy soft-paste porcelain enamelled in colours; h. 114
Mark: a circle centred by a dot all incised under the foot
VAM (C.265+A-1940)

The body in the form of a melon naturalistically painted in tones of green, yellow and brown, the cover similarly moulded and painted and with the stalk forming the knop, the handle irregularly formed as a green stalk, the spout formed as two overlapping leaves. The whole rests on an irregular triangular foot formed as leaves and stalks. Other coloured examples of this peculiar naturalistic form are in the Cecil Higgins Museum, Bedford (Watney, 1955, pp. 28-29 and Fig. 7) and formerly in the Dr and Mrs Hugh Statham Collection (Watney, 1957, pl. 35 as part of a group photograph, and Sotheby sale catalogue, London, October 16, 1956, 101 and illustration). A powder blue example, also formerly in the Statham Collection is illustrated by Watney (1957, pl. 22C). There is a white example in the VAM, No. C.267 and A-1918. W. Bemrose (1906, pl. III, fig. 1) illustrates a coloured example without handle or spout, evidently intended to contain sugar.

Prov: Arthur Hurst Collection
Lit: Bemrose 1906; Watney 1955 pp. 26-31; Watney 1957
JVGM

O29 *Block for a sauceboat*
Staffordshire, modelled by Aaron Wood. *c.*1757-65
Salt-glazed stoneware of pale greyish-buff colour; l. 188
VAM (3910-1852).

Of boat shape moulded with a 'mosaic' design interrupted by rococo scrollwork and with scroll border. At the base are stiff leaves and under the lip-spout is shell moulding. The whole thickly formed, apparently by press-moulding and with an oval aperture at the top. Convex moulds or 'blocks' of this type were used to take two-piece plaster moulds from which the actual ware was made. The blocks were themselves moulded objects and the present pattern for instance, survives in different sizes and a number of examples: three in the VAM, including a small block of this form but with plain panels under the spout and at the place where the handle would be fitted, incised at the top before firing with the initials *K.S.*, (Luxmore 1924, pl. 45); several also in Stoke-on-Trent Museum (Ibid, pls. 50, 56 and 61) and in the Wedgwood Works Museum, Barlaston (Ibid, pl. 68). The last example has presumably belonged to Wedgwood's ever since it was in use by the first Josiah Wedgwood. A salt-glazed dish in the VAM with the same mouldings as the present salt-glazed block was later refired by Enoch Wood with the following enamelled inscription: *This Dish was modelled by Aaron Wood about 1759 or 1760 . . .* Inscribed on a bust of Enoch Wood modelled by himself is: *My father Aaron Wood, died May 12th, 1785, aged 68, buried at Burslem 1785. He made the models for all the potters during the time Salt Glaze was in general use.* Blocks attributable to Aaron Wood were also used by porcelain makers at Longton Hall in Staffordshire (cat. O31) and at Bow in the outskirts of London (cat. O32). The provenance of this and of cat. O30 from the Enoch Wood Collection should not be taken as evidence that Aaron Wood was necessarily the modeller of the pieces, since Enoch Wood was a noted collector of all types of Staffordshire wares.

Prov: Wood Collection
Lit: Falkner 1912, chap. IV, p. 80, pl. XLIV; Luxmore 1924; Mallet 1967 II, pls. 142, 143; Mountford 1971
JVGM

O29

O30

O32

O31 *Sauceboat*

Staffordshire (Longton Hall factory) from a block modelled by Aaron Wood. *c.* 1759-60
Glassy soft-paste porcelain enamelled in colours; l. 195
The Syndics of the Fitzwilliam Museum, Cambridge (C.28-1973).

Of the same moulding as cat. O29, with added loop handle. The exterior enamelled with peonies and insects in Chinese style. See notes to cat O29. For further examples of this moulding see Watney, 1957, pls. 47B and 48B.

Prov: Mrs Statham Collection
JVGM

O32 *Sauceboat*

Bow (from a block modelled by Aaron Wood). *c.* 1759-60
Soft-paste porcelain containing bone-ash, decorated in underglaze blue; l. 101
Mark: two small parallel lines in underglaze blue
Private Collection

For the shape see cat. O29. The handle has thumb-piece, grooved sides and curled back lower terminal. The paste has a warm, slightly yellowish translucency, the glaze a turquoise tinge. The exterior is left unpainted except for the acanthus leaves at the foot, which are picked out with blue hatching, and the handle, which has a trailing flower-spray. The interior painted at the bottom and at the spout with peonies and at the rim with cell-diaper. See cat. O29. The use of a Staffordshire salt-glaze 'block' by a London porcelain firm is remarkable, though justified by the resultant crispness of moulding.

Prov: John Ainslie Collection (Sotheby's, March 7, 1961, 83)
Lit: Mallet 1967 II, p. 213, pl. 144b
JVGM

O30 *Sauceboat*

Staffordshire ? from a block modelled by Aaron Wood. *c.* 1759-65.
Salt-glazed stoneware of warm whitish-grey colour; l. 171
VAM (2199-1901)

The moulding similar to cat. O29.

Grooved loop-handle. For notes and bibliography see cat. O29.

Prov: Enoch Wood Collection, Museum of Practical Geology, Jermyn Street
JVGM

O33

O33 Jug (one of a pair)

Worcester, probably painted by James
Rogers, 1757
Steatitic soft-paste porcelain,
enamelled in colours; h. 299
Inscribed *1757* on a bale of goods
depicted on one of the jugs beneath a
Merchant's mark which has been
interrupted as a *W* in monogram
Worcester City Council

The ovoid body and cylindrical neck
are moulded with overlapping
cabbage-leaves; towards the rim is a
horizontal band of stiff leaves and an
undulating line of rococo scrolls.
Scroll handle. At the front of the body,
within an elaborate lilac cartouche are
the arms of the City of Worcester.
Flanking this are seated figures of
Britannia holding an olive-branch and
blind Justice with sword and scales,
both seated in a quayside landscape.
The shoulders and neck have
horizontal bands of pure rococo
scrolls and the stiff-leaves at the rim
are picked out in yellow and green.
Hugh Tait (1962 II) suggests that these
jugs are by the hand responsible for a
somewhat inferior Worcester Mug
with bird-painting now in the British
Museum and signed *I. Rogers/Pinxit/
1757*. The manner in which the date,
1757, is inscribed so exactly matches
the writing of the same date on one of
the present mugs that Tait is probably
right in attributing to Rogers a whole
group of painted Worcester porcelain,

including the Sandys mug at the
British Museum. This artist may be
identical with the James Rogers
'Engraver and Enameller' who
exhibited a ring at the Free Society of
Artists in London in 1756, giving his
address as 'Dobson China Shop, in St
Martin's Court, Leicester Fields'. Such
an address, close to the geographical
centre of diffusion for the Rococo in
England, might explain the artist's
quite sophisticated use of rococo
scrollwork and his evident links with
the style of J.H. O'Neale. Since both
the present jugs and the Lord Sandys
mug were for Worcestershire clients,
the chances are that between 1756 and
1757 James Rogers, if he it was,
moved to Worcester.

Lit: Tait 1962 II, pp. 223-233, figs. 3,4;
Tait 1972 pl. 40
JVGM

O34 Handleless cup and saucer

Worcester, the engraving probably by
Robert Hancock. *c.*1760
Steatitic soft-paste porcelain transfer-
printed and hand-painted over glaze
in reddish brown; cup diam 750
saucer diam 124
VAM C. 95+A-1948

Transfer-printed with *La Cascade* after
Watteau. The reverse of the cup with a
fountain group. The borders of both
cup and saucer enamelled free-hand
in reddish brown. The figure subject is
based on a painting by Antoine
Watteau now in the Wallace Collection,
engraved by G. Scotin (see Dacier &
Vauflart 1929, p. 28). A large version
of this print, on a bowl formerly in the
Sir William Mullens collection, was
attributed by Watney (1972 II, p. 825,
pl. 25) to Louis Philippe Boitard by
comparison with the signed print, *Les
Amusements Champêtres*, which occurs
on the other side of the same bowl.
On the other hand Cook (1948, Item
19, fig 2) illustrates a black-printed
saucer from his own collection signed
R. Hancock fecit rather indistinctly below
the base of the fountain. As Watney
points out, Hancock seems for a time
to have had a close connection with
Boitard so it is not unlikely that the
former reproduced on the smaller
scale suitable for teacups and saucers
the design Boitard had engraved
rather more sensitively on the large
scale requisite for bowls.

Prov: Mrs Ionides Bequest
Lit: Cook 1953, pp. 72-75; Watney
1972 II, pp. 818-826
JVGM

O34

O35 *Portrait*

General Henry Seymour Conway, his
wife Caroline, Countess Dowager of
Aylesbury and their daughter Anne.
John Giles Eckhardt (active 1746,
d. 1779). *c.*1755
Oil on canvas; 660 x 509
Private Collection

Painted for Horace Walpole, this is
one of six portraits by Eckhardt of
Walpole and his closest friends,
painted for the Blue Bedchamber at
Strawberry Hill. Most of them are
modelled after portraits by Van Dyck,
but the only other group, Col. Charles
Churchill and his wife and child, is
derived from Rubens (Lewis 1973, 46).
The present painting is modelled on
Watteau's *La Cascade*, engraved by
Scotin and published in Paris in 1729
(Dacier & Vauflart 1929, 28). *La
Cascade* was also used on transfer-
printed porcelain and enamels (cat.
O34, Q4) and on the Watteau
tapestries, now at Ham House, made
by the Bradshaw manufactory 1730-60
(MacColl 1917). A drawing by Walpole
himself after Audran's print of
Watteau's *Les Entretiens Badins*
(Dacier & Vauflart 1929, 95) is dated
1737 (Lewis 1973, 15). The Blue
Bedchamber portraits are described as
having 'frames . . . of black and gold,
carved after those to Lombard's prints
from Vandyke, but with emblems
peculiar to each person' (Walpole
1774). The present frame does not
have emblems, which may have been
restricted to the single portraits for
which no frames survive, but it is very

close to the running scroll frames on
Pierre Lambart's portraits after Van
Dyck, eg his engraving of Lucy,
Countess of Carlisle. Conway (1719-
1795) was Walpole's cousin,
correspondent and closest friend; his
daughter became the sculptress Mrs
Damer.

Prov: Horace Walpole; Strawberry Hill
Sale, 1842, 22nd day, 35; Sir
Alexander Johnston; by descent
Lit: Orleans House 1980, 16; Walpole
1774, p. 37 ('taken from Watteau')
MS

O36 *Mug*

Worcester, transfer-printed by John
Sadler at Liverpool from a copper-
plate attributable to Thomas Billinge.
c. 1763
Steatitic soft-paste porcelain transfer-
printed overglaze in brownish orange;
h. 152
The transfer-print signed *I. Sadler/
Liverpool*
VAM (C.50-1938)

Of cylindrical form, the loop handle
with a central ridge. Transfer-printed
at the front with a portrait of Queen
Charlotte, wife of George III; under
the truncation and rising to the level
of her head on either side is an
ornament of scrollwork, floral
garlands, a lion holding the Royal
Arms and a unicorn with the lion of
Scotland, as well as other emblems
and two scrolls inscribed *CHARLOTTE
QUEEN OF/GREAT BRITAIN.* Another
example of this mug is in the British
Museum (Hobson, 1905, p. 133,
X.14). A smaller (860mm) Worcester
mug with the image printed in reverse
in black was in the Wallace Elliot sale
(Sotheby's, May 25 1938, 189 and
illustration). These mugs have
sometimes in the past been attributed
to Liverpool rather than Worcester
because they bear prints by the
Liverpol firm of John Sadler. See for
example Rackham, 1927, p. 87 and
fig. VIII and Price, 1948, p. 67 and
pl. 15. Price is, however, probably
correct in dating these wares to 1763:
at least a similar print made for
Wedgwood quart mugs was described
as 'a new one' on April 29 of that year
(Ibid p. 48). The engraver of the plate
used on this mug and on the
companion mug of George III was
probably Thomas Billinge, the
freelance engraver recorded in

Liverpool directories from 1766-1800.
See Price, op cit, p. 23 and compare
pl. 9 figs 1 and 2, pl. II fig. 1, and
pl. 14 figs. 1 and 5. We do not know
the dates of T. Billinge's birth or
death, but a career stretching from
1766 to 1816 has been reconstructed
for him, on the basis of the Liverpool
directories, by H. Boswell Lancaster
(1942). While this is not altogether
inconceivable, even if we add to it the
prints for ceramics which appear to
date from the early 1760s, the very
diverse skills and addresses credited to
'Thomas Billinge' in the Directories
prompt the thought that we may be
confusing the activities of more than
one man: in 1766 there was an
engraver of this name at Rainsford's
Buildings; in 1767 an engraver and
glass flowerer of Pool Lane; in 1772 an
engraver and druggist in Castle Street
while two years later the profession of
'Copper plate printer' is added; in
1790 there is a printer, stationer and
engraver of this name at 64 Castle
Street; by 1803 the occupation of a
publisher of the Liverpool Advertiser
is added and the address changes to
62 Castle Street; this continues until
1816. Whatever the truth about
Billinge's other activities, we can form
an idea of his skill and style as an
engraver for the ceramic industry from
the following: Worcester porcelain
bell-shaped mug in the VAM (C.940-
1924), transfer-printed in black with
The Right Hon. William Pitt, Esq
inscribed *T. Billinge SC,* (illustrated by
Price, 1948, pl. 14, fig. 5; Williams-
Wood, 1981, pl. 64); Chaffers factory
porcelain jug formerly in the
E. Allman Collection with a black
print of George III, signed *T. Billinge
Sc.* (Lancaster, 1942, fig. IV; Price,
1948, pl. 14 fig. 1; Sotheby's January
12, 1965, 241). A different print of
George II, apparently not signed by
the engraver, appears on a creamware
jug with a painted date, 1798; but the
King is shown as a youngish man and
the potter evidently re-used an old
plate (see Price, 1948, pl. 18). Billinge's
designs often look as though they are
intended to be carved in wood like
those in engravings by Thomas
Johnson or in Chippendale's first
Director. The portrait of Queen
Charlotte is said wrongly by Rackham
(1927) to be after a painting by
Jeremiah Meyer. According to
information provided by Jacob Simon

of the National Portrait Gallery it derives instead from Thomas Frye's portrait, published in various editions in 1762. (See O'Donoghue, 1908, pp. 409-410).

Prov: Wallace Elliot Bequest
Lit: Hobson 1905; Boswell Lancaster 1942; O'Donoghue 1908; Rackham 1927; Price 1948; Williams-Wood 1981; Christie's, 8 December 1925 JVGM

O37

O37 *Plate*

Worcester (decorated in the London workshops of James Giles). *c.*1763-70
Steatitic soft-paste porcelain enamelled in colours and gilt; diam 226
VAM (C.880-1935)

Of wavy outline, the centre with a sliced lemon, a stippled plum and sprays of flowers and mushrooms. The border with a scale 'mosaic' pattern with blue, puce and gilding, outlined with irregular gilt scrollwork. This plate is one of four believed to have been passed down by descendants of James Giles, the independent decorator of porcelain and glass, and eventually given to VAM by Mrs Dora Edgell Grubbe in 1935. Honey (1937) used these 'Grubbe Plates' as a basis for identifying the style of James Giles' enamelling workshop. While accepting Mrs Grubbe's evidence that the pieces were associated with Giles, Honey considered them not necessarily by his own hand, and doubted the family tradition that they were specially made for the wedding of James Giles' daughter, Mary Giles, who married in 1763 John Hall, an ancestor of the Grubbes. Honey considered the date,

1763, 'perhaps too early', but since at least one of the Grubbe plates looks like a prototype never carried into general production, that date seems not altogether impossible for a London porcelain dealer and enameller in close touch with German and French fashion. The Grubbe plate here shown is closely modelled on a style of decoration with *Mosaik* borders evolved around 1760-1 at the great Meissen factory, near Dresden, apparently under the personal influence of Frederick the Great. Cut fruit and flower decoration is often found associated with *Mosaik* borders on Meissen porcelain of the 'Academic Period' (1763-74). In 1768 Giles particularly emphasised in his advertisements that the goods he had for sale were 'curiously painted in the Dresden, Chelsea, and Chinese Tastes'.

Prov: Mrs Dora Edgell Grubbe
Lit: Barett 1953, p. 33, pl. 62; Charleston 1965, pp. 292-316, pl. 222a; Coke 1983, pl. 61B; Honey 1937 I, pp. 7-16, pl. IIIa; Honey 1937 II, p. 88, fig. II; Marshall 1951, pp. 3-5; Marshall 1954, Chap. 7, pl. 7 JVGM

O38 *Part tea service comprising teapot and cover, tea canister and cover, sucrier and cover and two teacups and saucers.*

Worcester. *c.*1770
Steatitic soft-paste porcelain painted in enamel colours, underglaze blue and gilding; h. 159, 140, 112, 64 and diam 130 respectively
Mark: a fretted square in underglaze blue
VAM (C.379-383-1921)

Each piece with an underglaze blue scale 'mosaic' ground interrupted by reserved panels enamelled with Chinese musicians, flowers and insects bordered with gilt scrollwork; the neck of the tea canister has in addition paterae and square mosaic all in gilding. The slender Chinese figures on this set perhaps derive in the first instance from those on Chelsea; compare for instance the crimson ground Emily Thomson Teaset in the VAM (King 1922, pp. 54-5 and pl. 51). King suggests that the last would no doubt have been similar to a Chelsea service described as '*A very curious and matchless tea and coffee equipage,* crimson and gold, most inimitably enamell'd in figures, from the designs of *Watteau*', sold at Christie's, lot 70 on February 17, 1770, in Nicholas Sprimont's final sale. Even if, in the Worcester as in the Chelsea instance,

O38

there was no exact correspondence with any engravings from Watteau, the flimsy, wistful figures were no doubt intended to evoke the Cathay of Watteau rather than the more robust vision of Boucher. The scaly 'mosaic' ground on services such as the present develops and anglicises a Meissen fashion (Cat. O37). The scales, being in underglaze blue, must have been applied at the factory, but pieces with blue scale, but otherwise blank, seem sometimes to have been supplied to James Giles, who added overglaze enamels and gilding. The present set, however, seems likely to be wholly factory work.

Prov: David M. Currie Bequest
Lit: Godden 1966, pl. XVI
JVGM

O39 *Pieces from a Service*
Chelsea (Lawrence Street Factory).
Before March, 1763
Soft-paste porcelain containing bone-ash, decorated in underglaze 'Mazarine' blue, enamel colours and gilding; cut-glass bottles; some metal fittings; wooden support under the épergne. Épergne l. 670; tureen l. 320; stand l. 430; oil and vinegar stand h. 295; cruet h. 310; plates diam 216; sauceboat l. 214
Gold anchor marks
Her Majesty The Queen

The whole Service is decorated with areas of white porcelain enamelled in colours with exotic birds and insects or with swags of flowers, alternating with areas of mazarine blue gilded with moths and butterflies, each piece with raised scrollwork mouldings picked out in gilding. The epergne is surmounted by an oval dish with pierced lid and sides raised by four supports above a massive platform with four scroll-feet; from this base rise also four candle-holders with drip-pans, and four circular pierced dishes; the tureen is oval with domed lid and scroll-handles, and rests on an oval dish; the cruet comprises one large vase-like container with pierced cover and two smaller with unpierced covers; the oil and vinegar stand holds two glass bottles cut with hollow diamonds and surmounted by porcelain lids, besides two small circular spaces now unoccupied; the plates with exotic birds in the centres and each with five panels of mazarine blue at the rim; the sauceboat with four scroll-feet and with a handle shaped as two intertwining scrolls, attached to the vessel only at their lower end. The Service was made to the order of George III and Queen Charlotte as a present for the latter's brother, Duke Adolphus Frederick IV of Mecklenburg-Strelitz. It may be dated from Horace Walpole's letter to Horace Mann of March 4th, 1763: 'I saw yesterday a magnificent service of Chelsea china which the King and Queen are sending to the Duke of Mecklenburgh. There are dishes and plates without number, an épergne, candlesticks, salt-cellars, sauce-boats, tea and coffee equipages – in short, it is complete – and costs twelve hundred pounds! I cannot boast of our taste; the forms are neither new, beautiful, nor various. Yet Sprimont, the manufacturer, is a Frenchman: it seems their taste will not bear transplanting – But I have done; my letter has tumbled from the King of Prussia to a set of china – *encore passe*, if I had begun with the King of Poland, *ce roi de faïence*, as the other called him. Adieu!' (Lewis, 1960, Vol. 22, pp. 121-122).The Service remained at Strelitz until bought in the early 1920s by Sir Joseph Duveen for his private collection in the U.S.A., but was returned to the British Royal Family in 1948 when presented by Mr James Oakes to Her Majesty Queen Elizabeth, the Queen Mother.

The Chelsea branches from candelabra forming part of the service found their way in 1867 into the Schreiber Collection and are now in the VAM (Rackham, 1927, pp. 46-7, no. 210). 'Escaped' pieces apparently from the Mecklenburg-Strelitz Service also include a dish in the Katz Collection (Savage, 1952, p. 37a) and a plate formerly in the Smeathman Collection (English Ceramic Circle, 1949, no. 241 and pl. 52. In March 1764 the Chelsea factory advertised in its sale a near duplicate of the Mecklenburg-Strelitz Service, described as 'the same as the Royal Pattern which sold for £1150 Pounds'. This second service, promised as 'the last that will be made of the Pottery' was soon afterwards exhibited by the dealer, Williams, before it was 'sent abroad'. To it probably belonged the plates and dishes now in various collections, similar to those of the Mecklenburg-Strelitz Service, but with the Mazarine blue panels indented at the rim (eg see Mackenna, 1952, pl. 9, fig. 16). Plates and dishes with 'Mecklenburg-Strelitz' mouldings are found decorated with other patterns but the hollow-wares seem unique to the Service. Hence a biscuit fragment from the foot of a vase-like cruet found at the Factory site in 1970 is probably a failed piece intended for the Service.

Prov: Dukes of Mecklenburg-Strelitz until the early 1920s; Sir Joseph (later Lord) Duveen, U.S.A.; James Oakes Collection 1944-48, England
Lit: English Ceramic Circle 1949, no. 241 & pl. 52; Gardner 1937, pp. 24-25 & pl. lxc; Gardner 1942, p. 137, pl. XLVII; Hughes 1960, pp. 28-36; King 1922, pp. 49-50; Lewis (ed) Vol. 22, pp. 121-122; Mallet 1965 I, p. 37 & pl. 5A; Rackham 1927, pp. 46-47, nos. 210 & 211; Savage 1952 pp. 27, 213-4, pl. 37; Severne Mackenna 1952, pp. 13, 15, 16, 65, 66
JVGM

O39

O40 *Porcelain Clock*

Chelsea (Lawrence Street Factory); the movement dated 1755, the porcelain *c.*1760-69
Soft-paste porcelain containing bone-ash, painted in underglaze blue, coloured enamels and gilt; h. 521.
The woman at the top holds a sheet of music inscribed *Sung by Miss Young Ranelagh/Young Collin probe (?) . . . his joy and delight he ever . . . when I am by his sight he want to be with where . . .* The enamelled face of the clock inscribed, *STEPHEN RIMBAULT. LONDON,* the back of the clock inscribed *F E J Parsons, Londoni, fecit, 1755*

The Wernher Collection, by arrangement with the NACF

The case of rectangular shape and slightly curved outline raised on four scroll-feet, the sides elaborately pierced, at each corner is a music-making putto, the top of the clock rising to a domical platform on which sits a female figure attended by a boy playing a horn. The clock partly decorated in underglaze Mazarine blue with gilt flowers and partly left in the white but picked out in gilding, the figures naturalistically coloured, the domical platform at the top painted possibly by J. H. O'Neale with birds and flying cupids. This clock is shown in an advertisement by Messrs Albert Amor in the *Connoisseur,* February, 1925, on a lacquered stand which no longer exists. It is not now known whether this stand was contemporary or a later edition. Three other Chelsea gold anchor porcelain clocks are recorded by Gardner (1935) as well as a crest with four putti, evidently intended for a clock and perhaps identical with the 'Group of Boys for the top of a Clock' contained in a list of goods made prior to 1769 (Bemrose, 1898, p. 47). Gardner mentions that one of these clocks, also with a movement by Rimbault, was discovered at Soria in Spain in 1850 in the possession of a priest. That this piece should have been in Spain at such an early date raises the possibility that it might have been exported to the Iberian Peninsula at the time of its manufacture, like many of the most elaborate rococo clocks by Ellicot (see cat. I2) This second Rimbault clock is now in a private collection in London.

Lit: Bemrose 1898; Blunt 1924; Gardner 1935; Hayden 1932, no. 213; Severne Mackenna 1952, pl. 59, fig. 115
JVGM

O41 *Pair of Candlesticks*

Chelsea (Lawrence Street Factory). *c.*1760-69
Soft-paste porcelain containing bone-ash, enamelled and gilt; h. 400
Gold anchor marks

The Wernher Collection, by arrangement with the NACF

Each group comprised of an asymmetrical rococo terrace with scrollwork feet and covered at the top with applied and enamelled flowers and leaves. On one candlestick is a leopard hunt with five hounds, one of them lying wounded, on the other is a stag hunt with four hounds. From the back of each group rise three candle-nozzles and drip-pans attached to irregularly arranged scroll-work brackets, the whole further backed by flowering May trees. The remote ancestor of Chelsea *bocage* candlesticks such as these might be the 'projet de Chandelier à branche pour le Roy', in the eleventh book of Meissonnier's *Œuvre*. The English *bocage* candlestick groups like the present have no exact equivalent in continental Europe, but some of Kändler's Meissen porcelain chamber-candlestick groups contain the germ of the idea. Compare Rückert (1966) no. 1097.

Lit: Hayden 1932, nos. 203, 204; Rückert 1966
JVGM

O42 *Clock-case*

Chelsea (Lawrence Street Factory).
*c.*1760-70
Soft-paste bone-ash porcelain, decorated with a crimson ground-colour, other enamels and gilding; h. 43 8
Mark: an anchor in gold. The enamel dial of the clock inscribed *STRIGEL LONDON*
Her Majesty The Queen

The clock, which is scarcely more than a large watch, is fixed in an asymmetrical housing with a wing to symbolise the flight of time; this is set on an irregular arch which springs from a roughly oval base with moulded rococo scrollwork. The background parts of the group, where not left white or gilded, bear a crimson enamel ground. On the base reclines a

O41

O41

sleeping shepherdess accompanied by an ewe with two lambs, who is about to be woken by a shepherd. The model is probably due to Joseph Willems, in which case it must have originated before 1766, when he left Chelsea for Tournai. The earliest certain reference we have for the use of the crimson ground (sometimes described as 'claret' by modern writers) is in the 1761 Chelsea catalogue, though it may have been one of the 'new colours' advertised the previous year. The composition of this group may have been suggested, though only in very general terms, by one or other of the numerous engravings after Boucher representing awakening shepherdesses, (Jean-Richard 1978, nos. 282, 573, 713, 739, 1031, 1158, 1540). The design and symbolism of the housing, with its wing and flying Cupid, may not be wholly unrelated to a model in Kändler's manner produced at Meissen (Christie's, December 5, 1983, lot 146). The clock-housing, rococo architectural setting and base occur in white and gold on a gold anchor marked Chelsea example on which is set a polychrome-decorated shepherd embracing a lamb, and a shepherdess playing a flute (Sotheby's July 17, 1973, lot 109)

Prov: Queen Charlotte's Collection, sold 1819. George IV's Collection, bought back at the sale
Lit: King 1922 frontispiece; King 1935, p. 249, pl. IIb; Mallet 1980, p. 6, pp. 12-13
JVGM

O42

O43 *Clock-case*
Chelsea (Lawrence Street Factory).
*c.*1761
Soft-paste bone-ash porcelain, enamelled and gilt; h. 181
Mark: an anchor in gold, on the enamel clock-dial is the clockmaker's name, Fladgate
Museum of Fine Arts, Boston, Gift of Richard C. Paine

In the form of an upright bouquet of naturalistically coloured flowers and leaves, centred at the front by a sunflower in which the clock-face is set. The scroll-edged base picked out in gilding. The production of artificial flowers in porcelain was carried to extreme sophistication at Vincennes and Sèvres. There, however, the flowers were normally used as an adjunct to ormolu and a large assemblage of flowers into a porcelain clock-case like the present example is unknown. Already at Chelsea in 1756 there were included on the 16th day of the annual sale, lot 34: *'Two beautiful perfume pots in the shape of a bunch of flowers'*. A similar item was lot 78 on the same day of the 1756 sales. A sunflower clock, however, is only documented in the 1761 sale of the Chelsea factory, 1st day, lot 58: 'A fine *table clock* in a case of a bunch of flowers, curiously enamelled, the movement by Fladgate'. This last might either be the present example or else it might be the sunflower clock-case, now ormolu-mounted, with contemporary watch by Fladgate sold at Sotheby's on 18 November, 1952, 100 and 29 November, 1960, 14.

Prov: Hutton Collection (in 1924 No. 176)
Lit: Blunt (ed.) 1924, pl. 25, fig. 93; Severne Mackenna 1952, p. 83
JVGM

O44 *Bocage Group of the Dancing Lesson*
Chelsea (Lawrence Street Factory).
*c.*1762-9
Soft-paste porcelain enamelled and gilt; h. 407
Mark: an anchor in gold
The Museum of London C.1073

The young couple, their clothes elaborately enamelled and gilt, are shown seated beneath an elaborate flowering bocage background, he playing a hurdy-gurdy and she

teaching a dog in human clothing to dance on a pedestal. On scroll base applied with coloured flowers and picked out in gilding. Arthur Lane (1961, p. 72 and pl. 29) illustrates this group and dates it about 1762-3. No such group, nor the very similar group of the Music Lesson appears in the incomplete copy of the 1761 catalogue. The next catalogue that survives, that of February 1770, when Nicholas Sprimont was selling up his stock, much of which was probably some years old, includes two examples of the Music Lesson, 2nd Day, lot 41 and 3rd Day, lot 46 (Nightingale, 1881). In neither of these entries is the Music Lesson paired to the Dancing Lesson. These two groups do not seem to have formed a pair. The Dancing Lesson has a very differently shaped scroll base to the Music Lesson group. Both the Dancing Lesson and the Music Lesson appear to be in the style of the modeller Joseph Willems who left Chelsea in 1766. The model, if not this particular example, was presumably made before that date. Most *bocage* groups in English porcelain support candle-nozzles and drip-pans, unlike the present group.

Prov: Mrs M.E. Salting Collection, lent 1912, bequeathed in 1924
Lit: Hackenbroch 1958, fig. 73, Lane 1961; Nightingale 1881; Severne Mackenna 1952
JVGM

O44

O45 *Garniture of seven pot-pourri vases*

Chelsea (Lawrence Street Factory)
Soft-paste bone-ash porcelain
enamelled and gilt; h. 428; 393, 374
and 345.
Marks: gold anchors
The National Trust (Upton House).

Comprising one central ovoid vase,
two large pear-shaped vases, two
inverted pear-shaped vases and two
smaller pear-shaped vases. Each with a
pierced cover and neck, scroll handles
and feet. Each decorated within
reserved panels on a crimson ground
on one side with peacocks and other
fowl somewhat in the manner of
Hondecoeter (1636-95) and on the
other side with mythological scenes in
landscapes. The scenes represented on
the pieces (left to right) are as follows:
Diana and a Satyr from *Le Repos de
Diane* by Jean Pelletier after Boucher
(Jean-Richard 1978, no.
1454); Death of Adonis from a print
by Louis Surugue after Boucher
published in 1742 (Ibid No 1591);
Cupid and Psyche being garlanded by
cupids (source unidentified);
Alphaeus and Arethusa from an
engraving by Etienne Fessard after a
painting by Pierre-Charles
Trémolières; Leda and the Swan with
Nymphs and Cupids (source
unidentified); Venus on Clouds with
Cupids (source unidentified); A Nude
Woman playing with Cupid's Arrows,
the central figure after the engraving,
Le Trait Dangereux, published 1742 by
J.F. Poletnich after Boucher (Ibid No
1474). Mackenna (1952, p. 71, fig. 70)
illustrates a vase in the Huntingdon
Art Gallery, San Marino, of the same
shape and with the identical scene of
Cupid and Psyche as on the third vase
listed above, saying the scene is 'after
Boucher', but citing no reference. The
present set of vases, amongst the most
elaborate of their kind, came to be
known, after one of their Victorian
owners as 'the Dudley Vases'. Their
forms appear to be original to Chelsea
and it is hard to say whether they and
others like them are due to Joseph
Willems, Nicholas Sprimont or some
unknown designer or modeller. A
print published by Thomas Johnson
in 1758 (Hayward 1964, fig. 104)
anticipates the bizarre spirit of the
gold anchor Chelsea vases of the
1760s, but there is no evidence of
direct copying. The colour of the

ground may have originated in an
attempt to copy the paler pink *Rose
Pompadour* of Sèvres. However
'Crimson' is the term normally used
from 1760 onwards in the Chelsea
advertisements and sale catalogues of
Sprimont's time and two lots in the
1770 catalogue called respectively
'Pompadour' and 'laylock colour'd'
(lilac coloured) may describe different
grounds altogether (Nightingale 1881,
Appendix, p. 10). William King (1948)
writes of the Dudley Vases: 'they are
traditionally said to have been made
for George III as a present for Lady
Cope', who was married in 1767, a
date which would well suit the style of
the vases. After her husband's death
Lady Cope became the wife of Sir
Charles Jenkinson, later created Earl
of Liverpool. During her lifetime she
appears to have given them to her
daughter by her first husband,
Arabella Diana, Duchess of Dorset,
who predeceased her, dying in 1825,
and bequeathed them to her own
daughter, Mary, Countess of
Plymouth and later Countess
Amherst, who died in 1864. At some
time previous they had already been
sold . . .'. For the later and less
hypothetical provenance see below.

Prov: Sir Dudley Coutts Marjoribanks,
Bart, M.P. (in 1867); Messrs Falke &
Co, Bond Street; Lord Dudley; Lord
Burton; Lord Astor; Christie's, 1920;
Messrs Albert Amor; Lord Bearsted
Lit: Bunford 1937; Jean-Richard 1978;
King 1922, p. 54, pls. 57, 58; King
1948, pp. 141-2; Litchfield 1925, pl.
17; Manchester Guardian 1922;
Marryat 1854, pp. 284-5
JVGM

O46 *Vase and Cover*

Chelsea-Derby factory (probably at the
Chelsea, Lawrence Street site). *c.* 1771
Soft-paste porcelain containing bone-
ash, enamelled in colours and gilt;
h. 385
Mark: an anchor in gold
VAM (Illidge Loan)

Ovoid body with moulded gadrooning
at the base and elaborate rococo
handles. The short neck is supported
on a short stem with a central ring and
circular foot with moulded scrolls.
Domed cover, the finial replaced.
Apart from the white and gold
handles, the gadrooning and
moulded scrollwork, the vase is

O46

decorated with a crimson ground
enriched with gilt ribbon tie and
garlands of flowers and with an oval
reserved panel on either side of the
body. One side is painted with
Vertumnus and Pomona, the other
with a spray of mixed flowers. This
vase, which used to be mistaken for a
product of Sprimont's period at
Chelsea by reason of its rococo form
and gold anchor mark, can be proved
to be later. The subject painted on one
side, Vertumnus and Pomona repeats
an engraving by Augustin de Saint-
Aubin after Boucher. The engraving
was published in Volume IV of l'Abbé
Banier, *Les Métamorphoses d'Ovide*,
which only appeared in 1771, whereas
Sprimont sold the factory in 1769. See
Jean-Richard 1978, p. 376, no. 1564.
The present vase is almost certainly
one described in William Duesbury's
first annual sale of his Chelsea and
Derby factories' products held on
April 17th, 1771 and the three
following days. Lot 58 on the fourth
day reads 'A curious antique jar, with
the story of Vertumnus and Pomona,
from Ovid's Metamorphoses, with a
curious gold gadroon frame, and
entwin'd with ribbands and garlands
of chased gold flowers, on a crimson
ground, highly finish'd and burnish'd
gold. 20 1.' No buyer's name is given
and it is possible that the lot may have
been bought in because two years
later, in Mr Duesbury's sale of the
February 9, 1773 and following days
appeared 'A large antique jar and
pedestal, crimson ground, finely

enamelled in compartments, the story of Vertumnus and Pomona, and superbly finished with gold. 12 1 12 s.' Nightingale 1881, pp. 34 and 45. The second of these references may, however, refer to a different vase with separate 'pedestal'. The claret ground and the other enamels on this piece are somewhat softer in tone than pieces certainly attributable to Sprimont's time, and indeed bear certain resemblances to the late work of Giles who, in 1771-73 had close business links with Duesbury, even apparently acquiring undecorated porcelain from him. (Coke, 1983, pp. 20, 21.)

Lit: Bunford 1937, p. 26, pl. IVa + b; Charleston (ed) 1965, p. 38, pl. 7B; Coke 1983; Jean-Richard 1978; Nightingale 1881
JVGM

O47

O47 *Sauceboat*
Plymouth (William Cookworthy's factory). *c.*1768-70
Hard-paste porcelain enamelled in colours; l. 138
VAM (3096.1901)

Of boat shape with moulded scrollwork panels on either side, scroll-edged foot and rim. The handle formed as two opened C-scrolls with a leaf-shaped thumbpiece. The panels on either side and the space under the lip-spout and handle are painted with sprays of flowers. The *rocaille* ornament of the foot is picked out in puce; puce scrolls on the handle and interior of the lip-spout. Another Plymouth sauceboat with the same mouldings was in the Frank Arnold Collection (Mackenna 1946, pl. 22, fig. 33). In 1768 when William Cookworthy began to produce a true hard-paste

porcelain from the Cornish materials he had discovered, he showed himself an innovator in the chemistry of porcelain-making, whereas in style he remained attached to a somewhat *retardataire* rococo. The moulding of this jug particularly recalls the silver prototypes with which it would have been in competition.

Prov: given by W. Cookworthy Esq, presumably a relative of the founder of the factory, to the Museum of Practical Geology, Jermyn Street. Since this piece is not mentioned in the 1855 edition of de la Beche and Reeks it was presumably presented by him between that date and 1871
Lit: de la Beche and Reeks 1871, p. 165, no. K11; Severne Mackenna 1946
JVGM

O48 *Mug*
Bow. January 1770
Soft-paste porcelain containing bone-ash, enamelled and gilded; h. 111
Inscribed under the base in enamel:
This Pint was/Painted for Mrs/Mary Bromley/of Campden Gloc:shire/by her Loving Son/John De Lanauze/January 1770

The Trustees of the British Museum (1938, 3-14, 112)

Cylindrical with a lobed handle ending with a heart-shaped terminal. Painted on one side with a Turk smoking and on the other with a shepherd in European clothes talking to a standing milkmaid. Both the male figures recline on elaborate scrollwork supports. Gilt dentil rim. The extreme rococo decoration on this piece is directly copied from two prints by J.E. Nilson of Augsburg, from the series of prints entitled 'Caffe, The und Tobac Zieretten'. The engravings of Nilson were influential in diffusing an extreme version of the rococo through the porcelain and faïence factories of Germany. In England Birmingham Enamel snuff-boxes were transfer-printed with a coffee-drinking and a smoking subject (Watney and Charleston 1966, pl. 102b) and wood-block tiles were printed after this same set by John Sadler of Liverpool (Cat. P1). For Nilson prints of the coffee, tea and tobacco series see Ray 1973, pl. 30 and Ducret 1973 figs. 88, 90, 94 and 127. A number of prints from this set are in the Print Room at the VAM. A further Bow mug painted

after the same series of prints and, though unsigned, clearly by John De Lanauze, is at Luton Hoo (Hayden 1932, No. 117 and Adams and Redstone 1981, p. 190 and fig. 118). Nothing is known about John De Lanauze apart from the evidence supplied by this mug, though Tait (1959) recorded a number of people named Bromley in the parishes of Campden and Welford. William Bowyer (1936) and Adams and Redstone (1981, p. 190) consider the possibility that he may have worked for an independent decorator such as James Giles, and the prominent, jagged gilt dentil pattern at the rim would be compatible with such an attribution. However, the relationship between inside and outside decoration at Bow may have been complex: we know that Thomas Craft, the Bow factory enameller, sent the 'Craft Bowl' now in the British Museum 'to Kentish Town, and had it burned there in Mr Gyles's kiln, cost me 3s . . .'.

Prov: J.R. Cookson of Kendal (at Antique Dealers' Fair 1936); Wallace Elliot Collection
Lit: Adams and Redstone 1981; Bowyer 1936, p. 229; Charleston 1966; Ducret 1973; Hayden 1932; Tait 1959, no. 120, figs. 47-49
JVGM

O48

Earthenware

P1-6

P1 *Tile*
Liverpool (factory of John Sadler).
1756-7
Tin-glazed earthenware transfer-
printed in manganese-purple from a
wood-block 127 square
VAM (C.1432-1924)

A lady and gentleman in hunting
costume by a *rocaille* scroll
ornament with two dogs and a putto.
The design is taken from the series of
prints entitled *Caffe, The und Tobac
Zieretten* by J.E. Nilson of Augsburg.
John Sadler's first transfer-printed tiles
were printed from wood-blocks but
although of a very high standard he
found it difficult to achieve delicate
detail with this technique. In 1758 he
started printing exclusively from
copper plates. John Sadler was a
printer by profession and his works in
Harrington Street, Liverpool, were
next to a pottery run by Frederick
Fisher. Although others had pioneered
the process of decorating porcelain
and enamels by applying transfer-
prints, Sadler was the first to do so on
to tin-glazed tiles. For this and the
following tiles see Ray 1973 II. He
supplies a useful bibliography on print
sources.

Prov: given by Lt Col K. Dingwall,
DSO
Lit: Ray 1973 I, No. A1-1
MA

P2 *Tile*
Liverpool (factory of John Sadler).
1758-61
Tin-glazed earthenware transfer-
printed in black. 127 square
Signed *Sadler*
VAM (C.582-1922)

A gentleman helping a girl over a stile.

Prov: given by R. Holland-Martin
Lit: Ray 1973 I, No. B4-2
MA

P3 *Tile*
Liverpool (factory of John Sadler).
1758-61
Tin-glazed earthenware transfer-
printed in black. 127 square
Signed *J. Sadler Livero¹.*
VAM (C.137-1981)

A gallant offering a bird's nest to a
seated girl. The design appears to be

taken from a number of prints issued
as a drawing book by John Bowles in
1756-7.

Prov: L.L. Lipski Collection; given by
R.J. Charleston
Lit: Ray 1973 I, No. B3-2
MA

P4 *Tile*
Liverpool (factory of John Sadler).
1758-61
Tin-glazed earthenware transfer-
printed in manganese-purple. 127
square
VAM (931-1892)

A ship seen from inside a rocky grotto.

Lit: Ray 1973 I, No. B9-1
MA

P5 *Tile*
Liverpool (factory of John Sadler).
1758-61
Tin-glazed earthenware transfer-
printed in black. 127 square
VAM (C.54-1967)

Two young men and a girl fishing.
The design is adapted from Robert
Sayer's *Ladies' Amusement,* 1759 or
1760, plate 32.

Prov: Mrs M.B. Sargeant Bequest
Lit: Ray 1973 I, No. B4-7
MA

P6 *Tile*
Liverpool (factory of John Sadler).
1756-7
Tin-glazed earthenware transfer-
printed in blue from a wood-block.
127 square.
VAM (C.134-1981)

A shepherd and shepherdess seated
on a bank with a dog. This tile is
found in blue monochrome or printed
in black and painted in enamel
colours. The same design appears
printed from copper-plates.

Prov: L.L. Lipski Collection; given by
R.J. Charleston
Lit: Ray 1973 I, No. A2-3
MA

P7 *Tureen, cover and stand*
Staffordshire (probably made by
Josiah Wedgwood). 1759-65
Lead-glazed cream-coloured
earthenware transfer-printed in over-
glaze black probably by Sadler and
Green with peacocks and other birds;
h. 215, l. 368
VAM (2291-B-1901)

The shell-like moulding on this piece
and the naturalism of the artichoke
knob and twig handles are both
rococo characteristics. The knob and
the moulding of the stand derive
directly from a Sèvres tureen, cover
and stand in the Duchess of Bedford's
service, which is still at Woburn
Abbey. In May 1759 Josiah
Wedgwood spent three days 'takeing
pattns. from a set of French China at
the Duke of Bedford's'. The Sèvres
service is painted with exotic birds,
which may have suggested the use of
similar decoration to Wedgwood,
although peacocks were also a popular
motif on printed textiles of the period
(Cat. N29). The prints on the
ceamware tureen, cover and stand are
very close to counterparts on marked
Wedgwood pieces (cf. VAM Schreiber
Collection II.353), suggesting that they
are by Sadler and Green.

Prov: Jermyn Street Collection, 1876
(G.213)
Lit: Mallet 1975
MA

P8 *Coffee-pot*
Staffordshire (mould perhaps made by
William Greatbatch). *c.*1755-65
Lead-glazed earthenware, the lowest
part decorated in under-glaze green;
h. 254
*City of Stoke-on-Trent Museum and Art
Gallery (2225)*

The naturalism of the cauliflower
forming the body of this pot is not in
itself a particularly rococo
phenomenon, but when a spout and
handle are added of such radically
contrasting type, the bizarre and
frivolous product of the union has a
claim to be so.
MA

P8

P9

P9 Coffee-pot
Staffordshire. *c.1760*
Red unglazed stoneware with applied
and moulded decoration; h. 239
VAM (C.25&A-1947)

The spout and handle were press-
moulded and applied to the main
body of the pot which would have
been hand thrown. The ornament on
the pot itself was press-moulded in
separate pieces and applied to the pot
when damp. Both the shape and
applied decoration clearly derive from
a silver prototype.
MA

P10 Wall flower-holder
Staffordshire (perhaps made by Josiah
Wedgwood and the mould by William
Greatbatch). *c.1760*
Lead-glazed earthenware decorated in
under-glaze green, yellow-ochre and
brown with a moulded figure perhaps
representing Flora; h. 279, w. 264
VAM (C.45-1944)

Fragments corresponding to part of
the upper edge and lower part of the
cornucopia have been found on the
site of the Greatbatch factory. They
come from the lowest layer indicating
a date in the early 1760s. There is
evidence that the popularity of green
glazed wares was declining by the mid
1760s. The cartouche enclosing the
figure, the twisting asymmetric
cornucopia form and the distribution
of the coloured glazes are all rococo
qualities. The purpose to which
objects of this type were put is
uncertain. They all have flat backs
pierced with one or more holes
allowing attachment to the wall or
other flat surface. This particular
example is moulded with a figure of
Flora (?) holding flowers, suggesting
that it may have been a receptacle for
dried or fresh flowers. However, other
wall-pockets are known of a similar
shape but decorated with a bird or in
the form of a fish. No contemporary
picture or print is known showing
such wall-pockets in a domestic
setting.

P10

Prov: Miss Helena Hill Bequest
Lit: Towner 1963
MA

P11 *Wall flower-holder*
Staffordshire (perhaps made by Josiah
Wedgwood and the mould by William
Greatbatch). *c.*1765
Undecorated white salt-glazed
stoneware moulded in the form of a
face surrounded by scrolls and foliage;
h. 306, w. 210
*The Syndics of the Fitzwilliam Museum,
Cambridge*

Prov: Milner-Gibson-Cullum
Collection, Suffolk, 1924; Glaisher
Collection, 540
Lit: Towner 1963
MA

P12 *Punch bowl*
Probably Bristol. 1759
Tin-glazed earthenware painted in
blue; diam. 387
Inscribed *WBM 1759* City of Bristol
Museum and Art Gallery (G.2155)

The hen and chickens inside the bowl
derive from a print by Thomas Barlow
(published *c.*1658, British Library No.
433.b.13) a drawing for which is in the

Cecil Higgins Museum, Bedford. The
rococo scrolls surrounding it are the
invention of the pot painter. The
exterior is painted with a church
amongst trees and a man and a
woman leading a procession of twelve
boys and girls walking in pairs.

Prov: gift of Mr and Mrs Hall Warren,
1924
Lit: Bristol n.d., 18; Britton 1982, pp.
152-3; Garner & Archer 1972, pls. 76,
77
MA

P13 *Sauceboat*
Probably London. *c.*1760-70
Tin-glazed earthenware painted in
blue; l. 216
VAM (C.88-1947)

The asymmetric handle and the C-
scrolls of the cartouches, which appear
on both sides containing harbour
scenes, are markedly rococo in
character. With the exception of the
handle the general form is close to a
slightly earlier Liverpool porcelain
prototype of which an example is in
the VAM (770-1924).

Prov: Mellor Bequest
MA

P12

P14 *Jug*

Yorkshire. 1769
Lead-glazed cream-coloured
earthenware painted in overglaze red
and black colours. The applied flower-
sprig terminals to the twisted handles
are also painted in pink, green, yellow
and blue overglaze colours; h. 190
Inscribed *God Speed the Plough* and *Thos;
Stonier 1769*
VAM (C.14-1952)

The form of this jug could in no way
be described as rococo but the
primitive asymmetric painting of
scrolls is clearly intended to be so. The
piece was probably made at one of the
small factories which preceded the
opening of the Leeds pottery. The
enamel painting is of the type
associated with David Rhodes but was
probably carried out by his one-time
partner Jasper Robinson.

Prov: A.B. Morgan Bequest
Lit: Towner 1974; Towner 1978,
pp. 128-32, pl. 86; Walton 1976, cf.
No. 716
MA

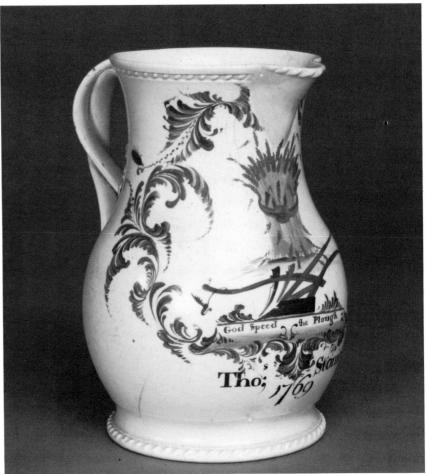

P14

P15 *Dish*

Staffordshire, Etruria, Josiah
Wedgwood. *c.*1776-80
Lead-glazed cream-coloured
earthenware printed in black and
hand coloured in green by Guy Green
of Liverpool; l. 305.
Mark: *Wedgwood* and *C* impressed.
VAM (C.19-1945)

The asymmetric form and shell-like
mouldings are clearly rococo
characteristics as well as the random
arrangement of the naturalistic
decoration. Wedgwood, who was
much interested in conchology, wrote
that this pattern was intended chiefly
for foreign markets which would
tolerate 'higher colouring and more
forcible contrasts than the English'.

Prov: given by Commander J.A.L.
Drummond, RN, from the Lily
Antrobus Collection
Lit: Mallet 1974
MA

P15

Q1

Q1 Snuff-box
The lid probably Battersea, the walls
and base Birmingham. c.1756-60
The lid of copper enamelled and
transfer-printed, the walls and base of
'aventurine' glass, mounted in copper
gilt; l. 86
VAM (C.129-1963)

Rectangular snuff-box, the lid of
which is printed in brown with Paris
presenting the apple to Hibernia,
from a plate by S.F. Ravenet after a
design by James Gwyn, and inside
with a portrait of Maria Gunning,
Countess of Coventry, probably from
a plate engraved by John Brooks after
Francis Cotes's portrait, painted in
1751, and the walls and base of which
are of 'aventurine' glass mounted in
copper-gilt, pierced and chased with
scrolls, beading and ropework. The lid
of the box was probably printed at the
York House, Battersea factory of
Stephen Theodore Janssen, Henry
Delamain and John Brooks, which was
in business from the third quarter of
1753 until probably not later than 28
February 1756 and certainly not after
8 June 1756. At the later date the stock
of the factory was sold, together with
'a great Number of Copper Plates
engraved by the best Hands'. Since the
'aventurine' glass of the rest of the box
suggests a Midlands, probably
Birmingham, origin, it is likely that the
lid was purchased at the Battersea sale
and mounted in Birmingham.
Alternatively the lid could have been
printed in Birmingham from plates
bought at the sale. However, the

quality of the reproduction suggests
that the plaque was bought already
decorated.

Prov: The Hon. Mrs N. Ionides
Lit: Charleston 1967 II, pp. 1-12, figs
3a-b; Hughes 1951, pl. 7; Watney and
Charleston 1966, pp. 57-123
CT

Q2 Snuff-box
Birmingham or South Staffordshire
(Bilston or Wednesbury). c.1761
Copper, enamelled and gilt; h. 35,
w. 60, depth 83
Lettered on the base with a verse, and
on the lid *K. GEORGE the IIId* and *Q.
CHARLOTTE.*
Her Majesty The Queen

Rectangular snuff-box of copper
enamelled white and printed in purple
with a portrait of George III on the
lid, and Queen Charlotte inside the
lid. Around the sides are cartouches
enclosing representations of the Prince
of Wales encouraging the Arts, flanked
by images of plenty, Britannia
receiving a torch from Cupid, flanked
by images of trade, and Neptune, and
two amorini with a globe. This box
commemorates the coronation on 22
September 1761 of George III and
Queen Charlotte of Mecklenburg-
Strelitz. The verse on the base is from
Thomas Parnell's translation of
Pervigilium Veneris and the portrait of
George III is after an engraving by
William Woollett. The use of raised
white enamel is considered to have
been a speciality of the South

Staffordshire enamellers, and was
certainly used as early as 1757, the
date on a snuff-box in the VAM (C.24-
1953). However, the printing of this
box suggests a Birmingham origin.
The side prints occur on boxes which
can be dated between 1756 and 1770
and in conjunction with
engravings of *Fêtes Venitiennes* after
Watteau, *La Bonne Aventure, Les
Amusements champêtres, Le Panier
Misterieux* and *Les Amours Pastorales* all
after Boucher, and *L'Amour* after
Cochin, *Autumn* by Thomas Major,
1754, after Paul Ferg, and a *Boar Hunt.*
A comparable box with printing and
raised white enamel, also probably of
Birmingham manufacture is illustrated
in Watney 1966, pl. 60c and an almost
identical box, but with a different
mount is illustrated by Mew 1926, pls.
60, 61.

Lit: Benjamin 1978, p. 63; Hughes
1951, fig. 24; Mew 1926, pl. 60 and
61; Watney and Charleston 1966,
pl. 60c
CT

Q3 Set of tea caddies and sugar box
South Staffordshire (probably Bilston
or Wednesbury). c.1770
Copper, enamelled and gilt; h. 180, w.
210, depth 120
VAM (C.424-1914)

Rectangular case comprised of six
panels of copper, enamelled with
landscapes in reserves bordered by gilt
scrolls and flowers against a ground of
pink decorated with white scrolls and
dots, mounted in copper, chased with
scrolls, shells, and flowers and gilt.
The lid is set with a cartouche-shaped
handle of copper-gilt and the front
panel contains a lock with a copper-
gilt escutcheon. The inside of the case
is fitted with wood covered in green
velvet and contains two canisters and a
sugar box enamelled *en suite* with the
case. Enamelling was undertaken in
the small towns of Bilston and
Wednesbury from the 1740s and
pieces with raised gilding and white
enamel are usually attributed to them.
However, Birmingham was by far the
largest centre of production of enamel
in the eighteenth century and the great
number of pieces in this style make it
impossible to exclude a Birmingham
origin for the whole group. The pink

ground with gilt cartouches and reserves painted with landscapes derives from the porcelain of Sèvres where 'roze' was introduced as a ground colour in 1757. That the central box was intended for sugar, not for mixing teas as sometimes supposed, is confirmed by *The Cabinet-Makers' London Book of Prices* (London 1793) p. 235, where a set of this type in wood is described.

Prov: C.S. Kennedy; M.B. Kennedy
Lit: Benjamin 1978, pp. 75-87
CT

Q4 *Scent bottle*
South Staffordshire (Bilston or Wednesbury). *c.* 1765
Copper, enamelled and gilt, and silver; h. 820, w. 285
The Museum of London (A9800)

Rectangular scent bottle with tapering neck of copper enamelled with panels of green and pink overpainted by a white diaper pattern enclosed by gilt scrolls, and two printed and painted reserves, that on the front with two figures and that on the back with a ship being loaded with barrels. The neck is mounted in silver chased with scrolls and is sealed by a silver stopper shaped as a foliate scroll. The style of enamelling of this scent bottle is typical of that attributed to the workshops of South Staffordshire. The two figures in the front reserve are taken from Antoine Watteau's *La Cascade* engraved by G. Scotin (see also cat. O35). The same reserves appear on a very similar scent bottle in the Schreiber Collection at the VAM (Sch III/219).

Prov: J.G. Joicey
Lit: Rackham 1924 pp. 47-48
CT

Q5 *Candlestick*
South Staffordshire (Bilston or Wednesbury). *c.* 1775
Copper, enamelled and gilt; h. 333, w. 163
The Museum of London (A7611)

Candlestick of raised copper in white enamel rising from a shaped, spiralling domed base decorated with flowers and reserves in pink, yellow, mauve and green overpainted with scrolls and diapers of white enamel with gilt scrollwork and husks. The

stem is formed of a scrolling twisted baluster similarly decorated and attached to the base and the nozzle by a copper-gilt ring. The nozzle is formed as a twisted scrolled vase and supports a drip pan similarly decorated with flowers and bordered by gilding. The inspiration for this candlestick is presumably the silver versions found in the 1740s and 50s such as that by James Shruder of 1740-41 (Clayton 1971, fig. 78) and ultimately from Meissonnier's *Livre de Chandeliers*.

Prov: Messrs Duveen Bros
CT

Q6 *Wine glass*
Decorated by William Beilby (1740-1819). *c.* 1765
Lead glass with painted enamel decoration; h. 184
Signed in red enamel *Beilby pinxit.*
VAM (C.623-1936)

Newcastle wine glass with round-funnel bowl on a light baluster stem rising from a slightly domed foot. The front of the bowl bears an asymmetrical scrolling cartouche in mauve and white, flanked by long tapering leaves and hung with garlands of flowers, in the centre of which is a fictitious shield of arms.

The reverse is painted in white enamel with a landscape comprising a ruined temple and a pyramid among trees and shrubs. The rim of the bowl was formerly gilt. At least four members of the Beilby family of Newcastle are recorded as enamellers on glass. Of these William is the most important. In 1755 he was apprenticed to an enameller John Haseldine in Birmingham, where the enamelling on glass is recorded in 1756 and was very probably practised there earlier. The first datable pieces by William Beilby are the goblets enamelled in celebration of the birth of the Prince of Wales in 1762, at least one of which is signed: *W Beilby Junr NCastle inv't & pinxt*. It has been suggested that the inclusion of the word 'junior' in Beilby signatures indicates a date before 1765 when his father, also William, died. By 1779 William Beilby had moved to London and between about 1778 and 1814 he is said to have lived in Fifeshire, after which he is said to have lived in Hull until his death in 1814.

Prov: Collection Wilfred Buckley
Lit: Bewick 1762; Delomosne 1978, pp. 40-41; Laing Art Gallery 1980, no. 59; Rush 1973, pls. 34 & 35
CT

Q7 *Trade card of George Maydwell and Richard Windle's cut-glass warehouse*
Robert Clee. 265 x 187. Before 1765
The Trustees of the British Museum (Heal 66.44)

At the cut-glass warehouse, King's Arms the Strand. On the verso is a bill dated 1765.

Lit: Charleston 19XX, p. 4; Hughes 1956, pl. 28
MS

Chinoiserie and Gothic

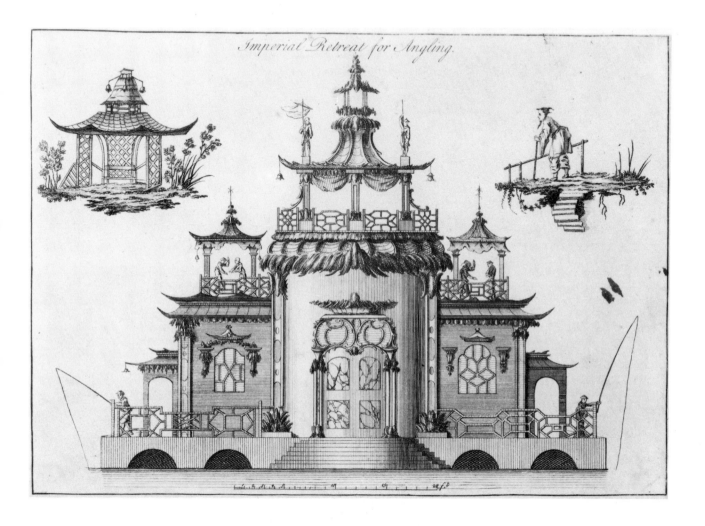

Imperial Retreat for Angling.

Imperial retreat for angling. Matthew Darly and George Edwards. See Cat. R9.

R1 *Tea Canister*

Paul De Lamerie (1688-1751). London
hallmarks for 1747/8
Silver-gilt; gilding renewed; h. 140
Engraved with an unidentified
coat of arms
The Worshipful Company of Goldsmiths

Cast, chased and embossed, originally
one of a pair. Oblong with rippled
angles, the shoulders topped with
helmeted putti. The side panels depict
a Chinaman cutting sugarcane
between a palm and a nut tree, the
end panels a coconut palm above a
hut, all on matted grounds, below
central moth-like scalloped wings. The
handle of the hinged lid is two cast
tea-plant sprays on a matted ground.
Figure panels on Chinese themes,
peculiarly appropriate to a tea
equipage, such as growing and
consuming tea and sugar, occur on
De Lamerie's silver from early in the
1740s. A tea service purchased from
De Lamerie for David Franks of
Philadelphia between 1742 and 1744
(tea and sugar canisters, bowl, kettle
on stand, basket and salver, split
between various American collections)
uses the same elements of baroque
helmeted putti, coconut palms and
Chinese scenes as this canister.
Identical pairs (1744) and another with
a sugar box (1747 and 1750) are
known (Grimwade 1974, pl. 66B).
Many goldsmiths picked up the
Chinese theme from the late 1740s.
The seven-piece Oranjenbaum tea and
coffee service at the Hermitage is the
work of three goldsmiths (Heming,
Fuller White and Sprimont; c. 1745-
1758) united by its Chinese figure
scenes. Peter Kaell Green cites other
examples.

Prov: John Dunn Gardner
Lit: Carrington and Hughes 1926,
p. 98, pl. 64; Goldsmiths's Hall 1951,
no. 241; Phillips 1958, pl. CLIV;
Kaellgren 1982; McNab Dennis 1967
PG

R2 *Pair of Busts of Mongolians*

Bow *c.* 1750-54
Glazed white soft-paste porcelain
containing bone-ash; h. of man 274;
h. of woman 267
*Geoffrey Freeman collection of Bow Porcelain
on loan to Pallant House Gallery, Chichester.*

He wears a cap with many projecting
points each terminating in a pom-
pom, a lace collar and a tunic with
elaborate frogging; she wears a
plumed cap with pom-poms and a
fur-fringed jacket with embroidered
frogging. Each on a rocaille-moulded
socle terminating in a mullet-shaped
base. Dr Bellamy Gardner (1929
p. 260) was surely right in reclaiming
these spirited early Bow busts, which
had become known to Collectors as
'the Roumanian (or Hungarian)
Minister and his wife' as fanciful
chinoiserie productions. Adams and
Redstone (1981 p. 142) claim the
Mongolian busts as 'examples of
excellent modelling which has nothing
in common with the Muses figures'
though the apparent difference may,
in the opinion of the present writer,
have more to do with scale and
subject-matter than with style.

Prov: Lord Suffield Collection, Gunton
Park, sale by Ireland's 16 September,
1980 774
Lit: Adams & Redstone 1981, p. 142
and fig. 69; Gabszewicz & Freeman
1982; Gardner 1929, p. 26, pl. VII;
George 1982, No. 63; Hackenbroch
1957, fig. 242 and pl. 79; King 1925,
fig 4; Savage 1952, pl. 42
JVGM

R3 *Design for a Seat at Strawberry Hill*

Richard Bentley (1708-1782). *c.* 1753
Pen and ink; 200 x 255.
Inscribed with title
Lewis Walpole Library, Yale University

This drawing is taken from Walpole's
folio scrapbook *Drawings and Designs by
Richard Bentley* (p. 33). T. Morris
engraved only the front view for the
1784 description of Walpole's villa
(p. 82). The unengraved side view
nicely emphasises the depth of
Bentley's rococo innovation. Carved in
oak (1754), but symmetrically with a
flat bench like seat, not as Bentley had
designed it, the seat was placed at 'the
end of the winding walk' in the
southeast corner of the garden where
it is shown in 'View of the Shell Seat',
a watercolour and chalk drawing by
J.H. Muntz (1755), and in the 'General
Ground Plot of the Gothic Mansion'
c. 1790. Both pasted into Walpole's
extra-illustrated 1784 description.
Possible sources are Botticellis's *Birth of
Venus,* Jacques de Lajoue's *rocaille*
decorations (engraved by Huquier) in
*Livre nouveau de divers morceaux de
fantaisie* (1736), and the shell cartouche
shown in a print of Thomas Howard,
Duke of Norfolk, engraved in 1735 for
Houbraken's Heads, (see Cat. D7) a
copy of which Walpole owned. Below
the portrait a weeping child sits in a
shell. On 2 June 1759, Walpole wrote
to Montagu that 'Strawberry Hill is
grown a perfect Paphos' for there
'never was so pretty a sight' as to see
the Countess of Ailesbury and the
Duchesses of Hamilton and
Richmond seated in Bentley's shell: 'a
thousand years hence . . . I shall . . .
tell young people how much
handsomer the women of my time
were . . .' (Lewis 1937, 9.237, 10.93,
168).

Prov: Horace Walpole; Strawberry Hill
Sale vii, 57 to William Knight; Spenser
(bookseller) to W.S. Lewis, 1926;
bequeathed by W.S. Lewis to Yale,
1979
Lit: Hazen 1969, .3585; Lewis 1934,
pp. 85, 87; Toynbee 1972, pp. 5, 65;
Walpole 1784 p. 82
LJ

R4 *Master's Chair of the Joiners' Company*

Mahogany with leather upholstery.
1550 x 690 x 990
On the back a brass plaque inscribed,
*This chair was carved in 1754 by Edward
Newman.*

*The Worshipful Company of Joiners and
Ceilers*

The scrolling crest rail with scallop-
shell cartouche is surmounted by the
Company's coat-of-arms and
supporters, (some of this carving now
missing). The uprights are formed as
scroll-edged pilasters ornamented with
quatrefoils, and fleuron finials. The
design of the back is essentially
formed as a two-tiered triple arcade of
gothic arches crowned by crocketed
pinnacles, the whole rising from a
central splat framed by angled
pilasters. The many C-scrolls of which
this complex design is formed are
ornamented with acanthus and
dripwork. The arms terminate in lion
heads. The seat frame, legs and
stretchers display a variety of blind
tracery. Edward Newman, chairmaker
of Golden Square, Liveryman of the
Joiners' Company in 1720, and Master
in 1749, supplied this 'Proper
Handsome Master's Chair' for the
Court Parlour, at a price of £27.6.0.

273

He also supplied furniture to the Vintners Company 1741/3 and to Temple Newsam House, Leeds in 1753. In 1754 Horace Walpole had designed a parlour chair, whose back is based relatively accurately on Gothic window tracery. By comparison the rusticated hybrid gothicism of Newman's chair is flamboyantly rococo.

Lit: Edwards 1924, Vol. I, p. 283, fig. 181; Edwards and Jourdain, 1955, p. 101, p. 237, fig. 225
JH

R5 *Punch pot*
Staffordshire. c. 1755-60
White salt-glazed stoneware painted with Chinese figures in landscapes in overglaze enamel red, blue, pink, yellow, green and blackish brown colours; h. 188, diam. 178
VAM (c. 81 & A - 1938)

The asymmetric cartouches round the lid, the bizarre chinoiserie figures are all rococo features. The crabstock spout and handles derive from Chinese Yixing red stonewares.

Prov: Wallace Elliot Bequest
Lit: Charleston & Scheurleer 1978, pl. 36
MA

R6 *Title page*
Jean Pillement (1728-1808). 1755
Etching and engraving; 425 x 262
Lettered *A New Book of Chinese Ornaments Invented & Engraved by J. Pillement. J. Pillement inv. & Sculp* and with a copyright line dated 1755
VAM (28639.A)

Pillement, born in Lyons, the centre of the French silk industry, worked as a textile designer at the Gobelins factory and elsewhere, and as a decorative painter in Spain and Portugal in the 1740s. His first suites of prints seem to

have been published in England, including this suite and *A New Book of Chinese Designs* published in 1755 by D. Voisin, a printseller in Holborn (Yale Center for British Art, L. 210.14, 80), which may indicate that Pillement had arrived in London by that date. Between 1757 and 1761 many suites and individual prints after his designs and paintings were published in London and (perhaps simultaneously) in Paris (see Berlin 1939, 449). They included Italianate landscapes as well as Chinese figures and chinoiserie grotesques of the type shown here, the most notable being *Etudes de differentes figures Chinoises*, 1758 and an untitled suite of large Chinese figures emblematic of the months, published 1 March 1759. Most characteristic, however, are the prints of flowers, many of them imaginary, at least four suites of which, engraved by P.C. Canot, were published in the summer of 1760, aimed principally at the textile market. Also published in 1760 was a suite of flowers engraved by Anne Allen, who later married the artist. The trade card of Wickes and Netheron (Barr 1980, fig. 108) includes similar fantasy flowers but certainly pre-dates the published suites, so may have been designed by Pillement, as may Cat. R7c, which shows flowers of the same character. Pillement seems to have left England in about 1760, but he exhibited landscapes sporadically in London until 1780.
MS

R7 *Trade cards and ephemera*
The Trustees of the British Museum, unless otherwise stated

a) John Oliver, coffin plate chaser. Matthew Darly after I. Rousset. *c.* 1755? (Heal 124.56). An example of a popular type of trade card, often chinoiserie, in which the side elements incorporate trees (see also Cat. R7c). It was re-used by Robert Legg, upholder, and has been mistakenly attributed to Chippendale. (Gilbert 1978, p. 7, pl. 14).

b) John Platt, cabinet maker, chair maker and upholder. Matthew Darly and George Edwards (1694-1773). *c.* 1755? (Heal 28.175) A chinoiserie card incorporating figures similar to

those in Cat. R9. A 'Mr Platts' subscribed to the 2nd edition of Chippendale's *Director*, 1755. (Heal 1953, repr. p. 140).

c) Invitation card to Caesar Crouch's at the Black Swan. Matthew Darly after Thomas Chippendale (1718-1779). *c.* 1754. (*The Chippendale Society*). Crouch was a cabinet maker who had subscribed to Chippendale's *Director* in 1754. He took in charitable subscriptions on Chippendale's behalf when the latter's workshops in St Martin's Lane were damaged by fire in 1755. (Gilbert 1978, I, pp. 10-11, II, pl. 12). The design of the card is similar to Cat. R7a. An impression in the Banks Collection is inscribed '1791 (suppose very old?)'.

d) William Henshaw, cabinet maker. Morrison (active 1760s). After 1753 (Heal 28.90). A design with some chinoiserie elements. The ribband-back chair in the centre is taken from Chippendale's *Director*, 1753, pl. XVI or a later edition. (Heal 1953, p. 79 repr.).

e) Simon Lesage, goldsmith and jeweller. Anonymous. *c.* 1755-60 (Heal 67.259). The flowers are very close to those after Pillement published in 1760, and used on a trade card before that date (see Cat. R6). Lesage was made free in 1755 and left off business in 1761 (Grimwade 1976, pp. 580-581).

f) Richard Coffin, print seller and seller of coffee, chocolate, tea, china and glass, of Broad Gate, Exeter. Probably by Richard Coffin (active 1759-1770). *c.* 1765? (Heal 59.39). The Chinese figures and cartouche are taken from two plates in J.E. Nilson's *Caffe, The und Tobac Zieretten* (see also Cat. P1.). In 1772 Coffin published a print of William Peckitt's west window in Exeter Cathedral, made in 1766.

g) Dominicus Negri, confectioner. J. Fougeron probably after Pierre-Edmé Babel (1720-1770). The firm was founded in 1757; for other work by Babel see Cat. L22. (Heal 1925, pl. XX; Dasent 1920, p. 218).

h) William Webb, garden chair maker. Anonymous. *c.* 1790? (Banks 28.148). Shown on the card are various types including gothic and windsor chairs and a rural seat made of rough branches. (Heal 1953, p. 197).

i) Henry Scott, nurseryman, at Weybridge, Surrey. Francis Vivares (1707-1780) after Samuel Wale (?1721-1786). 1754. (Heal 74.39). Scott and the figures of the Four Elements are shown in a garden. The scene, which is lettered 'Henry Scott invt.' is framed in restrained strapwork. Some figures and settings were used again on the card of James Gordon, seedsman. MS

R8 *A garden with a gothic temple*

Thomas Robins (1715/16-1770)
Later 1750s.
Body- and water-colour on vellum;
417 x 620
Private collection

Robins was a fan painter and a botanical and topographical artist. His views of gardens are the best surviving record of that whimsical gardening style, with its winding paths and scattering of Chinese, gothic and other structures, which has been called rococo. The location of this curious steepled garden building has not been determined, but it is almost certainly in the lower Thames Valley. The building is in the lighter and more correct gothic style which was promoted by, among others, Horace Walpole and his friends, and which replaced the clumsier gothic of William Kent. Robins was using rococo ornaments in his drawings in 1748; the open-work tendril frame of this drawing is characteristic of his paintings of the 1750s.

Lit: Harris 1978, I pp. 34-5, II pl. 10
MS

R9 *Imperial Retreat for Angling*

Matthew Darly (1741-1780) and George Edwards (1694-1773). 1754, with additions of 1759
Etching and engraving; 187 x 251
Lettered with title and numbered.
VAM (29347-4)

From *Chinese Architecture, Civil and Ornamental . . . by P. Decker Architect*, 1759, a collection of reissues, with additions, of plates originally published in Darly and Edwards's *A New Book of Chinese Designs, Calculated to Improve the present Taste*, 1754. This plate was no. 103 in the latter, described as a 'Water Summer House'. Decker (probably a pseudonym) added two details and a scale. *The New Book*, both the earliest and one of the finest chinoiserie pattern books, coincided with the height of the craze about 1750. It included flowers and landscapes close to Chinese originals as well as more fanciful and rococo buildings, and root and other furniture. Edwards was an eminent ornithologist and book illustrator, but Darly and Edwards's joint productions, which began in the early 1750s and included printed ephemera and satirical prints, do not differentiate between their individual contributions. Darly's own career as an engraver seems to have begun in 1741 with satirical prints; he became the most prolific engraver in the field in the later 1750s. His activities as an engraver of furniture designs began with his own suite in 1751 (Cat. L21). He engraved plates for Chippendale's *Director* in 1753 (when he seems to have been sharing a house with Chippendale), for Ince and Mayhew, 1759-60 (Cat. M21) and for the collection of designs for the Society of Upholsterers published by Robert Sayer in 1760. In 1771 he styled himself 'The Political Designer of Pots, Pans and Pipkins'. His later work concentrated on neo-classical architecture and ornament; from 1765 he called himself 'Professor and Teacher of Ornament'.

Lit: Atherton 1974; Gilbert 1975; Gilbert 1978, pp. 5-7; Ward-Jackson 1958, p. 37
MS

R10 *Epergne*

Thomas Pitts I (active 1744-1773)
London hallmarks for 1762/3
Silver; h 673
The Colonial Williamsburg Foundation

Cast, chased and pierced. An openwork floral frame on four scrolled legs, rising to a central pierced basket surrounded by four scrolled branches with detachable saucers; four slender vine-entwined columns rise to support a bell-hung pagoda-like canopy with a pineapple on top, between four further columns supporting a second smaller pagoda canopy. Removable scrolled plugs on the legs conceal sockets for a lower tier of baskets, or perhaps for candle-holders. The chinoiserie element, that is the double bell-hung pagoda canopy, is superimposed on a centre-piece whose form had been well-established in English silver for at least twenty years. The maker Thomas Pitts specialised in epergnes and at least twelve made after 1761 with identical feet and frames, the feet related to designs by Lock published in 1746 (Cat. L18, pl. 2 and 5), are known although three only of these have pagoda canopies and two, openwork pagodas. The basic canopied form was familiar from Kent's design (published 1744) and had been anticipated in Paris-made epergnes (Cat. A10). Lock and Copland could have supplied the source for the entwined columns; e.g. *A New Book of Ornaments* 1752 (pl. 3, Cat. L24).

Prov: Christie's, 14 May 1902, 117.
Lit: Davis 1976, p. 111-113; Gaines 1965, 462-65; Gaines 1967, 748-53; Heckscher 1979, Vol. XV, 1-24
PG

R11 *Shutter panel*
Luke Lightfoot (1722-1789). *c. 1765*
Carved pine; 1465 x 470
The National Trust (Claydon House)

The adjoining gothic and Chinese
rooms at Claydon are both decorated
with astonishing carved woodwork by
Luke Lightfoot (see Cat. M25). They
show how the rococo could assimilate
other styles with ease and demonstrate
how well-suited it was to the bizarre
and exotic fantasies of the mid-century
reaction against the dictatorial
Palladianism of Lord Burlington. The
three shallow domes in the ceiling of
the gothic room are adorned with little
tabernacles or temples, behind which
trees are growing. The shutters are
carved with the same sort of ogival
panels, scrolls and crockets. They are
far from the archaeological accuracy of
Strawberry Hill, and are used purely
as light-hearted surface decoration.

Lit: Jackson-Stops 1981, pp. 23, 29.
G J-S

R12 *Printed cotton furnishing:*
'*Chinese Figures*'
After Jean Pillement (1728-1808).
Printed at Bromley Hall after 1774.
Cotton plate-printed in blue, blue
threads in the selvedge; 1900 x 720.
Museum of Fine Arts, Boston
Mrs. Samuel Cabot's Special Fund
(47.1549)

Two Chinese figures with a parasol
mount an unsupported stair to a
pagoda hung with bells. They are in
the curve of a large fantastic plant of a
type made popular by Pillement's
Fleurs de Caprice and *Fleurs de Fantasie
dans le goût chinois*, of 1760. The design
is close to Pillement's compositions
published in *The Ladies Amusement* of
Robert Sayer, first edition 1759 or

early 1760, known from the second
edition of 1762. It is possible that
Pillement drew some designs for
English textile manufacturers, but
more likely that his designs were
plagiarised. This, if an imitation, is a
particularly fine one.

Lit: VAM 1960, cat. 91
WH

276

Sculpture

Design for the monument to General Wolfe. T. Cook after L.F. Roubiliac. See Cat. S42.

Rococo styles in eighteenth century English sculpture

Malcolm Baker

1. Monument to Jane Rodney, Alresford, Hants. Attributed to Sir Henry Cheere.

2. Monument to Katherine Bovey, Westminster Abbey. By James Gibbs and Michael Rysbrack, *c.* 1727.

In August 1742 the *Gentleman's Magazine* published some verses entitled 'Greenwood Hall or Colin's Description (to his Wife) of the Pleasures of Spring Gardens' in which the naive observer describes the wonders of Vauxhall, among them Roubiliac's statue of Handel (Cat. F10).

> As still amaz'd, I'm straying / O'er this inchanted grove, / I spy a HARPER playing / All in his proud alcove. / I doff my hat, desiging / He'd tune up BUXOM JOAN / But what was I admiring! / Odzooks! a man of stone.

As well as playing on a familiar 18th century antithesis between town and country, more subtly developed by Pope in his *Epistle to Miss Blount on her leaving Town after the Coronation*, the author is here employing a commonplace about statues being mistaken for living figures that occurs frequently in accounts of sculpture. Conventional though it is, however, the surprise registered here may also be interpreted as a recognition of the dramatic and illusionistic qualities of the first fully-fledged example of the rococo in English sculpture. The spectator is thus shown responding to the effects of verisimilitude achieved through the startling informality of the sitter's dress, with its unbuttoned shirt and loose slippers, his jaunty, asymmetrical pose and the virtuoso carving of the drapery, suggesting a shifting play of light on a figure who is just about to change his position.

These qualities together constitute a rococo figure style distinct from the late baroque manner that had held sway until the Handel was executed in 1738. However, whereas most of the applied art in this exhibition draws on a readily recognisable vocabulary of rococo ornament, none of these motifs is found on the Handel or indeed on most of Roubiliac's sculpture. Thus, despite the apparently obvious rococo nature of the Handel statue, the definition of the rococo in sculpture is more intangible than in other areas. To what extent did any distinctively rococo sculpture exist in England? What different manifestations did it take? In what ways does English rococo differ from rococo sculpture in France and Germany?

The existence of a rococo style distinct from the late baroque manner that dominated English sculpture in the early 18th century may be seen by comparing Sir Henry Cheere's monument to Jane Rodney at Alresford (Hants) (Fig. 1) with Rysbrack's monument to Katherine Bovey (d. 1724) in Westminster Abbey designed by Gibbs and included in his *Book of Architecture* in 1728 (Fig. 2). The Rysbrack represents a classicizing version of late baroque that is fundamentally Flemish though the models for the design lie in Florentine late baroque sculpture and earlier Roman papal monuments.[1] The female allegories seated on the sarcophagus have draperies with broad diagonal folds while the architecture is grand and substantial. The same pattern is used by Cheere but the draperies of the figures are now broken into small folds and their forms made lighter. More significantly, however, the weighty architecture has been replaced by something more fanciful while the coloured marbles and delicate ornamental details give it an essentially decorative quality. But in this respect the Cheney monument differs not only from the Bovey but also from Roubiliac's Montagu or Nightingale monuments. Even in this work, the figure style plays a lesser role than the decorative elements.

From this comparison it is apparent that a shift in taste did indeed take place in English sculpture in the mid 18th century but this was not simple or consistent. Although the rococo became the dominant style between about 1740 and 1760 it remained only one of various alternatives and itself had different manifestations. Some of the various possibilities are seen in three standing figures shown in contemporary dress: Rysbrack's Sloane (c.1737; Fig. 3), Cheere's Pole (1745-6; fig. 4) and Roubiliac's Cass (1751; fig. 5). Rysbrack's figure is shown in a relaxed but static pose, his coat and gown casually arranged but falling in broad folds in an Antwerp late baroque manner. By contrast, Roubiliac's Cass is shown apparently moving forwards, his gaze fixed ahead and his clothes untidily crumpled with broken outlines and irregular surfaces. The Pole is also recognisably rococo but, unlike Roubiliac's figure, through essentially decorative devices, such as the undulating edge of the coat, the ornament of the cuffs and coat. Cheere's figure also differs from the others in the rather cruder cutting of the face which reflects the sculptor's training in the tradition of the earlier English mason-sculptors. Indeed, despite its rococo features, the Pole is best seen as a direct descendent of the standing figures on English monuments by sculptors such as Stanton.

The full length statue was well-established elsewhere in Europe but these English examples are unusual in that they are of figures other than monarchs, nobility or military heroes,[2] and they reflect the distinctive nature of English society in the 18th century. The patronage of sculptors was not dominated by the court or the church but by the middle and professional classes and this, together with the attitudes to images implicit in a protestant tradition, meant that the classes of sculpture required in England differed markedly from those that enjoyed popularity in France or Germany. Nothing equivalent to the elaborate programme of garden sculpture at Marly or the altarpieces at Berg am Leim is to be found in England, sculptors here found opportunities to develop original and distinctive types, above all, in the form of portrait busts and monuments. The classicizing portrait bust, which developed at such an early date in England, has been recognised as an expression of the aspirations and sense of identity of one section of English society. In a comparable way the forms and conventions developed by sculptors working in a rococo style may be regarded as a response to the attitudes of a rather different social group.

The pattern of patronage underlying the evolution of rococo sculpture in England has yet to be systematically analysed but certain sections of society appear to have cultivated the new style. Not surprisingly, the Huguenot community played a major role and many of Roubiliac's most substantial commissions came through this group. Some of these were professional figures, particularly doctors, and so also belonged to another circle important for rococo portrait sculptors. There also seem to have been close connections between Cheere's patrons and Roubiliac's. The related families of Brownlow, Cust and Bertie commissioned monuments from Roubiliac, Cheere and Roubiliac's follower, Tyler as well as paintings by Mercier (Cat. C2) and Hogarth. The commissioning of sculptors working

3. Sir Hans Sloane, Chelsea Physick Garden. By Michael Rysbrack, c. 1737.

4. William Pole. Shute, Devon. Probably by Richard Hayward working in the studio of Sir Henry Cheere, c. 1745.

5. Sir John Cass. Cass Institute, London.
By Louis François Roubiliac, c. 1751.

in a rococo manner did not preclude the employment of artists working in a late baroque style. The pattern of patronage, like the stylistic account apparent from Vertue's notebooks, suggests that contemporaries made no clear distinction between rococo and late baroque.

Another social factor of importance in the emergence of the rococo in sculpture was the nature of the activities at Vauxhall over which Roubiliac's Handel presided. As a place of illusion, fantasy and amusement (all present in Colin's description) Vauxhall gave Roubiliac a freedom to evolve new forms that were not possible in the 1730s either in an ecclesiastical setting or even a country house interior. The close association of this emergent style with Vauxhall meant that it was developed within a close and relatively small group of artists, writers and musicians and it is therefore probably no coincidence that the subjects of most of the early rococo portrait busts are of sitters associated with the arts, rather than the nobility.

Associated with the pattern of patronage and the links between artists in different media is the changing position of the sculptor in relationship to architects and craftsmen in the decorative arts. It is significant that Roubiliac, Taylor and Cheere frequently sign their monuments 'invenit' as well as 'sculpsit' for, unlike Rysbrack, many of whose monuments were executed to the designs of architects, those sculptors responsible for developing the rococo style in England appear to have conceived their works as integral wholes. The integration of architectural, ornamental and figurative elements is indeed one of the characteristics of the rococo style not only in England but also in France and Germany.

The unity of the various visual arts is also reflected in the close collaboration between sculptors, goldsmiths and others in works such as Clay's 'Temple of the Four Monarchies' in which Amiconi, Roubiliac and Rysbrack combined with a silversmith and the maker of the machinery that played music composed by Handel and Corelli. The extent of the involvement of sculptors in such projects is as yet unclear but a number of specific connections and the geographical proximity of the various workshops suggest that this may have been more extensive than has usually been assumed. Roubiliac apparently purchased bronzes from his fellow Huguenot, Pierre Harrache,[3] a goldsmith, while the strangely German qualities of Channon's furniture may possibly be explained by the closeness of his workshop to that of the Dresden-trained sculptor.[4] Although the association with Roubiliac of designs for certain figures thought to be Chelsea has now been convincingly rejected, Roubiliac's personal links with Sprimont still make his involvement in this area a possibility. A connection with porcelain factories may also perhaps be implied by the sculptor's apparent familiarity with piece moulding techniques. Whereas Rysbrack regarded the taking of plaster casts as 'entirely out of my way'[5] Roubiliac's use of plaster and casting techniques for both busts and models is evident from the 1762 sale catalogue and indeed from surviving works executed in the mid 1740s (Cat. S6).

The most important documentary source for the emergence of the rococo style is in the notebooks of George Vertue who evidently came to know fellow artists such as Roubiliac well. From Vertue's extensive account of the Argyll monument it is clear that Roubiliac was recognised as the most deeply inventive and technically able sculptor at this date. Born in Lyons, probably in 1702, Roubiliac rather unusually received his early training in Dresden where a relative was a court official. He probably arrived there around 1718 where Balthasar Permoser and his workshop were completing the sculptural decoration of the Zwinger, one of the major complexes of late baroque sculpture north of the Alps, and may also have known Permoser's follower, Paul Egell who was to play a leading part in the evolution of the rococo style in German sculpture. Some time in the 1720s he arrived in Paris where it is likely that he worked under one of the Coustou brothers, the influence of whose drapery style may be seen later on the Argyll figures. This unusually varied training in which he would have become acquainted with current developments in two of the most vital centres of sculptural activity in the early eighteenth century appears to have been supplemented by a knowledge, either through prints or at first hand, of Roman late baroque. Together these factors may in part account for those exceptional qualities that distinguish Roubiliac's work from that of his more straightforward Flemish-trained contemporaries.

No works executed by Roubiliac in France (with the possible exception of a drawing in the École des Beaux Arts, Paris) have been traced but in 1730 he was awarded second prize by the Academie Royal for his Daniel Saving Susannah. Between this date and his marriage to Catherine Helot in 1735 he moved to London and, according to Vertue at first received little encouragement. Several nineteenth century sources record that he worked for Thomas Carter and then for Henry Cheere but it is difficult to detect Roubiliac's role in any works by these sculptors during the 1730s. Although various works have been attributed to him in his early years in England, his first certain sculpture is the Handel statue. Two lost works from the same year were a marble Venus made for Sir Andrew Fountaine and a group of Tarquin and Lucretia about which a poem was published in 1738. The latter is probably the 'gentleman surprising a lady on a couch' of which moulds appear in the 1762 catalogue (4th day, lot 70) and the group of which was a subject for figure drawings submitted to the Society of Arts in 1765.[6] The subject suggests that this is a group in the same late baroque tradition as both the Daniel composition and the Hercules and Atlas bronze surmounting the Temple of the Four Monarchies which was also probably executed during the late 1730s. Following the success of the Handel, Vertue lists in 1738 and 1741 various busts including Pope (Cat. S5), Hogarth (Cat. E2), Ware (Cat. E15) and Handel. Rather surprisingly, however, little is known of Roubiliac's activities in the early 1740s, the only recorded works being lost portraits of 'worthies' which Pope inspected at the sculptor's workshop on behalf of his friend Ralph Allen, whose house at Bath they were intended to decorate.[7] During this period, however, he presumably received the commission for the Hough monument at Worcester, finished in April 1747, though the circumstances of this important project, which was Roubiliac's first important monument in England, have yet to be investigated. Although the fame of the Handel statue and even the knowledge of his work on the Hough tomb may both have had some influence, it is equally uncertain how the sculptor received the commission for the Argyll monument in 1745. By the late 1740s Roubiliac began to receive commissions for the various large-scale portraits that begin with Lady Murray in 1747 (Cat. S6), continue with Folkes (Cat. S11) and Swift (Cat. S10) and culminate in the Trinity College series (Cat. S34, S35) in the 1750s. The success of the Argyll monument, of 1749, apparently led to Roubiliac being chosen for monuments in Westminster

Abbey and elsewhere, beginning with the Duke of Montagu's at Warkton (Cat. S14, S15), that is among the most inventive achievements in 18th century English art and in contemporary European sculpture.

Another figure who made a contribution to the rococo style in England who occurs in Vertue is the medallist Jacques Antoine Dassier. Born in Geneva in 1715 he came to England in 1740. In that year Vertue reports his projected series of medals of 'famous men then living in England'.

Informative though Vertue is, his notebooks give a somewhat partial account of the figures involved with the rococo style in sculpture. Seeing a rise in the standard of the visual arts in England as concomitent with an improvement in the status and training of artists he tends to neglect figures who were trained in the English tradition of the mason-sculptor. As a result the contributions of Sir Henry Cheere, William Collins and especially Sir Robert Taylor have not received their full due.

Cheere was apprenticed to Robert Hartshorne in 1711 and by 1726 had established his own workshop near St Margaret's Westminster.[8] By 1729 he was working with Henry Scheemakers, with whom he signed various monuments including that to the 1st Duke of Ancaster at Edenham. Although Scheemakers vanishes after 1733, the fundamentally Flemish design of their joint works remains a feature of Cheere's later work. Another continuing thread in Cheere's career was the connection with the Abbey and its masons, particularly the Tufnell family. However, despite the sparseness of Vertue's references to him, Cheere also seems to have been associated with the St Martins Lane set, thus apparently belonging to two different circles that only slightly overlapped. As early as 1734 a lightness of drapery anticipating the rococo appears in the Codrington statue at All Souls, Oxford[9] and this was developed during the 1740s in monuments such as that to Bishop Willis at Winchester and the statue of Sir George Cooke and its reliefs at Stoke Park, which has sometimes been attributed to Roubiliac (fig. 6). The most clearly rococo of Cheere's works appear in the late 1740s in a series of monuments in Westminster Abbey which appointed him 'carver' in 1743. The essentially decorative nature of these works is continued with variations in the many monuments and chimneypieces produced by his large workshop during the 1750s and 60s. By this date, however, Cheere's involvement in financial and political affairs meant that much of his work must have been left to assistants, among them Richard Hayward, who probably executed the Pole,[10] and William Collins. Although little is known of this latter figure, J.T. Smith's praise of his reliefs, their exhibition at the Society of Artists in the early 1760s and the quality of the plaster relief at Magdalen College, Cambridge suggests that he probably played an important role in both the design and execution of the central parts of many of Cheere's chimneypieces and some monuments.

Sir Robert Taylor came from the same mason-sculptor background as Cheere and like him acquired considerable wealth and a knighthood. The son of a Master of the London Masons Company, Taylor was apprenticed to Cheere and was working for him in 1736-7.[11] Shortly afterwards, however, he travelled to Rome and, unlike his master, apparently became acquainted at first hand with recent architecture and sculpture in France and Italy. On his return he was chosen in 1744 to execute the Mansion House pediment (almost certainly because of his city connections) and in 1747 given by Parliament the commission for the monument to Captain

6. Relief from the monument to Sir George Cooke (d. 1740), Stoke Park, Northants. Attributed to Sir Henry Cheere.

Cornewall. The originality of his architecture, to which he devoted much of his energies later in his career, has recently been made clear by Marcus Binney but his sculpture has received little attention. However, his designs for monuments that survive in the Institution founded with money left by him (significantly perhaps for the study of *European* languages) show a thorough understanding of rococo style that occurs in the work of no other sculptor working in England except Roubiliac. Despite Vertue's silence and the poor execution of his surviving works he may be regarded as a major figure in the evolution of the rococo style in English sculpture.

Roubiliac remains the dominant and most richly inventive of these sculptors and the prominence given to him by Vertue no doubt reflects the impact of his work on contemporary observers. A different picture of the evolution of the rococo style from that based solely on Vertue emerges if we examine two major classes of sculpture, the bust and the monument, chronologically, rather than separated among the *œuvres* of different artists.

Although both Cheere and Roubiliac sometimes employed the classicizing convention used for Pope (Cat. S5), the type far more frequently adopted was the bust *en négligé*. This form, showing the sitter informally dressed with open shirt and the soft cap that would have replaced a wig, was initially considered appropriate for artists and poets. It was used by Jonathan Richardson for his self-portrait of 1717 and its adoption by sculptors was probably stimulated by Coyzevox's bust of Prior (cf. Cat. S29). Rysbrack portrayed Kneller in this way in 1730 and during the following decade the convention becomes more widespread. In its informality, however, it was especially suited to the rococo style and was developed by sculptors into a series of ever more virtuoso forms.

Among the earliest were Roubiliac's Handel and the brilliantly idiosyncratic portrait of Hogarth (1741). However, a wholly rococo version of the same convention had been evolved by Cheere as early as, if not earlier than, 1741 in his bust of George Pitt (Cat. S1). We know that the conception of this portrait involved the sitter's son John Pitt, an amateur architect of some distinction and probably in contact with artistic circles in London. It is significant that almost all these rococo busts *en negligé*, including Hogarth, Handel and Roubiliac's lost portrait of the castrato Farinelli, are of persons connected with the arts. Although there are French precedents for the sculptural use of the *en negligé* convention, these are relatively few (and include, perhaps significantly, an Englishman) and the possibilities for developing this convention in England, with its wider range of potential sitters, were considerably greater. In England the interconnecting worlds of St Martin's Lane, Vauxhall and the circle of the Italian opera in London in particular provided an especially sympathetic context in which it could evolve into a rococo form of a distinctively English type. Thus, while Roubiliac's Hogarth in its vitality recalls Coustou's portrait of his brother, neither the striking informality nor the wit in the decoration of the socle has any parallel in French sculpture.

Roubiliac further develops this convention in the busts of the late 1740s. However, some of the qualities of these are anticipated, even before the Hogarth, in Dassier's portrait of Martin Folkes, produced as the first of his 'eminent men' in 1740. Though of small size, the portrait is conceived on a broad scale and the modelling of both the face and the rippling drapery surfaces is rococo in the same way as Roubiliac's bust of the same sitter, executed nine years later. Many sitters were common to both artists and the likelihood that Dassier belonged to the Slaughter's set (suggested by both the references in Vertue and the patronage of sitters such as Abraham de Moivre) makes it probable that Roubiliac would have known these medals. It is tempting to think that the immediacy that could be achieved by modelling in wax (the preliminary process in producing a medal) would have appealed to a sculptor whose terracottas have a comparable spontaneity. Beginning with the Lady Murray (Cat. S6), Roubiliac's portraits from the late 1740s onwards are less intimate and on a larger scale than those of the early group; the *en negligé* form has now been transformed into a more powerful, but still informal form, though the distinctively English qualities remain. The Mrs Aufrere (Cat. S9), for example, recalls Boucher in his drapery configurations but has no equivalent among the more consciously grand female portraits by Le Moyne or Pigalle, though some by Adam are akin to it. The culmination of this development is Roubiliac's portrait of Wilton which, has the authority of one of the most original portraits of the eighteenth century.

The evolution of the rococo monument is more ambiguous and is perhaps best charted by looking chronologically at the examples in Westminster Abbey, though this excludes important works such as the Hough and Montagu monuments. The earliest works in the Abbey in which any recognisably rococo elements occur are those to Sir Thomas Hardy (Fig. 7) and John Conduitt by Henry Cheere. The 'fines' for both were paid in 1738 but neither is mentioned in the 1742 edition of the *Antiquities of St Peters*, suggesting that they were not yet completed. The cutting of Hardy's drapery already has small rococo folds, while the putto resembles those who play around the cartouches of Houbraken's *Heads* (Cat. D12), prints of which were circulating during the late 1730s. Similarly, the rocaille details on the feet and the cartouche above recall some motifs in Brunetti (Cat. B5, B6). However, despite these individual rococo features, the overall design follows a well-established baroque pattern, perhaps not surprisingly since the two monuments were clearly intended to balance Rysbrack's Newton (for which Conduitt paid) and Stanhope at the opposite end of the nave. Like most monuments before this date with the exception of the Newcastle tomb, these two Cheere works were designed to fit, at least approximately, with the scale of the Abbey's architecture. But with the completion of Roubiliac's Argyll monument in 1749 and Taylor's Cornewall in 1755 (described by Grosley in 1765 as a 'huge machine')[12] a scale of monument was introduced that anticipated the late 18th and early 19th century works that dominate the interior of the Abbey today.

In its dramatic intensity, swift movement and illusionistic drapery, so admired by Vertue, the Argyll monument contrasts strikingly with both the baroque manner of Rysbrack and the tentative rococo of Cheere. Although all its elements except the writing Fame may be paralleled in earlier monuments, the theatricality of the action and the virtuosity of the carving create an illusionistic effect characteristic of Vauxhall but unprecedented in the context of an English church. As yet we know little about the circumstances in which Roubiliac was awarded this much sought-after commission but it marks a turning point in the development of the English monument. In comparison the carving of the Cornewall monument (Fig. 8) appears very perfunctory, particularly in its present state, cut down and repositioned in an entrance to the cloisters instead of

7. Monument to Sir Thomas Hardy, Westminster Abbey. By Sir Henry Cheere, *c.* 1742.

near the West end of the nave where Grosley described it as 'the first that catches the eye'. Nevertheless the figures have a dramatic swiftness of movement akin to the Argyll while the palm and laurel trees 'both of which issue from the natural barren rock, as alluding to some heroic and uncommon event'[13] recall the tradition of French *pompes funèbres*.

The rococo quality of the Hardy, Argyll and Cornewall monuments lies in the figure style or overall conception rather than in any specifically rococo ornamental motifs. However, another distinctive variety of English rococo monument that involved prominent rococo decoration and which was to spread throughout the country through the smaller monuments of Cheere, Taylor and their followers, appears in the Abbey shortly before 1750. The earliest example is that to Archbishop Boulter (Fig. 9) who was 'translated to the Archbishop of Armagh 1723, and from thence to Heaven Sep.br the 27th 1742'. The fine was paid in 1745 and the monument said to be 'now erecting' in 1748; it was presumably completed shortly afterwards. In its fulsome account of 1754 the *Historical Description* describes it as 'of the finest Marble, and of new-invented Polish' and asserts that the 'Ensigns of his Dignity wherewithal the Monument is ornamented, are most exquisitely fine, and every part of it discovers a masterly Genius in the Sculptor'. Contemporary admiration for the monument is also reflected in Earl Verney's will of 1752 in which £200 is left for a monument 'after the model set up in Westminster Abbey for Archbishop Boulter'.[14] The elaborate, randomly placed attributes and coloured marbles to which the 1754 description is referring and which were presumably to be imitated for Verney are prominent features of a group of other Cheere monuments in the Abbey including the Atkyns (*c.* 1755), Prideaux (mid 1750s) and Sausmarez (mid 1750s) and occur on numerous Cheere works elsewhere. Surprisingly the one surviving drawing (Fig. 10) for the Boulter monument does not include any of these distinctive ornaments. However, they figure prominently in several designs by Taylor that may well represent unsuccessful schemes for the same project (Fig. 11). Although the Cheere drawing may of course be merely the simplest of various proposals, some of which did include elaborate ornament, it is also conceivable that some of the decorative devices that distinguish Taylor's designs were taken over by Cheere or at least acted as a stimulus to him. Cheere's connections with the Slaughter's group, his visit to Paris with Hayman and others in 1748 and the way in which some of the ornamental motifs on the Sausmarez monument appear to derive from the Houbraken *Heads* which appear complete in 1747, all indicate Cheere's active involvement in the mature rococo style around this period. Nevertheless, his designs are usually quite static and frequently lack asymmetry, consisting of conventional architectural forms in coloured marbles to which rococo ornament is applied. On the evidence of his remarkably inventive designs, Taylor, by contrast, seems by 1750 to have fully absorbed a variety of continental, particularly French, sources such as Oppenord and Meissonnier, both of whose works were in his library. Although the figural elements are often crudely executed, the rococo ornament on his monuments has not merely been applied externally but determines the conception as a whole. The Guest monument (fig. 12), completed in December 1751 and so probably almost contemporary with the Boulter, has a three-dimensional movement that is difficult to match in Cheere's work, except in the Sausmarez monument. Perhaps therefore

8. Monument to Captain James Cornewall, engraving in the London Magazine, 1755. After Sir Robert Taylor.

9. Monument to Archbishop Boulter, Westminster Abbey. By Sir Henry Cheere, *c.* 1748.

10. Design for the Boulter monument, Society of Antiquaries of London. By Sir Henry Cheere, *c.* 1745-48.

11. Design for the Boulter monument (?), Taylorian Institution, Oxford (fol. 136r). By Sir Robert Taylor, *c.*1745-48.

credit should be given to Taylor rather than Cheere for the creation of this ornamental type of English rococo monument.

This class of decorative rococo monument has much in common with contemporary plasterwork and even furniture, the *bombé* form of Taylor's sarcophagi being close to that used for rococo commodes. They may in one sense be interpreted as a reduced and contained form of rococo interior decoration transported into an ecclesiastical context, a transition that was possible only given certain underlying secular attitudes in the mid-eighteenth century English church. Another contrasting aspect of eighteenth-century spiritual life, however, finds expression in the monuments executed by Roubiliac in the Abbey during the 1750s, which represent a very different variety of rococo. In their treatment of eschatological themes, monuments such as the Hargrave and Nightingale (S40 and Fig. 13) that so impressed Wesley, are related to literature such as Young's *Night Thoughts* and conceits such as Denbies, Tyers's other garden devoted to the themes of death and melancholy.[15] Although possessing the verisimilitude seen in the Handel statue and illusionistic qualities characteristic of Vauxhall, these works also anticipate the Christian imagery that was to be developed for monuments at the end of the century. The same seriousness and intensity are apparent in Roubiliac's design for the Wolfe monument where the central group, no doubt coincidentally, recalls late medieval *Andachtsbilder* of angels with the dead Christ.[16] The successful design by Wilton in some ways looks forward in its use of modern dress to West's painting of the same subject while the almost nude figure anticipates Pigalle's slightly later statue of Voltaire. In the dramatic responses of its participants and its flurried drapery patterns however, it remains the Abbey's last rococo monument.

The differences between the types of monument evolved by Roubiliac, Cheere and Taylor are partly accounted for by the artists' diverse training and their different relationship to continental sculptural traditions. Although the imagery of Roubiliac's monuments results from the English cultural context in which he worked,[17] their scale and sophisticated figure style reveal a familiarity with both French and German court and ecclesiastical sculpture. Convincing connections, interestingly reciprocal, have been made between the monuments of Slodtz and Roubiliac.[18] However, the distinctive architectural elements in the latter's work, which are wholly rococo in their movement but rarely employ devices such as *rocaille*, seem to have more in common with German sculpture, presumably because of his Dresden training. For example, a slimmer version of the background to the Fleming monument appears in two of Straub's designs for the Graf Ignaz von Törring-Jettenbach.[19] Similarly, some of the frames, that ever-varying rococo form, of Roubiliac's smaller monuments resemble forms used in altarpieces or monuments by Egell, a fellow pupil of Permoser with whom Roubiliac has considerable affinities. Monuments do not constitute an important aspect of German sculpture so that close parallels are difficult to find. Nevertheless, it is only in Permoser or rococo altarpieces such as Rohr and Weltenberg that we encounter drama comparable to the Hargrave or Nightingale monuments. Both types of sculpture, in other ways so different, share the same total integration of figures and architecture. Although produced in a completely different context with different aims, Roubiliac's monuments may be seen as rococo in the same way as the work of the Assam brothers, Straub and Günther.

12. Monument to General Guest, Westminster Abbey. By Sir Robert Taylor, completed 1751.

By contrast, Taylor appears to draw on largely decorative sources, predominantly French, in which the figural elements are subsidiary. The way in which these are assimilated implies a first-hand knowledge of contemporary French work, to which Taylor's designs are the closest English equivalent. Cheere, on the other hand, though developing an accomplished rococo figure style, appears to base the decorative parts of his work mainly on sources available in England he applies these motifs to designs that develop from the native tradition in which he was trained. In such varying ways these sculptors adapted a range of sculptural traditions to meet different needs within the context of an English culture, thus producing a variety of rococo styles in sculpture.

If we turn again to the statue of Handel we see this same process at work. Modifying a drapery style in large part developed from that of Guillaume Coustou, Roubiliac gives it an informality unthinkable in France. Likewise he draws on a precedent such as the Parnasse François,[20] on which revered men of genius are gathered around Apollo, to portray a composer still alive who, though middle-aged, is playfully shown as Apollo, parodying the tradition of representing monarchs in the guise of gods. Combining diverse elements such as these in a cultural and social setting quite distinct from that in any continental country, English sculpture made its own varied, idiosyncratic and often subtle contribution to European rococo.

13. Monument to Mr and Mrs Nightingale, Westminster Abbey, By Louis François Roubiliac, 1761.

S1 *George Pitt MP*

Sir Henry Cheere (1703-81) *c.* 1738-41
Marble bust; h. 575
VAM (A.7-1981)

Formerly known as a portrait of the poet Matthew Prior by Roubiliac, this bust is a more finely finished version of the portrait on the monument to George Pitt (?1663-1735) at Stinsford, Dorset. Pitt was MP for various Dorset and Hampshire constituencies between 1694 and 1727; a distant relative of William Pitt, Earl of Chatham, he was the father of John Pitt, a distinguished amateur architect. Between August 1738 and April 1741 three payments, amounting to £146.8.0, were made to Henry Cheere by Pitt's widow from her account at Hoare's Bank; these probably refer to the bust, the monument and perhaps some chimney pieces at Enscombe House, designed by John Pitt from 1734 onwards. The version shown here was probably executed for the house, being less summary in its modelling than that on the monument. According to Hutchins (1792, II p. 164) the bust on the monument was 'executed from a model made after his death from recollection by his son John Pitt'. Although the monument is based on a design in Gibbs's *Book of Architecture* (1728, p. 123) the bust is far less conventional. The informal male portrait, with open shirt and loose cap was established in England by the mid 1720s, but the decorative effect of the shirt front and the fluttering tie are signs of a newly adopted rococo manner. With Roubiliac's Hogarth (Cat. E2), this is among the earliest of English rococo busts. Within the context of Cheere's own work the drapery style may be paralleled by the figure of Sir Thomas Hardy in Westminster Abbey (executed *c.* 1740) and the bust of Sir Orlando Humphreys (died 1736) at Barking.

Prov: W. Moreton Pitt; Street of Brewer Street; Webb; Duke of Buckingham; Stowe sale, 1848, 751; Sir Robert Peel; Peel Heirlooms sale, 10 May 1900, 133; Duveen; unknown private collection; John Pinkerton, from whom it was purchased by the Museum.
Lit: Esdaile 1928, p. 52; Baker 1983 (2); Sainte-Croix 1882, p. 108
MCB

S1

S2 *The Temple of the Four Monarchies*

C. Grignion after H. Gravelot
Engraving; 440 x 262
Lettered *H. Gravelot, delin.* and *C. Grignion, Sculpt.*
Royal Borough of Kensington and Chelsea, Libraries & Arts Services (Local Studies Section QGC 2233)

The clock illustrated here survives in a modified form in the Royal Collection at Kensington Palace. Another impression of the engraving (see Cat. G46) is accompanied by a French translation of an English advertisement dated 31 December 1743 (*Lyson's Collecteana*, British Museum, 1889 e 5) which describes 'a most magnificent and curious MUSICAL MACHINE CALL'D The Temple of the Four Monarchies of the World . . . Begun by the late ingeneous Mr CHARLES CLAY, and finish'd by Mr PYKE'. This extensive account describes the group of 'Hercules taking the celestial globe off the shoulders of Atlas compos'd and executed by Mons. Roubiliac' and 'the four Figures likewise in Bronze, being Emblems of the four Monarchies . . . also by Mons. Roubiliac', the four 'Avenues' containing 'the subjects relating to each Monarchy finely represented in Historical Paintings by Signior Amiconi' and at the entrance to each avenue, the 'Genii of the Arts and Sciences . . . made of Silver in Alto Relievo, by Mr Rysbrack'. The music played was by 'the three Great Masters Geminiani, Handel and Corelli'. The clock is possibly that described in Clay's obituary (*Gent's Mag*, x (1740), pp. 92f) as 'a Musical Machine which had cost him 20 years Time and expence of £2000 to bring to Perfection', although he had ordered this to be destroyed 'to prevent further expence of Time and Money of anyone who should attempt to finish it after his Death'. As Amiconi did not arrive until late in 1729 and Roubiliac probably only in the 1730s it is likely that the design for the case dates from *c.* 1735-40. The iconographical programme of the four Monarchies appears to be unusual in England but the theme enjoyed considerable popularity in Germany from engravings of Lucas Kilian in the 17th century (information from Marjorie Trusted) to Meissen figures by Kändler (Kramer, 1965). Here, however, the personifications are not male and standing but female and seated, like allegorical figures on monuments. Other clocks by Clay are known (including examples with reliefs by Rysbrack and paintings by Amiconi) but it is uncertain to what extent Clay was responsible for the design of their case, as distinct from their mechanisms. However, the coherence of design and iconography suggests a single designer. This project is the outstanding example of the involvement of English rococo sculptors and painters in the decorative arts and it is noteworthy that three artists of such different backgrounds should produce a wholly consistent work. However, Rysbrack's contribution is somewhat untypical of his work, although he collaborated with goldsmiths on the Jerningham wine cooler (Cat. B9). Plaster moulds for Roubiliac's Hercules and Atlas appear in the sculptor's 1762 sale (4th Day, Lot 70) and a model of it was drawn by Nathaniel Smith for a premium awarded by the Royal Society of Arts in 1759 (Dossie 1782, III p. 416). The group is probably among Roubiliac's earliest English works and as a small mythological group may be associated with the lost Tarquin and Lucretia, executed before 1738 (Esdaile 1928, p. 43). Its

invention by Roubiliac (implied by 'compos'd' in the description) may reflect the influence of Permoser's Hercules Saxonicus which dominates one of the pavilions of the Zwinger (Asche 1978, p. 88) and also served as the basis of an Atlas by Egell (Lankheit 1954, p. 81).

Lit: Croft-Murray 1943; Hayes 1975, p. 40; Murdoch 1982, p. 93; Murdoch 1983, p. 43
MCB

S3

S3 *Persia and Rome*
By Louis François Roubiliac (1702/5-62); *c.* 1735-40.
Bronze; Persia h. 285, Rome h. 311
Her Majesty The Queen

Two of the four monarchies which were detached from Clay's musical clock (Cat. S43) when it was modified, possibly by Vulliamy, in the 19th century. The two companion figures of Chaldea and Macedonia are recorded in a Royal collection inventory of 1870 but have not been traced. With their exotic head-dresses and attributes these personifications are comparable to figures of the four continents. The facility with which the surviving figures and the Hercules group are modelled suggests that he may have already become familiar with techniques of bronze sculpture in France. The use of the relief modelled by Rysbrack on another of Clay's clocks indicates that this was available before the latter's death, suggesting a

date before 1740 for the overall composition.

Prov: Acquired as part of the clock by Princess Augusta, wife of Frederick Prince of Wales
Lit: Murdoch 1983, pp. 31 and 43
MCB

S4 *Alexander Pope*
Louis François Roubiliac (1702/5-62). *c.* 1738.
Terracotta bust; h. 620
Trustees of the Barber Institute of Arts, University of Birmingham

In 1741 Vertue recorded that Roubiliac 'had Modelld from the Life several Busts or portraits extreamly like Mr Pope. more like than any other sculptor has done I think.' This terracotta was the model for four marble versions (see Cat. S3), the earliest being that at Temple Newsam House, Leeds, dated 1738. The Temple Newsam marble may have belonged to Pope's friend, William Murray, 1st Lord Mansfield, and it is possible that he was responsible for the original commission, although for his own portrait bust he chose Rysbrack (Webb 1954, p. 220). Appropriately for the translator of Homer, Pope is shown in the classical manner, introduced by Rysbrack in his bust of Daniel Finch (1723); the Barber terracotta is apparently Roubiliac's earliest use of this pattern. More striking than the form of the bust, however, is the immediacy of the portrait in which the poet's physical frailty and intellectual dignity are vividly evoked. According to Reynolds in 1742 (Prior, 1860, p. 429), Roubiliac 'observed that his countenance was that of a person who had been much afflicted with headache, and that he should have known the fact from the contracted appearance of the skin above the eyebrows, though he had not been otherwise apprised of it'. Although more highly finished than the models for monuments (Cat. S46, S47), this portrait illustrates Roubiliac's outstandingly sensitive handling of clay. Plaster casts, including that purchased for the British Museum by Dr Maty were listed in the sculptor's posthumous sale and reduced variants produced in plaster (Cat. S29) bronze (Cat. S45) and earthenware (Wimsatt 1964, pp. 254-266).

S4

S5

Prov: Roubiliac's sale, 14 May 1762, 76; John Belchier, a surgeon who also sat to Roubiliac; Belchier sale, 29 March 1805, 119; Samuel Rogers; Samuel Rogers sale, 5 May 1856, 836; John Murray: by descent to Christopher Murray; purchased by the Barber Institute at Christie's, 19 June 1970, 47
Lit: Barber Institute 1983, p. 79; Esdaile 1929, pp. 47-9; Riely & Wimsatt 1979, p. 144; Vertue III, p. 105; Whinney 1964, pp. 104-5; Wimsatt 1965, p. 231-3 (with full bibliography)
MCB

S5 *Alexander Pope*
Louis François Roubiliac (1702/5-62).
1741.
Marble bust; h. 490 (without socle)
Inscribed (below sitter's right shoulder) *Anno Dom./MDCCXLI/L.F. Roubiliac/Sc^{it}. ad vivum* and (below left shoulder) *Alex pope nat^s. LONDINI,/die 8°. junii anno MDCLXXXVIII./Obiit in vico Twickenham prope/Urbem. die 8°. maii MDCCXLIV.*

Earl of Rosebery collection, Dalmeny House, Edinburgh

One of four early autograph marbles (others at Temple Newsam House, Leeds (1738), Earl Fitzwilliam collection (1740) and Shipley Art Gallery, Gateshead (1741)) carved after the terracotta (Cat. S4) and the only example from this group to show the sitter's shoulders, as in the model. Other undated marbles include a

version in the VAM (A.14-1947). Apparently retaining its original surface, the Dalmeny bust shows particularly well Roubiliac's ability to carve marble without any loss of the delicate effects of modelling achieved in the clay model. Although all four early dated marbles are inscribed 'ad vivum', this phrase may refer to the modelling of the terracotta. However, Pope's correspondence confirms that he visited Roubiliac's studio at least once in 1741 (Pope 1956, IV, pp. 351, 360) so that additional sittings for the marbles are conceivable. The apparent contradiction between the date 1741 and the reference to the poet's death in 1744 is puzzling, since there is no clear disparity in style between the two inscriptions. Despite the fact that Vertue's note about the clay model was made in the same year as that recorded on the Dalmeny bust, this date cannot refer to Pope's sitting to Roubiliac for the model since there are two earlier marbles. If the 1741 date refers to the carving of the marble, the inscription giving the dates of the poet's birth (following the erroneous date given in Curles 1737 edition of Pope's *Letters*) and death was presumably added later, perhaps by Roubiliac's studio. The four early marble versions were probably produced for close friends of Pope. According to Thomas Moore in 1834, the Dalmeny portrait was executed for the Tory statesman Lord Bolinbroke, a friend of the poet and closely

associated with the Huguenot community (Murdoch 1983, pp. 38-9). But, although Roubiliac was later to carve Bolinbroke's monument, the evidence for the commissioning of the Pope is uncertain, since the politician spent most of his time in France between 1739 and 1743 and, following Pope's death, was to revise his former good opinion of his friend.

Prov: Lord Bolinbroke (?); James Bindley; Bindley sale, 5 March 1819, 243; Watson Taylor; Watson Taylor sale, July 1832, 162; Sir Robert Peel; Peel Heirlooms sale, 10 May 1900, 142
Lit: British Institution 1820, no. 45; Cunningham 1830, p. 58; Esdaile 1928, pp. 47-48, 50; Jameson 1844, p. 380; Ruscoe 1824, frontispiece; Sainte-Croix 1822, pp. 106-7; Whinney 1964, p. 104; Whinney 1971; Wimsatt 1965 (with full bibliography)
MCB

S6 *Design for the monument to John, 2nd Duke of Argyll and Greenwich*
Anonymous (after Roubiliac). 1745
Pen and ink, black and white chalks; 725 x 430
Signed *L.F. Roubiliac Inv^{it}*
VAM (8381)

This drawing is probably that described by Jupp, on the verso of which was a witnessed statement by Roubiliac referring to the contract between Roubiliac and the Duchess signed on 25 May 1748. This date is almost certainly a misreading by Jupp of 1745 (which is the date given in the Nollekens sale catalogue) but since the drawing is mounted on card this cannot be verified. The high finish, absence of any scale and the recorded inscription indicate that this is a presentation drawing, intended as a record of the agreed design and probably referred to in the contract. Although it shows the main elements in the finished composition already established, various modifications were to be made in the surviving terracotta model (Cat. S7) and the monument itself. The use in the signature of 'invenit' alone implies that this is not by Roubiliac's hand but probably by an artist in the St Martin's Lane circle, working under the influence of Gravelot with whose work it shows considerable similarities.

Prov: Joseph Nollekens sale 4 Dec.
1823, 252, bt. Evans (?); Edward Jupp;
E. Parsons from whom purchased by
the museum in 1878
Lit: Esdaile 1928, p. 62; Jupp 1871;
Physick 1967; Physick 1969,
p. 119; Whinney 1971, p. 84.
MCB

S7 *Model for the monument to John, 2nd Duke of Argyll and Greenwich*

Louis François Roubiliac (1702/5-
1762)
Terracotta mounted on a modern slate
support; 895 x 502
Inscribed on base, *L F Roubiliac in^t et
Fecit 1745*
VAM (21-1888)

The Duke reclines on a sarcophagus,
supported by Fame (or History,
according to some contemporary
descriptions) who writes an inscription
on the pyramid behind him; below,
Eloquence and Pallas, exemplifying
the Duke's oratorical and military
achievements, flank a relief showing
the presentation of his coat-of-arms to
Liberty. This model, which was
damaged in firing and has
contemporary repairs including that to
the top of the pyramid, may be the
'Design' for the Duke's monument
which appeared in the 1762 sale

catalogue (3rd Day, Lot 70) along with
a mould and plasters of the relief
(3rd Day, Lot 57; 4th Day, Lots 34-5)
and plaster busts of Eloquence
(4th Day, Lots 2 and 19). The scale at
the bottom and the precise signature
and date indicate that it is connected
with a contract. In June 1734
Sir Henry Fermor bequeathed £500
for the erection in Westminster Abbey
of a monument to Argyll (d. 1743)
within two years of his decease (PRO,
Prob 11, 665 fol 262v) and in 1745 a
'fine' of £50 was paid to the Dean and
Chapter for permission to erect the
monument in the south transept. The
contract between the Duchess and
Roubiliac was signed on 25 May 1745
(see Cat. S33) and on 31 May
Roubiliac was paid £250 by the
Duchess (Coutts & Co, George
Middleton Ledger 1744-5, fol 2;
information from Mary Cosh); a
further payment of £100 was made on
6 August 1748 (Ledger 1747-9, fol 2).
(According to Wilton (Farington's
diary 5 Jan. 1796) Roubiliac charged a
total of £1200 but, despite an
additional payment of £200 was still
£300 out of pocket). In early 1749
various inscriptions were proposed in
the *Gentleman's Magazine* (XIX, p. 76),
the *General Advertiser* (17 Feb.) and the
Scots Magazine (pp. 87, 164) and the
Gentleman's Magazine (XIX, p. 233)
reported the monument 'opened' on
18 May 1749. Further accounts in the
Gentleman's Magazine (XXXIV, p. 558)
and the *General Advertiser* (19 May
1749) reflect the impression made by
the monument. Vertue, who gives an
unusually full account (III, p. 146, 148
& 9) describes it as 'much admired by
the Publick' and outshining 'for
nobleness and skill all those done
before, by the best sculptors. This fifty
years past'. The exact circumstances of
the commission are otherwise
undocumented but no less than 22
Rysbrack drawings, divided between
Plymouth (Eustace 1982, pp. 128-32),
Sir John Soane's Museum (Designs for
monuments vol fols. 23, 27, 28, 30),
Chicago (Harris 1971, p. 190, as
designs for Marlborough monument)
and the London art market (Christie's,
14 June 1983, Lots 131 and 133), may
be associated, with varying degrees of
probability, with this project. It is
unclear why Roubiliac, who had yet to
complete a major monument, was
chosen in preference to Rysbrack who

had already executed busts of the
Duke and Duchess (Vertue, III, p. 56).
According to Horace Walpole (1771,
IV, p. 99) Roubiliac was
recommended by Sir Edward
Walpole; possibly some influential
suppport also came from one of
Fermor's executors (Sir William
Ewisden, Charles Amherst,
Dr Thomas Thomson and Charles
Worsley) or even the writer of the
inscription, Paul Whitehead (*Historical
Description*, 1754, p. 110) who was a
friend of Hogarth and Hayman and
later sat to the sculptor (see Cat. S33).
Designs involving a reclining figure
flanked by two allegories were already
well established in Roman late
baroque tomb sculpture and known in
England from Monnot's Exeter
monument (Eustace 1982, p. 115) and
later adaptations in Westminster
Abbey. Similar elements appear in
Rysbrack's drawings, one of which
(Eustace 1982, fig 43) depends, like
Roubiliac's seated Pallas, from
Rusconi's monument to Gregory XIII,
probably familiar to both sculptors
through Freij's engraving. The
originality of Roubiliac's composition
lies in the writing Fame, the figure of
Eloquence and the unprecedentedly
dramatic movement which
characterises the monument as a
whole. Although a writing History
occurs on Rysbrack's Marlborough
monument at Blenheim (Whinney
1964, pl. 706), Roubiliac's figure,
whose inscription breaks off in the
middle of the title that became extinct
on the Duke's death, is probably
derived from the Fame (with similarly
incomplete inscription) on Fischer von
Erlach's monument to Jan Vaclav
Vratislav of Mitrovice in St James,
Prague, engraved in the English
edition of the *Entwurff Einer Historischen
Architectur* (1730, IV, taf. 21; Laing
1984). A familiarity with mid-
European baroque, acquired during
Roubiliac's Dresden stay, may partly
account for the remarkable forward
movement of Eloquence, which was
praised by Walpole (1771, IV, p. 99) as
'very masterly and graceful' and has
continued to impress later observers,
including Canova (Cunningham 1830,
p. 46). Equally striking is the virtuoso
carving of drapery; according to
Vertue (III, p. 149), 'the Draperys and
foldings truly natural and excells all
others in skill and softness of plaits

S8

S9

really more like silk than marble'. A considerable number of changes took place in the development of the composition: in the final version History's forward movement becomes more urgent and the relationship with the Duke is clarified; similarly, both Eloquence and Pallas assume more dynamic poses with more crumpled drapery surfaces. The evolution of the relief in particular indicates that the terracotta represents an intermediary stage although certain details, such as the scales of justice, were apparently abandoned in the terracotta but re-introduced from the drawing in the finished monument.

Prov: Purchased from Benjamin Webb, 1888
Lit: Brinckmann 1925, III, pp. 110-1; Esdaile 1928, pp. 62-5; Eustace 1982, p. 132; Physick 1966; Physick 1969, p. 119; Whinney 1964, p. 105; Whinney 1971, pp. 84-5
MCB

S8 *Lady Murray of Stanhope*
Louis François Roubiliac (1702/5-62). 1747
Marble bust; h. (including socle) 730
Inscribed in the medallion on the socle, *GRISEL BAILLIE/LADY MURRAY/ AETAT. 55 A.D./MDCCXLVII.*
The Lord Binning, Mellerstain, Gordon

Lady Murray (1693-1759) was a prominent member of London musical and literary circles and friend of Pope (Cat. S4) and is described in *Mr Pope's Welcome from Greece* as 'the sweet-tongued Murray'. Appropriately she is shown here in an informal manner, almost as a female equivalent to Roubiliac's busts of male *virtuosi* such as Dr Martin Folkes (Cat. S11). A payment to Roubiliac of £31.10.00 for this bust is recorded in an entry of 14 July 1748 in the account book kept by Lady Grisel Baillie and continued by her daughter. This entry also refers to a marble of her mother (still at Mellerstain), the two terracotta models

(at Tyninghame) and two plasters, including that of Lady Murray also at Mellerstain. The distinctive drapery around the head is parelleled approximately in contemporary French portraits such as Louis Tocqués' Mme de Grafigny (Doria 1929, fig 108), although the tasselled shawl worn by Lady Murray is fanciful rather than a representation of a contemporary garment. The same convention was adopted by the sculptor for the figure of Religion on the Hough monument at Worcester (1746) and the relief of Elizabeth Harvey at Hempstead (1753). In all three the sculptor loosely knots the drapery to create an asymmetrical pattern of apparently shifting, crumpled material, an essentially rococo effect.

Prov: by family descent to present owner
Lit: Baker 1984 II; Royal Academy 1956, p. 82, no 230; Webb 1957, pp. 87-8; Whinney 1964, p. 113
MCB

S9 *Arabella Aufrere*

Louis François Roubiliac
(1702/5-62)
Marble bust; h. (without later socle),
690
Inscribed *ARABELLA AUFRERE/*
MDCCXLVII/L.F. Roubiliac
Earl of Yarborough

Mrs Aufrère was the niece of the
Countess of Exeter, a notable patron
of Huguenot craftsmen who
commissioned the monument to
Thomas and Mary Chambers,
executed in 1737 probably by
Roubiliac (Murdoch 1983, p. 29). This
strikingly virtuoso exercise in the
carving of different drapery textures
perhaps reflects Roubiliac's familiarity
with the textiles produced in his native
Lyons. However, the precisely
executed embroidered linen shift does
not apparently follow known 18th
century examples while the flurried
outer drapery forms a richly inventive
abstract pattern recalling Smith's
remark (1828, II, p. 90) that Roubiliac
'seldom modelled his drapery . . . but
carved it from the linen itself, which
he dipped into warm starch-water, so
that when he had pleased himself, he
left it to cool and dry'. Approximate
precedents for the wind-swept drapery
occur in the busts of Guillaume
Coustou (eg Samuel Bernard, Souchal
1980, pl. 27d) and engravings after
Boucher but Roubiliac's modification
of his French rococo sources remains
highly individual. The distinctive
knotted motif is developed further in
his variation on Bernini's lost Charles
II (Mann 1931, pp. 7-8) and the late
portrait of George II (Esdaile 1928,
pp. 91-2).

Prov: by family descent to present
owner
Lit: Murdoch 1983, pp. 29-30; Royal
Academy, 1956, p. 166, no 534;
Whinney 1964, p. 113
MCB

S10 *Jonathan Swift (1667-1745)*

Louis François Roubiliac (1702/5-62).
1749
Marble bust; h. 851
Inscribed (on socle) D^n *SWIFT* and (on
the reverse) *EX DONO QUARTAE*
CLASSIS AN: 1745 PROCURANTE
DIGBAEO FRENCH
The Provost, Fellows and Scholars of Trinity
College Dublin

S10

The arrival in Dublin of this apparently
posthumous portrait by 'Mr Ruvilliac'
(*sic*) is recorded in Faulkner's *Dublin*
Journal for 21 March 1749 which
mentions its purchase by the senate of
Senior Sophisters with 'the money that
is usually laid out on an
entertainment'. According to this
report it 'is done with exquisite skill
and delicacy and . . . looked on by
persons of taste as a masterpiece'. The
commission is otherwise
undocumented but the reputation
gained by his portraits of Pope
(Cat. S3) may have made Roubiliac an
appropriate choice for the Swift.
Although Walpole's statement (1771,
p. 99) that Roubiliac executed 'half the
busts at Trinity-college, Dublin' is
exaggerated, portraits of Bacon and
Pembroke have recently been
attributed to him by Tessa Murdoch
and he later carved the statue of
Sir Thomas Molyneaux for Dublin
(Potterton 1975, p. 75). Since Swift's
last visit to England was in 1727
Roubiliac's bust was presumably
based on a painted portrait, possibly
that by Charles Jervis, although this
shows the sitter more formally
dressed. The bust's arresting vivacity,
however, shows the effect Roubiliac
could achieve even when a portrait
was not modelled *ad vivum*. Although
it shares many common elements with
the Folkes, the Swift is given a very
different character, suggesting,
according to Whinney, 'a more volatile
and indeed a more venomous spirit

. . . than in the cautious, watchful
Folkes'.

Prov: Commissioned for Trinity
College
Lit: Esdaile 1928, p. 186; Royal
Academy 1961; Strickland 1916, p. 73;
Whinney 1964, p. 112
MCB

S11 *Martin Folkes*

Louis François Roubiliac
(1702/5-62). 1749
Marble bust; h. (with socle) 780
Inscribed (on the right side) *Martin*
Folkes of Hillington in Norfolk, Esqr; (on
left side) *L.F. Roubiliac/Scu.^{lt} ad vivum/*
1749; (on socle) *M. Folkes Arm/Socic.*
Regal. Lond./Praeses./MDCCXLIX.

Earl of Pembroke, Wilton House

Folkes was a distinguished scientist
and antiquarian, serving as President
of the Royal Society between 1741 and
1753 and as President of the Society of
Antiquaries from 1750. He was also a
vice-president of the Foundling
Hospital and often to be seen with the
St Martin's Lane group at Slaughter's.
It was probably through him that
Roubiliac received the commission for
the Duke of Montagu's monument
(Cat. S14; Murdoch 1980) as well
as portrait commissions from
professional figures who formed a
significant part of the sculptor's
clientele.
This bust is one of four marbles
commissioned by the 9th Earl of
Pembroke and a payment of £35 in
'full of all demands' was made to
Roubiliac on 16 November 1749.
Before it was sent to Wilton the

marble was seen by Vertue who described it as 'a most exact likeness of him – as much as any work of that kind ever seen – equal to any present or former ages'. Among the most boldly characterised of Roubiliac's elderly men, Folkes, like Swift (Cat. S10), Belchier (Esdaile 1928, p. 111) and Cheselden (ibid.), shows the *en negligé* convention evolved from the early portraits (Cat. E2) into a large scale, powerful form characteristic of the sculptor's work in the late 40s and 50s. In both marble and plaster (Cat. S12) versions, particular play is made of the contrast between textures of drapery and flesh. The medallion on the original socle closely resembles medal reverses (eg Sir Andrew Fountaine; Grueber 1911, pl. CLXIV, 4) by Dassier, whose medal of Folkes (Cat. S17) in some ways anticipates Roubiliac's portrait.

Lit: Esdaile 1928, p. 90; Royal Academy 1956, p. 65, no 1756; Webb 1964; Whinney 103-5
MCB

S12 *Martin Folkes*
Louis François Roubiliac (1702/5-62). 1749
Plaster bust; h. 660
The Trustees of the British Museum

Purchased from Roubiliac's posthumous 1762 sale (4th Day, Lot 15) by Dr Maty, the Huguenot Under-Librarian of the British Museum, together with plasters of Socrates, Plato, Demosthenes, Cicero, Marcus Aurelius, Milton, Pope, Dr Mead, Chesterfield, terracottas of Ray and Willoughby and clay models of Dr Barrow and Dr Bentley. Tessa Murdoch has suggested that they may have been purchased partly with the intention of displaying them in the library. The plaster, which differs from the marble (Cat. S11) in having incised eyes, is presumably taken from the lost terracotta. However, the possibility that Roubiliac was using a 'waste-mould' technique that involved the casting of an 'original plaster', thus avoiding the risks inherent in the firing of a clay model, should not be excluded.

Prov: Purchased at Roubiliac's 1762 sale
Lit: Esdaile 1928, pp. 103-5, 111, 182; Whinney 1964, p. 112
MCB

S13 *Princess Amelia*
By Louis François Roubiliac (1702/5-62). *c.* 1740
Marble bust; h. 750
Inscribed *L.F. Roubiliac Sc^{it} ad vivum*. *The Syndics of the Fitzwilliam Museum, Cambridge*

The second daughter of George II, Princess Amelia (1711-86) is shown in her mid-thirties, suggesting a date of around 1740-45. Although undocumented, it may have been bought by Lord Radstock from one of the Princess's sales and is possibly Roubiliac's sole royal commission, the portrait of George II (Esdaile, 1928, pp. 81-2) having entered in the Royal Collection only in 1817 with the Lord Ligonier to which it probably formed a pendant (Kerslake, 1977, p. 168). Comparison with his two other approximately contemporary female portraits (Cat. S8, S9) demonstrates Roubiliac's inventiveness in handling drapery, each arrangement being quite distinctive yet equally rococo in spirit. In 1757, however, he was to re-employ the pattern created for the portrait of Amelia in the bust of the Countess of Pembroke (Webb, 1956).

Prov: Princess Amelia (?); Lord Radstock; Lady Caroline Waldegrave; Messrs T.H.W. Lumley; purchased by the Fitzwilliam Museum, 1955
Lit: Esdaile 1928, pp. 97-8; Royal Academy 1956, p. 181, no 586; Whinney 1964, p. 113
MCB

S14 *Model for the monument to John 2nd Duke of Montagu*
Louis François Roubiliac (1702/5-62). 1749-50
Terracotta; h. 348; w. 318
VAM (A.6-1947)

Although without an early provenance, this terracotta may have been among the 'Five designs' for the Duke's monument included in Roubiliac's 1762 Sale catalogue (3rd Day, Lot 67) Roubiliac's work on the monuments to the Duke (b. 1688) and his widow, placed in the new chancel at Warkton, Northants, is recorded in detail in an undated bill indicating the sculptor's responsibility for the architectural setting as well as the monuments. According to a letter from Dr Thomas Birch of 8 September 1750, 'the whole care of a monument'

to the Duke, following his death in July 1749, was entrusted to Martin Folkes (Cat. S11) whose associations with the St Martin's Lane group perhaps led to the selection of Roubiliac for this commission. On 19 December 1749 the *Dublin Courant* reported the sculptor at work on the monument and Birch's letter implies that by September 1750 several models had been produced. The final design was presumably worked out before Roubiliac's departure for Italy in October 1752 but it is uncertain whether the monument was in place by this date. Comparison with the plaster version (Cat. S15) and a sketchiness exceptional among English 18th century models indicate that this terracotta represents an early stage in the evolution of the design. Although the final disposition of the mourning Duchess and the figure of Charity with the Duke's medallion portrait is already established, the protagonists are still dominated by the architecture which is more conventional than on the finished monument. The vertical incisions on the right, however, perhaps hint at a proposed reduction in its width that is realised in Cat. S15.

Prov: possibly Roubiliac's 1762 sale, 3rd Day, Lot 67; given by Dr W.L. Hildburgh to the Museum in 1947
Lit: Hodgkinson 1947; Murdoch 1980; Physick 1969, p. 34; Whinney 1964, p. 260; Whinney 1971, pp. 92-3
MCB

S15 *Model for the monument to John, 2nd Duke of Montagu*

Louis François Roubiliac
(1702/5-62). *c.* 1750-52
Painted wood and plaster; h. 632
*The Dean and Chapter, Westminster Abbey
(on loan to the Victoria and Albert Museum)*

Discovered in Westminster Abbey with Cat. S16 and S40 this model does not apparently appear in the 1762 sale catalogue although reference is made there to plaster 'mould' for the Duke's monument (2nd Day, Lot 57). Painted wood and plaster were employed to simulate the effect of the marbles used for the completed monument, for which this was probably the final model. By comparison with Cat. S14 the architecture (described in *The Spectator* of 1753 as a 'temple of fame') is more boldly three-dimensional and the figures somewhat increased in size. The tendency towards greater plasticity is also reflected in the translation of the trophies of arms into three-dimensions, emerging dramatically from dark arches. The monument itself was apparently modified, after its installation, by the addition of the ogee dome and finial, described in the bill as 'an additional peice of work'; this upper section, which is not shown on the terracotta, forms a separate piece on the wood model, and may well be a slightly later addition. The iconographical elements of the mourning wife, a portrait of the deceased and allegorical figures were already common in English

monuments but the interaction between them and the free, almost pictorial, quality of the compositions must have appeared strikingly novel, perhaps explaining Walpole's appraisal (1771, . 99) of the Warkton monuments as 'well perform'd and magnificent, but wanting simplicity'. Comparably open compositions involving figures and architecture are to be found in the work of Slodtz, whose Vienne monument (Souchal 1967, pp. 666-8) with its use of a figure standing alongside a sarcophagus anticipates similar devices used by Roubiliac here and on the Hough monument (Worcester Cathedral). However, the relationship between a chain of figures and architecture may also be paralleled in the monuments of Paul Egell (eg Lankheit 1954, pl. 14) whom Roubiliac may have known in Dresden; in the architectural form of the Duke's monument we find the most obvious reflection of this early German training (Baker 1984 I).

Prov: discovered in the triforium of Westminster Abbey in 1870
Lit: The *Builder*, XXVIII, July 1870; Esdaile 1923; Edsaile 1928, pp. 70f; Murdoch 1980; Whinney 1964, p. 200 MCB

S16 *Model for the monument to Mary, Duchess of Montagu*

Louis François Roubiliac
(1702/5-62); *c.* 1752
Painted wood and plaster;
h. 632, w. 457
*The Dean and Chapter, Westminster Abbey
(on loan to the Victoria and Albert Museum)*

Although found at Westminster Abbey, this model may possibly be identified with the 'Duchess of Montagu's monument in plaister' in Roubiliac's 1762 sale (1st Day, Lot 73) where 'moulds' (2nd Day, Lot 58) and two 'designs' (3rd Day, Lot 68) are also recorded. The commission for this monument, like that of the Duke was supervised by Martin Folkes and the details recorded in an undated bill (see Cat. S14). The project's chronology is uncertain. The Duchess died in May 1751 and according to *The Spectator* (XVI, 1753) the monument was still in Roubiliac's studio in December 1753. The materials employed and the close resemblance to the finished monument indicate that this model was the final version, but it is unclear

whether it was executed before or after the sculptor's Italian visit in October 1752. However, its compatability in both composition and figure style with that for the Duke and the absence of any features reflecting the impact of sculpture seen in Rome suggest that this design was worked out before that date. Although the right hand seated Fate recalls the flanking figures on papal tombs, particularly those by late baroque sculptors such as Rusconi, the Argyll monument (Cat. S7) shows that Roubiliac was already familiar with this type. The iconography of the three Fates occurs frequently in 18th century literary sources but it is unusual, if not unique, on a monument, suggesting that it was chosen by Folkes. The change from the traditionally aged hags on the model to the more elegant and decorous young women on the monument may reflect his intervention.

Prov: discovered in the triforium of Westminster Abbey in 1870
Lit: The *Builder*, XXVIII, 2nd July 1870; Esdaile 1923; Esdaile 1928; Murdoch 1980; Whinney 1964, p. 260 no 26 MCB

S17 *Louis Francois Roubiliac*

Andrea Soldi (*c.* 1703-71). 1751
Oil on canvas; 975 x 832
Signed and dated *A. Soldi/Pinx. Ao. 1751*

Governors of Dulwich Picture Gallery

A Florentine who had executed
portraits of English residents in the
Holy Land, Soldi came to London
around 1735 where he enjoyed
considerable success in the 1730s and
40s as one of the '*exotics* from abroad'
described by Hogarth (Nichols and
Steevens 1808, I, p. 106). He painted
portraits of various English artists,
including Ware and Rysbrack; this
portrait may be identified with that
mentioned by Vertue in November
1751 and was followed in 1758 by
another showing the sculptor with his
bust of Garrick (Garrick Club). The
characteristically alert Roubiliac is here
seen working on a model for the
Charity on the Duke of Montagu's
monument (Cat. S14, S15) but this
shows substantial differences from
those on the surviving models and the
finished monument, notably in the
figure's reversed pose, her draped
head, the rocky base and the pose of
the child. Although work on the
monument was well advanced by
November 1751, this figure apparently
represents an early idea that was later
rejected in favour of the composition
used on both surviving models.
Possibly Soldi's sketch was executed
earlier and the portrait only finished in
November 1751.

Prov: this (or in the Garrick Club
portrait) in Sir Henry Gott's sale
(Christie's, 2 Feb 1810, 26); Matthews

coll., Birmingham; Fairfax Murray Gift
to Dulwich, 1917
Lit: Esdaile 1928, pp. 67, 69, 190;
Finberg 1929, p. 159; Ingamells 1974,
pp. 178ff; Ingamells 1980, p. 14;
Kerslake 1977, p. 238; Murray 1980,
p. 120; Royal Academy, 1960, no 55;
Vertue III, pp. 84, 109, 120 and 132;
Whinney 1964, p. 107
MCB

S18 *Martin Folkes*

Jacques Antoine Dassier (1715-59)
1740
Bronze medal; diam. 545
Inscribed *MARTINUS FOLKES
ARM.R. (obv)* and *SOCIETATIS REGALIS
LONDINI SODALIS. M.DCC.XL*

VAM (A.11-1971)

One of a series celebrating 'some of
our great men then living . . . sold in
copper at seven shillings and sixpence
each' (Walpole 1771, p. 101) and
executed during Dassier's stay in
England between 1740 and 1757
(Demole 1917, p. 117). In February
1740 Vertue (III, p. 101), giving a full
list, reported that Dassier 'has publishd
proposals for cutting several medals or
Dies – the portraitures of famous men
living in England – Martin Folkes Esq.r
is done very like him – but was struck
in Geneva. from the Die done here
because there is not engines allowed
for that purpose. or because it is
cheaper'. In 1741 (III, p. 104) he
describes the medals of Folkes, Pope
and the mathematician Abraham de
Moivre as 'done from the life
and . . . free and boldly cutt but not so
elaborately, nor as high finisht. as
others, there appears a little of the fa-
presto'. Walpole (1771, p. 102) thought
them 'very good performances, though
inferior to the popes by Hamaroni and

more inferior to those of St Urbain,
medallist to the last dukes of Lorain'.
By contrast with the late baroque
compositions of Christopher Tanner
and Laurence Natter, medallists
resident in England in the 1740s,
Dassier's portrait of Folkes shows a
light, rococo handling of the drapery
that exploits the effects possible in the
modelling of the wax from which the
medal was cast. This essentially rococo
style of portraiture, which anticipates
Roubiliac's busts of the same sitter
(Cat. S11, S12), may derive from
French painting and sculpture that
Dassier would have seen while learning
die-sinking with the Germain family in
Paris. In many cases (eg Cat. S19) the
same sitter sat to both Roubiliac and
Dassier (Murdoch 1982, p. 187) and a
number of them appear to have
belonged to the Slaughter's set of
which Dassier too may well have been
a member.

Prov: purchased from B.A. Seaby Ltd.
Lit: Franks and Grueber 1885, p. 558,
no. 185; Forrer 1899; Forrer 1904, I,
p. 511; Grueber 1911, pl CLIX, no 13
MCB & LMC

S19 *Philip Dormer Stanhope, 4th Earl of Chesterfield*

Jacques Antoine Dassier (1715-59)
1743. Bronze medal diam. 545
Inscribed, *'COMES DE CHESTERFIELD.
MDCCXLIII' (rev)*
The Trustees of the British Museum (M8480)

One of the series of medals of eminent
men, with Cat. S18. Unlike the severe
design imitated by Roubliac on his
bust of Folkes (Cat. S9), this reverse
is more characteristic of Dassier's
medals; it bears a decorative cartouche
that employs some rococo motifs
though arranged in a restrained,
symmetrical form. The portrait on the
obverse may be compared with
Roubiliac's bust, known in plaster and
bronze versions (Whinney 1971, p. 86).

Prov: purchased from Edward
Hawkins. (*c.* 1855)
Lit: Franks and Grueber 1885, p. 582,
no 222; Forrer 1899; Forrer 1904 I,
p. 511; Grueber 1911, pl. CLXIII, no 2
MCB & LMC

S20 *Frederick, Prince of Wales*

Jacques Antoine Dassier (1715-59);
c. 1750. Bronze medal, parcel gil;
diam. 55 Inscribed *ICH DIEN* (*rev*)
VAM (310-1880)

The reverse shows the Prince's coronet
and feathers supported by two putti.
Similar in size and form to, but
independent of, the series of eminent
men (Cat. S18, S19) this medal does
not apparently commemorate a
specific event but was probably issued
at a time when the Prince was
attempting to gain popularity. It is
closely related to Dassier's medal of
George II (Grueber 1911, pl. CLXIV,
no 5), dated 1750.

Prov: purchased from Miss M.L. Miller
Lit: Franks and Grueber 1885, p. 660,
no. 366; Forrer 1899; Forrer 1904 I,
p. 512; Grueber 1911, pl CLXXIV,
no 8
MCB & LMC

S21 *Monument to Captain James Cornewall*

J. Hinton (active *c.* 1750-60). *c.* 1756
Engraving; 90 x 111
Lettered *Engraved for the Universal
Magazine for J. Hinton, Newgate Street.*

*National Portrait Gallery (Macdonnell
collection)*

Cornewall died in 1743 and was
acclaimed as one of the heroes of the
naval battle off Toulon, an encounter
which led to the court martial of
various other officers involved. On
28 May 1747 the Commons resolved
that a monument to him should be
erected at Parliament's expense (*Journals
of the House of Commons*, XXV, p. 397)
and on 8 June Horace Walpole
commented to Conway, 'In the present
dearth of glory he is canonised; though
poor man, he had been tried twice the
year before for cowardice' (Lewis 1937,
37, p. 271). Taylor was apparently
selected without a competition. The
scaffolding around the monument
'Designed and executed by Mr Taylor'
was removed on 8 February 1755
(*Gent's Mag*, XXV, pp. 89f) and
payment approved by the Commons
on 15 March and 8 April 1756
(*Journals*, XXVII, pp. 525 and 572).
According to J.T. Smith (1828, i,
p. 180), the figures of Fame and
Britannia were in fact carved by
Benjamin Cheney. The monument
originally stood between the two most

westerly columns on the south side of
the nave but in the 1930s it was
removed and re-erected in a truncated
form in the cloister Parlour. The
Taylor monument volume contains
various designs for naval figures
(cf Cat. S23) but none appears related
obviously to the Cornewall project.
Although naval monuments formed a
conspicuous feature of Westminster
Abbey by the early 18th century, the
Cornewall monument, described by
the *Gent's Mag* as 'an illustrious instance
of national gratitude as well as of good
policy', was the first to a naval or
military figure to be erected with
Parliamentary funds, foreshadowing
many late 18th and early 19th century
examples, among them the monument
to Wolfe (Cat. S42, S43). The relief
depicting the battle of Toulon is in the
tradition of earlier naval reliefs
(eg Esdaile 1946, figs 134 and 137) but
other elements are far less familiar.
The form of the rocks and stalactites
used for the base has close parallels in
contemporary carver's work but their
arrangement to form a double arch
may reflect Taylor's awareness of
French fountain designs, notably
Le Brun's Fontaines des Muses et des
Arts illustrated in his *Receuil de divers
desseins de fontaines . . .* which he almost
certainly owned (Gilson 1973, no 25).
By 1750 both palm fronds and
complete trees formed part of a
widespread rococo decorative
vocabulary in England. As the central
element in a monument, however, the
palm tree here has a precise
iconographical role as a symbol of
fame (cf Cat. S24), suggesting that
Taylor was familiar with its use in
France in *pompes funèbres*, such as that
designed in 1735 by Sebastien-Antoine
Slodtz for Maréchal de Villars (Souchal
1967, pp. 393-4). Seeing it in 1765, the
Frenchman Grosley (1771 II, p. 67)
observed that the 'pomp and
magnificence displayed around it seem
rather to suit a funeral decoration, than
a standing monument'. The
combination of Fame and Britannia is
more familiar (cf. porcelain version,
Cat. O27); the arrangement of the two
figures with a medallion portrait
around a central vertical may be
compared with Roubiliac's far more
dramatic use of the same form in his
contemporary monument to General
Wade, erected in 1750 (Bindman 1981).
Although poorly executed, the

Cornewall monument in its original
state must have made considerable
impact in the Abbey, if only on
account of its size and position. This is
indicated by the production of this
engraving and two others in the
Macdonnell collection, one by Wale
and Grignion.
MCB

S22 *Design for a monument to a bishop*

Sir Robert Taylor (1714-88). *c.* 1745-50
Pencil; 280 x 195
*Taylor Institution, Oxford (Arch. Tay. 1,
fol 137r)*

One of 54 drawings, mainly for
monuments (including also Cat. S23,
S24, S50, S51) mounted in a quarto
volume with spine label reading 'SIR
R. TAYLOR'S DESIGNS'; this has an
early bookplate of the Institution
founded with money bequeathed by
him to the University (Gilson 1973,
A1). This unusually free sketch is
probably for a monument intended for
Westminster Abbey, the trefoil arcading
of which is lightly drawn around it; the
inclusion of a bishop's attributes
suggest that it may (like fols 36r, 53r,
122r and 136r) be an unsuccessful
design for Dr Boulter's monument, for
which the 'fine' was paid in 1745. The
existing monument by Cheere was
reported to be 'now erecting' in April
1748 (*Gent's Mag*, XVIII, p. 180) and
was complete by 1752; this differs
considerably from the surviving drawing

and may incorporate elements from Taylor's designs. The watermark (cf Heawood 1950, no 1827) of the paper bearing one of the alternative designs (fol 136r) is consistent with a date in the late 1740s. The composition which belongs to a group being evolved by Taylor at this period, is distinguished by the decorative cluster of mitre, book, censer and crozier and the characteristic waisted sarcophagus, supported on slender rococo scroll feet. The same form, the source of which is probably French, is frequently adapted by Taylor for hanging wall monuments, as in Cat. S51.

Prov: probably acquired from Taylor's estate when the Institution was founded in 1834 in accordance with his will
MCB

S23 *Design for a monument to a naval officer*
Sir Robert Taylor (1714-88) *c.* 1745-50
Pen and ink and wash; 510 x 380
Taylor Institution, Oxford (Arch. Tay. 1, fol 91r)

Characteristic of the finished compositions that comprise the majority of the drawings in the Taylor monument volume (cf Cat. S22), this design, with its anchor and navigational instruments, is presumably for a naval figure and is closely related to three other drawings with the same bust (fols. 92r, 93r and 95r); two pencil sketches (fol 134r) may also be connected. The sprays of laurel and palm around the niche are to be read as alternatives. No monument of this form by Taylor is known but, despite the absence of a trefoil frame, as in Cat. S24, the four designs may represent an unsuccessful attempt by Taylor for a Westminster Abbey commission, possibly the monument to Aubrey Beauclerk (d. 1740) commissioned by Scheemakers after the 'fine' was paid in 1744. The sarcophagus from Taylor's design was re-employed in his monument to General Guest (d. 1747), the 'fine' for which was paid in 1749. 'Opened' by 21 December 1751 (*Gent's Mag* XXI, p. 571) this was seen in 1752 by Vertue (III, p. 161) who commented that 'the ornaments to the Bust and various beautyes of the Marble have obtained some reputation to Mr. Taylor the sculptor – who has infinitely polishd his work beyond comparison this being another English artist who made the tour of Italy'. The combination of a sarcophagus, trophies, pyramid and bust within a niche was already being used for other naval and military monuments in the Abbey during the 1740s. In Taylor's adaptation, however, the sarcophagus, with its *bombé* form, becomes more boldly three-dimensional and the trophies more numerous and apparently placed at random; equally rococo, the decorativ motifs show an awareness of sources such as Brunetti and contemporary plaster work.

Prov: as Cat. S22
Lit: Esdaile 1948, p. 64
MCB

S24 *Design for a monument to a military officer*
Sir Robert Taylor (1714-88). *c.* 1750
Pencil; 370 x 280
Taylor Institution, Oxford (Arch. Tay. 1, fol 84r)

The trefoil setting suggests that the monument was intended for

Westminster and this design may be a rejected sketch for the Guest monument (cf Cat. S23). The combination of a medallion portrait surrounded by trophies was already well-established in Westminster Abbey monuments. Taylor's composition differs from earlier examples in its rich profusion of attributes and its French characteristics. The form of the base, with its carved fluting and undulating cornice, recalls the mirror heads (probably designed by Oppenord in the late 1730s) in the Hotel d'Evreux (Kimball 1943, fig 181) while the combination of trophies and palms is found as early as 1717 in designs for the Salon à l'Italienne at the Palais Royal (*ibid*, fig 123). By the 1750s, however, the latter feature had crossed the Channel and a complete palm tree, with armour and weapons, as in Taylor's design, were used by Clay in the overmantel at Blair Castle in 1751 (Beard 1975, pl. 145).

Prov: as Cat. S22
MCB

S25 *Design for the monument to Captain Philip de Sausmarez*

Sir Henry Cheere (1703-81). *c.* 1750
Pen and ink and wash; 350 x 215
VAM (4910.25)

Included (with Cats. S26 and S27) in one of four books of designs, copy drawings and tracings associated with the Cheere workshop, this design is for the monument to Sausmarez (d. 1747) in Westminster Abbey. A 'fine' of £10 was paid in 1748 and letters to John de Sausmarez from Cheere between 19 January and 13 March 1750 refer to a total cost of £270 of which £100 was to be paid in advance (Webb 1958, pp. 239-40). However, its absence from the 1754 *Historical Description* (though it is added in 1761) suggests that it was not erected by this date. Cheere carried out various other commissions for Channel Island families (Legouix 1975) including lead gate decorations for De Sausmarez Manor and a monument to Lady de Cartaret (cf Cat. S27). The putti in this drawing follow those seen earlier on the Hardy and Conduitt monuments but they are employed here in a composition which, in its asymmetry, rippling drapery and decorative motifs, is thoroughly rococo. These features receive greater emphasis in the executed monument which differs from the design in the addition of a book with ruffled pages, a shell-shaped cartouche and volutes on the bracket supports, all of which enhance the three-dimensional effect and perhaps reflect the influence of Brunetti's engravings. The shell swags, though characteristic of Cheere's rococo vocabulary, in this case reproduce the ormer shells native to the Channel Islands.

Prov: purchased with 59 others 'by Rysbrack' from Mr B. Quaritch, 1867
Lit: Physick 1969, pp. 122-3
MCB

S26 *Design for a monument to David Polhill*

By Sir Henry Cheere (1703-81)
c. 1755-60
Pen and ink and wash; 330 x 185
VAM (4910.41)

This design is for the monument at Otford, Kent, to David Polhill (d. 1754), MP and Keeper of the

Records in the Tower of London who in his youth was Dr Richard Mead's travelling companion in Italy (*DNB*). A variant design (4910.2) was used for the monument to Lord Carpenter at Owlesbury, Hampshire. In form it is characteristic of many wall-monuments by Cheere, which employ similar sets of three cherub heads and distinctive socles of splaying form with volutes and shell ornament. In the executed Polhill monument the classicising bust shown here is replaced by a more rococo portrait *en negligé*.

Prov: as cat. S25
Lit: Physick 1969, pp. 126-7

S27

S27 *Design for a monument*

Attributed to Henry Cheere (1703-81)
c. 1750-60
Pen and ink and watercolour;
442 x 297
Inscribed 'Hone'
VAM (4910.17)

From the same source as Cats. S25 and S26, this design is probably for the monument to Lady de Cartaret at St Helier, erected with £300 left in 1747 by her nephew, Captain de Sausmarez (Cat. S23) and convincingly attributed to Cheere (Legouix 1975, p. 282). Compositions with women seated within an arched and pedimented setting form a popular Cheere type; closest to this design is the monument to Matthew Humberston (d. 1709) at Humberston

but other examples include those to Viscount Tyrconnel (d. 1754) at Belton (Webb 1958, p. 278) and Lord Donneraile at Donneraile, County Cork, executed 1759 (Potterton 1975, p. 40). The architectural settings recall both Cheere's earlier work with Henry Scheemakers as well as monuments (eg Esdaile 1946, pl. 118) by early 18th century London mason-sculptors, in which tradition Cheere was trained. This conventional type, however, is transformed by the drapery style of the figure used earlier on the Willis monument at Salisbury (Webb 1958, p. 274), and the rococo form of the flying putto, urn, swags and lamps, which occur in the same combination on monuments such as that to John Brown (d. 1750) at Frampton, Dorset. The use of variously coloured marbles is also very characteristic of Cheere's work.

Prov: as Cat. S25
MCB

S28 *Alexander Pope (1688-1744)*

John Cheere (1709-87). 1749
Bronzed plaster statuette; h. 460
Inscribed on pedestal, *POPE* and *Cheere Ft 1749*
Castel Museum, York (on loan to City of York Art Gallery)

With 18 other plasters, including Cat. S29, this statuette, though dated considerably earlier, was probably supplied to Sir Charles Turner when Kirkleatham Hall was refurbished around 1765. During the 1750s and 60s both Henry and John Cheere received commissions from Yorkshire families, including Henry's monument to Chomley Turner (1761). This figure, known also in a lead version VAM (A4-1955), evidently formed part of a standard set that also included a reduction of Scheemakers' Shakespeare monument. This latter work was the source for the Pope which was probably John Cheere's own invention, although the similarity of reliefs used on some of the other, apparently original, statuettes, to those on Henry Cheere's statue of Sir George Cooke hints at his brother's involvement.

Prov: Kirkleatham sale, 1951
Lit: Friedman 1973, p. 925; Temple Newsam 1974; Wimsatt 1965, p. 258
MCB

S29 *Matthew Prior*

John Cheere (1709-1787). *c. 1750*
Bronzed plaster bust; h. 440
Inscribed on the integral socle *PRIOR*.
York Castle Museum, (on indefinite loan to York City Art Gallery)

Formerly at Kirkleatham Hall (see Cat. S28), this bust of the celebrated poet and diplomat is based on Coyzevox's portrait, executed about 1700 possibly after Rigaud. Placed on the monument designed by Gibbs and executed by Rysbrack in 1723, this bust was by 1734, 'justly esteemed one of the best things in England' (Ralph, 1734) and proved an influential source for busts *en négligé* by English sculptors. A lead statuette, probably by Cheere, showing the poet standing beside a low bookcase (Esdaile, 1928, pl. XLII), is adapted from the Coyzevox portrait.

Prov: Kirkleatham sale, 1951
Lit: Friedman 1973, p. 926; Temple Newsam 1974, no 57
MCB

S30 *Bracket*

Attributed to John Cheere (1709-87).
c. 1750
Plaster; 500 x 330
York Castle Museum (on indefinite loan to York City Art Gallery)

One of four brackets with masks of Comedy and Tragedy, apparently associated with the plasters from Kirkleatham, together with Cat. S31 and another set of two with caryatid mermaids and mermen. All are probably to be attributed to John Cheere who produced the figures they supported; this set was perhaps intended for the statuettes of Shakespeare, Milton, Pope and Spenser. The decorative elements have their origins in the ornament of Gravelot and the St Martin's Lane Circle but have been developed into a full, somewhat heavier form, which by about 1750, was becoming more widespread, partly as a result of this type of mass production. Embeded in the reverse is a mutton bone, evidently intended to strengthen the cast.

Prov: probably presented by Cholmley Turner to Sir William Turner's Hospital, Kirkleatham; purchased, September 1950, by the Castle Museum, York
Lit: Leeds, Temple Newsam, 1974

S31 *Bracket*

Attributed to John Cheere (1709-87).
c. 1750
Plaster, 265 x 170
York Castle Museum (on indefinite loan to York City Art Gallery)

One of three small brackets intended to support the figures from Kirkleatham (Cat. S28, S29; cf Cat. S30). A further set of three follows this pattern but on a larger scale. By the mid century this combination of scrollwork, cartouche and floral sways had become a standard component of rococo architectural decoration, appearing, for example, on chimney pieces by John's brother Henry (eg Grimsthorpe, Lincs). A somewhat similar form, though with different ornamental elements, is also known in porcelain (Cat. O27).

Prov: as Cat. S26
MCB

S32 *Wine cistern*

Thomas Carter the Elder (d. 1756).
1751
Marble; l. 900, h. 450
His Grace The Duke of Atholl's Collection, Blair Castle

A payment of £35.15s was made to Carter in 1751 for 'a richly carved cistern' (Duke of Atholl archives, cited Gunnis and Physick 1975). This was presumably intended for the dining room at Blair Castle for which Carter suplied a chimney piece and Clayton

S32

produced plaster work in the same year (Beard 1975, p. 87). Between 1751 and 1756 Carter carved a considerable number of chimney pieces for the remodelled interiors commissioned by James, 2nd Duke of Atholl. Other craftsmen patronised included Chippendale and John Cheere who supplied 19 lead garden statues and probably executed the gilt lead bust of the Duke. Carter and Cheere's workshops were geographically close and the two sculptors often had common patrons The marine motifs of dolphins, masks and swags of shells entwined with pearls are common rococo decorative elements, particularly in silver as in Crespin's centrepiece of 1741 (Cat. G17). However, although silver was more usual for a wine cistern and both silver and ceramic forms probably provided models for this marble vessel, both the style of the carving and the individual decorative details may be paralleled by the chimney pieces produced by the Carter family. In both, the rococo elements are subordinated to a fundamentally symmetrical form.
MCB

S33 *Sir Mark Pleydell*

Louis François Roubiliac
(1702/5-62). 1755
Marble bust; h. 550
Inscribed on reverse across the shoulders *Sʳ Mark Stuart Pleydell Bᵗ 1755. det. 63* and on left side of the support *ad vivum scᵗ/L.F. Roubiliac.*
The National Trust (on loan to the VAM)

S33

Pleydell owned Coleshill House, designed by Sir Roger Pratt 1650-62, the ceilings of which were recorded by Isaac Ware (Cat. E15). Through the marriage of his daughter to Viscount Folkestone he had close Huguenot connections. An entry in his account book for February 1756 records a payment to Roubiliac of £86; Pleydell sat from 12 to 17 May 1755 and the bust arrived at Coleshill on 3 February 1756. Although the house was destroyed by fire in 1952, the bust may be identified with the portrait on the chimneypiece in the saloon, shown in photographs of 1909. The chimneypiece appears to conform in style to the baroque decoration of the interior; it is possible that the chimneypiece was adapted to receive the bust but this work cannot be related to any payments recorded in the account book. Roubiliac is here employing a convention first used by Rysbrack for his bust of Daniel Finch in 1723 and based on Roman Republican portraits, with short hair and classical drapery. The small folds and asymmetrical arrangement of the drapery, however, show Roubiliac transforming this classical convention into something thoroughly rococo. Almost identical drapery was used on a bust of Paul Whitehead, convincingly attributed to Roubiliac (Kerslake 1977 II, pl. 881).

Prov: by family descent to Miss Katherine Pleydell-Bouverie; Cook; bequeathed to the National Trust with Coleshill House
Lit: Murdoch 1983, p. 39; Webb 1954, p. 176
MCB

S34 *Dr Richard Bentley*
Louis François Roubiliac (1702/5-62). 1756
Marble bust; h. (without socle) 620
Inscribed (on the socle) *BENTLEY* and *Pos.nt Bentleii Filia e/MDCCLVI 1756* and on the left side *L.F. Roubiliac Sc!.*
Master & Fellows of Trinity College, Cambridge

A distinguished classical scholar, Bentley (1662-1742) was the controversial Master of Trinity College between 1700 and 1734, far-seeing in his promotion of the natural sciences but arrogant and quarrelsome by nature. His portrait, given by his daughters, is one of ten busts executed by Roubiliac for the college between 1751 and 1757. A model, apparently of unfired clay, was purchased for the British Museum by Dr Maty from the 1762 sale (3rd Day, Lot 81) and a plaster is at Lambeth Palace. According to Elizabeth Montagu in 1753 no less than 48 busts of 'considerable persons that have been of the college' were originally envisaged and the master, Robert Smith (who commissioned Roubiliac's statue of Newton) evidently intended that scientists should be strongly represented. The choice of Roubiliac for what was to be

S34

S35

his most extensive group of portraits may be due to Daniel Lock, a Fellow of Trinity and friend of Hogarth, whose monument in the college chapel was executed by the sculptor. Although plaster busts of ancient and modern 'worthies' were by this date common in libraries (see Cats. S28, S29) such a major series of portrait busts is exceptional. A French precedent, probably known to the sculptor, was the Bibliothèque Ste. Geneviève (Brice 1725, II, p. 510) containing busts by Girardon and Coyzevox, among them the latter's Robert de Cotte (Souchal, 1977, p. 211). Roubiliac's debt to such French portraits is seen in the virtuoso carving of the wig, a convention of dress used on relatively few of his busts. The treatment of the shifting drapery, with its small angular folds, shows a rococo concern with the momentary play of light on different textures, first seen in the statue of Handel (Cat. F10).

Lit: Bindman 1982; Esdaile 1924, p. 23; Esdaile 1928, p. 98; Whinney 1964, p. 113
MCB

S35 *Sir Robert Cotton*

Louis François Roubiliac
(1702/5-62)
Marble; h. (without socle) 580
Inscribed (on left side) *L.F. Roubiliac* and (on the socle) *ROB. COTTON/ Baronettus, Posuit Eliab Harvey/1757* and *1757*
Master and Fellows of Trinity College, Cambridge

Although among the last four of the Trinity series, Cotton (who was unconnected with the College) may have been included in the original scheme in an attempt by Dr Smith to secure the Cottonian Library; by 1753, however, this has passed to the newly founded British Museum. It was apparently based on an earlier printed portrait in the College. A virtuoso example of Roubiliac's marble carving, this bust (a terracotta model for which is in the British Museum) is exceptionally vivacious for an historicising portrait. By exploiting the contrast between different drapery textures and giving the ruff an unexpected lightness and movement, Roubiliac translates his early 17th century source into a wholly rococo idiom. The portrait reflects the taste

for 'Van Dyck' and other period costume that also found expression in, for example, some Gainsborough portraits (Cherry and Harris 1982) and Rysbrack's busts of Van Dyck and others (Eustace, 1982, pp. 138-47).

Lit: Bindman 1982; Esdaile 1924, p. 33; Esdaile 1928, pp. 3, 98, 101, 165; Whinney 1964, p. 113
MCB

S36

S36 *Joseph Wilton*

After Louis François Roubiliac
(172/5-62). *c.* 1825 after a model of 1761
Plaster bust; h. 840
Later socle inscribed *JOSEPH WILTON ESQ. RA/ died November 25th 1803. This bust, by Roubiliac, is presented to the Royal Academy by his Daughter Lady Chambers.*
Royal Academy of Arts, London

This bust has hitherto been identified with 'Ditto [ie bust] of Mr Wilton' shown at the Socity of Artists in 1761 (no 154), together with Wilton's portrait of Roubiliac (cf Cat. S37). However, recent examination by Anne Brodrick and John Larson (Dept of Conservation, VAM) has revealed casting lines that run down the shoulders and arms and continue down the sides of the socle, indicating that both bust and socle were cast together. As the inscription, referring to the presentation of the portrait of Wilton to the Royal Academy, is not carved on the plaster but cast from an

earlier carved inscription, the cast must post-date this gift which was probably made shortly before 1824, when it is recorded in the Academy's Minute Book (Esdaile 1923). The plaster cannot therefore be the bust exhibited in 1761. The somewhat sketchy quality of the hair indicates that the original was modelled rather than carved and the pink surface that lies beneath the later overpainting of the cast suggests an imitation of unfired clay or terracotta rather than of plaster. Similarly, although the material is not stated in the Society of Artists' catalogue, the description of the following entry as a bust in marble perhaps implies that the preceding work was in some other medium. According to J.T. Smith (1829, II, p. 184) Roubiliac's bust was sent to 'Mr Nolleken's to be repaired' and the carved socle could have been added at this date. The original appears to have disappeared as early as 1830 when Allen Cunningham unsuccessfully attempted to trace it for illustration in his Life of Wilton, published in that year; the present plaster came to light in 1923 at Burlington House. In its scale and form, showing the sitter with arms rather than truncated below the shoulders, this portrait is exceptional among 18th century English busts. Possible sources may be found in the well-established French tradition of three-quarter-length painted portraits showing sculptors with their tools, notable examples being Largellière's portrait of Nicolas Costou now in Berlin (Souchal 1980, pl. 1d) and Lambert-Sigisbert Adam's self-portrait drawing in Oxford (Kalnein and Levey, 1972, pl. 66). In boldly adapting this convention into three dimensions Roubiliac may also have been aware of the form of Roman late baroque busts, such as that on Maratti's monument to Carlo Maratta which he may have seen in 1752 and which Scheemakers had drawn earlier. The illusionism of the Wilton portrait, however, perhaps owes more to Bernini whose impact may also be seen in the illusionistic devices employed in the slightly earlier monument to Viscount Shannon (Esdaile 1928, pl. XXXVII).

Prov: Lady Chambers; presented to the Royal Academy before 1824
Lit: Allen 1983; Esdaile 1923; Esdaile 1928, p. 89; Radcliffe 1969, p. 44;

Royal Academy 1951, p. 22; Sainte-Croix 1882, p. 118; Smith 1829, II, p. 115; Society of Artists 1761, no 154; Whinney 1964, pp. 112-3
MCB

S37 *Louis Francois Roubiliac*
Attributed to Joseph Wilton (1722-1803). *c.* 1761
Marble bust; h. 650
National Portrait Gallery, London

Although the bust is undocumented before 1851, the identity of the sitter as Roubiliac is supported by comparison with portraits by Carpentiers, Soldi (Cat. S17) and Vispré. However, an attribution to Roubiliac himself, proposed by Esdaile and followed by Whinney, is unacceptable. Although the sculptor's 1762 sale catalogue includes a self-portrait in oils and several examples of 'Mr *Roubiliacs* mask' and 'a head' of himself, no mention is made of a proper sculptural self-portrait and in style this bust is not compatible with Roubiliac's own later work. The rather dry modelling of the face (and particularly the eyes) instead suggest an attribution to Wilton, whose busts (eg an unidentified man, Bromley-Davenport collection) show comparable handling. This attribution is supported by the exhibition by Wilton in 1761 at the Society of Artists of 'A Bust of Mr Roubiliac' (no 167) and a reference in the sitter's 1762 sale catalogue (Lot 8, 2nd Day, under 'BUSTS in Plaister') to 'Mr *Roubiliac* by Mr *Wilton*'. Although the material of the portrait exhibited in 1761 is unspecified the description of the succeeding exhibit as 'Ditto in marble of Oliver Cromwell' suggests that it was not in marble and may perhaps have been the plaster that appeared in Roubiliac's sale in the following year. The National Portrait Gallery's marble may well be a version based on the model shown in 1761.

Prov: James Thomson sale, 18 July 1851, Lot 162 (as Voltaire); Colnaghi; Francis Roubiliac Corder (sitter's great grandson); Dr A.F.R. Corder sale, 3 December 1926; Shilliter; presented to National Portrait Gallery by the National Art-Collections Fund
Lit: Esdaile 1928, pp. 191-2; Kerslake 1977, pp. 236-7; Whinney 1964
MCB

S38

S38 *Design for a monument*
Attributed to Louis François Roubiliac (1702/5-62) or his workshop. *c.* 1753
Pencil, pen and ink and wash; 330 x 200
VAM (D.628-1887)

First associated with Roubiliac by John Physick and exhibited in 1966 with an attribution to his workshop, this drawing is apparently related in its form to the monument to Thomas and Arabella Myddleton at Wrexham and may be one of two 'Designs' (medium unspecified) for 'Mr and Mrs Middleton' in the 1762 sale catalogue (2nd Day, Lot 71). However, the medallion portraits are closer to those of George and Elizabeth Harvey (1753) at Hempstead (Whinney 1964, pl. 81), so that it is possibly a rejected design for the Harvey monument that was later re-used for the Myddletons. Significant differences (notably in the shape of the console panel and the disposition of the drapery) between drawing and monument, together with alterations made when the pencil under-drawing was inked in, suggest that this is a preliminary design rather than a copy. However, it has few similarities with the only other drawing that may plausibly be attributed to Roubiliac, (Murdoch 1983, p. 27) if we exclude Cat. S6, and

may possibly be by a workshop assistant rather than from his own hand. In 1767 Wedgwood purchased from the sculptor's widow a volume of sketches but the description of it as containing 'any momentary thought or vision in connection with his art' implies that it did not contain worked-out designs for monuments. The imprecise nature of this sketch and the absence of comparable examples support the view that Roubiliac preferred to model in clay without preliminary drawings. The Myddleton work belongs to a group of modest wall monuments which sometimes share common features, (cf the curtain on the Bolinbroke monument, Battersea), but never apparently follow the same pattern. Characteristic are the medallion portraits, reflecting not only earlier French monuments (eg Souchal II, p. 47) but also perhaps Roubiliac's contact with Dassier (Murdoch 1982, p. 187), and the idiosyncratic architectural frames in which the fluid, three-dimensional forms hint at his Dresden training.

Prov: purchased from E. Parsons, 1887
MCB

S39 *General Hargrave's Monument in Westminster Abbey*
Philip Dawe (active *c.* 1760-*c.* 1806) 1806
Mezzotint; 621 x 382
Lettered with title, and *Roubiliac Statuary Pubd. by R Pollard June 5 1806 Engraved by P. Dawe*

The Trustees of the British Museum (1851-9-8-19)

Hargrave (d. 1751) was an undistinguished colonel in the Royal Fuseliers and a friend of General Fleming, whose nephew (who served under Hargrave) commissioned the monuments to the two men, placed adjacently in Westminster Abbey (Bindman 1981). 'Fines' for the erection of both monuments were paid in 1751 but the Hargrave was not finished until 1757 (dated on the monument), three years after the Fleming (cf. *Gent's Mag.*, Aug. 1754, p. 352). A 'design for General Hargrave' is included under 'Designs . . . in *Terra cotta*, etc' in the 1762 sale catalogue (4th Day, Lot 63). The iconography is complex and apparently draws on a wide range of sources. The motif of the deceased emerging from the tomb at the Last Trump, already employed in the monuments to Lord Petre (cf Cat. S36; Penny 1975) and Mary Myddleton (Allan 1973) probably depends from French works such as the monument to Le Brun's mother (Souchal 1979, I, p. 108) and Dedieu's Bishop Gaspard des Laurens (*ibid*, p. 229) but Roubiliac may also have been aware of 17th century English precedents (eg Sir John Denham, Egham; Kemp 1980, fig 150). The symbolism of the collapsing pyramid, signifying the end of Time, apparently implies a thorough understanding of the broken pyramid in Fischer von Erlach's Mitrowitz monument earlier used as a source for the Argyll composition (Cat. S5; Laing 1984). Further possible sources include Schlüter (whose figures entangled in drapery Roubiliac may have seen in Berlin) Bernini and Permoser (reflected in the personifications of Time and Death) and Le Gros (whose group of Religion and Heresy on the St Ignatius Altar provides a precedent for the falling arrangement of the latter two figures) (Baker 1984 I). In its dramatic exposition of an eschatological theme the monument forms a counterpart to passages in Handel's Messiah (first performed 1741) which may possibly have had an indirect influence. (Bindman 1981, p. 15).

Lit: Esdaile 1928
MCB

S40 *Model for the monument to Joseph and Elizabeth Nightingale*

Louis François Roubiliac
(1702/5-62). 1758
Terracotta; h. 350
Inscribed (on left edge of base) *1758 Roubiliac. in.*
Dean and Chapter of Westminster Abbey (on loan to the VAM

This model for the monument to Joseph (d. 1752) and Elizabeth Nightingale (d. 1731) in Westminster Abbey shows the husband embracing his wife while, below, a draped skeleton of Death (now fragmentary) emerges from the doors of a tomb, stepping from a sarcophagus within. Discovered in the Abbey's Triforium in 1870 it may be identifiable with 'One ditto [ie design] for

S40

Mr *Nightingale*'s', listed in the 1762 sale catalogue (3rd Day, Lot 71) under 'DESIGNS for Monuments . . . etc'. Also included were busts of 'Mr *Nightingale* and his Lady' in both terracotta (2nd Day, Lot 85) and plaster (4th Day, Lot 28) and a plaster mould for 'Mrs *Nightingale*' (1st Day, Lot 44). This terracotta or another model was sold by a Mr Jackson at Christie's 22 July 1807, Lot 88 (Gunnis 1968, p. 330). Included (with Cat. S4) in Lot 252 of Nollekens' sale of 4 December 1823 were 'two other Designs for the Nightingale Monument &c by *ditto* [ie Roubiliac]' which were presumably drawings rather than models since the Lot is listed under the heading 'Drawings'. The monument was erected under the terms of their son's will but as he died in 1754 the project was probably supervised by his sister. The emphasis given to the mother, unusual in a monument ostensibly to both parents, may be explained by her death occurring while giving birth to the daughter (Bindman 1981, p. 13). An unusually high 'fine' of £80 was paid in 1758 for the erection of the monument which is signed and dated 1761. The presence of a precise date, signature and scale suggests that the terracotta (like Cat. S5) was directly related to a contract. The architectural setting of the monument follows the

model closely but several significant changes are made to the figures. In the model Nightingale embraces his wife rather than wards off Death, while Death itself does not apparently threaten the couple with his spear but instead grasps the door of the tomb. Correspondingly, Lady Nightingale's left breast is not yet uncovered to receive the dart. The angular drapery of the model, reminiscent of Egell's designs becomes in the marble more rounded and classical. Its iconographical sources are apparently complex and varied. The motif of Death emerging from a doorway derives from Bernini's Alexander VII monument and belongs to a varied tradition of monuments involving the door of death (Biatostocki 1973). By giving Death a spear in the finished monument, however, Roubiliac may have been influenced by Hayman's *Death of an Unbeliever*, placed alongside his own sculpture at Denbies (Allen 1982, pp. 227-9) or Miltonic illustrations, such as Hogarth's *Satan, Sin and Death* (Bindman 1981, p. 13) but Anthony Radcliffe suggests that the relationship between the swooning woman and her adversary shows the impact of Bernini's *Ecstasy of St Teresa*. For Nightingale's defensive response Roubiliac may have been indebted not only to Hayman but also to Pigalle's monument to the Maréchal de Saxe (Brinckmann 1925, III, pp. 114-5), the model of which was produced by 1756 and widely discussed (Eurcy-Raymond 1927, p. 272); Lady Nightingale's bare breast and more classical drapery were perhaps prompted by Pigalle's figure of France there. The arched setting is probably taken from the engraving of the Mitrovice monument (cf Cat. S5; Laing 1984) but in Roubiliac's composition it serves almost as a proscenium arch beneath which is enacted the most dramatic action of any 18th century English monument. Conceivably this reflects the 'forced conceits' characteristic of the acting of Roubiliac's friend Garrick (Murdoch 1983, p. 38).

Prov: Jackson sale, Christies, 22 July 1807, 88 (?); discovered in Westminster Abbey, 1870
Lit: Esdaile 1923; Esdaile 1928, p. 157
MCB

S41 Monument to Joseph and Elizabeth Nightingale

Attributed to E.F. Burney (1760-1848)
Watercolour; 540 x 340
Inscribed in pencil, *2201, ROUBILIAC INV^t* and *DRAWN BY E.F. BURNEY*
VAM (P5Q-1982)

Closely related in style to signed works by E.F. Burney, this watercolour was probably intended as the basis for an engraving. By the early 19th century earlier admiration of the monument, apparent in both the judgment of a writer in the *Gent's Mag* (1772, p. 517) that this was 'the finest piece of sculpture' in the Abbey and John Wesley's comment (Esdaile 1928, p. 157) that it was the 'one tomb that showed common sense', had given way to disapproval of its baroque qualities. Although Cunningham (1830, p. 58) could describe the monument as 'more generally praised than any of his works', an attitude presumably reflected in the execution of this watercolour, Flaxman was by this period criticising Roubiliac's work for its use of 'epigrammatic conceit and frequent meanness of parts' (1838. p. 50).

Prov. purchased from Mr Stirling, London, in 1982
MCB

S42 Design for the monument to General Wolfe

T. Cook after L.F. Roubiliac (1702/5-62); 1789 after a model of *c.* 1760
Engraving; 220 x 160
Lettered *Roubiliac fecit, Cook sculp., Model of an original Design for a Monument to the Memory of Gen. Wolfe, in the possession of Charles Theomatyr Crane, Merch.^t London*

The Trustees of the British Museum

Engraved in the *Gentleman's Magazine* for January 1789 (pl. I) Roubiliac's terracotta model for the Wolfe monument was described in the previous year (LVIII, pp. 668-9). Wolfe is shown in the arms of Victory flanked by Magnanimity, (with laurel wreath, shield, eagle and Hercules's club) and 'the British lion triumphing over the savage, a map of Quebec, on which the Indian prostrate rests his right-hand, and in his left his bow, with a beaver peeping out underneath'. Said in 1783 to belong to Edward Bridgen, the model was given

to Charles Theomatyr Crane before 1789. Another 'design' appeared in Roubiliac's 1762 sale (1st Day, Lot 71) and subsequently passed through the silversmith Panton to Nollekens (Smith 1828, I, p. 188; Nollekens sale 1823, 3rd Day, Lot 43, sold to the sculptor Behnes). One of these models was offered by Roubiliac to the Duke of Newcastle in a letter of 18 January 1760 (BL MS Add 32, 901, fol 361). A drawing in a volume owned by Nollekens in Sir John Soane's Museum (fol 41) has been attributed to Roubiliac (Esdaile 1928, p. 164) but this is unconnected with Bridgen's model and does not resemble Cat. S38 in style; it might conceivably relate to Tyler's proposed design. Although described in 1783 (*Gent's Mag* LIII, p. 54) as 'far preferable to that in the Abbey' Roubiliac's composition appears from the engraving to lack unity, with the central group placed on a plinth almost as a freestanding statue. Enclosed within a proscenium arch recalling that around the Nightingale monument (Cat. S40), the illusionistic background of the tent (perhaps fired separately as in Cat. S46) and the cannon closely resembles features of Roubiliac's Shannon monument (Esdaile 1928, pl. XXXVII). The motif of the 'Indian' derives from a well-established baroque tradition of rulers or saints crushing personifications of Discord or Heresy (eg Permoser's Apotheosis of Prince Eugen) which was earlier employed by Rysbrack in one of his designs for the Newton monument (Eustace 1982, cat. 45). An example probably known to Roubiliac when in Paris was Guillaume Coustou's group for the bridge at Juvisy-sur-Orge (erected 1728; Souchal 1980, pp. 150-2, 262) but the closest parallel is Rusconi's group St Ignatius Trampling Heresy in St Peter's, Rome (Enggass 1976, pl. 226). For the central group, however, a possible source may have been an Ajax and Patrocolus group akin to the well-known Pasquino (Haskell and Penny 1981, pp. 291-6).

Lit: Esdaile 1928, pp. 161-4; O'Donoghue 1914, p. 526; Whinney 1964, p. 265
MCB

S43 Monument to General Wolfe

E.W. Thomson (1770-1847) after Riley.
(*c.* 1752-98). 1798
Engraving; 279 x 209
Lettered *Riley del, E W Thomson sculp.* and *London. Published by R. Bowyer Historic Gallery, Pall Mall, April 1798*

The Trustees of the British Museum

Wilton's monument in Westminster Abbey shows the dying Wolfe, with his officers, looking towards Fame who flies towards him with a wreath; below a bronze relief by Capitsoldi depicts the taking of Quebec on 13 September 1759. Following Wolfe's death, Parliament voted money for the erection of a monument on 21 November 1759 (*Journals of the House of Commons*, xxviii, p. 643) but this was not opened until November 1773 (*Gent's Mag*, XLIII, pp. 524, 616). However, the competition for the commission was apparently held in mid 1760 for on 1 August 1760 Horace Walpole wrote to Horace Mann that 'designs have been laid before my Lord Chamberlain several months; Wilton, Adam, Chambers, and others, all gave in their drawings immediately and I think the Duke of Devonshire decided for the first'. (Lewis 1937, 21, p. 428). Both contemporary comments and the number of the sculptors submitting proposals indicate the prestige attached to the commission and public interest is registered in a satirical print inscribed 'The Vanity of Human Glory A Description of the Monument to General Wolfe 1760' (BM: S. 3696). The 'others' mentioned included Roubiliac (Cat. S41), Rysback (who on 11 December 1759 told Sir Edward Littleton that he had 'made some Drawings for it but know not how they will succeed', Webb 1954, p. 204; Lambert 1984), Tyler (who exhibited a model at the Society of Artists in 1760) and possibly Cheere (whose design may have been included in his 1770 sale, Esdaile 1928, p. 162). Carlini showed a 'Design for General Wolfe's Monument' at the Society of Artists in 1760 (no 77) which may be the 'Death of Wolfe' in his sale of 13 January 1791. Designs by unidentified artists are in the Huntington Library (Harris 1971, p. 326) and Sir John Soane's Museum (Cat. S42) while Adam's relief from his design was re-employed for the Townsend monument (Fleming 1962). The chronology of the monument's evolution is uncertain. Walpole's report implies that Wilton had been chosen for the commission by August 1760 (perhaps partly because of his bust of Wolfe; Cat. S42) but it is unclear whether the executed monument follows the design submitted then. A finished design (Parsons cat. no 40, no 456; undated cutting in Sculpture Department archive), showing it in its final form, except for the omission of the relief, is of uncertain date and status. However, Walpole's angry (and effective) protest to the Dean in July 1761 (cf Lewis 1937, 38, p. 110) about the proposed removal of Aymer de Valence's monument suggests that proportions at least were already determined and Grosley's detailed description of the model he saw in Wilton's studio in 1765 (1771, II, p. 102f) confirms that the final design was established by this date. Smith's statement (1828, II, p. 176) that his father spent three years carving the figures indicates that carving had begun by late 1768 and in November 1772 the monument was reported to be 'now erecting' (*Gent's Mag* X, p. 517). The work is transitional, certain elements anticipating the large neo-classical monuments erected in the Abbey towards the end of the century but the main composition remaining largely rococo in its treatment of the subject and its figure style.

Lit: O'Donoghue 1914, p. 567; Stevenson 1976, p. 79
MCB

S44 *General James Wolfe*
After Joseph Wilton (1722-1803). Early 20th century after a model of *c.* 1760
Plaster; h. 740
VAM

The type cast of a plaster edition listed in the VAM 1939 catalogue of plaster reproductions as a cast from a bronze in the National Portrait Gallery; this modern bronze was case from an apparently early plaster formerly in the collection of Lord Harmsworth and said to have been acquired from the grandson of Rev Richard Board, Vicar of Westerham, where Wolfe is buried. As Kerslake has demonstrated (1959, pp. 40-2), this early plaster is related to the marble (which has a gorget added) now in the National Gallery of Canada, Ottawa, and formerly in the collection of the Earl of Rosebery, acquired by the third Earl (1847-1929). This marble may well be that sketched in 1872 by Sharf in the collection of Lord Charlemont, a patron of Wilton. According to Horace Walpole (Lewis 1937, p. 156), 'The duke of Richmond had a mind to have a statue of General Wolfe. Wilton the statuary went down to Portsmouth, and opened his coffin, when it was brought over, to try to take off his face, but it was too much distorted. They found out a servant of Lord Gower, who was like Wolfe, and Wilton was ordered to model his face, and Lord Edgcumbe was to correct it by memory.' If Walpole was accurate, this must have taken place between 17 and 20 November 1759 (cf *Gent's Mag.* 29 pp. 548f) suggesting that the model for these busts was executed about 1760. However, Wilton also probably made use of a profile sketch (Royal United Services Institution), attributed to Henry Smyth, Wolfe's officer, which was made shortly before the general's death and, according to a pencil inscription on the verso, is the sketch 'from which his bust was principally taken'. This may explain the striking, almost caricature-like profile of the Wolfe portrait. In the asymmetry of the drapery, flowing hair and the twist of the shoulders it shows Wilton working in a wholly rococo manner.

MCB

S45 *George Frederick Handel*
Louis François Roubiliac (1702/5-62); *c.* 1755-60
Bronze portrait relief; h. 263
Cheng Huan

This relief, representing an elderly Handel, is closely related to bronze reliefs of Conyers Middleton (Cheng Huan coll., probably from a model for an unexecuted bust for Trinity College), Pope and a gilt bronze of Garrick (Garrick Club) based on Roubiliac's portrait. Although differing from each other in technique and facture, all share features characteristic of Roubiliac's modelling style and probably belong to a group of 'basso relievos' represented in the 1762 sale catalogue by an Inigo Jones, Cromwell, Pope and Handel (2nd Day, Lots 92-3). The inclusion of the elderly Handel in the group suggests a late date in Roubiliac's career. This relief differs from the Pope and Middleton in handling and facture, notably in its less highly finished surface and the casting of bust and backplate as one piece. Two other differently finished versions of this model are known (as busts only), suggesting that aftercasts were produced after Roubiliac's death. Unlike some reliefs in this group, the Handel does not appear to follow a three-dimensional portrait, although it resembles the terracotta roundel (Cat. F12). Versions of Pope, Handel and Newton, 'in bronze finely repared by the late ingenious Mr Roubiliac' appear in an early Christie's sale (1766 or 67), the use of 'repared' suggesting that they were worked up by the sculptor after casting. Although little is known about 18th century English bronze casting, the quality of the Pope, the bronze bust of Chesterfield (Whinney 1971, pp. 86-7) and the figures from the Kensington Palace clock (Cat. S44, assumes a sophisticated casting technique, also evident in cast components of contemporary silver, as well as, on Roubiliac's part, a training that involved the finishing of bronzes.

Lit: Mallet 1962
MCB

S46

S46 *Model for the monument to George Frederick Handel*

Attributed to Louis François Roubiliac (1702/5-62). *c.* 1760
Terracotta; h. 980
The Visitors of the Ashmolean Museum, Oxford

Fired in two parts consisting of (1) the composer and table on a plinth and (2) the architectural setting, with central arch masked by the figure, mounted on slate. Traces of gesso remain below the composer's coat. Probably the final model for the Westminster Abbey monument (Whinney 1964, p. 110) and developed from Cat. S47, this terracotta does not appear in the 1762 sale catalogue although lot 61 (2nd Day, under 'Moulds in Plaister') lists 'Mr Handell's monument', suggesting that one or more plaster models were made. In 1766 the Royal Society of Arts awarded John Kitchingman third prize under 'Drawings . . . from *Models, casts in Plaster*' for a copy of one of these models (Dossie 1782, III, p. 417). The monument was erected with £600 left in the composer's will. A fine of £25 was paid to the Abbey in 1759 and the monument 'opened' on 10th July 1762 (*Gent's Mag*, XXXII, p.

340), after the sculptor's death. Unlike Cat. S47 which shows the composer wearing a soft cap and apparently involved with his score, this later model presents Handel in an attitude of inspiration, pointing to the winged figure (described by the *Gentleman's Magazine* as David) above. Although still boldly naturalistic in its drapery and facial expression, the composition now has a more markedly noble theme; the architecture has become more spacious, suggesting a theatrical backdrop, particularly in the handling of the clouds. The executed monument follows the Ashmolean terracotta closely but modifications are made to the music and the perspectival effects of background to allow the composition to fit more comfortably into its setting.

Prov: Given by James Wyatt to the University of Oxford in 1848
Lit: Burke 1976, p. 190; Esdaile 1928, p. 154
MCB

S47 *Model for the monument to George Frederick Handel*

Attributed to Louis François Roubiliac (1702/5-62) *c.* 1759
Terracotta; h. 357
Gerald Coke Handel Collection

Apparently an early design for the monument, preceding Cat. S46. Compact in scale, it is more tentatively modelled, with the relationship between composer and winged figure not yet clearly defined. The composer's profile view emphasises his bulbous nose, often ridiculed in contemporary caricatures, and the change of pose in Cat. S46 may have been made partly to avoid this.

Prov: purchased from a Bristol antique shop; John Kenworthy-Browne
Lit: Kerslake 1977; Whinney 1961, pp. 84-5; Whinney 1964, p. 260 n 35
MCB

S48 *Fame*

John Michael Rysbrack (1694-1770). 1760
Terracotta, h. 581
Inscribed (on the base), *Michl. Rysbrack fecit 1760*
VAM (A.1-1969)

Probably identifiable with 'a sketch of *Fame* for Admiral *Vernon's Monument*' in

Rysbrack's sale, 25 January, 1766, Lot 9. The 'fine' for the erection of the monument in Westminster Abbey, one of Rysbrack's last works, was paid in 1759 and the finished work dated 1763. Various alternative pen and ink designs survive (Eustace 1982, p. 184 n. 1) but this model shows the figure in its final form. Figures in such vigorous movement are unusual in Rysbrack's work; Whinney detected in the pose the influence of Roubiliac's History on the Argyll monument but Eustace has suggested that Rysbrack was more indebted to early 18th century Franco-Flemish sculpture and classical works such as the Borghese gladiator. Whatever the specific source of the pose, however, the heightened drama and smaller drapery folds reflect the impact of the rococo manner on an artist whose sculpture was rooted in an Antwerp late baroque tradition. A readiness to respond to the new style, seen earlier in his figures of Van Dyck and Rubens (Eustace 1982, pp. 141-6), is also implied by his subscription to the 1736 edition of Brunetti (see Cat. B10) and his ownership of Johnston's *Ornaments* (Cat. L48) (Christie's, 7 February 1774, 55).

Prov: Rysbrack sale, 25 January 1766, Lot 9 (?); Peter Hollins, sculptor (information from Hollins' descendant) purchased by the Museum with the assistance of the Bryan and Hildburgh Bequests
Lit: Eustace 1982, pp. 182-4; Physick 1969, fig 73; Webb, 1954, pp. 91, 167, 226; Whinney 1971, pp. 54-5
MCB

S49 *Relief of a shepherd and shepherdess*

Attributed to Henry Cheere (1703-81) or William Collins (1721-93). *c.* 1760
White marble on giallo marble ground, within later gilt wood frame, 41 x 640
VAM (1951-1882)

Probably intended for a chimneypiece, the relief is carved *à jour* and applied to the coloured ground, but there is no evidence that it was ever in fact mounted *in situ*. This technique was frequently used by Cheere (most notably in the chimneypiece of the Great Drawing Room at West Wycombe) and exploits the contrast

307

between differently coloured marbles that are characteristic of his monuments too. The similarity of the shepherd and the tree to those found in Cat. S52 (no 24) support an attribution to Cheere and this relief may have been among the 'Marble Basso Relievos &c' sold at his sale on 26 March 1770 (Lots 40-50). However, reliefs with very similar subjects to those in designs and documented chimneypieces by Cheere were exhibited at the Society of Artists from 1760 onwards by William Collins who may well have executed examples in chimneypieces for which Cheere received payment. Collins, who is listed in Kirby's *Perspective* among the members of the St Martin's Lane Academy (Girouard 1966, p. 189), is described by J T Smith (1828, II, p. 313) as 'the most famous modeller of chimney tablets, of his day', executing 'pastoral scenes which were understood by the most common observer'; these included 'shepherds and shepherdesses seated on a bank, surrounded by their flocks'. This relief may therefore have been executed by Collins, rather than Cheere, and the grimacing expression of the man make it conceivable that it was the 'Ditto [bas-relievo], for a chimney-piece; a clown and country girl' exhibited at the Society of Artists in 1761 (no 144).

Prov: Jones Bequest to VAM, 1882
Lit: Jones Catalogue 1924, II, no 394 (as Bacon)

S50 *Design for a monument*

Sir Robert Taylor (1714-88),
c. 1760-5
Pencil; 325 x 210
Taylor Institution, Oxford (Arch. Tay. 1, fol. 85r)

Probably a design for the monument to Richard Emmott (d. 1761) at Colne, Lancashire, which employs an identical putto on a rocaille base but is set within a round-headed niche, without a sarcophagus. The inscription describes Emmott as 'late of Basinghall-Street London', a city connection that explains the commissioning of Taylor, many of whose clients were city merchants (Binney 1984). Small monuments with similar *putti*, surrounded by assorted books, skulls, rocaille work and cartouches, form a distinctive group within Taylor's sculpture and a variant composition on fol. 88r (Esdaile 1948, fig 8) appears to relate to a monument to Theophilus Salwey (d. 1760) at Ludlow. Both designs are characteristic of monuments dating predominently from the 1750s and early 60s. Taylor's putti are quite distinct from those of Cheere or the Anglo-Flemish children of Rysbrack and Scheemakers and may perhaps be derived from a French tradition seen in the contemporary work of Pigalle (eg Réau 1950, pl. 27).

Prov: as Cat. S22
MCB

S51 *Design for a monument to a poet*

Sir Robert Taylor (1714-88).
c. 1755-60
Taylor Institution, Oxford (Arch. Tay. 1, fol. 130r)

A more finished version of this unidentified monument is on fol. 61r in the same volume. The apple tree branch suggested to Mrs Esdaile (MS note in the volume) that this was a preliminary design for a monument to John Philips (d. 1708), author of the poem *Cyder*, but the existing monument to him, in Westminster Abbey is of considerably earlier date. It might conceivably, however, be a design for the monument to James Thomson, executed in 1762 by Spang. With its cluster of asymmetrically arranged poetical attributes and the draped medallion portrait it is a characteristic example of a small rococo wall monument, the most distinguished example of which is probably Roubiliac's Daniel Lock in Trinity College, Cambridge, although this has a full portrait bust. Typical of Taylor's work are the heavy scrolls, the urn and the supporting console panel which in outline recalls the tailpieces used in rococo book decoration.

Prov: as Cat. S22
MCB

S52 *Book of designs for chimneypieces*

Sir Henry Cheere (1703-81).
c. 1750-60
28 pen and ink and watercolour drawings, silhouetted, on 16 leaves bound in vellum; 315 x 229
VAM (D.715-1887)

These designs, which represent a distinctive form of English rococo developed by Cheere, include chimneypieces executed by him at Picton Castle (no 13 Girouard 1960), Langley Park (no 27) and Grimsthorpe. The two examples shown here illustrate two contrasting types. No 15 follows a conventional Palladian pattern although the delicate floral sways are typical of Cheere's workshop. Like a number of Cheere's Gothic designs, no 16 derives its clustered column supports and shaped inner edge from a design in Batty Langley's *Gothic Architecture Improved* (pl. XLVIII) which was used as the basis for various existing chimneypieces including that supplied *c.* 1757 by 'Daniel Sephton to Tissington Hall, Derbyshire (Rowan 1975, pl. 87). However, in place of Langley's background of blank arcading, Cheere substitutes the quatrefoils frequently employed on his chimneypieces and monuments (eg VAM 4910.2) and adds a relief of three hounds savaging a fox beneath a tree. This composition, which was intended to be carved *à jour* in white marble and applied to a coloured ground (cf Cat. S49) is apparently loosely adapted from Jean Baptiste Oudry's Wolf Hunt in the Musée Condé, Chantilly, which was engraved by the artist in 1725 (Opperman 1977, Cat. P180). A chimneypiece based on this design survives at Beauport, Massachusetts, one of various works by Cheere (including the monument to Charles Apthorpe, Boston) exported to America.

Prov: purchased from E. Parsons, 1887
Lit: Physick 1982; White 1983
MCB

S53 *Design for a chimneypiece at Barlaston Hall*
Sir Robert Taylor (1714-88).
c. 1756
Pen and ink and watercolour;
250 x 140
Taylor Institution, Oxford (Arch. Tay. 2, fol. 7r).

This design is one of 13 included in an octavo volume of chimneypieces drawings with the label 'SIR R TAYLOR'S DESIGNS' (Gilson 1973, A2). An existing chimneypiece following this design is in the west room of Barlaston Hall, Staffordshire, (building 1756-8) which, on the basis of its plan and architectural details, has been convincingly attributed to Taylor (Gomme 1968). The over-mantel mirror was apparently not executed. The distinctive moulding of the upper edge, with its strongly modelled rocaille ends, corresponds closely with mouldings used on Taylor's monuments (cf George Hinde's monument, Kingston, Jamaica; Lewis 1972, p. 77) while the plaster swags are characteristic of the rococo ornament employed in the interiors of his early buildings (Binney 1984).

Prov: as Cat. S22
Lit: Gomme 1968
MCB

S54 *Design for a chimneypiece*
Sir Robert Taylor (1714-86).
c. 1750-60
Pen and ink and watercolour;
250 x 140
Taylor Institution, Oxford (Arch. Tay. 2, fol. 9r).

This design, from the same volume as Cat. S53, has sides showing alternative decorative schemes, intended to be viewed with a mirror to make up two complete chimneypieces with balanced sides. With its elaborate rocaille work and scrolls, it resembles the most flamboyant of English rococo carver's work. The accumulation of small scrolls seen on the lower border of the overmantel is also found on many of Taylor's wall monuments (eg Richard Freeman d. 1756, Batsford, Glos). A related chimneypiece design is in the Metropolitan Museum of Art, New York (67.707.5).

Prov: as Cat. S22
MCB

S55 *Pair of wall brackets*
Attributed to John Cheere (1709-1787). *c.* 1755
Gilt plaster; 660 x 460 x 300
The National Trust (Felbrigg Hall)

Apollo, God of Poetry and Music, appears on one bracket seated

amongst foliage, flowers, scrolls and rocaille, which represent Mount Parnassus. He wears a laurel crown, a sign of his supremacy in the arts, and holds a lyre in one hand while the other is stretched out to command attention. A swan stands next to him above a fall of water, which represents the stream of Castalia. According to classical writers, the swan loved music and was believed to utter a beautiful song at its death; it thus became an attribute of Apollo. A winged figure of Victory appears on the other bracket holding a wreath and palm branch. Clouds are above her head and an exotic bird emerges from a rocaille cartouche at the base of the bracket. The brackets formed part of William Windham's furnishings of the Cabinet Room at Felbrigg Hall, Norfolk and hung on either side of the bay window. They may have supported bronzed plaster busts, which were supplied by Henry Cheere. This type of bracket with elaborate scrolls inhabited by figures and animals, is reminiscent of the ormolu brackets for wall-clocks, produced by French craftsmen, such as Charles Cressent (1685-1768) or Jacques Caffieri (1678-1755).

Lit: Jackson-Stops 1980, pp. 30, 31
JH

Bibliography

Published in London unless otherwise stated.

Adams & Redstone 1981, E. Adams and D. Redstone, *Bow Porcelain*, 1981.
Agnews 1971, Agnews, *English Life and Landscape*, exhibition, 1971.
Allan 1968, D.G.C. Allan, *William Shipley, Founder of the Royal Society of Arts*, 1968.
Allan 1973, D. Allan, 'A Roubiliac Contract', *Connoisseur*, CLXXIV, 1973, pp 102-104.
Allan 1973-4, D.G.C. Allan, 'The Society of Arts and Government, 1754-1800', *Eighteenth Century Studies 7*, 1973-4.
Allen 1981, B. Allen, 'Jonathan Tyers' Other Garden', *Journal of Garden History*, I, 1981, pp 215-238.
Allen 1983, B. Allen, 'Joseph Wilton, Francis Hayman and the chimney-pieces from Northumberland House', *Burlington Magazine*, CXXV 1983, pp 195-202.
Allen 1937, B.S. Allen, *Tides in English Taste*, Cambridge, Mass., 1937.
Allen 1967, D.E. Allen, 'John Martyn's Botanical Society. A Biographical Analysis of Membership,' *Proceedings of the Botanical Society of the British Isles*, vol 6 pt 4 May 1967.
Anon 1897, 'Some Relics of David Garrick,' vol 1, 1897, pp 266-7.
Antal 1962, F. Antal, *Hogarth*, 1962.
Arnold 1832, *Library of the Fine Arts*, published by M. Arnold, iii, 1832.
Arnold 1871, W. Arnold, *The Life and Death of the Sublime Society of Beef Steaks*, 1871.
Arts Council 1975, Arts Council, *The Georgian Playhouse*, exhibition, 1975.
Asche 1978, S. Asche, *Balthasar Permoser*, Berlin, 1978.
Ashmolean 1836, *A Catalogue of the Ashmolean Museum*, Oxford, 1836.
Ashmolean 1969, *Eighteenth Century Master Drawings from the Ashmolean*, exhibition 1979-80. Shown at Baltimore, Minneapolis, Fort Worth, Cincinnati, Amsterdam.
Atheron 1974, H. M. Atherton, *Political Prints in the Age of Hogarth*, Oxford, 1974.
Atkins 1931, C. E. Atkins, *Register of Apprentices of Company of Clockmakers*, privately printed, 1931.
Aurenhammer 1973, Hans Aurenhammer, *J.B. Fischer von Erlach*, 1973.
Austin 1977, J. C. Austin, *Chelsea Porcelain at Williamsburg*, Williamsburg, Virginia, 1977.
Avray Tipping 1916, H. Avray Tipping, 'The Royal Fort, Gloucestershire', *Country Life*, 27 May 1916, 646-52.
Ayrton & Denvir 1948, M. Ayrton & B. Denvir, *Hogarth's Drawings*, 1948.
Baker 1984 I, M. Baker, 'Roubiliac and his European background', *Apollo*, CXIX.
Baker 1984 II, M. Baker, 'Henry Cheere's bust of George Pitt of Stratfieldsaye', *Burlington Magazine*, forthcoming.
Baker 1984 III, Baker, 'Roubiliacs portrait's of Lady Grisel Baillie and Lady Murray', *Burlington Magazine*, forthcoming.
Baker 1984 IV, 'Roubiliac's portraits of Handel', *Country Life*, forthcoming.
Banister 1981, J. Banister, 'In the Cause of Liberty', *Country Life*, 12 November 1981, CLXX, pp 1671-2.
Banister 1983, J. Banister, 'Pottery and Porcelain of "Silver Shape",' *Antique Dealer and Collectors' Guide*, February, 1983.
Bapst 1887, G. Bapst, *Les Germain*, Paris and London, 1887.
Barnard 1924, H. Barnard, *Chats on Wedgwood Ware*, 1924.
Barnett (ed.), R. D. Barnett, *Catalogue of the Collections of the Jewish Museum London*, 1974.
Barr 1980, E. Barr, *George Wickes, Royal Goldsmith 1698-1761*, 1980.
Barr 1983, E. Barr, 'The Bristol ewer and basin', *Art at Auction — The year at Sotheby's*, 1982-83, 1983.
Barrett 1953, F. Barrett, *Worcester Porcelain*, 1953.
Beard 1975, G. Beard, *Decorative Plasterwork in Great Britain*, 1975.

Beard 1975 I, G. Beard, 'Babel's 'A New Book of Ornaments', 1752', *Furniture History*, XI, 1975, pp 30-31.
Beard 1975 II, G. Beard, 'William Kent and the Cabinet Makers', *Burlington Magazine*, CXVII, December 1975, pp 867-871.
Beard 1981, G. Beard, *Craftsmen and Interior Decoration in England, 1660-1820*, Edinburgh 1981.
Beckett 1949, R. B. Beckett, *Hogarth*, 1949.
Bemrose 1898, W. Bemrose, *Bow, Chelsea and Derby Porcelain*, 1898.
Bemrose 1906, W. Bemrose, *Longton Hall Porcelain*, 1906.
Benjamin 1978, S. Benjamin, *English Enamels*, 1978.
Benton 1976, E. Benton, 'Payments by Sir Everard Fawkener to Nicholas Sprimont', *Transactions of the English Ceramic Circle*, vol 10, pt 1, 1976.
Berain (n.d.), J. Berain, *Ornamens Inventez par J. Berain*.
Beresford Chancellor 1909, E. Beresford Chancellor, *Lives of the British Architects*, 1909.
Berlin 1939, Staatliche Muzeen zu Berlin, *Katalog der Ornamentstichsammlung des Staatlichen Kunstbibliothek, Berlin*, Berlin & Leipzig, 1939.
Berliner & Egger 1981, R. Berliner & G. Egger, *Ornamentale Vorlageblätter*, München, 1981.
Berry-Hill 1953, H. & S. Berry-Hill, *Antique Gold Boxes*, New York, 1953.
Bewick 1762, T. Bewick, *A Memoir of Thomas Bewick written by himself*, Newcastle, 1762.
Bialostocki 1973, J. Bialostocki, 'The Door of Death', *Jahrbuch der Hamburger Kunstsammlungen*, 18, 1973, pp 7-32.
Bindman 1970, D. Bindman, *European sculpture from Bernini to Rodin*, 1970.
Bindman 1981, D. Bindman, 'Roubiliac in Westminster Abbey', *Oxford Art Journal*, 4, 1981, pp 10-16.
Bindman 1981, D. Bindman, *Hogarth*, 1981.
Bindman 1982, D. Bindman, 'Roubiliac's Busts at Trinity College, Cambridge' (Unpublished paper given to the Mellon Seminar on British Art, London 1982).
Binney 1984, M. Binney, *Sir Robert Taylor 1714-88. Architect to merchants and bankers*, 1984.
Binyon 1898, L. Binyon, *Catalogue of Drawings by British Artists*, the British Museum, 1898-1907.
Birch 1756, T. Birch, *The Heads of Illustrious Persons of Great Britain*, 1756.
Blakemore 1976, K. Blakemore, *Snuff Boxes*, 1976.
Blackmore 1965, H. L. Blackmore, *Guns and Rifles of the World*, 1965.
Blondel 1737, J.F. Blondel, *De la distribution des maisons de plaisance*, 1737.
Blunt 1972, A. Blunt, *Some uses and misuses of the terms Baroque and Rococo as applied to Architecture*, 1972.
Blunt 1924, R. Blunt (ed), *The Cheyne Book of Chelsea China and Pottery*, 1924 and reprint of 1973.
Blunt & Gardner 1924, R. Blunt & Bellamy Gardner, 'Some Finely Modelled Chelsea Figures', *Country Life*, May 17th, 1924.
BN: Fonds, Paris, Bibliothèque Nationale, *Inventaire du Fonds Français, Graveurs du dix-huitième siècle*, 1930 (continuing) (the numbers refer to the works of each artist).
Bordeaux 1977, Galerie des Beaux-Arts, Bordeaux, *La peinture Britannique, de Gainsborough à Bacon*, exhibition, 1977.
Bolling Hall 1979, Bolling Hall, Bradford, *Thomas Chippendale*, exhibition, 1979.
Borsay 1977, P. Borsay, 'The English Urban Renaissance — the Development of Provincial Culture c.1688-c.1760', *Social History* 2, 1977.
Lancaster 1942, H. Boswell Lancaster, 'Neglected Liverpool Engravers', *Apollo*, May, 1942.
Boulle (n.d.), A. C. Boulle, *Nouveaux Desseins de Meubles et Ouvrages de Bronze et de Marquetrie* (n.d.).
Bowyer 1936, W. Bowyer (alias W. B. Honey), 'A Ceramic Problem', *Connoisseur*, October 1936.
Boynton 1966, L. Boynton, 'Luke Lightfoot (?1722-1789)', *Furniture History*, II, 1966, pp 7-17.
Boynton 1980, L. Boynton, 'William and Richard Gomm',

Burlington Magazine, CXXII, June 1980.

Bradshaw 1981, P. Bradshaw, *18th Century English Porcelain Figures, 1745-1795,* 1981.

Bramsen 1965, B. Bramsen, *Nordiske Snusdåser,* Copenhagen, 1965.

Brewer 1976, J. Brewer, *Party Ideology and Popular Politics at the Accession of George III,* Cambridge, 1976.

Brighton 1983, Brighton Museum (and Manchester City Art Gallery), *The Inspiration of Egypt,* exhibition, 1983.

Brinckmann 1925, A. E. Brinckmann, *Barock-Bozzetti,* Frankfurt-am-Main, 1925.

BM:S, British Museum, *Catalogue of Political and Personal Satires,* 1877-1954.

British Museum 1910, British Museum, *A Guide to the English Pottery and Porcelain in the Department of British and Medieval Antiquities,* 2nd edition, 1910.

British Museum 1978 I, British Museum, *The Jewellers Art,* exhibition, 1978.

British Museum 1978 II, British Museum, *Gainsborough and Reynolds in the British Museum,* exhibition, 1978.

Bristol 1965, City Art Gallery, Bristol, *English Silver 1600-1850,* exhibition, 1965 (later shown in Germany as *Englisches Silber 1600-1850).*

Bristol 1979, Bristol, City Museum and Art Gallery, *Ceramics in Bristol: The Fine Wares* (exhibition catalogue), 1979.

Bristol (n.d.), Bristol, City Art Gallery, *Delftware,* (n.d.).

Britton 1801, J. Britton, *The Beauties of Wiltshire,* vol 1, 1801.

Britton 1982, F. Britton, *English Delftware in the Bristol Collection,* London, 1982.

Brown 1757, J. Brown, *An Estimate of the Manners and Principles of the Times,* 1757.

Brown 1982, D. Blayney Brown, Ashmolean Museum, *Catalogue of the Collection of Drawings, the earlier British drawings,* vol IV, Oxford, 1982.

Bruand 1960, Y. Bruand, 'Hubert Gravelot et L'Angleterre', *Gazette des Beaux-Arts,* LV, 1960, pp 35-44.

Brusa 1978, G. Brusa, *L'Arte dell'Orologeria in Europa,* Busto Arsizio, 1978.

Buck 1979, A. Buck, *Dress in Eighteenth-Century England,* 1979.

Bunford 1937, A. H. S. Bunford, 'Some Remarks on Claret Colour', *Transactions of the English Ceramic Circle,* No 5, 1937.

Burke 1976, J. Burke, *English Art 1714-1800,* Oxford 1976.

Burlington Magazine 1978. Burlington Magazine, CXX, November 1978, p LXXII.

Burt 1816, W. Burt in *Review of Merchantile Trading,* 1816.

Bury & FitzGerald 1969, Shirley Bury & Desmond FitzGerald, 'A Design for a candlestick by George Michael Moser, *VAM Yearbook,* 1969, pp 27-29, fig 1.

Bury & Lightbown 1970, S. Bury & R. W. Lightbown, English silver-new pieces and new facts, *Victoria & Albert Museum, Year Book,* 1970.

Cable 1939, M. H. Cable, 'The Idea of a Patriot King in the Propaganda of the Opposition to Walpole, 1735-39' *Philological Quarterly,* 18, 1939.

Cailleux 1967, J. Cailleux, 'Newly Identified drawings by Watteau', *Burlington Magazine,* February 1967, CIX, p 59.

Calman 1977, G. Calman, *Ehret Flower Painter Extraordinary,* 1977.

Camerer Cuss 1976, T. P. & T. A. Camerer Cuss, *The Camerer Cuss Book of Antique Watches,* Woodbridge, 1976.

Campbell 1747, R. Campbell, *The London Tradesman,* 1747.

Came 1961, R. Came, *Silver,* 1961.

Carrington & Hughes 1926, J. B. Carrington and G. R. Hughes, *The Plate of the Worshipful Company of Goldsmiths,* 1926.

Carsix 1909, R. Carsix, 'Juste-Aurèle Meissonnier' *Revue de l'Art ancien et moderne,* vol XXVI, 1909.

Carswell and Dralle 1965, J.Carswell and L.A. Dralle (eds.), *The Political Journal of George Bubb Dodington,* Oxford 1965.

Carver & Casey 1978, B. S. Carver and E. M. Casey, *Silver by Paul de Lamerie at the Sterling and Francine Clark Art Institute,* Williamstown, Mass., 1978.

Chambers 1728, E. Chambers, *Cyclopaedia,* 1728.

Chambers 1763, Sir W. Chambers RA, *Plans, elevations, sections and perspective views of the Gardens and Buildings at Kew, in Surrey,* 1763.

Champeaux n.d., Champeaux, *Portefeuille des Arts Décoratifs,* n.d.

Charleston 1965, R. J. Charleston, 'A Decorator of Porcelain and Glass — James Giles in a New Light', *Transactions of the English Ceramic Circle,* vol 6, part 1, 1965.

Charleston 1966, R. J. Charleston, 'Petitions for Patents concerning Porcelain, Glass and Enamels with special reference to Birmingham, "The Great Toyshop of Europe", *Transactions of the English Ceramic Circle,* vol 6, part 2, 1966.

Charleston 1967 I, R. J. Charleston, 'Porcelain in the Collection of Earl Spencer at Althorp, Northamptonshire: 1. English Porcelain', *Connoisseur,* January 1967.

Charleston 1967 II, R. J. Charleston, 'Battersea, Bilston and Birmingham; the Ionides Gift and other English enamels''. *Victoria and Albert Museum Bulletin,* vol 3, no 1, 1967.

Charleston 1982, R. J. Charleston, 'Some English Glass Engravers', *The Glass Circle,* vol IV, 1982, pp 4-12.

Charleston & Mallet 1971, R. J. Charleston and J. V. G. Mallet, 'A Problematical Group of Eighteenth Century Porcelain', *Transactions of the English Ceramic Circle,* vol 8, part 1, 1971.

Charleston and Mallet 1972 & 1973, R. J. Charleston and J. V. G. Mallet, 'Nicholas Crisp, Founding Member of the Society of Arts, *Journal of the Royal Society of Arts,* December 1972, January and February 1973.

Charleston & Scheurleer, 1978, R. J. Charleston and D. F. Lunsingh Scheurleer, *Masterpieces of Western Ceramic Art, English and Dutch Ceramics,* vol VII, Tokyo, 1978.

Charleston & Towner 1977, R. J. Charleston and D. Towner, *English Ceramics 1580-1830, a Commemorative Catalogue to Celebrate the 50th Anniversary of the English Ceramic Circle,* 1977.

Cherry & Harris 1982, D. Cherry and J. Harris, 'Eighteenth-century portraiture and the seventeenth-century past: Gainsborough and Van Dyck', *Art History,* 5, 1982, pp 287-309.

Chippendale 1762, T. Chippendale, *'The Gentleman and Cabinet-Maker's Director,* 1st ed. 1754, 3rd ed. 1762.

Christies 1969, Christies *Review of the Year* 1969.

Christies 1977, Christies *Review of the Year,* 1977, p 55.

Citroen 1975, K. A. Citroen, *Amsterdam Silversmiths and their Marks,* Amsterdam, 1975.

Clarke 1959, T. H. Clarke, 'French Influences at Chelsea', *Transactions of the English Ceramic Circle,* vol 4, part 5, 1959.

Clayton 1971, M. Clayton, *The Collectors' Dictionary of the Silver & Gold of Great Britain & North America,* 1971.

Clifford-Smith 1931, H. Clifford-Smith, *Buckingham Palace,* 1931.

Clifford & Friedman 1974, T. Clifford and T. Friedman, *The Man at Hyde Park Corner, Sculpture by John Cheere, 1709-1789,* Leeds, 1974.

Clouston 1904, R. S. Clouston, 'Claydon House, Bucks', *Burlington Magazine,* V, April, July, 1904.

Clouzot 1928, H. Clouzot, *Histoire de la Manufacture de Jouy et de la Toile Imprimée en France,* 2 vols, Paris 1928.

Clutton & Daniels 1971, C. Clutton and G. Daniels, *Watches,* 2nd edn., 1971.

Clutton & Daniels 1975, C. Clutton and G. Daniels, *Clocks and Watches, The Collection of the Worshipful Company of Clockmakers,* 1975.

Cochin 1754, C. N. Cochin, 'Supplication aux Orfèvres, Ciseleurs, . . . par une société d'Artistes', *Mercure de France,* December 1754 (Eriksen, 1974, Appendix II).

Cochin 1755, C. N. Cochin, Lettre à M. L'Abbé R**. . . par une société d'Architects', *Mercure de France,* 1755 (reprinted in Eriksen 1974, p 238 *et seq.)*

Cock 1746, *A Catalogue of the Entire Collection of that ingenious Artist Mr. Ishmael Parbury,* sold by Mr. Cock, 17-18 December 1746.

Coke 1983, G. Coke, *In Search of James Giles,* Wingham, 1983.

Coke 1978, D. E. Coke, *The Muse's Bower, Vauxhall Gardens 1728-1786,* exhibition, Gainsborough's House Society, Sudbury, 1978.

Coleridge 1960, A. Coleridge, 'Chippendale, the Director and some Cabinet Makers at Blair Castle,' *Connoisseur,* 1960.

Coleridge 1962, A. Coleridge, 'John Vardy and the Hackwood Suite', *Connoisseur,* CXLIX, Jan 1962, pp 12-17.

Coleridge 1967, A. Coleridge, 'Georgian cabinet-makers at Uppark, Sussex', *Connoisseur*, November 1967, p 161, fig 11.

Coleridge 1968, A. Coleridge, *Chippendale Furniture*, 1968.

Colley 1977, L. Colley, 'The Loyal Brotherhood and the Cocoa Tree: The London Organisation of the Tory Party, 1727-1760', *Historical Journal* 20, 1977.

Colley 1982, L. Colley, *In Defiance of Oligarchy: The Tory Party 1714-60,* Cambridge 1982.

Coulton 1979, I. Coulton, *The Parnasse François, Titon du Tillet and the origins of the Monument to Genius*, New Haven, 1979.

Colvin 1955, H. M. Colvin, 'Roubiliac's Bust of Isaac Ware', *Burlington Magazine*, XCVII, 1955, p 151.

Colvin 1978, H. Colvin, *A Biographical Dictionary of British Architects*, 1978.

Connaissance des Arts 1965, Connaissance des Arts, *Les Grands Orfèvres de Louis XIII à Charles X*, Paris, 1965.

Constable 1927, W. G. Constable, 'Canaletto in England, some further work', *Burlington Magazine*, I, January 1927, p 18-19, pl IIb.

Constable 1962, W. G. Constable, *Canaletto, Giovanni Antonio Canal, 1697-1768*. Oxford 1962. Revised 1976 by J. G. Links.

Cook 1946-1952, C. Cook, 'The Art of Robert Hancock', *Transactions of the English Ceramic Circle*, vol III, part I, 1946-1952.

Cook 1953, C. Cook, 'Louis P. Boitard and his Designs on Battersea Enamels', *Apollo*, March 1953.

Cook 1955, C. Cook, *Supplement to the Life and Work of Robert Hancock*, London, 1955.

Cooper 1979, J. C. Cooper, 'The Gibbs Collection of English Silver', *Connoisseur*, October 1979, vol 202, 135.

Cormack 1970, M. Cormack, *The Drawings of Watteau*, 1970.

Cornforth 1967, J. Cornforth, 'Art in the cause of London Charity', *Country Life*, November 16, 1967, p 1260, fig 4.

Cornforth 1977, J. Cornforth, 'Kirkleatham, Cleveland' II', *Country Life*, 20 January, 1977, pp 134-7.

Country Life 1926, 'The Furnishings of Hagley', *Country Life*, LIX, 16 January 1926.

Coxe 1799, Archdeacon Coxe, *Anecdotes of George Frederick Handel and John Christopher Smith, 1799*. Extra-illustrated edition, including 'A Descriptive Catalogue of the Celebrated Statue of Handel, by Roubiliac . . .'

Cox-Johnson 1961, A. Cox-Johnson, *John Bacon RA, 1740-1788,* 1961.

Croft-Murray n.d., E. Croft-Murray; *British Museum Catalogue of British Drawings*, part II (in preparation).

Croft-Murray 1943, E. Croft-Murray, 'The ingenious Mr Clay', *Country Life*, 31st December, 1943.

Croft-Murray 1953, E. Croft-Murray, 'John Devoto, a Baroque Scene Painter', *The Society for Theatre Research, pamphlet series, 2*, 1952, 1953.

Croft-Murray 1970, E. Croft-Murray, *Decorative Painting in England 1537-1837,* vol II, 1970.

Cruickshanks 1979, E. Cruickshanks, *Political Untouchables: The Tories and the '45,* 1979.

Cunningham 1830, A. Cunningham, *Lives of the most eminent British Painters, Sculptors and Architects*, 1830.

Curran 1967, C. P. Curran, *Dublin Decorative Plasterwork*, 1967.

Cust 1909, Lady E. Cust, *Records of the Cust Family*, series ii, 1909.

Dacier and Vauflart 1929, E. Dacier and A. Vauflart, *Jean de Julienne et les Graveurs de Watteau au XVIII siécle*, 1929.

Dale 1913, W. Dale, *Tschudi The Harpsichord Maker*, 1913.

D'Allemagne 1942, H. R. D'Allemagne *La Toile Imprimée et les Indiennes de Traite* 2 vols, Paris, 1942.

Dasent 1920, A. Dasent, *Piccadilly*, 1920.

Dauterman 1965, C. Dauterman, 'English Silver in an American Company Museum Part I', *Connoisseur*, 1965, vol 159, 206-11.

Davis 1970, F. Davis, *French Silver*, 1970.

Davis 1976, J. Davis, *English Silver at Williamsburg*, Colonial Williamsburg, Virginia, 1976.

Davies 1946, M. Davies, *National Gallery Catalogues: The British School,* 1946.

Dawe 1909, G. Dawe RA, *The Life of George Morland*, 1909 reprint.

De Baudicour, Prosper de Baudicour, *Le Peintre-Graveur Français Continué*, vol I, Paris, 1859.

De Bellaigue 1974, G. de Bellaigue, *The James A. Rothschild Collection at Waddesdon Manor. Furniture, Clocks and Gilt Bronzes*, 1974.

Deelman 1964, C. Deelman, *The Great Shakespeare Jubilee*, 1964.

De la Beche & Reeks 1871, Sir Henry de la Beche and Trenham Reeks, *Catalogue of Specimens in the Museum of Practical Geology*, 1871 edition.

Delevingne 1963, D. Delevingne, 'The Bust of George II', *Transactions of the English Ceramic Circle*, vol 5, part 4, 1963, pp 236-248.

Delomosne 1978, Delomosne Ltd, London, *Gilding the Lily*, 1978.

Demole 1917, E. Demole, 'Jacques-Antoine Dassier', *Schweizerisches Künstler-Lexikon* (ed. C. Brun), IV, 1917.

Denvir 1983, B. Denvir, *The Eighteenth Century: Art, Design and Society 1698-1789*, 1983.

Deshairs (n.d.), L. Deshairs, *Dessins originaux des maîtres décorateurs: Nicolas et Dominique Pineau*, n.d.

Detroit Institute of Arts 1954, Detroit, Institute of Arts, *English Pottery and Porcelain 1300-1850*, Detroit, 1954.

De Vesme 1971, A. de Vesme, *Stefano Della Bella*, with Additions by Phyliss Dearborn Massar, New York, 1971.

Dickson 1967, P.G.M. Dickson, *The Financial Revolution in England 1688-1756*, 1967.

Dickson 1978, E. Dickson, 'Petworth House in Sussex', *Architectural Digest*, vol 35, November 1978, p 183.

Dictionary of National Biography 1921-2. *Dictionary of National Biography*, xvi, reprinted 1921-2, 386-8.

Dimier 1928, L. Dimier, *Les Peintres Français du XVIIIe Siècle*, Paris and Brussels, 1928, 2 vols.

Dobson 1892, A. Dobson, 'Old Vauxhall Gardens', *Eighteenth Century Vignettes*, 1892.

D'Oench 1980, E. G. D'Oench, *The Conversation Piece: Arthur Devis & His Contemporaries*, Yale Center for British Art, New Haven, 1980.

Doria 1929, A. Doria, *Louis Tocqué*, Paris, 1929.

Dossie 1782, R. Dossie, *Memoirs of Agriculture and other Oeconomical Arts, iii,* 1782.

Ducret 1973, Siegfried Ducret, *Keramik und Grafik des 18ten Jahrhunderts*, Brunswick, 1973.

Durham (n.d.), *Treasures from Durham Cathedral*, pp 35-39.

Edelstein 1983, T.J. Edelstein, *Vauxhall Gardens*, New Haven, 1983.

Edwards 1808, E. Edwards, *Anecdotes of Painters*, 1808.

Edwards 1924, R. Edwards, *Dictionary of English Furniture*, vol 1, 1924.

Edwards 1951, R. Edwards, *English Chairs*, 1951.

Edwards 1954, R. Edwards, *Early Conversation Pictures*, 1954.

Edwards 1955, R. Edwards, 'Devon Painters', *The Listener*, 15th December, 1955.

Edwards 1958, R. Edwards, 'Two Versions of Gravelot's Le Lecteur', *Apollo*, June 1958, p 212

Edwards 1960, R. Edwards, preface to *Ince and Mayhew's Universal System of Household Furniture*, reprint, 1960.

Edwards 1965, R. Edwards, 'Patrons of Taste and Sensibility, English Furniture of the Eighteenth Century,' *Apollo*, LXXXII, December 1965.

Edwards 1974, R. Edwards, *Shorter Dictionary of English Furniture*, 1974.

Edwards 1977, A. C. Edwards, *The account books of Benjamin Mildmay, Earl Fitzwalter*, 1977.

Edwards and Jourdain 1955, R. Edwards and Margaret Jourdain, *Georgian Cabinet-Makers*, 3rd ed., 1955.

Eldelberg 1968, M.P. Eidelberg, 'Watteau and the Fountains of Oppenord', *Burlington Magazine*, CX, August 1968, pp 447-456.

Enggass 1976, R. Enggass, *Early Eighteenth Century Sculpture in Rome*, 1976.

English Ceramic Circle 1949, English Ceramic Circle, *English Pottery and Porcelain, Exhibition Catalogue*, 1949, no 241 and pl 52.

Eriksen 1974, S. Eriksen, *Early Neo-Classicism in France*, 1974.

Esdaile 1923, K.A. Esdaile, 'A Renowned Masterpiece by

Roubiliac', *Burlington Magazine*, XLIII, 1923, pp 138-139.
Esdaile 1924, K.A. Esdaile, *Roubiliac's Work at Trinity College, Cambridge*, 1924.
Esdaile 1928, K.A. Esdaile, *Louis François Roubiliac*, 1928.
Esdaile 1944, Mrs. A. Esdaile, 'A signed drawing by Sprimont', *Apollo*, XXXIX, 1944, p 134.
Esdaile 1946, K.A. Esdaile, *English Church Monuments 1510 to 1840*, 1946.
Esdaile 1948, K.A. Esdaile, 'Sir Robert Taylor as sculptor', *Architectural Review*, 103, 1948, pp 63-66.
Eustace 1982, K. Eustace, *Michael Rysbrack*, Bristol, 1982.
Evans 1921, J. Evans, *English Jewellery*, 1921, p 136.
Evans 1931, J. Evans, *Pattern: a Study of Ornament in Western Europe from 1180 to 1900*, vol II, 1931.
Falkner 1972, F. Falkner, *The Wood Family of Burslem*, 1912 and reprint of 1972.
Farington 1923, J. Farington, *The Farington Diary*, ed. J. Greig, 1923.
Farnham 1982, *Colour and the Calico Printer, an exhibition of printed and dyed textiles, 1750-1850*, Farnham College of Art and Design. Catalogue by Deryn O'Connor and Hero Granger-Taylor, 1982.
Faulkner 1960, R. K. Faulkner, 'The Ellicotts: A family of clockmakers', *Antiquarian Horology*, vol 3, no 4, September 1960.
Fénaille 1903, M. Fénaille, *Etat Général des Tapisseries de la Manufacture des Gobelins*, ii, Paris, 1903.
Finer & Savage 1965, A. Finer and George Savage, *The Selected Letters of Josiah Wedgwood*, 1965, p 237.
The Lord Fisher 1944, The Lord Fisher, 'Some notes on the 1743 Chelsea Jug', *Apollo*, December 1944.
Fitz-Gerald 1968, D. Fitz-Gerald, *Georgian Furniture*, 1968.
Fitz-Gerald 1969, D. Fitz-Gerald, 'Gravelot and his influence on English furniture', *Apollo*, XC, August 1969, pp 145-6, fig 24.
Fitz-Gerald 1973, D. Fitz-Gerald, *The Norfolk House Music Room*, Victoria and Albert Museum, 1973.
Fleming 1962, J. Fleming, *Robert Adam and his circle*, 1962.
Fleming 1962, J. Fleming, 'Robert Adam, Luc-François Breton and the Townshend monument in Westminster Abbey', *Connoisseur*, CL, 1962, pp 163-171.
Florence 1974, P. P. Florence, *The Twilight of the Medici, late Baroque Art in Florence, 1670-1743* (exhibition cat.), Florence and Detroit, 1974.
Floud 1957 I, P. Floud, 'English Printed Textiles I. Copperplate pictorials', *Antiques*, LXXI, March 1957, pp 238-241.
Floud 1957, II, P. Floud, 'English Printed Textiles III. Copperplate floral designs', *Antiques*, LXXI, May 1957, pp 460-463.
Floud and Morris 1957, P.C. Floud and B. Morris. Articles on English printed textiles in *Antiques*, March 1957 — April 1958, and in *The Connoisseur*, October 1957-February 1959. — P.C. Floud. Articles on the history of English printed textiles in *The Journal of the Society of Dyers and Colourists*. Vol 76, May-July 1960. P.C. Floud. English Chintz in *CIBA Review*. Basle 1961/1. Revised by Barbara Morris.
Foley 1911, E. Foley, *Book of decorative Furniture*, 1911, vol II, p 14.
Forrer 1904, L. Forrer, *Biographical Dictionary of Medallists*, 1904.
Franks & Grueber 1885, A.W. Franks, H.A. Grueber, *Medallic Illustrations of the History of Great Britain and Ireland to the death of George II*, 1885.
Freeman 1937, A. Freeman, 'The Beckford-Fonthill organ at Towcester parish Church', *The organ world*, June 1937.
Friedman 1973, T. Friedman, 'John Cheere's Busts and Statuettes from Kirkleatham Hall, *City of York Art Galley Quarterly*, (1973), pp 992-97.
Friedman 1975, T.F. Friedman, 'Two Eighteenth Century Catalogues of ornamental Pattern Books, *Furniture History*, XI, 1975, pp 66-75.
Friedman 1981, T. Friedman, 'A convenient and pleasant habitation', *Leeds Art Calendar*, 89, 1981, pp 5-13.
Friedman 1984, T. Friedman, *J. Gibbs*, Yale, 1984.
Friedman & Clifford 1974, T. Friedman and T. Clifford, *The man at Hyde Park Corner, Sculpture by John Cheere, 1709-1787*, Leeds, 1974.

Fuessli 1774, J.C. Fuessli, *Geschichte der besten Künstler in der Schweiz*, Zurich, 1774, iv, pp 129-138.
Furcy-Raymond 1927, M. Furcy-Raymond, *Inventaire des sculptures executées en XVIIIe siécle*, Paris, 1927.
Gabszewicz and Freeman 1982, Anton Gabszewicz and Geoffrey Freeman, *Bow Porcelain, the Collection formed by Geoffrey Freeman*, 1982.
Gaines 1965, E. Gaines, 'Powell? Potts? Pitts!, The TP Epergnes', *Antiques*, 87, April, 1965.
Gaines 1967, E. Gaines, 'More by — and about — Pitts of the Epergnes', *Antiques*, 90, June 1967.
Galbraith 1972, L. Galbraith, 'Garrick's Furniture at Hampton', *Apollo*, 1972, XCV, July, p 47, fig 3.
Gardner 1929, Dr Bellamy Gardner, 'Chinoiserie Models in Porcelain and Wood', *Transactions of the English Porcelain Circle*, no II, 1929.
Gardner 1932, Dr Bellamy Gardner, 'Sir Hans Sloane's Plants on Chelsea Porcelain', *Transactions of the English Porcelain Circle*, no IV, 1932.
Gardner 1935, Dr Bellamy Gardner, 'Chelsea Porcelain Clocks', *Connoisseur*, December, 1935.
Gardner 1937 I, Dr Bellamy Gardner, 'English China Collectors of the Past', *Transactions of the English Ceramic Circle*, vol 1, no 4, 1937.
Gardner 1937 II, Dr Bellamy Gardner, 'Sir Hans Sloane's Chelsea Porcelain Heirlooms', *Antique Collector*, April, 1937.
Gardner 1937 III, Dr Bellamy Gardner, 'Old Chelsea Plates', *Country Life*, 20th November, 1937.
Gardner 1939, Dr Bellamy Gardner, ' "Silvershape" in Chelsea Porcelain', *Transactions of the English Ceramic Circle*, vol 2, no 6, 1939.
Gardner 1940, Dr Bellamy Gardner, 'Origins of Designs on Old Chelsea Porcelain', *Connoisseur*, July 1940, pp 3-6.
Gardner 1942, Dr Bellamy Gardner, 'Further History of the Chelsea Porcelain Manufactory', *Transactions of the English Ceramic Circle*, vol 2, no 8, 1942.
Garner & Archer 1972, F.H. Garner and M. Archer, *English Delftware*, London, 1972.
Garrard Inventory 1911, The Royal Collection, *Garrard Inventory*, privately printed, 1911.
Gascoigne 1978, B. Gascoigne, *Images of Richmond*, Richmond, 1978.
Geffrye Museum 1972, London, Geffrye Museum, *George Dance the Elder 1695-1768, the Younger 1741-1825*, 1972.
Gentleman's Magazine, XXI, 1751.
Gentleman's Magazine, XL, 1770.
Gentleman's Magazine, LIII, 1783.
Gentle & Field 1975, R. Gentle & R. Field, *English Domestic Brass*, 1975.
George 1982, A. M. George, Catalogue of a *Loan Exhibition of Bow Porcelain in Memory of Geoffrey Freeman*, 1982.
Gervers 1977, V. Gervers (ed.), 'John Holker's mid-18th century 'Livere d'Echatillons'', *Studies in Textile History*, Ontario, 1977.
Gibbs 1728, J. Gibbs, *A Book of Architecture*, 1728.
Gilbert 1968, C. Gilbert, 'The Temple Newsam Suite of early-Georgian Gilt Furniture', *Connoisseur*, CLXVII, February 1968, pp 844-8, fig 5.
Gilbert 1969, C. Gilbert, 'Thomas Chippendale at Dumfries House', *The Burlington Magazine*, CXI, November 1969, pp 663-77.
Gilbert 1973, C. Gilbert, 'An Exceptional Bureau-Plat by B.V.R.B.', *Leeds Art Calendar*, 73, 1973.
Gilbert 1973 II, C. Gilbert, 'Thomas Chippendale as Undertaker', *Furniture History*, IX, 1973, pp 114-8.
Gilbert 1975, C. Gilbert, 'The Early Furniture Designs of Matthias Darly', *Furniture History*, XI, 1975, pp 33-39.
Gilbert 1978 I, C. Gilbert, *The Life and Work of Thomas Chippendale*, 1978.
Gilbert 1978 II, C. Gilbert, *Furniture at Temple Newsam House and Lotherton Hall*, 1978, p 256.
Gilson 1973, D.J. Gilson, *Books from The Library of Sir Robert Taylor*, Oxford, 1973.
Girouard 1960, M. Girouard, 'Picton Castle', *Country Life*, 14 January, 1960.

Girouard 1966, I, II, & III, M..Girouard, 'English Art and the Rococo.'; I. 'Coffee at Slaughter's.' *Country Life*, January 13, 1966, p 58-61; II. 'Hogarth and his Friends'. *Country Life*, January 27, 1966, p 188-190; III. 'The Two Worlds of St Martins Lane'. *Country Life*, February 3, 1966, pp 224-227.

GLC 1960, Greater London Council, Iveagh Bequest, Kenwood, *Paintings, Drawings and Prints by Francis Hayman RA, 1708-1776*, 1960.

GLC 1965, Greater London Council, The Iveagh Bequest,Kenwood, *The Conversation Piece in Georgian England*, exhibition, 1965.

GLC 1968, Greater London Council, Iveagh Bequest, Kenwood, *The French Taste in English Painting*, 1968.

GLC 1975, Greater London Council, *To Preserve and Enhance*, GLC exhibition, Marble Hill, 1975.

GLC 1980, Greater London Council, Marble Hill House, *Alexander Pope's Villa*, 1980, exhibition, 1980.

Glendenning 1931, Oliver Glendenning, 'Porcelain Wall-brackets', *Transactions of the English Porcelain Circle*, vol 1, no 3, 1931.

Godden 1966, G. Godden, *An Illustrated Encyclopaedia of British Pottery and Porcelain*, 1966.

Godden 1974, G. Godden, *British Porcelain — An Illustrated Guide*, 1974.

Goldsmiths' Hall 1951, Goldsmiths' Hall, *Exhibition of Historic Plate from the City of London*, 1951.

Goldsmiths' Hall 1978, Goldsmiths' Hall, London, *Touching Gold and Silver*, 1978.

Gomme 1968, A. Gomme, 'The architecture of Barlaston Hall, *Country Life*, 18 April, 1968, pp 975-9.

Gomme, Jenner & Little 1979, A. Gomme, M. Jenner and B. Little, *Bristol. An architectural history*, 1979.

Goncourt 1875, E. de Goncourt, *Catalogue raisonné de l'oeuvre peint, dessiné et gravé d'Antoine Watteau*, Paris, 1875.

Goncourt 1882, E. and J. de Goncourt, *L''Art du Dix-Huitième Siècle*, 3rd ed., 1882.

Griffith 1962, H. Griffith, *Alexander Pope: a bibliography*, 1962.

Goodison 1975, N. Goodison, 'The Victoria and Albert Museum's Collection of Metal-Work Pattern Books', *Furniture History*, vol II, 1975, pp 1-30.

Goodison 1977, J. W. Goodison, *Fitzwilliam Museum Cambridge, Catalogue of Paintings Vol III, The British School* Cambridge, 1977.

Goodwin 1903, C. Goodwin, *James McArdell*, 1903.

Gould 1912, A. W. Gould, *History of the Worshipful Company of Fruiterers of the City of London*, 1912.

Gould 1949, C. Gould, 'The English Conversation Piece, *Country Life Annual*, 1948.

Gowing 1953, L. Gowing, 'Hogarth, Hayman and the Vauxhall Decorations', *Burlington Magazine'*, January 1953, vol XCV, no 598, p 4-19.

Grandjean 1981, S. Grandjean, *Catalogue des tabetières, boîtes et étuis des XVIIIe et XIXe siècles du musée du Louvre*, Paris, 1981, no 474.

Grandjean, Piacenti, Truman & Blunt, *The James A. De Rothschild Collection at Waddesdon Manor:* S. Grandjean, K.A. Piacenti, C. Truman, A. Blunt, *Gold Boxes and Miniatures of the Eighteenth Century*, Fribourg, 1975.

Graves 1905-6, A. Graves, *The Royal Academy of Arts*, 1905-6, I, p 112.

Graves 1907, A. Graves, *The Society of Artists of Great Britain, 1760-91, The Free Society of Artists, 1761-1783*, 1907.

Griffiths 1980, A. Griffiths, *Prints and Printmaking*, 1980.

Grimwade 1956, A. Grimwade, 'Royal toilet services in Scandinavia', *Connoisseur*, 1956, vol 137, p 175-8.

Grimwade 1963, A. Grimwade, 'Silver at Althorp: II Candlesticks and Candelabra', *Connoisseur*, vol 152, March 1963, p 159-165.

Grimwade 1969, A. G. Grimwade, *Crespin or Sprimont? An unsolved problem of Rococo silver*, Apollo XC, 1969.

Grimwade 1974, A. G. Grimwade, *Rococo Silver*, 1974.

Grimwade 1976, A. G. Grimwade, *The London Goldsmiths, 1697-1837*, 1976, revised 1982.

Gruber 1982, A. Gruber, *Silverware*, Paris and New York, 1982.

Grueber 1911, H. A. Grueber, *Medallic illustrations to the history of Great Britain and Ireland to the death of George II*, 1911.

Guilmard 1880, D. Gulmard, *Les maîtres ornemanistes*, Paris, 1880, 1881.

Gunnis 1968, R. Gunnis, *Dictionary of British Sculptors 1660-1851*. 2nd Edit. 1968.

Gunnis & Physick 1975, R. Gunnis and J. Physick, *Dictionary of British Sculptors 1660-1851*. Revised ed., typescript (VAM library), 1975.

Haase 1983, G. Haase, *Dresdener Möbel*, Leipzig, 1983, p 291.

Habsburg 1983, G. von Habsburg-Lothringen, *Gold Boxes from the collection of Rosalinde and Arthur Gilbert*, 1983.

Hackenbroch 1958 I, Y. Hackenbroch, *English Furniture in the Irwin Untermeyer Collection*, Norwich, 1958.

Hackenbroch 1958 II, Y. Hackenbroch, *Chelsea and other English Porcelain, Pottery and Enamel in the Irwin Untermeyer Collection*, London 1957, Cambridge, Massachusetts, 1958.

Hackenbroch 1969, Y. Hackenbroch, *The Irwin Untermeyer Collection: English and other Silver*, Metropolitan Museum of Art, New York, 1969 (rev. ed.).

Hall 1982, I. Hall, 'William Constable and Burton Constable' — III and IV in *Country Life*, May 6 and 13, 1982.

Halliwell 1864, J. O. Halliwell, *An Historical Account of the New Place, Stratford-on-Avon*, 1864.

Hammelmann 1958, H. A. Hammelmann, 'Shakespeare Illustration: the earliest known originals', *Connoisseur*, CXLI, 1958, pp 144-9.

Hammelmann 1959, H. A. Hammelmann, 'Portrayer of 18th century Cockneys', *Country Life*, CXXVI, September 1959, pp 356-7.

Hammelmann 1975, H. A. Hammelmann, *Book illustrators in eighteenth-century England*, ed. T.S.R. Boase, New Haven, 1975.

Hardy 1973, John Hardy, 'The Discovery of Cosway's Chair', *Country Life*, CLIV, March 15, 1973.

Harris 1960, J. Harris, *English Decorative Ironwork*, 1960.

Harris 1961, J. Harris, 'Clues to the "Frenchness" of Woodcote Park', *Connoisseur*, 147, April 1961, pp 241-50.

Harris 1968, J. Harris, 'Pritchard redivivus', *Architectural History*, vol II, 1968, pp 17-24.

Harris 1969, J. Harris, 'Brightening up Palladio: A Design for a British Museum', *Apollo*, August 1969, pp 129-133.

Harris 1970, J. Harris, *Sir William Chambers*, 1970.

Harris 1971, J. Harris, *British Architectural Drawings in American Collections*, 1971.

Harris 1971 I, E. Harris, 'The Architecture of Thomas Wright', *Country Life*, August 26, September 2 and 7, 1971.

Harris 1977, E. Harris, 'Batty Langley: a Tutor to Freemasons '1696-1751)', *Burlington Magazine*, May 1977.

Harris 1978, J. Harris, *Gardens of Delight, the Rococo English Landscape of Thomas Robins the Elder*, 1978.

Harris 1979, J. Harris, 'The Flower Garden 1730-1830', in *The Garden* (guide to the exhibition at the Victoria and Albert Museum), London 1979.

Harris 1979 I, E. Harris, *Thomas Wright's Arbours and Grottoes*, 1979.

Halfpenny, Morris and Lightoler 1757, W. and J. Halfpenny, R. Morris and T. Lightoler, *The Modern Builders Assistant*, 1757.

Harrison-Wallace 1983, C. Harrison-Wallace, *P. Monamy, 1681-1749, Marine Artist*. Exhibition Catalogue, Pallant House Gallery, Chichester, 1983.

Haskell & Penny 1981, F. Haskell and N. Penny, *Taste and the Antique*, 1981.

Hawkins 1979, J. B. Hawkins, *Masterpieces of English and European Silver & Gold*, Sydney, 1979.

Hawley 1978, H. Hawley, 'Meissonnier's Silver for the Duke of Kingston', *Bulletin of The Cleveland Museum of Art*, December 1978.

Hayden 1932, A. Hayden, *Old English Porcelain, the Lady Ludlow collection*, 1932.

Hayes 1967, J. Hayes, 'British Patrons and Landscape Painting', *Apollo*, April 1967, pp 254-259.

Hayes 1969 I, J. Hayes, 'The Ornamental Surrounds for Houbraken's "Illustrious Heads"', 'Notes on British Art, no 13', *Apollo*, LXXXIX, 1969, pp 1-3.

Hayes 1969, II, J. Hayes, 'English Painting and the Rococo', *Apollo*, XC, August 1969, pp 114-125.

Hayward 1963, J.F. Hayward, *The Art of the Gunmaker*, 1963.

Hayward 1964, H. Hayward, *Thomas J.son and English Rococo*, 1964.

Hayward 1965, J. Hayward, 'English Brass-inlaid Furniture', *Victoria and Albert Museum Bulletin*, January 1965, vol I, no 1, fig 5.

Hayward 1969, Helena Hayward, 'The Drawings of Thomas J.son in the Victoria and Albert Museum', *Furniture History*, V, 1969, pp 1-115.

Hayward 1969-70, H. Hayward, 'English Rococo Designs for Silver', *Proceedings of the Society of Silver Collectors*, 1969-70.

Hayward 1975, H. Hayward, 'Newly Discovered Designs by Thomas J.son, *Furniture History*, XI, 1975.

Hayward 1980, J. Hayward, 'Furniture designed and carved by Matthias Lock at Hinton house, Somerset, *Connoisseur*, CXLVI, December 1980, pp 284-286.

Hayward and Kirkham 1980, H. Hayward and P. Kirkham, *William and J. Linnell: Eighteenth Century London Furniture Makers*, 2 vols, 1980.

Hayward 1973, H. Hayward, 'A unique Rococo Chair by Matthias Lock', *Apollo*, XCVIII, October 1973.

Hazen 1948, A. T. Hazen, *A Bibliography of Horace Walpole*, New Haven, 1948.

Hazen 1969, A. T. Hazen, *A Catalogue of Horace Walpole's Library*, 3 vols, New Haven, 1969.

Heal 1925, Sir A. Heal, *London Tradesmen's Cards of the XVIII Century*, 1925.

Heal 1931, Sir A. Heal, *The English Writing-Masters and their copybooks 1570-1800. A biographical dictionary and a bibliography*, Cambridge, 1931.

Heal 1935, Sir A. Heal, *The London Goldsmiths 1200-1800*, Cambridge, 1935.

Hébert & Sjöberg 1973, M. Hébert, Y. Sjöberg, *Inventaire du Fonds Français, Graveurs du XVIIIe Siècle*, XII, Paris, Bibliothéque Nationale, 1973.

Heckscher 1969, M. Heckscher, 'Gideon saint: An Eighteenth-Century Carver and His Scrapbook', *The Metropolitan Museum of Art bulletin*, XXVII, February 1969, pp 299-310.

Heckscher 1975, M. Heckscher, 'Eighteenth Century Rustic Furniture Designs', *Furniture History*, XI, 1975, pp 59-65.

Heckscher 1979, M. Heckscher, 'Lock and Copland', *Furniture History*, vol XV, 1979.

Hefford 1977, W. Hefford, 'Thomas Moore of Moorfields', *The Burlington Magazine*, CXIX, December, 1977.

Hefford 1984, W. Hefford, 'Soho and Spitalfields: little known Huguenot tapestry-weavers in and around London, 1680-1780.' *Proceedings of the Huguenot Society of London*, November 1984.

Henry 1958, S.A. Henry, 'A Further Note on the Engravings of the Oil Paintings of Francis Hayman in Vauxhall Gardens', *Burlington Magazine*, vol C, no 669, December 1958, p 439.

Hercenberg 1975, B. Hercenberg, *Nicolas Vleughels*, Paris, 1975.

Hermann 1962, W. Hermann, *Laugier and Eighteenth Century French theory*, 1962.

Hernmarck 1977, C. Hernmarck, *The Art of the European Silversmith 1430-1830*, 1977.

Hill 1976, B.W. Hill, *The Growth of Parliamentary Parties 1689-1742*, 1976.

Hill 1981 I, D. Hill, 'Archives and Archaeology at Temple Newsam House', *Leeds Art Calendar*, no 89, 1981, pp 26-32.

Hill II 1981, D. Hill, 'James Pascall and the Long Gallery Suite at Temple Newsam', *Furniture History*, vol XVII, 1981, pp 70-74, figs 49-56.

Hitchcock 1968, H.-R. Hitchcock, *Rococo Architecture in Southern Germany*, 1968.

Hobson 1905, R.L. Hobson, *Catalogue of the Collection of English Porcelain . . . of the British Museum*, 1905.

Hodgkinson 1947, T. Hodgkinson, 'A sketch in terracotta by Roubiliac', *Burlington Magazine*, 89, 1947, p 258.

Hodgkinson 1965, T. Hodgkinson, 'Handel at Vauxhall.' *Victoria and Albert Museum Bulletin*, vol I, no 4 October 1965, pp 1-13.

Revised in Victoria and Albert Museum Bulletin Reprints I, 1969.

Hofmann 1921-3, F. H. Hofmann, *Geschichte der bayerisches Porzellan-Manufaktur, Nymphenburg*, Leipzig, 1921-3.

Hogarth 1953, W. Hogarth, *Analysis of Beauty*, (ed. J. Burke), Oxford, 1953.

Hogarth 1955, W. Hogarth, *Analysis of Beauty*, 1955.

Holmes (ed.) 1969, G. Holmes (ed.), *Britain after the Glorious Revolution 1689-1714*, 1969.

Holmes 1982, G. Holmes, *Augustan England: Professions, State and Society, 1680-1730*, 1982.

Honey 1928, W. B. Honey, *Old English Porcelain*, London 1928 and reprint of 1977.

Honey 1937 I, W. B. Honey, 'The Work of James Giles', *Transactions of the English Ceramic Circle*, no 5, 1937.

Honey 1937 II, W. B. Honey, 'English Porcelain: Some Independent Decorators', *Apollo* XXV, 1937.

Honey 1977, See Honey 1928.

Honour 1969, H. Honour, *Cabinet-Makers and Furniture Designers*, 1969.

Honour 1971, H. Honour, *Goldsmiths and Silversmiths*, 1971.

Hooper 1762, S. Hooper, *A Description of Vauxhall Gardens*, 1762.

Howard 1974, D. S. Howard, *Chinese Armorial Porcelain*, 1974.

Howard and Ayers 1978, D. Howard and J. Ayers, *China for the West*, vol II, 1978.

Hughes 1951, T. and B. Hughes, *English painted enamels . . . illustrated from the collections of Her Majesty Queen Mary and the Hon. Mrs Ionides*, 1951.

Hughes 1956, G. B. Hughes, *English, Scottish and Irish Table Glass*, 1956.

Hughes 1960, G. B. Hughes, 'Masterpieces of Chelsea Porcelain, a Famous Table Service at Buckingham Palace', *Country Life Annual*, 1960, pp 28-36.

Hughes 1973, P. Hughes, 'The Williams-Wynn silver in the National Museum of Wales', *Connoisseur*, 1973, vol 184, 33-8.

Hulton 1980, P. Hulton, *Watteau Drawings in the British Museum*, 1980.

Humphries and Smith 1970, Charles Humphries and William C. Smith, *Music Publishing in the British Isles from the Beginning untill the Middle of the Nineteenth Century*, Oxford 1970.

Hurlbutt 1937, F. Hurlbutt, *Chelsea China*, London, 1937.

Hutchins 1792, J. Hutchins, *History and Antiquities . . . of Dorset*, 1792.

Hutchins 1783, J. Hutchins, *A Catalogue of the Museum of George Michael Moser . . .*, auction by Hutchins, 19-21 May 1783; *A Catalogue of the Collection of Plaister Casts . . .*, auction by Hutchins, 7 July 1783.

Hutchison 1968, S.C.Hutchison, *The History of the Royal Academy*, 1968.

Ingamells 1974 I, J. Ingamells, 'An existence à la Watteau', 'Rational and Elegant Entertainment', *Country Life*, February 7 and 14, 1974, pp 256-8, 315-7.

Ingamells 1974 II, J. Ingamells, 'Andrea Soldi', *Connoisseur*, CLXXXVI, 1974.

Ingamells 1980, J. Ingamells, 'A. Soldi — A Check-list of his Work', *Walpole Society*, 47, 1980.

Ireland 1799, S. Ireland, *Graphic Illustrations of Hogarth*, vol II, 1799.

Jackson 1911, Sir C. J. Jackson, *An Illustrated History of English Plate*, 2 vols, 1911 (reprinted 1967).

Jackson-Stops 1974 I, G. Jackson-Stops, 'Pre-Adam Furniture Designs at Nostell Priory', *Furniture History*, vol X, 1974.

Jackson-Stops 1974 II, G. Jackson-Stops, 'West Wycombe Landscape — I' *Country Life*, 20 June 1974.

Jackson-Stops 1977, G. Jackson-Stops, 'Furniture at Petworth House', *Apollo*, CV May 1977, p 362, fig 13.

Jackson-Stops 1978, G. Jackson-Stops, *Claydon House*, The National Trust, 1978.

Jackson-Stops 1980, G. Jackson-Stops, *Felbrigg Hall*, The National Trust, 1980.

James 1712, J. James, *The Theory and Practice of Gardening* 1712.

Jeanneret, 1950, P. Jeanneret, 'Thames-Side Masterpieces', *Daily Mail Ideal Home Book* 1950-51.

Jean-Richard 1978, P. Jean-Richard, *L'Oeuvre Gravé de François Boucher*, Paris, 1978.

Jessen 1924, P. Jessen, *Meister des Ornament-stichs; Das Rokoko*, 1924.

Jeudwine 1968, W. Jeudwine, *Stage designs*, The RIBA Drawings Series, 1968.

Jewitt 1878, L. Jewitt, *The Ceramic Art of Great Britain*, 1878, vol I.

J.ston 1970, E. Johnston, 'A Wilson for Manchester', *Burlington Magazine*, vol CXII, August 1970.

Jones 1911, E. Alfred Jones, *The Gold and Silver of Windsor Castle*, Letchworth, 1911.

Jones 1973, E. L. Jones, 'The Fashion Manipulators: Consumer Tastes and British Industries, 1660-1800', in Louis P. Cain and Paul J. Uselding (eds.), *Business Enterprise and Economic Change*, Ohio, 1973.

Jones 1979, W.E. Jones, *Monumental Silver: Selections from the Gilbert Collection*, Los Angeles County Museum, 1979.

Jourdain 1948, M. Jourdain, *The work of William Kent*, 1948.

Jourdain 1950, M. Jourdain, 'Furniture at Hagley Hall', *Apollo*, LI, January 1950, pp 8-10, fig IV.

Jourdain & Soan 1950, M. Jourdain and R. Soan Jennins, *Chinese Export Art in the 18th Century*, 1950.

Jupp 1871, *A descriptive list of original drawings, engravings . . . in the possession of Edmund Jupp*, 1871.

Kaellgren 1982, C.P. Kaellgren, 'The teapicker design on English rococo silver tea caddies', *Antiques*, February 1982, vol

Kalnein & Levey 1972, W. G. Kalnein & M. Levey, *Art and Architecture of the Eighteenth Century in France*, Harmondsworth, 1972.

Kemp 1980, B. Kemp, English Church Monuments, 1980.

Kent 1927, W. Kent, *The Designs of Inigo Jones with some additional designs*, 1727.

Kerslake 1959, J. Kerslake, 'The Likeness of Wolfe', *Wolfe: Portraiture and Genealogy*, 1959.

Kerslake 1966, J. Kerslake, 'Roubiliac's "Handel" a terra-cotta restored', *Burlington Magazine*, CVIII (1966), p 475.

Kerslade 1977, J. Kerslake, *National Portrait Gallery Early Georgian Portraits*, 2 vols, 1977.

Kimball 1933, F. Kimball, 'Wanstead House, Essex', *Country Life*, 2 December 1933, pp 605-7.

Kimball 1942, F. Kimball, 'J A Meissonnier and the Beginning of the Genre Pittoresque', *Gazette des Beaux Arts*, 6 Ser. XXII, October, 1942.

Kimball 1943, F. Kimball, *The Creation of the Rococo*, Philadelphia, 1943 (reprinted 1964).

King 1922, W. King, *Chelsea Porcelain*, 1922.

King 1925, W. King, *English Porcelain Figures of the Eighteenth Century*, 1925.

King 1930, W. King, 'A Chelsea Vase', *British Museum Quarterly*, vol V, no 1, 1930.

King 1931, W. King, British Museum Quarterly, vol 5, no 1, 1931.

King 1935, W. King, 'The Royal Collections: V. Ceramics', *Burlington Magazine*, vol LXVI, May 1935.

King 1942, W. King, 'Two Chelsea Porcelain Vases', *Collector*, May, 1942.

King 1948, W. King, 'The Dudley Vases', *Apollo*, June 1948.

King 1980, Ed. D. King, *British Textile Design in the Victoria and Albert Museum*, 3 vol , Tokyo, 1980.

Kirkham 1969, P. Kirkham, 'Samuel Norman', *Burlington Magazine*, CXL, August 1969, pp 503-13.

Kirkham 1974, P. Kirkham, 'The Partnership of William Ince and John Mayhew, 1759-1804', *Furniture History*, X, 1974.

Knight 1798, *The Works of Sir Joshua Reynolds*, Knight, 2nd edn, 1798.

Kramer 1965, E. Kramer, 'Die vier Monarchien, Der Traum Nebuchadnezars als Thema Keramischer Werke', *Keramos*, 28 1965.

Kunstmuseum Dusseldorf 1971, *Europäische Barockplastik Am Niederhein, Grupello und seine zeit*. Kunstmuseum Dusseldorf, 1971.

Kunze 1982, J. Kunze, 'Die Bedeutung des 'Englischen Handels'

der Miessner Manufaktur in der Ersten Hälfte des 19 Jahrhunderts', *Keramos*, no 95, January, 1982.

Laing 1979, A. Laing, 'French Ornamental Engravings and the diffusion of the Rococo', proceedings of the conference of the C.I.H.A., 1979 (to be published).

Laing 1984, A. Laing, 'Fischer von Erlach's monument to Wenzel, Count Wratislaw von Mitrowitz', *Umeni* (forthcoming).

Laing Art Gallery 1980, Laing Art Gallery, Newcastle upon Tyne, *The decorated glasses of William and Mary Beilby*, Newcastle, 1980.

Lambert 1984, S. Lambert, *Drawing, Technique and Purpose*, 1984.

Lane 1958, A. Lane, 'Unidentified Italian or English Porcelains: the A Marked Group', *Keramikfreunde der Schweiz*, 43, July 1958.

Lane 1960, A. Lane, 'Chelsea Porcelain Figures and the Modeller Joseph Willems', *Connoisseur*, May 1960.

Lane 1961, A. Lane, *English Porcelain Figures of the Eighteenth Century*, 1961.

Langley 1745, B. Langley, *The City and Country Builder's and Workman's Treasury of Designs*, 1745.

Lankheit 1954, K. Lankheit, *Die Zeichnungen des kurpfälzischen Hofbildhauers Paul Egell (1691-1752)*, Kurlsruhe, 1954.

Lankheit 1958, K. Lankheit, 'A pair of Bronze Vases by Massimiliano Soldani', *Connoisseur*, CXLII, 1958, pp 159-63.

Lankheit 1962, K. Lankheit, *Florentinische Barokplastik. Die Kunst am Hofe der letzen Medici, 1670-1743*, Munich, 1962.

Lankheit 1982, K. Lankheit, *Die Modellsammlung der Porzellanmanufaktur Doccia*, Munich, 1982.

Laran 1925, J. Laran, *François de Cuvilliés*, Paris, 1925.

Leeds 1950, Leeds Art Calender, No. 13, 1950, p 8.

Leeds 1957, Leeds Art Calender, No. 38, 1957.

Leeds Temple Newsam 1974, *The Man at Hyde Park Corner, Sculpture by John Cheere 1759-1787* (exhibition cat.), Leeds, 1974.

Legouis 1975, S. Y. Legouis, 'John Cheere's Statue of George II, *Connoisseur*, CLXXXVIII, 1975, pp 277-83.

Lenman 1980, B. Lenman, *The Jacobite Risings in Britain 1689:1746*, 1980.

Lever 1982, J. Lever, *Architect's designs for furniture*, 1982.

Levey 1959, M. Levey, 'Francesco Zuccarelli in England', *Italian Studies*, XIV, 1959, p 1-20.

Levey 1961, M. Levey, 'The Real Theme of Watteau's *Embarkation for Cythera*', *Burlington Magazine*, CIII, 1961, pp 180-185.

Lewis 1934, W. S. Lewis, 'The Genesis of Strawberry Hill', *Metropolitan Museum Studies*, vol V, pt 1, 1934, pp 57-92.

Lewis 1936, W. S. Lewis, *Bentley's Designs for Walpole's Fugitive Pieces*, Farmington, 1936.

Lewis 1937, *Horace Walpole's Correspondence*, ed W.S. Lewis, 48 vols, New Haven, 1937-1983.

Lewis 1961, W. S. Lewis, *Horace Walpole, The A.W. Mellon Lectures in the Fine Arts 1960*, 1961.

Lewis 1972, L. Lewis, 'English Commemorative Sculpture in Jamaica', *Jamaican Historical Review*, IX (1972).

Lewis 1973, W. S. Lewis, *A Guide to the Life of Horace Walpole*, New Haven, 1973.

Lenygon, F. Lenygon, *Furniture in England, 1660-1760*, 1914.

Lippincott 1983, Louise Lippincott, *Selling Art in Georgian London: The Rise of Arthur Pond*, 1983.

Litchfield, F. Litchfield, *Pottery and Porcelain*, 4th edition, 1925.

Liversidge 1972, M.J.H. Liversidge, 'An Elusive Minor Master, J.F. Nollekens and the Conversation Piece', *Apollo*, January 1972, pp 34-41.

Lockman 1751, J. Lockman, 'A Sketch of the Spring-Gardens, Vaux-Hall', *In a Letter to a noble Lord*, 1751.

Loers, V. Loers, Rokokoplastik und Dekorationssysteme, *Aspekte der süddentschen Kunst und des ästherischen bewusstsesns in 18. Jahrhunderts*, Munich, 1976.

London Museum 1973, London Museum, *Twenty five years of the London Museum*, 1937, pl 86.

London Museum 1983, Museum of London, *Masquerade*, 1983.

Long 1757, E. Long, *The Anti-Gallican: or, the History and Adventures of Harry Cobham, Esq., Inscribed to Louis XVth*, 1757.

Luxmoore 1924, C. F.C. Luxmoore, *'Saltglaze' with the Notes of a*

Collector, 1924, reprint 1971.

Le Blanc 1747, A. J.-B. le Blanc, *Lettres . . . concernant le gouvernement, la politique et les moeurs des Anglois et des François*, I-III, 1745 (English translation 1747).

Le Corbeiller 1966, C. le Corbeiller, *European and American Snuff Boxes 1730-1830*, 1966.

Le Corbeiller 1970, C. le Corbeiller, 'James Cox: a biographical review', *Burlington Magazine*, CXII, June 1970.

Lybbe Powis 1899, C. L. Powis, *Diaries*, ed. Climenson, 1899.

Mainstone 1976, M. Mainstone, 'Roubiliac's Handel', *Victoria and Albert Museum Masterpieces*, Sheet 4, 1976.

Mallet 1962, J.V.G. Mallet, 'Some Portrait Medallions by Roubiliac', *Burlington Magazine*, CIV, 1962, pp 153-58.

Mallet 1964, J.V.G. Mallet, *Upton House, the Bearsted Collection*, National Trust, 1964.

Mallet 1965 I, J.V.G. Mallet, 'Chelsea' in R.J. Charleston (ed), *English Porcelain 1745-1850*, 1965.

Mallet 1965 II, J.V.G. Mallet, 'A Chelsea Talk', *Transactions of the English Ceramic Circle*, vol 6, part 1, 1965, pp 15-29.

Mallet 1967 I, J.V.G. Mallet, 'John Baddeley of Shelton an Early Staffordshire Maker of Pottery and Porcelain, Part I', *Transactions of the English Ceramic Circle*, vol 6, part 2, 1967.

Mallet 1967 II, J.V.G. Mallet, 'John Baddeley of Shelton an Early Staffordshire Maker of Pottery and Porcelain, Part II', *Transactions of the English Ceramic Circle*, vol 6, part 3, 1967.

Mallet 1967 III, J.V.G. Mallet, 'Hogarth's Pug in Porcelain', *Victoria & Albert Museum Bulletin*, vol III, no 2, April 1967 (Revised and reprinted separately, 1971).

Mallet 1969, J.V.G. Mallet, 'Rococo English Porcelain, a study in Style', *Apollo*, August 1969.

Mallet 1973, J.V.G. Mallet, 'The Site of the Chelsea Porcelain Factory', *Transactions of the English Ceramic Circle*, vol 9, part 1, 1973.

Mallet 1974, J.V.G. Mallet, 'Wedgwood and the Rococo', *Apollo*, May 1974, pp 320-29, and reprinted with slightly altered illustrations, *Proceedings of the Wedgwood Society*, no 9, 1975, pp 36-62.

Mallet 1977, J.V.G. Mallet, 'A Chelsea Greyhound and Retrieving Setter', *Connoisseur*, November, 1977.

Mallet 1978, J.V.G. Mallet, 'Pottery and Porcelain at Erddig', *Apollo*, January 1978.

Mallet 1980, J.V.G. Mallet, 'Chelsea Porcelain — Botany and Time', *Catalogue of the Burlington House Antiques Fair*, 1980.

Manchester Guardian 1922, *Manchester Guardian*, 6 November, 1922.

Marble Hill Supplement 1969, G.L.C., *The Marble Hill Catalogue*, 1969, Supplement, No. 23.

Mariette 1727, J. Mariette, *L'Architecture Française, 1727.*

Mariette (n.d.), J. Mariette, *L'Architecture à la Mode*, (n.d.).

Mariette 1929, J. Mariette, *L'Architecture Française*, (1727), facsimile edition, 1929.

Marryat 1854, J. Marryat, *History of Pottery and Porcelain*, 1854.

Marshall 1951, H.R. Marshall, 'James Giles, Enameller', *Transactions of the English Ceramic Circle*, vol 3, part 1, 1951.

Marshall 1954, H.R. Marshall, *Coloured Worcester Porcelain of the First Period, (1751-1783)*, Newport, Monmouthshire, 1954.

Mathias 1979, P. Mathias, *The Transformation of England: Essays in the Economic and Social History of England in the Eighteenth Century*, 1979.

Mayne 1968, J. Mayne, 'Rowlandson at Vauxhall', *Victoria and Albert Museum Bulletin*, July 1968, vol 4, no 3, p 77-81.

Meissonnier, Oeuvre, *Oeuvre de Juste-Aurèle Meissonnier*, New York 1969, with an introduction by Dorothea Nyberg.

Mentmore 1884, Anonymous, *Mentmore*, privately printed, 1884.

Messelet 1937, J. Messelet, 'Musée des Art Decoratifs. Donation de M et Mme David-Weill', *Bulletin des Musées de France*, Paris, 1937.

Merchant 1958, W.M. Merchant, 'Francis Hayman's illustrations of Shakespeare', *Shakespeare Quarterly*, IX, 1958, pp 141-52.

Merchant 1959, W.M. Merchant, *Shakespeare and the artist*, 1959.

Metcalf 1977, P. Metcalf, *The Halls of The Fishmongers Company*, 1977.

Metropolitan Museum of Art, 1974-65, Metropolitan Museum

of Art, *The Grand Gallery*, New York 1974-75.

Mew 1928, E. Mew, 'Battersea Enamels and the Anti-Gallican Society', *Apollo*, 7, 1982.

Meyer 1983, V. Meyer, 'L'oeuvre gravé de Daniel Rabel', *Nouvelles de l'estampe*, 67, January-February, 1983, pp 6-15.

Michel 1952, M. Roland Michel, 'L'ornement rocaille quelques questions', *Revue de L'Art*, 55, 1982, pp 66-75.

Milan 1975, Palazzo Reale, Milan, *British Painting 1660-1840*, exhibition, 1975.

Millar 1963, O. Millar, *The Tudor, Stuart and Early Georgian Pictures in the collection of Her Majesty the Queen*, 1963.

Minneapolis 1971, *European Paintings from the Minneapolis Institute of Arts*, New York, Washington, 1971.

Moger 1980, V. Moger, *The Favour of Your Company*, 1980.

Montgomery 1970, F. M. Montgomery, *Printed Textiles, English and American cottons and linens, 1700-1850*, 1970.

Montgomery 1970, F. M. Montgomery I, John Holker's mid 18th century Livre d'Échantillons' in *Studies in Textile Hisory*, ed Gervers, Royal Ontario Museum 1977, pp 214-231.

Morris 1957 I, B. Morris, 'English Printed Textiles II, Copperplate Chinoiseries', *Antiques*, LXXI, April 1957, pp 360-363.

Morris 1957 II, B. Morris, 'English Printed Textiles IV, Copperplate bird designs', *Antiques*, LXXI, June 1957, pp 556-559.

Mortimer 1763, Mortimer, *Universal Director*, 1763.

Moss 1910, F. Moss, *Pilgrimages to Old Homes*, 1910.

Mountford 1971, A. Mountford, *The Illustrated Guide to Staffordshire Saltglazed Stoneware*, 1971.

Mudie 1822, R. Mudie, *A historical account of His Majesty's visit to Edinburgh*, Edinburgh, 1822.

Mulliner 1924, H.H. Mulliner, *The Decorative Arts in Britain*, 1924.

Munich 1980, *Zwei Jahrhunderte Englische Malerei*, exhibition, Munich, 1980.

Murdoch 1980, T. Murdoch, 'Roubiliac as an Architect? The bill for the Warkton monuments', *Burlington Magazine*, CXXII (1980), pp 40-46.

Murdoch 1983, T. Murdoch, 'Roubiliac and his Huguenot Connections', *Proceedings of the Huguenot Society*, 24, 1983, pp 26-45.

Murdoch 1982, T.V. Murdoch, *Huguenot Artists, Designers and Craftsmen . . .*, Univ. of London Ph.d. thesis, 1982.

Murray 1980, P. Murray, *Dulwich Picture Gallery, A Catalogue*, 1980.

Musée de l'Ermitage 1981, Musée de l'Ermitage, *Peinture de l'Europe Occidentale*, Catalogue 2, Leningrad, 1981.

Musée du Louvre 1958, *Catalogue de l'Orfevrerie du XVII, du XVIII et du XIX Siècle*, 1958.

Museo Poldi Pezzoli 1974, *Cataloghi del Museo Poldi Pezzoli I, Gli orologi a cura di Giuseppe Brusa*, Milan, 1974.

McNab Dennis 1967, J. McNab Dennis, 'London Silver in a Colonial Household', *Bulletin of the Metropolitan Museum of Art*, December 1967.

Macquoid 1928, T. Macquoid, *Old Furniture*, III, April 1928.

MacColl 1917, D.S. MacColl, 'Bradshaw's Tapestries at Ham House', *Burlington Magazine*, XXXI, June, October, 1917, pp 218-219, 148-157.

McCrory 1983, M.A. McCrory, 'A Proposed Exchange of Gem Impressions during the Period of the Directoire', *Studien zum europäischen Kunsthandwerk. Festschrift Yvonne Hackenbroch*, Munich 1983, pp 273-87.

McKendrick, Brewer and Plumb 1982, N. McKendrick, J. Brewer and J.H. Plumb, *The Birth of a Consumer Society: The Commercialization of Eighteenth-century England*, Bloomington, 1982.

National Portrait Gallery 1976, National Portrait Gallery, London, *Johan Zoffany*, 1976.

Nevill 1919, R. Nevill, *Lady Dorothy Nevill*, 1919.

Newman 1961, A.N. Newman, 'Leicester House Politics, 1748-1751', *English Historical Review*, 76, 1961.

Nichols 1786, J. Nichols, *Lambeth*, 1786.

Nichols 1808, J. Nichols, *The Genuine Works of William Hogarth*, 2 vols, 1808-10.

Nichols 1833, *Anecdotes of William Hogarth*, 1833 compiled by J.B.

Nichols, 1970 Facsimile, p 37.

Nichols and Wray 1935, R.H. Nichols and F.A. Wray, *The History of the Foundling Hospital*, 1935.

Nicholson 1972, B. Nicholson, *The Treasures of the Foundling Hospital*, 1972.

Nightingale 1881, J.E. Nightingale, *Contributions towards the History of Early English Porcelain*, Salisbury, 1881.

Nocq 1927, H. Nocq, *Le Poinçon de Paris*, vol I-V, Paris, 1926-31.

Nocq, Alfassa and Guérin, H. Nocq, P. Alfassa, J. Guérin, *Orfèvrerie Civile Française du XVIe au début du XIXe siècle*, Paris (n.d.).

Noon 1979, P. J. Noon, *English Portrait Drawings and Miniatures*, New Haven, 1979.

Norman 1977, A.V.B. Norman, 'Prince Charles Edward's silver hilted back-sword', *Proc. Soc. Antiq. Scot.*, CV, 1976-7, pp 324-6, pls 28-9.

Norman 1980, A.V.B. Norman, *The Rapier and Small-Sword 1460-1820*, 1980, pp 206, 207.

North 1982, A.R.E. North, *Introduction to European Swords*, 1982.

Norton 1938, R. & M. Norton, *A History of Gold Snuff Boxes*, 1938.

Nottingham 1973, Nottingham University Art Gallery, *Lord Burlington and His Circle*, Nottingham, 1973.

Nyberg 1969, D. Nyberg, *Meissonnier An Eighteenth-Century Maverick*, New York, 1969.

O'Donoghue 1908, F. O'Donoghue, *Catalogue of Engraved British Portraits preserved in the Department of Prints and Drawings in the British Museum*, vol I, A-C, 1908.

Oman 1954, C. Oman, 'Royal Plate from Buckingham Palace and Windsor Castle', *Victoria and Albert Museum Picture book*, 1954.

Oman 1957, C. Oman, *English Church Plate 597-1830*, 1957.

Oman and Hamilton 1982, Charles C. Oman and Jean Hamilton, *Wallpapers: A history and Illustrated Catalogue of the Collection in the Victoria and Albert Museum*, 1982.

Oppé 1947, A.P. Oppé, *The Drawings of Paul and Thomas Sandby in the Collection of His Majesty The King at Windsor Castle*, 1947.

Oppé 1948, A.P. Oppé, *The Drawings of William Hogarth*, 1948.

Oppé 1950, A.P. Oppé, *English Drawings at Windsor Castle. Stuart and Georgian Periods*, 1950.

Opperman 1977, H.N. Opperman, *Jean-Baptiste Oudry*, New York, 1977.

Orleans House 1980, Orleans House Gallery, Twickenham, *Horace Walpole and Strawberry Hill*, exhibition, 1980.

Orleans House 1982, Orleans House Gallery, Twickenham, *James Gibbs Architect*, exhibition, 1982.

Ormond 1968, R. Ormond, 'Silver shapes in Chelsea Porcelain', *Country Life*, February 1st, 1968, pp 224-226.

Oswald 1949, A. Oswald, 'Blair Castle II', *Country Life*, 18 November 1949.

Paris 1867, Catalogue of the Exhibition, Paris, 1867, British Section.

Paris 1950, Paris, Bibliothèque Nationale, *Dessins du Nationalmuseum de Stockholm*, exhibition, 1950.

Parker 1929, G. Parker, 'Tyndal's Park, Bristol, Fort Royal and the Fort House Therein', *Transactions of the Bristol and Gloucestershire Archaeological Society*, LI, 1929, 124-41.

Parker 1931, K.T. Parker, *The Drawings of Antoine Watteau*, 1931.

Parker 1938, K.T. Parker, *Catalogue of the Collection of Drawings in the Ashmolean Museum*, vol I, Oxford, 1938.

Parker & Mathey 1957, K.T. Parker & J. Mathey, *Antoine Watteau; catalogue complet de son oeuvre dessiné*, Paris, 1957.

Park Lane 1930, 25, Park Lane, London, *Conversation Pieces*, exhibition, 1930.

Parrott 1752, R. Parrott, *Reflections on Various Subjects relating to Arts and Commerce: particularly the Consequences of admitting Foreign Artists*, 1752.

Patte 1777, P. Patte, *Cours d'Architecture* 1777.

Paulson 1965, R. Paulson, *Hogarth's Graphic Works*, New Haven and London, 1965.

Paulson 1971, R. Paulson, *Hogarth*, 1971.

Penny 1975, N.B. Penny, 'The Macabre Garden at Denbies and its Monument', *Garden History III*, 1975, pp 58-61.

Penzer 1956, N.M. Penzer, 'The Jerningham-Kandler Wine-Cooler', *Apollo*, September, October, 1956, pp 80ff, *III* ff.

Percy 1874, Dr. J. Percy, MS catalogue of his collection of drawings, Department of Prints and Drawings, British Museum.

Pevsner 1955, N. Pevsner, *The Englishness of English Art*, 1955.

Pevsner 1973, N. Pevsner, *Northamptonshire*, 2nd ed 1973.

Phillips 1935, P. A.S. Phillips, *Paul de Lamerie, A Study of his Life and Work*, 1935.

Phillips 1964, H. Phillips, *Mid-Georgian London*, 1964.

Physick 1967, J. Physick, 'Some eighteenth-century designs for monuments in Westminster Abbey', *Victoria and Albert Museum Bulletin*, 3, 1967.

Physick 1969, J. Physick, *Designs for English Sculpture 1680-1860*, 1969.

Physick 1982, J. Physick, letter, *Country Life* 16 Dec. 1982.

Picart 1734, B. Picart, *Impostures innocentes . . . et le catalogue des ses ouvrages*, Amsterdam, 1734.

Pickford 1983, I. Pickford, *Silver Flatware*, 1983.

Pineau (n.d.), N. Pineau, *Nouveaux desseins de Plaques, Consoles, Torchères et Medailliers*, (n.d.).

Pinkerton 1973, J. Pinkerton, 'Roubiliac's Statue of Lord President Forbes', *Connoisseur*, CLXXXIII 1973, pp 274-279.

Pinto 1955, E.H. Pinto, 'The Furniture at Woburn Abbey', *Apollo*, LXIII, December 1955.

Pinto 1959, E.H. Pinto, 'The Furniture of William Vile and John Cobb', *Antiques*, January 1959.

Pitkin 1979, Pitkin Pictorials, *The Royal Mews, Buckingham Palace, The Queen's Horses and Carriages*, 1979.

Plumb 1967, J.H. Plumb, *The Growth of Political Stability in England 1675-1725*, 1967.

Plumb 1977, J.H. Plumb, *The Pursuit of Happiness*, exhibition, Yale Center for British Art, 1977.

Pope 1956, A. Pope, *Correspondence*, 1956, IV.

Pope-Hennessy 1964, J. Pope-Hennessy, *Catalogue of Italian Sculpture in the Victoria and Albert Museum*, 1964.

Pope-Hennessy 1967, J. Pope-Hennessy, 'Foggini and Soldani: some recent acquisitions', *Victoria and Albert Museum Bulletin*, III, 4, (1967), pp 135-144.

Populus 1930, B. Populus, *Claude Gillot, Catalogue de L'Oeuvre Gravé*, Paris, 1930.

Porter 1982, R. Porter, *English Society in the Eighteenth Century*, 1982.

Postlethwayt 1751, Malachy Postlethwayt, *The Universal Dictionary of Trade and Commerce*, 1751, vol I, article on engraving.

Potterton 1975, H. Potterton, *Irish Church Monuments 1570-1880*, Belfast 1975.

Pratt 1928, ed. R.T. Gunther, *The Architecture of Sir Roger Pratt*, 1928.

Praz 1971, M. Praz, *Conversation Pieces*, 1971.

Price 1948, E. Stanley Price, *John Sadler, a Liverpool Pottery Printer*, West Kirby, 1948.

Pye 1845, J. Pye, *Patronage of British Art*, 1845.

Pyke 1973, E.J. Pyke, *Biographical Dictionary of Wax Modellers*, Oxford, 1973.

Rackham 1923, B. Rackham, *Catalogue of the Herbert Allen Collection*, Victoria and Albert Museum (2nd ed), 1923.

Rackham 1924, B. Rackham, *Catalogue of the Schreiber Collection*, vol III, 1924.

Rackham 1927, B. Rackham, 'Mr Wallace Elliot's Collection of English Porcelain', *Connoisseur*, vol LXXVIII and LXXIX, 1927.

Rackham 1928, B. Rackham, *Catalogue of the Schreiber Collection*, vol 1, 1928 (2nd ed).

Radcliffe 1969, A. Radcliffe, 'Acquisitions of Sculpture by the Royal Academy', *Apollo*, 1969, LXXXIX.

Raines 1966, R. Raines, *Marcellus Laroon*, 1966.

Ralph 1734, J. Ralph, *A Critical Review of the Public Buildings, Statues and ornaments, In, and about London and Westminster*, 1734.

Rasmussen 1977, J. Rasmussen (ed) *Barockplastik in Norddeutschland*, Hamburg, Museum für Kunst und Gewerbe, 1977.

Ray 1965, A. Ray, 'A Collector examines the 'Flower Bowl' and the 'Musical Entertainer', *Connoisseur*, December 1965 pp 232-5.

Ray 1968, A. Ray, *English Delftware Pottery in the Robert Hall Warren Collection*, Ashmolean Museum, Oxford, 1968.

Ray 1973 I, A. Ray, *English Delftware Tiles*, 1973.
Ray 1973 II, 'Liverpool Printed Tiles', *Transactions of the English Ceramic Circle*, vol 9, part 1, 1973, pp 36-66.
Réau 1950, L. Réau, *J.-B. Pigalle*, Paris, 1950.
Redgrave 1878, S. Redgrave, *A Dictionary of Artists of the English School*, 2nd ed, 1878.
Residenz Museum 1958, Residenz Museum, Munich. Catalogue, *The Age of Rococo*. 4th Council of Europe Exhibition, 1958, Cat. 902, p 257.
RIBA 1972, *Catalogue of the Drawings Collection of the Royal Institute of British Architects*, vol B, 1972.
Ribeiro 1983, E. Ribeiro, *A Visual History of Costume. The Eighteenth Century*, 1983.
Rice 1983, D.G Rice, *Derby Porcelain, the Golden Years 1750-1770*, Newton Abbot, 1983.
Riely & Wimsatt 1979, J. Riely and W.K. Wimsatt, 'A Supplement to The Portraits of Alexander Pope', *Evidence in Literary Scholarship* (ed.) R. Wellek and A. Ribeiro.
Rogers 1896, H.A. Rogers: *Views of Some of the Most Celebrated By-Gone Pleasure Gardens of London*, 1896.
Rogers 1973, N. Rogers, 'Aristocratic Clientage, Trade and Independancy: Popular Politics in Pre-Radical Westminster', *Past and Present*, 61, 1973.
Roland-Michel 1975, M. Roland-Michel, 'Le Cabinet de Curiosité de Bonnier de la Mosson et la participation de Lajoue à son Decor', *Bulletin de la Société de l'Histoire de l'Art Français*, 1975, pp 211-21.
Roland-Michel 1979, M. Roland-Michel, 'Eighteenth-Century Decorative Painting: Some False Assumptions', *The British Journal for Eighteenth-Century Studies*, II, 1, 1979, pp 1-36.
Roland-Michel 1982, M. Roland Michel, 'L'ornement rocaille: quelques questions', *Revue de L'Art*, 55, 1982, pp 66-75.
Rosenberg 1928, M. Rosenberg, *Des Goldschmiede Merkzeichen*. Vols I-IV, Berlin, 1928.
Rosenberg 1972, P. Rosenberg, *French Master Drawings of the 17th and 18th centuries in North American collections*, 1972.
Rosenfeld 1981, S. Rosenfeld, *Georgian Scene painters and Scene Painting*, Cambridge 1981.
Rosenthal 1980, M. Rosenthal, *Hogarth*, 1980.
Roth 1971, Cecil Roth, 'The Amazing Clan of Buzaglo', *Transactions of the Jewish Historical Society of England*, vol XXIII, 1971, pp 11-21.
Rothstein 1964, N. Rothstein, 'Nine English Silks', *Bulletin of the Needle and Bobbin Club*, vol 4, nos 1 and 2, 1964, pl 11.
Rothstein 1967, N. Rothstein, 'Silks for the American Colonies', *Connoisseur*, October and November 1967 pp 90-94 and 150-156.
Roumier 1724, F. Roumier, *Livre de plusiers coins de Bordures*, 1724.
Rouquet 1755, J.A. Rouquet, *The Present State of the Arts in England*, 1755.
Rowan 1975, A. Rowan, 'Batty Langley's Gothic', *Studies in Memory of David Talbot Rice* (ed. G. Robertson and G. Henderson), Edinburgh, 1975.
Royal Academy 1907, Royal Academy, London, *Winter Exhibition*, 1907.
Royal Academy 1934, Royal Academy, *British Art*, exhibition, 1934.
Royal Academy 1954-5, Royal Academy, London, *European Masters of the Eighteenth century*, exhibition, 1954-5.
Royal Academy 1955-6, *English Taste in the 18th Century*, Winter 1955-6.
Royal Academy 1956, *British Portraits*, exhibition, 1956.
Royal Academy 1961, *Treasures of Trinity College Dublin* exhibition, 1961.
Royal Academy 1968, *France in the Eighteenth Century*, exhibition, 1968.
Ruch 1970, J. Ruch, 'A Hayman Portrait of Jonathan Tyers's Family', *Burlington Magazine*, CXII, August 1970.
Rückert 1963, R. Rückert, *Franz Anton Bustelli*, Munich, 1963.
Rückert 1966, R. Rückert, *Meissener Porzellan 1710-1810*, Munich, 1966.
Rush 1973, J. Rush, *The Ingenious Beilbys*, 1973.

Sainte-Croix 1882, Le Roy De Sainte-Croix, 'Vie et ouvrages de L.F. Roubiliac', Paris, 1882.
Savage 1952, G. Savage, *18th Century English Porcelain*, 1952.
Sayer c.1758-62, *The Ladies Amusement*, published by Robert Sayer c.1758-62, reprint Newport, Monmouthshire, 1966.
Schroder 1983, T. Schroder, *The Dowty Collection of Silver by Paul de Lamerie*, Cheltenham Art Gallery and Museums, 1983.
Scott Thomson 1949, G. Scott Thomson, *Family Background*, 1949.
Sedgwick 1970, R. Sedgwick, *The History of Parliament: The House of Commons 1715-54*, 2 vols, 1970, 1.
Sedlmayr 1956, H. Sedlmayr, *Johann Bernhard Fischer von Ehrlach*, Vienna and Munich, 1956.
Sedlmayr & Baur 1966, H. Sedlmayr & H. Baur, 'Rococo', *Encyclopaedia of World Art*, New York, London, Toronto, 1966, vol XII, pp 230-74.
Seelig 1977, L. Seelig, 'Das Bildnis in der Barockskulptur Norddeutschlands', *Barokplastik in Norddeutschland*, (exhibition cat), Hamburg 1977, pp 63-92.
Seling 1980, H. Seling, *Die Kunst der Augsburger Goldschmiede 1529-1868*, Munich, 1980.
Severne Mackenna 1942, F. Severne Mackenna, 'Chelsea or Plymouth?', *Apollo*, May, 1942.
Severne Mackenna 1944, F. Severne Mackenna, 'English Porcelain a Chelsea Rarity', *Apollo*, December 1944.
Severne Mackenna 1946, F. Severne Mackenna, *Cookworthy's Plymouth and Bristol Porcelain*, Leigh-on-Sea, 1946.
Severne Mackenna 1948, F. Severne Mackenna, *Chelsea Porcelain, the Triangle and Raised Anchor Wares*, leigh-on-Sea, 1948 (Reprinted 1969).
Severne Mackenna 1951, F. Severne Mackenna, *Chelsea Porcelain, the Red Anchor Wares*, Leigh-on-Sea, 1951.
Severne Mackenna 1952, F. Severne Mackenna, *Chelsea Porcelain, the Gold Anchor Wares*, Leigh-on-Sea, 1952.
Severne Mackenna 1972, F. Severne Mackenna, *The F. Severne Mackenna Collection of English Porcelain*, Leigh-on-Sea, 1972.
Sewter 1948, A.C. Sewter, 'Stephen Slaughter', *Connoissuer*, CXXI, March 1948, pp 10-15.
Shaw 1801, Rev. S. Shaw, *History and Antiquities of Staffordshire*, II, 1801.
Shugborough 1977, *Shugborough* Guide Book, 5th ed, 1977.
Sitwell 1936, S. Sitwell, *Conversation Pieces*, 1936.
Sitwell 1945, S. Sitwell, *British Architects and Craftsmen*, 1945.
Smith 1756, G. Smith, *Laboratory or School of Arts*, 1756.
Smith 1828, J.T. Smith, *Nollekens and His Times*, 1828.
Smith 1883, J. Chaloner Smith, *British Mezzotinto Portraits*, 1883.
Smollett 1771, T. Smollett, *The Expedition of Humphry Clinker*, 1771.
Snodin 1974, M. Snodin, *English Silver Spoons*, 1974.
Snodin 1983, M. Snodin, 'George Bickham Junior', *The VAM Album*, 2, 1983, pp 354-360.
Snowman 1966, A. Kenneth Snowman, *Eighteenth Century Gold Boxes of Europe*, 1966.
Society of Arts 1778, Society of Arts, *A Register of Premiums and Bounties given by the Society*, 1778.
Solon 1903, M. L. Solon, *A Brief History of Old English Porcelain*, London and Derby, 1903.
Souchal 1967, F. Souchal, *Les Slodtz*, Paris, 1967.
Souchal 1977-81, F. Souchal, *French Sculptors of the 17th and 18th centuries. The reign of Louis XIV, I & II*, Oxford, 1977-81.
Souchal 1980, F. Souchal, *Les Frères Coustou*, Paris, 1980.
Southwick 1982, L. Southwick, *The Price Guide to Antique Edge Weapons*, Woodbridge, 1982.
Southworth 1941, J.G. Southworth: *Vauxhall Gardens*, New York, 1941.
Sprague Allen, 1937 B. Sprague Allen, *Tides in English Tastes*, Cambridge, Massachussetts, 1937.
Standen 1983, E.A. Standen, 'A Parrot and a Squirrel in a Landscape', *Studien zum Europäischen Kunsthandwerk, Festschrift Yvonne Hackenbroch*, Munich, 1983, pp 251-256.
Starkie Gardner 1903, J. Starkie Gardner, *Old Silverwork*, 1903.
Stevenson 1976, S. Stevenson, *A Face for Any Occasion*, Edinburgh, 1976.

Stockholm 1980, Nationalmuseum, Stockholm, *1700-tal Tanke och form i rokokon*, exhibition, 1980.

Stoner 1955, F. Stoner, *Chelsea, Bow and Derby Porcelain Figures*, Newport, Monmouthshire, 1955.

Strickland 1916, W.G. Strickland, *A Descriptive Catalogue of the Pictures, Busts, and Statues in Trinity college, Dublin*, Dublin, 1916.

Stroud 1971, D. Stroud, *George Dance Architect*, 1971, pp 57, 74.

Strutt 1786, J. Strutt, *A Biographical Dictionary containing an historical account of all the Engravers*, 1786.

Sugden & Edmonson 1926, A.V. Sugden & J.L. Edmonson *A History of English Wallpaper*, 1926.

Sunderland & Camesasca 1971, J. Sunderland, E. Camesasca, *Watteau*, 1971.

Sutton 1969, D. Sutton, 'Le Bon Ton and le Roast Beef', *Apollo*, August 1969.

Sykes 1934, N. Sykes, *Church and State in the Eighteenth Century*, Cambridge 1934.

Symonds 1965, R.W. Symonds, 'A Magnificent Dressing Table', *Country Life*, February 16, 1965.

Synge-Hutchinson 1954, P. Synge-Hutchinson, 'Some Chelsea Porcelain in the Queen Mother's Collection', *Connoisseur*, August, 1954.

Synge-Hutchinson 1958, P. Synge-Hutchinson, 'G.D. Ehret's Botanical Designs on Chelsea Porcelain, *Connoisseur*, October, 1958.

Taft Museum, Taft Museum, Cincinnati, *Catalogue*.

Tate Gallery 1971, Tate Gallery, *Hogarth*, exhibition, 1971-2.

Tate Gallery 1982, Tate Gallery, *Richard Wilson's Early Contemporaries*, exhibition, 1982-3.

Tait 1957, G.H. Tait, 'Outstanding Pieces in the English Ceramic Collection of the British Museum', *Transactions of the English Ceramic Circle*, vol 4, part 3, 1957.

Tait 1959, H. Tait, *Bow Porcelain 1744-1776*, 1959.

Tait 1960 I, H. Tait, 'Some Consequences of the Bow Special Exhibition, Part I', *Apollo*, vol LXXI, February 1960.

Tait 1960 II, H. Tait, 'Some Consequences of the Bow Special Exhibition, Part III', *Apollo*, June, 1960.

Tait 1962 I, H. Tait, 'Handel and Bow', *Apollo*, July 1962, pp 384-390.

Tait 1962 II, H. Tait, 'James Rogers, A Leading Painter at Worcester c.1755-65', *Connoisseur*, April, 1962.

Tait 1963, H. Tait, 'The Bow Factory under Alderman Arnold and Thomas Frye (1747-1759)', *Transactions of the English Ceramic Circle*, vol 5, part 4, 1963.

Tait 1972, H. Tait, *Porcelain*, Revised edition, 1972.

Tapp 1937, Major W.H. Tapp, 'The Chelsea Fable Painter', *Transactions of the English Ceramic Circle*, no 4, 1937.

Tapp 1938 I, Major W.H. Tapp, *Jefferyes Hamett O'Neale*, 1734-1801, London, 1938.

Tapp 1938 II, W.H. Tapp, 'Joseph Willems, China Modeller, died 1766', *Connoisseur*, April 1938, pp 1-7.

Tapp 1941 I, Major W.H. Tapp, 'Porcelain Artists, the unrecorded Book of Engravings, Parts I and II', *Apollo*, 1941.

Tapp 1941 II, Major W.H. Tapp, 'Chelsea China Factory Catalogues and the Fable Painter, Parts I and II', *Apollo*, June and July, 1941.

Tattersall 1934, C.E.C. Tattersall 1934, *A History of British Carpets*, 1934.

Temple Newsam 1938, Temple Newsam, *Pictures and Furniture*, 1938 (237).

Temple Newsam 1951, Temple Newsam House, Leeds, *Thomas Chippendale*, 1951, Catalogue.

Temple Newsam 1968, Temple Newsam House, Leeds, *Thomas Chippendale and His Patrons in the North*, 1968.

Theuerkauff 1981, C. Theuerkauff, 'Einige Bildnisse, Allegorien und kuriositaten von Johann Christoph Ludwig Lucke (um 1703-1780)' *Alte und Moderne kunst*, no 174/175, 1981, pp 27-38.

Theuerkauff 1982, C. Theuerkauff, 'Johann Christoph Ludwig Lucke 'Ober model-meister und Inventions-Meister' in Meissen, 'Ober Direktor', Zu Wien', *Alte und Moderne kunst, no 183, 1982.*

Thornton 1958, P. Thornton. 'An 18th century silk designer's Manual'. *Bulletin of Needle and Bobbin Club* Vol 42, nos 1 and 2, 1958.

Thornton 1965, P. Thornton, *Baroque and Rococo Silks*, 1965.

Thornton & Rieder I, P. Thornton and W. Rieder, 'Pierre Langlois Ebeniste, Part 1, *Connoisseur*, CLXXVII, December 1971, pp 283-88.

Thornton & Rieder II, P. Thornton and W. Rieder, 'Pierre Langlois, Ebéniste, part 5', *Connoisseur*, CLXXX, February 1972, p 30, fig 1.

Thornton and Rieder III, P. Thornton and W. Rieder, 'Pierre Langlois, Ebéniste part 2, *Connoisseur*, CLXXIX, February 1972.

Tilley 1957, F. Tilley, *Teapots and Tea*, Newport, Monmouthshire, 1957.

Tomlin 1972, M. Tomlin, *Catalogue of Adam Period Furniture*, 1972.

Toppin 1946 I, A. Toppin, 'The Origin of Some Ceramic Designs', *English Ceramic Circle Transactions*, 1946.

Toppin 1946 II, A. J. Toppin, 'Battersea: Ceramic and Kindred Associations', *Transactions of the English Ceramic Circle*, vol 2, no 9, 1946.

Toppin 1948, A. Toppin, 'The Origin of Some Ceramic Designs', *Transactions of the English Ceramic Circle*, vol 2, no 1, 1948.

Toro 1719, J.B. Toro, *Desseins arabesques à plusieurs usages*, c.1719.

Towner 1963, D. Towner, 'William Greatbatch and the early Wedgwood Wares', *Transactions of the English Ceramic Circle*, vol 5, part 4, 1963, pp 180-193.

Towner 1974, D. Towner, 'Robinson and Rhodes, Enamellers at Leeds', *Transactions of the English Ceramic Circle*, vol 9, part 2, 1974, pp 134-139.

Towner 1978, D. Towner, *Creamware*, 1978.

Toynbee 1927, P. Toynbee, *Strawberry Hill Accounts*, Oxford, 1927.

Trevor 1955, J. Trevor & Sons, *Catalogue of Antique Silver, the property of Sir Lyonel Tollemache Bart*, sold London, 12 May 1955.

Turner 1927, L. Turner, *Decorative Plasterwork in Great Britain*, 1927.

Twyman 1971, M. Twyman, *Printing 1770-1970*, 1971.

Uppark, *Uppark, National Trust Guide Book*, 1976.

Valpy 1983, N. Valpy, 'Extracts from the Daily Advertiser 1745-1746', *Transactions of the English Ceramic Circle*, vol 11, part 3, 1983.

Valpy & Mallet 1982, N. Valpy, 'Extracts from Eighteenth Century London Newspapers', and J.V.G. Mallet, 'Vauxhall "Porcelain Ware" a Note', *Transactions of the English Ceramic Circle*, vol II, part 2, 1982.

VAM 1924, *Catalogue of the Jones Collection*, II, 1924.

VAM 1926, Victoria and Albert Museum, *Livery Companies Exhibition*, 1926.

VAM 1954, Victoria and Albert Museum, *Royal Plate from Buckingham Palace & Windsor Castle*, exhibition, 1954.

VAM 1960, Victoria and Albert Museum, *Catalogue of a loan exhibition of English Chintz, 1960.*

VAM 1962, Victoria and Albert Museum, *Third International Art Treasures Exhibition presented by C.I.N.O.A.*, 1962.

VAM 1968, Victoria and Albert Museum, *The British Antique Dealers Association Golden Jubilee Exhibition*, 1968.

VAM 1983, *Pattern and Design, Designs for the Decorative Arts*, exhibition, 1983.

VAM 1984, Victoria and Albert Museum, *From East to West, a celebration of the work of G.P. and J. Baker, exhibition, 1984.*

Vardy 1744, J. Vardy, *Some Designs of Mr Inigo Jones and Mr William Kent*, 1744.

Versailles 1963, Château de Versailles, *Charles le Brun*, exhibition, 1963.

Vertue, G. Vertue notebooks, *The Walpole Society*, XVIII (I), XX (II), XXII (III), XXIV (IV), XXVI (V), XXIX (index), XXX (VI).

Verlet 1982, P. Verlet, 'The James de Rothschild Collection at Waddesdon Manor', *The Savonnerie*, 1982, pp 144-5.

Vitruvius Britannicus 1739, J. Badeslade & J. Rocque, *Vitruvius Brittanicus Volume the Fourth*, 1739.

Volk 1981, P. Volk, *Rokoko Plastik*, Munich 1981.

Volk 1982, P. Volk, 'Johann Baptist Straubs Törring-Epitaph in Au am Inn', *Münchner Jahrbuch der bildendenkunst*, XXXIII (1982), pp 155-172.

Voltaire 1733, F.M.A. de Voltaire, *Le Temple du goût,* 1733.
Von Carolsfeld 1928, L.S. von Carolsfeld, *Porzellansammlung Gustav von Klemperer,* Dresden, 1928.
Wackernagel 1983, R. H. Wackernagel, 'Festwagen', *Reallexikon zur Deutschen Kunstgeschichte,* vol VIII, Munich 1983, pp 380-383.
Wainwright 1982, D. Wainwright, *Broadwood By Appointment,* 1982.
Walker Art Gallery 1958, Walker Art Gallery, Liverpool, *Painting and Sculpture in England 1700-1750,* exhibition, 1958.
Walpole 1774, H. Walpole, *A Description of the Villa of Horace Walpole,* Twickenham, 1774.
Walpole 1784, H. Walpole, *A Description of the Villa of Mr. Horace Walpole,* Twickenham, 1784.
Walton 1976, P. Walton, *Creamware and other English Pottery at Temple Newsam House, Leeds,* Bradford, 1976.
Ward-Jackson 1958, P. Ward-Jackson, *English Furniture Designs of the Eighteenth Century,* 1958.
Ward-Jackson 1969, P. Ward-Jackson, 'Some Main Streams and Tributaries in European Ornament from 1500 to 1750', *VAM Bulletin Reprints,* 3, 1969 (from *Bulletin,* vol III, 2-4, 1967).
Ware 1733, I. Ware, *Designs of Inigo Jones and others,* 1733.
Ware 1756, I. Ware, *A Complete Body of Architecture, with plans and elevations in which are interspersed some designs of Inigo Jones,* 1756.
Wark 1973, R.R. Wark, *Drawings from the Turner Shakespeare,* San Marino, California, 1973.
Wartski 1971, Wartski, *A thousand years of enamel,* 1971.
Washington 1976, National Gallery of Art, Washington, *The Eye of Thomas Jefferson,* exhibition, 1976.
Waterhouse 1941, E.K. Waterhouse, *Reynolds,* 1941.
Waterhouse 1946, E. Waterhouse, 'English Conversation Pieces of the Eighteenth Century', *Burlington Magazine,* LXXXVIII, June 1946, p 152.
Waterhouse 1953, E. Waterhouse, *Painting in Britain 1530-1790,* 1953.
Waterhouse 1968, E. Waterhouse, 'Reynolds "Sitters Book", for 1755', *Walpole Society XLI,* 1968.
Waterhouse 1981, E. Waterhouse, *The Dictionary of British 18th Century Painters in Oils and Crayons,* 1981.
Watney 1955, B. Watney, 'A Study of Longton Hall Teapots', *Antique Collector,* February, 1955.
Watney 1957, B. Watney, *Longton Hall Porcelain,* 1957.
Watney 1967. 'B. Watney, 'Pre-1756 Derby Domestic Wares Contemporary with the Dry-Edge Figures', *Burlington Magazine,* January 1967.
Watney 1968, B. Watney, 'The King, the Nun and other Figures', *Transactions of the English Ceramic circle,* vol 7, part 1, 1968.
Watney 1972 I, B. Watney, 'Origins of Designs for English Ceramics of the Eighteenth Century', *Burlington Magazine,* December 1972.
Watney 1972 II, B. Watney, 'A Hare, A Ram, Two Putti and Associated Figures; *Transactions of the English Ceramic Circle,* vol 8, part 2, 1972.
Watney 1972 II, B. Watney, 'Notes on Bow Transfer-Printing', *Transactions of the English Ceramic Circle,* vol 8, part 2, 1972.
Watney 1975, B. Watney, 'The Origins of Some Ceramic Designs', *Transactions of the English Ceramic Circle,* vol 9, part 3, 1975.
Watney & Charleston 1966, B. Watney and R.J. Charleston, 'Petitions for Patents concerning Porcelain, Glass and Enamels with special Reference to Birmingham, "The Great Toyshop of Europe",' *Transactions of the English Ceramic Circle,* vol 6, part 2, 1966.
Watson 1956, F.J.B. Watson, *Wallace Collection, Catalogue of the Furniture,* 1956.
Watson 1960, F. Watson, 'The Collections of Sir Alfred Beit', *Connoisseur,* CXLV, 1960, pp 156-63.
Watson 1976, F. Watson, 'An Historic Gold Box by Moser: Some problems of cataloguing gold boxes', *Burlington Magazine,* CXVIII, January 1976, pp 26-9.
Watson & Dauterman 1970, F.J.B. Watson, C.C. Dauterman, *The Wrightsman Collection,* III, New York, 1970.
Watts 1978, M.R. Watts, *The Dissenters,* Oxford, 1978.
Webb 1954, M.I. Webb, *Michael Rysbrack Sculptor,* 1954.

Webb 1956, M.I. Webb, 'Roubiliac Busts at Wilton', *Country Life,* CXIX (1956), pp 804-
Webb 1957, M.I. Webb, 'The French Antecedents of L.F. Roubiliac', *Gazette des Beaux-Arts,* 6th series, XLIX (1957), pp 81-88.
Webb 1958, M.I. Webb, 'Henry Cheere, Sculptor and Businessmen, and John Cheere', *Burlington Magazine,* C, 1958, pp 232, 274.
Webster 1970, M. Webster, 'Taste of an Augustan Collector, the collection of Dr. Richard Mead I', *Country Life,* 29 January 1970, pp 249-251.
Webster 1976, M. Webster, 'A Room of the Widow Bellmour's, *Country Life,* CLX, 1976, pp 1832-3.
Webster 1978, M. Webster, *Hogarth,* 1978.
Weiss 1982, L. Weiss, *Watch-Making in England 1760-1820,* 1892.
Wells-Cole 1974, A. Wells-Cole 'Two Rococo Masterpieces', *Leeds Art Calendar,* Leeds Art Gallery and Museum, 1974.
Wells-Cole 1983, A. Wells-Cole, *Historic Paper Hangings from Temple Newsam and other English Houses,* Leeds, 1983.
Westminster Abbey 1754, Westminster Abbey, *An Historical Description of Westminster Abbey, its Monuments and Curiosities,* 1754.
Whinney 1961, M.D. Whinney, 'Handel and Roubiliac', *Musical Times,* 102, 1961 pp 82-85.
Whinney 1964, M.D. Whinney, *Sculpture in Britain 1530 to 1830,* 1964.
Whinney 1971, M.D. Whinney, *English Sculpture 1720-1830,* 1971.
White 1983, R. White, 'The Architecture of Batty Langley', *A Gothick Symposium* (ed. J. Mordanut Crook), 1983.
Whitley 1928, W.T. Whitley, *Artists and their Friends in England 1700-99,* London and Boston, 1928.
Wildenstein 1924, G. Wildenstein, *Lancret,* Paris 1924.
Wilkinson 1825, R. Wilkinson, *Londina Illustrata,* 1825.
Willet 1899, H. Willett, *Catalogue of a Collection of Pottery and Porcelain,* London, 1899.
Williams 1933, C. Williams (Trans and introd), *Sophie in London 1786,* 1933.
Williams-Wood 1981, C. Williams-Wood, *English Transfer-printed Pottery and Porcelain,* 1981.
Williamson 1904, A.C. Williamson, *George Morland,* 1904.
Willis 1977, P. Willis, *Charles Bridgman and the English Landscape Garden,* 1977.
Wills, G. Wills, *English Furniture, 1760-1900,* 1971.
Wilson 1968, M. Wilson, *The English Chamber Organ,* 1968.
Wimsatt 1965, W.K. Wimsatt, *The Portraits of Alexander Pope,* New Haven, 1965.
Wittkower 1948, R. Wittkower, 'The Earl of Burlington and William Kent', *York Georgian Society, Occasional Papers,* v, 1948
Wroth 1896, Warwick Wroth, *The London Pleasure Gardens of the Eighteenth Century,* 1896.
Wroth 1898, Warwick Wroth, 'Tickets of Vauxhall Gardens', *Numismatic Chronicle,* XVIII Third Series, 1898, p 73-92.
Wrigley 1975, E.A. Wrigley, 'A Simple Model of London's Importance in Changing English Society and Economy 1650-1750', in Daniel A. Baugh (ed) *Aristocratic Government and Society in Eighteenth-Century England,* New York, 1975.
Wunder 1962, Richard Wunder, *Extravagant Drawings of the Eighteenth century* Cooper-Hewitt Museum, exhibition, 1962.
Wunder 1975, R. P. Wunder, *Architecture, ornament, Landscape and Figure Drawings Collected by Richard Wunder,* Middlebury College, Vermont, 1975.
Wyman 1979, C. Wyman, 'The Society of Bucks', *English Ceramic Circle Transactions',* X, 1979, pp 293-304.
Yale 1965, Yale University Art Gallery, *Painting in England, 1700-1850, From the Collection of Mr. and Mrs. Paul Mellon,* exhibition, 1965.
Yale 1983, Yale Center for British Art, *Vauxhall Gardens.* Exhibition catalogue with essays by T.J. Edelstein and Brian Allen, New Haven, Connecticut, 1983.
York 1969, City Art Gallery, York, Iveagh Bequest, Kenwood, *Philip Mercier 1689-1760,* exhibition, 1969.
Young 1983, H. Young, 'Thomas Heming and the Tatton Cup', *The Burlington Magazine,* May, 1983.

Zahle 1960, E. Zahle, 'Queen Caroline Mathilda's toiletset', *Virksomhed 1954-1959*, Danish Museum of Decorative Art, Copenhagen 1960, 14-34.
Zurich 1971, Schweizerisches Landesmuseum, Zurich, *80 Jahresbericht 1971,* Zurich 1971.

Notes

The English Rococo: historical background

1   Lippincott 1983, p. 14.
2   Porter 1982, pp. 381, 390; Mathias 1979, p. 118.
3   Holmes (Ed.) 1969; Lenman 1980; Plumb 1967.
4   Sykes 1934; Watts 1978.
5   Burke's composition for the inscription on the statue of William Pitt the Elder, now in the Guildhall of the City of London.
6   Dickson 1967.
7   Hill 1976; Colley 1982.
8   The putative Jacobitism of the Tory party is still a contentious issue among historians, see Colley 1982, pp. 25-50, and Cruickshank 1979.
9   Cable 1939, pp. 119-30; Colley 1982, pp. 204-62; Newman 1961, pp. 577-89.
10   Allan 1973-4, p. 439
11   The available biographies on Frederick, Prince of Wales, are without exception extremely limited in scope and quality. Kimerly Rorschach of Yale University is currently researching Frederick's role as an art patron. For one aspect of his rococo patronage see Grimwade 1974, pp. 21-33.
12   Girouard 1966 I, pp. 58-61; Girouard 1966 II, pp. 188-90; Girouard 1966 III, pp. 224-7.
13   For the questions surrounding this Lord Baltimore's contribution, see Harris 1961, pp. 241-50.
14   Sedgwick 1970, I, p. 518; II pp. 436, 560-1.
15   Doddington's diary is full of artistic exchanges: it shows, for example, that he introduced the Italian artist Servandroni to the Prince.

16   For these Tory politicians, see Hayward & Kirkham 1980, I, pp. 89-130: Sedgwick 1970, I, pp. 599, 605, 621; II, p. 431.
17   For Smithson, see Coleridge 1968, p. 81; Sedgwick 1970, II, pp. 428-9. For Courtenay see Girouard 1966 II, p. 188; Sedgwick 1970, p. 588.
18   In addition to these possible links between Opposition politicians and the rococo, there is some intriguing evidence that many London craftsmen in the St Martin's Lane area (the centre of rococo production in England) voted for Opposition candidates at general and by-elections. See Rogers 1973, pp. 70-106, especially p. 82.
19   Printed in Porter 1982, pp. 67-8
20   See Lippincott 1983, *passim.*
21   Campbell 1747; Wrigley 1975, pp. 62-5.
22   Holmes 1982. For Mead and middle class taste in the mid-eighteenth century, see Denvir 1983, pp. 7, 83-7.
23   Brewer 1976, pp. 7, 16, 139-60.
24   Humphries & Smith 1970, *passim.*
25   Heal 1925, pl. LXX.
26   *Ibid.*, pp. 9-11.
27   Porter 1982, pp. 251-2; Twyman 1971, p. 5.
28   Brewer 1976, p. 7.
29   Arnold 1871, p. xviii; McKendrick, Brewer & Plumb 1982, pp. 217-34.
29a   Harris 1977, pp. 327-35; McKendrick, Brewer & Plumb 1982, p. 218.
30   Colley 1977, pp. 77-95, and the Brotherhood's minute book in *Greater London Record Office* A/BLB/1-2.
31   Oman 1982, pp. 17-30; Porter 1982, p. 240. These

developments in the quality of eighteenth-century English life are best examined in McKendrick, Brewer & Plumb 1982, especially pp. 9-144, 265-85.

32 Borsay 1977, pp. 581-603; Edelstein 1983; Wroth 1896.
33 McKendrick, Brewer & Plumb 1982, pp. 275-6; Rosenfeld 1981.
34 Batty Langley employed this description in Langley 1745, p. 21.
35 Jones 1973, pp. 207-10 (Voltaire quoted at p. 208).
36 Quoted in Paulson 1971, II, p. 77.
37 Colley 1982, pp. 155-6. These slogans were chanted by a Bristol mob in 1754.
38 Lippincott 1983, p. 115; Paulson 1971, II, p. 202; Rogers 1973, pp. 100-1.
39 For example, the more French designs in Isaac Ware's *A Complete Body of Architecture* were attacked in the *Critical Review* iv)1758), p. 430; and see John Shebbeare's criticism of English cultural eclecticism, printed Denvir, *The Eighteenth Century*, pp. 57-8. Brown 1757.
40 Long 1757, p. 13. The whole of this atrocious novel is illuminating about the content of English francophobia in this period.
41 Hayward 1964. There is no published account of this Society. For its craft sponsorship in the 1750s see the *Gentleman's Magazine* 21, 1751, p. 520 22; 1752, pp. 381, 534; 23 1753, p. 245.
42 Mew 1982, pp. 216-21; Sedgwick 1970, II, p. 171.
43 Parrott 1752, pp. 9, 13-14, 89.
44 Hayward 1964, pp. 23-5 and the facsimile reprint of the frontispiece and dedication of *Collection of Designs*. I am grateful to Brian Allen of the Mellon Centre, London, for information on Moser and the Anti-Gallicans.
45 Brewer 1976, *passim*.
46 Mallet 1974, p. 327.

English Rococo and its Continental Origins

1   Kimball 1942, pp. 4, 5. It probably derives from *rocaille* and *barocco*, or *barocco* alone.
2   Kimball *op. cit.*, pp. 3-9, Laing 1979, Roland Michel 1982, Sedlmayr & Baur 1966 (with bibliographies).
3   Kimball *op. cit.*, p. 58.
4   Voltaire 1733 (written in 1731).
5   Listed in Hermann 1962. See also note 2 and Eriksen 1974.
6   e.g. Cochin 1755.
7   Kimball *op. cit.*, p. 160.
8   Blondel 1737.
9   le Blanc 1747, letter XXXVI.
10 Webster 1970, Ingamells 1974.
11 Phillips 1935, pls. LXX, LXXIII, LXXIX.
12 See especially Birch 1756, facing p. 185 (Sidney Godolphin) cf *Oeuvres* D22.
13 Snodin 1983.
14 and one signed by Jean Rocque, perhaps related to a suite by Chatelain of the same year (Berlin 1939, 406).
15 Willis 1977, pl. 109.
16 Vertue III, p. 127.
17 The Mansion House pediment (Vertue III, p. 122).
18 Girouard 1966, I, II, III.
19 Ward-Jackson 1958, 20-25.
20 He was apprenticed to the goldsmiths Charles Beard (14 July 1720) and Bishop Roberts (Oct. 1724) Goldsmiths' Hall, Apprenticeship Books 5, 6, pp. 105, 38).
21 Apart from Cuvilliés (see Friedman 1975) and Nilson, the evidence for the import of German prints is small.
22 It succeeded Cochin 1754.
23 Rouquet 1755, p. 85.
24 Le Blanc 1747, letter XXIII.
25 Willis 1977, *passim*.

Vauxhall Gardens

Some of the most useful primary sources of information on Vauxhall are the collections of news-cuttings, programmes, advertisements, engravings and other ephemera to be found at the Museum of London (Warwick Wroth Collection), The British Library (BM CUP 401 K7), the Bodleian Library (James Winston Collection) and the Guildhall Library (Fillinham Collection). Similar material is also held by the Minet Library, Lambeth, the Duchy of Cornwall Office, the Victoria and Albert Museum (Enthoven Collection) and the University of London (Harry Price Library).

1   There seem to be no clues about his professional background. His epitaph in the Whitehall Evening Post described him as 'the zealot of his country's cause . . . Friend of her King, and pupil of her laws'. Rogers 1896. p. 5.
2   News cutting in Wroth Collection, Museum of London.
3   Two copies of this manuscript are known; one at the Victoria & Albert Museum, and one, from which I quote here, in a private collection.
4   BM. CUP 401 K7. np.
5   Southworth 1941, p. 43.
6   Winston Collection, Bodleian Library, Vol. 1, np.
7   Suggested to me by the late Edward Croft-Murray.
8   London Daily Post. 18th April 1738.
9   'the hint of this rational and elegant *Entertainment* was given by a *Gentleman*, whose *Paintings* exhibit the most useful lessons of *Morality*, blended with the happiest strokes of *Humour*' (Lockman 1751, p. 2; see also Yale 1983, p. 25, and p. 33 (n4).
10 Scots Magazine, July 1739, p. 332. "An Evening at Vaux-hall."
11 Scots Magazine, August 1739, p. 409.
12 Girouard 1966 I, pp. 58-61.
13 Sprague Allen 1937, p. 81.
14 The Champion, No. 424, August 5th 1742. pp. 419-420.
15 Smollett 1771, pp. 129-130.
16 Vertue III p. 150.
17 (John Lockman): A Sketch of Spring-Gardens, Vaux-Hall. In a Letter to a Noble Lord. London (1752). p. 28.
18 Yale 1983. pp. 22, 24n.
19 Lockman 1751, p. 11
20 Williams 1933. p. 280.
21 Quoted Fleming 1962 p. 368.
22 The Champion, No. 424, August 5th 1742. p. 420.

Rococo Silver: design

1   Came 1961, pp. 95, 104-5. The third Earl of Berkeley had strong family ties with France, his wife being the grand-daughter of Charles II's mistress Louise de Kéroual, Duchesse d'Aubigny.
2   The model was the candelabrum to which Germain is pointing in his portrait painted by Nicolas de Largillière in 1736. A pair made by Kandler in 1738 was based on this design; two close copies were executed by Le Sage in 1744 and Wickes in 1745.
3   Rouquet, 1755, singled out Moser as the one artist in this branch [chasing] whose abilities really deserve the attention of the curious, and the approbation of his profession'. Moser's signed drawing of a candlestick and the unmarked Daphne and Apollo pair made to this design are included in the Exhibition (Cats. E13, E14).
4   Vertue wrote of him in 1741 as 'Mr Gravelot whose drawings for Engravings and all other kinds of Gold and Silver works shows [sic] he is endowed with a great and fruitful genius for designs, inventions of history and ornaments'.
5   Hayward 1969-70.
6   Sale at Mr Hutchins's Auction Rooms, King's Street and Hart Street, Covent Garden, 17th and 22nd March 1783.
7   Grimwade, 1974, pp. 5-6 & Plate 1.
8   Grimwade, 1974, Pl. 4.
9   Kunstmuseum Dusseldorf 1971.
10 P.R.O. C. 104/58. An account dated May 1807 in the Vulliamy

Silver Book (Client Levison Gower, Esq.) relating to shell pattern salts mentions 'shells to cast from'. I am indebted to Mr Geoffrey de Bellaigue for this reference.

11 Compare with the set of four mermaid salts made by Paul De Lamerie in 1739 in the Sterling and Francine Clark Art Institute, Williamstown, Massachusetts.

12 Tessa Murdoch, 'Louis François Roubiliac', Proceedings of the Huguenot Society of London, Vol. XXXVI No. 1, 1983.

13 Compare with Thomas Germain's tortoise/crab/scallop salt and spice box of 1734-36 in the Musée du Louvre, Paris.

14 The Paul De Lamerie inkstand of 1741 in the Collection of the Goldsmiths' Company is decorated with masks representing Athene and Hermes as well as Homer and Sappho.

15 See Nicholas Sprimont's kettle stand of 1745 in the Hermitage Museum.

16 Pineau c. 1725-30.

17 Kaellgren 1982, p. 487 & fig. 4.

Rococo Silver: patrons & craftsmen

1 Evans 1933; Grimwade 1976. A large number of people were engaged in the production and retail of silver; in 1773 well over 160 'Goldsmiths, Silversmiths and Plateworkers' active in London, with marks registered at the Hall, plus another five hundred specialists describing themselves as spoon and bucklemakers, haft and hiltmakers, goldworkers and watchcasemakers. The list excludes journeymen, both native-born and visitors, regularly employed in the trade and retailers without marks; *Report from the Committee appointed to enquire into the Several Assay Offices*, 1773. Earlier in the century numbers were much the same; some ran retail businesses large and small, others merely supplied the trade with specialized goods such as flatware, candlesticks, casters, epergnes or teapots.

2 For De Lamerie, Phillips 1968; Wickes, Barr 1980. Crespin Jones 1940.

3 Hayward 1966 (Courtauld) for Willaume I and II, Hayward 1959 and Honour 1971.

4 Letters (in French) at Welbeck from Crespin to John Achard, the Duke of Portland's agent, show of the goldsmith's attention to detail and the interest taken by the Duchess in her plate. 'I have received an order from M. the Duchess to make 6 silver sconces like the model sent to me for the 6 short ones . . . His Grace's wax chandler gave me a piece (of candle) as a sample, the sconce being bigger than the socket. I have been obliged to shape my leaves ('feuillies') into twelve instead of 6. I do not know if they will please' 25 Oct. 1754; Jones 1940.

5 For his long-running relationship as goldsmith to successive Viscounts Townshend, see the Townshend plate book at Goldsmiths' Hall and Lever 1975, 192/3. While David Willaume II initially supplied the Tollemache plate from 1729 to 1740, the more fashionable Crespin gradually took over, virtually monopolizing their large dinner service orders of the 1740s; Tollemache MSS, Goldsmiths bills 1729-1744; Trevor 1955.

6 Barr 1980; Grimwade 1960.

7 Grimwade 1961.

8 Between 1759 and 1762 the Philadelphia goldsmith, Joseph Richardson, repeatedly ordered teasilver from his London suppliers Thomas How and John Masterman; the teapots were to be 'Good Work and of the Newest fashion', and the sugar dishes 'Neatly Chast to suit the teapotts.' Stands to accompany coffee-pots were 'to weigh about 10 ounces with 6 Shells on the Border to suit the Coffe Potts' Fales 1974, 225, 231. In the 1760s simple candlesticks with shells or festoons were cast from London-made originals by both Jamaican and New York goldsmiths; information from Robert Barker.

9 For example, octagonal gilt dessert plates made for Lord Mornington in 1759 have cast and applied borders which alternate guilloche and shell pattern, a costly but restrained design for which Parker & Wakelin charged the high price of £2 per plate

for 'fashion' (on top of the metal price) plus £3 per plate for gilding. Butty and Dumée lifted wholesale both forms and aggressively modelled vine, reed and other plant motifs of the French goldsmiths Bailly, Joubert and Durand e.g. Grimwade 1974, 33b; Dennis 1960, 195 and 24.

10 Graham 1972, items 7 and 5; Schroder 1983, p. 16.

11 Moulds remained in use for many years; a candlestick by James Gould was reproduced, presumably to make up a set, by his ex-apprentice John Cafe 25 years later and De Lamerie's figure candlesticks reappear with the marks of Kandler (1752) and Le Sage (1758); Grimwade 1963.

12 Salts were consistently the most expensive items – (eg. Barr 1980, 147 and compare cat. G17). A less expensive alternative was to add applied cast scrollwork and substitute new handles and feet, as on a pair of De Lamerie tureens of 1722, brought up to date in this fashion around 1740; Jones 1977, 12. Even cheaper was the addition of chased ornament to old plate.

13 Grimwade 1974, 32b-35b.

14 Davis 1976, 120-1. These cost 10/6 an ounce.

15 But the milk or cream jug was often purchased separately as both Benjamin Mildmay and Lyonel Tollemache did. (Wickes sold less than a dozen between 1735 and 1747). One only of the snake-handled cups made by De Lamerie around 1740 can be tied to its original owner by his engraved armorials (Cat. G3) .See also the vine-wreathed cups made by Thomas Heming between 1753 and 1761; (Young 1982, 285; Cat. G40).

16 Edwards 1977, passim.

17 Warrington MSS, Dunham Massey: plate inventory 1750. William Kent's influence on silver continued alongside the current of French-derived naturalism; Crespin made up his owl candlestick in 1741 and again in 1745 for the Duke of Newcastle and other Kent designs recurred, such as that for the Pelham gold cup, throughout the 1750s and 1760s.

18 Cat. G11; Carrington and Hughes 1926, p. 00.

19 Dennis 1960, 127.

20 Walpole to Mann 1769.

21 Edwards 1977, De Lamerie's account. The personal taste for French art of Lyonel Tollemache, 4th Earl Dysart, is evident in the tapestry-hung Queen's Bedchamber at Ham House, redressed about 1740, for which his superb pair of Thomas Germain's male and female figure candelabra were perhaps intended (Trevor 1955).

22 Rouquet 1970, 'Of Goldsmiths' ware'. A direct comparison between the demand for porcelain and for silver in England is not easy; the former was decorative and a fashionable novelty but fragile and much cheaper. In 1770 a decorated Chelsea dessert service, complete with 24 plates, cost only £31; the equivalent in silver, a gilt centrepiece plus dessert plates, could cost nearly ten times as much. Dr Johnson's comment to Mrs Thrale, after his 1777 visit to the Derby porcelain factory, sums up the balance of aesthetic appeal and practicality 'The finer pieces are so dear that perhaps silver vessels of the same capacity may be sometimes bought for the same price and I am not yet so infected with the contagion of China-fancy as to like anything at that rate which can so easily be broken' quoted Mallet 1969, p. 101.

23 Production records for the London trade do not exist. The best evidence for assessing the demand for newly-wrought (as opposed to secondhand) silver are the Assayers' Books at Goldsmiths' Hall, kept from 1740 when the assaying procedure was overhauled. Daily totals both of the 'Betts', or items brought in, and the weight of 'Small Work', (items weighing less than four pounds) show a clearly marked rise for this category between the early 1740s and the late 1750s. The monthly assay totals for Small Work averaged just over a thousand pounds in the early 1740s, but double that amount by 1750 and quadruple by 1759 (eg for June 1741: 1316 lb; June 1756: 2,255 lb; March 1759: 5,818 lb). Direct comparison with earlier returns of the 1730s, which were compiled differently, is not possible but the total weight of sterling plate of all sizes assayed in 1732 was only thirty six thousand pounds.

24 Maker's (or more accurately sponsor's) marks have been both a

boon and a stumbling block to understanding craft organisation. Large businesses, such as those run by De Lamerie or George Wickes, made up substantial orders with stock from other goldsmiths' often specialists, as in Cat. G50 or in the presentation set Wickes supplied to the Prince of Wales for the city of Bath in 1738; the salver bore Lewis Pantin's mark and a date letter of 5 years earlier. The mark of the supplier might or might not be overstruck by the retailer, as De Lamerie did on a Crespin box of 1720.

25 Rouquet was disparaging about the English taste for sideboard plate, referring to 'the ridiculous ostentation with which they commonly display some trifling quantity of useless plate on a sideboard during the time of repast', seeing this as further evidence of its scarcity, 'even among persons of rank'. This abiding display role has ensured the preservation in both private and institutional hands of some magnificent commissions.

Gold Chasing

1 Chambers 1728, i, p. 306.
2 Grandjean, Piacenti, Truman and Blunt 1975, no. 5.
3 Eriksen 1974, pl. 249–54; p. 264.
4 Rosenborgsamlingen, Copenhagen.
5 Strutt 1786, ii, pp. 11–12.
6 Fuessli 1774, iv, pp. 132–3.
7 Knight 2nd edn. 1798, i, p. xlvii.
8 *Gentleman's Magazine*, liii, 1783, 180.
9 Fuessli 1774, iv, 134; Farington 1923, ii, 88.
10 Edwards 1808, p. xxii.
11 *The Plan of an Academy*, 1755, p. iv.
12 Whitley 1928, i, p. 165.
13 Pye 1845, p. 116, n. 27.
14 Hutchison 1968, p. 54.
15 Campbell 1747, p. 145.
16 Mortimer 1763, p. II.
17 Pyke 1973, p. 100.
18 Public Record Office, Kew, I.R.I./20/41.
19 Pyke 1973, pp. 102, 157; *Library of the Fine Arts*, iii, 1832, 95–101.
20 Edwards 1808, p. 91.
21 Edgcumbe *The Embossed Watchcase in England, c. 1700 to c. 1800* (unpublished doctoral thesis, Oxford University), 1980, i, pp. 175-7.

Rococo Furniture and Carving

1 Quoted in Gilbert 1978, p. 96
2 Ware 1733; Vardy 1744.
3 James 1712, p. 216.
4 Patte 1777.
5 Friedman 1975, pp. 66-75.
6 Heckscher 1969, pp. 299-311.
7 Berain (n.d.); Roumier, 1724; Boulle (n.d.); Berain (n.d.), Mariette (n.d.), Meriette 1727, Pineau (n.d.) Roumier (n.d.)
8 Fitz-Gerald 1969, pp. 140-47.
9 Heckscher 1975, pp. 59-65.
10 Boynton 1966, pp. 7-17.
11 Ware, 1733 pl. 36.
12 Peter Ward-Jackson (1958) publishes a summary of the various designers and illustrates many of their drawings and engravings.
13 Heckscher 1979, pp. 1-23.
14 His brother Thomas was a carver with premises in Grosvenor Square.
15 Morrison Heckscher (1979).
16 Hayward, 1964.
17 One clock case was ornamented with Father Time throttling the French cock. A reminder that the publication appeared during the Seven Years War with France.
18 The latter were inspired by Toro *c.*1719; q.v.: Helena Hayward,

'Newly Discovered Designs by Thomas Johnson, *Furniture History* XI Hayward 1975, pp. 40-42.
19 Helena Hayward 1964, p. 36.
20 Gilbert 1975, pp. 33-39.
21 Darly issued a second book of similar chair designs a short time later, and engravings from both books were reissued in Robert Manwaring, *The Chair Maker's Guide*, 1766.
22 An enlarged version appeared in 1762 and was reissued in 1763. It was then enlarged again in 1764/5. A facsimile of the 2nd ed. of 1762, *Genteel Household Furniture in the Present Taste by a Society of Upholsterers, Cabinet-Makers etc.* with an introduction by Christopher Gilbert, 1978.
23 Mr William Hubert's sale of stock, announced in *The Daily Journal* , 18 April, 1735.
24 Thornton + Rieder 1971, pp. 283-88.
25 Kirkham 1969, pp. 503-13.
26 Pat Kirkham 'The Partnership of William Ince and John Mayhew, 1759-1804, *Furniture History* X; Kirkham 1974, pp. 56-60.
27 Horace Walpole criticised them in 1768 for being 'absurdly like the King's coach' (Cat. L77) q.v. Hayward + Kirkham 1980, p. 112.
28 Gilbert 1978, fig. 11.

Rococo Architecture and Interiors·

1 Hogarth 1953 (ed.) preface, 3
2 Hitchcock 1968, p. 15.
3 Blunt 1973, p. 26.
4 Harris 1969, pp. 129-133.
5 Harris 1960, p. 10.
6 Harris 1979, p. 41.
7 Jackson-Stops 1974 II, 1618-1621, fig. 5.
8 Chambers 1763.
9 Croft-Murray 1970 II, pp. 14-15.
10 Evans 1931 II, p. 69.
11 Beard 1975, pp. 200, 203, 219, 248.
12 Thieme-Becker XXX, p. 506.
13 Croft-Murray 1970 II, p. 176.
14 Curran 1967, pp. 27-41.
15 Beard 1975, pp. 246-7.
16 Pratt 1928, p. 77.
17 Ware Book V Chap. 27, p. 522.
18 Beard 1975, pp. 210, 233.
19 RIBA Drawings Collection, O-R, 12-13 [I].
20 Fiske Kimball 1943, p. 227.
21 Halfpenny, Morris and Lightoler 1757 plate 80 – the basis for ceilings at Came House and Cranborne Lodge in Dorset.
22 Jackson-Stops 1981, pp. 11, 30.

Textiles and Dress

1 The royal accounts, representing a conservative customer show this taking place. LC9.287, 288, 289 (PRO) The Lord Chamberlain's accounts for 1721–1740.
2 Tablecloth. German; 18th century, given by Mrs Bernard Rakham. VAM. T.62–1929.
3 The sale use and wear of all-cotton cloth was illegal from 1721–1736. The 'Manchester' Act declared that fustian, made with a linen warp and a cotton weft could be legally woven in the United Kingdom. From then until 1774 such materials were also printed. As the linen took the dye less well, printed fustians have a speckled effect.
4 Inscription on a printed handkerchief commemorating the Grand Masquerade Ball in Soho Square in 1771. VAM. T.314–1960.
5 A striking example may be seen in a dress at the Museum of London 83.531 worn by a Lady Mayoress in 1753. The flowers are

in keeping with the styles of the time but the designer has clearly
been commissioned to add some appropriate extra details: bales
and an anchor are brocaded in silver thread and there are hops
among the brocaded flowers. The result is certainly striking!

6 Croft Murray 1962–70, vol II, p. 192.

7 The Public Advertiser, 18 April, 1755 (B.L. Burney 472b).
   Reference supplied by Lisa Clinton, who worked through some
   twenty years of this newspaper abstracting references for this
   exhibition.

8 Standen 1983, pp. 251–256. Fig. 1 illustrates two screens
   mentioned in the next sentence.

9 Residenz Museum 1958 p. 257, Cat. 902. The carpet is discussed
   and illustrated by Verlet 1982, pp. 144–5.

10 Postlethwayt 1751. Vol I article on engraving.

11 Rouquet 1755. Facsimile edition 1970 p. 71.

12 Pevsner 1955.

13 Ephraim Garthwaite, a pluralist with several livings had three
   daughters. He died in 1719 and in his will he divided his English
   books between the daughters leaving the Latin and Greek books
   to his son-in-law Robert Danny unless the younger daughters also
   married clergymen within 5 years. Mary the eldest daughter
   married first Thomas Johnson rector of Spofforth in 1710 who
   died in 1712 and then his successor to the living, Robert Danny in
   1714. He died in 1729.

14 No 2 Princelet Street, still awaiting its blue plaque.

15 Vincent Bacon had been a member of an early eighteenth century
   naturalists' club. See Allen 1967, p. 310. Wills Mary Dannye PCC.
   Middx. April 172. Caesar. Will proved April 6 1763.
   Anna Maria Garthwaite. PCC. Middx. October 471. Caesar. Will
   proved 24 October 1763.

16 Peter Campart was a weaver of striped and plain lustring, mantua,
   and tabby, according to Mortimer's Directory of 1763.

17 King (ed) 1980. Vol I p. XXVI.

18 Thornton 1958.

19 Smith. 1756 edition p. 39.

20 Smith, op cit. p. 39.

21 Nichols 1970 facsimile p. 37.

22 In VAM. T.393–1971 on p. 27 there is the design for this silk. It
   was woven by Captain John Baker, one of the most important
   English master weavers.

23 Birmingham Museum and Art Gallery 391–37. I am very grateful
   to Miss Emmeline Leary for her help on examining this dress.

24 Rouquet 1755, p. 30.

25 Museum of London 69–137, Heritage Foundation Deerfield
   Mass., and Cooper-Hewitt Museum, New York 1955. 16252.

26 Hogarth (1955 edition), p. 48.

27 The work is inscribed on the spitoon in the foreground of the
   opening scene in the engraving.

28 Two are illustrated in King(ed) 1980 Vol I pl. 235 1744, 242 1749.

29 Garthwaite's designs for 1746 have not been traced so a
   comparison must be made with those of 1745 and 7.

30 Smith 1756. The author admired French designers whose 'natural
   freeness of composition is really admirable and suited to the
   purposes intended . . . without crowding things together but . . .
   with a careless air, beauty and delicacy . . .' p. 36.

31 House of Commons Journals. Report on Silk Manufacture March
   4 1765 pp. 209 and 210, evidence of John Perigal and John Allen.

32 King (ed) 1980 pls. 215 1740, 223 1741, 230 1743 (no roots but a
   complete plant).

33 King (ed) 1980 pl. 245.

34 60.9.16. Worn by Hannah Allen, married Captain James Hooker
   1763 of Windsor Conn. ancestor of the donor.

35 Rouquet 1755, French edition p. 114.

36 This subject was pursued in 2 articles: Rothstein 1967 pp. 90–94
   and 150–156.

37 PRO Customs 3, until 1783 the Port Books list all imports and
   exports to and from London and the outports. Goods are
   distinguished when they are of British manufacture. Even if the
   values are distorted by the use of an out-of-date Book of Rates the

proportion and type of goods can be assessed. I have examined
every year until 1783.

38 Albany, New York, Institute of Arts. 1944. 60.1–3 Dress of
   Catherine Livingston. The silk woven from 5981.10b dated 1742
   by Mr Pully; Henry Francis Du Point Winterthur Museum, silk
   damask dress worn by Mrs Charles Willing painted by Robert
   Feke in 1746. The silk woven by Simon Julins from Garthwaite's
   design in VAM T.391–1971 p. 55; Boston Museum of Fine Arts
   471.1021. Buff damask dress said to have been worn by Ruth Eliot
   married to Jeremy Belknap of Dover in 1747, the silk woven by
   Simon Julins from 5988.28 in 1751, Boston MFA. 59.648 Blue
   damask dress, said to have come from a Boston family, the silk
   woven by John Sabatier from the design 5989.18. There is another
   example of this damask in red with a Scottish provenance in the
   VAM. T.346–1975 King (ed) 1980 Vol II Black and White plates 4
   and 5.

39 [Plumer] Reasons against the Bill now depending in Parliament . . . 1743
   pp. 12–13 '. . . the Revocation of the Edict of Nantz [sic] was a
   great Acquisition to us . . . by the Addition of People to this
   Nation, and the transplanting of their Manufactures to us . . .'

40 House of Commons Journals April 14th 1766. p. 725. Silk
   Manufacture, evidence.

41 Gentleman's Magazine 1749 p. 319.

42 King (ed) 1980, Vol I pl. 22 (black and white). Barbara Johnson's
   Album, VAM T.219–1973, contains samples of the fabrics of her
   clothes from 1746-1823. It is hoped to publish it as a facsimile.

43 They were also imitated by drawloom woven fabrics in the 17th–
   18th century and by wallpapers in the 18th century.

44 Catalogue of the Collections of the Jewish Museum London 1974.
   pl. XLIX no. 69.

45 Museum of London 83.844.

46 VAM T.179–1959.

47 One is illustrated pl. 39 Calman 1977.

48 The Holker samples are illustrated and discussed by Mrs Florence
   Montgomery. Gervers (ed) 1977 pp. 214–231.

49 Smith, 1756, p. 47.

50 King (ed) 1980 Vol II, p. XII.

51 2 volumes from the Bromley Hall factory on the river Lea in
   Poplar run by families who had been calico printers since the 17th
   century. One is in Mulhouse and one in the VAM and shown
   here. Three pattern books have survived from Nixon & Co of
   Phippsbridge near Merton, Surrey, and are in the Musée de
   l'Impression in Mulhouse, one belongs to GP and J Baker Ltd.
   (See VAM 1984).

52 14 Geo. III cap. 72.

53 Contained in a series of articles in Antiques and the Connoisseur, in 3
   articles in the Journal of the Society of Dyers and Colourists and,
   above all, in the Catalogue of the Loan Exhibition of English Chintz
   1960 which he did not live to see and was completed by Mrs
   Barbara Morris.

54 VAM T.166–1920.

55 Smith 1756, p. 39.

56 A typical selection may be seen in one of the pattern books from
   the Warner Archive, VAM T.373–1972, and in the dated Galy
   Gallien designs acquired at the same time, VAM T.399.430–1972.

57 '. . . all the childish and ridiculous absurdities of temples, dragons,
   pagodas, and other fantastic fripperies, which have been imported
   from China.' Nichols 1970 facsimile p. 37. John Baptist Jackson's
   views are quoted by Miss Hefford p. XV King (ed) 1980. 'Lions
   leaping from Bough to Bough like Cats . . . Men and Women, with
   every other Animal, turn'd Monsters, like the figures in a Chinese
   paper'.

58 Thornton 1965, compare pl. 63a of 1733 with pl. 65a. The latter is
   illustrated in colour in King (ed) 1980 Vol. 1 pl. 166.

59 VAM 442–1897.

60 The style provoked an intense reaction by the Arts and Crafts
   Movement. Their views were particularly relevant to the South
   Kensington Museum for William Morris and, no doubt other Art
   Referees, tried not to acquire eighteenth century textiles. The

greater part of the collection of eighteenth century printed and woven textiles has been acquired since the First World War.

61 Clouzot 1928. Clouzot had not studied the books of English block impressions. The same is true of D'Allemagne 1942. Both are standard, reliable authors otherwise.

62 There are some in the Cabinet des Estampes of the Bibliothèque Nationale and others in the Library of the Musée des Arts Décoratifs, Paris. Very few are dated compared with the large number from the 1720s, 1730s and 1760s. The French silk designs in the VAM date from the 1760s and early 1770s.

63 Three smuggled waistcoat shapes seized at Dover and bearing the Customs stamp G II R must, therefore, date from before 1760. All three are in mint condition and unfaded. They are beautifully worked in an unmistakably *French* colour scheme in pastel shades. Two are in a private collection and one belongs to the VAM T.12 & A–1981.

Porcelain

1 Rouquet Paris, 1755, p. 143. I have not here used the English translation published soon afterwards, since it is in small but quite significant respects inaccurate. The 1970 reprint of the English text will however be found useful because of the admirable introduction by my colleague, Ronald Lightbown.

2 Benton 1976, pp. 54-58.

3 See the Catalogue entry for No. O39.

4 Adams & Redstone 1981, p. 209, Appendix III.

5 Finer & Savage 1965, p. 237.

6 Lane 1961, Pls. 36, 37, 58, 84 and Colour Pl. D.

7 Tapp 1938, pp. 1-7. Lane 1960, pp. 245-51; Lane 1961, pp. 63-76 and pp. 133-38.

8 Mallet 1973.

9 Watney 1972, p. 821 and figs. 3 and 4.

10 Cox-Johnson 1961, pp. 3-6.

11 For bibliography on the A Marked porcelains and on Nicholas Crisp see Cat. D2, D12.

12 Clifford & Friedman 1974, especially pp. 17–22.

13 Mallet 1974, pp. 320-331.

14 Rasmussen (ed) Hamburg, 1977, pp. 568-594; Theuerkauff 1981; Theuerkauff 1982. Some busts after von Lücke were made by Chelsea-Derby ca. 1780.

15 Tait 1963, p. 209.

16 Falkner 1912, Chapter IV and Pl. 96. For the other inscribed dish see Mallet 1967, Pl. 142 a and b.

17 On a site discovered by Mr J L Evans, the finds are being worked on at Stoke Museum by David Barker, to whom and to Arnold Mountford, I am indebted for a sight of them. Towner 1978, pp. 34-42; *Transactions of the English Ceramic Circle*, Vol. 5, Part 4, 1963, pp. 180-93 and Vol. 10, Part 5, 1980, pp. 266-268.

18 Valpy 1983, p. 202.

19 Jewitt 1878, Vol. I, p. 172.

20 Rush 1973.

21 Toppin Vol. 2, No. 9, 1946, p. 177; Adams Redstone 1981, pp. 44-46.

22 Coke, Wingham, 1983.

23 Eg Arnold Mountford 1971, Pl. 82.

24 Rückert, Munich 1966, No. 469.

25 Mallet 1969, fig. 19.

26 Kunze 1982, pp. 37-50.

Sculpture

1 Cf. Lankheit 1962 pl. 32, brought to my attention by Anthony Radcliffe.

2 Seelig 1977, p. 69f.

3 Murdoch 1983, p. 31.

4 I owe this suggestion to Peter Thornton.

5 Webb 1954, p. 199.

6 Dossie 1782, III p. 417.

7 Pope 1956, IV, pp. 351, 360.

8 Webb 1958.

9 Cheere was paid £97.19.0 on 4 July 1734 for carriage and putting up the statue (New Titling Book; kindly communicated by Mr J.S.G. Simmons).

10 Webb 1958, p. 277.

11 Henry Cheere's account, Hoare's Bank; kindly communicated by Mr Lloyd.

12 Grosley 1771, p. 67.

13 *Gent's Mag.* (1755).

14 Gunnis 1968, p. 98.

15 Allen 1981.

16 By the late 18th century an intaglio with this subject was being reproduced, for which see McCrory 1983, p. 278.

17 Bindman 1981.

18 Souchal 1967.

19 Volk 1982, p. 162f.

20 Culton 1979; Handel's monument is cited here but not the statue.

List of Lenders

Her Majesty The Queen
C6, 21, E9, G17, L1, 60, N2, 23, O39, 42, Q2, S3

His Royal Highness the Prince of Wales
F5, 7

His Grace the Duke of Atholl
L31, 39, 46, S32

His Grace the Duke of Marlborough
D1, G6

Major General, His Grace the Duke of Norfolk
A19, C19, L35

The Most Hon. the Marquess of Hertford
L41

The Most Hon. the Marquess of Tavistock and Trustees of the Bedford Estates
E1, G13, L50, 51, 53, M14

The Right Hon. the Earl of Harewood
L73

The Right Hon. the Earl of Rosebery
S5

The Right Hon. the Earl of Pembroke and Montgomery
S11

The Right Hon. the Earl Waldegrave
L68

The Right Hon. the Earl of Yarborough
S9

The Lord Binning
S8

The Right Hon. Lord Egremont
L49

The Right Hon. Lord St. Oswald
M8, 9

Sir Alfred Beit Bart
A13

Sir Ralph Verney Bart
L55, M26, 29

American Institute of Architects Archives, Washington DC
M23

The Visitors of the Ashmolean Museum, Oxford
A6, 7, B6, D7, 15, 16, G9, 21, H9, 14, 20, S46

Musée des Arts Décoratifs, Paris
A10, 18, 20

G.P & J. Baker Ltd
N29

The Trustees of the Barber Institute of Fine Arts, University of Birmingham
S4

Birmingham, City Museums & Art Gallery
F1, 28

Claude Blair
K5

Blaise Castle House Museum (City of Bristol Museum and Art Gallery)
D29, L79

The Bodleian Library, Oxford
D4

Museum of Fine Arts, Boston
G8, 19, N16, 17, O43, R12

The Broadwood Trust
B14

The Trustees of the British Museum
B5, 13, C1, 8, 9, 13, 14, 16, 22-24, D13, 18, 29, G8, 10, 22, F4, 18, 20, 22, 24, 40, G31, 37, 42, 49, H17, I18, J3, K3, L17, 43, 47, 52, 75, 79, M19, 32, N1, 34, O7, 9, 13, 48, R7, S12, 19, 39, 42, 43

Burghley House Collection
L69

City of Bristol Museum and Art Gallery
F42, M20, P12

The British Architectural Library/RIBA
A4, C15, 18, M16

Master & Fellows of Trinity College, Cambridge
S34, 35

Cheng Huan
S45

The Chippendale Society
K6, L32, 71, R7c

The Worshipful Company of Coachmakers and Coach Harness Makers
L77

Gerald Coke Handel Collection
E17, S47

The Collection of the Worshipful Company of Clockmakers
H6, I12

The Colonial Williamsburg Foundation, Virginia
G35, N9, R10

The Cooper-Hewitt Museum, New York
The Smithsonian Institution's National Museum of Design
D5, L76, 78, N27, N28

The Thomas Coram Foundation for Children
L15

Country Life
M6

Courtauld Institute Galleries
F27

The Provost, Fellows and Scholars of Trinity College, Dublin
S10

Governors of Dulwich Picture Gallery
S17

The Dean and Chapter of Durham Cathedral
G45

The Worshipful Company of Fishmongers
G3, 33

The Syndics of the Fitzwilliam Museum, Cambridge
C20, D23, F9, G15, H12, 24, O15, 31, P11, S13

Folger Shakespeare Library, Washington DC
E7

Dr Terry Friedman
B2

Geoffrey Freeman Collection of Bow Porcelain on loan to Pallant House Gallery, Chichester
O14, 16, 17, 20, 21, R2

The Worshipful Company of Goldsmiths
G11, R1

Arthur and Rosalinde Gilbert
I 5, 8, 19

Guildhall Library, City of London
D29, L29w, E11, G29, I6, J8, N34e

Roger Fleetwood Hesketh
M1

Musée de l'Impression sur Etoffes
de Mulhouse
N26, 32

The Worshipful Company of Joiners
and Ceilers
R4

Royal Borough of Kensington and
Chelsea, Libraries & Fine Arts Service
S2

King's Lynn Museum
N15

Lady Lever Art Gallery, Port Sunlight
D22

Lambeth Archives Department
F3, 6, 8, 11, 13, 31-39

Leeds City Art Galleries
G1, L7-9, M12, O26

Museum of London
F15-17, 19, 41, O4, 44, Q4, 5

Musée du Louvre, Paris
H21, I16

City of Manchester Art Galleries
K7, M22, N10

The Mapledurham House Collection
L3

Marble Hill House (GLC)
B12, D20

Methuen Collection, Corsham Court
L19, L20

Metropolitan Museum of Art,
New York
G12, 14, I10, 14, 15, 17, L72, M4, 5,
N12

Minneapolis Institute of Arts
N14

National Museum of Antiquities
of Scotland
J1, 2

National Museum of Wales
D12, G50, N13

National Portrait Gallery London
E2, 15, F2, S21, 37

National Trust
Anglesey Abbey G22, 39, 44
Belton House C2
Claydon House M25, R11
Felbrigg Hall L26, 27, M10, 11, S55
Shugborough, L30
Uppark L29, 74

National Trust on loan to the VAM
O45, S33

Institute of Fine Arts, New York
University
D21

The Trustees of the Nostell
Settled Estate
L33

Nottingham Castle Museum
G43, N20

Private Collection
A5, 8, 22, B3, 7, C4, 7, 12, D6, 8-10,
17, 19, 24, 28, F14, 21, 26, G2, 7, 10,
23, 25, 32, 34, 36, H3, 5, 13, 18, 22,
23, 25, I3, 4, 7, 9, 11, L22, 36, 37, 40,
54, 56, 61, O1, 8, 10, 32, 35, R8

Procter and Gamble Company
G27

Royal Academy of Arts, London
S36

Royal Albert Memorial Museum,
Exeter
M3

The Royal Society of Arts
E21, K4

The Hon. P.M. Samuel
M31

City Museum & Art Gallery,
Stoke-on-Trent
P8

The Trustees of the Tate Gallery
E3, 5, F25, N24, 33
Taylor Institution, Oxford
S22, 24, 50, 51, 53, 54

The Armouries, HM Tower of
London
J5, 7

Dr Eric Till
L67

The Treasury (on loan to the
National Trust)
L29, M30

The Trustees of Sir Wm Turner's
Hospital, Kirkleatham
K1

Victoria and Albert Museum
A1, 2, 3, 9, 11, 12, 14, 15-17, 21, 23-
28, B1, 8-11, 15, 16, C3, 5, 10, 11, 17,
D2, 3, 14, 25, 27, E4, 6, 13, 14, 16-18,
20, F10, 12, 23, 43a, 43b, 43c, G4, 5,
16, 18, 20, 24, 26, 28, 38, 40, 46-48,
H4, 7, 8, 15, 16, 19, I 1, 2, 13, J4, 6,
K2, L2, 4-6, 10-14, 16, 18, 21, 23-25,
28, 34, 38, 42, 44, 45, 48, 57-59, 62-
66, M2, 13, 15, 17, 18, 21, 24, N3, 4-8,
11, 18, 21, 22, 25, 30, 35, 36, O2, 5, 6,
11, 12, 18, 19, 22-25, 27-29, 30, 34,
36-38, 46, O47, P1-7, 9, 10, 13, 14, 15,
Q1, 3, 6, R5, 6, 9, S1, 6, 7, 14, 18, 20,
25-27, 38, 41, 44, 45, 48,
49, 52

Lewis Walpole Library, Yale University
D26, R3

The Wernher Collection by
arrangement with the NACF
F43d, e, f, g, h, i, O3, 40, 41

The Dean and Chapter of
Westminster Abbey
S15, 16, 40

Westminster City Libraries,
Archives Department
G41, D29e, 29r

The Henry Francis du Pont
Winterthur Museum, Delaware
N31

The Trustees of the late
H.C. Wolleston
B7

Worcester Art Museum, Massachusetts
N19, O33

Worcester City Council
O33

Paul Mellon Collection, Yale Centre
for British Art, New Haven
D11, E12, F29, 30, G30, H1, 2, 10, 11,
M7

York Castle Museum (on indefinite
loan to York City Art Gallery)
S28-31

York City Art Gallery
B4

Index